# MANAGING ORGANIZATIONS

# EDITORIAL BOARD

# MANAGING ORGANIZATIONS

*Current Issues*

Edited by

STEWART R. CLEGG,
CYNTHIA HARDY
AND WALTER R. NORD

SAGE Publications
London • Thousand Oaks • New Delhi

Chapters 1–12 originally published in *Handbook of Organization Studies*, 1996

First edition first published 1999

SAGE Publications Ltd
6 Bonhill Street
London EC2A 4PU

SAGE Publications Inc
2455 Teller Road
Thousand Oaks, California 91320

SAGE Publications India Pvt Ltd
32, M-Block Market
Greater Kailash – I
New Delhi 110 048

**British Library Cataloguing in Publication data**

A catalogue record for this book is available from the British Library

ISBN 0 7619 6046 5

**Library of Congress catalog record available**

Typeset by Mayhew Typesetting, Rhayader, Powys
Printed in Great Britain by Butler & Tanner Ltd, Frome and London

Stewart dedicates this book to Lynne who, as ever, was a great help in so many ways, but also to Jonathan and William as well as Bill and Joyce

Cynthia dedicates this book to all the wonderful friends she leaves behind in Canada and all the friends – old and new – she joins in Australia

Walt dedicates this book to three people who have helped so much in his life – Ann Nord, Arthur Nord and Elizabeth Nord

# Contents

Contributors      ix

Preface      xvii

Introduction      1
*Stewart R. Clegg, Cynthia Hardy and Walter R. Nord*

Chapter 1    Creative Deconstruction: Strategy and Organizations    11
*Richard Whipp*

Chapter 2    Leadership in Organizations    26
*Alan Bryman*

Chapter 3    Decision-Making in Organizations    43
*Susan J. Miller, David J. Hickson and David C. Wilson*

Chapter 4    Cognitions in Organizations    63
*Ann E. Tenbrunsel, Tiffany L. Galvin, Margaret A. Neale
and Max H. Bazerman*

Chapter 5    Diverse Identities in Organizations    88
*Stella M. Nkomo and Taylor Cox Jr*

Chapter 6    Putting Group Information Technology in its Place:
Communication and Good Work Group Performance    107
*Arthur D. Shulman*

Chapter 7    Metaphors of Communication and Organization    125
*Linda L. Putnam, Nelson Phillips and Pamela Chapman*

Chapter 8    Organizations, Technology and Structuring    159
*Karlene H. Roberts and Martha Grabowski*

Chapter 9    Organizing for Innovation    174
*Deborah Dougherty*

Chapter 10   Organizational Learning: Affirming an Oxymoron          190
             *Karl E. Weick and Frances Westley*

Chapter 11   Organizations and the Biosphere: Ecologies and
             Environments                                            209
             *Carolyn P. Egri and Lawrence T. Pinfield*

Chapter 12   Evolution and Revolution: from International Business
             to Globalization                                       234
             *Barbara Parker*

Epilogue: Now That It Has Been Said – What Do We Think?              257

Index                                                               259

# Contributors

**Max H. Bazerman** is the J. Jay Gerber Distinguished Professor of Dispute Resolution and Organizations at the Kellogg Graduate School of Management at Northwestern University. His research focuses on decision making, negotiation, fairness, social comparison processes and, most recently, environmental decision making and dispute resolution. He is the author or co-author of over ninety research articles, and the author, co-author, or co-editor of seven books, including *Judgement in Managerial Decision Making* (1994, 3rd edn), *Cognition and Rationality in Negotiation* (1991, with M.A. Neale), and *Negotiating Rationally* (1992, with M.A. Neale).

**Alan Bryman** is Professor of Social Research in the Department of Social Sciences, Loughborough University, England. His main research interests lie in research methodology and leadership studies, though he is currently co-director of a research project on the portrayal of social science research in the British mass media. He is the author of a number of books, including *Quantity and Quality in Social Research* (1988), *Charisma and Leadership in Organizations* (1992), and *Disney and his Worlds* (1995). He is editor or co-editor of *Doing Research in Organizations* (1988), *Analyzing Qualitative Data* (1994), and *Social Scientists Meet the Media* (1994).

**Pamela Chapman** is a doctoral student in organizational communication at Purdue University. She received her BA in communication from Rutgers University. Her research focuses on gender and organizational communication and is guided by critical and postmodern feminist perspectives. Her current interests include the discursive construction of sexual harassment and institutionalized sexism.

**Stewart R. Clegg** moved to Australia for a job in 1976 and has been there ever since, apart from an interregnum in Scotland in the early 1990s. He has held a Chair in Sociology at the University of New England, 1985–9; a Chair in Organization Studies at the University of St Andrews, 1990–3; and was the Foundation Chair of Management at the University of Western Sydney, Macarthur, 1993–6. He is currently Professor of Management at the University of Technology, Sydney. He was a founder of APROS (Asian and

Pacific Researchers in Organization Studies) in the early 1980s, and has been the co-editor of *The Australian and New Zealand Journal of Sociology*, as well as editor of a leading European journal, *Organization Studies*. He serves on the editorial boards of many other leading journals. Amongst the many books that he has published are *Frameworks of Power* (1989), *Modern Organizations: Organization Studies in the Postmodern World* (1990), and *Capitalism in Contrasting Cultures* (1990), *Constituting Management* (1996) and *The Politics of Management Knowledge* (1996) (both with Gill Palmer), *Transformations of Corporate Culture* (1998) (with Toyohiro Kono), *Changing Paradigms: The Transformation of Management Knowledge for the 21st Century* (1998) (with Thomas Clarke), and *Global Management: Universal Theories and Local Realities* (1998) (with Eduardo Ibarra and Luis Bueno). He has published widely in the journals. He researched the leadership and management needs of embryonic industries for the Taskforce on Leadership and Management in the Twenty First Century commissioned by the Federal Government of Australia, which reported in 1995.

**Taylor Cox Jr** is Associate Professor in the Organization Behavior and Human Resource Management Department of the School of Business at the University of Michigan. He is also founder and President of Taylor Cox & Associates, a research and consulting firm specializing in organization change and development work for employers with culturally diverse workforces. His work history includes nine years of management experience and twelve years of college and executive teaching. In addition to his work at the University of Michigan, he has held faculty appointments at Duke University and with the Industrial and Labor Relations School of Cornell University. He is author or co-author of more than twenty published articles on a variety of management topics including manufacturing strategy, performance appraisal, promotion systems and managing cultural diversity. His book *Cultural Diversity in Organizations: Theory, Research and Practice* (1993) was co-winner of the 1994 George R. Terry Book Award. His consulting practice has included education programmes, research, strategic planning and organization development work with more than a dozen organizations including Ford, Exxon and Philips.

**Deborah Dougherty**, after working in the trenches of several large bureaucracies for ten years, returned to school to study the prospects of innovation in large bureaucracies. She is now Associate Professor at McGill University, Faculty of Management, where she teaches policy and innovation management. Deborah also taught at the Wharton School, University of Pennsylvania, for five years, and at the Graduate School of Management, University of Melbourne. Her research papers on product innovation, understanding new markets, and organizing for innovation have been published in various journals. In addition to the review chapter in this handbook, she has contributed six other book chapters. Her current research concerns whether and how large, long-established organizations can transform to be more effectively innovative.

**Carolyn P. Egri** is an Assistant Professor in the Faculty of Business Administration at Simon Fraser University. Her research and writing have primarily been concerned with innovation, organizational power and politics, organizational change and development, as well as environmental and social issues in society and organizations. Recent publications concerning environmental issues include being guest co-editor (with P.J. Frost) of the *Leadership Quarterly* special issue on 'Leadership for environmental and social change', and a chapter in *Resistance and Power in Organizations: Agency, Subjectivity and the Labor Process* (eds J.M. Jermier et al.).

**Tiffany L. Galvin** is a PhD student in organization behaviour at the J.L. Kellogg Graduate School of Management at Northwestern University. Her research interests can be classified into two areas: understanding organizational change as influenced by social-structural and institutional processes and understanding organizational change within institutional environments. In the first area, Tiffany has worked on understanding corporate restructuring activity (e.g. divestitures and downsizing) through both economic and social influence/embeddedness processes. In the second area, Tiffany is pursuing questions surrounding how firms change and how new organizational forms emerge, particularly within institutional environments like health care and education. Her work seeks to explore organizational actions traditionally explained by economic-based rationales through more socially influenced explanations.

**Martha Grabowski** served as a shipboard merchant marine officer for El Paso Marine Company, Exxon Shipping Company, and Hvide Shipping. She subsequently spent ten years at GE, as a marketing and advanced programmes manager within GE Aerospace. Most recently, she was a programme integration manager for information systems and artificial intelligence research programmes at GE's Corporate Research and Development Center in Schenectady, New York. Currently, she is the Joseph C. Georg Chaired Professor at Le Moyne College in Syracuse, New York, and Research Associate Professor in the Department of Decision Sciences and Engineering Systems at Rensselaer Polytechnic Institute. Dr Grabowski also serves as a member of the National Research Council Marine Board, and as a member of the Secretary of Transportation's Navigation Safety Advisory Council. In 1993–4 she chaired the Marine Board study which investigated advances in marine navigation and piloting; that study report, *Minding the Helm: Advances in Marine Navigation and Piloting*, was released in October 1994. Over the past six years, she has developed a shipboard piloting expert system for oil tankers in Prince William Sound, which is an intelligent software module within an integrated ship's bridge system. She is currently developing similar systems for the St Lawrence Seaway and San Francisco Bay. Dr Grabowski's research interests include human and organizational error in large-scale systems; real-time knowledge-based systems; development methods for advanced information technology systems; and the organizational impacts of information technology.

**Cynthia Hardy** was previously Professor of Policy in the Faculty of Management, McGill University, Montreal, Canada, and is presently Professor and Head of the Department of Management at the University of Melbourne, Australia. Her research interests have spanned organizational power and politics; managing strategic change; retrenchment and downsizing; strategy making in universities; and interorganizational collaboration. She has published a number of books, including *Managing Strategic Action: Mobilizing Change* (1994), *Strategies for Retrenchment and Turnaround: the Politics of Survival* (1990), *Managing Strategy in Academic Institutions: Learning from Brazil* (1990), and *Managing Organizational Closure* (1985). An edited volume on *Power and Politics in Organizations* was published in 1995, and a book on retrenchment in Canadian universities in 1996. Dr Hardy has also published over forty articles in scholarly journals and books.

**David J. Hickson** is Research Professor of International Management and Organization at Bradford Management Centre, England. His principal research interests are how societal culture affects managerial decision-making in different nations, and what influences the success of major decisions. His previous research has included processes of managerial decision-making, power in organizations and bureaucratization. He was founding editor-in-chief of the international research journal *Organization Studies* from 1979 to 1990, and was a founder of the European research association in his field, EGOS (European Group for Organizational Studies). He has held appointments in university business schools and research institutes in Canada, the United States and The Netherlands, has an Honorary PhD from the University of Umeå in Sweden, and has lectured widely around the world. He has published numerous research journal papers and book chapters and is author or editor of eight books, most recently *Management in Western Europe* (1993) and *Management Worldwide: the Impact of Societal Culture on Organizations around the Globe* (1995, with Derek Pugh). Prior to becoming an academic, David Hickson worked in financial administration, and qualified professionally as a Chartered Secretary and in personnel management.

**Susan J. Miller** is currently Lecturer in Organizational Behaviour and Strategic Management at Durham University Business School, England. Her research interests include the making and implementation of strategic decisions in organizations, particularly focusing on reasons for decision success. She is also involved in the health sector, and recent work in this area has concentrated on the managerial/clinical interface, looking at the ways in which clinicians' contribution to the strategic direction of health service organizations can be identified and developed.

**Margaret A. Neale** is Professor of Organization Behavior at Stanford Graduate School of Business. Her research interests include: negotiation and dispute resolution, identifying a series of cognitive mechanisms such as the use of cognitive biases that systematically reduce the quality of potential agreements; the impact of cognitive biases on decision-making in the human resource management arena; factors that influence the cognitions of the decision-maker, such as relationships among the parties, what is being allocated (burdens or benefits), and the selection of allocation norms within groups; and *how* people collaborate, the selection of collaborative partners and the cognitive and affective mechanisms that enhance collaboration among successful teams. She is the co-author of three books: *Organizational Behavior: the Managerial Challenge* (1994, 2nd edn), *Cognition and Rationality in Negotiation* (1991), and *Negotiating Rationally* (1992).

**Stella M. Nkomo** is Professor of Management in the Belk College of Business Administration at the University of North Carolina at Charlotte. She is a former Bunting Fellow at the Mary Ingraham Bunting Institute at Radcliffe College. Her research has focused on human resource management practices in organizations with a special emphasis on strategic human resource planning. Her current research examines race, gender and diversity in the workplace. She and her colleague Dr Ella L. Bell are writing a book on the life and career experiences of black and white women managers in private sector corporations. She is also observing and evaluating diversity initiatives in eight not-for-profit organizations in the Southeast. Dr Nkomo is the past Chair of the Women and Management Division of the Academy of Management. Her research and writing have appeared in several journals. She is the co-author of the text *Applications in Human Resource Management*.

**Walter R. Nord** is currently Professor of Management at the University of South Florida. Previously he was at Washington University–St Louis (1967–89). His current interests centre on developing a critical political economics perspective of organizations, organizational innovation, and organizational conflict. He has published widely in scholarly journals and edited/authored a number of books. His recent books include *The Meanings of Occupational Work* (with A. Brief), *Implementing Routine and Radical Innovations* (with S. Tucker), *Organizational Reality: Reports from the Firing Line* (with P. Frost and V. Mitchell), and *Resistance and Power in Organizations* (with J. Jermier and D. Knights). He is currently co-editor of *Employee Responsibilities and Rights Journal* and a recent past book review editor for the *Academy of Management Review*. He has served as consultant on organizational development and change for a variety of groups and organizations.

**Barbara Parker** is an associate professor of management in the Albers School of Business and Economics, Seattle University, USA. Following a PhD in strategic management from the University of Colorado in 1985 she has taught and conducted research in a broad range of interest areas including managing diversity, gender roles, expatriate adjustment and managing small businesses in an international context. Teaching areas include strategy, international management, diversity management and globalization. She has published widely in various journals. Seattle University offers a required course in Globalization and Business Practices; writing the text for that course is a current project for Barbara Parker. Some of the ideas found in this contributed chapter emerged from the text project.

**Nelson Phillips** is an Assistant Professor in the Faculty of Management at McGill University. He completed a PhD in Organizational Analysis at the University of Alberta. He has published articles in the Academy of Management Journal, *Organization Science* and *Organization Studies*. His research interests include organizational legitimacy, organizational collaboration and a general interest in the intersection of cultural studies and organizational analysis.

**Lawrence T. Pinfield** is a Professor in the Faculty of Business Administration at Simon Fraser University, Burnaby, BC, Canada. His study of the internal labour market of a large forestry firm, *The Operation of Internal Labor Markets: Staffing Activities and Vacancy Chains*, was published by Plenum in 1995. Current interests include extensions of findings from his studies of ILMs: how patterns of vacancy chains support processes of organizational adaptation; how stock-flow models of human resources create and are modified by corporate cultures; what rules managers use to create and modify jobs; and how careers may be managed in organizations characterized by dynamic patterns of jobs.

**Linda L. Putnam** is Professor and Head of the Department of Speech Communication at Texas A & M University. Her current research interests include negotiation and organizational conflict, and language analysis in organizations. She has published over 60 articles and book chapters in management and communication journals. She is the co-editor of *Communication and Negotiation* (1992), *Handbook of Organizational Communication* (1987) and *Communication and Organization: An Interpretive Approach* (1983). She is the 1993 recipient of the Charles H. Woolbert Research Award for a seminal article in the communication field and is a Fellow of the International Communication Association.

**Karlene H. Roberts** is Professor of Business Administration at the University of California, Berkeley. Her research and teaching interests have been in organizational communication, research methodology, and cross-national management. More recently she has researched the design and management of organizations in which errors can lead to catastrophic consequences. She has studied organizations that both succeeded and failed at this challenge. In the last three years she has devoted much of her time to investigating management issues in the marine industry.

**Arthur D. Shulman** has over twenty-five years' experience as a teacher, researcher and international consultant on organizational communication planning and management. Art is concurrently Reader in the Graduate School of Management, University of Queensland, and the Principal Research Fellow of the Communication Research Institute of Australia. He is the author or co-author of over 90 scholarly publications. His current research activities focus on ways of improving R&D team management in the health, environmental, and information technology sectors. His prior academic appointments include Associate Professor and Director of the Interdisciplinary PhD Program in Organizational Psychology and Organizational Behavior, Washington University, and Associate Professor and Coordinator of Organizational Communication, Bond University.

**Ann E. Tenbrunsel** is an Assistant Professor in the Management Department at the University of Notre Dame. Her interests are concentrated in two research streams: one stream that aims at understanding why people engage in desirable versus undesirable behaviours, and another that investigates how decisions and behaviours are influenced by other people. In the first area, Ann has focused on understanding the factors that drive unethical behaviour, the influence of rules or standards on behaviour, strategic approaches to corporate philanthropy and the conceptual differences between the allocation of burdens and benefits. In the second area, Ann has examined the role that social comparison plays in job choice decisions, the influence of friendships in a matching market context, the transmission of sunk costs across negotiation partners, and the dual influence of family and work involvement.

**Karl E. Weick** is the Rensis Likert Collegiate Professor of Organizational Behavior and Psychology at the University of Michigan. He is also a former editor of *Administrative Science Quarterly*. Dr Weick has been associated with faculties at Purdue University, the University of Minnesota, Cornell University, and the University of Texas. He has also held short-term appointments at the University of Utrecht in The Netherlands, Wabash College, Carnegie-Mellon University, Stanford University, and Seattle University. In 1990 Weick received the highest honour awarded by the Academy of Management, the Irwin Award for Distinguished Lifetime Scholarly Achievement. In the same year, he also received the award for the Best Article of the Year in the *Academy of Management Review*. Dr Weick studies such topics as how people make sense of confusing events, the social psychology of improvization, high-reliability systems, the effects of stress on thinking and imagination, indeterminacy in social systems, social commitment, small wins as the embodiment of wisdom, and linkages between theory and practice. Weick's writing about these topics is collected in four books, including *The Social Psychology of Organizing* and the co-authored *Managerial Behaviour, Performance and Effectiveness*. In addition, he has written widely in the journals and elsewhere. Weick has also consulted with a variety of organizations in the public and private sector.

**Frances Westley** is Associate Professor of Strategy in the Faculty of Management at McGill University. She has published numerous articles on the subject of managing strategic change and is currently involved in research and teaching in the area of sustainable development.

**Richard Whipp** is Professor of Human Resource Management at Cardiff Business School, University of Wales, and the Deputy Director of the School responsible for research. He has taught and researched at Aston and Warwick Business Schools, the University of Uppsala and the Helsinki School of Economics. His book publications include: *Innovation and the Auto Industry* (with P. Clark), *Patterns of Labour: Managing Change for Competitive Success* (with A. Pettigrew) and *Competition and Chaos*. His current research centres on the relationship between the organization and strategy fields and the problem of time.

**David C. Wilson** was Professor of Organization Studies and Director of Research at the University of Aston Business School, Birmingham, UK, before returning recently to a Chair at the University of Warwick Business School, where he has previously worked (1985–93) for eight years in the Centre for Corporate Strategy and Change. His research interests include decision-making, strategy and change. He has published five books on these topics, the most recent of which include *A Strategy of Change* (1992) and *Strategy and Leadership* (1994, with B. Leavy). He was an original member of the Bradford Research Group studying decision-making in the 1970s and continues to research the processes and implementation of strategic decisions. He has also conducted research in the UK voluntary sector, assessing to what extent organization theory can apply to charitable and non-profit activities. He is Deputy Editor of the journal *Organization Studies*.

# *Preface*

This volume derives from the 1996 *Handbook of Organization Studies*. Originally, the *Handbook* was launched primarily for a research audience. Since its launch, the book's success has led to many requests for a paperback edition, particularly in a format that instructors and students might use. Recognition from the American Academy of Management which honoured the *Handbook* with its 1997 George R. Terry award for 'the most outstanding contributions to the advancement of management knowledge' has further increased interest in the *Handbook*. Accordingly, the editors and the publisher decided to launch a paperback version in 1999.

We decided to split the *Handbook* into two volumes. We wanted to produce a paperback version that would be more practical for teaching purposes. On the other hand, we also wanted to preserve the original integrity and structure of the *Handbook*. Volume 1, published as *Studying Organizations*, consists of the original Parts One and Three. It focuses on theoretical issues and the link between theory and practice. Volume 2 consists of the original Part Two and focuses on substantive organisational issues. Of course, there is some overlap between these categories but, nonetheless, each volume stands as a coherent entity with appeal to particular audiences.

The editors would like to thank Rosemary Nixon and the wonderful team at Sage, in both the UK and the US, who did so much to ensure the success of this project. We would also like to thank the contributors once again. We should point out that they did not have the opportunity to update their chapters owing to the pressures of the publication deadline. The desire to make the paperback version of the *Handbook* available as quickly as possible precluded revision. It was more important to make the existing material more readily available than to engage in the lengthy process of overhauling thirty, still very current, chapters.

Stewart R. Clegg, Cynthia Hardy and Walter R. Nord

# Introduction: Organizational Issues

## STEWART R. CLEGG, CYNTHIA HARDY AND WALTER R. NORD

It is instructive to recall the 1965 *Handbook of Organizations* edited by James G. March. At that time, March noted that 'the study of organizations has a history but not a pedigree' (1965: ix). Today, organization studies are even further removed from a pedigree in terms of a clear line of descent. Rather their history consists of multiple pasts and multiple presents. Organization studies have moved away from an unambiguous relationship between the word and the world in which the word was used to model the world and authorial authority exercised sovereign sway over the representation of reality. As alternative paradigms gained a foothold, multiple, conflicting realities started to emerge and the previously secure position of the researcher started to attract more critical attention. The task of any handbook today is no longer to construct one legitimate line of inquiry but to acknowledge and engage with the contemporary proliferation of approaches to the study of organizations.

Our intention in editing the original handbook (Clegg et al. 1996) was not to legislate but to engage conversationalists, new and old alike, in constructing multiple accounts of what organization studies have been and where they may be going. Some of those accounts – those that relate to broad theoretical themes – appear in Volume 1 of this edition. The chapters in this volume use those theoretical themes to address a specific range of issues facing individuals who work for and are affected by organizations. We present here a brief overview of these chapters.

### OVERVIEW OF CHAPTERS

An analysis of the pervasive use of the term 'strategy' opens Richard Whipp's chapter. He argues that we need to deconstruct and problematize the strategy concept. Noting the tensions between European and US thought and between economic and sociological approaches to strategy, he discusses how the term, and the arena of study, have evolved. One of the earlier incarnations derived from classical economics and concerned issues of competition, efficiency, and performance. Later, sociologists and political scientists entered the fray. Whipp, like Reed in his chapter in *Studying Organizations*, shows how different conceptualizations not only provide insight and illumination, but also produce silences around certain issues and themes, particularly issues pertaining to levels of analysis; the problem of strategic change and time; the non-reflexive nature of most strategy authors. Documenting the way the study of strategy has evolved over the years and the different approaches that comprise this subject, Whipp notes that strategy is far less reflexive and critical than organization theory. He calls for a melding of the two and more cross-disciplinary endeavour, particularly the use of insights derived from organization theory to deconstruct and challenge the assumptions that characterize strategy research. Finally, Whipp looks to the future, arguing that strategy research must consider more thoroughly the collective and interorganizational nature of 'industries' that exist today; the implications of new technology; the effects of globalization; the application of strategy to public sector contexts.

Alan Bryman addresses the subject of leadership in organizations. Previous work divides into four broad categories. The trait approach dominated the scene until the late 1940s; the style approach held sway from then until the late 1960s; the contingency approach had its heyday from the late 1960s; and the New Leadership approach revitalized research in the 1980s. As Bryman points out, these periods represent ascendancy of one particular approach, rather than the demise of all the others, since different approaches coexisted in the past and continue to do so today.

The New Leadership approach, with its focus on those transformational, charismatic, and visionary leaders thought to be responsible for major organizational change and success, has provided a 'shot in the arm' by offering an antidote to the waning interest in leadership research in the 1980s. It differs from earlier work in that the focus is on leaders of organizations rather than leaders of groups. The tendency to extol the virtues of transformational leadership heralds more universalistic thinking than that associated with the earlier contingency approach, although as Bryman points out, recent work has sought to combat this trend with a renewed interest in organizational context. This SuperLeadership approach emphasizes helping others to lead themselves. Other writers have focused on leadership practices, rather than the leader carrying out the practices.

Susan Miller, David Hickson and David Wilson examine decision-making in organizations, pointing out its practical and theoretical attraction. They start by exploring the concept of managerial rationality and the early critique of Simon's (1945) work on bounded rationality. Arguing that rational choice models have been the target of sustained criticism for over forty years, the authors then turn their attention to conceptions of decision-making as the enactment of power. They show how rational models break down and discuss both visible and less visible power dynamics. Covert aspects of decision-making raise methodological questions: if power is hidden, how can it be studied? The authors turn to a variety of empirical approaches to examine this issue.

Pointing out that an understanding of decision-making is incomplete without some consideration of implementation, the authors reflect on issues of implementation. Research has uncovered different approaches to implementation from top-down 'commander' interventions to bottom-up 'crescive' implementation. The authors conclude their chapter by classifying work on decision-making in two ways. Perspectives can be categorized in terms of whether they conceptualize decision-making as coherent or chaotic and as problem solving or political, which helps readers to make sense of the plethora of views that constitute this domain. The authors also provide a geographic analysis of the authors and research sites that comprise this body of work. The clear Northern/Western geographic bias of the work serves to remind us of the limitations of organization studies and the distance we must travel before we can call ourselves international.

The chapter by Ann Tenbrunsel, Tiffany Galvin, Margaret Neale and Max Bazerman focuses on how work on cognition draws from disciplines outside organization theory, especially the social cognitive psychology literature. The authors describe the way this area has grown as a result of developments elsewhere as well as through management interest in decision-making. This chapter reveals the permeability of organization studies, shaped both by other disciplines and by the world of practice. The emergence of negotiation as a central topic and the dominance of a cognitive orientation are key sites of these influences. The authors also outline the underlying assumptions of work on cognition: that researchers should understand the world as it is, not as how they would like it to be, and that people are not rational. They discuss the tensions between theory and practice, warning against those who make recommendations without the necessary empirical evidence. Nonetheless, they also argue that application strengthens descriptive research.

At the heart of this chapter is a detailed and comprehensive review of social cognition and behavioural decision theory that tracks new developments and recent findings. It provides readers with the substance of the subject: what one needs to know in order to understand where the research and theory on cognition stand today in the broader arena of organization studies. At a second level, the 'story' of cognition also shows how internal and external influences have a bearing on its research, discussion, practice and teaching. Thus, this chapter provides insight into the constitution of the subject that is 'organizational behaviour' and the colonization of the space that it occupies within organization studies. At a third level, the chapter provides insight into a particular sub-discipline: the problems the researchers see; how they define solutions; what their perceptions of progress are; and how they think the area will develop.

Stella Nkomo and Taylor Cox highlight a number of important issues that have emerged around diversity. They point out the tendency, especially among practitioners, to construe diversity as a 'problem', one that requires 'managing'. They also point to the lack of theoretical development that exists in this area. Nkomo and Cox expose some of the struggles that face 'new' areas of research: in this case, one that tries to give voice to identities that have, for most of the history of organization studies, remained nameless, faceless, genderless and colourless.

The authors first discuss the potential contribution of normal science. They review the work on social identity theory, embedded intergroup relations theory, organizational democracy, racioethnicity and gender, and ethnology. By drawing together the insights from these bodies of literature, and building on their empirical findings, the authors indicate ways to construct more sophisticated models of diversity and identity. The authors also discuss a very different approach to diversity, one that could be constituted as contra science (Marsden and Townley 1996). This approach challenges the idea that there are objective, essentialist characteristics that define gender, race, etc. Issues of measurement and scaling become irrelevant because there is nothing to measure, other than various ideological constructs. The production of such socially constituted categories occurs in a specific time, a specific space, and a specific location, serving to create identities into which people are forced to 'fit'. The language we use and the categories we create reflect power relations that permeate us to the extent that we can see no other way of being. This chapter reflects an increased interest in the individual and in identity, and it shows the alternative routes available to researchers of diversity (the normal and the contra) and the different challenges and contributions offered by each.

Arthur Shulman's chapter focuses on work group performance in relation to information technologies. Information technology is important not only in its impact on group performance, the dynamics of which relation are little understood, but also in surfacing those underlying assumptions about communication within the organizations in which work groups are partially embedded. A more informed view of work group performance emerges when these additional factors are included. The chapter suggests major implications for conceptualizing of the relation between technologies and the work groups that use them. These implications are related to a misunderstanding, not so much of group performance or of technology, but of the differences between information and communication. It is through communication that we negotiate the meanings of technological infrastructure. These negotiations are not neutral but morally based. It is within these moral frames that one understands good work group performance. Even seemingly technical and instrumental issues are not innocent of ethical dimensions.

Linda Putnam, Nelson Phillips and Pamela Chapman examine metaphors of communication and organizations. They point out that no other construct pervades organization behaviour more than the term 'communication'. Yet, opinions differ as to whether organizations determine the type and flow of communication; whether communication shapes the nature of organizing; or whether, and in what ways, the two processes co-construct each other. This confusion regarding the nature of the relationship between organizations and communication calls into question the traditional metaphors that we use to study organizations: our images of organizations are largely shaped by the metaphors that represent organizing, not the way communicating and organizing co-produce each other. The authors suggest new metaphors to deal with this dilemma. They draw on seven clusters of metaphors from communication theory and show how those clusters centre on different approaches to communication, recasting our images of organizations by viewing communicating and organizing as coterminous. After providing an overview of the history and development of organization communication, the chapter describes these clusters of related metaphors in the organizational communication literature. By exploring these metaphors, Putnam, Phillips and Chapman are able to demonstrate their implications for new insights about organizing.

Karlene Roberts and Martha Grabowski present a descriptive picture of what technology is and examine the relations between technology and organizations. They note that technology is both a process and a product and, using a selection of definitions, show how authors vary in their approach to technology and use different theories – scientific, economic and political – to explain technological developments. The authors argue that technology is a source of stochastic, continuous and abstract events which, together, involve a variety of challenges for organizational members. They examine three perspectives on technology. First, the technological imperative sees technology as an independent influence on human behaviour and organization properties. Second, strategic choice views technology as a product of ongoing human interaction. It encompasses socio-technical systems, shared interpretations, and Marxist labour process approaches. Third, the authors explore the link between technology and structural/organizational change. Drawing on structuration theory, they conclude that technology is both a cause and a consequence of structure. Roberts and Grabowski conclude their chapter by developing a research agenda for those interested in technology and organization.

Deborah Dougherty writes about innovation, specifically, how organizations can learn to innovate. The evidence, so far, is that organizations have difficulty in doing so, despite the wealth of research on this subject. (Weick and Westley make a similar observation in their chapter.) Dougherty argues that to address the shortcomings of practice, we need to address the shortcomings of research by confronting directly the difficulties that complex organizations have in innovating. Research which is grounded in the concrete activities of innovation, rather than focused on abstractions, and which connects the individual innovation project to the larger organization, offers a possible way forward. By locating the study of innovation within the broader context of organization studies, we can start to draw theory and practice closer together.

Dougherty uses these insights to draw attention to four tensions that arise when modern organizations attempt to innovate. The first tension arises between an internal and an external focus in the attempt to link technology to market needs. The second emerges between the old and the new, as would-be innovators struggle with creative decision-making. The third occurs between attempts to direct strategy and allowing it to emerge while monitoring and evaluating innovation. Finally, a tension between freedom and responsibility comes about in seeking to build a commitment for innovation. Such tensions aid creativity, so the aim is to 'manage' them not eradicate them. Innovative success comes from managing the routine and the mundane as much as the risky and the creative. The chapter offers some ideas for reconciling these tensions creatively by focusing on the microdynamics of culture. In this way, individuals can forge identities that provide them with capacities to bridge and manage the tensions.

Karl Weick and Frances Westley tackle organizational learning, an oxymoron since to learn is to disorganize and increase variety, while to organize is to forget and reduce variety. Consequently, in a similar manner to Dougherty's chapter on innovation, these contributors draw our attention to a series of tensions between organization and disorganization; exploration and exploitation; order and disorder; seeing and not seeing; forgetting and remembering. The authors note the importance of balancing these tensions, not eradicating them: it is *in* the paradox that learning occurs. The authors also relate the issue of learning to the broader context of organization studies: images of organization based on culture and its artifacts are particularly helpful to researchers trying to understand more about learning. Not only do the authors problematize the concept of organizations, they also show the difficulties that accompany the term 'learning'. The idea of collective learning is both more than and different from a straightforward accumulation of individual learning. This analysis also illuminates the central role that language plays in learning, as all learning occurs through social interaction in which language is both the tool and the repository of learning.

Finally, Weick and Westley discuss some of the factors that can help encourage and nurture organizational learning, such as humour, improvisation, and small wins.

Carolyn Egri and Lawrence Pinfield address the place of the natural environment in organization studies. They show how the meaning of the 'environment' has changed in recent years and still has different meanings in different parts of the world. The authors trace the roots of environmentalist theory and contrast different approaches to the natural environment in ecological theory. They contrast and critique the underlying assumptions of the dominant social paradigm with its strong anthropocentric values, various forms of radical environmentalism, and the reform environmentalism perspective. In the second half of the chapter, Egri and Pinfield examine the role of the 'environment' in organization theory and show, for the most part, the environment has meant other organizations rather than referring to the natural environment.

In integrating perspectives on eco-environments and organizations the authors offer two possible directions for the future. If the eco-environment is to take a more central place in organization studies the deep structure of society requires change. They show how a political perspective that focuses on self-interest might be a way to ensure change. In this respect, reform environmentalism offers considerable potential. A second prospect is a reconceptualization of systems theory that incorporates social, technical and ecological aspects. In this chapter, the authors review organization studies in the light of the pressing new demands of our world: notably a demand for appropriate and sustainable management of the natural environment.

Barbara Parker reminds us that the revolutionary aspects associated with globalization come from a variety of sources, occurring simultaneously and interactively. Despite the multiplicity, variety and complexity of these sources of globalization, she points out that business plays a unique role in globalization: business activities stimulate, sustain and extend globalization; the various globalization processes lead to unanticipated needs for alteration and adaptation on the part of business enterprises. Consequently, organizations both instigate global change and are on the receiving end of the global change process. Yet, despite the magnitude of the global 'revolution' and the degree to which business is implicated in it, business activities are, by no means, effectively organized for globalization. There are disagreements concerning the sources of globalization; about where global change is likely to lead; even about whether globalization is a phenomenon worth paying any attention to. Because writers cannot agree on how to define globalization, the ability to 'act global, think local' and become part of the 'global village' worldwide is hindered. If we are confused about what globalization means now, small wonder that we are perplexed about what it will mean for the future.

In her chapter, Parker describes how globalization has emerged from international business practices and research, showing how 'global' business comprises a very different set of activities than 'international' business. She then explores different aspects of globalization: the global economy, global politics, global culture, global technology and the globalization of natural resources. Only by understanding the complexity of globalization are we in a position to address some of the difficult questions that it raises, particularly those that relate to whether globalization offers potential and promise, or simply offers global opportunities for exploitation and abuse. Optimists argue that business centrality will create worldwide opportunities for growth and development; pessimists worry that business centrality will only lead to increased exploitation. The fact is that we do not even know what many of the effects, good or bad, of globalization are likely to be; hence the need for an intensified research agenda for this phenomenon.

## Contexts of Organizing

In this section, we explore the three conventional contexts of organizing: individual, organizational and environmental. These contexts highlight the major themes of the chapter. In particular, we examine the implications of the conversational and linguistic turn for research in these areas. That human beings use language to 'punctuate' (Weick 1969) the array of stimuli they receive is well accepted. Such punctuation has played an important role in defining the reality that researchers create as they explore the phenomena we call organizations. Since knowledge in the field is so closely tied to semantics and discourse, changes in language can be expected to signal important developments in the field of studies. Paradoxically, we use discourse and language to 'deconstruct' the very classification that we use to structure this section.

### The 'Individual' in Organization Studies

For many years, students of organizations divided their field of studies into two categories – micro and macro. This distinction presumed two levels of analysis. The micro level dealt with individual human beings and, to a somewhat lesser degree, individuals working together in groups. The macro level focused primarily on organizations as a whole, especially their structures, and interactions with an even larger system, i.e. the organization's environment. Although recognized as problematic because of the constraints and divisions it imposed on complex social systems, this distinction between micro and macro has long shaped conversation in organization studies. Indeed, it informs the structure of this introduction, and this section explores issues related to a number of chapters covering topics traditionally conceptualized as 'micro'.

Researchers have, however, become increasingly aware of how constant interaction taking place at these different levels blurs categories to the extent that the two levels often overlap. For example analysis of an entrepreneurial firm has, in many respects, turned out to be analysis of an individual. Similarly, Nord and Tucker (1987) found that, when investigating how a small financial organization made decisions, the best approach was to view the organization as a small group. Careful study of the 'micro' chapters in this book also reveals that traditional demarcations cannot be sustained: even though these topics have traditional roots at the micro level, the direction of current inquiry demands more flexible conceptualization.

Bryman (Chapter 2) notes considerable confusion about what leadership constitutes. In everyday discourse, leadership is generally thought to be a property of a person, and initial study of leadership focused on traits by examining personal qualities and characteristics of individuals. Attention in the 1960s shifted to more complex contingency approaches and away from universalistic theories of organizations, paralleling moves from universalistic theories of organization to the adoption of more particularistic frameworks. More recently, Bryman notes that attention has shifted to viewing the leader as a manager of meaning which, along with the development of a transactional approach to leadership, means that to study so-called 'leaders' we also need to study their so-called 'followers'. Contemporary research has shifted even further, to 'dispersed' leadership that is not lodged in formally designated leaders. In short, leadership research has developed in a way that undermines its traditional micro bent and, as Bryman suggests, will rely in the future on more diverse approaches as it engages with broader conversations and controversies within organization studies.

Chapter 4 by Tenbrunsel, Galvin, Neale, and Bazerman is, perhaps, as close to a traditional micro treatment as exists in this book. The authors give a great deal of attention to psychological topics but, even so, they note recent

efforts to apply psychological theories and cognitive perspectives to organizational level behaviour. We may observe that, over time, terms that
were originally treated as individual or micro
processes have been applied to organization level
or macro processes. We now talk of organizational cognition, organization goals and organizational learning. Similarly decision-making
is as much an organization level process as it is
something that individuals do, as Simon noted as
long ago as 1945.

Chapter 3 on decision-making in organizations by Miller, Hickson, and Wilson urges us to
understand decision-making as an organizational *process* even though the concept of
decision-making has roots in neo-classical economic theory, which focuses on rational individuals or entrepreneurs making 'maximizing'
decisions. A key problem for decisions in
organizations is that once they are made, they
have to be (or, at least, some people want them
to be) implemented. Thus, organizational decision-making adds an important new dimension
to the topic that is not directly derived from
individual oriented work and argues for a more
political orientation than the traditional rational
emphasis. Writers like Pfeffer (1992) voice an
extreme position that follows from this perspective, which these authors do not take. He argues
that, when it comes to organizations, decisions
are not made: they simply 'happen'. According
to this view, the decision-making metaphor does
not seem particularly helpful for understanding
organization processes.

The chapter by Nkomo and Cox (Chapter 5)
considers the topic of diversity as organizations
have attempted to react to societal pressures and
provide greater opportunity in the workplace for
individuals who are not white males. The initial
actions of organizations, at least in the US,
occurred in response to government regulations
that provided various incentives for changing
ways of dealing with people from different ethnic
backgrounds and genders. As a result, issues
became defined in terms of demographic classifications. While initially much of the focus was
on race, ethnicity and gender, before long other
demographic categories became involved and the
term 'diversity' emerged. While in some respects
this is a more adequate concept than its predecessors, Nkomo and Cox point out that even
this term is incomplete and they propose a
greater focus on an individual concept – identity.
However, since these issues concern social
categories, the authors argue that an individual
conceptualization of identity is also inadequate.
Hence, they move to social identity theory,
which they present as a cognitive theory that
concerns how individuals classify themselves.
They note that while this theory has traditionally

focused on the individual level, increasingly,
writers have focused on the social context.
Despite exploring several theoretical orientations that help to expand our conception of
diversity, these authors argue that none is
sufficiently complex to deal adequately with the
topic. Combining various individual approaches
offers a more sophisticated understanding, but
the authors suggest that diversity is best viewed
as a description of the total workforce, rather
than as a description of members of minority
groups. Consequently, they direct studies
towards the study of human group identities
more generally and further away from the
traditional ground of 'minority' research.

Chapter 6, 'Putting Group Information Technology in its Place: Communication and Good
Work Group Performance', reveals yet another
example of the blurring of micro and macro.
Traditionally, the study of group performance
was a micro level topic. But Shulman finds
important deficiencies in the tendency of scholars
to examine human work groups as if they are
separate from technology as well as a related
failure in the inability to distinguish between
information and communication. He suggests
that what is needed is an approach which considers
communication in a way that is quite different
from the last several centuries of mainstream
philosophical tradition, one which emphasizes the
importance of communication in negotiating the
meaning of technology (also see Chapter 8).

These chapters – on leadership, cognitions,
identities, and group information technology –
make a strong case for the point of view that
traditional microanalysis may fast be coming to
an end. This conclusion derives from the fact
that the authors of these chapters, researchers
who are at the forefront of inquiry into
traditional micro level questions, have been
forced outside traditional academic boundaries
to capture recent developments in their field.
Nord and Fox (1996) also noted this trend in
considering the treatment of the individual in
modern organization studies. As they evolve,
traditional micro topics are likely to be much
more concerned with macro matters of context
and philosophy, which previously lay hidden
under the frameworks and methods provided by
the traditions of American psychological thinking that provided a major impetus for the
development of organization behaviour.

## Organization as Conversation

A relatively recent way of thinking about
organizations is as conversation. For example,
in their chapter on organizational communication (Chapter 7), Putnam, Phillips and Chapman

argue that it is time to move organizational theory to discursive metaphors. Discursive approaches project a very different organization than the clearly defined and clearly visible entities found in much of the literature. According to Putnam et al., dis~ursive approaches posit equivalence between organization and communication: communicating *is* organizing and organizing *is* communicating. Organizations are texts, created through discourses, which have symbolic meaning for participants. These meanings are open to multiple and unlimited readings even when particular readings and meanings become sufficiently privileged to appear fixed and concrete (e.g. Clegg 1989).

The seeds of a discursive approach to organizing have already been widely sown; some of the fruits are harvested in this volume. For example, while many writers emphasize structural and behavioural prerequisites for technology, innovation and organizational learning, Chapters 8, 9 and 10 emphasize discursive orientations. Roberts and Grabowski (Chapter 8) use a structurational model of technology that collapses structure and technology into a single set of constructs. Technology is both created by human action and used to accomplish human action. Technology may seem like a 'part of the objective, structural properties of the organization' because 'once developed and deployed, technology tends to become reified and institutionalized, losing its connection with the human agents that constructed it and gave it meaning' (Orlikowski 1992: 406; quoted in Roberts and Grabowski, Chapter 8). Technology invites 'several possible or plausible interpretations and therefore can be esoteric, subject to misunderstandings, uncertain, complex and recondite' (Weick 1990: 2; quoted in Roberts and Grabowski, Chapter 8). In other words, to understand technology we must explore meaning and, specifically, how fluid meanings become fixed, reified, objectified and institutionalized. Discursive approaches, with their emphasis on language and multiple meanings, offer particular insight in this regard.

This theme is continued in the work of Dougherty (Chapter 9), who also challenges structuralist and determinist views of innovation. She reminds us that Burns and Stalker (1961) emphasized that innovation is embedded in cultural 'codes of conduct'. She draws our attention to the work of Swidler (1986), who argued that culture brings about change because it provides a 'tool kit' of symbols, stories, rituals, and worldviews that people can use in varying configurations to solve different kinds of problems. Individuals act because they have the tools or skills that make certain actions possible. In other words, actions capitalize on competen-

cies. These culturally situated skills are constituted in conversations that shape behaviour by providing context and frames of meaning (Hardy et al. 1998). Weick and Westley (Chapter 10) also emphasize the importance of language. 'To learn is to use language.' It allows for reflection which, along with action or behaviour, is a critical part of learning. Language is thus both the tool and the repository of learning. These discursive views emphasize learning as a form of meaning creation and sense-giving/making rather than a set of objective techniques designed to process information.

Discursive approaches do not only inform practices of organizational change and action; they also inform processes of theorizing. For example, Richard Whipp (Chapter 1) deconstructs the term 'strategy' to show how strategy constitutes a discourse that has implications for both theory and practice. Whipp reflects a newly evolving approach to the study of strategy that emphasizes strategy as a social and, in particular, a linguistic construction (see Hardy and Palmer 1997). 'Strategy' is thus a construction that serves to make sense of the world, and which is reproduced by a variety of texts and practices. Strategic plans, mission statements, academic papers, articles in *Fortune* and *The Economist*, and strategy task forces, as well as specific practices such as acquisitions, restructuring, and selling in overseas markets, make strategy what it is. Similarly, the way in which research questions are posed, methodologies selected, and publishing conventions imposed, helps to constitute strategy as a field of inquiry (Inkpen and Choudhury 1995). What we know about strategy, we know only because we talk and write about it, and because some activities get talked about as strategy, whereas others do not.

Whipp points out that the use of the term 'strategy' has become commonplace – in hospitals, universities, governments as well as businesses. Inkpen and Choudhury (1995) argue that the discovery of strategy has more to do with how academics theorize than how firms secure competitive advantage. In both cases, talk of strategy is pervasive. The aggregation of actions by researchers (and managers as they learn strategy from popular texts or business schools) in their search for strategy – by attributing a meaning to particular events – has produced a phenomenon from which it has become difficult to escape. In other words, the concept of strategy has become a universal sign which is assumed to exist regardless of whether it does or not, or whether others see it. Strategy has become a discourse so well ingrained in management language that it is commonly accepted as a determinant of success and failure. To have a good strategy, a bad strategy, or no strategy, can discursively make or break the esteem in which an organization is held.

As Whipp notes, strategy as discourse has political implications. Within strategic discourse, some subjects – senior managers, academics, business journalists – have a clear mandate to speak and act, while other actors are invisible. So, by conceptualizing strategy as a discursive construction, we can explore its political implications – by asking who gets to write and read the story (Barry and Elmes 1997). Strategy's widespread acceptance and association with organizational performance advantages those groups associated with 'performance-related' activities; at the same time, others, such as accountants and human resource managers, strive to make themselves more 'strategic' by redefining their work as 'performance-related' (Knights and Morgan 1991). Hence strategic HRM, strategic accounting, and so on.

Discursive approaches thus provide research with an opportunity to be more reflexive about its role in constituting the phenomenon that it studies. By understanding the study of organizations as a discursive enterprise, we are better placed to reflect upon the assumptions we make in studying them, and on the links and gaps between different approaches. In this way, more effective 'conversations' may emerge within the field, thereby improving the quality of teaching, research and practice.

## The Environment: Global Discourse, Local Practice

While the discursive focus discussed above helps to challenge dominant understandings of individual, organization and environment, we would not want to suggest that it is all a matter of language. Language is important because, as Wittgenstein (1972) remarked, it frames our form of life. But our forms of life are also embedded in the material world. Nowhere is this more evident than in matters related to the impact of organizations on their ecological and global environments, as the chapters by Egri and Pinfield and by Parker clearly show. The key issues of these chapters are sustainability and globalization, both relatively recent additions to the lexicon of organization studies.

At face value, who could be against sustainability? After all, to sustain means to support, to nurture, and to foster all positive aspects of the human condition. Yet, although sustainability is clearly a term with positive connotations, the world is mediated by what we produce. What we have produced in the last 200 years are modern organizations, organizations that have sustained people since the industrial revolution. But, while

these organizations have sustained humans, the contemporary meaning attributed to sustainability focuses attention on the considerable costs of doing so. Had current definitions of sustainability been applied earlier, maybe the coal would have stayed in the ground, the atom would have remained intact, and the rainforests would have stood unlogged. Modern, industrial organizations have allowed us to reinvent nature and transform the original site of the species, imprinting human dominance on the world. The dominant social paradigm in organization studies, as Egri and Pinfield point out, advocates unlimited human progress resulting from the exploitation of infinite natural resources. Humankind has been positioned at the centre of all life as the fusion of power and knowledge allowed the transformation of nature by the transformation of society, primarily through organizations that plundered and despoiled nature as they exploited people.

This anthropocentric attitude pervades much of everyday life: people's relationships with nature are based on exploitation and control. Through the domination of nature lies the way to the future, to progress, to growth. The idea of growth is central for organizations in all spheres of society. Thus the natural environment serves human needs, in which organizations are an important tool (Perrow 1979). However, in organization studies, more concern has been expressed for the project guiding the tool and less for the impact of the tool on the surrounding environment. Consequently, management theorists and practitioners work to improve the efficiency of these organizations. The differences between organization theories, even those deemed critical, and management practices, are marginal in this important respect: both have neglected the natural environment. The environment, as far as organization studies was concerned, was, at best, an abstracted phenomenon and, at worst, ignored altogether, as Egri and Pinfield point out.

Today, the environment garners far more attention, not simply in the form of some theoretical construct, but as a repository of material practices into which organizational effects literally spill over. Environmental organizations, such as Greenpeace and Friends of the Earth, have moved organization studies further in this direction through their effects on the way in which we think of the environment and on the consequences of material practices inflicted on the environment. Consequently, in responding to and creating new approaches to incorporate the ecological environment, organization studies have sought to break down traditional demarcations between organization and environment and between discourse and practice.

The ecological environment and the damage done to it respect no national boundaries, as oil-spills and other ecological disasters resulting from global exchange demonstrate. Nor do they respect political differences. Both capitalist and socialist societies use organizations to exploit resources and to reinforce political systems. While the impact of global capitalism is evident, so too is the impact of organizations in state socialist societies, which have produced, and continue to produce, even greater pollution than their capitalist counterparts. So, even where political systems remain relatively closed, their environmental effects do not. The widespread pollution of South East Asia in 1997, which was a result of massive, illegal burn-offs of forestry in Malaysia and Indonesia, continued unabated because of the late arrival of the monsoons. This, in turn, was partly due to El Niño, which makes the western rim of the Pacific unduly dry and the eastern rim unduly wet, and is – some scientists believe – linked to global warming. It is a case in point of how ecological degradation fails to respect national and political boundaries. Degradation of the environment is often one of the first signs of industrial globalization.

If progress is often used to justify natural exploitation, the same term may be as easily pressed into the service of globalization, which is also typically associated with growth and devel-opment. The concept of globalization suggests the phenomenal scale, accelerating speed, incredible diversity, and enormous complexity of international business. Globalization has come into being by incorporating more and more elements of the world into an organization system, creating one world economy that incorporates – *everything*. The concept conveys the integration of worldwide economic activities necessary to capture the expanding market opportunities that exist for businesses capable of coordinating and controlling their operations to maximum effect, as the chapter by Parker discusses. Globalization apparently presents the whole world as an option for identity: we are free to be who we want, where we want, how we want, when we want. In so doing, globalization opens up identities in a thoroughly postmodern way, rather than foreclosing them in conver-gence around one form. One consequence of this is a romanticization of narratives of self, society, and the globalizing world. Exotic stories lodge in different forms of consciousness, encoded in the lore of the elders, the wisdom of the tribe, the news on the airwaves, the sights and sounds that come down the tube, the transmissions through the satellites, optical cables and microwaves. In the postmodern world, are these not free-floating signifiers in dreamtime stories that imagine futures now rather than pasts? But for whom?

We are caught up in the drama of globaliza-tion but, like Plato's slaves, catch only the flickering representation of its appearance, rather than the 'real thing'. For the vast majority of supposedly global citizens who do not comprise part of the global elite, globalization is a word they may not hear and certainly will never experience. Some inhabitants of some countries, without access to modern technology or even old technology, such as phones, faxes, electricity, never even glimpse the global world. Many others, through the proliferation of television and satellite, may have a window through which to view a global world, but only as spectators. And as for the majority, they are far more likely to feel the negative effects of multinational enterprises than the benefits, much less to influence them. In this world, globalization is a one-way street. Global discourse and global practice are always inscribed with power: global power is never absent from global opportunity.

## Conclusions

The time-honoured distinctions between three levels of analysis – the individual, the organiza-tion, and the environment – are clearly breaking down. The previous certainty of discrete, self-contained individuals, fully formed by their roles in organizations, has been shattered. Now identity is a far more complex matter – formed inside and outside organizations, enduring multi-ple commitments and ties and only partially formed by organizational scripts. The light cast by organization studies on these identities refracts and splinters. What once were distinct organizations are now fluid, amorphous collec-tions of stories and conversations, not all of which are recorded by the conventions of research. The environment, which once barely intruded on our theoretical consciousness, now confronts us, demanding practical action.

As conversations in organization studies grow in their specialization, the consequent fragmen-tation renders them less able to deal with the new complexities and nuances. The challenge for the future of organization studies is to create arenas of research and practice where transla-tions of competing conversations can take place. It is to this task that *Managing Organizations* is dedicated.

## References

Barry, D. and Elmes, M. (1997) 'Strategy retold: towards a narrative view of strategic discourse', *Academy of Management Review*, 22(2): 429–52.

Burns, T. and Stalker, M. (1961) *The Management of Innovation*. London: Tavistock.

Clegg, S.R. (1989) *Frameworks of Power*. London: Sage.

Clegg, S.R., Hardy, C. and Nord, W.R. (eds) (1996) *Handbook of Organization Studies*. London: Sage.

Hardy, C. and Palmer, I.C. (1997) 'Re-directions in strategy theory and practice: walking the talk or talking the walk?', in *Management Theory and Practice: Proceedings of the 1997 Anzam Conference*. Melbourne: Monash University.

Hardy, C., Lawrence, T. and Phillips, N. (1998) 'Talking action: conversations, narrative and action in interorganizational collaboration', in D. Grant, T. Keenoy and C. Oswick (eds), *Discourse and Organization*. London: Sage.

Inkpen, A. and Choudhury, N. (1995) 'The seeking of a strategy where it is not: towards a theory of strategy absence', *Strategic Management Journal*, 16: 313–23.

Knights, D. and Morgan, G. (1991) 'Strategic discourse and subjectivity: towards a critical analysis of corporate strategy in organizations', *Organization Studies*, 12: 251–73.

March, J.G. (ed.) (1965) *Handbook of Organizations*. Chicago: Rand McNally.

Marsden, R. and Townley, B. (1996) 'The owl of Minerva', in S.R. Clegg, C. Hardy and W.R. Nord (eds), *Handbook of Organization Studies*. London: Sage.

Mintzberg, H. (1979) *The Structuring of Organizations*. Englewood Cliffs, NJ: Prentice-Hall.

Nord, W.R. and Fox, S. (1996) 'The individual in organizational studies: the great disappearing act?', in S.R. Clegg, C. Hardy and W.R. Nord (eds), *Handbook of Organization Studies*. London: Sage.

Nord, W.R. and Tucker, S. (1987) *Implementing Routine and Radical Innovations*. Lexington, MA: Lexington Books.

Orlikowski, W. (1992) 'The duality of technology: rethinking the concept of technology in organizations', *Organization Science*, 3: 398–426.

Perrow, C. (1979) *Complex Organizations: A Critical Essay*, 2nd edn. Glenview, IL: Scott, Foresman.

Pfeffer, J. (1992) *Managing with Power*. Boston: Harvard Business School Press.

Simon, H.A. (1945) *Administrative Behavior*, 2nd edn. New York: Free Press.

Swidler, A. (1986) 'Culture in action: symbols and strategies', *American Sociological Review*, 51: 273–86.

Weick, K.E. (1969) *The Social Psychology of Organizing*. Reading, MA: Addison-Wesley.

Weick, K.E. (1990) 'Technology as equivoque: sensemaking in new technologies', in P.S. Goodman and L. Sproull (eds), *Technology and Organization*. San Francisco: Jossey-Bass.

Wittgenstein, L. {1972) *Philosophical Investigation*, trans. Anscombe. Oxford: Blackwell.

# 1

# Creative Deconstruction:
# Strategy and Organizations

## RICHARD WHIPP

At a recent conference a sociologist was complaining of the pervasive use of the word 'strategy' during the proceedings. His remarks came close to a paraphrase of Goering's irritation with culture: 'when someone mentions strategy, I reach for my gun'. The episode illustrates the centrality of strategy to the field of organizational studies as well as its latent controversial power. The time is ripe therefore to take stock of the developments around what has become a core subject for social science in general. That the use of the word 'strategy', and its adjective 'strategic', has extended beyond managers and policy-makers to enter common parlance, makes the task all the more urgent.

This essay will explore the problem through four main stages. The first concerns the social construction of the term 'strategy' and its derivatives. The second and main stage examines the way in which the study of strategy has been pursued and its consequent intellectual evolution. The account will highlight the tensions between the economic and the social dimensions which have bedevilled those writing in the strategy and organization area. Stage three gives separate attention to some of the issues which seldom receive treatment in print, such as the differences between US and European approaches. The fourth stage sets out the challenges which the strategy domain faces in the form of major empirical research objects and their attendant problems. Each stage covers an important aspect of the strategy and organization area in the following way.

The first section has twin purposes. The primary task is to provide an account of the genesis and mutation of the term 'strategy'. The intention is not to provide a definitive etymology. Rather, in the spirit of *Keywords* (1976) by Raymond Williams, the section will dissect the layers of meaning which the word and its uses have carried. This will involve a discussion of the possibilities raised by the recent application of discourse analysis in the deconstruction of the language of strategy. The section sets out to demonstrate that these multiple constructions are a vital means of deciphering the varieties of academic use which have arisen. Above all, the section provides telling clues as to the intellectual contests which have ensued.

In the light of these issues, the job of the second section is to offer an overview of the treatment of the strategy and organization subject and its strengths and inherent tension. The distinctive feature of this tension has arisen from the way those involved have dealt with the economic and social aspects of strategy and organizations. An outline of the way the subject's treatment has unfolded will clarify the point. In its first incarnation the study of strategy leaned heavily on its neo-classical supports. The path-breaking work of Chandler (1962) and Ansoff (1965) was notable for its rationalism and driving economic determinism. In providing many of the basic building blocks of strategy studies these early authors held an essentially mechanistic appreciation of the operation of organizations. The 1970s saw sociologists and political scientists enter the domain. Their concerns swung towards the internal social character of organizations as a means of understanding strategy. Their preoccupations stemmed from the political and cognitive aspects of decision-making theory and an awareness of the combined political, cultural and educational processes which shape strategy at organizational level.

The late 1970s and the early 1980s constitute a separate period with two main strands of progress. The first arose directly from the work of Caves and Porter as they brought the techniques of neo-classical industry analysis to bear on 'business policy' (Barney 1986). The economic context of the strategic choices of the firm became the focal point, giving rise to models of 'extended competition' (Porter 1980), 'structure, conduct and performance' (Bourgeois 1984), and 'strategic groups' (Rumelt 1988). The interior processes of the firm remained largely unexplored. Followers subsequently reinforced the neglect by concentrating on the precise 'fit' of organizational form and action with industry and market type (Miles and Snow 1984) – a parallel line of thinking to the population ecologists. The second strand of this era was shaped by the so-called 'new competition' of the 1980s and the corporate trauma expressed in Ford's 'after Japan' project. An attempt was made to combine the economic and the social as a way of unravelling strategy as a means of organizational transformation. The result has been a mingling of those who had been extending the methods of the earlier decision-making approach, the work of institutional economists and the findings of second-generation business policy experts. The hallmark of strategy as a business tool has become its impermanence and fragility in the face of the technological and economic upheavals of the era.

The history of strategy and organization studies has produced a rich cacophony of intellectual and practical themes. However, there appears to have been a number of apparent silences, at least in the formal discussions of the strategy field. Such points are made in corridor and post-seminar exchanges rather than in print. The objective of the third section is to fill some of the silences. This will be attempted by addressing the issue of levels of analysis, the role of time, the non-reflexive character of strategy experts and, thereby, the relationship between the academic and the practitioner.

The challenge facing this diverse body of writers forms the centre-piece of the fourth and last section of the essay. Broadly speaking, the threat comes from new empirical research objects, all of which are wrapped in theoretical barbed wire. The major query has arisen from the received notion of 'global industries' (Bartlett and Ghoshal 1989) generated by business policy specialists on the one hand and yet the apparently enduring relevance of national business systems (Whitley 1992) asserted by organizational sociologists on the other. For some, inter-organizational forms or the transition from public to private sector in both West and East are set to rewrite our comprehension of strategy. The purpose of this fourth section is also to perform some intellectual brokering through the identification of the common problems facing strategy and organization scholars. In particular, the deepening of the interpretative perspective (in alliance with institutional economists) has had precious little impact on those conducting specialist research on strategy and organizations with respect to new technology, manufacturing, or employee relations. It is ironic, for example, how critical studies of post-Fordism and flexibility employ the same rational assumptions of the Porterians.

The overall aim of the piece is to problematize the strategy concept: in other words, to confront the construction of the term, to unravel the epistemological assumptions which have informed the growth of the field, to break the public silences which have overlain key issues, and then, by laying out the problems facing strategy scholars, to suggest future research directions. Put in terms of the need for a map of the area, the chapter will supply a linguistic scale, a conceptual key with which to chart the intellectual topography of the subject; it will also supply the theoretical contours with the main debates acting as grid points. The nature of the field of enquiry means that the cartography will be one which is international and yet, paradoxically, revealing of previously uncharted terrains.

## STRATEGY: BUZZWORD AND KEYWORD

The 1980s witnessed the entry of the word 'strategy' into popular parlance. Given the rise of neo-liberal economics and its political expression in 'Thatcherism' and 'Reaganomics' the *zeitgeist* of the age was acutely commercial. It is virtually unremarked in the 1990s therefore when trade unionists, public sector workers or journalists litter their everyday speech with the words 'strategy' or 'strategic'. The use is often straightforward and its connotations positive. The intention is to convey the importance of the project in question and the elevated status of the aims, and to suggest the sense of coherent thinking and planning which is associated with the label 'strategic'. In July 1994, in a piece of introspection the *Financial Times* (St George 1994: 11) discovered that its pages contained a wide variety of applications. These embraced not only a defensive strategy in US politics, and myriad business uses such as Schroders' investment strategy, but also the adoption of strategy versus technique, used to report the activities of the Soccer World Cup held in the USA that month.

Is this popular use of the word merely a generalized confirmation of the relevance of the term found among managers? Had it become so well rooted in managerial discourse that the new competitive and political conditions of the last decade led to its wider dispersal? Certainly the term promised much, as was shown by Marjorie Lyles's (1990: 363) comment to academics that: '"strategic" has became a buzzword for all disciplines trying to stress the importance of their work.' Schendel and Cool (1988) point out that there was little use of the word in a management context before 1979. In fact, the apparently commonplace use of the word 'strategy' and its derivatives masks the varieties of construction and the layers of meaning which have been generated historically.

Using the approach suggested by Raymond Williams (1976), 'strategy' can emerge as a key-word of modernity rather than just a buzzword. The word 'strategy' derives from the Greek *strategia*, meaning generalship, and was first used in English in 1688. According to *James's Military Dictionary* of 1810, 'strategy' concerns something done out of sight of the enemy whereas 'tactics' were immediate measures taken in front of an adversary. The words 'strategist' and 'stratagem' appear in 1825 and 1838 respectively and are more closely related to the medieval notion of stratagem as an artifice or trick (St George 1994: 11). The translation of strategy into commerce occurred largely through the common theme of competition. Indeed one of the most frequently used reference points for the strategy field has been Andrews's formulation of strategy as 'rivalry amongst peers, for prizes in a defined and shared game' (Andrews 1971).

The dominant figures in the practitioner and academic worlds which employ the term have drawn heavily on the military and competitive sources of the word. Hence Schendel and Hofer (1979: 11) summarized the landmark University of Pittsburgh conference on strategic management by defining the subject as one which 'deals with the entrepreneurial work of the organization, with organizational renewal and growth, and more particularly, with developing and utilizing the strategy which is to guide the organization's operations'. In 1993, Howard Thomas reflected on the subsequent University of Texas 'Strategic Management Frontiers' conference of 1988 and the recent annual meetings of the Strategic Management Society. He concluded that it was possible to identify a shared view of strategy as 'something an organization needs or uses in order to win, or establish its legitimacy in a world of competitive rivalry . . . strategy is what makes a firm unique, a winner, or a survivor' (1993: 3). As the two quotations confirm, the historic notions of generalship and competitive behaviour appear to have been sustained in the academic domain over the past three decades. For many practitioners the assumptions are often stronger. The consultants' newsletter *Strategic Directions* felt able therefore in 1991 to categorize the strategies being used in preceding years according to their principal aim. These included the conglomeration aims of the 1960s, the consolidation objectives in the following decade, through to the 'demassing' of the 1980s and the restructuring strategies of the 1990s (1991: 3). The efficiency of strategy was never in doubt.

Clearly, the leading authorities in the subject have constructed a meaning for the word 'strategy' which both exploits its purposive military origins and invests heavily in the rational expectations of those wishing to direct and manage an organization. However, whilst this representation of strategy, or the strategic management area, has gained widespread acceptance (notably in the USA) it does not reflect the true richness of the domain. In order to uncover the full character and potential of this keyword, it is necessary to go beyond its received usage and explore how it has been studied and researched. In this way, the contribution of organization writers becomes of vital significance.

Perhaps one of the most instructive attempts to link the fields of organization studies and strategy comes in the recent work of Knights and Morgan (1991). They argue that strategy is not simply a technique or body of knowledge. Instead, they apply linguistic theory to suggest that strategy is essentially a discourse. In other words, the very language, symbols and exchanges around the subject of strategy have important outcomes. Strategy is a mechanism of power. People within organizations may be identified according to their participation within the discourse around strategy and its related practices. Those who accept the constructs of strategy (such as market and industry analysis, for example) are able to enjoy the credentials of expertise and position within corporate hierarchies (1991: 251–3). The potency of the discourse around strategy is high because of the promise of complete knowledge. Those who subscribe to the rational, purposive notion of corporate strategy which dominates business schools and Western contemporary management rely on the belief that all is potentially knowable in commercial environments.

Clearly, the attraction of the rational model of strategy is considerable. Indeed, it is possible to point to those professional groups within organizations who have failed in their status and influence because of their inability to embrace the discourse of strategy. UK engineers and designers are cases in point. However, the use of linguistic theory by Knights and Morgan helps one to understand the cleavage among academics over strategy. Broadly speaking, in North America the strength of business schools and, of course, corporate power in society has enhanced the power effects of strategy as a subject. The result has been a market dominance of the rational model of strategy based firmly on neo-classical economics.

Organization writers have sought to enhance their status (and tenure) through clear identification with such orientations to strategy (see Burrell et al. 1994). In Europe, the converse has been true: organization analysts have not been confronted with such power effects. Strategy has been less central and more fragmented as a subject. The result, therefore, has been a deepening of the critical stance in organization studies. Credentials and preferment have simply not been given for competence in the strategy field until very recently. How this divergence has come about requires investigation in its own right.

## The Development of
## the Strategy Field

The fields of strategy and organization present very different profiles in contemporary university departments. As one might expect having read the previous section, strategy writers display an imposing conviction in both the certainty of their analytical frameworks and the relevance of their results to managers and policy-makers. Success, measured in sales and citation indexes, has been remarkable for leading authors such as Porter, fuelled by the management education boom of the 1980s. The keynote for the field's development has been a progressive extension of existing central areas of interest (such as industry analysis or acquisitions) to include new areas (such as alliances and cooperation). The vast majority of work has remained within the paradigm which gives purpose to strategy studies: neo-classical economics.

While the strategy area has its minority quota of renegades searching for alternative perspectives drawing on separate paradigms (see, for example, Bourgeois 1984; Weick 1987), organization studies has them in abundance. The core characteristic of organization scholars (especially in Europe) is the divergent strands of theoretical approaches, analytical frameworks

and empirical targets. Lex Donaldson (1985) described the collection of academics as anarchic. More recently, groups have not only celebrated such diversity but explicitly rejected the paradigm consensus of disciplines such as economics. Moreover, they celebrate the theoretical openness and pluralism of their subject (Burrell et al. 1994: 7–8).

At first sight the two fields of strategy and organization would appear to have conflicting aspirations and value systems. Yet as the successful migrants have shown (see for example Van de Ven et al. 1989) it is possible to apply techniques from one domain to another, to import novel conceptions of central problems and adopt fresh methodologies. Before explaining how such exchanges have been attempted and the prospect for future joint endeavours, there is a need to rehearse the unfolding of the strategy specialism and the opportunities produced.

In his recent book on business strategy, the economist John Kay (1993) is damning of the achievements of the field. In his words, 'the inability to distinguish sufficiently clearly between taxonomy, deductive logic, and empirical observations is responsible for the limited progress which is being made in the development of an organised framework for the study of business behaviour' (1993: 337–8). Casting his eye over the past thirty years, he is clear that the subject of strategy has suffered from the neglect of sociological, legal and alternative economic theory (1993: 362). Is Kay's conclusion appropriate (1993: 337–63)? If so, how can it be accounted for and what are the implications for organization analysts and others?

In many ways the appearance of Kay's challenge has unsettled the strategy field. It is certainly unusual in its attack on the certainties which characterize much strategy writing. The assault may appear to set up a contradiction. Why should a strategy writer and economist seek to undermine the edifice which his discipline had helped to create? The solution lies in the undifferentiated nature of his criticism. As the following pages will show, at various moments in the unfolding of the strategy literature leading works have differed greatly in their level of scholarship. Peters and Waterman (1982) made little use of formal methodologies or theoretical exploration. The same cannot be said of Chandler (1962) or Mintzberg (1978). Kay's assertions are useful though, since they alert us to the wide variations of technical accomplishment which are often concealed by the apparent relevance and potency of strategy texts.

Any reconstruction of the unfolding of strategic management thought is obliged to begin in the 1960s with the rise of strategic planning. It is important to note that the growth of the strategy area did not move through distinct and successive phases. Rather, approaches from the 1960s continued alongside new models which were established subsequently. In its first incarnation the study of strategy was inherently rational and unashamed of its economic determinism. Strategy and planning were synonymous. The essential aim was to assess the environment of the firm, forecast the future of the business and adjust internal structures and resources accordingly (Anthony 1965). Increasingly, high expectations were held of the application of computer technology and the reinforcing examples of planning apparatus erected by national governments. The portfolio matrix and product life-cycle were the most popular devices designed to aid the planning process (Levitt 1965). In many ways, the points made by Knights and Morgan in the previous section on the seductive power of such rational instruments of management are reinforced here. If the dominant, North American understanding of strategy is predicated on a 'knowable environment' then the planning techniques which emerged from the 1960s and 1970s illustrate the point admirably. It has been the simplicity of their core frameworks which has appealed to managers. The growth, maturity and decline of product demand over time in the 'product life-cycle' is one example. The apparently straightforward categorization of products or business areas according to a 2×2 matrix based on market share and market growth (the 'Boston Box') had enormous appeal to executives in multi-divisional firms.

Although planning approaches have continued through the use of information technology, both managers and commentators became impatient with the aridity of the financially driven frameworks and their disturbingly low level of use in practice. The 1970s saw a reaction against the mechanistic appreciation of strategy. Lindblom had offered his 'science of muddling through' in 1959. Yet his contention that planning and execution were seldom orderly and sequential but the victims of chance and the internal working of the firm, was only extensively taken up much later by, for example, March and Olsen (1976) or Mintzberg (1978). The debt to organizational decision-making theory was clear and it was in this era that the notions of strategy as a product of incremental, adaptive, emergent processes began (cf. Pettigrew 1973; Quinn 1980; Frederickson 1983).

The strengths of the processual tradition have been manifold. Taken together, it is the richness of the possibilities for development of the strategy idea which stand out. Mintzberg, for example, not only highlighted the inconsistent and often contradictory process of emergence but also drew attention to the way failed and aborted strategies litter the corporate world. Moreover, the processual writers opened up the opportunity for other organization writers to engage in the exploration of strategy. By exploding the assumption that strategic decisions evolve neatly from analysis through choice to implementation, writers such as Quinn and Pettigrew offered the chance for analysts of organizational power or culture to intervene.

The late 1970s and the 1980s constitute a readily identifiable phase in the evolution of the strategy domain. The diversification and corporate decentralization of the 1960s and 1970s failed to meet the demands of new international forms of competition (Best 1990). The emphasis shifted to a concentration on 'core businesses' (Peters and Waterman 1982) and the clarification of the objectives of the firm in the face of competitive pressures. It was here that Porter's (1980) 'generic strategies' of cost leadership and differentiation gained widespread acceptance. The preoccupations of the decade centred around the concepts of 'strategic intent' – the linking of narrow commercial actions with the broad aspirations of the firm (Prahalad and Hamel 1985) – and the problems involved in creating global strategies to meet world-wide competition (Bartlett and Ghoshal 1989).

The developments of the 1980s have an important contextual ingredient which conditioned the acceptance of the conclusions of Porter, Peters and Waterman and others. Given the epoch-making impact of Japanese manufacturers in Western markets, business people were virtually desperate for texts which offered hope of commercial salvation and, if possible, the restoration of self-belief. Porter's analysis of the extended competitive relations within industries and the resulting stark choices over cost or differentiation emphasis offered the first steps. His constructs took over from the earlier Boston Box frameworks in terms of appeal. Peters and Waterman's eight rules of excellence spoke most directly to the heartfelt need for Western businesses to discover what were the appropriate standards required to compete with the Japanese. Although fundamentally rationalist, Peters and Waterman skilfully combined an appreciation of superficial understandings of culture and structure with key features of the content of strategic choices. It is worth noticing that their work relied in part on the established techniques of the consulting firm McKinsey – a linkage which would repay further academic research more generally in Europe and North America.

In answering the questions posed at the start of this section, Kay's acerbic summary of the strategy field has validity. He is correct that the subject is a long way from exhibiting the characteristics of a discipline, that is, a broad organizing structure around key theories related to a corpus of empirical knowledge. There are many social scientists who pour scorn on the predominance of list-building, the rush to prescription and the statements of the obvious found in key strategy texts. Notwithstanding these doubts, it is possible to take a more generous position, one which recognizes the need to extract the implicit conceptual and analytical features of strategy writing. At the same time, it is necessary to admit the contribution (often indirect) made to the strategy field by earlier students of organization and sociology.

Zan has produced, in this spirit, a typology of the conceptions of strategy which is more helpful than blanket condemnation. The typology (Zan 1990: 96–7) relies on a set of distinctions between various orientations to strategy. These include a 'descriptive' tone concentrating on the reconstruction of events; an 'evaluative' aspect relying on the appraisal of management actions; the policy-making approach, concerned with how firms aspire to develop; and the interpretative perspective, aimed at examining how strategies come into being. Zan argues that it is possible to uncover four main meanings contained within the field over the last thirty years. The first is the 'evaluative policy-making' understanding of strategy which regards managerial volition as absolute; a core activity of strategic management therefore becomes evaluation of the internal and external conditions for the success of given policies. The second is 'descriptive policy-making' which concentrates on the intentions and choices of management from within the firm with a view to completing given projects but not necessarily as means to market dominance (Chandler 1962). The third version is labelled the 'evaluative/interpretative' approach. Here, as was suggested for the 1980s, strategy is seen as the means of achieving 'fit' between firm and environment and is judged according to how sustainable that conduct by management might be (cf. Miles and Snow 1984). The last category, the 'descriptive/interpretative', emerges from the writers we identified in the 1970s in the more processual orientation to strategy. In this category strategy is equated with the logic of the firm's behaviour within a 'stream of actions' (Mintzberg 1978). The logic is established by reference to the dialectical relationship between the firm, its internal systems and its environment.

As with all typologies the fourfold categorization says nothing of the scope of work completed under each type. Its main service though is to point to the wider range of constructions of meaning of the term 'strategy' in existence than most people in the organization studies and related areas assume. It is instructive that critical studies of post-Fordism and the flexible organization (Gilbert et al. 1992), for example, employ broadly similar rationalist notions of strategy as, say, Porter or Chandler. To take a current example, the debaters around the issue of 'flexible specialization' treat the statements and actions of managers in a very literal way. Seldom does one encounter an appreciation of the accidental emergent quality of a given production policy or the inherent contradictions of market understandings. More pointedly, the typology of Zan alerts one to the existence of more sophisticated conceptions of management and the firm in the strategy world than is commonly recognized. Moreover, these emergent understandings cry out for assistance from the organization camp. Some examples from strategy writers will illustrate the claims.

As far back as 1984 Bourgeois bemoaned the restrictive influence of industrial organization economics, contingency theory and population ecology models of organisation on the development of the strategic management field. As he put it, informed by these frameworks, management 'may as well resign itself to succumbing to the matrix of deterministic forces presented by the environmental, technical, and human forces that impinge upon its freedom of choice. At best, management becomes a computational exercise.' The reductionism of such models eliminated much of the richness that characterizes the strategic management process, and constrained the 'advancement of the strategic management discipline' (1984: 586). Above all, Bourgeois was arguing for basic recognition of the way organizational actors make strategic choices which in turn determine how a firm discovers itself within a given context. He went on to plead for the adoption of a dialectical view and the recognition of reciprocal causality. It is tantalizing that such strategy writers had made no use of Giddens or his concepts of structuration (Giddens 1981). The potential is almost breathtaking to contemplate. Rather than seeing structures within the organization or its environment as separate, 'out there', or distant from a social actor, it is possible to link the two intimately. In other words, managers do not only operate within corporate structures (such as divisions or business units): they are part of their creation. If this is accepted, then organizational sociologists have much to offer the strategy field in their techniques of researching action, perception and social construction.

Other students of strategy in the 1980s made equally telling *cris de coeur* which remained unanswered by organization scholars. Chaffee (1985) concluded that the strategy concept had emerged with three distinct 'mental models' – the linear, the adaptive and the interpretative – and that conflicting views abounded. In particular, she maintained that such differences were rarely analysed, and that the strategy construct was multi-faceted and evolving 'to a level of complexity almost matching that of organizations themselves' (1985: 89). Yet instead of seeking support from the emerging innovations in organizational analysis (outlined in the introduction) to pursue the potential in her questions, Chaffee stopped. Her rather tame conclusion was that the three models represented stages through which organizations pass (1985: 96).

In 1988, another strategy professional encapsulated the huge benefit of linking organization and strategy research. Wensley (1988: 21) considered that 'a concept of organisation is inevitably bound with most of what is written and researched in the field of strategic management.' Given the attempts to reveal the implicit richness of the strategy theme, together with the latent possibilities of bringing more recent organizational frameworks to the area, it would be unfortunate if the opportunity were missed again. An illustration of those possibilities is supplied by brief examination of the related empirical areas of markets and competition.

## Strategy and Organizations: Markets and Competition

From the vantage point of the UK especially, it would seem that hardly an aspect of the public or private sector has escaped the impact of the forces of market relations and competition. The two words 'market' and 'competition' became the hallmarks of one of the most powerful political imperatives to drive a series of government administrations over the past fourteen years. The core belief of the new right rested on the assumed superiority of market relations to deliver competitive efficiency. The effects have been widespread. Simultaneously, market mechanisms have been introduced within organizations (for example, through profit centres), across professions and 'knowledge workers', and throughout the public sector in the form of tendering or the 'internal market' of the British National Health Service (NHS) (McNulty et al. 1994). In spite of the profound economic and social implications of these programmes, in the UK and elsewhere, the strategy and organization scholars have mounted separate investigations of the phenomena. The contention of this section is that market relations and competition offer one of the most promising sites for cooperation between the two fields.

Much of the reason for the mutual antipathy of the work of strategy and organization analysts stems from the contribution of economic theory to the former. Those who constructed the world of *Homo economicus*, and supplied the basic concepts of monopoly, oligopoly and perfect competition, came predominantly from the micro-economics tradition (Jain 1985). Students of organizational behaviour have been virtually allergic to such work given the micro-economics training of many strategy specialists. The result has been strategists writing on competition with the reliance on: rational, profit-maximizing behaviour by all economic agents, the absence of chronic information problems, little time for the ignorance shown routinely by firms and consumers, and the preoccupation with equilibrium states (Hodgson 1988: 4–21).

Many of the conceptions of competition and markets displayed by the leading strategy writers of the 1980s (commonly referred to as the industrial organization or IO school) exemplify the economic rationalism of their trade and would try the patience of the most forbearing organization scholar (cf. Barney 1986). The emphasis among the strategy specialists of the last decade has been therefore on explaining the creation of strategies which exploit a firm's uniqueness (Lenz 1980), heed the rivalry among competing firms and suppliers/buyers (Porter 1980) and take account of the classification of the industry involved (Gilbert and Strebel 1988).

It is understandable that many social scientists have been repelled by the assumptions of the IO writers and expended no further effort on penetrating the field. However, if they had battled through the undergrowth of this part of the strategy territory they might have encountered more useful inhabitants: the 'new competition' school. These academics are interesting for their heretical attitudes to strategy and their deployment of not just alternative forms of economic theory but a range of disciplinary models and techniques. The arch-heretics were Hayes and Abernathy (1980) who accused corporate USA of 'managing our way to industrial decline' in a now celebrated *Harvard Business Review* article. The pair attacked the dominant logic of the strategy experts head-on. Their argument centred on the way return on investment-based financial controls and portfolio management techniques (supplied by the authors mentioned in the first section) had stifled innovation. They challenged the accepted notions of life-cycle models of the IO school and rejected the 'static optimization' paradigm. Above all, they mobilized the Schumpeterian theory of competition (Schumpeter 1950: 82–3) to argue that technological innovation within the firm could create new sources of demand which in turn might provoke wholesale restructuring of existing markets and industries (Abernathy et al. 1983).

Subsequently, their followers have gone further into the role of management and the problems of innovation. Sadly the intellectual demands which their heresies created have not been heard by organizational scholars. In spite of the opportunity to link strategic management, technological innovation and aspects of the social organization of production (in Bill Abernathy's shorthand, 'bringing together technological hardware and human software') few organization specialists picked up the gauntlet (Whipp and Clark 1986); most seemed unaware of it ever having been thrown down. What has the organization literature been missing?

In brief, the new competition writers were drawing on the institutional economists (Langlois 1986; Hodgson 1988), a group who rejected the deterministic and static models of neo-classical micro-economics. Institutional economists see market relations and competition as the product of human experience. Market relations are seen as informed by a variety of 'social institutions', that is, agreed forms of behaviour which specify conduct in recurrent situations (Schotter 1981: 11); examples include property rights or employment contracts. Moreover, institutionalists have sought to explain competition as a sequence of events taking place in real time, involving people who have highly imperfect information and for whom specific benefits are often transitory. Investigations of UK industry have been mounted by institutional economists using such a perspective. The results have been telling but isolated. Elbaum and Lazonick (1986) argued that social institutions in Britain restrained the growth of mass production techniques and the forms of corporate coordination found in the USA, Germany and Japan. The interlocking constraints included the retention of family-controlled firms, the absence of bank involvement within industry and the inability of education systems to provide managers and applied scientists (1986: 6). Lewchuk (1987), in the same vein, explained the differences in the technological base of the US and British motor industries by reference to the social institutions surrounding the effort bargain at shopfloor level (cf. Whipp 1990).

In truth, strategy experts and organization analysts have remained apart, to the detriment of all concerned. It is frustrating that the wealth of analytical tools and empirical material generated by organizational scholars has been so seldom engaged with the institutional and new competition work. Both groups would be beneficiaries of collaboration via, minimally, simple exchange. In broad terms, the organization specialist could supply much sharper tools for exploring the subjective dimension of economic agents, most notably management. Conversely, institutional economists would offer organization analysts an expanded set of frameworks for comprehending a market. Taken together the promise of unlocking the motors which drive the dynamic of competitive relations is considerable.

It is not the intention to suggest such cross-disciplinary endeavour is unknown; the point is its rarity. Gospel's (1993) work on British labour and management or Scott and Lodge's (1985) study of competition in the USA are worthy examples of the synthesis of institutional economics, organization theory and industrial sociology. Some of the commentators on strategy, grouped under the interpretative label in the first section, have made sporadic connections between their adaptive view of management and the social institutions which shape the market (for example, Teece 1987). The sceptic may well comment, 'does it matter?' The apparent dominance of market structures and the espousal of competition by the previous opponents of liberal capitalism led Fukuyama (1989) to proclaim 'the end of history'. The implications are non-trivial, to say the least. Given the commitment of resources in the name of market efficiency it smacks of negligence for academics to remain locked within their disciplinary stockades.

Perhaps some indication of the intellectual benefits and an example of the research involved will help support the need for more collaboration and exchange. In conceptual terms, bringing together institutional economics, an interpretative perspective on strategy and organizational theories, points to a more demanding appreciation of management and competition. Organizations may aspire to Chandler's (1962) original definition of strategy as the 'determination of the basic long term goals of an enterprise, and the adoption of courses of action and the allocation of resources necessary for carrying out those goals'. In practice, strategy is far more complicated. Allegedly objective decisions relating to finance or products are conditioned by the social character of an organization. Business strategy is by no means rational. Managerial action is notable for the limits of its impact and the way it is victim to chance. Organization specialists are well equipped to examine the intricacies of the interior life of the firm. Who better to deconstruct strategic management than the academics for whom structure, culture and politics are their stock-in-trade? Such forces transform given strategic intentions and account for the ambiguity of much managerial activity. The institutional economists have highlighted the impermanence of market relations. Organizational researchers should find it intriguing to supply complementary explanations of the instability and interdeterminacy of the behaviour of those responsible within organizations for activity in the market (Whittington and Whipp 1992). Studying the attempted creation of the internal market in the UK NHS reinforces the point. Our conclusion was that the market supplies no more unambivalent sources of managerial control than the earlier Fordist hierarchical variant. The strategy of employing market relations is characterized by compromise, contradiction and unintended consequences.

Research which draws on the range of conceptual and analytical devices offered by the specific types of organization, economics and strategy scholars outlined here, promises much. Put simply, the result would be an account of strategic management and market forms which reveals how they are socially constructed, their inherent irrationality and, not least, their conspicuous instability. Empirical targets for those willing to operate this intellectual equipment are growing apace. Nonetheless, if market relations and competition offer a strong example of a productive combined assault then the lost opportunities are equally apparent. In many ways the silences among strategy scholars over certain issues are almost deafening. Three examples of such silences may be instructive for both illustrating the essential character of the area and yet indicating possible lines of future development.

## RESOUNDING SILENCES

The silences or absences which stand out in the corpus of strategy and organization writing are threefold: they include the issues of levels of analysis, the problem of change and time, and the non-reflexive nature of most strategy authors.

### Levels of Analysis

The levels problem is ironic. The earlier strategy experts of the industrial organization literature (Barney 1986) were at pains to emphasize the goal of strategic management as the maximization of the unique strengths of a firm within its markets and industry settings. The general acceptance of Porter's (1985) form of industry analysis or the popularity of strategic intent (Prahalad and Hamel 1985) shaped by the industry context has been readily visible. Yet, very few strategy or organization experts have

sought to link systematically and investigate the multiple linkages which connect firm-level behaviour and the operation of markets *and* industries. Perhaps the silence is partly explained by the vested interests of specialists who have excavated the area along distinct channels such as industry groups or value chains. What is required to fill the silence is a more inclusive orientation which uses economic and social modes of analysis to open up the array of intersecting relationships.

Constructive steps in this direction are suggested by Boons and Roberts (1994) who align a resource-based view of the firm with industry-level understandings. As their recent work shows, making such linkages obliges them to combine economic laws with the subjective determinants of exchange relationships. In addition, such combinations require the study of an array of organization and external features. The result is a joining of: the technical resources of the firm and their means of conversion into final products or services; the highly indeterminate organization processes which mobilize the firm's tangible and intangible assets; the way resources and capabilities face often incomplete markets; and how each may fall victim to unpredictable outcomes arising from the contradictory perceptions of suppliers, new entrants, intermediaries and regulators.

### Change and Time

The second absence concerns the subject of change and time. To many the assertion that anything like silence exists around the words 'change', 'strategic change' or 'change management' would seem perverse. Such phrases appear almost universally in the subtitles of academic papers, while the cliché of managing change is applied to almost every management area from IT to supply chain development. Of course, strategic change has been researched by academics anxious to synthesize analytical perspectives from the economics, strategy and organization traditions (see, for example, Kanter 1990; Pettigrew and Whipp 1991).

Nevertheless, even allowing for the work of the process scholars outlined earlier in this chapter the central problem of time is at once generally acknowledged but not the subject of searching examination. The work of Miller and Friesen (1980) or more recently Greenwood and Hinings (1988) has made great strides in developing the conceptual framework necessary to describe the momentum of change, transition and adaptation in organizations. The problem has been that very few writers on strategic change have ever challenged their mathematically based, linear and Newtonian conceptions of time, either in their theory-building or in their empirical investigations (Whipp 1994; Wilson 1992). The resulting lacuna is disturbing for two main reasons. First, strategy analysts are missing the opportunity to mobilize the abundant richness of time ordering systems found within organizations (for example, subjective industry maps versus rational planning manuals). It is this diversity of understandings of time which goes a long way to explaining the uneven rhythms of the process of corporate change and its indeterminacy. Second, in the practical sphere, the claims that business processes are amenable to 're-engineering' along a single time dimension, for example, are in danger of reducing our appreciation of the multiple sources of time ordering by people in contemporary organizations.

## Reflexivity

The third major silence is perhaps the most serious and potentially debilitating for the strategy territory. It is no surprise that strategy scholars who predominantly regard their subject as applied and resting on neo-classical economic assumptions show little evidence of reflexivity. As the previous sections have shown, the aim of the majority of such writers is highly positivist: to understand the problem of renewal and growth in order to provide better guidance for the strategic direction of an organization (Lyles 1990: 363). Critical self-appraisal of motivations or core beliefs by those in the strategy literature is not widespread. *Pace* Kay's (1993) criticisms, the conviction of most North American strategy academics is that the industrial organization framework (see earlier) provides a common foundation for their work. The variety of their research objects, from 'intrapreneurship' to international strategic alliances, is made possible, they argue, precisely because of this common platform. It is telling that attempts to question the paradigmatic and theoretical starting-points of the strategy areas have come from those whose training lay outside (see, for example, Zan 1990; Johnson 1987). In a similar way, the questioning of the motives and assumptions which underpin the actions of those responsible for strategy within organizations has received correspondingly scant attention. Whilst process analysts take seriously the cultural and political diversity within an organization (see, for example, Kunda 1992) few of their number have addressed the wider social and political conditioning of the senior management. As Willmott (1993b) points out, the spread of corporate culture programmes, for example, has seen little attempt to scrutinize the

assumptions and prescriptions of the 'excellence' movement and its ideological base. The only exception currently to be found is in volume 9 of the 'Advances in Strategic Management' series (Shrivastava et al. forthcoming) – *Critical Perspectives on Strategic Management* – which observes that 'one source of progress in a scientific field is its ability to engage in critical self-reflection.'

The reason for emphasizing the seriousness of the need for greater reflexivity is partly due to the intellectual and practical opportunities which beckon. As will be apparent from the earlier pages of this chapter, the strategy specialists founded their work on the conviction that it was possible to capture the workings of markets and competition and to advise practitioners accordingly. The pervasive take-up of 'Boston Box' or 'product life-cycle' devices is testimony to the relevance of such work (Kay 1993: 340–9). However, it is arguably research which has questioned the fundamental nature of strategy (cf. Knights and Morgan 1991) which offers the most exciting practical insights. In short, reflexiveness could lead to more profound research and equally challenging applied projects.

Mintzberg's work provides an instructive example in the way he criticizes the narrowness of much strategy writing. His central argument is that organizations should engage in strategic thinking rather than the planning espoused by many experts. Strategic thinking is about synthesis, involving intuition and creativity; it is not constrained by established categories. To paraphrase Mintzberg, strategy-making should occur outside the 'boxes' or conventional perspectives. His iconoclastic approach attacks the fallacious assumptions that prediction is possible, that strategists can be detached from the subjects of their strategies and that the strategy-making process can be formalized (Mintzberg 1994). Others have offered practical advice by adopting a similar questioning of the taken-for-granted truths of strategic management (for a review of competing theories and multiple diagnoses, see Edmondson 1994). Extending such interrogation to include the highly active critical literature within organization studies would be invigorating in academic terms. Given the current experience of the disenchantment of managers with 'fad theories', a more reflexive mode of strategy and organization research could well appeal to practitioners for its candour.

## FUTURE POSSIBILITIES

Many of the silences in the strategy area are so resounding because of the needs which are not being met and the opportunities which risk being missed. In this sense, much of the foregoing argument about the dominant tendencies amongst strategy writers points to the future direction which the field may take. The potential avenues of study are vast, as surveys of academics and practitioners have found (Lyles 1990: 369). However, four areas give a strong indication of such future possibilities, namely: the nature of industries, new technology, global operations and the public sector.

Although micro-economists have been to the fore in the study of industries, alternative understandings have arisen from collaboration between strategy and organization specialists. Sometimes writers from either area have usefully employed one another's concepts and frameworks.

Management writers such as Huff (1982) and Spender (1989) argue that industries are informed by 'dominant logics' or 'recipes' that limit decision-making at firm level. Industry studies from within the broad strategy area have shed light on the collective mindset of an industry as a key influence on competition. Porac and Thomas (1992) maintain that managerial cognitive structures contain the consensually held beliefs within an industrial community. If they stabilize, the structures become interpretative frames which shape the way managers make sense of actions and circumstances outside the firm. The authors contend that industrial belief systems mature through 'strategic paradigms' as managers make resource allocation decisions and 'reputational orderings' as all involved evaluate the relative strength of firms. Meanwhile, others from outside the North American strategy stable have extended the coverage of the non-material features of an industry. Melin and Hellgren (1993) claimed that a specific 'industrial wisdom' has conditioned the strategic choices of firms in the Swedish paper industry over time. Durand (1993) has explored the dynamics of cognitive technological maps and how firms draw on them to adapt to market demands. Shearman and Burrell (1987: 330) point to the social structures which support such cognitive processes. The 'community' and 'formal and informal networks' and the 'club' forms represent the specific formations of power, status and negotiated order found at different stages of the industry life-cycle.

The outcome of these authors' work is that the meso-level phenomenon of the industry is a worthy object of enquiry for two main reasons: (1) it is a vital arena for understanding the interior life of organizations; and (2) it contains rich potential within its non-material aspects for comprehending the collective and inter-organizational aspects of economies. The sector concept has provided one means of releasing these possibilities (cf. Whipp and Clark 1986: Chapter 1; Child 1988; Rasanen and Whipp 1992). Furthermore, it might prove a useful meeting point where various organizational sociologists might apply their expertise to the issues of strategic management and competition.

The term 'sector' refers to a historical formation of complementary, co-evolving business activities. It is often, though not invariably, attached to specific locations, such as a region or country. A sector includes organizations which provide similar goods or services together with those who regularly transact with them in supplying, servicing, regulatory or customer roles (Rasanen and Whipp 1992: 47). Mature sectors may exhibit formal social networks but their capacity to coordinate the whole may be limited. Sectors cannot be taken as governance structures in a strong sense; rather they are arenas of cooperation and competition. Given this community of diverse actors, conventional IO economics is ill equipped to capture the social and political processes concerned.

The forest sector is a useful example (see Lilja et al. 1992). Forestry has certain economic features, such as vertical integration, capital intensity, and low and cyclically dominated returns, which shape the forms of business organization. In reality, the pattern of organization cannot be explained by reference to these economic aspects alone. National forest sectors (notably in Finland, Sweden, Canada and the USA) can be distinguished by the respective combination of social networks, ownership and control relationships and their relation to government. In many senses, the sector is an accomplishment of multiple actors with often diverse logics of action. The sector is never a completed project but is a contradictory whole in a state of relative impermanence and tension, with constantly emerging alternative organizational solutions.

Even in this brief rendition of the sector concept, one hopes the opportunities for intervention by organizational/industrial sociologists, historians and certain breeds of strategy scholars begin to appear. The linkage of cognitive, economic and socio-political perspectives raises the prospect of much fuller accounts than are currently available of not only nationally based sectors but their international operation (Porter 1990). In turn, these broader analyses of sectors could help clarify the character and emergence of national business systems (Whitley 1992: Chapter 1). This might take the form, for example, of testing the extent to which national institutions are able to shape the evolution of individual sectors, or conversely, how far the changes in national business systems or national systems of innovation are accounted for by the shifts in sector patterns of development.

The potential for collaborative research which blends the theories and techniques of strategy and organization studies is considerable. As the example of the sector shows, the research canvas is extensive. Allying analytical frameworks around such fundamental problems (as with industry form and operation) can be used with other major segments of economic life. New technology is a strong example. The strategy field has clearly identified information technology as a critical feature to be managed, given the aspiration of strategists to supply appropriate direction to the growth and renewal of the firm. Equally, organization scholars have been drawn to the rise of 'new organizational forms' which challenge many of the precepts behind previous notions of rational bureaucracy. It is interesting that both sets of writers have arrived at similar positions. Two parallel projects make the point. Rockhart and Short, in their 'management in the 1990s' programme at MIT, conclude that 'organizations today are disintegrating - their borders punctured by the steadily decreasing costs of electronic interconnection among firms, suppliers, and customers' (1989: 7). Meanwhile Lash and Urry (1987) are able to supply highly appropriate frameworks for the social and economic 'disorganization' of capitalist systems in the late twentieth century. The problem of technology is so quintessentially a defining feature of the postmodern age that the need for synthesis of strategic and organizational research has reached screaming point (for examples of bold attempts in this spirit, see Scott-Poole and Van de Ven 1989).

A similar pressure is building in the area of international business. The advent of 'globalization' has been trumpeted for some years. A rich vein of research from strategy academics has produced a mature appreciation of the international operations of business. A distinction is drawn now between the fragmented multinational strategies pursued by Western firms and the globally integrated approach of the Japanese. The technical debate over the optimum strategies has been pursued around the issues of global marketing, world-scale efficiencies and the use of cross-subsidization between markets. Put in a summary way, the current consensus emphasizes the study of 'corporate capabilities'. The aim is to generate global efficiency, national responsiveness and an ability to exploit knowledge on a world-wide basis simultaneously (Bartlett and Ghoshal 1989). The conclusions of the international business specialists are dripping with questions that could be explored by organization analysts. The core concept of organizational capabilities (Prahalad

and Hamel 1985), to take one instance, could be developed by such analysts applying their understanding of the processes of innovation, learning and adaptation – pressures which have been assumed rather than researched by their strategy colleagues. The critical excavation of the interior life of the transnational organization beckons as one of the overwhelming collaborative projects for the next decade.

The third example of the type of area where the strategy and organization fields may develop is in the public, or not-for-profit, sector. Here the work of organization experts had led the way but could well benefit from adopting the tools of strategic management. The attraction of the public sector as a laboratory of managerial experiment is well known. Public services have been reorganized through privatization, decentralization and the use of contractual and 'quasi-market' apparatus. The changes have occurred against a backcloth of government financial crises and have been legitimated by reference to the language of the sovereign consumer (McNulty et al. 1994). While organization departments have offered subtle interpretations of the combination of restructuring, improved efficiency and highly imperfect markets, their work is stunted by their crude appreciation of strategy. Quite apart from the pressing need for thorough empirical investigation of such a shift within Western economies, the chance to stretch and test strategy concepts established within the private sector offers a substantial prize.

Certainly, these three areas of future development in no way exhaust the schedule of research objects which have assembled in recent years. Others include the market and diffusion of managerial knowledge, the establishment of commercial and industrial entities *de nouveau* in former communist states, and the elevation of ethical and environmental dimensions of business life. All are amenable to the synthetic approaches described here.

## CONCLUSION

This chapter began with an acknowledgement of the sensitivities which bedevil the relationships across the academic division of labour. The hope of this review is that it might, at least, persuade some of our colleagues in the organization studies sphere to put away their metaphorical guns. Such tensions, however, are indicative of the vibrant character of the strategy debate.

The approach taken in this treatment of the area has been unambiguously positive. As the first part of the piece tried to show, military and one-dimensional views of 'strategy' have dominated its use. Yet it is the diversity of constructions of the term which give rise to contention and the hope of fruitful exchanges. The dialectic has not been well represented in the past. Instead, narrow conceptions of strategy have been allowed to dominate, almost by default. The time for a corrective therefore was overdue. The core of the chapter has been at pains to draw attention to the varieties of perspective and use of the strategy concept. The evolutionary path from mechanistic strategic planning, through cognitive decision-making formats, to the resurgence of business policy and processual orientations has been as fragmented as it has been divergent. It is unsurprising that reductionist versions of the subject of strategy are retailed across the business studies field.

The contention of this essay is that the term 'strategy' is usefully problematic. There is no denying the ideological turbulence which surrounds it and the difficulties which new entrants face in coming to terms with such cleavage. Yet if the past thirty years show anything, then it is that where specialists have combined or attempted to mix organization and strategy frameworks, genuinely searching progress has occurred. In short, strategy is too important to be annexed by a single discipline.

The signs for synthetic and boundary-crossing projects are currently good. The 'death of certainty' (Appleby et al. 1994) has been marked by the outbreak of epistemological doubt across many disciplines in North America. The challenges of multi-culturalism, a new world economic order and demographic turmoil have made certain academics receptive to alternative orientations. It is instructive that in the results of a recent questionnaire of strategic management, 'organization theory' was identified as the third main subject which will have 'the most impact on strategic research in the next ten years' (Lyles 1990: 370). In the previous pages, the examples of industry form, new technology, globalization and new public management provide an indication of the possible sites for stretching the joint endeavours of strategy and organization scholars.

The central assertion of the exchange or reshaping of the instruments of strategy and organization academics is uncomfortable for many. Ideology, epistemology and methodology separate and divide. Moreover, the calls for the strengthening of field boundaries in order to ward off 'hostile takeover' by leading figures such as Pfeffer (Burrell et al. 1994: 7) highlight the problems involved. Yet, rather than seeing openness and pluralism as weaknesses in these respective subject areas, the converse could be true. The defining character of organizations at the close of the twentieth century is the fragility of their shapes and the turbulence born of the co-existence of order and disorder (Sminia 1994: 53) in their strategic processes. Such ferment would be best approached by academics if they were to take seriously their own intellectual turmoil. Reference to Kuhn's model of the dynamics of scientific knowledge development may be of help. Those attempting to research such order and disorder should be prepared to work at the process of struggle which is impelled by an accumulation of anomalies in existing theories and which stimulates alternative theorizing (Willmott 1993a: 683). Such creative deconstruction is to be welcomed.

## REFERENCES

Abernathy, W., Clark, K. and Kantrow, A. (1983) *Industrial Renaissance: Producing a Competitive Future for America*. New York: Basic Books.

Andrews, K. (1971) *The Concept of Corporate Strategy*. Homewood, IL: Irwin.

Ansoff, H. (1965) 'The firm of the future', *Harvard Business Review*, 43(5): 162–78.

Anthony, T. (1965) *Planning and Control Systems: a Framework for Analysis*. Boston: Harvard University Press.

Appleby, J., Hunt, L. and Jacob, M. (1994) *Telling the Truth about History*. New York: Norton.

Barney, J.B. (1986) 'Types of competition and the theory of strategy: towards an integrative framework', *Academy of Management Review*, 11(4): 791–800.

Bartlett, C. and Ghoshal, S. (1989) *Managing across Borders*. Boston: Harvard Business Review.

Best, M. (1990) *The New Competition: Institutions of Industrial Restructuring*. Cambridge: Polity Press.

Boons, A. and Roberts, H. (1994) 'The resource-based view of the firm'. Paper presented to the 2nd Workshop on Accounting, Strategy and Control, EIASM, Brussels, September.

Bourgeois, L.J. (1984) 'Strategic management and determinism', *Academy of Management Review*, 9(4): 586–96.

Burrell, G., Reed, M., Alvesson, M., Calás, M. and Smircich, L. (1994) 'Why organization? Why now?', *Organization*, 1(1): 5–18.

Chaffee, E. (1985) 'Three models of strategy', *Academy of Management Review*, 10(1): 89–98.

Chandler, A. (1962) *Strategy and Structure*. Boston: MIT Press.

Child, J. (1988) 'On organizations and their sectors,' *Organizational Studies*, 9: 13–19.

Donaldson, L. (1985) *In Defence of Organisation Theory*. Cambridge: Cambridge University Press.

Durand, T. (1993) 'The dynamics of cognitive technological maps' in P. Lorange, B. Chakravarthy, J.

Roos and A. Van de Ven (eds), *Implementing Strategic Processes: Change, Learning and Co-operation*. Oxford: Blackwell. pp. 394–410.

Edmondson, A. (1994) 'Three faces of Eden: the persistence of competing theories and multiple diagnoses in organization intervention research'. Unpublished paper, Harvard Graduate School of Business Administration.

Elbaum, B. and Lazonick, W. (1986) *The Decline of the British Economy*. Oxford: Clarendon Press.

Frederickson, J. (1983) 'Strategic process research: questions and recommendations', *Academy of Management Review*, 8(4): 565–75.

Fukuyama, F. (1989) 'The end of history?', *Financial Times*, 19 October: 2.

Giddens, A. (1981) *A Contemporary Critique of Historical Materialism*. London: Macmillan.

Gilbert, N., Burrows, R. and Pollert, A. (eds) (1992) *Fordism and Flexibility: Divisions and Change*. London: Macmillan.

Gilbert, X. and Strebel, P. (1988) 'Developing competitive advantage', in J. Quinn, H. Mintzberg and R. James (eds), *The Strategy Process: Concepts, Contexts and Cases*. Engelwood Cliffs, NJ: Prentice-Hall. pp. 70–9.

Gospel, H. (1993) *Markets, Firms and the Management of Labour: the British Experience in Historical Perspective*. Cambridge: Cambridge University Press.

Greenwood, R. and Hinings, C. (1988) 'Organizational design types, tracks and the dynamics of strategic change', *Organization Studies*, 9(3): 293–316.

Hayes, R. and Abernathy, W. (1980) 'Managing our way to industrial decline', *Harvard Business Review*, July/ August, 69–77.

Hodgson, G. (1988) *Economics and Institutions*. Cambridge: Polity Press.

Huff, A. (1982) 'Industry influences on strategy-formulation', *Strategic Management Journal*, 3: 119–30.

Jain, S. (1985) *Marketing, Planning and Strategy*. Cincinnati: South Western.

Johnson, G. (1987) *Strategic Change and the Management Process*. Oxford: Basil Blackwell.

Kanter, R. (1990) *The Change Masters*. London: Unwin.

Kay, J. (1993) *Foundations of Corporate Success*. Oxford: Oxford University Press.

Knights, D. and Morgan, G. (1991) 'Strategic discourse and subjectivity: towards a critical analysis of corporate strategy in organizations', *Organization Studies*, 12(2): 251–73.

Kunda, G. (1992) *Engineering Culture: Control and Commitment in a High-Tech Corporation*. Philadelphia: Temple University Press.

Langlois, R.N. (ed.) (1986) *Economics as a Process: Essays in the New Institutional Economics*. Cambridge: Cambridge University Press.

Lash, S. and Urry, J. (1987) *The End of Organised Capitalism*. Oxford: Polity Press.

Lenz, R. (1980) 'Strategic capability: a concept and framework for analysis', *Academy of Management Review*, 5(2): 225–34.

Levitt, T. (1965) 'Exploit the product life-cycle', *Harvard Business Review*, November–December: 81–94.

Lewchuk, W. (1987) *American Technology and the British Vehicle Industry*. Cambridge: Cambridge University Press.

Lilja, K., Rasanen, K. and Tainio, R. (1992) 'A dominant business recipe: the forest sector in Finland', in R. Whitley (ed.), *European Business Systems*. London: Sage. pp. 137–54.

Lindblom, L. (1959) 'The science of muddling through', *Public Administration Review*, 19 (Spring): 78–88.

Lyles, M. (1990) 'A research agenda for strategic management in the 1990s', *Journal of Management Studies*, 27(4): 363–75.

March, J. and Olsen, J. (1976) *Ambiguity and Choice in Organisations*. Bergen: Universitetsforlaget.

McNulty, T., Whittington, R., Whipp, R. and Kitchener, M. (1994) 'Implementing marketing in NHS hospitals', *Public Money and Management*, April–June.

Melin, L. and Hellgren, B. (1993) 'Industrial wisdom: the case of the Swedish paper industry', Mimeo, University of Linköping.

Miles, R. and Snow, C. (1984) 'Fit, failure and the hall of fame', *California Management Review*, 3: 10–28.

Miller, D. and Friesen, A. (1980) 'Momentum and revolution in organization adaptation', *Academy of Management Journal*, 23: 591–614.

Mintzberg, H. (1978) 'Patterns in strategy formation', *Management Science*, 24(9): 934–48.

Mintzberg, H. (1994) *The Rise and Fall of Strategic Planning*. Hemel Hempstead: Prentice-Hall.

Peters, T.J. and Waterman, R.H. (1982) *In Search of Excellence: Lessons from America's Best Run Companies*. New York: Harper & Row.

Pettigrew, A. (1973) *The Politics of Organisational Decision Making*. London: Tavistock.

Pettigrew, A. and Whipp, R. (1991) *Managing Change for Competitive Success*. Oxford: Blackwell.

Porac, J. and Thomas, H. (1992) 'The cognitive construction of industries'. Unpublished paper, Department of Management, New York University.

Porter, M. (1980) *Competitive Strategy*. New York: Free Press.

Porter, M. (1985) *Competitive Advantage: Creating and Sustaining Superior Performance*. New York: Free Press.

Porter, M. (1990) *The Competitive Advantage of Nations*. New York: Free Press.

Prahalad, C. and Hamel, G. (1985) 'Strategic intent', *Harvard Business Review*, May–June: 63–76.

Quinn, J (1980) *Strategies for Change: Logical Incrementalism*. Homewood, IL: Irwin.

Rasanen, K. and Whipp, R. (1992) 'National business recipes: a sector perspective', in R. Whitley (ed.),

*European Business Systems*. London: Sage. pp. 46–60.

Rockhart, J. and Short, J. (1989) 'IT in the 1990s: managing organizational interdependence', *Sloan Management Review*, 30: 7–17.

Rumelt, R. (1988) 'The evaluation of business strategy', in J.B. Quinn, H. Mintzberg and R.M. James (eds), *The Strategy Process: Concepts, Contexts and Cases*. Engelwood Cliffs, NJ: Prentice-Hall. pp. 50–6.

Schendel, D. and Cool, K. (1988) 'Development of the strategic management field', in J. Grant (ed.), *Strategic Management Frontiers*. Greenwich, CT: JAI Press. p. 7032.

Schendel, D. and Hofer, C. (1979) *Strategic Management: a New View of Business Policy and Planning*. Boston: Little Brown.

Schotter, A. (1981) *The Economic Theory of Social Institutions*. Cambridge: Cambridge University Press.

Schumpeter, J.A. (1950) *Capitalism, Socialism, and Democracy*, 3rd edn. New York: Harper.

Scott, R. and Lodge, G. (1985) *US Competitiveness in the World Economy*. Boston, MA: Harvard Business School Press.

Scott-Poole, M. and Van de Ven, A. (1989) 'Toward a general theory of innovation processes', in A. Van de Ven, H. Angle and M. Scott-Poole (eds), *Research on the Management of Innovation*. New York: Harper & Row. pp. 637–62.

Shearman, C. and Burrell, G. (1987) 'The structures of industrial development', *Journal of Management Studies*, 24(4): 326–45.

Shrivastava, P., Stubbart, C., Huff, A. and Dutton, J. (forthcoming) *Critical Perspectives on Strategic Management. Vol 9. Advances in Strategic Management*. New York: JAI Press.

Sminia, H. (1994) *Turning the Wheels of Change*. Groningen: Wolters-Noordhoff.

Spender, J. (1989) *Industry Recipes*. Oxford: Blackwell.

St George, A. (1994) 'Strategy', *Financial Times*, 11 July: 11.

*Strategic Directions* (1991) April, 2–5.

Teece, D. (ed.) (1987) *The Competitive Challenge: Strategies for Industrial Innovation and Renewal*. Cambridge, MA: Ballinger.

Thomas, H. (1993) 'Perspectives on theory building in strategic management', *Journal of Management Studies*, 30(1): 3–10.

Van de Ven, A., Angle, H. and Scott-Poole, M. (eds) (1989) *Research on the Management of Innovation*. New York: Harper & Row.

Weick, K.E. (1987) 'Substitutes for corporate strategy', in D.J. Teece (ed.), *The Competitive Challenge: Strategies for Industrial Innovation and Renewal*. Cambridge, MA: Ballinger.

Wensley, R. (1988) 'Strategic management: avoiding economic errors and managerial myths', *University of Wales Review of Business and Economics*, 2.

Whipp, R. (1990) *Patterns of Labour: Work and Social Change in the Pottery Industry*. London: Routledge.

Whipp, R. (1994) 'A time to be concerned', *Time and Society*, 3(1): 99–116.

Whipp, R. and Clark, C. (1986) *Innovation and the Auto Industry: Product, Process and Work Organisation*. London: Frances Pinter.

Whitley, R. (ed.) (1992) *European Business Systems*. London: Sage.

Whittington, R. and Whipp, R. (1992) 'Professional ideology and marketing implementation', *European Journal of Marketing*, 26, 31(1): 52–63.

Williams, R. (1976) *Keywords: a Vocabulary of Culture and Society*. London: Fontana.

Willmott, H. (1993a) 'Breaking the paradigm mentality', *Organization Studies*, 14(5): 681–719.

Willmott, H. (1993b) 'Strength is ignorance; slavery is freedom: managing culture in modern organizations', *Journal of Management Studies*, 30(4): 515–52.

Wilson, D. (1992) *A Strategy of Change*. London: Routledge.

Zan, L. (1990) 'Looking for theories in strategy studies', *Scandinavian Journal of Management*, 6(2): 89–108.

# 2

# Leadership in Organizations

## ALAN BRYMAN

Leadership has long been a major area of interest among social scientists and in particular psychologists. However, the field of leadership in organizations seemed to be in a trough in the early 1980s. For some time there had been a feeling that the field lacked an agreed-upon framework (a paradigm) within which research took place and that the findings of a century of research were trivial or contradictory. New approaches continued to surface (e.g. Hunt et al. 1982) but the field seemed to lack coherence and there was a sense of despondency about its future direction. There was even a call for the temporary abandonment of the concept (Miner 1982), but such extreme views did not find many adherents, because, for all the undoubted problems with the area in those years (some of which have not gone away), the notion of leadership is one that continues to attract generations of writers, in large part because we tend to view leadership as an important feature of everyday and organizational affairs.

Leadership, as one might anticipate, is not an easy concept to define. Its widespread currency and use in everyday life as an explanation affects the way it is defined and indeed probably makes it more difficult to define than a concept that is invented as an abstraction *ab initio*. Most definitions of leadership have tended to coalesce around a number of elements which can be discerned in the following definition by a researcher whose work had a profound impact on one of the stages of theory and research to be encountered below:

Leadership may be considered as the process (act) of influencing the activities of an organized group in its efforts toward goal setting and goal achievement. (Stogdill 1950: 3)

Three elements can be discerned in this definition that are common to many definitions: influence, group and goal. First, leadership is viewed as a process of influence whereby the leader has an impact on others by inducing them to behave in a certain way. Second, that influence process is conceptualized as taking place in a group context. Group members are invariably taken to be the leader's subordinates and hence the persons for whom the leader has some responsibility. This focus on the leader in relation to a definable group is invariably translated into research in which sergeants and their combat units or supervisors and their work groups constitute the focus of analysis. Third, the leader influences the behaviour of group members in the direction of goals with which the group is faced. Effective leadership – the holy grail of leadership theory and research – will be that which accomplishes the group's goal(s).

This definition applies best to theory and research which was conducted up to the mid 1980s. While it by no means fell into disuse, later definitions, in so far as they were specifically articulated, tended to dwell on the leader as a *manager of meaning* – a term employed by Smircich and Morgan (1982). In a similar fashion, Pfeffer (1981) writes about leadership as symbolic action, by which he means that leaders engage in 'sense-making' on behalf of others and develop a social consensus around the resulting meanings. In both cases, leadership is seen as a process whereby the leader identifies for subordinates a sense of what is important – defining organizational reality for others. The leader gives a sense of direction and of purpose through the articulation of a compelling worldview. There is an irony in the use of the phrase 'manager of meaning', because one of the most intractable problems is that of distinguishing *leadership* from *management*. Many of the types of leader behaviour examined by leadership researchers, which are explored below, were underpinned by the previous definition of leadership as an influence process of moving a group to achieve its goal. These conceptions of leader behaviour might just as appropriately have been called 'managerial behaviour'. For writers like Zaleznik (1977) and Kotter (1990), the key to the difference between leadership and management lies in the orientation to change. Management is concerned with the here-and-now and does not ask broader questions about purpose and organizational identity; leaders by contrast 'change the way people think about what is desirable, possible and necessary' (Zaleznik 1977: 71). Thus, the phrase 'manager of meaning' (and the congruent notion of 'symbolic leadership') is meant to draw attention to the defining characteristic of true leadership as the active promotion of values which provide shared meanings about the nature of the organization. This emphasis has the further potential to differ from the earlier definition of leadership in that the focus on meaning might be taken to imply that a wider constituency of organizational members are implicated in leadership, in that meanings will tend to be the product of the interpretation by others of the messages intended by the leader. Influence, by contrast, implies a much more one-way leadership process. However, the definition of leadership in terms of influence, group and goal tended to hold sway, albeit in various guises, in much of the history of leadership theory and research. This history can be broken down into four main stages, which are the focus of the next section, and the influence-group-goal definition predominated in the first three of these stages.

## FOUR STAGES OF LEADERSHIP THEORY AND RESEARCH

Each of the four approaches to the study of leadership covered in this section is associated with a particular time period. The *trait approach* dominated the scene up to the late 1940s; the *style approach* held sway from then until the late 1960s; the heyday of the *contingency approach* was from the late 1960s to the early 1980s; and the *New Leadership approach* has been the major influence on leadership research since the early 1980s. Each of these stages signals a change of emphasis rather than the demise of the previous approach(es). Trait research, for example, is still very much alive in the 1990s: the point is that each of the time periods is associated with a change of prominence.

## The Trait Approach

The trait approach seeks to determine the personal qualities and characteristics of leaders. This orientation implies a belief that leaders are born rather than made – nature is more important than nurture. Research tended to be concerned with the qualities that distinguished leaders from non-leaders or followers. For many writers concerned with leadership in organizations the findings of such research had implications for their area of interest because of a belief that the traits of leaders would distinguish effective from less effective leaders, although relatively few trait studies examined this specific issue.

A host of different traits were examined by researchers. The bulk fall into three main groups: physical traits, such as physique, height, and appearance; abilities, such as intelligence and fluency of speech; and personality characteristics, such as conservatism, introversion–extroversion, and self-confidence. A key event in the history of the trait approach was the publication of an influential review of relevant findings by Stogdill (1948), who, along with a review by Gibb (1947), questioned the fruits of years of trait research. Both Stogdill and Gibb found the consistency of trait research to be questionable; this received confirmation in a later review by Mann (1959). While studies might find a certain trait to be significant, there always seemed to be considerable evidence that failed to confirm that trait's importance. Although it was not Stogdill's intention to bring trait research to a halt, writing in the *Handbook of Leadership* in 1974 he recognized that his review along with that of others 'sounded the seeming deathknell' of the approach (Bass 1990: 78). In fact, trait research did not grind to a halt and, in his 1974 review of the evidence, Stogdill appeared more sanguine about what had been accomplished within its purview (1990: 87).

Indeed, trait research enjoyed something of a renaissance in the late 1980s. A number of instances of this can be cited. Lord et al. (1986) reanalysed the studies on which Mann (1959) had drawn his pessimistic conclusions. They employed a technique called 'meta-analysis' which pools the findings of research in an area to generate an overall assessment of the impact of independent variables. Lord et al. found that the evidence for the importance of three of the six traits (intelligence, masculinity and dominance) was much stronger than Mann had recognized. However, the theoretical perspective taken by Lord et al. is different from that of the early trait researchers in that they argue that traits are important as 'perceiver constructs' (Lord and Maher 1991), that is, traits influence how people are perceived so that being a leader or a follower is inferred by people from evidence about traits that they exhibit. A further indication of the resurgence of trait thinking is an examination of evidence on real-life successful leaders which found that such leaders 'are strongly driven, have a strong desire to lead and exercise power, exhibit honesty and integrity, and are highly self-confident' (Locke et al. 1991: 34). Finally, a study of US presidents found a number of personality factors to be related to presidential performance; for example, need for power and activity inhibition both affected performance in a positive direction (House et al. 1991).

However, the key point is to recognize that the reviews by writers like Stogdill led to a disillusionment with trait investigations and from the late 1940s the trend shifted to the examination of leadership *style*.

## The Style Approach

The emphasis on leadership style from the late 1940s signalled a change of focus from the personal characteristics of leaders to their behaviour as leaders. As much as a change in what was to be studied, this shift denoted an alteration in the practical implications of leadership research. The trait approach drew attention to the kinds of people who become leaders and in the process had great potential for supplying organizations with information about what should be looked for when *selecting* individuals for present or future positions of leadership. By contrast, since leader behaviour is capable of being changed, the focus on the behaviour of leaders carried with it an emphasis on *training* rather than selecting leaders.

There are a number of possible exemplars of the style approach but arguably the best known is the stream of investigations associated with an approach generated by a group of researchers at the Ohio State University, one of whose main figures was Stogdill. Not only did the Ohio State researchers generate a large number of studies, but the concepts and methods that they employed were widely used well beyond the confines of the Ohio group, an influence that can still be felt in the 1990s. The chief approach taken by the Ohio researchers was to administer questionnaires to the subordinates of leaders in one or a number of organizations, which in the early years tended to be military organizations. The questionnaire comprised a battery of items each of which was a statement about a leader's behaviour. Each subordinate was asked to indicate how well each statement reflected the behaviour of his or her leader. Subordinates' replies were aggregated to provide an overall score for each leader on each of a number of aspects of leader behaviour. The two main components of leader behaviour that Ohio State researchers tended to focus upon were dubbed *consideration* and *initiating structure*. The former denotes a leadership style in which leaders are concerned about their subordinates as people, are trusted by subordinates, are responsive to them, and promote camaraderie. Initiating structure refers to a style in which the leader defines closely and clearly what subordinates are supposed to do and how, and actively schedules work for them. Leaders' scores on these two styles were then related to various measures of outcome like group performance and subordinate job satisfaction. Early findings tended to be that consideration was associated with better morale and job satisfaction among subordinates but lower levels of performance. Initiating structure tended to be associated with poorer morale but better group performance. Later research often suggested that high levels of both consideration and initiating structure were the best leadership style.

At quite an early stage in the development of the Ohio Studies, it was noted by Korman (1966) that they were plagued by inconsistent results. He noted also that insufficient attention was paid to the possibility that the effectiveness of the two types of leader behaviour is situationally contingent; in other words, what works well in some situations may not work well in others. Later research in the Ohio tradition reflected a greater sensitivity to this possibility (for example, Kerr et al. 1974), a trend that was consistent with the growing adherence to a contingency approach that marked the 1970s (see below). Other problems contributed to the gradual drift away from the Ohio State approach. The kind of research design typically used in Ohio research allows relationships between leadership style and various outcomes to be determined, but could not sustain the causal interpretations that were invariably inferred from findings, for example, that consideration influenced job satisfaction. Indeed, studies using experimental and longitudinal research designs often found the leader-causes-outcome inference to be highly questionable (e.g. Lowin and Craig 1968; Greene 1975). Second, the tendency for research to be conducted on formally designated leaders meant that informal leadership processes were rarely investigated, though such processes have rarely been the focus of researchers in later years either. Third, the aggregation of subordinates' ratings of their leaders tended to neglect the significance of intra-group differences in the perception of leaders. Finally, there was growing recognition of measurement problems with the Ohio scales to measure leadership. In particular, the recognition of the impact of people's 'implicit leadership theories' on how they rated the behaviour of leaders was very damaging to the Ohio researchers. Rush et al. (1977), for example, showed that when rating the behaviour of an imaginary leader, people generated ratings that were very similar to those pertaining to real leaders in Ohio investigations. In other words, Ohio research might merely be tapping people's generalized perceptions of the behaviour of leaders. The theoretical implications of such research have become an area of interest in their own right (Lord and Maher 1991).

The significance of the Ohio State approach is as much methodological as it is substantive. While the terms 'consideration' and 'initiating structure' were still being employed in studies many years after the approach had lost favour (for example, Fry et al. 1986), the general methodological strategy that was signalled continues to be used in a variety of guises. Ironically, research on one aspect of leader behaviour – leaders' reward and punishment behaviour – proved to be very robust in terms of both consistency of findings and the imputation of causal interpretations (for example, Sims and Manz 1984; Podsakoff et al. 1984; 1990). However, the main drift from the late 1960s was toward contingency models of leadership.

## The Contingency Approach

Proponents of contingency approaches place situational factors towards the centre of any understanding of leadership. Typically, they seek to specify the situational variables which will moderate the effectiveness of different leadership approaches. This development parallels the drift away from universalistic theories of organization in the 1960s and the gradual adoption of a more particularistic framework which reflected an 'it all depends' style of thinking (e.g. Lawrence and Lorsch 1967).

Arguably, one of the best known exemplars of contingency thinking is Fiedler's contingency model of leadership effectiveness (Fiedler 1967; 1993; Fiedler and Garcia 1987). Fiedler's approach has undergone a number of revisions and changes of emphasis over the years. At its heart is a measurement instrument known as the least preferred coworker (LPC) scale which purports to measure the leadership orientation of the person completing it. It comprises a number of pairs of adjectives – the number varies from eighteen to twenty-five – with each pair being separated by an eight-point scale. The respondent is asked to think about the person with whom he or she has least liked working, either currently or in the past, and then to describe that person in terms of each of the pairs of adjectives. Examples of the pairs of adjectives are: pleasant–unpleasant; friendly–unfriendly; rejecting–accepting; and distant–close. Each respondent's reply to each pair is scored one to eight, with a score of eight indicating a positive view of the least preferred coworker (pleasant, friendly, accepting, close, etc.) and a score of one indicating a negative view (unpleasant, unfriendly, rejecting, distant, etc.). Fiedler argues that the higher are people's LPC scores, the more relationship-motivated they are as leaders. This means that they are primarily concerned to foster good relationships with subordinates and are considerate. Leaders with low LPC scores are deemed to be task-motivated, that is, they are preoccupied with task accomplishment. In spite of an apparent similarity with the Ohio consideration and initiating structure pairing, it should be appreciated that for Fiedler there is a key difference between his and other conceptualizations like that of the Ohio researchers. Whereas for the latter there was a focus on consideration and initiating structure as contrasting styles of leadership, for Fiedler relationship and task motivation are *personality* attributes, a conceptualization which ties his work much more with earlier trait approaches.

From results relating to numerous studies conducted in a variety of work and non-work settings, Fiedler found that the effectiveness of relationship- and task-motivated leaders varied according to how favourable the situation was to the leader. More recently, this notion of situational favourableness has been dubbed 'situational control'. This idea has three components: leader–member relations; task structure; and position power. Fiedler's accumulated evidence led him to propose that task-oriented leaders are most effective in high control and low control situations; relationship-oriented leaders perform best in moderate control situations. The practical implication of Fiedler's work was that since a person's personality is not readily subject to change, it is necessary to change the work situation to fit the leader rather than the other way around.

Fiedler's model has been the subject of a great deal of controversy and debate. Much of this has centred upon the LPC scale, with many writers and researchers unconvinced by the link that is made between people's LPC scores and their approach to leadership. There has also been considerable unease over the conceptualization of situational control or favourableness. Many students of leadership asked why situational control was the only situational factor that was the object of attention and why the three components previously mentioned were the only crucial elements in situational control. Fiedler has responded to some extent to this kind of criticism by including stress within the model's purview in more recent years (Fiedler and Garcia 1987; Fiedler 1993). But probably most damaging of all is that there has been widespread disagreement over the model's validity, that is, whether results really are consistent with the model. The three dimensions of situational control are usually presented as dichotomies, which, when differentially weighted, yield eight 'octants' of situational control. The results relating to two of these octants tend to yield reasonably consistent results, but for the other six the degree of variability of findings is often great (Bryman 1986: 129). Thus, for octant 2 (good leader–member relations, presence of task structure, and weak position power), LPC–performance correlations varied between 0.60 and -0.55. However, a meta-analysis by Strube and Garcia (1981) concluded that there was strong support for the model, although Vecchio (1983) noted some technical problems with the analysis. A later meta-analysis by Peters et al. (1985), using a different set of techniques, generated a more mixed set of findings. For example, it was found that results were more likely to be consistent with the theory in laboratory studies than in field studies, where other non-specific variables seemed to moderate LPC–performance relationships. Fiedler's contingency approach shares with the Ohio Studies a tendency to emphasize formally designated leaders to the virtual exclusion of informal leadership processes.

In the end, contingency approaches like Fiedler's probably became less popular because of inconsistent results that were often generated by research conducted within their frameworks and problems with the measurement of key variables. The idea of a contingency approach still has considerable support, although research sometimes suggests that situational factors are not always as important as might be expected. A study by Kennedy (1982) of leaders with LPC scores in the middle of the range found them to perform better than low and high LPC leaders regardless of levels of situational control. Podsakoff et al. (1984) found that the reward and punishment behaviour of leaders related to various measures of outcome irrespective of a wide range of situational factors that were examined. Nonetheless, by the early 1980s, there was considerable disillusionment with contingency theories.

## The New Leadership Approach

The term 'New Leadership' has been used to describe and categorize a number of approaches to leadership which emerged in the 1980s which seemed to exhibit common or at least similar themes, although there were undoubtedly differences between them (Bryman 1992a). Together these different approaches seemed to signal a new way of conceptualizing and researching leadership. Writers employed a variety of terms to describe the new kinds of leadership with which they were concerned: transformational leadership (Bass 1985; Tichy and Devanna 1986), charismatic leadership (House 1977; Conger 1989), visionary leadership (Sashkin 1988; Westley and Mintzberg 1989); and, simply, leadership (Bennis and Nanus 1985; Kotter 1990). Together these labels revealed a conception of the leader as someone who defines organizational reality through the articulation of a vision which is a reflection of how he or she defines an organization's mission and the values which will support it. Thus, the New Leadership approach is underpinned by a depiction of leaders as managers of meaning rather than in terms of an influence process.

While many of the ideas associated with the New Leadership approach were presaged by some earlier writers like Selznick (1957) and Zaleznik (1977), its intellectual impetus derives in large part from the publication of Burns's study of political leadership in 1978. In this work, Burns proposed that political leaders could be distinguished in terms of a dichotomy of transactional and transforming leadership. Transactional leadership comprises an exchange between leader and follower in which the former offers rewards, perhaps in the form of prestige or money, for compliance with his or her wishes. In Burns's view, such leadership is not ineffective but its effectiveness is limited to the implicit contract between leaders and their followers. They are not bound together 'in a mutual and continuing pursuit of a higher purpose' (1978: 20). The transforming leader raises the aspirations of his or her followers such that the leader's and the followers' aspirations are fused. Burns's distinction was popularized by Peters and Waterman's (1982) hugely successful book *In Search of Excellence*, where they asserted that almost all of the highly successful companies that they studied had been influenced by a transforming leader at some stage in their development. The link between transforming leadership and vision was forged by a number of writers at around the same time and can be seen in the work of Bass (1985), Bennis and Nanus (1985), and Tichy and Devanna (1986). In the process, the nomenclature changed and transform*ing* became transform*ational* leadership.

Bennis and Nanus and Tichy and Devanna adopted a similar approach of interviewing successful chief executives to determine the nature of their approaches to leadership. Bennis and Nanus are somewhat different in that they also tracked a number of their subjects. They also viewed their chief executives as leaders rather than as managers, suggesting a parallel between transactional/transforming and manager/leader. In both cases, the importance of articulating a vision was found to be a central element of their leadership which invariably involved the transformation of followers and often of organizations in correspondence with their vision. Both pairs of writers recognized that the vision must be communicated and made intelligible and relevant to the leader's followers. Roberts (1985) provided an interesting case study of a single transformational leader, a school superintendent in the USA, who, shortly after taking office, found herself in the midst of a budgetary crisis which she overcame; indeed, she helped the school district to prosper through the articulation and promotion of a vision about the aims of schooling. Peters and Austin also formulated a view of leadership which saw the formulation of a vision as central to leadership:

> You have got to know where you are going, to be able to state it clearly and concisely – and you have got to care about it passionately. That all adds up to vision, the concise statement/picture of where the company and its people are heading and why they should be proud of it. (1985: 284)

Writers on charismatic leadership also depicted vision as central to such leadership in organizational settings. This emphasis is not surprising since a vision or mission is almost a defining characteristic of charismatic leadership. As Weber, whose writings are central to an understanding of charisma, wrote: 'The bearer of charisma enjoys loyalty and authority by virtue of a mission believed to be embodied in him' (1968: 1117). In his study of charismatic leaders in business, Conger (1989) broke down charismatic leadership into four stages. First, the leader recognizes opportunities and the need for change and formulates a vision in relation to those needs. Second, the leader communicates that vision, a process which entails depicting the status quo as unacceptable and generating a rhetoric which aids the understanding of the vision. Third, the leader builds trust in the vision. Last, the leader helps others to achieve the vision through leading by example (role modelling) and by empowering followers.

These various writings on the New Leadership can, then, be viewed as signalling a change of orientation towards the leader as a manager of meaning and the pivotal role of vision in that process. However, two other ingredients stand out. First, in the New Leadership most research is conducted on very senior leaders, often chief executive officers, rather than low- to middle-level leaders such as supervisors, sergeants, middle managers, foremen, and sports coaches, as in the Ohio and Fiedler research. For example, in their article on different types of visionary leader, Westley and Mintzberg (1989) base their distinctions on case studies of two founders of organizations (Jobs of Apple and Land of Polaroid), two chief executives (Carlzon of SAS and Iacocca of Chrysler), and one leader of a political party (René Lévesque of the Parti Québecois). Second, unlike the three earlier stages of leadership research, substantial use is made of qualitative case studies. Some writers, like Bennis and Nanus and Tichy and Devanna, employed informal, semi-structured interviews as their chief source of data; others, like Westley and Mintzberg, employed documentary evidence. The use of such methods represents a substantial methodological shift from the quantitative studies that were typical of earlier phases of leadership research. However, a stream of highly influential research inaugurated by Bass includes leaders at lower levels and uses a quantitative approach in the manner of much leadership style and contingency research.

## Bass's Research on Transactional and Transformational Leadership

Bass's approach (Bass 1985; Bass and Avolio 1990) draws heavily on Burns's (1978) work for its basic ideas, but goes much further in two respects. First, rather than as opposite ends of a continuum, Bass views transactional and transformational leadership as separate dimensions. Indeed, for Bass, the ideal approach exhibits both forms of leadership (Bass and Avolio 1993: 72). Second, in contrast to Burns's broad-brush style of discussing the two types of leadership, Bass has specified their basic components and has developed a battery of quantitative indicators for each component. His specification of these components has varied somewhat as his model has undergone development. Transformational leadership is made up of four components:

- *charisma* – developing a vision, engendering pride, respect and trust
- *inspiration* – motivating by creating high expectations, modelling appropriate behaviour, and using symbols to focus efforts
- *individualized consideration* – giving personal attention to followers, giving them respect and responsibility
- *intellectual stimulation* – continually challenging followers with new ideas and approaches.

Transactional leadership is conceptualized in terms of two components:

- *contingent rewards* – rewarding followers for conformity with performance targets
- *management by exception* – taking action mainly when task-related activity is not going to plan.

Each of these components is measured in a manner similar to the Ohio approach, in that followers complete questionnaires which specify types of leader behaviour each of which relates to one of these components. Leaders are then scored in terms of each component and their scores are correlated with various outcomes, which are usually a measure of performance and/or a measure of 'extra effort', which refers to the respondent's preparedness to expend extra effort on behalf of the leader and the organization. Much of the research up to 1991 is summarized in Bryman (1992a: 121–8), while Bass and Avolio's (1993: 67) summary includes the results of some of the more recent research. The research, which has been conducted on a host of different levels of leader in a variety of settings, typically shows charisma and inspiration to be the components of leader behaviour that are most strongly associated with desirable outcomes such as performance of subordinates. Individualized consideration and intellectual stimulation typically come next, while contingent reward usually exhibits quite a strong correlation. Management by exception produces inconsistent results in that in some studies it is positively and in others negatively related to desirable outcomes. Programmes for the selection and training of leaders which draw on this conceptualization and measurement of transactional and transformational leadership have been developed (Bass and Avolio 1990).

Bass's framework has generated an impressive set of findings and has made a great impact on the study of leadership. Some reflections about the approach can be found in the following overview.

## Overview of the New Leadership Approach

The New Leadership offers a distinctive approach which ties in with the great appetite for stories about heroic chief executives which was referred to above and with the growing self-awareness of many organizations about their missions. The New Leadership is at once cause, symptom and consequence of this self-reflection that can be seen in the widespread reference to visions and missions in newspaper advertisements and company reports. The approach has been critically examined in Bryman (1992a) from which the following selection of points has been gleaned.

With the exception of the research stemming directly or indirectly from Bass's work, the New Leadership approach can be accused of concentrating excessively on top leaders. While a switch toward the examination of the leadership *of*, rather than *in*, organizations is an antidote to the small-scale, group-level studies of earlier eras, it could legitimately be argued that the change in focus has gone too far and risks having little to say to the majority of leaders. Second, as with earlier phases of research, the New Leadership has little to say about informal leadership processes, though the qualitative case studies that have grown in popularity have great potential in this regard. On the other hand, quantitative approaches like Bass's work are likely to replicate the tendency to focus on formally designated leaders. Third, there has been little situational analysis. The tendency to extol the virtues of transformational leadership and other forms of New Leadership risks creating a return to universalistic thinking. Avolio and Bass (1987) depict situational factors as largely unimportant because transformational leaders are able to change the situation in their quest for the enhancement of subordinate performance. The problem with this position is that it comes perilously close to presenting a view which makes success an essential ingredient of transformational leadership. The neglect of situational factors seems to be changing. Keller (1992) reports the results of a study of R&D groups which uses Bass's measures and which shows that transformational leadership was a stronger predictor of project quality for research than for development projects. Bryman et al. (1996) show from a multiple case study of specialized transportation organizations in England how such factors as pre-existing levels of trust and resource constraint can have a pronounced impact on the prospects of transformational leadership. Similarly, Leavy and Wilson conclude from their investigation of four private and public sector Irish organizations that their leaders were 'tenants of time and context' (1994: 113). In so doing they draw attention to a wide range of contextual factors that can limit the room for manoeuvre of prospective transformational leaders. The contextual factors that they identified were: technology; industry structure; the international trading environment; national public policy; and social and cultural transformation. Therefore, there is growing evidence that situational constraints may be much more important in restricting the transformational leader's room for manoeuvre than is generally appreciated. Fourth, Bass's research approach probably suffers from some of the technical problems identified in relation to the Ohio research, such as problems of direction of causality and of implicit leadership theories (for a discussion of such issues, see Bass and Avolio 1989; Bryman 1992a). Fifth, there is a tendency for New Leadership writers to emphasize the exploits of successful leaders. This can generate a distorted impression since there may be important lessons to be learned from failed transformational leaders.

In spite of such problems, the New Leadership approach provided a 'shot in the arm' for leadership researchers. It enjoyed a broad swathe of support among both leadership researchers and writers of popular works on management, and broke with many aspects of earlier phases of the field. It is possible to exaggerate the differences. Like its predecessors, much if not most New Leadership writing is wedded to a rational model of organizational behaviour, while the growing popularity of a quantitative research approach within the New Leadership tradition (in particular the stream of research associated with Bass) seems to herald a return to a style of research associated with an earlier era.

## Dispersed Leadership

The New Leadership approach has not completely superseded previous approaches but more significantly other perspectives have emerged during the 1980s and 1990s that cannot be encapsulated by it. Indeed, at the time of writing a reaction seems to be developing to three tendencies exhibited by New Leadership writers (though these points do not apply to the bulk of the work inaugurated by Bass): a focus on heroic leaders; a preoccupation with leadership at the highest echelons; and a focus on individuals rather than teams. A separate tradition which focuses on 'dispersed leadership' seems to be emerging to offset these tendencies. Four strands in recent writing illustrate this development. First, Manz and Sims (1991) and Sims and Lorenzi (1992) have developed an approach which specifies the advantages of a type of leadership that is expected to supersede the 'visionary hero' image which is a feature of the perception of leaders in the New Leadership tradition. They develop the idea of SuperLeadership, which is 'the leadership culture of the future, the new leadership paradigm' (Sims and Lorenzi 1992: 296). A keynote feature of SuperLeadership is the emphasis that is placed on 'leading others to lead themselves' (1992: 295), so that followers are stimulated to become leaders themselves, a theme that was in fact a feature of Burns's (1978) perspective on transforming leadership. SuperLeadership is to do with both developing leadership capacity in others and nurturing them so that they are not dependent on formal leaders to stimulate their talents and motivation. A second example is Katzenbach and Smith's (1993) book in which they extol the virtues of 'real teams', that is teams with 'a small number of people with complementary skills who are committed to a common performance purpose, performance goals, and approach for which they hold themselves mutually accountable' (1993: 45). Katzenbach and Smith view the role of leaders of such teams in terms of developing leadership in others by building commitment and confidence, removing obstacles, creating opportunities and being part of the team. Thus, in a manner similar to the Super-Leader, the leader of real teams is a facilitator who cultivates the group and its members. As a result, leadership is dispersed throughout the team. Third, Kouzes and Posner (1993) argue that credible leaders develop capacity in others. They 'turn their constituents into leaders' (1993: 156). For Kouzes and Posner, the issue is not one of handing down leadership to others, but one of liberating them so that they can use their abilities to lead themselves and others. These three strands signal a change of focus away from heroic leaders, from the upper echelons, and towards a focus on teams as sites of leadership (see also Reich 1987).

The fourth expression of an emergent dispersed leadership tradition can be seen in the suggestion that there should be much greater attention paid to leadership processes and skills, which may or may not reside in formally designated leaders. Hosking (1988; 1991) conceptualizes leadership in terms of an 'organizing' activity and spells out some of the distinctive features of leadership in terms of such a perspective. For example, she identifies 'networking' as a particularly notable organizing skill among leaders, in which the cultivation and exercise of wider social influence is a key ingredient. But such skill is not the exclusive preserve of formally appointed leaders; it is the activity and its effects that are critical to understanding the distinctiveness of leadership. In like fashion, Knights and Willmott (1992) advocate greater attention to what they call the 'practices' of leadership. This emphasis means looking at how leadership is constituted in organizations, so that in their study of a series of verbal exchanges at a meeting in a British financial services company, they show how the chief executive's definition of the situation is made to predominate. Unfortunately, the distinctiveness of this research and Hosking's (1991) investigation of Australian chief executives is marred somewhat by a focus on designated leaders. As a result, it is difficult to disentangle leadership as skill or activity from leadership as position. However, the potential implication of these ideas is to project an image of leadership as much more diffuse and dispersed within organizations than would be evident from the tendency for leadership to be viewed as the preserve of very few leaders, as in many versions of the New Leadership approach. However, Vanderslice's (1988) investigation of the Mouse-wood restaurant collective in New York State shows that the functions of leadership can exist without formal leaders since they are dispersed throughout the collective. For example, authority and responsibility exist but are rotated and hence are dependent on the task at hand rather than on a formal leader. As Vanderslice observes, Mousewood is not leaderless but 'leaderful' since the functions of leadership are dispersed throughout the collective.

In these four sets of writings, we can see an alternative perspective which emphasizes the importance of recognizing the need for leadership to be viewed as a widely dispersed activity which is not necessarily lodged in formally designated leaders, especially the heroic leader who is a feature of much New Leadership writing.

## Leadership and Organizational Culture

There is an affinity in many discussions between the concentration on vision in the New Leadership approach and organizational culture. This tendency can be seen in the advantages which were seen as stemming from an organization's possession of a 'strong culture' (for example, Peters and Waterman 1982). Strong cultures were seen as providing organizational members with a sense of their distinctiveness, a sense of purpose and the 'glue' which binds people together. Companies became increasingly self-conscious and forthcoming about their values and traditions. Moreover, the visions of leaders were seen by many writers as making a distinctive contribution to cultures. The notion of leadership as having culture creation as a core (if not *the* core) element can be discerned in a number of writings, other than that of Peters and Waterman. Schein, for example, wrote that 'the unique and essential function of leadership is the manipulation of culture' (1985: 317). In Bass's model, changing organizational culture is an outcome of transformational leadership which in turn has an impact on the follower's level of effort and performance.

The connection between leadership and organizational culture is especially noticeable in the case of the founders of new organizations whose values and preoccupations often leave a distinctive imprint on their creations (Schein 1985). Leaders who follow in the founder's footsteps often see their role as that of maintaining and reinforcing the early culture. At a later stage in their development the distinctive cultures that were created might come to be seen as liabilities, as environmental realities change. Trice and Beyer (1990; 1993) helpfully distinguish between the maintenance and innovation aspects of 'cultural leadership'. Innovation takes place as the founder creates a new culture or when a new leader replaces an existing culture. Much of the New Leadership writing tended to concentrate on situations in which the leader is confronted with a culture that is in need of change because it is out of tune with current realities or because the culture is a barrier to a change of strategic direction. Such a view is exemplified by an investigation of Jaguar and Hill Samuel in the UK, which concluded that a transformation of the organization's culture was a prerequisite for radical strategic change (Whipp et al. 1989). Similarly, Kotter and Heskett's (1992) quantitative study of the links between organizational culture and firms' performance led them to conclude that the really critical factor is that a culture is adaptive, that is, it seeks to anticipate and adapt to environmental change. Leadership becomes a particular consideration for Kotter and Heskett in that it is needed to change cultures so that they are more adaptive. Here too, then, is a depiction of leaders as having a responsibility for culture creation.

It is striking that this perspective on leadership as culture management ties the study of leadership to 'value engineering': the leader comes to be seen as someone who moulds how members are to think about the organization and their roles within it. In this way, leadership theory and research become implicated in the drift in the study of organizational culture from essentially academic discussions towards more normative, managerial approaches (Barley et al. 1988). Willmott (1993) argues that in these managerial discussions, culture is little more than an extension of management control in which the aim is to colonize the minds of members of the organization. Therefore, the wider political and ethical ramifications of cultural manipulation tend to be marginalized. Equally, the predominant paradigm for examining leadership in relation to culture is imbued with what Martin (1992) refers to as an 'integration' perspective. Martin distinguishes this approach from two others – a differentiation and a fragmentation perspective. Each represents a unique way in which an organizational culture can be 'read'. None of the three perspectives can be absolutely valid and all of them should be employed to draw out the full complexity of images and themes. Martin's elaboration of different approaches to reading cultures provides a helpful framework for further exploring the link between leadership and culture.

In the integration perspective, there is consistency between the various components of culture and there is fairly widespread agreement and understanding of the culture's precepts. Leadership is about creating, maintaining or changing cultures along the lines that have just been encountered in the writings of Schein, Kotter and Heskett, Peters and Waterman, and Trice and Beyer. Alvesson (1992) provides an alternative position within an integration perspective which views leaders as transmitters of culture within organizations. He shows how subsidiary managers in a Swedish computer consultancy firm have a social integrative function in that they transmit the organization's culture to combat the potential for the firm to splinter due to the highly decentralized and heterogeneous nature of the work of consultants. In this case, leaders transmit rather than mould culture.

In the differentiation perspective, leadership occupies a quite different position. Culture is seen as pervaded by lack of consensus across the organization. The perspective particularly draws attention to subcultural diversity and the resulting enclaves of consensus that form within the wider organization. Martin suggests that when investigators have explored leadership within a differentiation perspective, they have typically examined leadership exercised by groups. Such a perspective brings into play informal leadership processes which have invariably been absent in organizational research. However, it is difficult to believe that individual leaders, albeit informal ones, do not exercise leadership to promote or express subcultural positions. The notion of a collective arrogation of leadership by a group is feasible, but it is hard to believe that individual leaders are not instrumental in the process. Indeed, Martin cites the illustration from her own research (Martin and Siehl 1983) of the way in which John DeLorean formed a contraculture in his division at General Motors. He employed alternative dress codes, physical arrangements, and formal practices to promote an oppositional culture within the company. It may be that leadership by individuals has a greater role to play in the fostering of contracultures than of subcultures, but studies of informal organization have frequently pointed to the important role played by leaders in the context of subcultures (Homans 1950). The issue of how senior organizational leaders deal with subcultural variety within organizations also needs greater attention than it has been given so far, but the main contribution of the differentiation perspective is that it departs from the naive view of consensus within organizations and of leaders as sources of that integration.

Martin distinguishes a third approach to reading organizational cultures – the fragmentation perspective. This approach seems almost to decentre if not eliminate the role of leadership in organizational cultures. The fragmentation perspective characterizes organizational cultures as suffused with ambiguity and confusion. The meaning of cultural artefacts and their relationships to each other are unclear and confusing to members of the organization. The sheer complexity and heterogeneity of modern organizations tends to engender cultures whose elements lack the capacity to provide 'sense-making' that was often attributed to them by earlier generations of culture researchers in the early 1980s and by the exponents of the integration perspective in particular. The decentring of leadership in the fragmentation perspective can be discerned through a number of themes in Martin's (1992) writing, though it is not confronted in a direct way. She argues that the perspective offers very few guidelines to those individuals (presumably mainly senior executives) who might wish to implement cultural change. Indeed, from the fragmentation perspective the attempt to impose a coherent culture by dint of one's organizational vision is futile and dishonest because it fails to acknowledge the diversity, ambiguity and fluidity of modern cultures. However, the fragmentation perspective need not marginalize leadership as much as Martin's analysis implies.

An important feature of leadership within the fragmentation perspective is that leaders, far from being the sources of a coherent world-view as in the integration perspective, may come to be sources of ambiguity themselves. Tierney (1989) notes how the presidents of thirty-two higher education establishments in which he conducted his research frequently sent out symbols which were inconsistent with other cultural elements or with other symbols in which they dealt. In another investigation, an ethnographic study of a Catholic liberal arts college in crisis, Tierney (1987) shows how the new leader's symbols and messages were consistently misunderstood by others. The new president, Sister Vera, attempted to change the organization's culture from a family orientation to a more professional one. She introduced an executive committee, a forum for the discussion of important decisions and for broadening the constituency of staff involved in decision-making. For Sister Vera, the executive committee was meant to symbolize a shift away from autocracy and towards a team approach to decision-making, but instead of signifying 'open communication and more team involvement' it actually signified the opposite (1987: 242). When she decided that the committee's agenda should be published as a further sign of her commitment to openness, this too was widely interpreted as the opposite of what was intended. Even her 'open door' policy was interpreted, not as a symbol of openness, but as indicative of a failure of communication. In large part, this misinterpretation (though within a fragmentation perspective it is questionable whether the notion of misinterpretation has any meaning) arose because of the clash between the open door and other signs and symbols that she emitted that indicated otherwise, such as her practice of not going into staff members' rooms to chat to them. Perhaps at one level, and from the frame of reference of the integration perspective, Sister Vera was simply a poor leader who was not able to influence the organization's culture. However, this case and the fragmentation perspective more generally may provide the lesson that leaders' signs and symbols may be inherently more tenuous and equivocal than has typically been appreciated. Equally, the case demonstrates how matters of leadership can have a significant role within the purview of the fragmentation perspective, but perhaps their chief frame of reference is not so much leadership through the management of meaning as the transmission of equivocality. The former is intentional and is indicated by attempts to impose clear-cut meanings on others; the second is often an unintended consequence of the management of meaning in that the resulting messages may be more ambiguous to the listener than is typically appreciated by writers within the integration perspective and leaders themselves.

## Imaginative Consumption of Culture

One of the implications of the fragmentation perspective is that the visions of leaders and their strategies for enshrining these visions in their organizations' cultures is problematized. Even though it has been suggested in the previous paragraph that leadership maintains its significance within a perspective on culture in which ambiguity is a central ingredient, the impact of the kinds of leader-inspired actions that were the focus of attention among New Leadership writers (and among those who emphasized leaders as creators and managers of cultures) are viewed within the fragmentation approach as less central and indeed as less effective than within an integration framework.

This tendency receives reinforcement from an emerging emphasis within organizational culture research on how culture is received. It is ironic

that writers who view the role of leaders as culture manipulators in largely positive terms (e.g. Peters and Waterman 1982; Schein 1985) share with critics of cultural manipulation like Willmott (1993) a belief that culture control is largely successful, that is values, beliefs and symbols are imbibed by those at whom these cultural artefacts are projected. In contrast, Linstead and Grafton-Small argue for greater understanding 'through the examination of users' meanings and the practice of *bricolage*' of the creativity that is involved in culture *consumption* (1992: 332). This orientation shifts attention away from examinations of culture production, which is the main interest of New Leadership, culture management and integration perspective writers, towards the investigation of the imaginative consumption of cultural messages. In the process the role of leadership in culture production shifts from the centre to the periphery of the empirical agenda. This kind of position can be discerned in Hatch's (1993) reworking of an ethnographic investigation of strategic change by the new president at a large US university who employed a 'symbolic vision' to propel the change (Gioia and Chittipeddi 1991). Hatch notes that the president's actions underwent modifications and were even resisted by many organizational members. She argues that

> although the president was a major player in the initiation of strategic change, his influence depended heavily on the ways in which others symbolized and interpreted his efforts. The outcome of the president's influence ultimately rested with others' interpretations and the effect these interpretations had on cultural assumptions and expectations. In this light, it is worthwhile questioning whether the president was as central to the initiation effort, or the organizational culture, as he first appeared to be. (1993: 681–2)

The implication which can be derived from Linstead and Grafton-Small and Hatch, as well as from the foregoing discussion of leadership within a fragmentation perspective, is that organizational members are not passive receptacles, but *imaginative consumers*, of leaders' visions and of manipulated cultural artefacts.

There is much that is attractive about this view of organizational members as imaginative consumers of culture. There is a kind of optimism in the view that people are able to carve out spheres of interpretative autonomy which distance them from the mind-games of leaders who attempt to control what others think and feel. It countervails the tendency for studies of organizational culture to adopt the managerialist, normative stance with an emphasis on the control which was identified by Barley et al. (1988). It also has affinities with the interpretative stance with which much culture research is imbued (for example, Louis 1991), but as Linstead and Grafton-Small (1992) recognize, it is inconsistent with the emphasis on shared meanings which is a feature of much interpretative thinking. Also, it is congruent with and probably requires the kind of in-depth ethnographic approach to which many culture researchers are drawn.

However, the implicit optimism of the imaginative consumer account of organizational culture and of the roles of leaders in relation to it requires an element of caution. It must not be forgotten that visions and the cultures which may spring from them are attempts to frame people's ways of thinking. This is to suggest not that organizational members passively absorb cultural messages, but that these messages set limits and boundaries on how people are supposed to think and respond. The very language within which visions and cultures are couched and the intentional privileging of some themes and issues over others frame how people think about organizational issues, even if it means that some people reject the message or react with cynicism. The rejection of the messages takes place within the frame of those messages. Organizational members can only respond to the messages that are transmitted. They cannot be imaginative consumers of cultural messages which are absent. Those messages which are transmitted will have been designed with certain effects (such as control, performance enhancement, or reorientation) at their core. They may have a greater impact on how members think about organizational issues than the emphasis on imaginative consumption implies, since senior leaders' control over the cultural agenda means that many potential themes do not surface. Organizational members cannot be imaginative consumers of wilfully omitted messages and symbols, and therefore the impact of cultural manipulation and of the part played by leaders in moulding organizational members' thinking should not be under-estimated. Instead, there should be direct examination of the extent to which leaders' attempts to manage culture are subverted in the act of consumption by others. This would involve attention being paid to the significance of leaders' control over the cultural agenda as well as to how the messages and symbols are consumed. A balance is needed in empirical investigation which assumes neither that people are cultural dopes who passively imbibe cultural messages emanating from leaders, nor that the manipulation of organizational culture is constantly being undermined through imaginative consumption on the part of organizational members. The former position also invites us to question the seeming omnipotence with which leaders are often imbued by New Leadership writers, whereby the capacity of leaders to effect fundamental change is barely questioned.

The examination of leadership in relation to organizational culture has been a fertile area for theory and research. After an initially rather naive view in which leaders were viewed as builders of cultures, which in turn had an impact on the thinking and behaviour of members of the organization, the role of leaders and the implications of culture were problematized. Leadership seemed to be marginalized as a focus for analysis. It is being suggested here that the processes whereby leaders frame the ways in which members conceptualize organizational concerns and how the ensuing culture closes down alternative discourses and modes of thinking should be major issues in their own right. When issues such as these have been touched on, it has been shown that even when a culture and the vision that maintains it is treated with considerable scepticism, the culture nonetheless has considerable implications for how people apprehend organizational matters (for example, Smircich and Morgan 1982; Smircich 1983). Interestingly, there is an affinity between the fragmentation perspective and the emerging focus on dispersed leadership in that both emphasize the diffusion of power. Also culture can be instrumental (or not) in conditioning people's responsiveness to such things as self-leadership. However, a fragmentation analysis invites us to question whether the symbols of a cultural emphasis on dispersed leadership will be unambiguously understood and whether it might sometimes be viewed as a political manoeuvre for securing greater effort from employees under the guise of handing over greater responsibility and empowerment.

## METHODOLOGICAL AND EPISTEMOLOGICAL ISSUES IN THE STUDY OF LEADERSHIP

There can be little doubt that the bulk of leadership research has been conducted within the tradition of quantitative research in which leadership variables are related to various outcomes. Qualitative research has had little influence on the field, in spite of its impact on the social sciences more generally .where its strengths relative to quantitative research have been a subject of considerable discussion (Bryman 1988). The drift towards the New Leadership approach in the 1980s and the growing interest in organizational culture resulted in greater use of qualitative research. The emphasis within the New Leadership approach on the leader as a manager of meaning has led to an awareness that the ways in which this process occurs requires in-depth understanding of particular cases and detailed probing among both leaders and subordinates of aims and impacts. To such ends, a methodological strategy seems required which involves observation, in-depth interviewing and the detailed examination of documents, all of which are closely associated with qualitative research. However, there are two forms of qualitative research in the New Leadership. One is to produce essentially hagiographic pen pictures of successful leaders from whom 'lessons' can be learned. Leaders' exploits serve as illustrations of the leadership or culture change principles that the writer endorses (for example, Tichy and Devanna 1986; Kotter 1990). The second type of qualitative research is more 'academic' and involves either detailed explorations of one or a small number of cases (for example, Alvesson 1992; Smircich and Morgan 1982; Roberts 1985; Gioia and Chittipeddi 1991; Tierney 1987) or semi-structured interviews with a number of leaders (for example, Bennis and Nanus 1985; Bensimon 1989; Tierney 1989).

The role that is typically given to qualitative research by quantitative researchers is as preparation; in other words, if it has a role at all, qualitative research has often been reduced to a source of hypotheses to be taken up by quantitative researchers for subsequent verification. Such a division of labour keeps quantitative research very much in the methodological driving seat. However, in the social sciences at large there is a growing recognition of the contribution that qualitative studies can make. In the process of generating such a recognition, it has been necessary to discard some of the baggage of epistemological debate that has sometimes held back discussions of quantitative and qualitative research. For some writers, quantitative research is ineluctably tied to the label of positivism, while qualitative research is similarly enjoined with phenomenology. As a result of such associations, quantitative and qualitative research are deemed to be irreconcilable paradigms because of their incompatible epistemological underpinnings (e.g. Smith and Heshusius 1986). An alternative view is to recognize that quantitative and qualitative research are simply different approaches to the research process, and as such can be mutually informative and illuminating about an area like leadership, and can even be combined (Bryman 1988; 1992b). In fact, as awareness of the strengths of qualitative research for the study of leadership becomes better known, future researchers may be drawn to the wider range of issues concerning leadership raised by qualitative investigations.

There can be little doubt that quantitative research on leadership offers huge advantages to the researcher who wants clear-cut specification of causal connections between different types of leader behaviour and various outcomes (like subordinate job satisfaction and performance) under specific conditions. The very fact that the New Leadership seems to be drifting towards a more quantitative research approach is a testament to these strengths, which can be seen in the stream of research deriving from Bass's work, as well as that of alternative quantitative research approaches such as those of Leithwood and Steinbach (1993) and Podsakoff et al. (1990). On the other hand, qualitative research brings to the study of leadership an approach which sees leadership through the eyes of leaders and followers. In the process, the very notion of leadership is problematized by depicting the variety of meanings associated with 'leadership' or 'good leadership' among leaders and followers (for example, Tierney 1989).

Qualitative research is also acutely sensitive to the contexts of leadership. Through the use of a single case over time or the judicious comparison of cases, the qualitative researcher is able to highlight specific features of context and how they impinge on leaders. Roberts and Bradley (1988) show that the charismatic school superintendent who had been the focus of Roberts's (1985) study lost the aura of charisma when she moved to a state-level post and that a number of specific situational factors can account for that change (such as her more limited authority). In the multiple case study by Bryman et al. (1988) of three construction projects in England, the specific circumstances of such projects and the variations in those circumstances proved to be important factors which influenced the styles of construction project leaders. For example, projects are of limited duration and vary considerably in the degree to which there is a sense of urgency. Some projects seem to have more leeway in this regard than others, while it is often found that there are variations within a project's life in terms of this sense of urgency. This was one of three contextual factors which are fairly specific to the construction industry which had a considerable impact on leaders' styles. Also, qualitative research can be especially instructive when it comes to the examination of processes of leadership. By 'process' is here meant how leadership is accomplished and how leadership impacts occur over time. In detailed case studies, both features of a processual investigation may be in evidence. An illustration is Roberts's (1985) account of how a school superintendent actually had an impact and how that impact was gradually fostered.

Equally, as in the social sciences generally, quantitative and qualitative studies can usefully be combined (Bryman 1988: 127–56). The use of quantitative and qualitative research in tandem is still quite unusual in leadership studies. Kirby et al. (1992) employed a combined approach in the context of an investigation of school leaders and found a slight difference between the two sets of findings. When they employed Bass's framework and measures, their findings were extremely similar to those typically found by researchers using this approach. By contrast, their analysis of narrative descriptions of 'extraordinary leaders' found that the capacity of leaders to provide opportunities for professional development was more prominent than the kinds of leadership orientation identified by Bass. It is easy to view these differences within a framework of 'triangulation' (Webb et al. 1966) and to ask which is right. However, a much more promising avenue is to ask why the different contexts of questioning produce contrasting results and to see them as having gained access to different levels of cognition about leadership – general behaviours in the case of the quantitative study and more specific behaviours in the qualitative one – and to recognize that the research question needs to be linked to the appropriate kind of research design and instruments.

The injection of qualitative research into the study of leadership has great potential for the field. It can allow a different set of questions to be addressed and can address issues that are not readily accessible to a quantitative approach. For example, informal leadership has typically been neglected by quantitative researchers but may be more accessible to qualitative research. In this connection, it is interesting to speculate that the ideas associated with the idea of 'dispersed leadership', in which leaders as such are decentred and the focus turns to leadership in terms of acts and processes, may require a qualitative approach if it is to turn into a major framework for systematic research. One of the reasons why quantitative researchers concentrate on leaders is that they provide a ready-made focus for the administration of questionnaires. If acts of leadership are indeed dispersed, an important issue for researchers is that of identifying leadership and the acts and skills associated with it. Qualitative research is much more likely to provide the open-endedness that such a stance requires.

## OVERVIEW

There is clearly much greater optimism about the field of leadership in organizations than in the early 1980s. In shifting towards a view of leadership as the management of meaning and

in recognizing the potential of a greater range of research styles, the subject is well placed as a major area within the field of organization studies. Here I want to suggest two issues that may need to be particularly high on the agenda of leadership researchers in the coming years. Each relates in different ways to wider issues and perspectives within organization studies. Leadership theory and research have been remarkably and surprisingly uncoupled from the more general field in which they are located, so that the raising of these issues is meant to point to possible ways of offsetting that tendency. First, one of the more influential theories in the field since the late 1970s has been the population ecology perspective (Hannan and Freeman 1984). This approach represents something of a critique of leadership theory and research, but has hardly been acknowledged as such by those working within the leadership field. Population ecology proposes that the environments within which populations of organizations operate have a limited carrying capacity and that as a result some organizations are 'selected out' and die. This perspective suggests that human agency is of limited help in effecting the survival of organizations. The implications for the study of leadership are considerable because population ecology seems to reduce the importance of leadership greatly. The specific issue of whether leadership can make a difference to organizational survival is an important one for students of leadership and cannot be ignored.

Secondly, much of the field is still imbued with the rational model of organizational thinking which is a product of the modernist stance within much of the field of organization studies and of leadership studies in particular (Bryman 1992a: 162–4; Reed 1993). The fragmentation perspective within organizational culture research may counteract this tendency to a degree, since its emphasis on ambiguity is clearly at odds with the means–end theorizing that is a feature of rational model thinking. The institutional perspective may offer some interesting insights which are less wedded to rational model assumptions (DiMaggio and Powell 1983; Meyer and Rowan 1977). This perspective draws attention to the ways in which organizations take on forms that serve to enhance their legitimacy in the eyes of important constituencies within their environments. As a result, organizational forms are deemed often to arise not purely as a result of a quest for efficiency, at least not in the later stages in the diffusion of a form, but for reasons of appearance and image. It is not inconceivable that leadership processes are susceptible to the same kinds of impulse. Alvesson (1990), for example, has drawn attention to the ways in which organizational images are managed. Accordingly, we might wonder whether the widespread predilection for superficial tokens of New Leadership ideas proliferated in the 1980s and 1990s for this kind of reason. During this period, many senior executives were keen to propound their 'visions', announce 'cultural change', explicate 'mission statements', induce staff to 'lead rather than manage', and implant 'new values'. Doubtless organizational functioning undergoes change in the process, but it is conceivable from an institutional viewpoint that in many cases their role has been as much about being seen to be doing the right things as out of a conviction of their effectiveness. Accordingly, the diffusion of leadership themes and practices through mimetic processes and their ramifications for organizations are a worthy area of research which would loosen the bonds of the rational model on leadership research.

The aim of this final section is to suggest a need for leadership researchers to engage more with broader ideas and controversies within organization studies as part of their enterprise. Leadership theorists and researchers must not let the study of leadership in organizations become a hermetically sealed sub-discipline and exponents of organization studies must not let it happen.

## REFERENCES

Alvesson, M. (1990) 'Organization: from substance to image?', *Organization Studies*, 11: 373–94.

Alvesson, M. (1992) 'Leadership as social integrative action: a study of a computer consultancy company', *Organization Studies*, 13: 185–209.

Avolio, B.J. and Bass, B.M. (1987) 'Transformational leadership, charisma and beyond', in J.G. Hunt, H.R. Baliga, H.P. Dachler, and C.A. Schriesheim (eds), *Emerging Leadership Vistas*. Lexington, MA: Heath.

Barley, S.R., Meyer, G.W. and Gash, D.C. (1988) 'Cultures of culture: academics, practitioners and the pragmatics of normative control', *Administrative Science Quarterly*, 33: 24–60.

Bass, B.M. (1985) *Leadership and Performance beyond Expectations*. New York: Free Press.

Bass, B.M. (1990) *Bass and Stogdill's Handbook of Leadership: Theory, Research and Managerial Applications*, 3rd edn. New York: Free Press.

Bass, B.M. and Avolio, B.J. (1989) 'Potential biases in leadership measures: how prototypes, leniency, and general satisfaction relate to ratings and rankings of transformational and transactional leadership constructs', *Educational and Psychological Measurement*, 49: 509–27.

Bass, B.M. and Avolio, B.J. (1990) 'The implications of

transactional and transformational leadership for individual, team, and organizational development', *Research in Organizational Change and Development*, 4: 231–72.

Bass, B.M. and Avolio, B.J. (1993) 'Transformational leadership: a response to critiques', in M.M. Chemers and R. Ayman (eds), *Leadership Theory and Research: Perspectives and Directions*. New York: Academic Press.

Bennis, W.G. and Nanus, B. (1985) *Leaders: the Strategies for Taking Charge*. New York: Harper & Row.

Bensimon, E.M. (1989) 'The meaning of "good presidential leadership": a frame analysis', *The Review of Higher Education*, 12: 107–24.

Bryman, A. (1986) *Leadership and Organizations*. London: Routledge & Kegan Paul.

Bryman, A. (1988) *Quantity and Quality in Social Research*. London: Routledge.

Bryman, A. (1992a) *Charisma and Leadership of Organizations*. London: Sage.

Bryman, A. (1992b) 'Quantitative and qualitative research: further reflections on their integration', in J. Brannen (ed.), *Mixing Methods: Qualitative and Quantitative Research*. Aldershot, Hants: Avebury.

Bryman, A., Bresnen, M., Beardsworth, A and Keil, T. (1988) 'Qualitative research and the study of leadership', *Human Relations*, 41: 13–30.

Bryman, A., Gillingwater, D and McGuinness, I. (1996) 'Leadership and organizational transformation', *International Journal of Public Administration*, 19: 849–72.

Burns, J.M. (1978) *Leadership*. New York: Harper & Row.

Conger, J.A. (1989) *The Charismatic Leader: Behind the Mystique of Exceptional Leadership*. San Francisco: Jossey-Bass.

DiMaggio, P.J. and Powell, W.W. (1983) 'The iron cage revisited: institutional isomorphism and collective rationality in organizational fields', *American Sociological Review*, 35: 147–60.

Fiedler, F.E. (1967) *A Theory of Leadership Effectiveness*. New York: McGraw-Hill.

Fiedler, F.E. (1993) 'The leadership situation and the black box in contingency theories', in M.M. Chemers and R. Ayman (eds), *Leadership Theory and Research: Perspectives and Directions*. New York: Academic Press.

Fiedler, F.E. and Garcia, J.E. (1987) *Improving Leadership Effectiveness: Cognitive Resources and Organizational Performance*. New York: Wiley.

Fry, L.W., Kerr, S. and Lee, C. (1986) 'Effects of different leader behaviors under different levels of task interdependence', *Human Relations*, 39: 1067–82.

Gibb, C.A. (1947) 'The principles and traits of leadership', *Journal of Abnormal and Social Psychology*, 42: 267–84.

Gioia, D.A. and Chittipeddi, K. (1991) 'Sensemaking

and sensegiving in strategic change initiation', *Strategic Management Journal*, 12: 433–48.

Greene, C.N. (1975) 'The reciprocal nature of influence between leader and subordinate', *Journal of Applied Psychology*, 60: 187–93.

Hannan, M.T. and Freeman, J.H. (1984) 'Structural inertia and organizational change', *American Sociological Review*, 49: 149–64.

Hatch, M.J. (1993) 'The dynamics of organizational culture', *Academy of Management Review*, 18: 657–93.

Homans, G.C. (1950) *The Human Group*, New York: Harcourt, Brace.

Hosking, D.M. (1988) 'Organizing, leadership and skilful process', *Journal of Management Studies*, 25: 147–66.

Hosking, D.M. (1991) 'Chief executives, organising processes, and skill', *European Journal of Applied Psychology*, 41: 95–103.

House, R.J. (1977) 'A 1976 theory of charismatic leadership', in J.G. Hunt and L.L. Larson (eds), *Leadership: the Cutting Edge*. Carbondale, IL: Southern Illinois University Press.

House, R.J., Spangler, W.D. and Woycke, J. (1991) 'Personality and charisma in the U.S. presidency: a psychological theory of leader effectiveness', *Administrative Science Quarterly*, 36: 364–96.

Hunt, J.G., Sekaran, U. and Schriesheim, C.A. (eds) (1982) *Leadership: Beyond Establishment Views*. Carbondale, IL: Southern Illinois University Press.

Katzenbach, J.R. and Smith, D.K. (1993) *The Wisdom of Teams: Creating the High-Performance Organization*. Boston, MA: Harvard Business School.

Keller, R.T. (1992) 'Transformational leadership and the performance of research and development project groups', *Journal of Management*, 18: 489–501.

Kennedy, J.K. (1982) 'Middle LPC leaders and the contingency model of leadership effectiveness', *Organizational Behavior and Human Performance*, 31: 1–14.

Kerr, S., Schriesheim, C.A., Murphy, C.J. and Stogdill, R.M. (1974) 'Toward a contingency theory of leadership based upon the consideration and initiating structure literature', *Organizational Behaviour and Human Performance*, 12: 62–82.

Kirby, P.C., King, M.I. and Paradise, L.V. (1992) 'Extraordinary leaders in education: understanding transformational leadership', *Journal of Educational Research*, 85: 303–11.

Knights, D. and Willmott, H. (1992) 'Conceptualizing leadership processes: a study of senior managers in a financial services company', *Journal of Management Studies*, 29: 761–82.

Korman, A.K. (1966) '"Consideration", "initiating structure", and organizational criteria – a review', *Personal Psychology*, 19: 349–61.

Kotter, J.P. (1990) *A Force for Change: How Leadership Differs from Management*. New York: Free Press.

Kotter, J.P. and Heskett, J.L. (1992) *Corporate Culture and Performance*. New York: Free Press.

Kouzes, J.M. and Posner, B.Z. (1993) *Credibility: How Leaders Gain and Lose It, Why People Demand It*. San Francisco: Jossey-Bass.

Lawrence, P.R. and Lorsch, J. (1967) *Organization and Environment*. Cambridge, MA: Harvard University Press.

Leavy, B. and Wilson, D. (1994) *Strategy and Leadership*. London: Routledge.

Leithwood, K. and Steinbach, R. (1993) 'Total quality leadership: expert thinking plus transformational practice'. Paper presented at the annual meeting of the American Educational Research Association, Atlanta, Georgia.

Linstead, S. and Grafton-Small, R. (1992) 'On reading organizational culture', *Organization Studies*, 13: 331–55.

Locke, E.A. and associates (1991) *The Essence of Leadership: the Four Keys to Leading Successfully*. New York: Lexington.

Lord, R.G., DeVader, C.L. and Alliger, G.M. (1986) 'A meta-analysis of the relation between personality traits and leadership perceptions: an application of validity generalization procedures', *Journal of Applied Psychology*, 71: 402–10.

Lord, R.G. and Maher, K.J. (1991) *Leadership and Information Processing: Linking Perceptions and Performance*. Cambridge, MA: Unwin Hyman.

Louis, M.R. (1991) 'Reflections on an interpretative way of life', in P.J. Frost, L.F. Moore, M.R. Louis, C.C. Lundberg and J. Martin (eds), *Reframing Organizational Culture*. Newbury Park: Sage.

Lowin, A. and Craig, C.R. (1968) 'The influence of performance on managerial style: an experimental object lesson in the ambiguity of correlational data', *Organizational Behavior and Human Performance*, 3: 440–58.

Mann, R.D. (1959) 'A review of the relationship between personality and performance in small groups', *Psychological Bulletin*, 56: 241–70.

Manz, C.C. and Sims, H.P. (1991) 'SuperLeadership: beyond the myth of heroic leadership', *Organizational Dynamics*, 19: 18–35.

Martin, J. (1992) *Cultures in Organizations: Three Perspectives*. New York: Oxford University Press.

Martin, J. and Siehl, C. (1983) 'Organizational culture and counterculture: an uneasy symbiosis', *Organizational Dynamics*, 12: 52–64.

Meyer, J.W. and Rowan, B. (1977) 'Institutionalized organisations: formal structure as myth and ceremony', *American Journal of Sociology*, 83: 340–63.

Miner, J.B. (1982) 'The uncertain future of the leadership concept: revisions and clarifications', *Journal of Applied Behavioral Science*, 18: 293–307.

Peters, L.H., Hartke, D.D. and Pohlmann, J.T. (1985) 'Fiedler's contingency theory of leadership: an application of the meta-analysis procedures of Schmidt and Hunter', *Psychological Bulletin*, 97: 274–85.

Peters, T. and Austin, N. (1985) *A Passion for Excellence*. New York: Random House.

Peters, T. and Waterman, R.H. (1982) *In Search of Excellence: Lessons from America's Best-Run Companies*. New York: Harper & Row.

Pfeffer, J. (1981) 'Management as symbolic action: the creation and maintenance of organizational paradigms', *Research in Organizational Behavior*, 3: 1–52.

Podsakoff, P.M., MacKenzie, S.B., Moorman, R.H. and Fetter, R. (1990) 'Transformational leader behaviors and their effects on followers' trust in leader, satisfaction, and organizational citizenship behaviors', *Leadership Quarterly*, 1: 107–42.

Podsakoff, P.M., Todor, W.D., Grover, R.A. and Huber, V.L. (1984) 'Situational moderators of leader reward and punishment behaviors: fact or fiction?', *Organizational Behavior and Human Performance*, 34: 21–63.

Reed, M.I. (1993) 'Organizations and modernity: continuity and discontinuity in organization theory', in J. Hassard and M. Parker (eds), *Postmodernism and Organizations*. London: Sage.

Reich, R.B. (1987) 'Entrepreneurship reconsidered: the team as hero', *Harvard Business Review*, 65: 77–83.

Roberts, N.C. (1985) 'Transforming leadership: a process of collective action', *Human Relations*, 38: 1023–46.

Roberts, N.C. and Bradley, R.T. (1988) 'Limits of charisma', in J.A. Conger and R.N. Kanungo (eds), *Charismatic Leadership: the Elusive Factor in Organizational Effectiveness*. San Francisco: Jossey-Bass.

Rush, M.C., Thomas, J.C. and Lord, R.G. (1977) 'Implicit leadership theory: a potential threat to the internal validity of leader behavior questionnaires', *Organizational Behavior and Human Performance*, 20: 93–110.

Sashkin, M. (1988) 'The visionary leader', in J.A. Conger and R.N. Kanungo (eds), *Charismatic Leadership: the Elusive Factor in Organizational Effectiveness*. San Francisco: Jossey-Bass.

Schein, E.H. (1985) *Organizational Culture and Leadership*. San Francisco, CA: Jossey-Bass.

Selznick, P. (1957) *Leadership in Administration*. New York: Harper & Row.

Sims, H.P. and Lorenzi, P. (1992) *The New Leadership Paradigm*. Newbury Park: Sage.

Sims, H.P. and Manz, C.C. (1984) 'Observing leader behavior: toward reciprocal determinism in leadership theory', *Journal of Applied Psychology*, 69: 222–32.

Smircich, L. (1983) 'Leadership as shared meanings', in L. Pondy, P. Frost, G. Morgan and T. Dandridge (eds), *Organizational Symbolism*. Greenwich, CT: JAI Press.

Smircich, L. and Morgan, G. (1982) 'Leadership: the management of meaning', *Journal of Applied Behavioral Science*, 18: 257–73.

Smith, J.K. and Heshusius, L. (1986) 'Closing down the conversation: the end of the quantitative-qualitative debate among educational inquirers', *Educational Researcher*, 15: 4–12.

Stogdill, R.M. (1948) 'Personal factors associated with leadership: a survey of the literature', *Journal of Psychology*, 25: 35–71.

Stogdill, R.M. (1950) 'Leadership, membership and organization', *Psychological Bulletin*, 47: 1–14.

Stogdill, R.M. (1974) *Handbook of Leadership: a Survey of Theory and Research*. New York: Free Press.

Strube, M.J. and Garcia, J.E. (1981) 'A meta-analytic investigation of Fiedler's contingency model of leadership effectiveness', *Psychological Bulletin*, 90: 307–21.

Tichy, N.M. and Devanna, M.A. (1986) *The Transformational Leader*. New York: Wiley.

Tierney, W.G. (1987) 'The semiotic aspects of leadership: an ethnographic perspective', *American Journal of Semiotics*, 5: 233–50.

Tierney, W.G. (1989) 'Symbolism and presidential perceptions of leadership', *Review of Higher Education*, 12: 153–66.

Trice, H.M. and Beyer, J.M. (1990) 'Cultural leadership in organizations', *Organizational Science*, 2: 149–69.

Trice, H.M. and Beyer, J.M. (1993) *The Cultures of Work Organizations*. Englewood Cliffs, NJ: Prentice-Hall.

Vanderslice, V.J. (1988) 'Separating leadership from leaders: an assessment of the effect of leader and follower roles in organizations', *Human Relations*, 41: 677–96.

Vecchio, R.P. (1983) 'Assessing the validity of Fiedler's contingency model of leadership effectiveness', *Psychological Bulletin*, 93: 404–8.

Webb, E.J., Campbell, D.T., Schwartz, R.D. and Sechrest, L. (1966) *Unobtrusive Measures*. Chicago: Rand McNally.

Weber, M. (1968) *Economy and Society* (1925), 3 vols, edited by G. Roth and C. Wittich. New York: Bedminster.

Westley, F.R. and Mintzberg, H. (1989) 'Visionary leadership and strategic management', *Strategic Management Journal*, 10: 17–32.

Whipp, R., Rosenfeld, R. and Pettigrew, A. (1989) 'Culture and competitiveness: evidence from two mature UK industries', *Journal of Management Studies*, 26: 561–85.

Willmott, H. (1993) 'Strength is ignorance; slavery is freedom; managing culture in modern organizations', *Journal of Management Studies*, 30: 515–52.

Zaleznik, A. (1977) 'Managers and leaders: are they different?', *Harvard Business Review*, 55: 67–78.

# 3

# Decision-Making in Organizations

SUSAN J. MILLER, DAVID J. HICKSON
AND DAVID C. WILSON

The area of organizational decision-making is part of the broader field of organization studies and organization theory. It has therefore followed a similar pattern of evolution, drawing on a variety of paradigms and perspectives and being characterized by a multiplicity of theories, models and methodologies.

This chapter charts its development as a subject of study. The chapter attempts to show how competing views and alternative theoretical frameworks of the way in which decisions are made have shaped both the methods of enquiry and subsequent explanations. The central concepts of rationality and power in decision-making are discussed. Further, the understanding of decision-making as an organizational *process* is explored in detail, as is the relatively neglected area of implementation. Decision-making overlaps other areas, notably strategic management, so the ways in which strategic decisions and strategies may be related are addressed.

Finally, the chapter recognizes that most work on decision-making implicitly assumes culturally bounded Western views of the world and its management processes.

## WHY DECISION-MAKING?

Why should decision-making be studied at all? Although its popularity has waxed and waned over time it has continually stayed on the stage of organizational debate, though not always in the spotlight. Why should this be so?

There are a number of reasons. Certainly the increasing complexity of 'modern organizations'

which needed both differentiation and integration (Lawrence and Lorsch 1967) meant that key decisions about the organization of central operational and transformational processes were required. The overarching paradigm of structural functionalism (which continues to be a dominant perspective) viewed management as being fundamentally concerned with rational decision-making in order to facilitate the smooth running and goal attainment of the modern, complex, structurally and functionally differentiated organization. Rational-legal authority (Weber 1947) appeared to both empower and compel managers to take rational decisions. This emphasis upon unemotional, impersonal, objective logic has persuasively shaped managerial beliefs and action, and will be discussed further in this chapter.

If the dynamics of organizing created a need for decision-making, studies of managerial work confirmed that this was indeed how managers spent a large proportion of their time. Mintzberg's (1973) early work and Stewart's (1967; 1976; 1983) ongoing studies have both placed decision-making high on the managerial agenda, while Simon (1945) has suggested that 'managing' and 'decision-making' are practically synonymous.

A further reason concerns the intrinsic nature of the decision-making process itself. Decisions can be viewed as being fundamentally concerned with the allocation and exercise of power in organizations. The making of decisions, especially the larger, consequential ones which govern what things are done and shape the future direction of the organization and the lives of people within it, are of vital significance to organizational stakeholders. The issues of who is involved in the making of decisions; who is left out or kept out; who is in a position to exercise influence; who is able to introduce items on to the decision-making agenda or keep them off; are all central to an understanding of the politics of organizational behaviour. The study of decision-making is crucial to the comprehension of how and why organizations come to be what they are and to control whom they do.

To summarize, there are a number of reasons why this topic is of interest to both practitioners and theorists. Modern organizations need decisions to be made in order that they can function effectively; managers spend much of their time in making decisions at both the operational and the strategic level; and decision-making can be seen to focus political activity in organizations and so provide a window on to a less observable but nonetheless influential 'underworld'. There is clearly a contrast here between seeing decision-making as a functional prerequisite of effective organization and seeing it as a maelstrom of political activity and sectional conflict, where power games are played out in an arena which is only partially open to view, and this accounts in part for the differences in approaches to research and discussion.

The variety of contrasting assumptions and preconceptions is compounded because the subject crosses several academic disciplines. Choice behaviour under optimum and sub-optimum conditions is examined using rational choice models from economics and modelling techniques from mathematics and statistics; the behavioural aspects of making decisions in organizations are discussed by organization theorists, sociologists and social psychologists; while psychologists concentrate on individual cognitive behaviour. This chapter will not and could not address all these perspectives. What it will do is focus on the way in which decisions are made and implemented in an organizational setting. It will therefore draw mainly on material from organization theory which takes the organization with its members as the subject of analysis. Drawing the boundary in this way does not mean that what is inside it is a discrete area of understanding; the influence of the other disciplines mentioned above still permeates the discourse.

The next section will begin our scrutiny in earnest, by looking at the beginnings of decision theory. The approach first taken, with its central notion of rational behaviour, still retains a pivotal position in the field: an orthodox, normative model of decision-making within a paradigm which many other approaches still need to acknowledge before they attempt to dismantle its arguments.

## MANAGERIAL RATIONALITY IN DECISION-MAKING

Neo-classical economic assumptions lie at the heart of rational choice models of decision-making. Predicated on the supposition that individuals normally act as maximizing entrepreneurs, decisions are thought to be arrived at by a step-by-step process which is both logical and linear. Essentially, the decision-makers identify the problem or issue about which a decision has to be made, collect and sort information about alternative potential solutions, compare each solution against predetermined criteria to assess degree of fit, arrange solutions in order of preference and make an optimizing choice. Often such models leave out, or assume, the implementation stage which in principle follows the formal decision itself. Throughout the thrust is to maximize rewards and minimize costs for those involved.

As Zey (1992: 9) has shown, this kind of logic, although by no means new, has increasingly dominated many areas of government and business over the last twenty years, especially in the United States and Western Europe. The implicit assumption is that if individuals behave in accordance with rationality then little or no interference is required by any superordinate bodies.

At the level of the organization, or firm, this view aggregates the behaviour of individuals and groups without compunction. Since individual managers make rational decisions, the decisions made by groups within organizations will be equally rational. At the macro level, a competitive economic environment is both efficient and equitable because of its inherent dynamic logic.

Such a view of organizations and decision-making represents a mainstay of functionalist thinking and has been elaborated by other writers, notably Williamson (1975) with his account of what he terms 'markets and hierarchies', hierarchies here meaning organizations. However, the limitations of the approach have long been recognized by theorists from inside and outside the neo-classical paradigm.

Simon (1945) was one of the earliest authors to provide a comprehensive critique of the limitations of 'rational economic man' or the 'rational actor' model. Simon asserted that, constrained as they were by the complexity of modern organizations and by their own limited cognitive capacities, decision-makers were unable to operate under conditions of perfect rationality. The issue for decision is likely to be unclear or open to varying interpretation; information about alternatives may be unavailable, incomplete or misrepresented; and criteria by which potential solutions are to be evaluated are often uncertain or not agreed. In addition, the time and energy available to decision-makers to pursue a maximizing outcome is both limited and finite. Searching for better choices can simply take too long. The net result of these constraints is that the outcome is likely to be a 'satisficing' rather than an optimizing choice: one which both satisfies and suffices in the circumstances, for the time being. The absolutely rational model is beyond reach. Decision-making does not work that way.

Simon accepts that managers have to operate within a 'bounded rationality'. They intend to be rational, and indeed their behaviour is *reasoned* – it is not *irrational*, which is an important distinction – but it is unrealistic to expect them to meet the stringent requirements of wholly rational behaviour. Human frailties and demands from both within and outside the organization limit the degree of rationality which can be employed.

Even so, Simon makes the important observation that different types of decisions can be processed in different ways. Some decision processes may approximate to rational prescriptions, others may not. Decisions which occur more frequently, which are familiar, almost routine, may be made in a relatively straightforward fashion. These decisions are comprehensible to managers and usually there exist tried and tested protocols, formulae or procedures for making them. They are 'programmed' (Simon 1960), in the sense that they can be made by reference to existing rubrics. Programmed decisions are often made lower down in the organizational hierarchy; they are the operational decisions which can be safely left to subordinates. It is likely that they can be made in a way which closely parallels the prescripts of rational choice models. In fact there may be little in the way of formal deciding to be done.

In contrast, 'non-programmed' decisions are those which are unfamiliar: they have not been encountered in quite the same way before, they are to some extent novel, unusual. They therefore present a challenge to managers, for there are no obvious well-trodden paths to follow. To make matters even more challenging, these decisions are usually about the more significant areas of organizational activities. They will have consequential repercussions and will set precedents for other decisions which follow. Since decisions are intended to shape actions for the future and since the future is inherently uncertain, the potential consequences of non-programmed, or *strategic*, decisions have worrying implications for managers. Because of their consequentiality, these decisions are usually

sanctioned or authorized by the most senior executives in the elite. Since there is less likely to be an existing template to shape the process by which they are made, what happens may differ considerably from what might be fully rational. The topic for decision may be complex, making definition problematic; information may be needed which is difficult both to collect and to categorize; potential solutions may be hard to recognize and may in turn create new problems. It is not easy to follow a step-by-step, smoothly escalating, sequential process under such conditions. 'Problemistic search' may occur, where activity is spurred by the immediate problem, rather than being an orderly collection of information prompted by foresight (Cyert and March 1963).

This continuum of decisions along a programmed/non-programmed dimension represents an early but significant step in distinguishing the characteristics of decisions and associating them with types of process. It is a field of enquiry that has been explored in greater detail since Simon, and we will return to this later in the chapter.

The issue of rationality in decision-making is therefore a vexed one. Decisions in organizations are subject to constraints endemic to the context in which they are made. The lone decision-maker making choices about his or her own interests might be thought to act rationally (although psychologists may argue the evidence here) but the complexities of managerial decision-making in concert with others have been well documented (for example, see Asch 1955; Janis 1972).

So rational choice models have been the target of sustained criticism for over four decades. Although there are those who continue to call for attempts at synthesis and reconciliation of contradictions (Schoemaker 1993), it has been suggested (Eisenhardt and Zbaracki 1992) that it is time for theorists concerned with organizational behaviour to drop such models in favour of a more realistic approach to decision-making, particularly one which recognizes how it is imbued with power.

## DECISION-MAKING AS THE ENACTMENT OF POWER

In Simon's definition of the term, 'bounded rationality' is the result of human and organizational constraints. It can be argued that this view underplays the role of power and political behaviour in setting those constraints. Many writers have pointed out that decision-making may be seen more accurately as a game of power in which competing interest groups vie with each other for the control of scarce resources.

Power is an ever-present feature of organizational life. Legitimate power is allocated to positions of authority in the hierarchy. This 'rational-legal' power (Weber 1947) is given according to status and regularizes access to the decision-making process. Those with the requisite authority can participate in what occurs. Some can both discuss decisions and authorize them. The contribution of others is relegated to just the providing or cataloguing of data, or the recording of outcomes. Still others do not take part at all, and in the majority of organizations they are the great majority.

However the use of power legitimately is not the only way in which influence is exercised. Power-holders may choose to behave in ways which further their own, or others', interests. They may frame the matter for decision in a way which suits their own ends or blocks the objectives of others. They push for preferred alternatives, whether or not these will lead to decisions which are of organizational benefit. They manipulate information, withhold it, ignore some or all of it. They negotiate for support and suppress opposition. This applies not only to those who are directly engaged in the process, but also to those who, although only indirectly involved, still have the power to influence the process in some way – such as by having access to those who are more closely involved, or by providing information for the process. Since all interest groups may be engaging in similar behaviour the process may be characterized by various forms of bargaining, negotiation and compromise that may lead to outcomes which are less than optimum for all parties. So although it might seem rational for each to pursue their own sectional interests in this way, from the perspective of neo-classical theory this can lead to outcomes which for the whole are less than rational. Thus the *means* by which decisions are made may be separably rational while the *ends* may not be.

Some writers have long considered power to be the key factor in explaining how decisions are made. Pettigrew's (1973) longitudinal analysis of a British retail business reached that conclusion. A similarly vivid example of politics at work has been described by Wilson (1982) in his account of a chemical manufacturer where a decision about electricity generation turned into an intense and sometimes bitter career struggle between two senior executives.

One way of explaining this kind of power play is to see it as the inevitable outcome of the way we organize. The intrinsic nature of organizations as entities which are driven by the imperatives of division of authority and division of labour leads inexorably to fragmentation. Differentiation, which is required to maintain efficiency and cope with turbulent, unpredictable environments, also creates sectional interests, each with their own needs and priorities. A functionalist paradigm has difficulty with the notion of goal dissensus, but the reality of organizations appears to be that once organizational groups are given different tasks they also begin to formulate their own sets of norms and goals. They either reinterpret objectives or construct personal goals which serve their own interests.

This notion of differentiation is at the heart of the resource dependence perspective (Pfeffer and Salancik 1978). This explores how some parts of the organization gain power as a result of their ability to control access to resources. In this view, an organization, being an 'open system' which interacts with its environment in order to survive, is crucially dependent on obtaining resources from suppliers. Power accrues to those parts of the organization that can control the flow of resources, especially if these are scarce and critical for organizational functioning.

In this vein Crozier's (1964) seminal study of a French tobacco company showed how the exclusive possession of expert knowledge allowed maintenance workers to gain and maintain control over production processes (although gender was also crucial since they were male and production workers female). The idea of expertise being a potential source of influence germinated even earlier with March and Simon (1958), and it is expertise rather than resources which underlies the strategic contingencies theory enunciated by Hickson et al. (1971) in their explanation of why some 'subunits' (departments and the like) within organizations exert more influence than others. They showed (Hinings et al. 1974) that if the differential allocation of tasks confronts a subunit in its specialist area with an uncertainty that is critical for its organization, and it copes in such a way as to buffer other subunits from any resulting instability, then it can widely influence decisions even beyond its own competence. This influence is conditional upon it being sufficiently central and non-substitutable for the others to be dependent upon it. So, for example, a marketing department which can iron out fluctuations in demand by shrewd pricing and advertising gains influence. It is this *coping with uncertainty* which confers power. Since organizations are beset by uncertainty arising from suppliers, customers, competitors, outside agencies, government and so on, as well as from internal difficulties, the ability to manage uncertainty on behalf of others provides a vital power base.

Hence organizations can be seen as *ensembles des jeux* (Crozier and Friedberg 1980) where individuals and groups jockey for position in a hierarchy which is mediated by ongoing negotiation and bargaining. There are shifting, multiple coalitions of interests and thus only 'quasi-resolution of conflict' as interests seek to impose their own 'local rationalities' on any given decision (Cyert and March 1963). The existing structural framework undergoes subtle (or even radical) change as a result of the day-to-day interactions of organizational members. It functions as a 'negotiated order' (Strauss et al. 1982). Particular decisions will enfold particular subsections, drawn into the game by the nature of what is being decided. The topics on hand will attract those who have something to protect: they will want to be involved because they are affected by what is being decided or they see a chance to influence matters in their favour. The matter for decision therefore shapes the interests which become involved and the way the game is played. In this way power positions are formed and transformed depending on what is on the agenda.

This acknowledges the increased political complexity of decisions made in organizational settings. The rational model of decision-making begins to break down when faced with this pluralist vision of multiple, competing interest groups vying for supremacy. Allison (1971) explores this by showing how both organizational interests and government influence can shape events. He also shows how different assumptions and ways of viewing the world provide different interpretations of, and explanations for, these events. Using as an example the Cuban missile crisis (when the USA and the Soviet Union, as it was then, teetered on the brink of war) Allison offers three alternative models for viewing what happened: the rational actor model (which views the situation as an outcome of logical and rational decisions), the organizational process model (which takes into account the complicating effects of the organizational context from which the events arose), and the governmental politics model (which focuses on the various bargaining games played out on the larger scale between actors at the level of government). The model produces alternative views of reality which sometimes complement one another, but often conflict. So ways of seeing produce ways of understanding, which has penetrating implications for the ways in which research is done.

Pluralist positions are predicated upon the notion of unequal but shifting power relations among elites, under the auspices of a largely neutral set of institutional arrangements. Here Schattsneider's statement begins to have reso-nance: 'All forms of political organisation have a bias in favour of some kinds of conflict and the suppression of others because organisation is the mobilisation of bias. Some issues are organised into politics while others are organised out' (1960: 71). This suggests that something else is happening 'behind the scenes' of even the pluralists' complex scenario – that the action is not all that it might seem at first glance. This in turn implies that to gain an even deeper understanding of power in organizations we need to look beyond what is readily observable. So attending solely to manifest conflict reveals only the most easily discernible 'face' of power. Ideally, what is going on beneath the surface also needs to be fully understood: the less explicit, more covert, subtle and insidious exercise of power which is used to suppress conflict in the first place. Conflict can be kept quiet; it is not allowed to surface into open debate and so does not become an item for discussion. This means that some decisions do not get onto the agenda. This is the 'second face' of power which Bachrach and Baratz (1962) argue has such import for organizational decision-making. This is the sphere of 'non-decisions'.

What then are non-decisions and do they have a place in the study of decision-making? Bachrach and Baratz maintain that non-decisions are equally if not more important than the decisions which are overtly made. Non-decisions are the covert issues about which a decision has effectively been taken that they will not be decided. They are the controversial topics which go against the interests of powerful stakeholders: they do not engender support, they do not fit with the prevailing culture, they are not considered acceptable for discussion, so they are quietly side-stepped or suppressed or dropped. A knowledge of what these issues are is likely to be as revealing, or more so, as knowledge of what is overtly being discussed. They are what is really going on, not just on the surface but underneath it. The decisions which are being discussed in the board room, in meetings, by executives and management represent the tip of the iceberg, according to this view. As the complete shape of the iceberg can only be revealed by going under the water, so the really key issues and problems are only partially apparent from studies of topics which are being decided. Each topic needs to be embedded in a wider picture which gives it a context – and future decisions may come from under the surface.

Bachrach and Baratz's ideas have been the spur to a broadening of debate about power and decisions. But they have come under criticism from those who ask questions about how the existence of non-decisions can be investigated. If even decision-making itself is a fairly ephemeral, intangible activity (how do you spot a decision, where are decisions made?) then the epistemological and methodological problems associated with the discovery and analysis of non-decisions are yet far more difficult. Bachrach and Baratz maintain that non-decisions are rooted in observable behaviour, that is in pre-existing conflict which leads to action to close off areas of decision-making, but those attempting to carry out empirical research in organizations have so far found this a difficult lead to follow.

Going beyond this position, Lukes (1974) developed a third dimension, or 'face', of power. He maintains that the weakness of Bachrach and Baratz's approach is that the second face of power is still primarily concerned with what should be intrinsically observable behaviour and conflict, even though it be so difficult to detect. Surely a more sinister, insidious and yet ultimately more effective way of exercising power would be to prevent any awareness of conflict in the first place? One way of achieving this would be to shape views and beliefs in such a way that one's own interests are not recognized by others. If all interests are perceived to be shared then conflict does not occur. This Orwellian view of the world echoes Marx's concept of 'false consciousness' whereby the hearts and minds of the proletariat are so manipulated by dominant institutions of state (abetted by the hegemony of religious institutions) that they only see things as others wish them to be seen. It also echoes Giddens's (1990) and Beck's (1992) view of society overall as 'unreflexive'. That is, the current state of affairs is left unquestioned. Firms can implement decisions which are hazardous, risky and detrimental to the environment. Yet, such corporate actions are, according to Giddens, largely taken for granted and left unquestioned. Awareness that such action might be in conflict with large sections of society is suppressed and rarely open to question.

Such non-reflexivity takes us a long way from the ideas of rational economic behaviour. Decision-making is far removed from the coolly logical appraisal and selection of alternatives. Rather it is at the centre of political machinations and intrigue, the true nature of which is not always fully recognized, even by those involved.

So although some may see conflict as an endemic, but controllable, part of organizational life, created by the dysfunctions of a functional drive for efficiency, others explain conflict as arising from inherently inequitable power relationships in wider society. In the former view, the context for decision-making is the ongoing power play between interest groups, in which situations of disharmony are an expected but usually reconcilable by-product of organizational structure. In the latter view, decisions are shaped in ways which are not always obvious, by unseen influential power-holders playing within a larger arena.

This has spurred some writers to press for a more radical organization theory (Burrell and Morgan 1993) which would show greater awareness of the macro factors beyond the organization. Radical organization theory recognizes that the nature of economic relations in any economic system must breed inter-class conflict since such relations are essentially exploitative. Under capitalism management serves the interests of capital and therefore subordinates enter into a relationship in which they exchange their labour power for subsistence. Radical theorists criticize conventional organizational analysis for neglecting the power of the state and of those who control capital in shaping wider social relations, maintaining that orthodox theories are 'locked into an acceptance of managerially defined problems' (1993: 366). Conventional theory acknowledges that conflict may occur, but both seeks and expects equilibrium in organizations, and looks for ways to reduce conflict to arrive at a sustainable balance. In contrast, radical theory expects conflict because it is the result of the incongruent objectives of management and labour. Decision-making theory should therefore take cognizance of this radical standpoint which throws a different light on how decisions arise and come to be taken 'at the top'.

Whilst the power perspective opens up the heart of organizational decision-making, it brings with it difficult methodological questions of its own, as mentioned earlier. How is power to be conceptualized and how is it to be studied? If much of power is employed covertly, how can it be reached? The fact that it is all-pervading does not help to make it any more tangible. Recognizing that political behaviour does shape decisional processes, what other factors besides power might be important?

For empirical researchers these are some of the issues with which they have to grapple and some of the questions they have attempted to answer. The following section looks at studies which try to understand the way power is enacted in the making of decisions.

## PROCESSES, PRESCRIPTIONS AND EXPLANATIONS

Empirical studies of decision-making have added weight to the criticisms of rational choice models as being idealized prescriptions, depicting an unreality.

Lindblom's early work in the American public sector (Lindblom 1959; Braybrooke and Lindblom 1963) quickly dispelled the myth that decision-making, in public institutions at least, was a linear, sequential process. Decisions here were made in a halting 'incremental' way with periods of recycling, iteration and reformulation. The process was a non-linear one.

So instead of final choices being arrived at after the full rational process of search and evaluation is completed, small adjustments are made to ongoing strategies. The full range of alternative solutions is not considered, only ones which do not differ markedly from the status quo. Decisions proceed by a series of small steps, rather than attaining and implementing the complete solution in one large step. For Lindblom the advantages of this approach are clear. Because each step, in itself, is not too dissimilar from what is already being done, it does not upset too many stakeholders. They do not feel threatened by radical change so it is possible to gain commitment for what is being done. The repercussions from changes which, initially at least, are relatively minor, are likely to be less serious and more predictable. Most importantly, the decision has more chance of being 'undone' if necessary; it is more reversible. Once each small step has been taken it gives a clearer picture of what has to be done and the future becomes more focused. If the chosen path now seems unlikely to lead to the desired destination, or if changing circumstances make the destination less appropriate, the step can be retraced with less difficulty than a larger one.

Lindblom argues that this is not only a description of what is done in organizations but also what ought to be done, given the inherent unpredictability of the context in which most decision-makers work. The incrementalist model is therefore in the interesting position of being both normative and descriptive as Smith and May (1980) have commented.

Some have suggested that incrementalism, or 'muddling through' as Lindblom has referred to it, is less a recipe for change, more likely a formula for inertia. It has been argued that small decisions which are only marginally different from the status quo are fine – if the current position is acceptable. But if change needs to be immediate and substantial, for example if the organization is in crisis, then incrementalism is not enough. Lindblom has countered that radical change can be equally swift whether it is effected by a series of small frequent steps or one large stride. In fact, smaller steps may be quicker since they may encounter less delaying opposition.

Although Lindblom's work began in public administration, further work in private sector organizations has come to similar conclusions.

Quinn's (1978; 1980) development of the concept into 'logical incrementalism' comes from the very similar processes which can be found in private sector organizations. It appears that all kinds of decision-makers operate in an incremental fashion.

When Mintzberg and his colleagues (1976) studied 25 strategic decisions in a variety of Canadian organizations they found even clearer evidence of cycling and recycling of information and alternatives, again showing that the making of this level of decision is likely to require constant adjustment and reappraisal. Their study distinguished seven kinds of process: simple impasse, political design, basic search, modified search, basic design, blocked design, and dynamic design processes. Most of these experience delays and interruptions, and repeated reconsideration. Nutt's (1984) work analysed 73 decisions in health-related organizations in the USA and noticed some similar patterns occurring in search processes.

On the other hand, Heller et al. (1988) were prepared to assume common sequential phases across decision processes in British, Dutch and (former) Yugoslav organizations. They examined 217 cases of medium- and long-term decisions in each of these three countries: 80 cases in the UK, 55 in the Netherlands and 82 in former Yugoslavia (in addition to lower-level operational decision-making, which is not relevant for our purposes here). Four distinct phases were identified, namely: start-up; development (which includes the search for alternatives); finalization; and implementation. Not everything may be circuitous. Indeed, it is claimed that in periods of crisis decisions can be made in a relatively speedy and straightforward way (Dutton 1986; Rosenthal 1986). When organizations are in trouble and urgent action is required, those in authority can be given great freedom to act, even by subordinates whose jobs may be affected, particularly if they are perceived to have the necessary grasp of the situation and are likely to be able to do something to help.

So whilst it has become a truism that decision-making by the elite takes place in a state of political excitation and is not at all straightforward, this is a view that can be taken too far. All decision-making need not be so. Not all decisions are made the same way. Why is this? Why are decision processes the way that they are? What factors influence process?

## The Bradford Studies: Finding Explanations for Process

The Bradford Studies (Hickson et al. 1986; also Cray et al. 1988; 1991) set out to try and answer these questions. The Bradford team investigated the making of 150 decisions in 30 organizations in England (5 decisions in each), covering manufacturing and service industries in both public and private sectors. Examples include glass and engineering manufacturers, brewers, electricity and water utilities, insurance companies and financial institutions, universities and polytechnics, and local government. Using face-to-face interviews with senior executives as well as a number of in-depth case studies with a range of informants, the research built up a picture of decision-making from initiation to authorization. That is, from 'the first recalled deliberate action which begins movement towards a decision (when, for example, the matter is discussed in a meeting, or a report is called for)', to a point 'when the decision and its implementation are authorized'. A further development of the research, discussed later in this chapter, focuses on the implementation and outcomes of a subset of 55 of these decisions.

As the researchers recognize, decision start and end points are not easy to identify. The beginnings and endings of organizational processes commingle and it is no simple matter to carve out a slice of time for detailed investigation. Nevertheless, the limits of time and attention which hamper all research necessitate selection. Given this caution, an interesting statistic emerges from the Bradford work. The mean time that it takes to make a strategic decision is just over twelve months. An unexpectedly short time perhaps? The range, however, is from one month to four years. Immediately then, a wide variation along this dimension – duration – emerges. How else did decision-making differ and why?

Three kinds of processes were found, labelled *sporadic*, *fluid* and *constricted*. The sample of cases divided almost evenly between each cluster, so about a third of all the decisions studied were made in sporadic ways, a third were made in a fluid manner, while a third followed a constricted path.

Sporadic processes are subject to more disrupting delays than either fluid or constricted processes. The information used will be uneven in quality, some good, some bad, and will come from a wide range of sources, and there will be scope for negotiation. This kind of process is 'informally spasmodic and protracted' (Hickson et al. 1986: 118). The tale of electricity generation already referred to in this chapter (Wilson 1982) is a colourful example.

Fluid processes are almost the opposite of sporadic ones. There is much less informal interaction and the process flows more through formal meetings with fewer impediments and delays. These processes are rather faster and the decision is likely to be made in months, rather than years. In short, a fluid process is 'steadily paced, formally channelled and speedy' (Hickson et al. 1986: 120).

Lastly, constricted processes share some of the characteristics of each of the other two but have features distinctive from both. They are less fluid than the fluids and less sporadic than the sporadics, but constrained in a way that neither of the others is. They tend to revolve around a central figure such as a finance or production director who draws on a wide range of expertise in other departments before arriving at a decision. In short, they are 'narrowly channelled' (1986: 122).

Although public sector organizations and manufacturing firms each show some bias towards sporadic processes, each process is found in every type of organization. So the managements of organizations in any sector or type of business, making strategic decisions about any aspect of their products or services, may go through any of the three kinds of process, sporadic, fluid or constricted. The type of organization is not the strongest determinant of process. So what is? The Bradford team found that the primary and 'dual' explanation is the degree of *politicality* and *complexity* inherent in the matter for decision itself.

In other words, it is the political and complex nature of what is being decided which is all-important. With regard to politicality, all decisions draw in a specific 'decision set' of interests: those who have a stake in the outcome. These are drawn from inside and outside the organization: individuals, departments, divisions, owners, suppliers, government agencies and so on. But not all interests are equally influential and not every decision draws in the same number or configuration of them. Some decisions attract less attention: they are less controversial, perhaps, or require work to be done by relatively fewer people. Others are a whirl of interested activity. So every decision is shaped to some degree by the influence of the decision set. Politicality refers to the degree of influence which is brought to bear on a decision and how this influence is distributed within and without the organization.

Complexity refers to the problems which making the decision encompasses. The reasons for complexity are varied. Some decisions are more unusual than others: they may require information to be garnered from more diverse sources, they may have more serious or widespread consequences, or set more fundamental precedents for the future. Since each decision process is made up of various problems – some of which are more complex than others – decisions will vary in terms of how comprehensible they are. Some will be relatively straightforward while others will be more problematic, depending on the nature of the issues involved.

Together, these concepts of politicality and complexity are the primary explanation of why strategic decisions follow the processes they do. The strength and distribution of influence, coupled with the complexity of what is being decided, shape the process which ensues. As the authors put it, in accounting for what happens 'the matter for decision matters most' (1986: 248).

By their comprehensive mapping of decision processes the Bradford team demonstrate that not all decision-making is politically tumultuous. Far from it. Sporadic processes are most inclined that way, perhaps a third of all decisions at most. The greater proportion of decisions are more deliberative and less contentious.

Yet below what was reached empirically must have lain the concealed second and third faces of power. Were there no signs of what lay beneath? The research did show that in at least a third of all decisions the outcome was a foregone conclusion. The results were known before the process of deciding was completed, indeed often before it began. The Bradford team call this 'quasi-decision-making' (1986: 52). Sometimes this occurred because there was only one realistic alternative, but on other occasions quasi-decision-making must have been the result of prior manoeuvres by powerful parties involved. This strongly suggests that overt, aware decision-making frequently does 'go through the motions' within limits set by pre-existent positions.

A great deal of influence is exercised overtly, of course, and this research also has much to say about who has it and who does not. Generally, trade unions do not influence decisions, neither does the personnel function nor the purchasing department, nor government in most cases. The most influential interests (apart from the CEO) come from production (or the equivalent), sales and marketing, and accounting. This core triad of 'heavyweight' functions is involved more often and exerts most influence whatever the type of organization. Although external power-holders do take part in the game the balance of power is held internally. And this remains true throughout the process, for these same interests hold sway over implementation.

Building on the Bradford Studies, Butler et al. (1993) studied seventeen cases of a specific decision topic – strategic investment decisions. Reflecting Thompson and Tuden (1959), they argued that four elements were important in realizing effective investment decisions, namely, computation, judgement, negotiation and inspiration. They found that inspiration alone was not a recipe for effectiveness, since decision-making not only had to have accurately analysed the complexity of the situation (judgement and computation) but also had to steer a course through the political reality of persuading others of the inspirational idea (negotiation).

But does what happens in the process leading to the formal decision have any effect on the subsequent outcomes? What factors lead to success during implementation and beyond?

## IMPLEMENTATION AND OUTCOMES

Getting things done in an organizational setting is not always easy, and many writers have drawn attention to the problems of 'collective action' (for example, Pressman and Wildavsky 1973). The act of deciding may not be trouble-free, but implementing the decision can be worse![1]

Several authors have looked at the way in which implementation is carried out. It has been suggested (Nutt 1986; 1987; 1989) that managers choose from a repertoire of implementation tactics. These are the ways managers get others to action decisions. According to Nutt, they comprise *intervention*, where key executives justify the need for change by introducing new norms to identify performance inadequacies; *participation*, where task forces are set up to develop implementation and identify stakeholders; *persuasion*, when implementation strategies are delegated to technical staff or experts who then 'sell' their ideas back to the decision-makers; and finally, *edict*, where decision-makers use control and personal power while avoiding any form of participation (1986: 249). In Nutt's American sample, persuasion has been shown to be the most popular form of implementation tactic (it was used in 42 per cent of the cases), followed by edict (23 per cent), then intervention (19 per cent), and least of all participation (17 per cent). But if the measure of success is taken as being whether decisions are fully 'adopted' (that is, implemented) at the end of this process, then intervention with a 100 per cent success rate is clearly the most successful tactic. Persuasion and participation were moderately successful and edict was the least successful with a success rate of 43 per cent. One conclusion from this work is that managers only rarely hit on implementation strategies which are likely to lead to complete success.

But since there are so many dicta as to what managers need for strategic success it is unsurprising if they are perhaps rather nonplussed at how to act for the best . Some have argued that 'ownership' of the original strategy is crucial (Giles 1991), but so too is the need to gain acceptance (Piercy 1989). Setting clear objectives and 'milestones' is thought to be helpful (Owen 1993), while the 'excellence' literature (Peters and Waterman 1982) stresses the importance of a cohesive corporate culture.

Bourgeois and Brodwin (1984) have made a useful assessment of some of the literature and have distinguished five approaches to implementation. Each approach has its own view of the challenges of strategic action and thus the priorities to be tackled to implement successfully. Each therefore suggests a different way to put strategies into effect.

The first of these schemata is entitled the commander model. In this form of implementation the reliance is on centralized direction. The decision is made and others implement in accordance with instructions. The change model emphasizes the role of structure and of control and rewards systems in effecting change. The third approach sees strategy as a negotiated outcome at a senior level and is called the collaborative model. The cultural model relies on a strong culture which infuses the whole organization. The fifth and final model, the crescive model, advocates '"growing" strategy from within the firm' (1984: 242) and encourages managers to champion good strategies.

Bourgeois and Brodwin suggest when each of these approaches may be more or less appropriate. For example the commander model may work best when the change is unthreatening, when senior management already has a great deal of power and when existing systems and behaviours do not get in the way of what is required for implementation. In addition, objective planners and good information systems are called for. In contrast, the cultural model needs decentralized power and shared goals. This model may work best when the organization is stable and growing (1984: 252).

These several approaches lead to the conclusion that it is still not clear what factors influence successful implementation. With this in mind the Bradford Studies work has been extended by the authors of this chapter to cover what happened when the decisions were put into effect during the years following the original fieldwork. As already mentioned, a subset of 55 of the original 150 decisions has been chosen to search for any identifiable factors which might have affected the success of what was done. Success in implementing is assessed primarily by performance in terms of what was intended by the decision-makers, that is 'achievement'.

It has been found that decisions, once taken, are carried out. Very rarely are decisions left undone once they have been authorized. Suspicions that senior executives are preoccupied by taking decisions and then overlook whether anything is done about them are not borne out, at any rate in these British organizations. So once a formal decision is made, something happens. Many also achieve more or less what was intended. But not all; things do go wrong, there are unforeseen happenings, and decision-makers can get surprises.

The example of a regional brewer in the UK shows this. Seeking to expand capacity the company (a small owner-managed firm) discovered another brewery far larger than itself was for sale and bought it. An opportunistic decision which appeared to be a fortuitous answer to the firm's needs initially worked out well. The purchase price was very favourable, there were few production problems and the demand for the product was clear and sustainable. Yet over time, and with hindsight, it was evident that the buying and running of such a disproportionately larger second brewery had put insupportable strain on the whole operation. Cash flow problems ensued, were met by an injection of funds from outside, arose again when these funds proved insufficient, eventually leading to the take-over of the company and its disappearance as an entity. This was not at all what its owner-managers had intended when they set out to expand it as an independent firm. This shows how unexpected outcomes can result from decisions which at first seem to be wholly successful, and that a long time frame is needed to evaluate what transpires.

This study may be able to shed some light on some of the prescripts for success discussed earlier. As we have seen, a prime tenet of the 'excellence' debate, and one which has been greatly enlarged upon elsewhere in the literature, is the need to have a strong corporate culture. It is also felt to be particularly helpful to have a *champion* – someone in a powerful position who can foster support and drive implementation through the organization. The idea of the 'powerful leader' is one which is mythologized in management literature; witness the wealth and popularity of material written by impassioned entrepreneurs and sundry captains of industry in recent years. Indeed, the 'edict' mode of implementation and the 'commander model' both recognize the attraction of dynamic, charismatic centralized control – both in theory and in actuality. Several of our cases tell a different story. A champion can lead an organization to a series of failures, pushing on to realize his own vision but taking no heed of uncomfortable facts or doubting colleagues. This we call the 'blinkered' champion. How much worse the potential consequences if the culture is so cohesive, or the champion so powerful, that no one else sees the danger ahead, or dares to speak out.

In manufacturing firms we have found a tendency to 'over-reach' (Wilson et al. 1996) whereby firms stretch themselves beyond the limits of what they can manage and are forced to retract, if they can. The example of the regional brewer cited above provides an apt illustration here. Over-reach can easily lead to failure, depending on the degree to which decisions can be 'undone' once the danger is recognized. If the decision is largely irreversible, and if the scale or scope of the decision is too disproportional to the size of the company, then the likelihood of failure increases.

There is another body of thought, to which this chapter now turns, that stands distinct from both rational models and politicized views. Both of these are attempts to elucidate causal relationships between events and outcomes. From this other more challenging perspective, both are misunderstandings of the world in general and organizations in particular.

## STRATEGIES AND GARBAGE-CANS: CHAOS AND DISORGANIZED ORDER

The most imaginative, coherent and penetrating perspective is that of the evocatively named 'garbage-can' model (Cohen et al. 1972). This is a depiction of decision-making which turns much of what we have previously discussed on its head. Garbage-cans are found predominantly in 'organized anarchies', complex organizations whose internal processes are not really understood, even by people working in them. In these situations the means and ends of decisions become 'uncoupled' (Weick 1976) so that actions do not lead to expected outcomes, but are hijacked along the way by other decisions and other actions. The main components of decisions – problems, solutions, participants and choice situations – pour into the organizational garbage-can in a seemingly haphazard way, a stream of demands for the fluid attention and energy of decision-makers. If problem, solution, participant and choice situation happen to collide appropriately, then a decision occurs. It may not be foreseen. It may not be one which actually solves the problem to which it has been attached. For not only are the means and ends of decisional processes disconnected, but solutions to problems are in existence before the problems themselves are recognized.

All the while participants move in and out of decision-making processes since 'every entrance is an exit somewhere else' (March and Olsen 1976), which creates discontinuity. Perversely, actors jostle for the right to get involved and then appear uninterested either in exercising it,

or in whether decisions are carried out. The conventionally accepted order of things is transformed, put back to front, jumbled beyond recognition. The picture is one of seeming chaos, of disorder. And yet there are some patterns under the confusion and these can be modelled once the parameters are known. The process is not truly random and can be predicted to some extent, although it can feel like chaos to participants. Decisions do get made, although the process is about as far removed from rational choice prescriptions as it is possible to get.

Outside direct research into decision-making in organizations, chaos theories have received increasing attention in recent years. Beginning with iconoclastic revelations in the natural and physical sciences, their provocative and rather disturbing conclusions have thrown many orthodox assumptions into turmoil. With the basic postulate that small changes can, by means of complex feedback cycles, result in ever more complex, dynamic changes of unpredictable and epic proportions, it asks fundamental questions about the nature of cause-and-effect mechanisms. As yet, these ideas are feeding slowly into theories about organizations and management. 'Normal', positivistic, and functional orthodoxies still have a central place in organization theorizing, although other positions are generating increasing interest. The garbage-can model, together with the work of authors such as Weick (1976) and Brunsson (1985), can be seen as forerunners of this growing interest in chaos and complexity.

## MAPPING THE TERRAIN OF DECISION PROCESS RESEARCH

The range of work on decision-making covered in this chapter may be contrasted along two key dimensions. One is concerned with the nature of the decision process itself over time, the other with the involvement of various interests in the process. They may be termed the dimension of process *action* and the dimension of political *interest*. The principal researchers are 'mapped' on them in Figure 1 to present an overview of research and researchers. This is as we see it, of course, and others, especially the researchers and theorists themselves, may have differing views on where particular work should be positioned. Such a diagram is illustrative rather than precise.

### The Action Dimension

On the action dimension, decision-making processes may be viewed as running from the

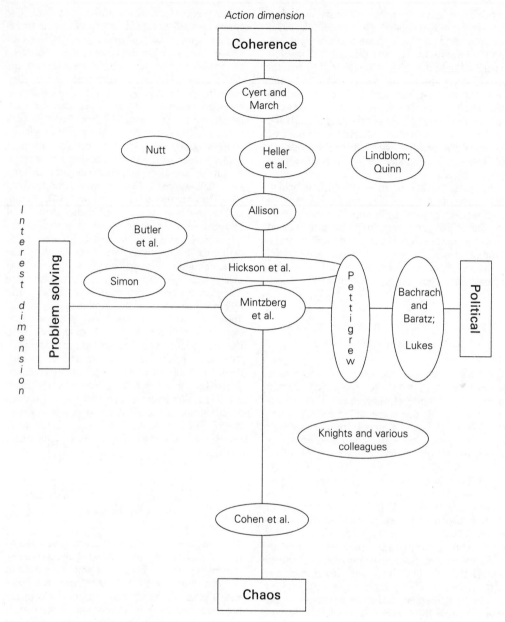

Figure 1   *Mapping decision studies*

more *coherent* to the more *chaotic*. Authors who take a predominantly coherent view of process subscribe to the notion that decision process trajectories can be relatively sequenced and linear, and reflect attempts by decision-makers to achieve step-by-step progress toward stated goals or objectives. Lindblom's (1959) incrementalism and Quinn's (1980) description of progressive change through step-by-step actions are examples of the coherent approach, as are Heller et al.'s (1988) linear phases. Coherence implies 'intended rationality' (Cyert and March 1963). Individuals strive to achieve rational decision-making, but are prevented from achieving this through lack of perfect knowledge, through cognitive limits and so on. Nevertheless, the intention is coherence. Butler et al. (1993) show how coherence can be better achieved by attention to specific factors (inspiration, judgement and computation). Hickson et al. (1986) claim to have uncovered a spectrum of process characteristics, so logically they also tend toward the coherent view, since their characterizations presuppose some degree of detectable order in the process.

A diametrically opposite perspective on process is adopted by those who argue that coherence is a myth derived from rational economics. Neat and precise its descriptions may be, but they do not describe the reality of decision processes which are not necessarily linear, sequenced or intendedly rational. At the extreme of this chaotic view of decision process lie the garbage cans of Cohen et al. (1972). Here, solutions are generated prior to processes and are attached to problems in a seemingly random fashion. Cohen et al. (1972) stand alone to define the chaos end of the action dimension. Processes are part of the embeddedness of the organization and are not always under control (e.g. Knights and Morgan 1991; Knights and Murray 1992). Chaotic action can also be seen in less extreme form in Mintzberg et al.'s (1976) recycling and discontinuous processes. Here, decisions stop, start again, and revisit their point of origin. They are still processes occurring over time, yet they lack the apparent linear sequential characteristics of their more coherent counterparts. It is very visible that this lower half of Figure 1 is least filled (or most empty). The intellectual boldness and empirical ingenuity to follow where Cohen et al. (1972) led does not come easily.

## The Interest Dimension

The more political interest dimension runs from a purely *problem-solving* view to a negotiated order view in which diverse interests give a *political* colour to decision-making.

The problem-solving view is perhaps best typified by Simon's (1960) description of decision-making as a 'new science'. It is 'new', because Simon rejected the prevailing orthodoxy of his coeval economists, who believed economic models of individual choice behaviour could be applied directly to organizational decision processes. It is 'scientific', however, since Simon still held centrally the notion of problem-oriented behaviour from those involved. Goals were specified, targets were set and the overall problem was held in view, whilst decision participants sought solutions which were satisfactory and which were sufficient to address the problem. This 'satisficing' behaviour is firmly rooted in the problem-solving perspective. Radical though Simon's ideas may have been to economists at the time, his relative orthodoxy is revealed when reflected against the more political perspectives which gained momentum in the 1970s. At the other extreme are the analyses of Bachrach and Baratz (1962;

1970), who completely eschew problem-solving approaches. All activity is politically driven, they argue, to the extent that certain items are deliberately kept off decision agenda. Whoever defines the agenda or the problem holds the key to decision-making. Bachrach and Baratz are clear about emphasizing politics over problem-solving perspectives, yet reveal far less detail about the action dimension of the decision process. Presumably to them this could be either chaotic or coherent. To them the most important dimension is the extent to which decisions are either made in advance, or kept off the agenda altogether by powerful interests. Pettigrew (1973; 1985; 1987) is less extreme, taking problems as given and overt, but agreeing that the predominant focus is political, as gatekeepers screen information or as interests negotiate in the decision arena. This places Pettigrew's work firmly on the political end of the interest dimension, but there is a similar lack of attention in his work to the relative degrees of coherence and chaos in the process. Hence his location on Figure 1 spans only a small range on the action dimension.

Since the explanation of differences in process advanced by Hickson et al. (1986) includes both the nature of the problem and its politics, their work is shown as extending in both directions along the interest dimension.

All the authors in Figure 1 have focused on decision-making *per se*. They have started from the decision as the unit of analysis around which other factors might vary. Decisions may vary in content (what they are about) and in process (how the decision moves through the organization) and they may vary in importance (operational or strategic). The common feature, however, is that the concept of decision is the primary unit of analysis. Suppose that the decision itself cannot be taken for granted? Suppose that the very idea of 'a decision' is misleading?

## THE CONCEPT OF 'A DECISION'

The realism of much of the decision-making research has been called into question by those who feel that the very concept of decision has outlived its usefulness. According to writers such as Mintzberg and Waters (1990) it 'gets in the way' of understanding organizational processes. They argue that there are inherent problems with the concept, one of these being that while decisions imply a commitment to action there are situations where actions are taken without decisions having been made. They argue that to see organizational shifts in terms of the deliberate making of decisions over-concretizes the rather ambiguous, uncertain processes of change and underplays the continual redefinition, reshaping and reformulation which commitments to action constantly undergo. It is possible that the 'quasi-decisions' about foregone conclusions mentioned earlier (Hickson et al. 1986) are an empirical verification of this.

Mintzberg and Waters (1990) claim the notion of decision is particularly unhelpful when thinking about strategies which organizations pursue. This opens up a large area which has not yet received full attention. For although the literature on strategic decisions often discusses corporate strategy (and vice versa) the links between the two are implicit rather than defined. Do strategic decisions implement some overarching strategy, are they made within the context of pre-existing strategies, and what is the interactive effect of decisions and strategies? Are decisions more successful if they are part of a 'global' strategy, or do they exist separately, and does this matter?

Mintzberg and Water's (1982) earlier work on strategy formulation prompted their subsequent musings. In this earlier work they defined strategy as a 'pattern in a stream of decisions'. Yet further ruminations along the lines discussed above refined the description to a 'pattern in a stream of actions' (Mintzberg and Waters 1985). Thus strategies may *emerge* rather than be deliberately decided in advance. Organizations may find themselves going in a particular strategic direction without anyone explicitly having decided that they should do so. The way this happens is that a strategy materializes from the combined effects of various actions which may or may not be directly connected. Over time, and with hindsight, these may be sufficiently consistent to be viewed as forming some kind of pattern. In this case it is possible to talk of the organization having a strategy, although it may not have been intentional.

For students of decision-making, this casts fresh doubt on the validity of the idea of decisions being deliberate, purposeful and planned, even on their 'happening' at all in an explicit way at particular points in time. Some authors in the area of strategic management have linked this with chaos theories (for example, see Stacey 1993a; 1993b). Yet this view may go too far. Others have countered (Butler 1990; Pettigrew 1990) that to discard the concept of a decision altogether 'throws the baby out with the bath water'. They maintain that the usefulness of the concept outweighs its limitations.

Subsuming the analysis of individual decisions into the patterns made by planned or emergent strategies is one example of the different levels of analysis in decision theory. Another in sharp contrast rests on the premise that decision-making is best studied by looking at interactions, interpretations of meaning and the significance of symbols, given by common-sense accounts by individuals of how and why they acted in certain ways. Such accounts produce a richness of data, largely consisting of definitions of the situation and interpretations by individuals (see Silverman 1970; Clegg 1975; Goffman 1982). What would such an analysis do to some of the research we have described earlier? It would have radically changed our own account of the expansion decision in the regional UK brewer, for example. Instead of giving a single picture of this decision process composed from managers' recollections, at the level of political balance and financial capacity, as we did, an interactionist perspective would have described in detail each manager's own account of the situation. In this way, the overarching constructs of 'decision' are removed. The account of what happened (and why) is expressed and contained only in the eyes and language of participants.

Although these perspectives draw heavily from earlier works concerned with existentialism (e.g. Sudnow 1965), concerns with postmodernity have also prompted decision theory to re-examine its basic assumptions. As Jeffcutt (1994: 241) says, 'the understanding of organization is inseparable from the organization of understanding.' Understanding decisions, therefore, is a process of analysing narratives, interpreting actions and identifying meaning in symbols as articulated by individuals. Such a perspective questions the constructs of late modernity (such as organizational size, technology, subunit power and characterizations of decision processes as incremental or sporadic) and argues that trying to draw conclusions about the relative contribution of such constructs to comprehending decision-making is fruitless. How different, then, would be our understanding (and data base) for decision theory had this perspective gained dominance whilst Simon, Cyert and March and Lindblom were first uncovering the details of decision process in the 1960s? Characterizations and aggregations of organizational and process data would be replaced by tales, folklore, dreams, symbols and myths. Case studies of decisions would not exist in their current form since they are argued to be imposed narrative, corresponding more to the logical constructs of an author rather than reflecting the 'reality' of the situation. It remains to be seen whether decision theory will look like this in the future, or whether it could even exist, then, as a separate focus of research since a decision is a false construct itself through postmodern eyes.

At a macro level, organizations can be seen to be imitative whereby their managements follow leads taken by other organizations in the sector and sometimes outside it (see Grinyer and Spender 1979; Hinings and Greenwood 1988; Fombrun and Shanley 1990). This follow-my-leader approach has some appeal, since competing firms within the same business sector will be likely to adapt and react to each other's strategies and may be seen to be following one another. For example, in our case of the regional brewer, it would be plausible to argue that growth in scale of operations was a 'recipe' prevalent in the brewing sector at the time (Grinyer and Spender 1979). The directors were merely following the trend. Similarly, Cyert and March's (1963) characterizations of 'satisficing' or 'sequential attention to goals' could be interpreted as cautious corporate action taken with an eye on the competition in the sector (rather than as managerial limitations). The electricity generation undertaken by a chemical company (Wilson 1982) could equally be seen as an example of a diversification strategy, prevalent in the chemical industry at the time, as much as an example of political careerism which is how it was presented.

Keat and Abercrombie (1990) go further and imply that the study of individual decisions in an organization is inappropriate since they fit into a pattern determined largely by socio-political factors. They cite the emergence of the 'enterprise culture' in Britain (1979 onwards) whereby particular strategic decisions in firms are framed by interventionist government policies such as privatization (for public sector organizations), reduction of dependencies (on suppliers and government agencies) and an increased emphasis on the customer as a major influence in product and service decisions. They argue that although individual strategic decisions may vary in topic content they will fit into this overall pattern if a wide enough frame of reference is adopted.

Yet even at this level of analysis, Child (1972) argues that managers do have a choice. They are not, he argues, deterministically led by the actions of other organizations. The regional brewer described above could have chosen to stay small and on a single site, and the chemical company could have chosen not to diversify into unrelated activity.

Voluntarist–determinist debates are provoked here. Do managers have the content and process of decision imposed upon them, or do they exercise a degree of strategic choice?

One final challenge to the contentious but stimulating area of research that this chapter has described arises from the differences in socio-economic context around the world. Yet the knowledge base from which virtually all decision theory emanates is socio-culturally North American or Western European. The implications of this partiality are examined next.

## NORTH, SOUTH, EAST AND WEST: THE CULTURE SHOCK FOR RESEARCHERS ON DECISION-MAKING PROCESSES

Take another look from a different angle at the main empirical research into the overt, empirically traced, processes of decision-making, *and* at the researchers who did it. Working around Figure 1 (in a clockwise direction) is revealing. What it reveals is shown in Table 1. It is startling when listed in this way.

Table 1 *Researcher nationality and research location*

| Researchers | Research nationality | Research location |
|---|---|---|
| Cyert and March | American | American firms |
| Lindblom | American | American public administration |
| Quinn | American | American and European firms |
| Pettigrew | British | British firms |
| Knights and colleagues | British | British firms |
| Cohen et al. | American, Norwegian (Olsen) | Scandinavian and American organizations |
| Simon | American | American, mainly business |
| Butler et al. | British | British firms |
| Nutt | American | American health services organizations |
| Heller et al. | British (Heller), Dutch, Yugoslavian (Rus) | British, Dutch, and Yugoslavian organizations |
| Allison | American | American government |
| Hickson et al. | British, American (Cray), Swedish (Axelsson) | Diverse organizations in England |
| Mintzberg et al. | Canadian, Indian (Raisinghani) | Diverse Anglo-Canadian organizations |

The researchers are almost all Westerners, from the United States, Canada, Britain, and Scandinavia. They are almost all Northerners, from North America and Northern Europe. The data themselves are drawn almost exclusively from managers of the same genre. So here are researchers and research subjects all from the distinctively individualistic, most coolly impersonal cultures of what is loosely called 'the West'. The only exceptions are Rus, who contributed data from two organizations in the former Yugoslavia to the work by Heller et al., and Raisinghani, an Indian in Canada with Mintzberg.

Of course, even among these Westerners and Northerners there are societal differences. There are cultural variations within 'the West'. It is tempting to think that some part of the differences in ideas about decision-making is traceable to this.

For example, Anglo-Canadian society is held to be more considerate and less urgently impelled to action than its giant American neighbour (e.g. Hofstede 1980; 1991; Carroll 1990; Lipset 1986). Could this be why recycling features in Mintzberg et al.'s (1976) findings? Are Canadian managers more willing than Americans to cautiously refer to matters so that they can be reconsidered over and over again?

How then, it might be asked, could Lindblom (1959) have discerned step-by-step incrementalism in American practice? It does not fit the bold decisiveness of the 'Yankee' stereotype. Speculatively, this could be because the politicality which Pettigrew (1973) and Hickson et al. (1986) found pronounced in processes in organizations in England was at an extreme in the government administration observed by Lindblom (1959), so that in this kind of organization the need to manoeuvre issues along thwarted the underlying American desire for quick decisions. Societal culture is not the only explanation for what happens.

Yet it can hardly be surprising that self-assertive political activity is a feature of the managerial echelons of the individualistic Anglo nations (especially the English?). Nor that the only work influenced by the careful, thorough, Dutch (Lawrence 1991), that by Heller et al. (1988), should have divided processes into conspicuously orderly phases.

Quite the opposite is the most radical notion of all, 'the garbage-can model' put forward by Cohen et al. (1972). As described earlier in the chapter, this is imaginative, even fanciful, in supposing that decisions can occur by the chance coinciding of their ingredients. Could its conception have been influenced by one author being Norwegian and all the authors being in continual contact with other Scandinavian researchers (as in March and Olsen 1976), who bring from that part of the world the vivid if not outlandish imagery of its traditional literature?

Further, research emanating from that by Hickson et al. (1986) has shown specific differences in the handling of time between Western decision-making processes. The British take more time over a decision than the Americans do (Mallory et al. 1983), and the Swedes are even slower than the British (Axelsson et al. 1991). Or, to put it the other way around, the Americans are faster than either (which does fit their stereotype).

In so far as these differences among the Westerners could be due in some measure to differences in societal cultures, attention is alerted. For if this is so, then how very different again must be processes in the wider world. Do the typological concepts and the models which have been examined in this chapter apply only to the organizations of 'Northern/Western' societies? Although that is probably too pessimistic a suggestion since there will be commonalities across societies, yet differences of degree, and inadequacies of concept, must surely be anticipated in other societies with other cultures. Indeed, it is possible that some completely fresh ideas might be needed.

This is no criticism of the researchers concerned. For decades they have had their hands full – or, rather, their heads full – of trying to make sense of something as elusive empirically and theoretically as powerful elite decision-making, just using organizations in the nearest available society. It would have been too much to take on the subtleties of cultural variation in addition. Moreover, only now are the beginnings of a truly world view of organizations and the organized taking shape (e.g. Hickson and Pugh 1995).

Since it is predominantly Western researchers who have had a rare tradition of fundamental research, some money for it, and some accessible organizations, the main ideas about decision-making have come from within their pluralistic, bluntly competitive, impersonal cultures. So there is nothing in this chapter that emphasizes, say, personal loyalties or the very personal wielding of supreme authority, or harmony-preserving devices, which are more pronounced in the wider world. The prevalence of the impersonal bureaucratic norms and forms whose early stages Weber (1947) analysed so insightfully is taken for granted, together with cultures that in their work-related aspects are comparatively individualistic and of low power distance, as Hofstede (1980; 1991) has termed them.

Yet most of the world struggles to reconcile this Western view of organization and management, carried by its expatriate managers and its exported teaching, with ways of managing more appropriate to Easterners and Southerners in Asia, Africa, Arabia, and South America. In their more person-centred approach it is people to whom loyalty is owed, often overriding any loyalty to the abstract fictions of organizational roles and departments. Harmony and consideration for others on the job moderate the drive for self-assertive achievement. Respect for higher authority is inconsistent with the idea that an ultimately uncontrollable chaos could be at the core of organizational behaviour (even where organizational practice may malfunction chaotically). For these are the relatively personalistic, collectivistic, higher power distance cultures (e.g. Hofstede 1980; 1991; Alston 1986; Lincoln and McBride 1987; Redding 1990; Child 1994; Jaeger and Kanungo 1990; Muna 1980) whose managerial decision-making processes might well not be adequately encompassed by concepts of satisficing search, incrementalism, rationality and politicality, recycling, sporadic or fluid or constricted movement, or coinciding garbage.

Although there is very little direct evidence to go on for that, what there is does signal the significance of non-Western, non-Northern cultures for decision-making, as the broad theoretical framework for cultures postulated by Lachman et al. (1994) predicts it should.

Management in the Arabian Middle East, for example, share the higher regard for status-based authority, especially when it goes with seniority and family position, which is general outside the West (e.g. Muna 1980; El-Ashker 1987; Attiyah 1992). So decision-making tends to be more centralized. Yet this hold on power can be felt to carry an obligation to personally consult underlings, even if this be what Westerners call 'pseudo-participation' in which no real power is shared. The well-known Japanese *ringi* system of confirming concurrence with a decision can also be 'pseudo' in that sense, but it does affirm at worst that those concerned will go along with a decision, at best that they fully support it. This is the practice of circulating among appropriate managers a document to which they may (or may not) affix an assenting personal signature stamp, *after* a prolonged period of largely informal discussion or *nemawashi* (Alston 1986; Lincoln and McBride 1987).

The Latin world has something of both the centralization and the personal touch, and more. Brazil, for instance, adds the immediatism of a 'New World' culture which has no time to wait for the future. Compared to English decision-making processes, those of Brazil are inclined to be far shorter, even hasty, yet despite that they are much more personal and sociable with management meetings inclined to meander and decisions not infrequently taking shape at weekend barbecues (Oliveira 1992; Amado and Brasil 1991).

By contrast, decision-making in sub-Saharan Africa, where government involvement is closer and instability usually greater, is widely authoritarian and politicized (e.g. Kiggundu 1989; Jaeger and Kanungo 1990; Blunt and Jones 1992). Indeed, planned or controlled economies of a kind not found in the Western nations always reduce the scope for decisions to be taken by the managers of operating organizations, and centralize those decisions that are allowed to them, as for instance in countries as different as Egypt (Badran and Hinings 1981) and China (Child 1994).

Is it then really conceivable that where there is an authoritative hand holding down the lid, there could be Anglo-Scandinavian chancy garbage-can processes? How could there be as many politically imbued sporadic processes as were found in England when there is not the same underlying individualistic pluralism? As yet, who knows?

The trite conclusion to this chapter therefore can only be that more research is needed. Trite it may be, but specifically it means more research beyond the confines of the (Northern) Western world. Of course, work should continue within that world on patterns of process, their conclusions, implementations, and consequences, and hopefully researchers doing this will become more cognizant than hitherto of the cultures they are working within. But research on decision-making at the managerial apex should extend to organizations in other societies. In this it is lagging behind the rest of organization theory. More has been done in more societies on the use of authority, on bureaucratization, on commitment and loyalties, on the use of time, and so on. Perhaps this is because of the empirical obstacles. Even Western managers accustomed to talking impersonally to all comers in comparatively open societies are cautious enough when asked to reveal to strangers something as sensitive as how a major decision is arrived at. Many managers elsewhere in the world would see no reason for doing anything so peculiar. Researchers in this difficult area will have to find means to break its culture bounds, nonetheless. Unless they can, Western models of decision-making will remain bounded by Western thinking and by Western constituted organizations. Although these organizations do make up a large proportion of the world's most developed economies, they are managed by and employ only a small proportion of humankind. Those who research their decision-making have come from an even smaller minority of human societies. Conceptual progress needs the stimulus of both non-Western data and non-Western researchers.

NOTE

1 Away from studies which specifically focus on the implementation of strategic decisions there is a range of work in other areas, including the broad area of change management, which can be considered to be related to this subject. This is not the place to deal with this material in any depth and readers are advised to refer to Chapter 9 in this *Handbook*.

REFERENCES

Allison, G.T. (1971) *Essence of Decision: Explaining the Cuban Missile Crisis.* Boston: Little Brown.

Alston, Jon P. (1986) *The American Samurai: Blending American and Japanese Managerial Practices.* De Gruyter.

Amado, Gilles and Brasil, Haroldo Vinagre (1991) 'Organizational behaviour and cultural context: the Brazilian "Jeitinho"', *International Studies of Management and Organization*, 21(3): 38–61.

Asch, S.E. (1955) 'Studies in independence and conformity: a minority of one against unanimous majority', *Psychological Monographs*, 20 (whole no. 416).

Attiyah, Hamid S. (1992) 'Research in Arab countries, published in Arabic', *Organization Studies*, 13(9): 105–10.

Axelsson, Runo, Cray, D., Mallory, G.R. and Wilson, D.C. (1991) 'Decision style in British and Swedish organizations: a comparative examination of strategic decision making', *British Journal of Management*, 2(2): 67–79.

Bachrach, P. and Baratz, M.S. (1962) 'The two faces of power', *American Political Science Review*, 56: 947–52.

Bachrach, P. and Baratz, M.S. (1970) *Power and Poverty: Theory and Practice.* London: Oxford University Press.

Badran, Mohamed and Hinings, Bob (1981) 'Strategies of administrative control and contextual constraints in a less developed country: the case of Egyptian public enterprise', *Organization Studies*, 2(1): 3–21. Reprinted in D.J. Hickson and C.J. McMillan (eds) (1981), *Organization and Nation: the Aston Programme IV.* Gower.

Beck, V. (1992) *The Risk Society.* London: Sage.

Blunt, Peter and Jones, Merrick L. (1992) *Managing Organizations in Africa.* De Gruyter.

Bourgeois, L.J. and Brodwin, D.R. (1984) 'Strategic implementation: five approaches to an elusive phenomenon', *Strategic Management Journal*, 5: 241–64.

Braybrooke, D. and Lindblom, C.E. (1963) *A Strategy of Decision.* New York: Free Press.

Brunsson, N. (1985) *The Irrational Organization.* New York: Wiley.

Burrell, Gibson and Morgan, Gareth (1993) *Socio-logical Paradigms and Organisational Analysis: Elements of the Sociology of Corporate Life.* Hants, UK: Ashgate.

Butler, R.J. (1990) 'Studying deciding: an exchange of views between Mintzberg and Waters, Pettigrew, and Butler', *Organization Studies*, 11(1): 2–16.

Butler, R.J., Davies, L., Pike, R. and Sharp, J. (1993) *Strategic Investment Decisions.* London: Routledge.

Carroll, Barbara W. (1990) 'Systemic conservation in North American organizations', *Organization Studies*, 11(3): 413–34.

Child, J. (1972) 'Organizational structure, environment and performance: the role of strategic choice', *Sociology*, 6: 1–22.

Child, J. (1994) *Management in China during the Age of Reform.* Cambridge University Press.

Clegg, S. (1975) *Power, Rule and Domination.* London: Routledge and Kegan Paul.

Cohen, M.D., March, J.G. and Olsen, J.P. (1972) 'The garbage can model of organizational choice', *Administrative Science Quarterly*, 17 (March): 1–25.

Cray, David, Mallory, Geoffrey R., Butler, Richard J., Hickson, David J. and Wilson, David C. (1988) 'Sporadic, fluid and constricted processes: three types of strategic decision-making in organizations', *Journal of Management Studies*, 25(1): 13–39.

Cray, David, Mallory, Geoffrey R., Butler, Richard J., Hickson, David J. and Wilson, David C. (1991) 'Explaining decision processes', *Journal of Management Studies*, 28(3): 227–51.

Crozier, Michel (1964) *The Bureaucratic Phenomenon.* London: Tavistock.

Crozier, Michel and Friedberg, Erhard (1980) *Actors and Systems.* Chicago: University of Chicago Press (published in French in 1977 by Editions du Seuil).

Cyert, R. and March, J.G. (1963) *A Behavioural Theory of the Firm.* Englewood Cliffs, NJ: Prentice-Hall.

Dutton, Jane E. (1986) 'The processing of crisis and non-crisis strategic issues', *Journal of Management Studies*, 23(5): 501–17.

Eisenhardt, K. and Zbaracki, M.J. (1992) 'Strategic decision making', *Strategic Management Journal*, 13: 17–37.

El-Ashker, Ahmed Abdel-Fattah (1987) *The Islamic Business Enterprise.* Beckenham: Croom Helm.

Fombrun, C. and Shanley, M. (1990) 'What's in a name? Reputation building and corporate strategy', *Academy of Management Journal*, 33(2): 233–58.

Giddens, A. (1990) *The Consequences of Modernity.* Cambridge: Polity Press.

Giles, William D. (1991) 'Making strategy work', *Long Range Planning*, 24(5): 75–91.

Goffman, E. (1982) *The Presentation of Self in Everyday Life.* Harmondsworth: Penguin.

Grinyer, P.H. and Spender, J.C. (1979) 'Recipes, crises and adaptation in mature businesses', *International Studies of Management and Organization*, IX(3): 113–33.

Heller, F., Drenth, P., Koopman, P. and Rus, V.

(1988) *Decisions in Organizations – a Three Country Comparative Study*. London: Sage.

Hickson, D.J., Butler, R.J., Cray, D., Mallory, G.R. and Wilson, D.C. (1986) *Top Decisions: Strategic Decision-Making in Organizations*. Oxford: Basil Blackwell. San Francisco: Jossey-Bass.

Hickson, D.J., Hinings, C.R., Lee, C.A., Schneck, R.C. and Pennings, J.M. (1971) 'A strategic contingencies theory of intra-organizational power', *Administrative Science Quarterly*, 16(2): 216–29.

Hickson, D.J. and Pugh, D.S. (1995) *Management Worldwide: the Impact of Societal Culture on Organizations Around the Globe*. Harmondsworth: Penguin.

Hinings, C.R. and Greenwood, R. (1988) 'The normative prescriptions of organizations', in L.G. Zucker (ed.), *Institutional Patterns and Organizations: Culture and Environment*. Cambridge, MA: Ballinger.

Hinings C.R., Hickson, D.J., Pennings, J.M. and Schneck, R.E. (1974) 'Structural conditions of intraorganizational power', *Administrative Science Quarterly*, 19(2): 21–44.

Hofstede, Geert (1980) *Culture's Consequences: International Differences in Work Related Values*. London: Sage.

Hofstede, Geert (1991) *Cultures and Organizations: Software of the Mind*. McGraw-Hill.

Jaeger, Alfred M. and Kanungo, Rabindra N. (1990) *Management in Developing Countries*. London: Routledge.

Janis, I.L. (1972) *Victims of Groupthink: a Psychological Study of Foreign Policy Decisions and Fiascos*. Boston: Houghton Mifflin.

Jeffcutt, P. (1994) 'From interpretation to representation in organizational analysis: postmodernism, ethnography and symbolism', *Organization Studies*, 15(2): 241–74.

Keat, R. and Abercrombie, N. (eds) (1990) *Enterprise Culture*. London: Routledge.

Kiggundu, M.N. (1989) *Managing Organizations in Developing Countries*. Kumarian Press.

Knights, D. and Morgan, G. (1991) 'Corporate strategy, organizations and subjectivity', *Organization Studies*, 12(2): 251–73.

Knights, D. and Murray, F. (1992) 'Politics and pain in managing information technology: a case study from insurance', *Organization Studies*, 13(2): 211–28.

Lachman, Ran, Nedd, Albert and Hinings, Bob (1994) 'Analyzing cross-national management and organizations: a theoretical framework', *Management Science*, 40(1): 40–55.

Lawrence, Peter (1991) *Management in the Netherlands*. Oxford: Clarendon Press.

Lawrence, P.R. and Lorsch, J.W. (1967) *Organization and Environment*. Cambridge, MA: Harvard Graduate School of Business Administration.

Lincoln, James R. and McBride, Kerry (1987) 'Japanese industrial organization in comparative perspective', *Annual Review of Sociology*, 13: 289–312.

Lindblom, C.E. (1959) 'The science of "muddling through"', *Public Administrative Review*, 19(2): 79–88.

Lipset, Seymour Martin (1986) 'Historical traditions and national characteristics: a comparative anlaysis of Canada and the United States', *Canadian Journal of Sociology*, 11: 113–55.

Lukes, S. (1974) *Power: a Radical View*. London: Macmillan.

Mallory, G.R., Butler, R.J., Cray, D., Hickson, D.J. and Wilson, D.C. (1983) 'Implanted decision-making: American owned firms in Britain', *Journal of Management Studies*, 20(2): 191–211.

March, J.G. and Olsen, J.P. (1976) *Ambiguity and Choice in Organizations*. Bergen, Oslo, and Tromsø: Universitetsforlaget.

March, J.G. and Simon, H.A. (1958) *Organizations*. New York: Wiley.

Mintzberg, H. (1973) *The Nature of Managerial Work*. New York: Harper and Row.

Mintzberg, H., Raisinghani, D. and Theoret, A. (1976) 'The structure of "unstructured" decision processes', *Administrative Science Quarterly*, 21: 246–75.

Mintzberg, H. and Waters, J.A. (1982) 'Tracking strategy in an entrepreneurial firm', *Academy of Management Journal*, 25(3): 465–99.

Mintzberg, H. and Waters, J.A. (1985) 'Of strategies, deliberate and emergent', *Strategic Management Journal*, 6: 257–72.

Mintzberg, H. and Waters, J.A. (1990) 'Studying deciding: an exchange of views between Mintzberg and Waters, Pettigrew, and Butler', *Organization Studies*, 11(1): 2–16.

Muna, Farid A. (1980) *The Arab Executive*. London: Macmillan.

Nutt, Paul C. (1984) 'Types of organizational decision processes', *Administrative Science Quarterly*, 29(3): 414–50.

Nutt, Paul C. (1986) 'Tactics of implementation', *Academy of Management Journal*, 29(2): 230–61.

Nutt, Paul C. (1987) 'Identifying and appraising how managers install strategy', *Strategic Management Journal*, 8: 1–14.

Nutt, Paul C. (1989) 'Selecting tactics to implement strategic plans', *Strategic Managment Journal*, 10: 145–61.

Oliveira, Beto (1992) 'Societal culture and managerial decision-making: the Brazilians and the English'. PhD thesis, University of Bradford Management Centre, England.

Owen, Arthur A. (1993) 'How to implement strategy', in C. Mabey and B. Mayon-White (eds), *Managing Change*. London: Paul Chapman.

Peters, T. and Waterman, R. Jr (1982) *In Search of Excellence: Lessons from America's Best-Run Companies*. New York: Harper and Row.

Pettigrew, A.M. (1973) *The Politics of Organizational Decision-Making*. London: Tavistock.

Pettigrew, A.M. (1985) 'Examining change in the long term context of culture and politics', in J.M. Pennings (ed.), *Organizational Strategy and Change*. San Francisco: Jossey-Bass.

Pettigrew, A.M. (1987) 'Context and action in the transformation of the firm', *Journal of Management Studies*, 24(6): 649–99.

Pettigrew, A.M. (1990) 'Studying deciding: an exchange of views between Mintzberg and Waters, Pettigrew, and Butler', *Organization Studies*, 11(1): 2–16.

Pfeffer, J. and Salancik, G.R. (1978) *The External Control of Organizations: a Resource Dependence Perspective*. London: Harper and Row.

Piercy, Nigel (1989) 'Diagnosing and solving implementation problems in strategic planning', *Journal of General Management*, 15(1): 19–38.

Pressman, J.L. and Wildavsky, A. (1973) *Implementation*. Berkeley, CA: University of California.

Quinn, James B. (1978) 'Strategic change: logical incrementalism', *Sloan Management Review*, Fall: 7–21.

Quinn, James B. (1980) *Strategies for Change: Logical Incrementalism*. Homewood, IL: Irwin.

Redding, S. Gordon (1990) *The Spirit of Chinese Capitalism*. De Gruyter.

Rosenthal, U. (1986) 'Crisis decision-making in the Netherlands', *The Netherlands Journal of Sociology*, 22(2): 103–29.

Schattsneider, E. (1960) *Semi-Sovereign People: a Realist's View of Democracy in America*. Holt, Rinehart and Winston. Quoted in Anthony G. McGrew and M.J. Wilson (eds) (1982), *Decision-Making: Approaches and Analysis*. Manchester University Press.

Schoemaker, Paul J.H. (1993) 'Strategic decisions in organizations: rational and behavioural views', *Journal of Management Studies*, 30(1): 107–29.

Silverman, David (1970) *The Theory of Organizations*. London: Heinemann.

Simon, Herbert A. (1945) *Administrative Behaviour*, 2nd edn. New York: Free Press.

Simon, Herbert A. (1960) *The New Science of Management Decision*. New York: Harper & Row.

Smith, G. and May, D. (1980) 'The artificial debate between rationalist and incrementalist models of decision-making', in Anthony G. McGrew and M.J. Wilson (eds) (1982), *Decision Making: Approaches and Analysis*. Manchester University Press.

Stacey, Ralph (1993a) *Strategic Management and Organizational Dynamics*. London: Pitman.

Stacey, Ralph (1993b) 'Strategy as order emerging from chaos', *Long Range Planning*, 26(1): 10–17.

Stewart, R. (1967) *Managers and their Jobs*. Maidenhead: McGraw-Hill.

Stewart, R. (1976) *The Reality of Management*. London: Pan.

Stewart, R. (1983) 'Managerial behaviour: how research has changed the traditional picture', in M. Earl (ed.), *Perspectives on Management: a Multi-disciplinary Analysis*. Oxford: Oxford University Press. pp. 82–98.

Strauss, A., Schatzman, L., Ehrlich D., Bucher R. and Sabshin, M. (1982) 'The hospital and its negotiated order', in *People and Organisations*. Essex, UK: Longman.

Sudnow, D. (1965) 'Normal crimes: sociological features of the penal code in a public defender office'. *Social Problems*, 12(3): 255–76.

Thompson, J.D. and Tuden, A. (1959) 'Strategies, structures and processes of organizational decision', in J.D. Thompson et al. (eds), *Comparative Studies in Administration*. Pittsburgh, PA: University of Pittsburgh Press.

Weber, Max (1947) *The Theory of Social and Economic Organization*, translated by A. Henderson and T. Parsons. Glencoe, IL: Free Press.

Weick, Karl E. (1976) 'Educational organizations as loosely coupled systems', *Administrative Science Quarterly*, 21(1): 1–19.

Williamson, O.E. (1975) *Markets and Hierarchies*. New York: Free Press.

Wilson, D.C. (1982) 'Electricity and resistance: a case study of innovation and politics', *Organization Studies*, 3(2): 119–40.

Wilson, D.C., Hickson, D.J. and Miller, S.J. (1996) 'Decision overreach as a reason for failure: how organizations can overbalance', *American Behavioral Scientist*, 39(8): 995–1010.

Zey, Mary (1992) *Decision Making: Alternatives to Rational Choice Models*. London: Sage.

# 4

# Cognitions in Organizations

ANN E. TENBRUNSEL, TIFFANY L. GALVIN,
MARGARET A. NEALE AND MAX H. BAZERMAN

Over the last decade, the study of organizational behavior has witnessed a dramatic shift toward a more cognitive perspective. This change in perspective has influenced both research and application in the field, and, more recently, has redefined topics typically viewed under the heading of organizational behavior (OB). Through the years, organizational behavior, particularly that segment of OB that is based on the study of the individual, has been chastised for lacking a central set of theories, for offering limited theoretical development of the theories it imports from psychology, and for covering topics that are over-researched and lacking connection to issues of interest to practitioners (O'Reilly 1991). We believe that these criticisms are the result of a traditional definition of the field that consists of a narrow set of topics that is more reflective of the table of contents of textbooks than the actual activity and interest of organizational scholars and practitioners. To remedy this problem a broader definition of organizational behavior is needed that includes the study of psychological issues that are relevant to understanding behavior in organizations. We see the cognitive perspectives and theories of psychology as central to this definition. By expanding the topics that the field encompasses, barriers that limit inquiry will be reduced and researchers in the field will be allowed to use and develop the very best psychological and cognitive ideas available to facilitate our knowledge about individual behavior in organizations.

In the 1988 *Annual Review of Psychology*, Ilgen and Klein wrote about what Markus and Zajonc (1985) term 'a shift of near revolutionary proportions in the behavior sciences: the cognitive perspective'. Ilgen and Klein documented the ways in which many traditional topics in organizational behavior were being influenced by this cognitive revolution. While their review is important, we believe that the cognitive revolution has created even more dramatic changes by altering the perception of what constitutes an OB topic to incorporate decision-making processes. The journal *Organizational Behavior and Human Performance* reflected this transition with a name change to *Organizational Behavior and Human Decision Processes*, clarifying the increasing importance of decision behavior to the study of OB. Indicative of the change taking place in the field, decision processes emerged as a mainstream topic within OB, with researchers focusing on how decisions influence managerial behavior (Bazerman 1994; Gioia and Sims 1986). In addition, negotiation has emerged as a new, central topic of OB, and has been dominated by a cognitive orientation (Neale and Bazerman 1991). As evidence of these changes, negotiation has become the most commonly published topic in *Organizational Behavior and Human Decision Processes*, and both decision processes and negotiation have been institutionalized as part of the field by the creation of new divisions within the Academy of Management that specifically address these topics.

We believe that these developments are not random. Rather, the tension between research and practice in business and management schools has resulted in a demand for research in OB that provides managers with more levers for change. This requires that researchers provide practitioners with new skills, and there is no skill more central to managerial behavior than decision-making. As a result, decision-making, and the broader topic of cognition, have gained centrality in OB in the 1990s, fueled by the demands of both researchers and practitioners.

The purpose of this chapter is to provide the background for researchers to appreciate the cognitive revolution in OB, to see its advantages, and to provide direction for future research. First, we discuss our underlying research values which bias the material that is reviewed and the conclusions that we reach. Next, we examine the psychological foundations for a cognitive perspective to organizations; specifically, we overview the development of the areas of social cognition and behavioral decision theory (BDT). We then examine and evaluate the contributions of the cognitive perspective to micro and macro OB topics. Finally, we conclude with an overall evaluation of the application of the cognitive perspective to organizations and discuss an agenda for future research possibilities.

## VALUES AND ASSUMPTIONS BEHIND OUR COGNITIVE PERSPECTIVE

Much of our own research, and that of other cognitive researchers in OB, is affected by a series of underlying values and assumptions (Bazerman 1993). We choose to be explicit about these goals since we believe that these underlying values distinguish cognitive from noncognitive work in OB and motivate much of the cognitively based research in OB (Bazerman 1993).

*Research should attempt to understand the world as it is, not as we would like it to be or think that it should be.* The assumption of rationality or utility maximization on the part of human actors is a hallmark of economics, but also is ubiquitous among organizational theories and researchers. The rationality assumption characterizes many micro-level OB theories, including virtually all of expectancy theory research (Lawler 1971) and the path-goal theory of leadership (House 1971). This assumption is also extended to the more macro-level rationality of organizational selection in population ecology (Hannan and Freeman 1989). Further, many behavioral researchers offer advice that is based on their assumptions rather than on the empirical realities of the organizations. For example, the field of OB has long conveyed the importance of participation, cooperation, collectivism, and empowerment before sufficient empirical support for these notions exists. Indeed, much of OB has been based on the way we think the world should be. In contrast, we believe that the field should be based on a more accurate understanding of human behavior as it is observed.

*Descriptive research is strengthened by comparisons to normative benchmarks.* The descriptive nature (the study of what we actually do) of the OB literature is a natural extension of the descriptive orientation of the disciplines, social psychology and sociology, from which such literature is traditionally drawn. This predisposition toward a descriptive orientation is exacerbated by organization scholars who view prescription/application as being of lesser value, often associated with instrumental pursuits rather than scientific values. Yet, many of these same scholars will offer prescriptions when they change from the role of researcher to that of teacher or consultant. Rather than foster such dualistic thinking or sacrifice one component for another, we believe there should be a more direct connection between the empirical and theoretical literature of OB and the prescriptive base we offer. We will return to this value in the behavioral decision research section, and outline what this interaction would look like. For now, we simply note that the tension between these two perspectives may increase our ability to communicate with other disciplines (e.g. economics), improve the theoretical base of organizational research, and help create a defensible, empirically based position from which to inform practitioners.

*Descriptive research can provide important adaptations to normative prescriptions.* Just as normative benchmarks serve to direct improvements in descriptive models, descriptive research can enhance the quality of normative models. If one assumes that actors are not typically rational utility maximizers, then the predictive quality of the normative models is enhanced by knowledge of the way in which individuals deviate from rationality. This argument is central to Raiffa's (1982) argument that prescriptive models need to better incorporate descriptive models of human behavior.

*Decisions are a core unit of activity for both understanding and changing individual behavior in organizations.* Historically, behavioral researchers have debated whether the person or the situation is more influential in the particular behavioral responses of individuals. This debate has led to the proposal that the way in which the individual perceives, filters, and conceptualizes information is critical to how he or she responds to situations; these responses in turn change the nature of their interaction and enact their perceptions of the environment (Weick 1992). This view emphasizes the importance of developing better models of decision making and cognition to understand behavior in organizations.

The values described above underlie many of the judgments that we will make throughout the chapter. We will return to these values when we evaluate the cognitive perspective of OB near the end of the chapter.

## PSYCHOLOGICAL FOUNDATIONS OF COGNITIVE RESEARCH IN ORGANIZATIONS

Two primary research areas of psychology – social cognition and behavioral decision theory – have served to inform organizational researchers in their attempts to understand the influence of human cognitions on OB. While there may be overlap between these two perspectives, there are also some sharp differences in orientation. Social cognition research is a purely descriptive field which tries to explain how people make sense of the world. Behavioral decision research, while also being a descriptive field, uses normative models such as 'straw men' to explain imperfections in human decision processes. Where the broader interpretative process is the focus of the social cognition area, the decision is the key unit of action in BDT. Our review of these two areas will highlight some of the key differences between BDT and social cognition in terms of their influence on OB. As our goal is to provide a sufficient appreciation of the backgrounds of these basic literatures to evaluate the developments that have occurred within OB, we will not provide comprehensive reviews of these two fields. However, we will suggest where such reviews can be found.

## Social Cognition

Social cognition has been defined as the study of how people make sense of other people and themselves, and how cognitive processes influence social behavior (Fiske and Taylor 1991). The social cognition approach attempts to understand the storage of social behavior in our cognition, the aspects or dimensions of stored social knowledge that affect our information processing, inferences, judgments, decisions, and actions, and the factors that influence changes in stored social information or knowledge (Sherman et al. 1989). Traditionally, this line of study has been associated with the proposition that people perceive and think about the social world differently than what would be expected based solely on stimulus information and principles of formal logic (Higgins and Bargh 1987).

Over the last decade, social cognition has become the dominant perspective in social psychology (Schneider 1991). Within this domain, social cognition has been applied to several phenomena including oneself, others, imaginary persons, interpersonal relationships, groups, and memory of social information (see Leyens and Codol 1988). Despite the breadth of applicability that the field offers, several limitations to its approach should be noted. As Schneider (1991) points out, the research is often driven more by model testing than by traditional social psychological efforts to explain social phenomena. In addition, there is often the argument that the 'social' aspect of social cognition is missing. Many critics share Schneider's complaint that 'at less than its best, however, social cognition research can be more concerned with the latest fashions from cognitive psychology than with social phenomena' (1991: 553). The implication is that social cognition researchers borrow cognitive psychology models originally developed for nonsocial objects and test their generalizability to social objects (Levine et al. 1993). In defense of these limitations and weaknesses, Higgins (1992) argues that there have been several cognitive models originated by social psychologists, such as the study of attribution processes, which have in turn been imparted into the field of cognition.

Research in the field of social cognition can be categorized into the following areas: (1) attribution theories, (2) memory, (3) knowledge structures (schemata, person perception, categorization, and stereotyping), (4) self-concepts, (5) attitudes and attitude changes, and (6) mental control (Schneider 1991; Sherman et al. 1989). While a complete review of each area would be impossible within the context of this chapter, we will provide definitions and examples of research to overview each of the areas of social cognition.

### Attribution Theories

Many scholars categorize attribution theory as the core of social cognitive psychology. Attribution theory is concerned with the way that people associate behavior with discrete causes, and thus focuses on the everyday, common-sense explanations that individuals construct for social events or actions of others. Theories in this field examine how the social perceiver gathers, combines and uses information to arrive at causal explanations for events (Fiske and Taylor 1991). While work in this area dates back to the mid 1940s, current research continues to be undertaken in quantity. There are three main theories which are considered to be the defining contributions to attribution theory. These theories stem from the works of Heider (1944), Jones and Davis (1965), and Kelley (1967). Combined, their work and resulting theories share a concern with common-sense explanations and answers to the question 'why,' while attempting to formalize the rules people might be using to make causal attributions.

Heider's (1944) work on naive psychology treated the lay person as a naive scientist who linked observable behavior to unobservable causes. Naive psychology maintained that the natural language people use to characterize causal action can form the basis for a theory of causal inference. Heider's major contribution to attribution theory was the division of potential sources of action into internal (personal) and external (environmental) types. Heider asserts that social perception research must consider attributes of the target person and the perceiver as well as the context and manner in which the perception occurs. The perceiver is proposed to decide whether an action results from something within the person who is performing the action or from some external source.

A second main contribution to attribution theory involves Jones and Davis's (1965) correspondent inference theory. This theory maintains that the goal of the causal attribution process is to infer that the observed behavior and the intention that produced it correspond to stable, underlying attributes of individuals, and thus to explain their behavior across situations. There are two major stages in the process of inferring personal dispositions: the attribution of intention and the attribution of dispositions. A noncommon effects principle is also at work, which maintains that a perceiver makes a correspondent inference by identifying the distinctive (noncommon) consequences of an actor's chosen course of action. The fewer the distinctive consequences, the more confident the inference about the causal attribution. According to the theory, the perceiver processes information backwards from effects, through action, to inferences about knowledge and ability. Behaviors/actions that are believed (by the perceiver) to be unconstrained, freely chosen, out of character/role, socially undesirable, violating prior expectations, and producing distinctive consequences are all believed to reveal underlying attributes.

The third main cornerstone of attribution theory involves Kelley's (1967) theories about the process of ascribing causes. His covariation model explores how individuals form causal inferences when they have access to multiple instances of similar events. In order to attribute the outcome to a stable cause or pattern of causes, individuals employ a covariation principle to determine how the outcome in question varies across entities, time, and people. However, if the perceiver is faced with only a single

observation, then he/she must take account of the plausible causes of the observed effect, employing what are known as causal schemata. These schemata are ready-made beliefs, preconceptions, and theories, formed by experience, that help an individual ascertain how certain kinds of causes interact to produce a specific effect. Thus, for a given attribution, the perceiver may have to interpret information and events by comparison and integration of schemata.

Outside of the three theories mentioned, there have been other lines of work that influenced early attribution formulations. For example, Weiner's (1986) work on attribution theory develops dimensions of attributional experience, integrates attributions with emotional processes, and enlightens the attributional and affective experience that underlies concrete domains of experience (see Fiske and Taylor 1991 for a more detailed discussion of other perspectives in attribution theory).

Attribution research has been extensive and varied and represents one of social cognition's most popular exports to other fields (see Harvey et al. 1976; 1978; 1981; Kelley and Michela 1980; Ross and Fletcher 1985; and Fiske and Taylor 1991 for more extensive reviews of the attribution field). Hundreds of empirical studies were prompted by the theories previously discussed and various other social phenomena have been analyzed within a causal attribution framework. Tests of attribution theory have uncovered various biases that people employ during the attribution process (e.g. fundamental attribution error, use of consensus information, and the self-serving attributional bias: see Ross 1977; Marks and Miller 1987; Zuckerman 1979; cf. Harvey, et al. 1976; 1978; 1981 for further discussion). The empirical research that has been conducted has been used as a basis for many attributional theories that analyze a variety of social and personal issues.

### Memory

Memory extends itself as both a theoretical and a methodological orientation throughout various areas within the realm of social cognition research. Issues surrounding memory have been examined in conjunction with other cognitive areas such as schemata, knowledge structures, categories, and encoding processes, and have been used as an approach to understanding other more social psychological concerns such as attitudes, person perception, stereotypes, judgment and decision making, and the self (see Sherman et al. 1989). The study of memory extends itself across various other topics and, as such, is seen as representing a central totem of modern social cognition (Schneider 1991) as well as ranking as a top cognitive export from the field. The importance of memory is seen in the several books and reviews that thoroughly cover the research in this area (see Martin and Clark 1990; Ostrom 1989; and Wyer and Srull 1988, for example).

The area of memory can be thought of as the examination of the manner in which people remember other individuals and complex social events (Fiske and Taylor 1991). Over the years, there have been several models proposed and tested which hold importance for different types of memory (or memory as viewed in different situations or contexts). More recently, research has drawn away from testing these models and has extended to explaining other social phenomena. Specifically, research on the accuracy, efficiency and representation of affect, mood, and emotion in memory has been increasing (Sherman et al. 1989).

### Knowledge Structures: Schemata, Person Perception, Categories and Stereotyping

Social objects, when they are targets of perception and cognition, are distinct from natural objects in a number of ways that influence the processing of information about them (Markus and Zajonc 1985). A major assumption of classic social cognition is that because our information-processing apparatus is resource-limited, we develop highly abstract knowledge structures (Schneider 1991). One such knowledge structure is a schema, which may be defined as a cognitive structure that represents knowledge about a concept or type of stimulus, including its attributes and the relations among those attributes (Fiske and Taylor 1991). Categories and schemata refer to people's expectations about themselves, other people, the situations they encounter, and the effects of these expectations. People have available to them a repertoire of schemata representing situations as well as a catalog of actors or personality types (person schemata) which encompass our organized knowledge (or knowledge structures) of other people (Bazerman and Carroll 1987). The basic premise of schema research has been that individuals simplify reality by storing knowledge at a broader, inclusive level rather than acquiring specific experiences and incorporating these on an individual basis.

The schema concept originated in person perception research with Asch's (1946) configural model of impression formation and Heider's (1958) balance theory of relationship. Their work focused on people's tendency to form unified overall impressions from discrete social elements (Fiske and Taylor 1991). Person schemata were proposed to constitute a knowledge structure which, when evoked, influences social judgments, behavior, and responses to that individual (as dictated in part by the characteristics of the person schema). Person schemata are believed to represent classifications that contain a great deal of information about traits, preferences, and goals that enable the perceiver to understand exhibited behavior, predict future behavior, and develop appropriate responses (Bazerman and Carroll 1987). The field of person perception has been built around the assumption that information about others includes both instances and abstractions, and that these abstract judgments in impression formation can be an overall evaluation of the target derived either from trait attributes or from behaviors performed by the target (Sherman et al. 1989). Research in this area continues to explore the role of information processing and the storage of information during schema formation and person perception.

Before schematic prior knowledge can be applied to social perception, the person or situation has to be classified into a category (Fiske and Taylor 1991). Categories are useful in distinguishing among people, interpreting information, and evaluating others and thus play an important role in providing meaning for social perceivers (Fiske 1993). While schema research is more concerned with the application of organized, generic prior knowledge to the understanding of new information, the domain of categorization research is more concerned with the classification of instances (Fiske and Taylor 1991). Categorization does not merely serve cognitive purposes; it also operates within a social and motivational context and can have important evaluative implications (Fiske 1993). Categorization research is abundant (see Hamilton and Sherman 1993), and has focused on a variety of areas, including an exploration of the information basis of knowledge structures, the cognitive representation of categories, the processing of category relevant information, the choice of categories, an understanding of the categorization process and how it can be controlled, and the relation of categorization to other processes such as attributions (see Schneider 1991). The resulting research has explored models of social categorization, identified core categories used by people to portray other people, and, in contrast, identified the use of concrete representation, exemplars, and target cases instead of person schemata (or stereotypes) (see Fiske 1993).

Significant advances have also been made in the area of stereotyping and prejudice (Markus and Zajonc 1985). Tajfel (1969), one of the first to bring more of a cognitive focus to the social phenomenon of stereotyping, proposed that stereotypes can be viewed as special cases of categorization which accentuate similarities within groups and differences between groups. Categorization models of stereotyping focus on the pragmatic implications for perceivers who use the stereotypes as a rich resource for making sense of their world (Fiske 1993). People use stereotypes when they seem to have explanatory value, give information, provide motivation, or comply with social norms. The effects of categorization on stereotyping have been a major concern, particularly with the attribution of characteristics to in-groups/out-groups, inter-individual and inter-group relationships and conflict, and work on illusory correlation (see reviews, e.g. Messick and Mackie 1989; Hamilton and Sherman 1989; Mullen and Johnson 1990). As social categorization and stereotyping extend to other areas and topics, the cognitive antecedents of these areas can also be explored from the basis of knowledge structures and schemata research.

## Self-Concepts

Understanding the concept of the self has been one of the oldest and most pursued goals in psychology. Social psychologists did much of the work in this area during the 1950s. For the next twenty years, however, it appeared that self-concept declined while other issues took center stage with experimental social psychologists. By the late 1970s, the concept of the self 'leaped back into the limelight' (Higgins and Bargh 1987). In the past decade or so, social cognition researchers have taken up the challenge of understanding the self-concept, and have thus added to our fundamental understanding of its structure and functioning (Fiske and Taylor 1991).

Much theory and empirical evidence have been offered in support of the self-concept as a multifaceted, diverse, and complex concept (see Cantor et al. 1986; Greenwald and Pratkanis 1984; and Markus and Wurf 1987 for reviews). Encompassing roles and attributes as key elements, self-concept has been viewed and explained as a collection of schemata, conceptions, and/or images arranged in a system or space. The self-concept has been defined and redefined structurally, thought of in its relation to ego, and considered in terms of its temporal qualities (Sherman et al. 1989). Though much of the early work concerning the self-concept was devoted to specifying its contents, more recent attention has turned to its structure and how it is cognitively represented (Sherman et al. 1989). Through a cognitive analysis of the self-concept and an emphasis on the nature of the knowledge

structures relevant to the self-concept, researchers have been able to empirically validate many of the assumptions of the early self theorists about the referencing, channeling and distorting functions of the self-concept (see Markus and Zajonc 1985).

The dominant position in the literature has been that the self is an unusually rich and highly organized structure (Higgins and Bargh 1987). Researchers have debated, however, whether the self is actually a unique cognitive structure (particularly in terms of its effects) or if it is even a cognitive structure at all. Much of the argument about the special quality of the self has been based on experimental evidence of the information-processing effects of the self and has centered around the research done on Rogers' (1977) self-referent effects (Higgins and Bargh 1987). At present, however, there is still insufficient information available to determine whether the self has unique cognitive properties. There is, however, a recognition that the self-concept is one of the most highly articulated and differentiated constructs that any individual has. Thus the self-concept is clearly important in producing reliable effects on processing (Fiske and Taylor 1991).

## Attitudes and Attitude Change

Attitudes are believed to be an intervening variable or a nonobservable link between an observable stimulus and an observable response. Attitudes are defined as an evaluation of the attitude object that often includes cognitive and behavioral tendencies (Fiske and Taylor 1991). Traditional attitude research focused on first defining attitude as a construct and then developing descriptive models and acceptable indicators or measurements of the construct (as discussed in Stahlberg and Frey 1988). Historically, attitude has mainly been defined as a set of overt responses to a questionnaire; consequently, several acceptable scales have been developed in accordance with this approach (e.g. the Likert and equal appearing scales), and other measurement techniques have also been explored. It is believed that most attitude theorists would agree that evaluation constitutes a central aspect of attitudes, that attitudes are represented in memory, and that affective, cognitive, and behavioral antecedents and consequences of attitudes can be distinguished (Olson and Zanna 1993).

The structure, measurement, and functions of attitude and the relationship between attitudes and behavior have become a renewed research interest in recent years (after a decline in interest in the late 1960s and 1970s). The level of activity in the attitude literature is visible in the number of books that have appeared recently (numerous texts, specific books on attitude measures, social judgment, propaganda, and prejudice: see Olson and Zanna 1993) and the comprehensive reviews of attitude literature (e.g., Eagly and Chaiken 1992). Recent research has focused on exploring the formation of attitudes and how such attitudes (as cognitive representations in long-term memory) can be evaluated, altered, or changed (Sherman et al. 1989). As the interest in attitude attributes has grown, more integrative models of the attitude–behavior relationship, as well as the relation of attitude to other topics such as persuasion, prejudice, and stereotyping, are being explored (Olson and Zanna 1993). There has also been a recent trend toward exploring attitude change as a strategy which influences behavior (Stroebe and Jonas 1988).

Various cognitive approaches have also been taken toward attitudes. From traditional theories to those exploring new processes, those emphasizing attitudes as a thoughtful, conscious process versus a more automatic process, and those debating the role of cognition versus motivation in attitude formation, the field of attitude research continues to thrive.

## Mental Control

The extent to which our cognitive processes are automatic continues to be a major focus of social cognition research (Schneider 1991). Outside of a level of consciousness, various tasks tend to be encoded without intention or effort. In this sense, the associated actions occur in a relatively automatic fashion. Bargh (1984; 1990) has done extended reviews of automatic processes and its dimensions. Research on proceduralized inference suggests that practice seems to be the crucial foundation for developing automatic responses (Fiske and Taylor 1991).

At a basic level, automaticity can be considered a form of behavior in which people attempt to gain control over their thoughts. Exploration about the varying kinds and degrees of mental control continues to spark research, and extends itself to studies on thought suppression and will-power in social and personality psychology (Schneider 1991).

Social cognition is a rich and broad perspective represented in various fields and disciplines, particularly within social and cognitive psychology. As Schneider (1991) points out, 'social cognition is alive and well and feeling strong.' Because of the blend of various issues and methodologies used throughout research in the field, many of the concepts and developments are easily applicable to understanding the cognitions

and behavior of people in structured social contexts such as organizations. We will return to the relevance of these theories when we consider their application to OB later in the chapter.

## Behavioral Decision Theory

The standard of economic rationality has long been the cornerstone of the formal study of decision making. Individuals were assumed to act in accordance with their self-interest and make choices that were consistent with the predictions of maximizing this self-interest. The tenets of rational action, however, have not proved particularly useful in describing the actual choice or decision behavior of individuals, nor were they particularly useful in prescribing or predicting actual choice behavior. Real decision makers typically behaved in ways that deviated from the predictions of economic models, made decisions that were not Pareto efficient, and were inconsistent in their choices or made decisions based on normatively irrelevant factors (Bazerman 1994). From the perspective of economic rationality, these errors were assumed to be the result of ignorance, lack of correct incentives, or unrevealed preferences.

What was presumed to be a result of inattention, ignorance, or error by those subscribing to the notion of rational decision-making was viewed by another group of researchers as systematic variations that were, in their own right, deserving of attention. The systematic study of choice, especially in the behavioral sciences, had as its roots the publication, almost forty years ago, of two seminal pieces. First, Edwards (1954) introduced behavioral scientists to the work on decision behavior conducted by economists, statisticians, and philosophers. Second, Simon's (1957; March and Simon 1958) work on bounded rationality suggested that if economists wanted to understand real decision behavior, they had to focus on the perceptual, psychological, and cognitive factors that caused human beings to make decisions that deviated from the predictions of the 'rational man'.

The discrepancies between the formal prescriptions of economists and the descriptive observations of Simon's bounded rationality result, according to Simon, from our inability to evaluate decision alternatives simultaneously (rather than sequentially), from failing to choose the optimal alternative (preferring, instead, to select an alternative that is 'good enough' – to satisfice), and from using simplifying rules or heuristics to reduce the cognitive demand of decision making. Thus, Simon's (1957) concept of bounded rationality highlighted the differences between what normative models predict and what people actually do. As suggested by Bell et al. (1988), behavior decision theory's primary focus encompasses the normative, descriptive and prescriptive perspectives of decision making, with a somewhat greater emphasis on the latter two. That is, BDT research seems more concerned with the empirical validity of descriptive models and the pragmatic value of prescriptive models than with the development of normative models.

A central question in the area of behavioral decision research, then, is how decision makers actually go about making decisions, using as a comparison the benchmark of optimal (i.e. rational) performance. Juxtaposing the standard of rationality against actual behavior, several researchers in the decision arena began mapping the systematic deviations from rationality that they observed. Behavioral decision researchers focus on these systematic inconsistencies in the decision-making process that prevent humans from making fully rational decisions. Kahneman and Tversky (1979; Tversky and Kahneman 1974) have provided critical information about specific systematic biases that influence judgment. This work has elucidated our modern understanding of judgment.

When making decisions, people rely on a number of simplifying strategies, or rules of thumb, called heuristics. Although heuristics often prevent us from finding the optimal decision by eliminating the best choice, they do have some benefits: the expected time saved by using them could outweigh any potential loss resulting from a full search strategy. By providing people with a simple way of dealing with a complex world, heuristics produce correct or partially correct judgments more often than not. In addition, it may be inevitable that humans will adopt some way of simplifying decisions. The only drawback is that individuals frequently adopt these heuristics without being aware of them. The misapplication of heuristics to inappropriate situations, unfortunately, often leads people astray.

The three most important heuristics are the availability heuristic, the representativeness heuristic, and anchoring and adjustment. Decision makers assess the frequency, probability or likely causes of an event by the degree to which instances or occurrences of that event are readily 'available' in memory (Tversky and Kahneman 1973). To the extent that an event evokes emotions and is vivid, easily imagined, and specific, it will be more 'available' from memory than equally occurring events which are unemotional in nature, bland, difficult to imagine, or vague. For example, the subordinate in close proximity to the manager's office will receive a more

critical performance evaluation at year-end, since the manager is more aware of this subordinate's errors (Bazerman 1994).

People also assess the likelihood of an event's occurrence by the similarity of that occurrence to their stereotypes of similar occurrences. As Nisbett and Ross note, 'A botanist assigns a plant to one species rather than another by using this judgment strategy. The plant is categorized as belonging to the species that its principal features most clearly resemble' (1980: 7). In this case, the degree to which the unknown plant is representative of a known species of plant is the best information available to the botanist.

People also make assessments by 'anchoring' on an initial value and adjusting to yield a final decision. The initial value, or starting point, may be suggested from historical precedent, the way in which a problem is presented, or random information. For example, managers make salary decisions by adjusting from an employee's past year's salary. In ambiguous situations, a trivial factor can have a profound effect on our decision if it serves as a starting point from which we make adjustments (Dawes 1988). Frequently, people will realize the unreasonableness of the anchor (e.g. 'the other firm was *only* paying her $22,000 a year'), yet their adjustment will often remain irrationally close to this anchor.

Unfortunately, heuristics lead to predictable biases. A number of the predominant biases described in this literature are reviewed below (this summary is based on Bazerman [1994]):

*Ease of recall*  Individuals judge events which are more easily recalled from memory, based upon vividness or recency, to be more numerous than events of equal frequency whose instances are less easily recalled (Tversky and Kahneman 1974).

*Retrievability*  Individuals are biased in their assessments of the frequency of events based upon how their memory structures affect the search process (Tversky and Kahneman 1983).

*Presumed associations*  Individuals tend to overestimate the probability of two events co-occurring based upon the number of similar associations which are easily recalled, whether from experience or social influence (Chapman and Chapman 1967).

*Insensitivity to base rates*  Individuals tend to ignore base rates in assessing the likelihood of events when any other descriptive information is provided – even if the information is irrelevant (Kahneman and Tversky 1972).

*Insensitivity to sample size*  Individuals frequently fail to appreciate the role of sample size in assessing the reliability of sample information (Tversky and Kahneman 1974).

*Misconceptions of chance* Individuals expect a sequence of data generated by a random process to look 'random', even when the sequence is too short for those expectations to be statistically valid (Kahneman and Tversky 1972).

*Regression to the mean* Individuals often ignore the fact that extreme events tend to regress to the mean on subsequent trials (Kahneman and Tversky 1973).

*The conjunction fallacy* Individuals falsely judge that conjunctions, i.e., two events co-occurring, are more probable than a more global set of occurrences of which the conjunction is a subset (Tversky and Kahneman 1983).

*Anchoring* Individuals make estimates for values based upon an initial value (derived from past events, random assignment, or whatever information is available) and typically make insufficient adjustments from that anchor when establishing a final value (Slovic and Lichtenstein 1971).

*Conjunctive and disjunctive events bias* Individuals exhibit a bias toward overestimating the probability of conjunctive events and underestimating the probability of disjunctive events (Bar-Hillel 1973).

*Overconfidence* Individuals tend to be overconfident of the infallibility of their judgments when answering moderately to extremely difficult questions (Alpert and Raiffa 1969).

*The confirmation trap* Individuals tend to seek confirmatory information for what they think is true and neglect the search for disconfirmatory evidence (Wason 1960).

*Hindsight* After finding out whether or not an event occurred, individuals tend to overestimate the degree to which they would have predicted the correct outcome (Fischhoff 1975).

*Framing* Individuals are influenced by irrelevant information concerning how questions are framed (Kahneman and Tversky 1979).

During the 1980s and 1990s, these biases have had a profound influence on the field of OB. They have been used to help organizational members better understand their limitations, and have been extended to the organizational level of analysis to help account for the systematic errors of organizations.

However, it should be noted that BDT is not without its critics. Garb (1989) and Kagel and Levine (1986) suggest that experience may eliminate or at least attenuate decision bias as performance feedback can correct the inappropriate use of information and decision heuristics. These researchers see these well-replicated effects as the artificial creation of one-shot experiments. While much of the seminal work in the area of BDT was conducted in the relatively context-free environment of the laboratory, it is not so clear that real-world experience would provide decision makers with superior information or useful feedback. As Tversky and Kahneman (1986) suggest, responsive learning requires accurate and immediate feedback which is rarely available because:

1   Outcomes are commonly delayed and not easily attributable to a particular action.
2   Variability in the environment degrades the reliability of the feedback.
3   There is often no information about what the outcome would have been if another decision had been made.
4   Most important decisions are unique and therefore provide little opportunity for learning: 'any claim that a particular error will be eliminated by experience must be supported by demonstrating that the conditions for effective learning are satisfied' (see Einhorn and Hogarth 1978: 274–5).

In fact, recent research has shown that most of the effects described above occur with real managers, with multiple trials available for learning, and with rewards for successful performance. In virtually all cases, these biases are robust to the tests that critics have provided (Bazerman 1994).

The research in social cognition and BDT is theoretically and empirically rich. The two fields have both unique and overlapping topic areas. Together, these two literatures will provide the basic structure for reviewing and evaluating the development of a cognitive perspective within OB.

## COGNITIVE PERSPECTIVES IN MICRO ORGANIZATIONAL BEHAVIOR

### Social Cognition in Micro Organizational Behavior

Social cognition can be characterized as the application of cognitive research methods to social contexts, with the organization being one of these contexts (Brewer and Kramer 1985). Micro organizational research, a central component of organizational research, has been criticized in the past for the relatively passive role it affords to individuals (Brief and Aldag 1981). In response to this charge, it has been argued that this research could be enhanced by addressing the interaction among employee behavior, cognitions and the environment (Brief and Aldag 1981). Indeed, Cummings (1982) goes as far as stating that 'the work on cognitive processing of stimuli comes as close as organizational behavior has come to date in understanding the processes which underlie so many of the functional relationships central to the discipline.'

Our literature search for social cognitive research in micro OB found this research most commonly connected to three central domains of research: leadership, motivation, and performance appraisals. Each of these topics will be addressed by investigating the impact that social cognition has had in these areas.

## Leadership

Leadership is an old topic in OB, yet our review shows the area to be alive in producing new empirical research, with social cognition playing an active role. Social cognition has been applied to the study of leadership in a number of ways. An attributional perspective on leadership has been hailed as one of the most important cognitive applications (Cummings 1982). In addition, the simultaneous study of attitudes and leadership has been the focus of numerous studies. Finally, memory, self-concepts and stereotyping have also been linked, albeit to a lesser degree, to the study of leadership.

Attributional studies of leadership have incorporated leadership attributions, subordinate attributions, or some combination of these two. Heneman et al. (1989) found that internal, but not external, attributions were significantly related to critical performance incidents and leader–member exchange. An effort (versus ability) attribution has been shown to influence the variance in performance evaluations (Knowlton and Mitchell 1980).

In addition to influencing evaluations, attributions made by the leader also influence actions taken by that leader. Green and Mitchell (1979) proposed an attributional model of leader behavior that suggested that a leader's attributions influenced their subsequent actions. Evidence suggests that the belief about the cause of a subordinate's performance affects the choice of supervisory actions (Tjosvold 1985) and the extent to which organizational policy is implemented (Green and Liden 1980). This relationship has been shown to be impacted by the type of situation (James and White 1983), the gender compatibility between the leader and the subordinate (Dobbins et al. 1983), and the nature of the relationship (Heneman et al. 1989).

An attributional perspective has also been used to address attributions made by subordinates about their leader. Meindl et al. (1985) propose that leadership is a romantic concept that individuals utilize to make causal attributions about organizational outcomes. Meindl and Ehrlich (1987) provide support for this proposition in their findings that performance evaluations of leaders were better when the cause was attributed to leadership rather than nonleadership factors.

There has been a recognition that both leader and member attributions may have important implications for organizational research. Integrating these two concepts, Martinko and Gardner (1987) proposed a model that combines the attributions of members and leaders. The simultaneous study of self-serving biases in both leader and member decision-making processes suggested that leaders attributed poor performance to internal subordinate factors while subordinates attributed poor performance to internal leader factors (Dobbins and Russell 1986).

Attitudinal research has also enhanced leadership research. Wexley and Pulakos (1983) found that the more aware a subordinate was of their manager's work-related attitudes, the more favorable they were in evaluating the leader. In addition, attitudes, such as intrinsic job satisfaction, have been proposed as substitutes for leadership behavior, thus negating the leader's ability to influence the subordinate (Kerr and Jermier 1978). Leadership styles and employee attitudes have also been used together as independent variables. For example, work group effectiveness has been found to be positively associated with the match between leadership style and the members' attitude toward the leader's style (White and Bassford 1978).

Memory and self-concept have also been integrated with leadership research. Specifically, the attitudes ascribed to leader behavior have been studied from a memory perspective. Phillips (1984) found that leader behavior that was consistent with the initial leadership labels of subordinates influenced the frequency with which subordinates assigned a particular behavior to a leader. Memory (selective encoding specifically) has also been proposed as a mediator of the performance/leader-ratings relationship (Larson et al. 1984). Finally, the idea of self-concept has been used to separate leaders from nonleaders (Peppers and Ryan 1986).

## Motivation

Motivation has paralleled leadership as a topic rich in history in OB and yet disappointing to many. Again, we found many contemporary research efforts centering on this topic, with social cognition playing a critical role. Attributions of behavior in organizations have been shown to have important implications for explaining employee motivation (Knowlton and Mitchell 1980). Addressing this assertion, frameworks that integrate models of motivation and attributional processes have been proposed (for example, see Teas and McElroy 1986). One such framework examines the impact of attributions on affective, cognitive and behavior reactions to goals and feedback (Klein 1989). Within these models, there is some debate as to whether attributions are antecedent to cognitions and behavior or are in fact determined by them (Lord and Smith 1983).

The effect of attributions on motivation has also been empirically tested. Arnold (1985) found that the level of task performance was related to perceived competence and attributions, which in turn were related to intrinsic motivation. Attributions for failure have also been shown to influence the direction of motivation, in that salespeople worked harder if they attributed failure to lack of effort and worked smarter (changed the direction and focus of their work) if they attributed failure to the use of poor strategies (Sujan 1986). Supervisors and subordinates were found to have similar causal schemata; both attributed success to intrinsic motivation and ability while attributing failure primarily to low motivation (Huber et al. 1986). Performance trends also have attribution consequences, with descending or ascending performance attributed more to motivation than to consistently average performance (Karl and Wexley 1989).

In certain situations, memory has been proposed as an alternative to the role of attributions. Cellar and Barrett (1987) found that the use of a play script affected intrinsic motivation. As a result, they asserted that people may not make attributions in situations where automatic processes, such as scripts, serve as behavioral guides. Staw (1984) concurs with the notion that scripts are a valuable means for studying motivation.

Attitudes have also been linked up with motivation in OB research. Some of this research investigates causal relationships between these two constructs, such as the impact of motivation on attitudes and/or the impact of attitudes on motivation (Feldman and Weitz 1988). Bagozzi et al. (1992) investigated the attitude–motivation relationship, and posited that changing people's attitudes toward the process of learning may improve their motivation to learn. Job satisfaction is one attitude that is often studied in conjunction with motivation, with respect to job enrichment (Katerberg et al. 1979), union strength (Hammer 1978), job characteristics (Hackman et al. 1978), and corporate savings (Mirvis and Lawler 1977). Attitudes and motivation have also been compared against each other, as seen in a study by Drake and Mitchell (1977) which found that differences in power between members and leaders affected attitudes rather than motivation.

Self-concept research has been proposed as an important addition to the study of motivation. Sullivan (1989) states that theories about the self as a source of motivation may have implications for employee motivation. Shamir (1991) also agrees that motivation theories could be enhanced by incorporating a theory of self-concept. Implications of this inclusion are that job motivation could be enhanced if (1) job-related identities are salient in an employee's self-concept, (2) the job offers opportunities for the enhancement of self-esteem and self-worth, (3) actions required on the job are consistent with the employee's self-concept, and (4) career opportunities are congruent with a person's possible selves.

## Performance Appraisals

The topic of performance appraisal has a long history of research in OB and in industrial/organizational psychology. Through the 1970s, this research largely ignored the role of the appraiser, focusing instead on instrument development. In the 1980s, the focus changed, and the cognitions of the appraiser came to dominate performance appraisal research (Feldman 1981). A summary of this type of research is provided by Ilgen et al. (1993). Their review is focused around a three-stage process model emphasizing the gathering, storing and retrieving of performance information.

Research has investigated the underlying cognitive structures involved in the performance appraisal process. For example, Jolly et al. (1988) proposed and tested a model designed to uncover a summary cognitive map of performance appraisals. Results of this type of research have revealed consistent cognitive structures with regard to appraisals. Gioia et al. (1989) discovered that there were shared cognitive structures, or scripts, used in appraisal interviews. Similarly, Borman (1987) found that there was a core set of categories or schemata used in the formation of personal work constructs, although different people may emphasize different combinations of this core set.

A significant portion of the study of attributions in performance appraisals has examined the differences in causal attributions of success and failure between subordinates and superiors. Disagreement within dyads between the subordinate and superior may lead to disagreements over performance evaluations (Huber et al. 1986). In recognition of this, Bannister and Balkin's (1990) performance evaluation and compensation model identifies causal attributions made by the superior and recipient as a central component of these processes. One common attribution studied involves the judgment of a cause as either internal (i.e. personality, lack of motivation) or external (i.e. job environment) to the actor. These studies have emphasized that actors (typically the subordinates) and observers (the superiors) make different attributions with regard to the internal/external distinction (Huber et al. 1986; Bannister and Balkin 1990). Bernardin (1989) found that actors attributed performance failures to external factors beyond their control while observers attributed failures to internal factors. Similarly, Harrison et al. (1988) found that superiors' initial attributions were internal relative to the subordinate and that they were more inclined to seek out information on internal factors. The feedback provided to the subordinate has been shown to be distorted by these types of attributions. Knowlton and Ilgen (1980) found that the nature of feedback varied as a function of the performance attributions; more positive feedback was provided to low performers when ability was diagnosed as the cause.

Factors influencing the relationship between attributions and performance appraisal have also been studied. James and White (1983) found that managers' attributions of the cause of performance varied according to the situation. Knowledge of the outcome of the behavior has also been shown to influence the attribution process, with knowledge of a negative outcome resulting in more internal attributions than behaviors not associated with an outcome (Mitchell and Kalb 1981). Similarly, Gioia and Sims (1986) found that managers showed different patterns of attribution toward subordinates in a failure condition as opposed to a success condition. Managers in the failure condition tended to seek reasons for the failure by asking attribution-seeking questions.

Attributions have also been studied from a subordinate perspective. Larson (1989) posits that employee feedback-seeking behavior can influence the nature of feedback given, particularly when the feedback is sought to mitigate attributions of personal responsibility and blame. Rose (1978) found that sex moderated effort attributions made by subordinates, with greater effort attributed to managers whose subordinates were of the opposite sex than to those of the same sex.

Obstacles to accurate performance are attributed in part to limitations in human processing capacity (Bernardin and Cardy 1982). Consequently, the study of memory has been incorporated into performance appraisal research. DeNisi et al. (1984) proposed a model that described the performance appraisal process as a set of social cognitive operations that include the acquisition of information, the organization and storage of that information in memory, the retrieval of the information from memory and the integration of the information to formation of a judgment. Performance appraisal researchers who incorporate memory in their studies often examine the organization of performance information in memory. DeNisi et al. (1989) found that raters stored unorganized performance information in memory patterns consistent with organizational diaries. Support has also been found for the systematic distortion hypothesis which asserts that raters' semantic conceptual similarity schemata serve to guide and constrain the rating judgment process (Kozlowski and Kirsch 1987). In their examination of appraisal salience on information processing, Williams et al. (1990) discovered that high appraisal salience was related to online information processing while low appraisal salience was related to memory-based processing.

Memory structures have also been used as an independent variable in examining performance rating accuracy. Raters are seen to be more accurate if they have high memory capacity (Heneman et al. 1987) and high selectivity (Cardy and Kehoe 1984). Williams et al. (1990) found that certain organizational strategies used during the encoding process were able to improve rating accuracy. Performance observation with delays between observations has been found to affect the accuracy of behavioral ratings and recognition memory (Murphy et al. 1989). Memory biases, such as recall of behavior that is consistent with impression of the ratee (Murphy et al. 1986), the halo effect, the leniency/stringency effect, and racial, sexual, ethnic and personalistic influences, have also been found to affect assignment and recall (Feldman 1981).

Performance appraisal research has also joined forces with attitudinal research. The effect of performance appraisals and feedback on attitudes has been one of the results of this union, including studies on the effects on organizational commitment (Pearce and Porter 1986), job satisfaction (Daley 1985), the development of professional attitudes (Yeager et al. 1985) and perceptions of unfairness (Dailey and Kirk 1992). Similarities between rater and ratee job attitudes have been found to increase rating accuracy (Zalesny and Highhouse 1992). Attitudes toward the appraisal system have also been studied. Worker involvement in the appraisal system has been shown to positively impact perceptions of the appraisal system (Cummings 1973; Daley 1988) as well as the manner in which feedback is received (Harris 1988).

Research on stereotyping and person perception has also enhanced performance appraisal research. Evaluations have been shown to be influenced by age and sex stereotpying (Schwab and Heneman 1978; Pazy 1986; Ferris et al. 1985), while person perception and performance appraisals were found to be significantly affected by nonverbal cues (De Meuse 1987).

## Behavioral Decision Theory in Micro Organizational Behavior

Behavioral decision theory has developed into a recognized topic of the field of organizational behavior. This can be seen in the existence of OB textbook chapters on the topic (Northcraft and Neale 1994), a mainstream OB journal that focuses much attention on the topic (*Organizational Behavior and Human Decision Processes*), and faculty courses in organizational behavior departments devoted to BDT at many leading management schools (e.g. MIT, Cornell, Duke, Northwestern, and Chicago). From a theoretical and empirical standpoint, BDT has been used as a basic component in the development of the literatures on negotiation, group decision making, and human resource management. A review of each of these application areas is provided below.

### Negotiation

The last decade has seen a proliferation of interest in the topic of negotiation by OB researchers. Many scholars outside the BDT area have argued that the central negotiation perspective by OB researchers has been Neale and Bazerman's (1991) BDT perspective which focuses on the decisions made by negotiators (Greenhalgh 1993).

The development of this descriptive literature, which accounts for the limitations in negotiator decision making, is closely connected to the leading prescriptive work on negotiation (Raiffa 1982). Raiffa argues for an asymmetrically prescriptive/descriptive approach. This approach suggests that the decision analyst should asymmetrically (to only one of the actors) provide prescriptions to the negotiator based on the best possible description of the likely behavior of the opponent. In contrast to mainstream economic and game theoretic approaches, Raiffa explicitly acknowledges that the actual behavior of the opponent may fall far short of rationality.

Raiffa's work was a key turning point in negotiation research for a number of reasons. First, in the context of developing a prescriptive model, he explicitly realizes the importance of forming accurate descriptions of the opponent rather than assuming them to be fully rational. Second, his realization that negotiators need

advice implicitly acknowledges that negotiators do not intuitively follow purely rational strategies. Most importantly, he initiated the ground for dialogue between prescriptive and descriptive researchers. His work utilizes descriptive models which allow the focal negotiator to anticipate the likely behavior of the opponent. In addition, we argue that a central focus of the decision analyst should be to realize that the focal negotiator may have decision biases that limit his/her ability to follow such advice.

Our research has addressed some of the questions that Raiffa left behind. For example, if the negotiator and his or her opponents do not act rationally, what systematic departures from rationality can be predicted? Initial research has addressed some of the questions and has provided a set of empirical studies that integrate the value of existing descriptive and prescriptive research in creating a decision perspective of negotiation.

Building on BDT, a number of deviations from rationality that can be expected in negotiations have been identified. Specifically, research on two-party negotiations suggests that negotiators tend to: (1) be inappropriately affected by the frame in which risks are viewed (Huber et al. 1987a; Neale and Bazerman 1985; Bazerman et al. 1985), (2) anchor their judgments in negotiation based on rationally irrelevant information (Tversky and Kahneman 1974; Huber and Neale 1986; Northcraft and Neale 1987), (3) overweigh readily available information (Neale 1984), (4) be overconfident (Neale and Bazerman 1985; Bazerman and Neale 1982), (5) nonrationally assume that negotiation tasks are fixed-sum, and thus miss opportunities for mutually beneficial trade-offs (Bazerman et al. 1985), (6) nonrationally escalate commitment to a previously selected course of action (Northcraft and Neale 1986; Bazerman and Neale 1983), (7) ignore the valuable information that is available by considering the cognitions of others (Bazerman and Carroll 1987), (8) devalue any concession that is made by the other side, i.e. reactive devaluation (Stillinger et al. in press), (9) erroneously assume that opponents' interests are completely opposed to their own, when in fact negotiators' interests are perfectly compatible with those of the other party (Thompson and Hastie 1990), and (10) egocentrically interpret what would be fair in a negotiated agreement (Thompson and Loewenstein 1992; Loewenstein et al. 1993).

These results have had a strong influence on research and teaching in negotiation; BDT-influenced negotiation research is now commonly seen in organizational behavior journals and negotiation has been the fastest new topic in organizational behavior courses during the 1980s and 1990s. Many of these courses try to provide students with useful prescriptions based on descriptive models rooted in BDT.

## Group Decision Making

As characterized in the description of BDT, individuals often use heuristics to make decisions. Often, these heuristics are incorrectly used, resulting in biased decision making. Several researchers have extended the concept of biases in individual decision making to a group context. Specifically, group decision making research has influenced BDT research in two ways: (1) the application of 'individual' biases to a group context, and (2) the identification of group-specific heuristics and biases.

One of the individual biases that has been applied to group research is the framing bias. In an attempt to explain Stoner's (1961) finding that groups are more risk-seeking, Bazerman (1984) offered framing as an alternative interpretation which focused on group discussion as a mechanism for mitigating any one individual's frame. Following this line of reasoning, Bazerman predicted that a positive frame would mitigate risk-averse behavior displayed by individuals, thus creating an apparent risk-seeking tendency on the part of groups. Likewise, a negative frame in a group context would appear to create risk-averse behavior for groups when they were compared to individuals. Neale et al. (1986) find support for this prediction.

The tendency to adhere to the representativeness heuristic has also been studied in groups. Argote et al. (1986) found that this heuristic is used by both individuals and groups, with groups exhibiting an even greater biasing effect than individuals. This result was later clarified in a paper by Argote et al. (1990), who tested subjects' ability to judge the probabilities that an individual belonged to a certain category. They found that groups tend to judge primarily by representativeness when individuating information is informative, but were less affected by this heuristic when descriptions were not representative of categories. Overconfidence is also characteristic of both groups and individuals. Specifically, Sniezek and Henry (1989) found that groups, while perhaps more accurate in their judgments regarding uncertain ends, fell prey to the overconfidence bias just as often as individuals. Egocentrism appears to occur at both the individual and the group level, with group-serving biases having an even greater effect than self-serving biases (Taylor and Doria 1981).

Bazerman et al. (1984) discovered that groups exhibited a similar tendency to nonrationally escalate to a course of action as individuals. Whyte (1991), however, found that when responsibility was varied, groups in a group-responsibility condition actually exhibited a decrease in the escalation of commitment as compared to individuals in a responsibility condition. The explanation for this effect centers around the ability of members of a group to diffuse responsibility for a decision which is not a possibility in individual decision making.

The formation, maintenance and interaction of coalitions has also been informed by BDT research. Mannix and White (1992) found that the anchoring and adjustment heuristic characterized the distribution of resources within a coalition. In particular, in the absence of a distribution rule, past performance information served as an anchor for distributive outcomes. Bazerman (1994) suggests that coalitions may also be influenced by other biases. For example, Bazerman asserts that the reemergence of successful coalitions may be because of a reliance on the availability heuristic. In addition, the escalation of commitment bias and the positive framing effect imply that individuals may stay in a coalition longer than they should. Furthermore, individuals may be overconfident in their ability to form a new coalition.

Janis's (1972) work on groupthink suggests that groups may also exhibit biases unique to a group context. The eight symptoms of groupthink (illusion of invulnerability, collective rationalization, a belief in the group's inherent morality, stereotypes of outgroups, direct pressure on dissenters, self-censorship, illusion of unanimity and the use of self-appointed mind guards) are believed to lead to deficiencies in the decision-making process of groups, including an incomplete survey of alternatives and objectives, a failure to examine the risks of choices and reappraise initially rejected alternatives, poor information search, biased processing of information, and a failure to work out contingency plans (Janis and Mann 1977). Thus, groupthink can be thought of as a heuristic within highly cohesive groups that interferes with rational decision making (Bazerman 1994).

## Human Resource Management

Another important area to which BDT has contributed is human resource management (HRM). Decision-making research is considered to be a fruitful source of knowledge for HRM (Northcraft et al. 1988). Part of the reasoning behind this claim focuses on the inadequacy of human decision makers who face two impediments: cognitive limitations and biases from social influence (Northcraft et al. 1988). The review of BDT's influence in human resources thus involves an understanding of how biases can influence decisions made in this domain.

One bias that is particularly relevant in personnel decisions is the anchoring and adjustment bias (Slovic and Lichtenstein 1971). This bias reflects the tendency to insufficiently adjust away from a chosen reference point. The anchoring and adjustment bias is particularly prevalent in performance appraisals, which can be influenced by a halo effect (favorable performance in one area leads to favorable ratings in all job performance categories) and a pitchfork effect (behavior related to a trait that the rater doesn't like leads to negative performance rating) (Kelley 1950; Lowe 1986). Past performance can also be an anchor that influences judgments about current performance (Huber et al. 1987b). Furthermore, the order of the performance appraisal format can serve as an anchor, such that information presented early in the job description has a disproportionate influence on the entire evaluation (McArthur 1983).

In addition to the influence of anchors on raters, it has also been shown that ratees are subject to the anchoring and adjustment bias. People believe initial impressions of their performance and ignore or discount future evaluations (Ross et al. 1975). Similarly, Cervone and Peake (1986) discovered that self-efficacy, subsequent performance and persistence in solving novel problems were influenced by a random anchor of a performance rating. Salespeople's call selection decisions were found to be influenced by their position in relation to established quotas (Ross 1991). Locke et al. (1983) found that subjects adjusted goals in the direction shown by performance, suggesting that assigned goals may serve as an anchor by influencing perceptions of what is possible (Northcraft et al. 1988).

Anchoring also influences applicant selection and compensation. Huber et al. (1990) presented evidence that the number of openings in a firm anchored subjects' judgments of the number of suitable candidates. Similarly, the salary level of one's supervisor can also serve as an anchor in decisions regarding employee compensation (Goodman 1974).

The representative heuristic has also had an impact in HRM research. This heuristic involves the process through which people assess the likelihood of an event's occurrence by the similarity of that occurrence to their stereotypes of similar occurrences (Bazerman 1994). Common in selection and evaluation decisions, this heuristic can lead an organization to select their 'type' of employee (Dipboye and Macan 1987), resulting in a homogeneous workforce. Indeed, job classifications have been shown to influence stereotypes (Jackson et al. 1982). Huber (1986) provides further evidence that

people are in fact insensitive to base rates in their judgments of qualified applicants.

One negative implication of the representativeness heuristic is discrimination (Bazerman 1994). Use of this heuristic can lead to inappropriate hiring decisions based on sex and attractiveness of the candidate, with male and attractive applicants preferred (Cann et al. 1981). Job evaluations can also be biased, with more points given to job criteria drawn from male job evaluation plans than those drawn from female job evaluation plans (Cascio and O'Reilly 1982). Conversely, females are found to be awarded more in grievance settlements than men (Dalton and Todor 1985). The representativeness heuristic may also result in biases in instances where physical disabilities (Rose and Brief 1979; Czajka and DeNisi 1988), age (Haefner 1977), and race (Wendelken and Inn 1981) are considered in HRM decisions.

## An Evaluation of Cognition Perspectives in Micro Organizational Behavior

We concur with Ilgen and Klein's (1988) conclusion about the important and growing role of cognitive perspectives in OB. In general, we consider our review of the social cognition area to be extremely consistent with the perspectives of Ilgen and Klein. Both regard social cognitive research as critical to the continued development of traditional micro OB topics (e.g. leadership, motivation, and performance appraisal). Our review of BDT research in the micro OB literature suggests that in addition to helping with the advancement of traditional OB areas (e.g. group decision making and human resource management), BDT has also been instrumental in creating new topics in the field of OB, namely, decision making and negotiation. Both are now common topics of leading OB journals, textbooks, and courses. This was not true two decades ago.

We believe that the success of BDT in creating new topics is tied to the values and assumptions that we offered at the beginning of this chapter. We argued that research should understand the world as it is, not as we would like it to be. Both the social cognition and BDT literatures achieve this objective by avoiding the limitations of making obviously false assumptions about humans. We also argued that descriptive research is strengthened by comparison to a normative benchmark. We believe that this is an important lever of the BDT approach which highlights areas in which we can see limitations in behavior in organizations. We further argued that descriptive research can inform prescriptive frameworks. We believe that this aspect of BDT has been critical to its level of influence in the negotiation area. People want to know how to negotiate better, and BDT provides useful insights. Finally, we argued that decisions are a core activity in organizations. This obvious yet ignored perspective is critical to the emergence of decision making as a topic of inquiry by OB scholars.

Collectively, we see both social cognition and BDT playing a crucial role in contemporary micro OB. We believe that BDT has been particularly important in helping to identify the topics that define OB as we head into the next decade.

## COGNITIVE PERSPECTIVES IN MACRO ORGANIZATIONAL RESEARCH

The last decade has also witnessed the influence of cognitive perspectives on macro research. Efforts to apply psychological theories and cognitive perspectives to organization-level behavior began with the work of Katz and Kahn (1966; 1978), Weick (1969; 1979a; 1979b), Pondy and Mitroff (1979) and Daft and Weick (1984). This perspective describes organizations as 'enacting bodies' or 'interpretation systems', emphasizing the importance of language and symbols in the social construction of reality in organizations (Pfeffer 1981) and drawing parallels between schema concepts and strategy (Weick 1979a; Schwenk 1986; 1988). This work established the groundwork for general cognitive concepts to be adapted to the descriptions of organizations and their actions and to the diagnosis of organizational properties and problems.

Subsequent research has examined how the organizational context can be influenced by individual behaviors. Autonomous individuals are seen as posing as organizations (Staw and Sutton 1992), taking actions that reflect their own preferences, and yet disguising them as actions reflecting organizational policies and/or procedures (Staw 1991). As such, psychological and social cognitive theories are useful for explaining the behavior of organizations. As of yet, however, such concepts have not been explicitly studied (Mowday and Sutton 1993).

Related research focusing on the role of leaders suggests that, while leaders of organizations are not completely powerful in scope, they have at least a modest influence on organizations, particularly on small and young firms (Bass 1990; Pfeffer and Davis-Blake 1986; Thomas 1988). There are numerous ways that leaders and other key individuals can influence organizations, including shaping thoughts, feel-ings, perceptions, and actions of people inside and outside the organization and making decisions that affect the organization (Mowday and Sutton 1993). In addition to shaping the set of members who make up the organization, leaders also create conditions that influence members' emotion, behaviors, and cognitions (Staw and Sutton 1992).

Closely related to our cognitive focus is the stream of literature that focuses on the leader's role of providing explanations, legitimization, and rationales for organizational activities (symbolic management as proposed by Pfeffer 1981). Several studies have related concepts of attribution theories to leadership, including an examination of explanations provided by CEOs in regard to corporate performance (Staw et al. 1983; Salancik and Meindl 1984; Bettman and Weitz 1983). They suggest that CEOs use self-serving attributions to explain their own behavior by attributing good performance to internal organizational actions and factors and unsuccessful performance to events external to the organization. Staw et al. (1983) found that these self-serving attributions affected shareholders' perceptions, resulting in improved stock prices. Similarly, Salancik and Meindl (1984) found that management, particularly in unstable firms, strategically manipulated causal attributions to manage impressions of their control.

Another way in which powerful people influence organizations is through the decisions that they make. Strategy formulation is often treated as a process in which decisions are incremental, interdependent, and shaped by a variety of contextual and psychological influences (see Bateman and Zeithaml 1989). The study of strategists' cognition provides information about the workings of these informed minds and, therefore, the factors which contribute to the successes and failures of organizations (Schwenk 1988). This stream of research tends to focus more on cognitive structures and processes which may be shared by multiple strategists than on individuals and their differences in cognition. It calls for more detailed descriptions of the ways that individual-level cognitions contribute to organization-level strategies.

Drawing from the literature on social cognitive influences, there has been a stream of articles relating organizational decision making to cognitive structures and processes. This research addresses such topics as a decision maker's frame of reference (e.g. Mason and Mitroff 1981; Shrivastava and Mitroff 1983; 1984), strategic assumptions (e.g. Schwenk 1988), knowledge structures (Prahalad and Bettis 1986; Lyles and Schwenk 1992), categorization (Dutton and

Jackson 1987), and the concepts of scripts, cognitive maps, schemata, organizational learning, and interpretive systems (see Lyles and Schwenk 1992). Specific examples of the application of social cognitive concepts include Dutton and Jackson's (1987) model which integrates interpretive views of organizational decision making with categorization theory. It attempts to explain why organizations in the same industry respond differently to the same environmental trends and events. Prahalad and Bettis (1986) and Lyles and Schwenk (1992) suggest that the shared perspectives of organization members create knowledge structures for environmental events and organization capabilities. These structures can store a shared dominant general management logic which influences strategic actions and organization learning within the firm. Analysis of executives' strategic schemata is thought to help explain strategic choices in response to environmental and industry forces (Schwenk 1988).

Other research concentrates on the cognitive shortcomings that can affect the decisions made by top managers, which in turn affect the organization. This research stems directly from BDT literature and the notion that decision heuristics – including representativeness, framing, availability, anchoring, the hindsight bias, and overconfidence – influence managerial behavior (Bazerman 1994). As Schwenk (1988) supports, decisional biases found in many laboratory contexts can also affect strategic decision making. He lists applicable biases, such as those previously mentioned, along with selective perception bias, illusory correlation, conservatism, the law of small numbers, regression bias, illusion of control, logical reconstruction and wishful thinking. It is argued that such heuristics allow organizational experts to make sense of strategic issues quickly and respond in an efficient and effective manner (Day and Lord 1992).

Zajac and Bazerman (1991) integrated theory concerning cognitive shortcomings with insights from the strategy literature to develop hypotheses about why and how decision makers in competitive situations make nonrational judgments. They provided explanations for the persistence of poor strategic decisions that result in industry overcapacity, new business failures, and acquisition premiums. Their perspective illustrates how leaders' and key decision makers' cognitive limitations can lead to decisions or actions that affect organizational attributes such as size, mission, and performance. Duhaime and Schwenk (1985) support this notion with their theory that business decision makers may use cognitive simplifying processes in defining ill-structured problems

such as acquisition and divestment decisions. Other examples include Staw et al.'s (1981) work on the threat-rigidity model which suggests that distress can hinder the cognitive processes of leaders and cause them to make poor decisions.

Next steps in strategic decision-making agendas include more integration of psychological and cognitive research through the exploration of which heuristics are most relevant to strategic decision makers, how they work, why they work, and when they are most appropriate (Eisenhardt and Zbaracki 1992). In addition, researchers are attempting to describe the ways that individual biases interact to affect strategic decisions (Schwenk 1986).

In addition to the influence of individual members, there also exists the argument that organizations are influenced by the aggregation of individual attributes, thoughts, feelings, and behaviors (Mowday and Sutton 1993; Staw and Sutton 1992). Using a cognitive perspective to understand more about the sum of individual beliefs is seen as a way to provide better explanations for organizational-level actions. Work on organizational learning and memory, for example, draws parallels between individual processes and organizational processes. As Staw and Sutton (1992) note, the classic work of March and Simon (1958) illustrates this analogy through its treatment of organizational information processing as synonymous with individual information processing. Another example is present in Walsh and Ungson's (1991) review and integration of the literature on organizational memory. They suggest that an organization's memory is an individual-level phenomenon since it is determined partly by the aggregation of individuals' remembered information and records.

In summary, the topic of cognition has reached the agendas of several macro organization behavior researchers, from the field of strategic management to more interdisciplinary areas, focusing on the states and traits of individuals as explanations of collective behavior. The extension of applicable findings within the areas of BDT and social cognition provides more than alternative explanations; in many contexts, it is possible that it brings a more realistic interpretation of organizational action than traditional sociological approaches. Cognitive-based theories can add theoretical substance to existing macro models by supplying missing mechanisms to explain the behavior of organizations (Staw and Sutton 1992). More importantly, the integration of nontraditional disciplines in the development of theoretical ideas in macro organizational behavior also helps to make the existing lines between micro and macro organization behavior a little less obvious. This represents a realm for future research as well as a renewal of ideas within the field of organization behavior.

## THE FUTURE OF COGNITION IN ORGANIZATIONS

As is evident in our review, social cognition and BDT have had a significant influence on micro and macro organizational research. We do not view this as a fad but rather strongly believe that these two theoretical frameworks will continue to impact the field of OB. We see this influence as coming from several directions, including additional theoretical and empirical research in topic areas previously mentioned in this chapter, in the identification of additional topics that are important to the field, and in the integration of concepts from social cognition and BDT.

As previously discussed, memory and self-concept have been identified as important factors in the topics of leadership, motivation, and performance appraisal. This research is still in the recognition phase, with many propositions offered but little empirical evidence presented. Further theoretical clarification and additional empirical research will enhance our understanding of these areas and in turn present useful recommendations to organizations. For example, additional research on the role of memory in the evaluation of leaders and in performance appraisals of employees promises to identify sources of errors in these processes which in turn may indicate potential areas for improvement. Similarly, an understanding of self-concept differences in leaders versus nonleaders and motivated employees versus unmotivated employees will result in the development of propositions and suggestions aimed at self-concept improvement, which will in turn enhance leadership and productivity in organizations.

One of the primary contributions of BDT research has been the identification of biases that lead to a decrement in decision performance. The identification of new biases is expected to continue, albeit at a diminishing rate. Increased attention is expected to be directed at how this information can be used to increase decision-making ability. Heuristics are helpful shortcuts only when they are appropriately applied; identification of the factors that result in misapplication will enhance the usefulness of this research. Furthermore, inquiry into the process of 'unbiasing' decision-makers promises to increase individual and organizational performance. The increased popularity of the use of groups in organizations suggests that the identification of unique group biases will also be a focus of BDT research in the future.

A consideration of the integration of BDT and social cognition theories raises several questions, the answers to which could further augment micro organizational research. For example, a relatively untouched but nonetheless important question centers around the influence of attitudes on the prevalence of biases. Are some attitudes influential in promoting the inappropriate use of heuristics? What role do anchoring and adjustment play in the attribution process? What is the connection between memory and the representativeness heuristic?

From a macro standpoint, both BDT and social cognition will be influential in the development of new research paradigms. Theories from memory and attribution research may open up new avenues for research in the organizational learning area. Similarly, the identification of biases (i.e. anchoring and adjustment) instrumental in retarding organizational change is certain to expand our knowledge of this organizational phenomenon.

In conclusion, a new definition of OB that encompasses both social cognition and BDT addresses many of the criticisms aimed at this field. As evident in both past research and potential future research, these perspectives give new light to old issues and open up new doors to additional topics. Incorporating the theories of social cognition and BDT into the OB domain will ensure that OB remains a field that is alive and here to stay.

## REFERENCES

Alpert, M. and Raiffa, H. (1969) 'A progress report on the training of probability assessors'. Unpublished manuscript, Harvard University.

Argote, L., Devadas, R. and Melone, N. (1990) 'The base-rate fallacy: contrasting processes and outcomes of group and individual judgment', *Organizational Behavior and Human Decision Processes*, 46: 296–310.

Argote, L., Seabright, M.A. and Dyer, L. (1986) 'Individual versus group: use of base-rate and individuating information', *Organizational Behavior and Human Decision Processes*, 38: 65–75.

Arnold, H.J. (1985) 'Task performance, perceived competence, and attributed causes of performance as determinants of intrinsic motivation', *Academy of Management Journal*, 28: 876–88.

Asch, S.E. (1946) 'Forming impressions of personality', *Journal of Abnormal and Social Psychology*, 41: 1230–40.

Bagozzi, R.P., Davis, F.D. and Warshaw, P.R. (1992)

'Development and test of a theory of technological learning and usage', *Human Relations*, 45: 659–86.

Bannister, B.D. and Balkin, D.B. (1990) 'Performance evaluation and compensation feedback messages: an integrated model', *Journal of Occupational Psychology*, 63: 97–111.

Bargh, J.A. (1984) 'Automatic and conscious processing of social information', in R.S. Wyer Jr and T.K. Srull (eds), *Handbook of Social Cognition*, vol. 3. Hillsdale, NJ: Erlbaum.

Bargh, J.A. (1990) 'Auto-motives: preconscious determinants of social interaction', in E.T. Higgins and R.M. Sorrentino (eds), *Handbook of Motivation and Cognition: Foundations of Social Behavior*, vol. 2. New York: Guilford Press.

Bar-Hillel, M. (1973) 'On the subjective probability of compound events', *Organizational Behavior and Human Performance*, 9: 396–406.

Bass, B.M. (1990) *Bass and Stogdill's Handbook of Leadership*. New York: Free Press.

Bateman, T.S. and Zeithaml, C.P. (1989) 'The psychological context of strategic decisions: a test of relevance to practitioners', *Strategic Management Journal*, 10: 587–92.

Bazerman, M.H. (1984) 'The relevance of Kahneman and Tversky's concept of framing to organization behavior', *Journal of Management*, 10: 333–43.

Bazerman, M.H. (1993) 'Fairness, social comparison, and irrationality', in J.K. Murnighan (ed.), *Social Psychology in Organizations: Advances in Theory and Research*. Prentice-Hall.

Bazerman, M.H. (1994) *Judgment in Managerial Decision Making*. New York: Wiley.

Bazerman, M.H. and Carroll, J.S. (1987) 'Negotiator cognition', *Research in Organizational Behavior*, 9: 247–88.

Bazerman, M.H. and Neale, M.A. (1982) 'Improving negotiation effectiveness under final offer arbitration: the role of selection and training', *Journal of Applied Psychology*, 67: 543–8.

Bazerman, M.H. and Neale, M.A. (1983) 'Heuristics in negotiation: limitations to dispute resolution effectiveness', in M.H. Bazerman and R.J. Lewicki (eds), *Negotiating in Organizations*. Beverly Hills: Sage.

Bazerman, M.H., Giuliano, T. and Appelman, A. (1984) 'Escalation in individual and group decision making', *Organizational Behavior and Human Performance*, 33: 141–52.

Bazerman, M.H., Magliozzi, T. and Neale, M.A. (1985) 'The acquisition of an integrative response in a competitive market', *Organizational Behavior and Human Performance*, 34: 294–313.

Bell, D.E., Raiffa, H. and Tversky, A. (1988) *Decision Making: Descriptive, Normative, and Prescriptive Interactions*. Cambridge: Cambridge University Press.

Bernardin, H.J. (1989) 'Increasing the accuracy of performance measurement: a proposed solution to erroneous attributions', *Human Resource Planning*, 12: 239–50.

Bernardin, H.J. and Cardy, R.L. (1982) 'Appraisal accuracy: the ability and motivation to remember the past', *Public Personnel Management*, 11: 352–7.

Bettman, J.R. and Weitz, B.A. (1983) 'Attributions in the board room: causal reasoning in corporate annual reports', *Administrative Science Quarterly*, 28: 165–83.

Borman, W.C. (1987) 'Personal constructs, performance schemata, and "folk theories" of subordinate effectiveness: explorations in an Army officer sample', *Organizational Behavior and Human Decision Processes*, 40: 307–22.

Brewer, M.B. and Kramer, R.D. (1985) 'The psychology of intergroup attitudes and behavior', *Annual Review of Psychology*, 36: 219–43.

Brief, A.P. and Aldag, R.J. (1981) 'The "self" in work organizations: a conceptual review', *Academy of Management Review*, 6: 75–88.

Cann, A., Siegfried, W.D. and Pearce, L. (1981) 'Forced attention to specific applicant qualifications: impact on physical attractiveness and sex of applicant biases', *Personnel Psychology*, 34: 65–75.

Cantor, N., Markus, H., Niedenthal, P. and Nurius, P. (1986) 'On motivation and the self-concept', in R.M. Sorrentino and E.T. Higgins (eds), *Handbook of Motivation and Cognition: Foundations of Social Behavior*. New York: Guilford Press.

Cardy, R.L. and Kehoe, J.F. (1984) 'Rater selective attention ability and appraisal effectiveness: the effect of a cognitive style on the accuracy of differentiation among ratees', *Journal of Applied Psychology*, 69: 589–94.

Cascio, W.F. and O'Reilly, C.A. (1982) 'Comparable worth and job evaluation: the biasing effect of subfactors and contextual cues'. Paper presented at the 89th Annual Meeting of the American Psychological Association.

Cellar, D.F. and Barrett, G.V. (1987) 'Scripts processing and intrinsic motivation: the cognitive sets underlying cognitive labels', *Organizational Behavior and Human Decision Processes*, 40: 115–35.

Cervone, B. and Peake, P.K. (1986) 'Anchoring, efficacy, and action: the influence of judgmental heuristics on self-efficacy judgments and behaviors', *Journal of Personality and Social Psychology*, 50: 492–501.

Chapman, L.J. and Chapman, J.P. (1967) 'Genesis of popular but erroneous diagnostic observations', *Journal of Abnormal Psychology*, 72: 193–204.

Cummings, L.L. (1973) 'A field experimental study of the effect of two performance appraisal systems', *Personnel Psychology*, 26: 489–502.

Cummings, L.L. (1982) 'Organizational behavior', *Annual Review of Psychology*, 33: 541–79.

Czajka, J.M. and DeNisi, A.S. (1988) 'Effects of emotional disability and clear performance standards on performance ratings', *Academy of Management Journal*, 31: 394–404.

Daft, R.L. and Weick, K.E. (1984) 'Toward a model of

organizations as interpretation systems', *Academy of Management Review*, 9: 284–95.

Dailey, R.C. and Kirk, D.J. (1992) 'Distributive and procedural justice as antecedents of job dissatisfaction and intent to turnover', *Human Relations*, 45: 305–17.

Daley, D. (1985) 'An examination of the MBO/performance standards approach to employee evaluation: attitudes toward performance appraisal in Iowa', *Review of Public Personnel Administration*, 6: 11–28.

Daley, D. (1988) 'Profile of the uninvolved worker: an examination of employee attitudes toward management practices', *International Journal of Public Administration*, 11: 65–90.

Dalton, D.R. and Todor, W.D. (1985) 'Gender and workplace justice: a field assessment', *Personnel Psychology*, 38: 133–51.

Dawes, R.M. (1988) *Rational Choice in an Uncertain World*. New York: Harcourt Brace Jovanovich.

Day, D.V. and Lord, R.G. (1992) 'Expertise and problem categorization: the role of expert processing in organizational sense-making', *Journal of Management Studies*, 29: 35–47.

De Meuse, K.P. (1987) 'A review of the effects of non-verbal cues on the performance appraisal process', *Journal of Occupational Psychology*, 60: 207–26.

DeNisi, A.S., Cafferty, T.P. and Meglino, B.M. (1984) 'A cognitive view of the performance appraisal process: a model and research propositions', *Organizational Behavior and Human Performance*, 33: 360–96.

DeNisi, A.S., Robbins, T. and Cafferty, T.P. (1989) 'Organization of information used for performance appraisals: role of diary-keeping', *Journal of Applied Psychology*, 74: 124–9.

Dipboye, R.L. and Macan, T.M. (1987) 'A process view of the selection/recruitment interview', in R. Schuler, S. Youngblood and V. Huber (eds), *Readings in Personnel and Human Resources Management*. St Paul: West Publishing.

Dobbins, G.H., Pence, E.C., Orban, J.A. and Sgro, J.A. (1983) 'The effects of sex on the leader and sex of the subordinate on the use of organizational control policy', *Organizational Behavior and Human Performance*, 32: 325–43.

Dobbins, G.H. and Russell, J.M. (1986) 'Self-serving biases in leadership: a laboratory experiment', *Journal of Management*, 12: 475–83.

Drake, B. and Mitchell, T. (1977) 'The effects of vertical and horizontal power on individual motivation and satisfaction', *Academy of Management Journal*, 20: 573–91.

Duhaime, I.D. and Schwenk, C.R. (1985) 'Conjectures on cognitive simplification in acquisition and divestment decision making', *Academy of Management Review*, 10: 287–95.

Dutton, J.E. and Jackson, S.E. (1987) 'Categorizing strategic issues: links to organizational action', *Academy of Management Review*, 12: 76–90.

Eagly, A.H. and Chaiken, S. (1992) *The Psychology of Attitudes*. California: Harcourt Brace Janovich.

Edwards, W. (1954) 'The theory of decision making', *Psychological Bulletin*, 51: 380–417.

Einhorn, H.J. and Hogarth, R.M. (1978) 'Confidence in judgment: persistent illusion of validity', *Psychological Review*, 85: 395–416.

Eisenhardt, K.M. and Zbaracki, M.J. (1992) 'Strategic decision making', *Strategic Management Journal*, 13: 17–37.

Feldman, D.C. and Weitz, B.A. (1988) 'Career plateaus reconsidered', *Journal of Management*, 14: 69–80.

Feldman, J.M. (1981) 'Beyond attribution theory: cognitive processes in performance appraisal', *Journal of Applied Psychology*, 66: 127–48.

Ferris, G.R., Yates, V.L., Gilmore, D.C and Rowland, K.M. (1985) 'The influence of subordinate age on performance ratings and causal attributions', *Personnel Psychology*, 38: 545–57.

Fischhoff, B. (1975) 'Hindsight foresight: the effect of outcome knowledge on judgment under uncertainty', *Journal of Experimental Psychology: Human Perception and Performance*, 1: 288–99.

Fiske, S.T. (1993) 'Social cognition and social perception', *Annual Review of Psychology*, 44: 155–94.

Fiske, S.T. and Taylor, S.F. (1991) *Social Cognition*, 2nd edn. New York: McGraw-Hill.

Garb, H.N. (1989) 'Clinical judgment, clinical training, and professional experience', *Psychological Bulletin*, 105: 387–96.

Gioia, D.A., Donnellon, A. and Sims, H.P. (1989) 'Communication and cognition in appraisal: a tale of two paradigms', *Organization Studies*, 10: 503–29.

Gioia, D.A. and Sims, H.P. (1986) 'Cognition–behavior connections: attribution and verbal behavior in leader–subordinate interactions', *Organizational Behavior and Human Decision Processes*, 37: 197–229.

Goodman, P. (1974) 'Effect of perceived inequity on salary allocation decisions', *Journal of Applied Psychology*, 21: 372–5.

Green, S.G. and Liden, R.C. (1980) 'Contextual and attributional influences on control decisions', *Journal of Applied Psychology*, 65: 453–8.

Green, S.G. and Mitchell, T.R. (1979) 'Attributional processes of leaders in leader–member interactions', *Organizational Behavior and Human Performance*, 23: 429–58.

Greenhalgh, L. (1993) 'Discussant remarks'. Negotiating in Organizations Conference, Georgetown University, Washington, DC.

Greenwald, A.G. and Pratkanis, A.R. (1984) 'The self', in R.S. Wyer Jr and T.K. Srull (eds), *Handbook of Social Cognition*, vol. 3. Hillsdale, NJ: Erlbaum.

Hackman, J.R., Pearce, J.L. and Wolfe, J.C. (1978) 'Effects of changes in job characteristics on work attitudes and behaviors: a naturally occurring quasi-experiment', *Organizational Behavior and Human Performance*, 21: 289–304.

Haefner, J.E. (1977) 'Race, age, sex and competence as factors in employer selection of the disadvantaged', *Journal of Applied Psychology*, 62: 199–202.

Hamilton, D.L. and Sherman, J.W. (1993) 'Stereotypes', to appear in R.S. Wyer Jr and T.K. Srull (eds), *Handbook of Social Cognition*, 2nd edn. Hillsdale, NJ: Erlbaum.

Hamilton, D.L. and Sherman, S.J. (1989) 'Illusory correlations: implications for stereotype theory and research', in D. Bar-Tal, C.F. Graumann, A.W. Kruglanski and W. Stroebe (eds), *Stereotypes and Prejudice: Changing Conceptions*. New York: Springer-Verlag.

Hammer, T.H. (1978) 'Relationships between local union characteristics and worker behavior and attitudes', *Academy of Management Journal*, 21: 560–77.

Hannan, M.T. and Freeman, J. (1989) *Organizational Ecology*. Cambridge, MA: Harvard University Press.

Harris, C. (1988) 'A comparison of employee attitudes toward two performance appraisal systems', *Public Personnel Management*, 17: 443–56.

Harrison, P.D., West, S.G. and Reneau, J.H. (1988) 'Initial attributions and information-seeking by superiors and subordinates in production variance investigations', *Accounting Review*, 63: 307–20.

Harvey, J.H., Ickes, W.J. and Kidd, R.F. (eds) (1976) *New Directions in Attribution Research*, vol. 1. Hillsdale, NJ: Erlbaum.

Harvey, J.H., Ickes, W.J. and Kidd, R.F. (eds) (1978) *New Directions in Attribution Research*, vol. 2. Hillsdale, NJ: Erlbaum.

Harvey, J.H., Ickes, W.J. and Kidd, R.F. (eds) (1981) *New Directions in Attribution Research*, vol. 3. Hillsdale, NJ: Erlbaum.

Heider, F. (1944) 'Social perception and phenomenal causality', *Psychological Review*, 51: 358–74.

Heider, F. (1958) *The Psychology of Interpersonal Relations*. New York: Wiley.

Heneman, R.L., Greenberger, D.B. and Anonyuo, C. (1989) 'Attributions and exchanges: the effects of interpersonal factors on the diagnosis of employee performance', *Academy of Management Journal*, 32: 466–76.

Heneman, R.L., Wexley, K.N. and Moore, M.L. (1987) 'Performance-rating accuracy: a critical review', *Journal of Business Research*, 15: 431–48.

Higgins, E.T. (1992) 'Social cognition as a social science: how social action creates meaning', in D.N. Ruble, P.R. Costanzo and M.E. Oliveri (eds), *The Social Psychology of Mental Health*. New York: Guilford Press.

Higgins, E.T. and Bargh, J.A. (1987) 'Social cognition and social perception', *Annual Review of Psychology*, 38: 369–425.

House, R.J. (1971) 'A path-goal theory of leadership', *Administrative Science Quarterly*, 16: 321–38.

Huber, V.L. (1986) 'Managerial applications of judgmental biases and heuristics', *Organizational Behavior Teaching Review*, 10: 1–24.

Huber, V.L. and Neale, M.A. (1986) 'Effects of cognitive heuristics and goals on negotiator performance and subsequent goal setting', *Organizational Behavior and Human Decision Processes*, 38: 342–65.

Huber, V.L., Neale, M.A. and Northcraft, G.B. (1987a) 'Decision bias in personnel selection decisions', *Organizational Behavior and Human Decision Processes*, 40: 136–47.

Huber, V.L., Neale, M.A. and Northcraft, G.B. (1987b) 'Judgment by heuristics: effects of rater and ratee characteristics and performance standards on performance-related judgments', *Organizational Behavior and Human Decision Processes*, 40: 149–69.

Huber, V.L., Northcraft, G.B. and Neale, M.A. (1990) 'Effects of decision contexts and anchoring bias on employment screening decisions', *Organizational Behavior and Human Decision Processes*, 45: 276–84.

Huber, V.L., Podsakoff, P.M. and Todor, W.D. (1986) 'An investigation of biasing factors in the attributions of subordinates and their supervisors', *Journal of Business Research*, 14: 83–98.

Ilgen, D.R., Barnes-Farrell, J.L. and McKellin, D.B. (1993) 'Performance appraisal process research in the 1980s: what has it contributed to appraisals in use?', *Organizational Behavior and Human Decision Processes*, 54: 321–68.

Ilgen, D.R. and Klein, H.J. (1988) 'Organization behavior', *Annual Review of Psychology*, 40: 327–51.

Jackson, D.N., Peacock, A.C. and Holden, R.R. (1982) 'Professional interviewers' trait inferential structures for diverse occupational groups', *Organizational Behavior and Human Performance*, 29: 1–20.

James, L.R. and White, J.F. (1983) 'Cross-situational specificity in managers' perceptions of subordinate performance, attributions, and leader behaviors', *Personnel Psychology*, 36: 809–56.

Janis, I.L. (1972) *Victims of Groupthink*. Boston: Houghton Mifflin.

Janis, I.L. and Mann, L. (1977) *Decision Making*. New York: Free Press.

Jolly, J.P., Reynolds, T.J. and Slocum, J.W. (1988) 'Application of the means-end theoretic for understanding the cognitive bases of performance appraisal', *Organizational Behavior and Human Decision Processes*, 41: 153–79.

Jones, E.E. and Davis, K.E. (1965) 'From acts to dispositions: the attribution process in person perception', in L. Berkowitz (ed.), *Advances in Experimental Social Psychology*, vol. 2. New York: Academic Press.

Kagel, J.H. and Levine, D. (1986) 'The winner's curse and public information in common value auctions', *American Economic Review*, 76: 894–920.

Kahneman, D. and Tversky, A. (1972) 'Subjective probability: a judgment of representativeness', *Cognitive Psychology*, 3: 430–54.

Kahneman, D. and Tverksy, A. (1973) 'On the psychology of prediction', *Psychological Review*, 80: 237–51.

Kahneman, D. and Tversky, A. (1979) 'Prospect theory: an analysis of decision under risk', *Econometrica*, 47: 263–91.

Karl, K.A. and Wexley, K.N. (1989) 'Patterns of performance and rating frequency: influence on the assessment of performance', *Journal of Management*, 15: 5–20.

Katerberg, R., Hom, P.W. and Hulin, C.L. (1979) 'Effects of job complexity on the reactions of part-time employees', *Organizational Behavior and Human Performance*, 24: 317–32.

Katz, D. and Kahn, R.L. (1966) *The Social Psychology of Organizations*. New York: Wiley.

Katz, D. and Kahn, R.L. (1978) *The Social Psychology of Organizations*, 2nd edn. New York: Wiley.

Kelley, H.H. (1950) 'The warm–cold variable in first impressions of persons', *Journal of Personality*, 18: 431–9.

Kelley, H.H. (1967) 'Attribution theory in social psychology', in D. Levine (ed.), *Nebraska Symposium on Motivation*, vol. 15. Nebraska: University of Nebraska Press. pp. 192–240.

Kelley, H.H. and Michela, J.L. (1980) 'Attribution theory and research', *Annual Review of Psychology*, 31: 457–501.

Kerr, S. and Jermier, J.M. (1978) 'Substitutes for leadership: their meaning and measurement', *Organizational Behavior and Human Performance*, 22: 375–403.

Klein, H.J. (1989) 'An integrated control theory model of work motivation', *Academy of Management Review*, 14: 150–72.

Knowlton, W.A. and Ilgen, D.R. (1980) 'Performance attributional effects on feedback from superiors', *Organizational Behavior and Human Performance*, 25: 441–56.

Knowlton, W.A. and Mitchell, T.R. (1980) 'Effects of causal attributions on a supervisor's evaluation of subordinate performance', *Journal of Applied Psychology*, 65: 459–66.

Kozlowski, S.W. and Kirsch, M.P. (1987) 'The systematic distortion hypothesis, halo, and accuracy: an individual-level analysis', *Journal of Applied Psychology*, 72: 252–61.

Larson, J.R. (1989) 'The dynamic interplay between employees' feedback-seeking strategies and supervisors' delivery of performance feedback', *Academy of Management Review*, 14: 408–22.

Larson, J.R., Lingle, J.H. and Scerbo, M.M. (1984) 'The impact of performance cues on leader-behavior ratings: the role of selective information availability and probabilistic response bias', *Organizational Behavior and Human Performance*, 33: 323–49.

Lawler, E.E. (1971) *Pay and Organizational Effectiveness: a Psychological View*. New York: McGraw-Hill.

Lawrence, P.R. and Lorsch, J.W. (1967) *Organization and Environment: Managing Differentiation and Integration*. Boston: Graduate School of Business Administration, Harvard University.

Levine, J.M., Resnick, L.B. and Higgins, E.T. (1993) 'Social foundations of cognition', *Annual Review of Psychology*, 44: 585–612.

Leyens, J.P. and Codol, J.P. (1988) 'Social cognition', in M. Hewstone, W. Stroebe, J.P. Codol, and G. Stephenson (eds), *Introduction to Social Psychology: A European Perspective*. Oxford: Basil Blackwell.

Locke, E.A., Frederick, E., Buckner, E. and Bobko, P. (1983) 'Effects of previously assigned goals on self-set goals and performance', *Journal of Applied Psychology*, 69: 694–9.

Loewenstein, G., Issacharoff, S., Camerer, C. and Babcock, L. (1993) 'Self-serving assessments of fairness and pretrial bargaining', *Journal of Legal Studies*, 23: 135–59.

Lord, R.G. and Smith, J.E. (1983) 'Theoretical, information processing and situational factors affecting attribution theory models of organizational behavior', *Academy of Management Review*, 8: 50–60.

Lowe, T.R. (1986) 'Eight ways to ruin a performance review', *Personnel Journal*, 65: 60–2.

Lyles, M. and Schwenk, C. (1992) 'Top management, strategy, and organization knowledge structures', *Journal of Management Studies*, 29: 155–74.

Mannix, E.A. and White, S.B. (1992) 'The impact of distributive uncertainty on coalition formation in organizations', *Organizational Behavior and Human Decision Processes*, 51: 198–219.

March, J.G. and Simon, H.A. (1958) *Organizations*. New York: Wiley.

Marks, G. and Miller, N. (1987) 'Ten years of research on the false-consensus effect: an empirical and theoretical review', *Psychological Bulletin*, 102: 72–90.

Markus, H. and Wurf, E. (1987) 'The dynamic self-concept: a social psychological perspective', *Annual Review of Psychology*, 38: 299–337.

Markus, H. and Zajonc, R.B. (1985) 'The cognitive perspective in social psychology', in G. Lindzey and E. Aronson (eds), *The Handbook of Social Psychology*. New York: Random House.

Martin, L.L. and Clark, L.F. (1990) 'Social cognition: exploring the mental processes involved in human social interaction', in M. Eysenck (ed.), *Cognitive Psychology: An International Review*, vol. 1. Chichester: Wiley.

Martinko, M.J. and Gardner, W.L. (1987) 'The leader/member attribution process', *Academy of Management Review*, 12: 235–49.

Mason, R.O and Mitroff, I.I. (1981) *Challenging Strategic Planning Assumptions*. New York: Wiley.

McArthur, L.Z. (1983) 'Social judgment biases in comparable worth analyses'. Paper presented at the

Committee on Women's Employment and Related Social Issues Seminar on Comparable Worth Research.

Meindl, J.R. and Ehrlich, S.B. (1987) 'The romance of leadership and the evaluation of organizational performance', *Academy of Management Journal*, 30: 91–109.

Meindl, J.R., Ehrlich, S.B. and Dukerich, J.M. (1985) 'The romance of leadership', *Administrative Science Quarterly*, 30: 78–102.

Messick, D.M. and Mackie, D.M. (1989) 'Intergroup relations', *Annual Review of Psychology*, 40: 45–81.

Mirvis, P.H. and Lawler, E.E. (1977) 'Measuring the financial impact of employee attitudes', *Journal of Applied Psychology*, 62: 1–8.

Mitchell, T.R. and Kalb, L.S. (1981) 'Effects of outcome knowledge and outcome valence on supervisors' evaluations', *Journal of Applied Psychology*, 66: 604–12.

Mowday, R.T. and Sutton, R.I. (1993) 'Organizational behavior: linking individuals and groups to organizational contexts', *Annual Review of Psychology*, 44: 195–229.

Mullen, B. and Johnson, C. (1990) 'Distinctiveness-based illusory correlations and stereotyping: a meta-analytical integration', *British Journal of Social Psychology*, 29: 11–28.

Murphy, K.R., Gannett, B.A., Herr, B.M. and Chen, J.A. (1986) 'Effects of subsequent performance on evaluations of previous performance', *Journal of Applied Psychology*, 71: 427–31.

Murphy, K.R., Philbin, T.A. and Adams, S.R. (1989) 'Effect of purpose of observation on accuracy of immediate and delayed performance ratings', *Organizational Behavior and Human Decision Processes*, 43: 336–54.

Neale, M.A. (1984) 'The effect of negotiation and arbitration cost salience on bargainer behavior: the role of arbitrator and constituency in negotiator judgment', *Organizational Behavior and Human Performance*, 34: 97–111.

Neale, M.A. and Bazerman, M.H. (1985) 'The effects of framing and negotiator overconfidence on bargainer behavior', *Academy of Management Journal*, 28: 34–49.

Neale, M.A. and Bazerman, M.H. (1991) *Cognition and Rationality in Negotiation*. Free Press.

Neale, M.A., Bazerman, M.H., Northcraft, B.G. and Alperson, C.A. (1986) '"Choice shift" effects in group decisions: a decision bias perspective', *International Journal of Small Group Research*, 2: 33–42.

Nisbett, R. and Ross, L. (1980) *Human Inference: Strategies and Shortcomings of Social Judgment*. Englewood Cliffs, NJ: Prentice-Hall.

Northcraft, G.B. and Neale, M.A. (1986) 'Opportunity costs and the framing of resource allocation decisions', *Organizational Behavior and Human Decision Processes*, 37: 348–56.

Northcraft, G.B. and Neale, M.A. (1987) 'Expert, amateurs, and real estate: an anchoring-and-adjustment perspective on property pricing decisions', *Organizational Behavior and Human Decision Processes*, 39: 228–41.

Northcraft, G.B. and Neale, M.A. (1994) *Organizational Behavior: a Management Challenge*. Fort Worth, TX: Dryden Press.

Northcraft, G.B., Neale, M.A. and Huber, V.L. (1988) 'The effects of cognitive bias and social influence on human resources management decisions', *Research in Personnel and Human Resources Management*, 6: 157–89.

Olson, J.M. and Zanna, M.P. (1993) 'Attitudes and attitude change', *Annual Review of Psychology*, 44: 117–54.

O'Reilly, C.A. (1991) 'Organizational behavior: where we have been, where we're going', in *Annual Review of Psychology*. Palo Alto, CA: Annual Reviews.

Ostrom, T.M. (1989) 'Three catechisms for social memory', in P.R. Solomon, G.R. Goethals, C.M. Kelley, and B.R. Stephans (eds), *Memory: Interdisciplinary Approaches*. New York: Springer-Verlag.

Pazy, A. (1986) 'The persistence of pro-male bias despite identical information regarding causes of success', *Organizational Behavior and Human Decision Processes*, 38: 366–77.

Pearce, J.L. and Porter, L.W. (1986) 'Employee responses to formal performance appraisal feedback', *Journal of Applied Psychology*, 71: 211–18.

Peppers, L. and Ryan, J. (1986) 'Discrepancies between actual and aspired self: a comparison of leaders and nonleaders', *Group and Organization Studies*, 11: 220–8.

Pfeffer, J. (1981) 'Management as symbolic action: the creation and maintenance of organizational paradigms', *Research in Organizational Behavior*, 3: 1–52.

Pfeffer, J. and Davis-Blake, A. (1986) 'Administrative succession and organizational performance: how administrator experience mediates the succession effect', *Academy of Management Journal*, 29: 72–83.

Phillips, J.S. (1984) 'The accuracy of leadership ratings: a cognitive categorization perspective', *Organizational Behavior and Human Performance*, 33: 125–38.

Pondy, L.R. and Mitroff, I.I. (1979) 'Beyond open system models of organizations', *Research in Organizational Behavior*, 1: 3–39.

Prahalad, C.K. and Bettis, R.A. (1986) 'The dominant logic: a new linkage between diversity and performance', *Strategic Management Journal*, 7: 485–501.

Raiffa, H. (1982) *The Art and Science of Negotiation*. Cambridge, MA: Belknap.

Rogers, T.B. (1977) 'Self-reference in memory: recognition of personality items', *Journal of Research in Personality*, 11: 295–305.

Rose, G.L. (1978) 'Sex effects on effort attributions in

managerial performance evaluation', *Organizational Behavior and Human Performance*, 21: 367–78.

Rose, G.L. and Brief, A.P. (1979) 'Effects of handicap and job characteristics on selection evaluation', *Personnel Psychology*, 32: 385–92.

Ross, L. (1977) 'The intuitive psychologist and his shortcomings: distortions in the attribution process', in L. Berkowitz (ed.), *Advances in Experimental Social Psychology*, 35: 485–94.

Ross, L., Lepper, M. and Hubbard, M. (1975) 'Perseverance on self perception and social perception: biased attributional processes in the debriefing paradigm', *Journal of Personality and Social Psychology*, 32: 880–92.

Ross, M. and Fletcher, G.J.O. (1985) 'Attribution and social perception', in G. Lindzey and A. Aronson (eds), *The Handbook of Social Psychology*, 3rd edn, vol. 2. Reading, MA: Addison-Wesley.

Ross, W.T. (1991) 'Performance against quota and call selection decision', *Journal of Marketing Research*, 28: 296–306.

Salancik, G.R. and Meindl, J.R. (1984) 'Corporate attributions as strategic illusions of management control', *Administrative Science Quarterly*, 29: 238–54.

Samuelson, W.F. and Bazerman, M.H. (1985) 'The winner's curse in bilateral negotiations', in V. Smith (ed.), *Research in Experimental Economics*, vol. 3. Greenwich, CT: JAI Press. pp. 105–37.

Schneider, D.J. (1991) 'Social cognition', *Annual Review of Psychology*, 42: 527–61.

Schwab, D.P. and Heneman, H.G. (1978) 'Age stereotyping in performance appraisal', *Journal of Applied Psychology*, 63: 573–8.

Schwenk, C. (1986) 'Information, cognitive biases, and commitment to a course of action', *Academy of Management Review*, 11: 298–310.

Schwenk, C. (1988) 'The cognitive perspective on strategic decision-making', *Journal of Management Studies*, 25: 41–55.

Shamir, B. (1991) 'Meaning, self and motivation in organizations', *Organizational Studies*, 12: 405–24.

Sherman, S.J., Judd, C.M. and Park, B. (1989) 'Social cognition', *Annual Review of Psychology*, 40: 281–326.

Shrivastava, P. and Mitroff, I.I. (1983) 'Frames of reference managers use: a study in applied sociology of knowledge', in R. Lamb (ed.), *Advances in Strategic Management*, vol. 1. Greenwich, CT: JAI Press.

Shrivastava, P. and Mitroff, I.I. (1984) 'Enhancing organizational research utilization: the role of decision makers' assumptions', *Academy of Management Review*, 9: 18–26.

Simon, H.A. (1957) *Models of Man*. New York: Wiley.

Slovic, P. and Lichtenstein, S. (1971) 'Comparison of Bayesian and regression approaches to the study of information processing in judgment', *Organizational Behavior and Human Performance*, 6: 649–764.

Sniezek, J.A. and Henry, R.A. (1989) 'Accuracy and confidences in group judgment', *Organizational Behavior and Human Decision Processes*, 43: 1–28.

Stahlberg, D. and Frey, D. (1988) 'Attitudes I: structure, measurement and functions', in M. Hewstone, W. Stroebe, J.P. Codol and G. Stephenson (eds), *Introduction to Social Psychology: A European Perspective*. Oxford: Basil Blackwell.

Staw, B.M. (1984) 'Organizational behavior: a review and reformulation of the field's outcome variables', *Annual Review of Psychology*, 35: 627–66.

Staw, B.M. (1991) 'Dressing up like an organization: when psychological theories can explain organizational action', *Journal of Management*, 17: 805–19.

Staw, B.M., McKechnie, P.I., and Puffer, S.M. (1983) 'The justification of organizational performance', *Administrative Science Quarterly*, 28: 582–600.

Staw, B.M., Sandelands, L.E., and Dutton, J.E. (1981) 'Threat-rigidity effects in organizational behavior: a multilevel analysis', *Administrative Science Quarterly*, 26: 501–24.

Staw, B.M. and Sutton, R.I. (1992) 'Macro organizational psychology', in J.K. Murnighan (ed.), *Social Psychology in Organizations: Advances in Theory and Research*. Englewood Cliffs, NJ: Prentice-Hall.

Stillinger, C., Epelbaum, M., Keltner, D. and Ross, L. (in press) 'The "reactive devaluation" barrier to conflict resolution'. Working Paper.

Stoner, J.A.F. (1961) 'A comparison of individual and group decisions involving risk'. Unpublished master's thesis, Massachusetts Institute of Technology, School of Industrial Management.

Stroebe, W. and Jonas, K. (1988) 'Attitudes II: strategies of attitude change', in M. Hewstone, W. Stroebe, J.P. Codol and G. Stephenson (eds), *Introduction to Social Psychology: a European Perspective*. Oxford: Basil Blackwell.

Sujan, H. (1986) 'Smarter versus harder: an exploratory attributional analysis of salespeople's motivation', *Journal of Marketing Research*, 23: 41–9.

Sullivan, J.J. (1989) 'Self theories and employee motivation', *Journal of Management*, 15: 345–63.

Tajfel, H. (1969) 'Cognitive aspects of prejudice', *Journal of Social Issues*, 25: 79–97.

Taylor, D.M. and Doria, J.R. (1981) 'Self-serving and group-serving bias in attribution', *Journal of Social Psychology*, 113: 201–11.

Teas, R. and McElroy, J.C. (1986) 'Causal attributions and expectancy estimates: a framework for understanding the dynamics of salesforce motivation', *Journal of Marketing*, 50: 75–86.

Thomas, A.B. (1988) 'Does leadership make a difference to organizational performance?', *Administrative Science Quarterly*, 33: 338–400.

Thompson, L.L. and Hastie, R. (1990) 'Negotiator's perceptions of the negotiation process', in B.H. Sheppard, M.H. Bazerman and R.J. Lewicki (eds), *Research in Negotiation in Organizations*, vol. 2. Greenwich, CT: JAI Press.

Thompson, L.L. and Loewenstein, G.F. (1992) 'Egocentric interpretations of fairness and interpersonal conflict', *Organizational Behavior and Human Decision Processes*, 51: 176–97.

Tjosvold, D. (1985) 'The effects of attribution and social context on superiors' influence and interaction with low performing subordinates', *Personnel Psychology*, 38: 361–76.

Tversky, A. and Kahneman, D. (1973) 'Availability: a heuristic for judging frequency and probability', *Cognitive Psychology*, 5: 207–32.

Tversky, A. and Kahneman, D. (1974) 'Judgment under uncertainty: heuristics and biases', *Science*, 185: 1124–31.

Tversky, A. and Kahneman, D. (1983) 'Extensional versus intuitive reasoning: the conjunction fallacy in probability judgement', *Psychological Review*, 90: 293–315.

Tversky, A. and Kahneman, D. (1986) 'Rational choice and the framing of decisions', *Journal of Business*, 59: 251–84.

Walsh, J.P. and Ungson, G.R. (1991) 'Organizational memory', *Academy of Management Review*, 16: 57–91.

Wason, P.C. (1960) 'On the failure to eliminate hypotheses in a conceptual task', *Quarterly Journal of Experimental Psychology*, 12: 129–40.

Weick, K.E. (1969) *The Social Psychology of Organizing*. Reading, MA: Addison-Wesley.

Weick, K.E. (1979a) 'Cognitive processes in organizations', *Research in Organizational Behavior*, 1: 41–74.

Weick, K.E. (1979b) *The Social Psychology of Organizing*. Reading, MA: Addison-Wesley.

Weick, K.E. (1992) 'Sensemaking in organizations: small structures with large consequences', in J.K. Murnighan (ed.), *Social Psychology in Organizations: Advances in Theory and Research*. Englewood Cliffs, NJ: Prentice-Hall.

Weiner, B. (1986) *An Attributional Theory of Motivation and Emotion*. New York: Springer-Verlag.

Wendelken, D.J. and Inn, A. (1981) 'Nonperformance influences on performance evaluation: a laboratory phenomenon?', *Journal of Applied Psychology*, 66: 150–8.

Wexley, K.N. and Pulakos, E.D. (1983) 'The effects of perceptual congruence and sex on subordinates' performance appraisals of their managers', *Academy of Management Journal*, 26: 666–76.

White, H.C. and Bassford, G. (1978) 'Industrial effectiveness: leadership style and small groups', *Industrial Management*, 63: 277–88.

Whyte, G. (1991) 'Diffusion of responsibility: effects on the escalation tendency', *Journal of Applied Psychology*, 76: 408–15.

Williams, K.J., Cafferty, T.P. and DeNisi, A.S. (1990) 'The effect of performance appraisal salience on recall and ratings', *Organizational Behavior and Human Decision Processes*, 46: 217–39.

Wyer, R.S. and Srull, T.K. (1988) 'Understanding social knowledge: if only the data could speak for themselves', in D. Bar-Tal and A.W. Kruglanski (eds), *The Social Psychology of Knowledge*. Cambridge: Cambridge University Press.

Yeager, S.J., Rabin, J. and Vocino, T. (1985) 'Feedback and administrative behavior in the public sector', *Public Administration Review*, 45: 570–5.

Zajac, E.J. and Bazerman, M.H. (1991) 'Blind spots in industry and competitor analysis: implications of interfirm (mis)perceptions for strategic decisions', *Academy of Management Review*, 16: 37–56.

Zalesny, M.D. and Highhouse, S. (1992) 'Accuracy in performance evaluations', *Organizational Behavior and Human Decision Processes*, 51: 22–50.

Zuckerman, M. (1979) 'Attribution of success and failure revisited, or: the motivational bias is alive and well in attribution theory', *Journal of Personality*, 47: 245–87.

# 5

# Diverse Identities in Organizations

## STELLA M. NKOMO AND TAYLOR COX JR

In the last few years with the release of the Workforce 2000 Report and other publications predicting a more diverse workforce in the United States and throughout the world (Fullerton 1991; Johnston and Packer 1987; Johnston 1991), diversity has gained currency as a topic in the study of organizations. The most attention has come from practitioners interested in how to 'manage diversity' in light of these predictions (Cross et al. 1994; Morrison 1992; Loden and Rosener 1991; Thomas 1991). Organizational researchers have only recently turned their attention to the topic (Cox 1993; Cox and Blake 1991; Ferdman 1992; Jackson and associates 1992; Watson et al. 1993). For the most part the concept of diversity lacks rigor, theoretical development, and historical specificity.

The current state of theoretical knowledge and research on diversity in organizations might be likened to the situation of discovering the many tributary streams to a larger body of water but being uncertain about the very nature of the larger body of water. There are a number of theoretical and research areas which influence current understandings of diverse identities in organizations. The vastness of what might be assumed under the rubric of diversity reflects one of its major theoretical dilemmas – the lack of specificity of the concept. Diversity is underdeveloped as a scientific construct and has largely drawn its present meaning from the work of organizational practitioners. It is also very much a contested term. Current definitions of diversity range from narrow to very broad, expansive conceptualizations.

Narrow definitions emphasize race, ethnicity, and gender. For instance, Cross et al. (1994:

xxii) view diversity as 'focusing on issues of racism, sexism, heterosexism, classism, ableism, and other forms of discrimination at the individual, identity group, and system levels'. Cox (1993: 5–6) focuses on cultural diversity, which he defines as 'the representation, in one social system, of people with distinctly different group affiliations of *cultural* significance'. Examples of very broad definitions include Thomas (1991: 10) who states: 'Diversity includes everyone, it is not something that is defined by race or gender. It extends to age, personal and corporate background, education, function, and personality. It includes lifestyle, sexual preference, geographic origin, tenure with the organization, exempt or nonexempt status, and management or nonmanagement.' In a like fashion, Jamieson and O'Mara (1991: xvi) argue for a 'broadened view of diversity, adding values, age, disabilities, education to the more common interpretation that focuses exclusively on women and people of color'. Even more generally, Jackson et al. (1993: 53) use diversity 'to refer to situations in which the actors of interest are not alike with respect to some attribute'. Loden and Rosener (1991) also take a broad view but distinguish between primary dimensions consisting of immutable human differences like age, ethnicity, gender, race, sexual orientation, and physical abilities; and secondary mutable differences like educational background, geographic location, and work experience.

Broad definitions imply that the term refers to *all* individual differences among people – that is, everyone is different. This conceptualization mirrors the individualism that structures much of our thinking about organizations. On the other hand, narrow approaches which constrict diversity to race, ethnicity, and gender, tend to be interpreted as referring only to people who are in a particular gender or racioethnic[1] minority group in a social system (i.e. diversity refers to white women and racial minorities).

To achieve conceptual clarity in the language and meaning of diversity we have to begin with framing the concept itself. The specifics of how the term is defined and treated will go a long way toward establishing the ideology that will shape thinking about the topic in important ways. Indeed the very term is incomplete because it immediately raises the question: diversity in what? Despite the confusion over what constitutes diversity, it is somewhat clear that scholars are referring to 'diversity in identities' based on membership in social and demographic groups and how differences in identities affect social relations in organizations. We define diversity as a mixture of people with different group identities within the same social system. The concept of identity appears to be at the core of understanding diversity in organizations. Thus, our discussion of diversity in this chapter is centered around the very meaning of *identity* and its treatment in the study of organizations.

Because diversity is perceived to be such a new issue, an implicit assumption appears to be that there is little available knowledge relevant to its development as a topic. However, a close review of the organizational literature indicates a number of bodies of work relevant to diversity in identities. Our belief is that in order for theory and research on diversity to advance, it is important to critically review in one chapter theories and research which currently qualify as major orientations. The work reviewed includes social identity theory, embedded intergroup theory, racioethnicity and gender research, organizational demography, and ethnology. We do not undertake an exhaustive review of the empirical research each has generated. Our main concern is how identity has been conceptualized in each body of work. For each theory/body of work reviewed, we focus on six dimensions of the treatment of identity: (1) explicitly versus implicitly defined; (2) physically versus culturally defined; (3) proposed measurement; (4) self versus other defined; (5) levels of analysis; and (6) effects of diversity (see Table 1). Additionally, we review three recently proposed meta-theoretical diversity frameworks (Cox 1993; Jackson et al. 1995; Triandis et al. 1994). We end our review with prescriptions for how identity might be reframed and expanded. Finally, we explore the methodological and research implications of these prescriptions. We begin first, however, with a review of the relevant literature.

## LITERATURE REVIEW

### Social Identity Theory

We have defined diversity as a mixture of people with different group identities within the same social system. Intergroup perspectives have been one of the major frameworks for understanding human interactions involving individuals perceiving themselves as a member of a social category or being perceived by others as belonging to a social category (Taylor and Moghaddam 1987). These perspectives cover a range of concerns from intergroup conflict to prejudice (Brewer and Kramer 1985; Hewstone and Brown 1986; Kramer 1991; Messick and Mackie 1989; Sherif and Sherif 1953; Tajfel 1982). One of the most prominent intergroup theories informing us about group identity effects on human behavior has been social identity theory (SIT). SIT is a cognitive theory which holds that individuals tend to classify themselves and others into social categories and that these classifications have a significant effect on human interactions. The foundational work on social identification was done in the field of social psychology principally by Henry Tajfel and John Turner (Tajfel 1972; Turner 1975; Tajfel and Turner 1979). The treatment of group identity in social identity theory is somewhat inconsistent. For example, major contributors to the development of the theory differ on how much members must share in common in order to constitute a social identity group (Rabbie and Horwitz 1988). Thus, it is not entirely clear whether social identity categories are assumed to have cultural implications or simply represent different phenotypes or social categories. However, most SIT writers seem to lean toward the latter interpretation. It should be emphasized however that SIT does not treat group identity as a nominal scale measure. On the contrary, one of the most important contributions of SIT to the field of diversity research is the notion that people within social groups differ in the relative importance that any particular social identity has in their self-concept (Jackson 1981). Hence, one of the implications of SIT is that group identity should ideally be operationalized for research as a continuous scale measure.

There is also some ambiguity as to the extent to which how one is defined by others is relevant to one's social identity. For example Turner defined social identification as 'the process of locating oneself *or another person* within a system of social categorizations' but simultaneously defined 'social identity' as the 'sum total of the social identifications used by a person to define him or herself' (1982: 18). We believe that the categorical 'locations' attributed to one

Table 1  *Summary of approaches to identity in organizations*

| Treatment of identity | Embedded group theory | Social identity theory | Race/gender research | Organization demography | Ethnology | Suggested |
|---|---|---|---|---|---|---|
| Explicitly addressed vs implied | Explicit | Explicit | Implied | Explicit | Explicit | Explicit |
| Physical vs cultural | Physical | Physical | Physical | Physical | Cultural | Cultural/ historical/ political |
| Nominal vs interval/ratio | Nominal | Both | Nominal | Nominal | Interval/ratio | Both |
| Self-definition vs defined by others | Self | Self | Others | Self | Self | Both |
| Levels of analysis (individual, group, organization) | Group/ organization | Individual/ group/ organization | Individual/ group | Organization | Group | Individual/ group/ organizational/ societal |
| Effect of diversity | Depends on congruency with subsystem and suprasystem | Conflict; competition; in-group favoritism; stereotyping | Exclusion of minorities and women; discrimination | Adverse effects on cohesiveness, turnover, commitment, communication; enhances creativity, innovation and decision quality | Misunderstanding; conflict; stress; ethnocentrism | All potential effects should be understood; focus on understanding cirumstances under which positive effects can be increased; dysfunctions decreased |

person by other people are crucial to understanding the full implications of social identity. On balance, however, the clear emphasis of SIT is on self-definition, a fact that we find poses limitations for the usefulness of the concept as the focal point in diversity research. We believe that how one is defined by others both influences one's self-identity to some degree and has group affiliation effects in its own right (i.e. independent of one's self-definition). For example, the fact that a person does not identify strongly with being male or female does not mean that her/his gender will not be important in how other people relate to him/her, and thus gender identity can affect life experiences whether one self-identifies by gender or not. In light of this, to the extent that social identity is to be understood as limited to a person's self-conception (Abrams and Hogg 1990), some other concept is needed to capture the role that others play in defining the relevant group identities of a person.

Although well developed in the social psychology literature, social identification theory has only recently been applied to the organizational setting. Ashforth and Mael (1989) and Wharton (1992) present theoretical work which addresses the interaction of social identity with one or more aspects of the social context. Ashforth and Mael (1989) note that a combination of factors prevalent in organizations work to intensify the effects of group identification. These factors include the presence of numerous formal and informal groups and the distinctiveness of traits of the various groups (e.g. differences in goals and processes between work units).

Wharton (1992) and Ridgeway (1991) take a social construction approach to show how social identity is specifically applicable to the topic of workforce diversity in organizations. Wharton (1992) argues that gender and race should be viewed as socially constructed categories in organizational research. For her, one implication of this approach is that identification with gender and race groups should be understood as evoked by contextual stimuli rather than as fixed components of an individual's self-concept. This view follows closely previous work on situational ethnicity and emergent ethnicity (e.g. Yancey et al. 1976; Okamura 1981; McGuire et al. 1978; Stayman and Deshpande 1989). A central contribution of this body of work is to illuminate the contextual forces that determine identity salience such as the type of task to be performed and the demographic make-up of work groups.

Ridgeway's (1991) work focuses on the status value of nominal characteristics. Using the structural theory of Blau (1977) and the expectation-states theory of Berger and Zelditch (1985), she explains why group identities like gender and race impact levels of social interaction with persons who have access to resources and thereby become independent status indicators (i.e. independent of possession of resources or other status relevant traits). The core of her argument is that when group identifications become highly correlated with a difference in exchangeable resources, the group identification becomes an indicator of status which is then used to determine inclusion or exclusion from important social networks and ultimately is taken as a proxy for general competency. Using equations developed by Skvoretz (1983) she predicts that gender is a group identity which is especially vulnerable to the cycle because men and women are about equally represented in the population.

One noteworthy contribution of these social construction theorists to the work on diversity is that they discuss the applicability of social identity on multiple levels of analysis. Traditionally, SIT has focused on the individual level, but by emphasizing the social context, these writers make clear the importance of group- and organization-level social identity phenomena.

We now come to the central question of what SIT has to say about the effects of diversity on work group and organizational processes and outcomes. For the most part, this body of work seems to suggest that social identification and related processes produce mainly detrimental effects on the group-level outcomes of diverse groups. The following comment by Brewer is illustrative:

> The common goals and cooperative interdependence characteristic of work teams should provide a context for breaking down barriers to communication and exploiting the benefits of diverse skills and perspectives. However, various aspects of intergroup relations (in-group loyalties, implicit intergroup rivalries, negative stereotypes and distrust of out-groups) often conspire to impede coordination among members of diverse work teams and reduce effective performance. (1995: 10)

On a similar note, Ashforth and Mael (1989) identify three general consequences of group identification which are especially relevant to organizational behavior/outcomes as follows: (1) individuals tend to choose activities and institutions which are congruent with their salient identities; (2) identification affects outcomes such as intragroup cohesion and cooperation; and (3) identification reinforces attachment to the group and its values and increases competition with out-groups. The second and third consequences suggest that the existence of diversity in group identifications may lead to some difficulty in relations between people of different salient group identities. To the extent that identities with sub-groups (micro-identities in the organization context) take precedence over the common organizational identity (macro-identity), the ability of people to work together in teams composed of members from different group identities may be hampered by the consequences of group identification.

## Embedded Intergroup Relations Theory

Like SIT, embedded intergroup relations theory also falls under the general rubric of intergroup perspectives. However, Alderfer and Smith (1982) have developed a theory of embedded intergroup relations specifically for organizations which explicitly integrates identity group membership and group membership resulting from organizational categorization. Their theory posits that two types of groups exist within organizations: identity groups and organization groups.

An identity group is a group whose members share some common biological characteristic such as sex, have participated in equivalent historical experiences, are currently subjected to similar social forces, and as a result have consonant world views (Alderfer 1987). The most commonly recognized identity groups are those based on gender, family, ethnicity, and age (Alderfer and Smith 1982). While there is little choice about physical membership in identity groups, there is some degree of choice about psychological membership. Like SIT, embedded intergroup theory argues that individuals may feel more or less identified with their identity group. The focus is on self-identification.

An organization group is one in which members share common organization positions, participate in equivalent work experiences and as a consequence have consonant world views. Identity group membership precedes organization group membership. Thus, the identity of people in organizations is a function of their identity group membership and their organization group membership.

The theory contains a rather complex set of interactions for understanding the effects of diversity in identities in organizations. Identity group and organization group membership are seen as highly related in their effects on social relations in organizations. Certain organization groups tend to be populated by members of particular identity groups. For example, positions in upper management in organizations in the United States and other industrialized

countries tend to be concentrated with older white males. According to embedded intergroup theory, individuals and organizations are constantly attempting to manage potential conflicts arising from the interface between identity groups and organization group membership. How tensions are managed depends on several factors, the most important of which is how the groups are embedded in the larger 'suprasystem' (Alderfer and Smith 1982). Alderfer and Smith (1982) use the term 'embedded intergroup relations' to capture the dynamics among identity groups, organization groups, and the suprasystem in which they are embedded. Embeddedness can be either congruent or incongruent. Congruent embeddedness exists when power relations among groups at one level are reinforced by power relations at the suprasystem and subsystem level (Alderfer 1987). Incongruent embeddedness exists when power relations are not consistent with suprasystem dynamics. Understanding diverse identities in organizations therefore requires an understanding of the group affiliation profile of the parties as well as the larger context within which the parties interact.

Embedded intergroup theory has been used to study women and minorities in predominantly white male organizations (Alderfer et al. 1980; Thomas 1990). Exemplary of research using the theory is the work of Alderfer et al. (1980). Alderfer and his colleagues studied race relationships among managers of a large business corporation. Their research demonstrated how racial group identity influenced cognitions of race relations within the organization. One significant finding was the existence of both parallel and nonparallel perceptions between black and white racial groups. Each racial group reported that members of the other group socialized more with each other than with members of the other race. Each racial group tended to see this pattern as weaker in its own group than in the other group. Identity group membership was the most powerful predicator even when there were objective facts about an issue.

The significance of embedded intergroup theory for understanding identity is its attention to the effects of diverse identities within a larger organizational context. The identity of individuals in organizations is said to be determined not only by organizational categorization but also by identity group membership. It recognizes that individuals don't leave their racial, gender, or ethnic identities at the door when they enter an organization. Embedded intergroup theory also suggests that identity group categorization will always be relevant in an organization context.

## Organizational Demography

Organizational demography research refers to the study of 'the causes and consequences of the composition or distribution of specific demographic attributes of employees in an organization' (Tsui et al. 1995: 4). The origin of organizational demography as a field of study is often attributed to Pfeffer (1983). The review of organizational demography research by Tsui et al. (1995) identifies fifteen empirical studies and one edited volume published since Pfeffer's seminal article. Their review indicates that organizational demographers have focused primarily on the group identities of age, tenure, education and functional background. Of the fifteen empirical studies located by their review, tenure was addressed in thirteen, age in nine, and education and functional background in six each. By contrast, gender and race were included in only three studies each (Tsui et al. 1995).

Our study of this work suggests that group identity is generally treated as a nominal scale variable which signifies social categories based on physical or work history characteristics. In addition, it relies largely on self-definitions of group identity most commonly taken from surveys or company background data files. As implied by the name 'organizational demography', this work focuses on the macro level of analysis more so than the group or individual level. A notable exception is the work of Tsui and O'Reilly (1989) on relational demography which focuses attention on the demographics of superior–subordinate dyads.

One limitation of organizational demography research which is suggested by the early theory on diversity in organizations (and the work presented earlier on social identity theory) has to do with how the dimensions of difference are operationalized. Writers on workforce diversity have emphasized the cultural significance of demographic categories such as gender, race and work function and the notion of differential levels of identification with the group within categories. For example, Cox (1993) notes that many identity groups represent both physical distinctiveness (phenotypes) and cultural distinctiveness (cultural identity). He also argues that members of identity groups vary in the extent to which they display both the cultural and, for certain types of diversity, even the physical characteristics which are prototypical of the group. One implication of this treatment is that identity should be measured as a continuous variable rather than as a nominal variable. Alternatively, organizational demography writers have typically treated the dimensions of difference as simply physical categories.

Tsui et al. (1992) argue that a distinction between diversity research and organizational demography research is that the former limits attention to the effect of group identity differences on members of minority groups while the latter is interested in effects on all workers. However, we believe that research which addresses the impact of identity on minority group members simultaneously reveals effects for majority group members. For example, research which reveals that being female has a negative effect on promotion prospects or on compensation also reveals that being male (the majority group) has a positive effect. In this regard, even research which focuses on a single dimension of diversity (e.g. gender) provides information that is relevant to all workers rather than only to members of minority groups. Also theory and research on diversity are increasingly addressing multiple dimensions of group identity, a trend that we expect to continue.

Of all the research areas discussed here, the work on organizational demography offers the most direct and extensive research on specific effects of diversity on work outcomes and performance. Indeed, the central thrust of empirical work on organizational demography has been to determine the impact of the demographic composition of organizations or work groups on work outcomes (Tsui et al. 1995). A review of the empirical research suggests that demographic heterogeneity potentially has both positive and negative effects on work outcomes of interest to practitioners. On the one hand, heterogeneity (compared to homogeneity in groups) reduces intragroup cohesiveness, lowers member satisfaction (at least for members of the majority group) and increases turnover (Jackson et al. 1991; Tsui et al. 1992; Wharton and Baron 1987). On the other hand, heterogeneity, at least under certain conditions, increases creativity, decision-making quality and innovation (Jackson and associates 1992; Ancona and Caldwell 1992; Bantel and Jackson 1989).

It is significant to note that this body of research addresses what we call 'unmanaged diversity', that is, no apparent efforts were made to reduce the potential negative effects of difference in work groups or to accentuate the potential positive effects. The question which therefore arises is: can steps such as education about cultural differences, allowing more time to reach decisions, and other interventions be used to reduce the negative effects of heterogeneity and increase the positive effects? We believe the answer is yes. There is some empirical research which seems to support this conclusion. Adler (1986) reports on an experimental study in which culturally diverse teams were compared to culturally homogeneous teams on productivity.

Results indicated that conscious attention to the dynamics of diversity may be the difference between positive and negative overall effects on group performance outcomes. In another study, the creativity scores of heterogeneous dyads (defined as different in attitudes) were compared to those of homogeneous dyads. Findings indicated that when there was no intervention to address the attitude differences, the heterogeneous dyads were less creative than the homogeneous dyads, but when there was some training given to increase understanding and communication among the members, the results were reversed (Triandis et al. 1965).

## Research on Racioethnicity and Gender

Prior to the late 1960s, little attention was paid to issues of race and gender in the study of organizations (Cox and Nkomo 1990) suggesting that employees were void of these identities. Large-scale attention to issues of race and gender in organizations began after the passage of equal employment opportunity and anti-discrimination legislation in the late 1960s and early 1970s in the United States and to a lesser degree in countries of Western Europe, especially Britain (Cox and Nkomo 1990; Nkomo 1992; Sivanandan 1985). The literature that sprung up revolved around those categories covered by the legislation: sex, race, national origin, religion, and age. Since the greatest amount of research has been accumulated on racioethnicity and gender, we focus our attention on those two areas. Much less attention has been given to sexual orientation and physical ability (Hall 1989; Harris 1994; Munyard 1988; Stone et al. 1992; Woods 1993).

The goal of much of this research has been to document differential treatment in organizations based on racioethnicity and gender. The early research on racioethnicity and gender was heavily influenced by assimilation theories found in the work of scholars like Allport (1954), Myrdal (1944), and Park (1950). The emphasis was on psychological expressions of racism, sexism, and other forms of discrimination. The major issue was assumed to be assimilating white women,[2] racial minorities and those who were 'different' into organizations.

For the most part identity has not been explicit in the treatment of race and gender in organizations. Indeed the concepts of *racial identity*, *ethnic identity*, and/or *gender identity* are rarely found in the work. Yet, implicitly the literature suggests the notion of identity embedded in research on racioethnicity and gender is one of identity as a variable. Race and gender have largely been studied as objective,

fixed properties of individuals that can be operationalized into measurable levels (e.g. 1 = white and 2 = black; 1 = male and 2 = female). Researchers have largely relied on nominal measures in carrying out their research. The bulk of the research on racioethnicity in organizations in the US has compared blacks and whites. This narrow focus is problematic in itself. Other racioethnic groups have received much less attention (Knouse et al. 1992).

Two major strands of research can be identified. One strand focuses on uncovering objective, quantifiable evidence of race and gender discrimination in organizational practices. Although results of these studies are mixed, taken as a whole they suggests that blacks and women face both access and treatment discrimination in organizations (Collins 1989; Kraiger and Ford 1985; Greenhaus et al. 1990). The literature is replete with studies documenting negative effects on the careers of racial minorities and white women, including tokenism, differential access to mentoring, exclusion from informal networks, glass ceilings, and other forms of restricted career mobility (Antal and Izraeli 1993; Bell 1990; Collins 1989; Cox and Nkomo 1991; Fernandez 1981; Greenhaus et al. 1990; Ibarra 1993; Iles et al. 1991; Morrison et al. 1987; Pettigrew and Martin 1987; Thomas 1990; Cahoon and Rowney 1993; Freedman and Phillips 1988; Stroh et al. 1992; Raggins and Cotton 1991).

A second strand of research focuses on race and gender differences in a host of traditional organizational behavior topics. The types of studies done reflect an assumption that racioethnicity and gender are objective, essentialist properties of individuals. That is, differences in identity reflect innate differences between racioethnic groups and men and women. For example, researchers have tested for racial differences in job satisfaction and job attitudes (e.g. O'Reilly and Roberts 1973; Weaver 1978), leadership styles (e.g. Bartol et al. 1978) and motivation (e.g. Brenner and Tomkiewcz 1982; McClelland 1974). Despite a sizable quantity of work, the results are largely inconsistent, with little evidence of systematic differences between blacks and whites in job attitudes and motivation. In the case of gender differences, a number of studies have raised the question of whether women managers have different leadership styles compared to men (Eagly and Johnson 1990; Powell 1990; Rosener 1990). Some researchers suggest that women do not use hierarchical styles of leadership but have more democratic, participative styles (Rosener 1990). Still other researchers have found that successful women managers do not differ in style from successful male managers (Powell 1990). Despite a proliferation of studies focusing on gender differences, cumulatively it is difficult to make blanket state-ments about what systematically differentiates female managers from male managers in atti-tudes toward work, personality, and behavior.

Explanations for the negative consequences for racial minorities and white women in organizations range from prejudice and discrimi-nation stemming from stereotyping to structural explanations centering on their proportional representation in organizational hierarchies (Kanter 1977). The influence of assimilation theory is evident in the kinds of questions studied and solutions proposed. Much of the work suggests that the solution to the negative effects of diversity lies in the successful integra-tion of racial minorities and white women into organizations. Implicitly, for the minority group, successful assimilation means a loss of identity – adapting to the norms and behaviors of the dominant group.

## Ethnology

Another part of the foundation of research on diversity is ethnology. Ethnology is the branch of anthropology which deals with the social and cultural characteristics of different 'tribal' group-ings of people. We prefer the term 'ethnology' rather than 'ethnography' because it includes the comparison and analysis of cultures rather than merely their description. Although historically the term has referred to cultural characteristics of different race or ethnic groups, we intend a somewhat broader application here to refer to any group identity to which distinctive cultural traits may be identified by systematic research. Therefore, in this context, ethnology represents work which identifies cultural similarities and differences between identity groups, as well as analysis of cultural phenomena such as cultural distance and culture clash. In our view this work is central to understanding the effect of diversity in organizations.

In applying ethnology to organizational settings and organizational issues, researchers have mainly concentrated on the group identity of nationality. Among the most influential work is that of Hofstede (1980; 1984), Hall (1976; 1982), Laurent (1983), and Tung (1988a; 1988b).

Hofstede's studies of value differences among people of more than forty countries of the world identified four core values which differentiated people of different nationality groups and which he argues hold implications for work behavior in organizations. The values were power distance, uncertainty avoidance, individualism–collecti-vism and masculinity–femininity.

Using measures adjusted for language and other cultural differences in the countries involved, Hofstede determined that the popula-tions of different nations of the world differ significantly on these four values and that these differences have important implications for application of management theories and con-cepts in cross-national work groups. A signifi-cant amount of empirical research has been done using one or more of these cultural dimensions (e.g. Yu and Murphy 1993; Farh et al. 1991; Davidson 1993; Cox et al. 1991).

Edward T. Hall (1976; 1982) has written extensively about the impact of culture and cultural differences on human behavior. His work is noteworthy for providing concrete examples of how specific, especially nonverbal-ized, cultural differences can become barriers to communication and understanding between people. For example his concept of action chains helps us to understand how behavioral choices are constrained by rituals and norms which are seldom made explicit. An example is the expectation that the existing members of a community are expected to initiate acquaint-anceship with newcomers rather than the other way around. This norm makes it possible for those already in the in-group to exclude newcomers without overtly rejecting them. This insight may be applicable to the often cited problem of unequal accessibility across identity groups to informal networks in organizations.

Other writers have made extensions and applications of Hall's work to the work setting, especially in the areas of marketing research (e.g. Graham 1981; Cote and Tansuhaj 1989), and preferred work styles (e.g. Cox 1993).

André Laurent (1983) is among a growing number of European scholars who have con-tributed to work on diversity (others include Stamp 1989; De Vries 1992; Essed 1991). Laurent's work has focused on identifying cul-tural differences in expectations of managers. His research is helpful in identifying specific ways in which cultural misunderstanding can lead to ineffective relationships in organizations especially in dyadic relationships between a supervisor and his/her direct reports. For example, according to his survey data of 1,762 respondents from ten countries, only 13 per cent of United States' workers expect that a manager should have precise answers to questions that subordinates may raise about their work, compared to 59 per cent in France, 67 per cent in Indonesia and 77 per cent in Japan. This suggests that the definition of competence to manage will vary greatly among persons of these different nationalities and that management theories and practices cannot be universalized. Similarly, Tung (1988a; 1988b) found in her study of motivation patterns among Chinese workers that the Chinese are much more tolerant and accepting of rule enforcement. She relates this to the existence of a rigidly planned socialist economy, and notes that Chinese employees (both managers and nonmanagers) are accustomed to receiving very detailed prescriptions of their work roles (Tung 1988a).

It is important to note that in view of high rates of immigration in the United States (and increasing rates in many other parts of the world), and because individuals with roots in micro-culture groups (groups within a particular national culture such as Chinese-Americans) are influenced by cultural norms and values of their root cultures, the work on nationality differences is relevant to domestic workforces in many parts of the world as well as to organizations with multinational operations. In addition, the basic principle behind this research, that differences in culture are central to understanding intergroup dynamics, is applicable to group identities beyond nationality.

Another area of theory and research in ethnology which is highly relevant to work on diversity in organizations is that on acculturation. This work focuses on the processes for resolving cultural differences among members of a nation at the societal level (e.g. Berry 1987; Padilla 1980), between organizations with different cultures (e.g. Nahavandhi and Malekzadeh 1988; Sales and Mirvis 1984), between organizations and their members (e.g. Cox and Finley-Nickelson 1991), and within individuals (e.g. Hazuda et al. 1988; Wong-Reiger and Quintana 1987). By resolving cultural differences 'within individuals' we mean the process by which individuals establish a cultural identity that responds to the differences between norm and value systems of the different cultural groups of which she/he is a part. For example, Cox (1993) reviews nine empirical studies addressing the extent to which members of racioethnic minority groups in the United States identify with their racioethnic group versus the Anglo majority group. This body of work links ethnology to social identity theory, a combination which offers a rich and substantial base of knowledge for understanding the cultural dynamics of diversity in organizations.

In general, ethnology researchers have focused less attention than organizational demographers on specifying the effects of diversity on work processes and outcomes. However it is fair to say that their work is more revealing of the potential difficulties, such as miscommunication, intergroup conflict, loss of effectiveness, and stress, than the potential benefits of cultural diversity. For example Hall (1976) points out that many instances of ineffective management, even among people of the same nationality and working for the same organization, are due to failure to recognize intercultural differences, and both Hofstede (1984) and Laurent (1983) make the point that ignorance of cultural differences has led to the misapplication of management theories of motivation and leadership.

In summary, the concept of group identity is explicitly addressed in the ethnology literature. Cultural aspects of identity are emphasized and identity is treated as a continuous measure recognizing the intragroup differences in how strongly one identifies with the group. The focus is on self-identification with the group rather than how others define one. The work on ethnology gives greatest attention to the group level of analysis through intergroup comparisons of cultural traditions. However, in the work on acculturation, individual identity structures and the interplay between individual identity and organizational identity as well as inter-organizational cultural differences are beginning to receive attention. Thus, ethnology is making a contribution on all three levels of analysis in organization behavior. Finally, because of the possibility of culture clash, ethnology research suggests that mixing people of different group identities in one social system may lead to a variety of dysfunctional outcomes unless steps are taken to overcome this problem.

## Theoretical Models of Diversity

Taken in isolation, none of the research streams reviewed here are sufficiently complex to do justice to the topic of diversity. Several scholars have recently published conceptual models of diversity which specifically combine and translate the information from these older streams of research. We were able to identify three such models. They are those of Cox (1993), Jackson et al. (1995), and Triandis et al. (1994). Each of these will be briefly reviewed next. We chose these models because they each make an attempt to utilize the information from the relevant contributing disciplines, they are comprehensive in scope, acknowledging the complexity of the topic, and they were specifically designed to explicate the impact of diversity in identities for organizational behavior and organizational outcomes.

The interactional model of cultural diversity (IMCD) developed by Cox (1993) holds that differences in group identities among individuals (both physical and cultural identities) interact with a complex set of individual, intergroup, and organizational factors (the diversity climate) to determine the impact of diversity on both individual and organizational outcomes. The individual outcomes which are predicted by the model are divided into affective response variables (satisfaction, organizational identification, and job involvement) and achievement variables (performance, job mobility, and compensation). Organizational outcomes are divided on the basis of the expected directness of impact into first level (e.g. attendance, turnover, and work quality) and second level (e.g. profits). Central to this model is the notion that the presence of diversity in organizations will impact measures of effectiveness at both the individual and the organizational levels, and that the organizational context for diversity is pivotal in determining whether the overall impact of group identity differences on effectiveness will be positive or negative. Other salient features of the model are that it is structured around social psychological phenomena which have clear applicability across many dimensions of group identity (i.e. not only gender and race but nationality, work function, religion, class and so on), and it has application to the experience of both majority and minority group members of organizations. For example, the tendency for unmanaged diversity to lead to heightened intergroup conflict between majority and minority group members will potentially lower the affective outcomes of work for members of both groups.

A second comprehensive theoretical model is that of Triandis et al. (1994). The model (labeled simply 'A theoretical model for the study of diversity') defines and specifies interrelationships among nineteen variables. A full list of the variables and their definitions will not be attempted here. However, some of the major linkages will be specified. Core concepts in the model include perceived similarity, degree of interaction and rewards. The primary outcome variable is positive intergroup attitudes. Following a Skinnerian line of reasoning (Skinner 1981), positive intergroup attitudes are posited to occur when transactions between people of different groups are experienced as rewarding. A sense of obtaining rewards, in turn, will occur when the parties perceive one another as similar, when they have opportunity to have positive contact, when they have a shared sense of goals, and when the society or recognized authorities in the social setting are encouraging of contact. The specifications of the model indicate that all of these factors have independent (main) effects on rewards.

A pivotal concept in the Triandis et al. (1994) framework is perceived similarity. Although this point of emphasis suggests that increasing diversity will tend to hinder work group and organization performance, the authors are careful to point out types of interventions which may avoid this.

The final theoretical model to be discussed here is Jackson et al.'s 'framework for understanding the dynamics of diversity in work teams' (Jackson et al. 1995). The model explicitly names more than thirty variables and some of these have multiple components. In recognition of this complexity, the authors do not attempt to specify the interrelationships among the numerous variables but rather present a collection of relevant concepts organized into a conceptual framework. The three main parts to the framework are aspects of diversity, mediating states and processes, and behavioral manifestations/consequences. All three are analyzed on three levels of analysis – individual, interpersonal and team – and within a broader context of organizational and societal forces. According to their framework, one can analyze 'diversity' as a characteristic: of individuals, of the difference between an individual and his/her work group, and as a characteristic of the work group itself. Also, dimensions of diversity are listed as either task-related (tenure, education, etc.) or relations-oriented (sex, race, etc.). The combination of individual attributes, interpersonal similarity and team composition is posited to affect outcomes like personal performance, power balance and team creativity. However, this relationship is mediated by a multitude of task and relational variables like attention, recall, stage of socialization, and cognitive and affective responses.

In summary, all three of these models have similar architectures in that they are collections of learnings about what is important and not parsimonious theoretical statements which are easily adapted to mathematical equations for testing with linear statistics. Also, as might be expected, there is considerable overlap in the concepts included although the definitions and positioning of the concepts within the frameworks differ considerably. The level of complexity of the models, while appropriate to the phenomena, will likely preclude empirical testing of the full models. Instead, it seems that they are best used as heuristic models which can guide empirical research designed to test various sub-configurations. To facilitate such utilization, Cox (1993) offers more than forty testable theoretical propositions which are derived from the IMCD framework.

## REFRAMING DIVERSE IDENTITIES IN ORGANIZATIONS

Having now reviewed some of the theory and research which largely forms the foundation for diversity research, in the last column of Table 1 we offer our suggested treatment of the concept of identity. To advance the theoretical development of diversity in organizations, we must begin with reframing the concept of identity. Specifically, the understanding of diversity identities will be advanced by theoretical perspectives which: (1) explicitly define and measure the group identity of individuals; (2) attend to the cultural, historical, and social meaning of identity; (3) treat identity as a continuous scale measure rather than merely as discrete categories, thereby allowing for members of groups to differ in the extent to which a specific identity is salient for them; (4) address the relevance of the social categorization by others to one's group identity; (5) address affects of identity on multiple levels of analysis (individual, group, organizational, and societal); and (6) address explicitly the effects of diversity without assuming the inevitability of negative consequences. Our alternative framing requires elaboration.

The main implication of this set of prescriptions is that identity should be understood as a complex, multifaceted, and transient construct (Bhavnani and Phoenix 1994). The fact that individuals have multiple identities and not a single identity contributes to the complexity of identity in organizations. Individuals are not just African, European, Korean, white, black, women, men, marketing managers, or operations managers. Identities intersect to create an amalgamated identity. The ways in which identities interact or become salient are important in an organizational context. Thus, the study of one identity necessarily involves attending to its interaction with other identities.

Distinctions should be made, however, between identities based on social categories like race, gender, ethnicity, and class, and identities based on categories like organization function or tenure. Social identity theory may appear to be a general model for examining the consequences of all types of group identities. However, its original empirical grounding in minimal group experiments limits its application to the understanding of group identities based upon socially marked categories like racioethnicity, gender, and class (Henriques 1984; Lloyd 1989; Michael 1990). According to Michael (1990) intergroup theories and social identity theory, in particular, have systematically neglected content, preferring to illuminate the processes or mechanisms underlying intergroup behavior. Consequently, exclusion of content tends to elevate process suggesting that the processes are universal regardless of the basis for identity. However, identity based on organization function or tenure may be donned or shed

or lost when an individual exits an organization. When sociohistorical identity categories are equated with less socially marked categories like organization function, the significance of racism, sexism, and other forms of domination in organizations and the broader society is overlooked.

Accordingly, the study of diverse identities in organizations should be situated in their cultural context and the specific content of different social categories should be explicated (Duveen and Lloyd 1986). Specifically, to establish the dialectic between intergroup content and process, there is a need for some theory of the relation that exists between particular groups, and for the sociohistorical circumstances that have given rise to relevant identities. In other words, this means identifying and describing the content of racial identity, gender identity, ethnic identity, cultural identity, etc. versus a generic social identity, or at a minimum to think in terms of the social identity of a particular group (e.g. the social identity of women). There is some research in other disciplines on racial identity (e.g. Helms 1990; Cross 1991; Tinsley 1994); the meaning of race (e.g. Omni and Winant 1986); the meaning of gender (e.g. Acker 1990; Calás and Smircich 1992; Mills and Tancred 1992); the social identity of women (e.g. Skevington and Baker 1989); and homosexual identity (e.g. Cass 1979) which has relevance for research on diverse identities in organizational settings. For example, there is an emerging body of work exploring the meaning of white racial identity and the social construction of whiteness (e.g. Carter et al. 1994; Frankenberg 1993; Helms 1990; Roediger 1991).

At the same time, we must avoid essentialism in our treatment of identity, recognizing its variability. Identity is socially constructed and not innate. It cannot be measured nominally as an objective property of an individual. As Stuart Hall (1992) has emphasized, identity is not stable or fixed but socially and historically constructed and subject to contradictions, revisions, and change. A social construction view emphasizes understanding the processes through which identity distinctions emerge and become salient to individuals and groups in organizations (Wharton 1992).

Identity needs to be understood at four levels of analysis: individual, group/intergroup, organizational, and societal. This is particularly important in order to avoid the tendency for research on diverse identities to imply that the burden of change rests solely on individual members of the organization. And to avoid the assumption that the negative effects of diverse identities are rooted in the faulty cognition processes of individuals. If we confine our analysis to the individual level, then the more systemic intergroup, organizational, and societal dynamics will be left underexplored and consequently the possibility of real organizational change is diminished. Important aspects of identity as a group position can also be overlooked if researchers confine their analysis to the individual level. On the other hand, sole reliance upon group-level analysis fails to recognize there may be individual differences in group identity. Identity is also not homogeneous within social groups. That is, attention must be paid to within-group differences in identities. Many individuals may not share the norms, values, and language of a group despite similarity in a demographic or cultural sense. At the organizational level, attention must be given to the broader contextual factors that affect and shape identity. Societal meanings and constructions of identity and identity formation also permeate organizational boundaries. For example, new legislation, political developments, and demographic changes have all affected how identity is perceived and understood.

Finally, much of the work on diversity in identities has been dominated by the negative effects of differences. There has been a tendency to universalize the conditions for intergroup conflict and to view diversity in identities as a 'problem' that cannot be avoided. This suggests that the negative consequences of categorization are a default condition of human nature and that little can be done to change group phenomena. However, we argue that all potential effects should be understood, and the focus must be on understanding categorization as a discursive practice (see Marshall and Wetherell 1989).

## METHODOLOGICAL ISSUES AND DILEMMAS

### Dichotomous Thinking

The aforementioned prescriptions give rise to a number of practical methodological issues and dilemmas. Understanding these is important to moving beyond the research paradigms that have dominated organizational research on diversity and identity. For the most part, the research that has grown out of the theories and bodies of literature reviewed in this chapter reflect dichotomous thinking about identity (e.g. black versus white; Anglo versus Latino, male versus female, etc.). Oppositional thinking is problematic for several reasons. Fixed oppositions conceal the extent to which things presented as oppositional are, in fact, interdependent and relational.[3] Hall points out that 'For example, there are differences between the ways in which genders are socially and psychi-

cally constructed. But there is no fixity to those oppositions. It is a relational opposition; *it is a relation of difference*' (1991: 16, emphasis ours). Oppositional thinking implies not only difference but hierarchy where one group is usually superior and the other inferior (Derrida 1976). The dominant group in fact derives its privilege from the curtailment or suppression of its opposite. Martin (1992: 136) further notes that oppositional thinking cannot value diversity in all of its complexity because it cannot account for mixed attributes which may fall between polar opposites.

Related to the above discussion is the whole question of representation. It raises two related issues. First, who is the 'diverse' in organizations? Who indeed is being studied? Current research and theoretical approaches imply traditional employee populations – white, male, Western, heterosexual, middle/upper class, abled – are the norms against which some become 'diverse' or 'others'. Second, to the extent our understanding of 'others' is embedded in notions of a dominant identity, it sets limits on the possibility of the representation of 'others' outside of this knowledge (Calás 1992). Research and theoretical frames are needed that allow scholars to 'notice the diverse under their own representational logic' (1992: 205).

This project is particularly pressing given that much of current rhetoric is framed within the notion of 'managing diversity' as a problem. Underlying the discourse are assumptions like 'minority workers are less likely to have had satisfactory schooling and training. They may have language, attitude, and cultural problems that prevent them from taking advantage of the jobs that will exist' (Johnston and Packer 1987: xxvi) or that it is important to have 'productive diversity and turn it to the advantage of the organisation' (Office of Multicultural Affairs, 1994). By implication such descriptions suggest that unmanaged diversity is unproductive and disadvantageous to organizations. Such constructions can end up serving particular purposes, often maintaining the existing pattern of social relations. Research emphasis should also be placed on examining how organizations produce and reproduce differences between social groups. This requires researchers to understand the social construction of diversity in organizations rather than viewing it as a reflection of natural category differences. In much of the research on diversity in organizations, the legitimacy and basic values of the organization are not in question. Organizations are regarded *a priori* as fundamentally sound and neutral sites. Inevitably, attention must be paid to what sustains and maintains the pattern of power relations in organizations.

## The Measurement of Identity

Much of the work on the effects of diversity and heterogeneity in identity (particularly those premised upon intergroup theory) has been done as laboratory studies. More work is needed in field settings. Among the questions needing attention are the following: How do group identities operate in practice? What factors determine the salience given to different group identities? How do people think about their group identities in organizations? How do people make sense of themselves in relation to their jobs and their identity(ies)? How do organizational practices and policies produce and reproduce diverse identities, valuing some and devaluing others? An example of an effort to address the last question can be found in the work of Collinson et al. (1990). In their study of forty-five companies in five industries in the United Kingdom, they show how sex discrimination can be reproduced, rationalized, and resisted by those in positions of both domination and subordination within the recruitment and selection processes (see also Cockburn 1991).

The study of identity is especially difficult because identity does not lend itself to discrete measurement. Quantitative survey methods may fail to capture the complex meaning and construction of identity. Scales can only measure quantity (or strength) of identity, answering the question: how much identification (Condor 1989)? They cannot measure the question of quality: in what way is identity manifested? To understand the cultural meaning and the variability in the meaning of identity among social groups within organizations, researchers need to expand their methodologies to include ethnographic approaches. In traditional research approaches, categorization of groups is seen as a natural phenomenon rather like breathing (Potter and Wetherell 1987). In more linguistically oriented approaches like ethnomethodology and discourse analysis, the interest is in how categories are constituted in everyday discourse and the various functions they satisfy (Potter and Wetherell 1987). Categorization is regarded as a complex and subtle social accomplishment. Discourse theory and analysis cover the study of all types of written texts and spoken interaction (formal and informal), with particular attention to the functions served by language and the implications of particular linguistic constructions. It asks how categories are flexibly articulated in the course of certain sorts of talk and writing to accomplish particular goals such as exclusions, blamings or justifications (Parker 1992; Potter and Wetherell 1987). Studying the language we use to talk about diversity in identities is so important because, as Parker (1992: xi) points out, 'Language is so structured to mirror power relations that often we can see no other ways of being, and it structures ideology so that it is difficult to speak both in and against it.'

There are ready examples of the application of discourse analysis in the study of identity. Open-ended interviews have been used by some scholars to focus on the content of identity categories and their construction from social experience (e.g. see Condor 1986). Discourse analysis has been used as a way of understanding how gender identity is constituted in discourse (Skevington and Baker 1989; Marshall and Wetherell 1989). The emphasis is upon examining how people talk about a particular identity. In a 1989 article, Marshall and Wetherell examined how a group of women and men students, just embarking on their careers as lawyers, construct their identity and their image of themselves in relation to their gender. They found many inconsistencies and contradictions across their sample of interviewees. Most respondents developed an essentialist model of gender and many also argued that men and women were the same in outlook and abilities. This kind of variability, argued Marshall and Wetherell (1989), is commonplace in natural discourse. Such analyses help capture the fluid and contradictory nature of identity.

Wetherell and Potter (1992) used discourse analysis to map the language of racism in New Zealand. Their case-study of white New Zealanders' accounts of relations with Maori New Zealanders revealed the heterogeneous and layered texture of practices, arguments and representations which make up the taken for granted in a particular society. They concluded that racism is a manifestation of the pattern of uneven power relations in New Zealand and not the result of one ethnic group having irrational delusions in relation to another ethnic group.

Related to the measurement of identity is how to account for intragroup differences. We cannot assume sameness in identity within a group. Not all members of a group may construct or respond to their group identity in the same way. Instead of assuming homogeneity in identity, research designs must explicitly test for within-group differences in identity. The question of how to treat multiple identities remains relatively underexplored. Although scholars have echoed the need to examine the interactions between different social categories, there are few empirical studies which demonstrate how this might be achieved. Measurement is problematic because the interactions are synergistic rather than additive. Additionally, little attention has been paid to the relationship between group identities based on socially marked categories like race and gender and other bases of identity like work style or career. However, Marshall and Wetherell's (1989) study does shed light on the interaction between women's and men's construction of their professional/occupational identity and their gender identity. In their study, the relation between women and occupational identity became problematized, whereas the relation between men and occupational identity became normalized. Women *and* lawyers were portrayed as dissonant, the identity relationship became a site of struggle; but, in contrast, the masculine *and* the law became synonymous, with the masculine personality portrayed as identical with the legal personality. There is some research suggesting members of subordinated groups have a more limited range of acceptable behavior than majority group members. Eagly et al. (1992: 16), in a review of data from sixty-one research studies on gender and leadership concluded that 'men have greater freedom than women to lead in a range of styles without encountering negative reactions.'

## Terminology

Finally, a word must be said about the very use of the term 'diversity'.[4] It should be recognized that diversity is a description of the total workforce, not a name for members of minority groups. Additionally, diversity should be distinguished from related concepts such as affirmative action, gender research, and racioethnicity research while at the same time preserving the legitimacy of these areas. Researchers must be careful to make clear how diversity relates to such topics as equal opportunity, discrimination, research on racioethnicity and gender, and affirmative action. Perhaps the greatest difficulty so far has occurred around affirmative action. While affirmative action is within the umbrella of diversity, the two concepts are clearly not equivalent. Those doing work on diversity in organizations are more comprehensive in the types of human group identities addressed, and affirmative action applies specifically to a remedial tool legislated to achieve equal opportunity. Diversity represents a much more expansive concept aimed at understanding the multidimensional structure and effects of differences in organizations. To avoid conflation of diversity with more traditional topics, researchers might use the label of 'diversity research' when addressing multiple dimensions of difference and phenomena which are common across dimensions. For instance, it seems appropriate to label a paper which addresses gender, race, and nationality as 'diversity research'. On the other hand a paper which examines the decision styles of Latinos and Anglos seems to fall with the domain of 'racioethnicity research' or, at the very least, should be specified as 'racioethnic diversity'.

## Conclusion

We have attempted to map the terrain for examining diverse identities in organizations. We reviewed several bodies of literature that have been the dominant bases for research on diversity in organizations. Our review suggests the need to move beyond traditional modes of thinking about the concept of identity which lies at the heart of this research. The breadth of our review reflects the complexity of the topic and the challenges that lie ahead.

## Notes

1 There are contradictions in how people use race and ethnicity. For example, African-Americans in the United States are said to be a 'racial group', while Latinos and Asians are sometimes viewed as ethnic groups. Ethnicity has been traditionally used for immigrants who came to the United States from Europe. However, in Britain and some other European countries, immigrants from Africa, the Caribbean, India and Pakistan are often viewed as 'blacks'. Taylor Cox Jr (1990) notes that 'classifications are often inappropriate because they imply a group is either biologically or culturally distinct from another, whereas it generally is both'. He has suggested the use of the term 'racioethnic' to refer to biologically (we personally prefer 'phenotypical' instead of 'biological') and/or culturally distinct groups. Further, scholars of race and ethnic relations often wind up espousing a theory of racial and ethnic relations.'

2 We explicitly use the terms 'white women' and 'racial minorities' to avoid the tendency of writers to refer to 'women and minorities'. The latter terminology does not acknowledge that women have both race and gender. It also omits the category of racial minority women.

3 A quote from Stuart Hall (1991) elegantly captures the relational nature of identity: 'Only when there is an other, can one know their identity'.

4 Much of this discussion is drawn from Taylor Cox Jr (1994) and Stella M. Nkomo (1993). The title of the latter paper, 'Much to do about diversity', is used not to suggest that the topic of diversity is frivolous, but to stress that researchers have much work to do towards understanding diversity in organizations. If this challenge is not met, then perhaps diversity will join the archives of other short-lived management fads.

## REFERENCES

Abrams, D. and Hogg, M. (1990) *Social Identity Theory: Constructive and Critical Advances*. New York: Harvester Wheatsheaf.

Acker, J. (1990) 'Hierarchies, jobs, bodies: a theory of gendered organizations', *Gender and Society*, 4: 139–58.

Adler, N. (1986) *International Dimensions of Organizational Behavior*. Boston: P.W.S. Kent.

Alderfer, C.P. (1987) 'An intergroup perspective on group dynamics', in Jay W. Lorsch (ed.), *Handbook of Organizational Behavior*. Englewood Cliffs, NJ: Prentice-Hall. pp. 190–222.

Alderfer, C.P. and Smith, K.K. (1982) 'Studying intergroup relations embedded in organizations', *Administrative Science Quarterly*, 27: 35–65.

Alderfer, C.P., Alderfer, C.J., Tucker, L. and Tucker, R. (1980) 'Diagnosing race relations in management', *Journal of Applied Psychology*, 16: 135–66.

Allport, G. (1954) *The Nature of Prejudice*. New York: Doubleday.

Ancona, D.G. and Caldwell, D.F. (1992) 'Demography and design: predictors of new product team performance', *Organization Science*, 3(3): 321–41.

Antal, A.B. and Izraeli, D. (1993) 'A global comparison of women in management: women managers in their homelands and as expatriates', in Ellen Fagenson (ed.), *Women in Management: Trends, Issues, and Challenges in Managerial Diversity*. Newbury Park, CA: Sage. pp. 52–96.

Ashforth, B.E. and Mael, F. (1989) 'Social identity theory and the organization', *Academy of Management Review*, 14: 20–39.

Bantel, K.A. and Jackson, S.E. (1989) 'Top management and innovations in banking: does the composition of the top team make a difference?', *Strategic Management Journal*, 10: 107–24.

Bartol, K.M., Evans, C.L. and Stith, M. (1978) 'Black versus white leaders: a comparative review of the literature', *Academy of Management Review*, 3: 294–304.

Bell, E. (1990) 'The bi-cultural life experience of career-oriented black women', *Journal of Organizational Behavior*, 11: 459–77.

Berger, J and Zelditch, M. Jr (eds) (1985) *Status, Rewards, and Influence*. San Francisco: Jossey-Bass.

Berry, J.W. (1987) 'Acculturation and psychological adaptation: a conceptual view', in J.W. Berry and W. Annis (eds), *Ethnic Psychology: Research and Practice with Immigrants, Refugees, Native Peoples, Ethnic Groups and Sojourners*. Lisse, Netherlands: Swets and Zeitlinger. Berwin, PA: Swets North American.

Bhavnani, K.K. and Phoenix, A. (eds) (1994) *Shifting Identities; Shifting Racisms: a Feminism and Psychology Reader*. London: Sage.

Blau, Peter (1977) *Inequality and Heterogeneity*. New York: Free Press.

Brenner, O.C. and Tomkiewcz, J. (1982) 'Job orientation of black and white college graduates in business', *Personnel Psychology*, 35: 89–103.

Brewer, M.B. (1995) 'Managing diversity: the role of social identities', in S. Jackson and M. Ruderman (eds), *Diversity in Work Teams: Research Paradigms for a Changing Workplace*. New York: American Psychological Association. pp. 47–68.

Brewer, M.B. and Kramer, R.M. (1985) 'The pyschology of intergroup attitudes and behavior', *Annual Review of Psychology*, 36: 219–43.

Cahoon, A.R. and Rowney, J. (1993) 'Valuing differences: organization and gender', in R.T. Golembiewski (ed.), *Handbook of Organizational Behavior*. New York: Marcel Dekker. pp. 339–54.

Calás, M. (1992) 'An/other silent voice? Representing "Hispanic woman" in organizational texts', in A. Mills and P. Tancred (eds), *Gendering Organizational Analysis*. Newbury Park, CA: Sage. pp. 201–21.

Calás, M. and Smircich, L. (1992) 'Using the "F" word: feminist theories and the social consequences of organizations', in A. Mills and P. Tancred (eds), *Gendering Organizational Analysis*. Newbury Park, CA: Sage. pp. 222–34.

Carter, R.T., Gushue, G.V. and Weitzman, L.M. (1994) 'White racial identity development and work values', *Journal of Vocational Behavior*, 44(2): 185–97.

Cass, V.C. (1979) 'Homosexual identity formation: a theoretical model', *Journal of Homosexuality*, 4(3): 219–35.

Cockburn, Cynthia (1991) *In the Way of Women: Men's Resistance to Sex Equality in Organizations*. Ithaca, NY: ILR Press.

Collins, S. (1989) 'The marginalization of black executives', *Social Problems*, 36(4): 317–31.

Collinson, D.L., Knights, D. and Collinson, M. (1990) *Managing to Discriminate*. London: Routledge.

Condor, S. (1986) 'From sex categories to gender boundaries: reconsidering sex as a stimulus variable in social psychological research', *BPS Social Psychology Section Newsletter*, Spring.

Condor, S. (1989) '"Biting into the future": social change and the social identity of women', in S. Skevington and D. Baker (eds), *The Social Identity of Women*. London: Sage. pp. 15–19.

Cote, J.A. and Tansuhaj, P.S. (1989) 'Culture bound assumptions in behavior intention models', *Advances in Consumer Research*, 16: 105–9.

Cox, T. Jr (1990) 'Problems with doing research on race and ethnicity', *Journal of Applied Behavioral Science*, 26(1): 5–24.

Cox, T. Jr (1993) *Cultural Diversity in Organizations: Theory, Research, and Practice*. San Francisco: Berrett-Koehler.

Cox, T. Jr. (1994) 'A comment on the language of diversity', *Organization*, 1(1): 51–8.

Cox, T. Jr. and Finley-Nickelson, J. (1991) 'Models of acculturation for intraorganizational cultural diversity. *Canadian Journal of Administrative Sciences*, 8(2): 90–100.

Cox, T. Jr and Nkomo, S.M. (1990) 'Invisible men and women: a status report on race as a variable in organizational behavior and research', *Journal of Organizational Behavior*, 11: 419–31.

Cox T.H. and Nkomo, S.M. (1991) 'A race and gender group analysis of the early career experience of MBAs', *Work and Occupations*, 18(4): 431–46.

Cox, T. Jr, Lobel, S. and P. McLeod (1991) 'Effects of ethnic group cultural differences on cooperative and competitive behavior of a task group', *Academy of Management Journal*, 34(4): 827–47.

Cross, E.Y., Katz, J.H., Miller, F. and Seashore, E.W. (1994) *The Promise of Diversity*. Burr Ridge, IL: Irwin.

Cross, W.E. (1991) *Shades of Black: Diversity in African-American Identity*. Philadelphia: Temple University Press.

Davidson, M.N. (1993) 'The effect of racioethnicity on beliefs about coping with interpersonal conflict: a comparison of African-American and European Americans'. Working paper 298, Amos Tuck School of Business, Darmouth College.

Derrida, J. (1976) *Speech and Phenomenon*. Evanston IL: Northwestern University Press.

De Vries, S. (1992) *Working in Multi-Ethnic Groups: The Performance and Well Being of Minority and Majority Workers*. Amsterdam: Gouda Quint bu-Arnhem.

Duveen, G. and Lloyd, B. (1986) 'The significance of social identities', *British Journal of Social Psychology*, 25: 219–30.

Eagly, A.H. and Johnson, B.T. (1990) 'Gender and social influence: a social psychological analysis', *American Psychologist*, 38(9): 971–81.

Eagly, A.H., Makhijani, M.G. and Klonsky, B.G. (1992) 'Gender and the evaluation of leaders: a meta-analysis', *Psychological Bulletin*, 111(1): 3–22.

Essed, P. (1991) *Understanding Everyday Racism: an Interdisciplinary Theory*. Newbury Park, CA: Sage.

Farh, J.L., Dobbins, G.H. and Cheng, B. (1991) 'Cultural relativity in action: a comparison of self-ratings made by Chinese and U.S. workers', *Personnel Psychology*, 44: 129–47.

Ferdman, B. (1992) 'The dynamics of ethnic diversity in organizations: toward integrative models', in K. Kelley (ed.), *Issues, Theory and Research in Industrial/Organizational Psychology*. Amsterdam: North Holland. pp. 339–84.

Fernandez, John (1981) *Racism and Sexism in Corporate Life*. Lexington, MA: Lexington Books.

Frankenberg, R. (1993) *White Women, Race Matters: the Social Construction of Whiteness*. Minneapolis: University of Minnesota Press.

Freedman, S.M. and Phillips, J.S. (1988) 'The changing nature of research on women at work', *Journal of Management*, 14(2): 251.

Fullerton, H.N. (1991) 'Labor force projections: the baby boom moves on', *Monthly Labor Review*, 114(11): 31–44.

Graham, R.J. (1981) 'The role of perception of time in consumer behavior', *Journal of Consumer Research*, 7(March): 335–42.

Greenhaus, J., Parasuraman, S. and Wormley, W. (1990) 'Effects of race on organizational experiences, job performance evaluation, and career outcomes', *Academy of Management Journal*, 33: 64–86.

Hall, E.T. (1976) *Beyond Culture*. New York: Double-day.

Hall, E.T. (1982) *The Hidden Dimension*. New York: Doubleday.

Hall, M. (1989) 'Private experiences in public domains: lesbians in organizations', in A. Mills and P. Tancred (eds), *Gendering Organizational Analysis*. Newbury Park, CA: Sage. pp. 125–38.

Hall, S. (1991) 'Ethnicity: identity and difference', *Radical America*, 23(4): 9–20.

Hall, S. (1992) 'The question of cultural identity', in S. Hall, D. Held and T. McGrew (eds), *Modernity and its Futures*. Cambridge: Polity. pp. 273–316.

Harris, C. (1994) 'Acknowledging lesbians in the workplace: confronting the heterosexuality of organizations'. Paper presented at the 1994 Academy of Management Meeting, Dallas.

Hazuda, H., Stern, M. and Haffner, S.M. (1988) 'Acculturation and assimilation among Mexican-Americans: scales and population-based data', *Social Science Quarterly*, 69(3): 687–706.

Helms, J.E. (ed.) (1990) *Black and White Racial Identity*. New York: Greenwood Press.

Henriques, J. (1984) 'Social psychology and the politics of racism', in J. Henriques, W. Hollway, C. Urwin, C. Venn and V. Walkerdine (eds), *Changing the Subject: Psychology, Social Regulation and Sub-jectivity*. London: Methuen. pp. 60–90.

Hewstone, M. and Brown, R. (eds) (1986) *Contact and Conflict in Intergroup Encounters*. Oxford, New York: Basil Blackwell.

Hofstede, G. (1980) 'Motivation, leadership and organization: do American theories apply abroad?', *Organizational Dynamics*, 9 (Summer): 43–62.

Hofstede, G. (1984) 'The cultural relativity of the quality of life concept', *Academy of Management Review*, 9: 389–98.

Ibarra, H. (1993) 'Personal networks of women and minorities in management: a conceptual frame-work', *Academy of Management Review*, 18(1): 56–87.

Iles, P., Keynes, M. and Auluck, R. (1991) 'The experience of black workers', in M. Davidson and J. Earnshaw (eds), *Vulnerable Workers: Psychosocial and Legal Issues*. London: Wiley.

Jackson, S.E. (1981) 'Measurement of commitment to role identities', *Journal of Personality and Social Psychology*, 40: 138–46.

Jackson, S.E. and associates (1992) *Diversity in the Workplace: Human Resource Initiatives*. New York: Guilford Press.

Jackson, S.E., Brett, J.F., Sessa, V.I., Cooper, D.M., Julin, J.A. and Peyronnin, K. (1991) 'Some differences do make a difference: individual dissimilarity and group homogeneity as correlates of recruitment, promotion, and turnover', *Journal of Applied Psychology*, 75(5): 675–89.

Jackson, S.E., May, K. and Whitney, K. (1995) 'Diversity in decision-making teams', in R.A. Guzzo and E. Salas (eds), *Team Decision Making Effectiveness in Organizations*. San Francisco: Jossey-Bass. pp. 204–61.

Jackson, S.E., Stone, V. and Alvarez, E.B. (1993) 'Socialization amidst diversity: the impact of demographics on work team oldtimers and new-comers', in L.L. Cummings and B. Staw (eds), *Research in Organizational Behavior*, vol. 15. Greenwich, CT: JAI Press.

Jamieson, D. and O'Mara, J. (1991) *Managing Workforce 2000*. San Francisco: Jossey-Bass.

Johnston, W. (1991) 'Global workforce 2000: the new world labor market', *Harvard Business Review*, 69: 115–27.

Johnston, W. and Packer, A. (1987) *Workforce 2000: Work and Workers for the 21st Century*. Indianapolis: Hudson Institute.

Kanter, R.M. (1977) 'Some effects of proportions on group life: skewed sex ratios and responses to token women', *American Journal of Sociology*, 82: 965–91.

Knouse, S.B., Rosenfeld, P. and Culbertson, A.L. (eds) (1992) *Hispanics in the Workplace*. Newbury Park, CA: Sage.

Kraiger, K. and Ford, J. (1985) 'A meta-analysis of ratee race effects in performance ratings', *Journal of Applied Psychology*, 70: 56–65.

Kramer, R. (1991) 'Intergroup relations and organizational dilemmas: the role of categorization processes', in L.L. Cummings and B.M. Staw (eds), *Research in Organizational Behavior*, vol. 13. Greenwich, CT: JAI Press. pp. 191–228.

Laurent, A. (1983) 'The cultural diversity of western conceptions of management', *International Studies of Mananagement and Organization*, 13(1–2): 75–96.

Lloyd, Barbara (1989) 'Foreword', in Suzanna Skevington and Deborah Baker (eds), *The Social Identity of Women*. London: Sage. pp. vii–x.

Loden, M. and Rosener, J. (1991) *Workforce America*. Homewood, IL: Business One Irwin.

Marshall, H. and Wetherell, M. (1989) 'Talking about career and gender identities: A discourse analysis perspective', in S. Skevington and D. Baker (eds), *The Social Identity of Women*. London: Sage. pp. 106–29.

Martin, J. (1992) *Culture in Organizations: Three Perspectives*. New York: Oxford University Press.

McClelland, D.A. (1974) 'Effects of interviewer–respondent race interactions on household interview measures of motivation and intelligence', *Journal of Personality and Social Psychology*, 29: 392–7.

McGuire, W.J., McGuire, C.V., Child, P. and Fujioka, T. (1978) 'Salience of ethnicity in the spontaneous self-concept as a function of one's ethnic distinctiveness in the social environment', *Journal of Personality and Social Psychology*, 36(5): 511–20.

Messick, D.M. and Mackie, D.M. (1989) 'Intergroup relations', *Annual Review of Psychology*, 40: 45–81.

Michael, M. (1990) 'Intergroup theory and deconstruction', in Ian Parker and John Shotter (eds), *Deconstructing Social Psychology*. London: Routledge.

Mills, Albert J. and Tancred, Peta (eds) (1992) *Gendering Organizational Analysis*. Newbury Park, CA: Sage.

Morrison, A.M. (1992) *The New Leaders: Guidelines on Leadership Diversity in America*. San Francisco: Jossey-Bass.

Morrison, A.M., White, R.P., Van Velsor, E. and the Center for Creative Leadership (1987) *Can Women Reach the Top of America's Largest Corporations?* Reading, MA: Addison-Wesley.

Munyard, T. (1988) 'Homophobia at work and how to manage it', *Personnel Management*, June: 46–50.

Myrdal, G. (1944) *An American Dilemma*. New York: Harper & Row.

Nahavandi, A. and Malekzadeh, A. (1988) 'Acculturation in mergers and acquisitions', *Academy of Management Review*, 13(1): 79–90.

Nkomo, S.M. (1992) 'The emperor has no clothes: rewriting "race" in the study of organizations', *Academy of Management Review*, 17(3): 487–513.

Nkomo, S.M. (1993) 'Much to do about diversity'. Paper presented at the Society for Industrial Psychology Conference, San Francisco.

Nkomo, S.M. and Cox, T. Jr (1989) 'Gender differences in the upward mobility of black managers: double whammy or double advantage', *Sex Roles*, 21: 825–39.

Okamura, J.Y. (1981) 'Situational ethnicity', *Ethnic and Racial Studies*, 4(4): 452–65.

Omni, M. and Winant, H. (1986) *Racial Formation in the United States: from the 1960s to the 1980s*. New York: Routledge and Kegan Paul.

O'Reilly, C.A. and Roberts, K.M. (1973) 'Job satisfaction among whites and nonwhites: a cross-cultural approach', *Journal of Applied Psychology*, 57: 295–9.

Padilla, A.M. (1980) *Acculturation: Theory, Models, and Some New Findings*. Boulder, CO: Westview.

Park, R.E. (1950) *Race and Culture*. Glencoe, IL: Free Press.

Parker, I. (1992) *Discourse Dynamics*. London: Routledge.

Pettigrew, T.F. and Martin, J. (1987) 'Shaping the organizational context for black American inclusion', *Journal of Social Issues*, 43(1): 41–78.

Pfeffer, J. (1983) 'Organizational demography', in L.L. Cummings and B. Staw (eds), *Research in Organizational Behavior*, vol. 5. Greenwich, CT: JAI Press. pp. 299–357.

Potter, J. and M. Wetherell (1987) *Discourse and Social Psychology: Beyond Attitudes and Behavior*. London: Sage.

Powell, G. (1990) 'One more time: do female and male managers differ?', *The Academy of Management Executive*, 4: 68–75.

Rabbie, J.M. and Horwitz, M. (1988) 'Categories versus groups as explanatory concepts in inter-group relations', *Journal of Social Psychology*, 18: 117–23.

Raggins, B.R. and Cotton, J.L. (1991) 'Easier said than done: gender differences in perceived barriers to gaining a mentor', *Academy of Management Journal*, 34(4): 939–51.

Ridgeway, C. (1991) 'The social construction of status value: gender and other nominal characteristics', *Social Forces*, 70(2): 367–86.

Roediger, D. (1991) *The Wages of Whiteness: Race and the Making of the American Working Class*. London: Verso.

Rosener, J.B. (1990) 'Ways women lead', *Harvard Business Review*, November–December: 119–25.

Sales, A.L. and Mirvis, P.H. (1984) 'When cultures collide: issues of acquisition', in J.R. Kimberly and R.E. Quinn (eds), *Managing Organizational Transition*. Homewood, IL: Irwin. pp. 107–33.

Sherif, M. and Sherif, C. (1953) *Groups in Harmony and Tension*. New York: Harper & Row.

Sivanandan, A. (1985) 'RAT and the degradation of black struggle', *Race and Class*, 26: 1–34.

Skevington, S. and Baker, D. (eds) (1989) *The Social Identity of Women*. London: Sage.

Skinner, B.F. (1981) 'Selection by consequences', *Science*, 213: 501–4.

Skvoretz, J. (1983) 'Salience, heterogeneity and consolidation of parameters: civilizing Blau's primitive theory', *American Sociological Review*, 48: 360–75.

Stamp, G. (1989) 'Tokens and glass ceilings: the real issues of "minorities" in organisations', *International Journal of Career Management*, 1(2): 1–9.

Stayman, M.H. and Deshpande, R. (1989) 'Situational ethnicity and consumer behavior', *Journal of Consumer Research*, 16: 361–71.

Stone, E.F., Stone, D.L. and Dipboye, R.L. (1992) 'Stigmas in organizations: race, handicaps, and physical attractiveness', in E. Kelley (ed.), *Issues, Theory and Research in Industrial/Organizational Psychology*. Amsterdam: North Holland.

Stroh, L.K., Brett, J.M. and Reilly, A.H. (1992) 'All the right stuff: a comparison of female and male managers' careers' progression', *Journal of Applied Psychology*, 77: 251–60.

Tajfel, H. (1972) 'Social categorization', English version of 'La catégorisation sociale', in S. Moscovici (ed.), *Introduction à la psychologie sociale*, vol. I. Paris: Larousse.

Tajfel, H. (ed.) (1982) *Social Identity and Intergroup Relations*. Cambridge: Cambridge University Press.

Tajfel, H. and Turner, J.C. (1979) 'An integrative theory of intergroup conflict', in W.G. Austin and S. Worchel (eds), *The Social Psychology of Intergroup Relations*. Monterey, CA: Brooks/Cole.

Taylor, D.M. and Moghaddam, M. (eds) (1987) *Theories of Intergroup Relations: International Social Psychological Perspectives*. New York: Praeger.

Thomas, D.A. (1990) 'The impact of race on managers' experiences of developmental relationships: an intraorganizational study', *Journal of Organizational Behavior*, 11(6): 479–92.

Thomas, R.R. Jr (1991) *Beyond Race and Gender: Unleashing the Power of your Total Work Force by Managing Diversity*. New York: AMACOM.

Tinsley, E.A. (1994) 'Racial identity and vocational behavior', *Journal of Vocational Behavior*, 44(2): 115–17.

Triandis, H.C., Hall, E.R. and Ewen, R.B. (1965) 'Member heterogeneity and dyadic creativity', *Human Relations*, 18: 33–55.

Triandis, H.C., Kurowski, L.L. and Gelfand, M.J. (1994) 'Workplace diversity', in H.C. Triandis, M.D. Dunnette and L.M. Hough (eds), *Handbook of Industrial and Organizational Psychology*. Palo Alto, CA: Consulting Psychologists Press.

Tsui, A.S. and O'Reilly, C.A. (1989) 'Beyond simple demographic effects: the importance of relational demography in superior–subordinate dyads', *Academy of Management Journal*, 32: 402–23.

Tsui, A.S., Egan, T.D. and O'Reilly, C. (1992) 'Being different: relational demography and organizational attachment', *Administrative Science Quarterly*, 37: 549–79.

Tsui, A.S., Egan, T. and Xin, K. (1995) 'Diversity in organizations: lessons from demography research', in M. Chemers, S. Oskamp and M. Costanzo (eds), *Diversity in the Workplace*. Thousand Oaks, CA: Sage. pp. 37–61.

Tung, R.L. (1988a) 'People's Republic of China', in R. Nath (ed.), *Comparative Management: A Regional View*. Cambridge, MA: Ballinger. pp. 139–68.

Tung. R.L. (1988b) 'Toward a conceptual paradigm of international business negotiations', *Advances in International Comparative Management*, 3: 203–19.

Turner, J.C. (1975) 'Social comparison and social identity: some prospects for intergroup behaviour', *European Journal of Social Psychology*, 5: 5–34.

Turner, J.C. (1982) 'Towards a cognitive redefinition of social group', in H. Tajfel (ed.), *Social Identity and Intergroup Relations*. New York: Cambridge University Press.

Watson, E.E., Kumar, K. and Michaelson, L.K. (1993) 'Cultural diversity's impact on interaction processes and performance: comparing homogeneous and diverse task groups', *Academy of Management Journal*, 36: 590–602.

Weaver, C.N. (1978) 'Black–white correlates of job

satisfaction', *Journal of Applied Psychology*, 63: 255–8.

Wetherell, M. and Potter, J. (1992) *Mapping the Language of Racism: Discourse and the Legitimation of Exploitation*. New York: Columbia University Press.

Wharton, A.S. (1992) 'The social construction of gender and race in organizations: a social identity and group mobilization perspective', *Research in the Sociology of Organizations*, 10: 55–84.

Wharton, A.S. and Baron, J.N. (1987) 'So happy together? The impact of gender segregation on men at work', *American Sociological Review*, 52(5): 574–87.

Wong-Reiger, D. and Quintana, D. (1987) 'Comparative acculturation of Southeast Asian and Hispanic immigrants and sojourners', *Journal of Cross-Cultural Psychology*, 18(3): 345–62.

Woods, J.D. (1993) *The Corporate Closet: The Professional Lives of Gay Men in America*. New York: Free Press.

Yancey, W.L., Ericksen, E.P. and Juliani, R.N. (1976) 'Emergent ethnicity: a review and reformulation', *American Sociological Review*, 41: 391–403.

Yu, J. and Murphy, K.R. (1993) 'Modesty bias in self-ratings of performance: a test of the cultural relativity hypothesis', *Personnel Psychology*, 46: 357–63.

# 6

# Putting Group Information Technology in its Place: Communication and Good Work Group Performance

## ARTHUR D. SHULMAN

This chapter examines the relationships between good work group performance and information technologies in the light of current work group theory and research. I focus on information technologies for two reasons: firstly, their roles in effecting group performance are claimed to be of increasing importance, yet they are little understood; and secondly, by focusing on the question of what are the relationships between good work group performance and information technology, it becomes apparent that the answers rely on our underlying assumptions about communication within the organizations in which these work groups are partially embedded. By reflecting upon these assumptions, a more informed view of work group performance emerges.

My approach builds upon prior arguments that focused on the interface of information technology systems with human systems at the individual level by Shulman et al. (1990) and at the organizational level by Orlikowski (1992), but does it with regard to recent work group theory and communication theory. In common with these past reviews, I take the position that how researchers conceptualize the interface between technology and the work groups that use them has major implications for our understandings. The chapter argues that these implications are related to a misunderstanding not so much of group performance or of technology, but of the differences between information and communication. It is through the human communication infrastructure that

we negotiate the meanings of the technological infrastructure. These negotiations are not neutral but morally based. It is within these moral frames that our understandings of good work group performance can be advanced. This argument is philosophically constructionist in the sense of reducing indeterminacy of possible meanings and directions and in the constitutive sense of creating possibilities (Philp 1985).

The examination is presented in four sections. In the first section, I consolidate the major themes that consistently occur in reviews of work group theory and research. In the second section, these themes are used as a background for examining research efforts that have attempted to address the relationships between work group performance and information technologies. The third section addresses the assumptions about communication processes that underlie these research programs. The last section focuses on future pathways.

## MAJOR THEMES IN WORK GROUP PERFORMANCE RESEARCH

Since the late 1980s there has been an upsurge of reviews of work group research. These reviews include Ancona and Caldwell (1988), Campion et al. (1993), Guzzo and Dickson (1996), Guzzo and Shea (1992), Hackman (1986; 1987), Levine and Moreland (1990) and Sundstrom et al. (1990).

With regard to work group performance, all the reviews have at least the following seven explicit themes in common.

## Reviewers Recognize that Good Work Group Performance is Important, but Assume that What is Good Performance is Self-Evident

The first theme is that understanding what fosters good work group performance is of increasing importance to organizations, at least within the industrialized countries where work groups or work teams are increasingly being used. (Consistent with the above reviews, I combine the terms 'work groups' and 'work teams' – because they are often used interchangeably.) For instance, one often quoted survey suggests that 47 per cent of the *Fortune* 1000 firms are using self-managing work teams with at least some employers and that they have been increasingly doing so for some time (Lawler et al. 1992). Rationales for this growth range from it being a response to increased pressures and complexities that can no longer be adequately handled by individuals, to a form of organizational structuring that fosters empowered and motivated workers at a time when changes such as automation and downsizing are also occurring. However, the reviews also point out that forming and using work groups do not always lead to better performance; it depends upon the coexistence of an enabling context, group design, and resource factors. At the same time these reviews give scant attention to the more fundamental issue of what are the standards for good work group performance. Hackman's proposition that a good outcome of the interaction of enabling conditions would be 'full exploitation of favourable performance conditions' (1987: 332), and Guzzo and Shea's adoption of the socio-technical school's definition of good performance as 'the joint optimization of social and task goals' (1992: 279), are examples of the current understandings of what is good performance. But how are groups to know when such optimization has occurred? They probably don't. What groups often have access to are judgments from their constituents as to whether the group outputs are adequate. The importance of managing this access with external constituents is highlighted in such studies as Ancona and Caldwell (1990) and reviews by Sundstrom et al. (1990). However, throughout the literature, it is almost as if there is a shared understanding of what is good performance.

## There is a Lack of Consistency of Findings across Studies of Work Group Performance

Results across studies are inconsistent. The field 'though quite vigorous, is badly fragmented' (Levine and Moreland 1990: 586). The reviewers claim that this has occurred because work group behaviors are complex, dynamic and context dependent. The inconsistencies also are associated with how and what researchers attend to. These inconsistencies are summarized in the next five themes.

## Work Groups are Multi-Functional Open Systems, but are Often Defined by Researchers as Single Purpose and Closed

There is a lack of consistency across research in what is a work group or work team. How researchers construe work groups is quite variable, reflecting what they choose to study. These vary from normative definitions such as

> a team is a small number of people with complementary skills who are committed to a common purpose, set of performance goals, and approach for which they hold themselves mutually accountable. (Katzenbach and Smith 1993: 112)

to more descriptive definitions such as

> Groups are assumed to be complex, intact social systems that engage in multiple, interdependent functions [production, member support, and group well being] on multiple concurrent projects, while partially nested within and loosely coupled to surrounding systems. (McGrath 1991: 151)

McGrath's definition provides further insight into the lack of consistency of findings across work group performance studies. For McGrath, groups are engaged in a messy array of projects, tasks and steps operating simultaneously. And as McGrath (1990: 28), points out, a group is playing several games at once, with different agendas for different audiences and different functions. These functions include: to support its members; to maximize its well-being; and to contribute to the organization it is embedded in. With regard to the last, there is a distinct shift to emphasize the difference between outputs and outcomes. Good group performance requires that the outputs are acceptable to those who receive or review them. These three functions are highlighted to different degrees in the above reviews. In comparison to McGrath (1991) and Hackman (1987), most investigators have assumed that groups are engaged in (almost) independent functions with group members being solely engaged in a single project with a single agenda. The lack of consistency across studies may be because different investigators are choosing to focus on different functions, at different levels, at different times, and to be more output oriented than outcome oriented. An implication of this is that if researchers were able and willing to specify a more complex 'contingency' model of context, that presumably matches the underlying complexity of work groups, then progress in understanding work group performance would occur. Hackman (1987), however, suggests that more complex models are not likely to be useful if they are deterministic. Groups are messy because they are open systems that possess human agency – a human quality that, by definition, cannot be completely predicted. Because of this quality, reviewers such as Hackman (1987) are recognizing that studies which employ deterministic methodologies based on logical positivism are likely to have limited value in advancing our understandings of ways of improving work group practices.

## Work Group Performances are Dependent upon Social and Organizational Contexts

What is meant by context differs from study to study, hence, overall generalizations are problematic. Recognizing that work groups operate within layers of socially constructed aggregates of organizations and communities, researchers are now attempting to develop understandings of the ways in which sets of actions within meetings are related to activities that are associated with the completion of projects (see Hackman 1987 and McGrath 1991 for an expansion of this theme).

An important implication of this is that much of the past research on groups that has focused on single meetings, and/or studies that failed to address the group's contribution and costs to its embedding system, may have added little to our understanding of how work groups go about achieving their objectives. All reviews point out the implication of this for the researcher's choice of methods. Groups in organizations are not like the *ad hoc* aggregates of individuals brought together in a laboratory for the occasion of research. As pointed out by McGrath (1991), group members have a history together, and they expect to have futures, but their memberships change from one occasion to another. If we want to understand work group performance we are going to have to use non-laboratory methods and build in ways of examining the group's contribution and costs to its embedding system.

## Temporal Contexts Shape Work Group Performance

All reviews except one have emphasized that what work groups do, and how they do it, changes over time. (The one review where temporal context is not an explicit theme is Campion et al. 1993, who do address change over time in a follow-up study: see Campion and McClelland 1993.) Such changes over time appear to be related to the task requirements and the time constraints under which groups operate. An illustrative study of this is Gersick's (1988) study of eight groups, each of which had a single mission and a predetermined life span, throughout their life course. The eight project groups varied in lifespan from a few days to fourteen weeks, but each had, from its beginning, a definite time deadline and an expected product. She provides evidence that every one of the groups made a major shift in what they did and how they did it at a point almost halfway through its lifespan. Regardless of the progress a given group made during the first half of the group life, each group had a more or less dramatic meeting at about the midpoint of its projected life, and as a consequence changed the course and pattern of its activity. After this midlife crisis, each group moved in a fairly direct way to complete their task. This study, perhaps more than others, has led group researchers such as Hackman (1987; 1990) and McGrath (1991) to further question and explore developmental and time-based theories of functional groups. However, as classification schemes for organizational contexts, tasks and time constraints are often not comparable across studies, further generalizations are problematic. This is amply demonstrated in studies such as Ginnett (1990), which reports where a new work group (in her case a flight crew) become effective immediately, largely due to organizational context. But most reviewers do acknowledge that what a group does has a beginning, an execution and an end stage. Depending upon the group studies, these stages are sometimes interspersed with stages that focus on technical issues and other stages that focus on political choices. There are also acknowledgements that these temporal sequencings are somehow related to the development of perceived capacity of the group to work together in the future (see, in particular, Levine and Moreland 1990).

Other insights into non-linear processes can be gleaned from research which focuses on bad work group practices which can lead to escalation of commitment to an inappropriate course of action. In the most relevant work of Ross and Staw (1986; 1993) the investigators describe an array of forces (project, organiza-tional, social, psychological) that interact dyna-mically to lead to escalation problems. Ross and Staw (1986) used a case analysis of the top team managing Expo 86 to lay out the temporal unfolding of the determinants of escalation of commitment to paths which subsequently were judged as too costly. Their major thesis is that project variables (e.g. cost/benefit analyses) are most important at early stages of the escalation episode. Psychological variables (e.g. individual motivations and biases) and social variables (e.g. cultural norms favoring consistent, strong leadership) are dominant at the middle stages, while both project variables and organizational variables (e.g. level of political support, or showcasing of a project as a symbol of the firm's values) become most important at the late or ending stage of the typical escalation episode. Recognizing the weaknesses of their data, and the *post hoc* interpretation of these data, Ross and Staw (1993) engaged in another case study to provide an *a priori* test of their temporal model of escalation and to extend the model to account for the exit of organizations from escalation. The case they selected was the building of the Shoreham nuclear power plant on Long Island, New York. This plant eventually incurred expenditures of over US$5.5 billion before it was abandoned in 1989. Like the Expo 86 case, it involved large expenditures of resources for construction. Using a mixture of archival material and interviews with top team members, they were able to test whether their hypothesized sets of determinants were present before, and during, the escalation of commitment, and if these sets of determinants were indeed ordered as pre-dicted. An iterative theory–data checking approach was used to extend their model to capture some of the determinants of exiting from escalation. In general, their analyses confirmed their temporal model. However unpredictively, organizational determinants appeared as an early influence of escalating commitment. That is, nuclear power became an important part of the firm's long term strategy at a relatively early phase. Moreover, they found that a fifth set of determinants, which they labeled contextual forces – which included the role of government and alliances with other utilities – seemed to account for much of the continuing escalation. An important implication of all of these lon-gitudinal studies is that much of the past research, which has assumed that group pro-cesses are linear or consist of a fixed sequence of phases, may have added little to our under-standing of how work groups go about achieving their objectives. These studies concerned with temporal context also reinforce the previous theme that studies which failed to address the group's contribution and costs to its embedding system may have added little to our under-standing of how work groups actually go about achieving their objectives.

## Groups Derive their Competitive Advantage from Better Sharing and Coordination

'Sharing' is a key to good work group per-formance. The authors all stress the importance of shared norms, with differential emphasis on shared visions, shared meanings, a sense of shared responsibility for group outcomes and coordination amongst group members. Though what they emphasize differs, they state that these sharings can be facilitated by 'shared' experiences, with a canvassing of options that lead to a shared understanding amongst group members of the ways each will need to behave. However, these reviewers also acknowledge that sharing of ideas is not always productive. For instance the sharing of low productivity norms can lead to poor performance, and too much sharing of views can lead to premature closure and group think. That is, well performing groups are proposed to manage their commu-nication so that a canvassing of views is encouraged as well as sharing a view for going forward. The question of whether there is a universal temporal ordering of seeking diversity versus sharing of views was raised under the preceding theme.

Sharing is also presented as a means of facilitating the coordination of actions. Along this line, most of the reviewers point to McGrath's (1984; 1991) work in which problem solving and conflict resolution are hypothesized to occur through the coordination, synchroniza-tion (or 'entertainment') of behaviors. The exception is Campion and McClelland (1993: 830) who do not mention coordination. Instead they point out that the related concepts of cooperation/communication (which Beer et al. 1990; Smith et al. 1995 have proposed as prerequisites of coordination) have not been extensively field tested.

Unfortunately, though some studies (for example Fulk 1993) operationalize sharing of views in terms of statistical analysis of central tendencies of five-point rating scales, none of the studies reviewed question the basic assumption of whether the sharing of views is possible. This is an assumption which I will question seriously in the third section of this chapter.

## Group Performances are not due Solely to the Group Processes that its Members Jointly Engage in

Many studies are now focusing on antecedent factors which directly impact upon performance and/or act in combination with group processes to affect performance. The vast majority of these follow a contingency hypothesis in which performance is seen as contingent on the match between the 'requisite variety' of characteristics of group members and task demands. Such member characteristics include the homogeneity of values, experience and skills that members have, or that others assume they possess. The models taking these alternative paths to group effectiveness are summarized in Guzzo and Dickson (1996), Guzzo and Shea (1992) and Hackman (1987). While studies are now showing that homogeneity of values and skills is related to various performances of top management teams (for instance, Daboub et al.'s 1995 examination of top management team characteristics and corporate illegal activity), an assumption underlying most of these studies is that these demographic combinations affect performance by first changing the engagement processes employed by the teams. Unfortunately there are few studies that have employed methodologies that allow an examination of the validity of this assumption. That is, they use archival records of top team makeup and then correlate differences in the degree of homogeneity across team members with differences of organizational performance. One implication of these models and studies of work group performance is that non-process factors can affect performance; however how such antecedent factors lead to the choice of paths members use in engaging in group tasks and projects is unknown.

In summary, these seven themes suggest that research has yet to address the fundamental issue of what constitutes good work group performance, except it requires that the outputs are acceptable to those who receive or review them. There is consensus that work group performance is dependent upon social, organizational and temporal contexts, though there is a lack of agreement on specific contexts. Furthermore, researchers are increasingly viewing work groups as open systems, that operate episodically, within multiple levels addressing multiple functions. There is also a growing consensus on the methodological implications of these understandings of work group performance: work group performance cannot be understood from studies of single meetings, or from studies which do not focus on the nexus between the work group and the organization in which it is embedded. There are also paradoxical implications for improving group performance: leaders of work groups need to encourage diversity of possible ways of achieving objectives, and at the same time foster 'shared' views on how to proceed. Changing the available mix of non-process skill bases can be used to influence group performance. These thematic generalizations form the basis for examining the impacts of electronic information technologies on work group performance.

### IMPACTS OF ELECTRONIC INFORMATION TECHNOLOGIES ON WORK GROUP PERFORMANCE

With few exceptions, the above reviews do not link work group performance with the use of electronic information technologies. Levine and Moreland (1990: 588) briefly review this area and conclude that there is little evidence that electronic communication improves productivity. The review by Guzzo and Shea suggests (in passing) that one of the topics that will appear as a center of attention in the future is the capacity of group computerization and software to change 'how information is communicated, stored and combined in the service of effective decision making' (1992: 307). Likewise, Guzzo and Dickson call (in passing) for future research to focus on 'team effectiveness under different ways of utilizing available technologies' (1996: 333). This theme about the potential impacts of electronic information technologies on work group performance is not mentioned in any of the other above reviews. The absence or relegation of technology to a minor category has recently been commented on by Polley and Van Dyne (1994) in their review of the limits and liabilities of self-managing work teams. They point out that given the central position that technology has in job design models (Hackman and Oldham 1980) and socio-technological systems models of work groups (Emery and Trist 1965), it is surprising that the impact of technologies on team performance has received relatively little attention. Their interpretation of this is that many of the followers of these models appear to concentrate on motivation, training and leadership with 'the assumption that work reorganization and change in technology will be considered by the work team after the team has been given training and autonomy' (Polley and Van Dyne 1994: 5).

While these recent reviews of work group performance do not place emphasis on the role of information technology at the work group level, there are models and studies of work groups that do. This section focuses on these studies. I limit this review to studies that concentrate on the nexus of work group performance with information technologies that are commonly called interactive, whether asynchronous as computer networking, or synchronous as teleconferencing, video conferencing, mobile telephone, etc. I also include hardware, software, and the programmed procedures as components of these technologies.

This review is also limited because most researchers who focus on the nexus have not addressed the major themes that emerged in the previous section. That is, they have tended to study a single meeting of a group without any attention to its social, organizational and temporal contexts, and without attention to multiple functions, and without attention to how changes in process are related to group performance. Furthermore, the researchers who do focus on the impact of information technologies on group performance also tend to focus on prototypes of a new technology and not on technologies that appear to be variants of commonly used existing systems. Hence, much more attention has been given to e-mail (for a review of e-mail research see Garton and Wellman 1995) than to mobile telephones – though the impact of mobile telephones on work group practices and performance is probably much more substantial than that of e-mail. This tendency of work-group/information-technology researchers to avoid the obvious has also been raised by Kiesler and Sproull (1992). It took fifty to seventy-five years for researchers to acknowledge the ways in which the ordinary telephone allowed the creation of the city landscape and different physical layout of organizations. For instance, without the telephone, buildings would have had wider stairways and fewer floors in order to accommodate the large number of runners needed to convey messages between departments. It also is obvious that the presence of the telephone had major impacts on the ways of doing business. For example, the telephone created new possibilities for centralized control in organizations with physically separate operations (Brooks 1976).

Within these limiting contexts, the majority of studies that have focused on the nexus of work group performance and information technology can be categorized as those that portray the nexus as if the link was a mostly closed system, a mostly open system or a mixture of both.

## Mostly Closed System Approaches

Researchers that appear to follow a closed system approach tend to focus on the ways in which various external factors affect the internal dynamics of the work groups and how these dynamics affect the groups' output. All the research that has followed Steiner's (1972) model of group process loss, and most of the research that falls into the input–process–output model of group effectiveness, is grouped within this approach (see Guzzo and Shea 1992 for an excellent review of these models). There are at least two variations of this approach. One focuses on electronic information systems as substitutes for face to face processes in which the underlying assumption is that modes do not matter. The other focuses on the ways electronic information systems can act as a substitute for the content of what a group does, such as controlling, developing, and monitoring expertise, and therefore change what the work group does and the output it produces.

For those following a process substitution approach, the emphasis is often on identifying those input factors that lead to better cooperation, often subsequently leading to better coordination, and eventually better performance. When information technology use is included within these studies, most assume that information technology acts as a substitute for face to face communication, or at least part of it. (See Shulman et al. 1990 and Nohria and Eccles 1992 for a review of limits of the substitution hypothesis when applied to the use of electronic networks when other modes of communicating are possible.) For substitution process researchers, context is often something that resides in the group as shared knowledge of the tasks, roles, habits and group norms, or comprises psychological motivational factors such as trust that are hypothesized as antecedents to cooperation and coordination (Beer et al. 1990; Smith et al. 1995: 11). In this sense, information technologies are a means of coordination, and coordination is taken to be equivalent to communication (McGrath 1990). For researchers such as Rice (1992), it is only when these contextual elements are certain and unambiguous that electronically mediated exchanges are chosen or preferred over face to face exchanges. Like the majority of studies of group processes, as summarized above, almost all of the electronic communication studies which have been guided by the process substitution hypothesis have tended to focus on single meetings and avoided examining the group's contribution and costs to its embedding system. There are notable exceptions. An example of a study that examined the context of use and functions of electronically mediated exchanges in ongoing work groups is McKenny et al.'s (1992) study of e-mail use by a systems design team. They followed Daft et al.'s (1987) elaboration of an information processing perspective. In this perspective the work group was construed as 'a set of actors exchanging information to accomplish tasks and build knowledge' (McKenny et al. 1992: 263). Their analyses were based on the pattern of interactions and on the content of those interactions in situations where the problem could be defined versus situations where the problem itself defied interpretation – that is, where equivocality existed. For these researchers, a building of shared understanding of a situation was necessary before group members can act. They hypothesized that managers exchanging information with their staff would be more likely to use e-mail for situations where problems did not exist or were well defined, than for situations where problem solving was necessary. The logic for this choice of mode follows the view that face to face interaction is a richer mode, allowing more flexibility of format, the use of simultaneous non-verbal channels, and more back and forth exchanges in which ambiguities can be resolved. However, face to face modes can be more costly in coordination and travel, and because of a bias to 'appropriately match' tasks with communication mode, people will choose to use a less costly mode, as e-mail, when the richness of face to face is not really needed. (See Rice 1992 for a summary of the history and status of media richness theory.) McKenny et al. (1992) also predicted that a pattern or program of combined use of these modes would occur that reflected the work routines of the group. As predicted, e-mail was primarily used to monitor status, send alerts, broadcast information and invoke action. These uses were often followed by face to face meetings by subgroups of staff who then discussed problems and maintained context under shifting priorities. Weekly face to face meetings also served as a routine context building process.

Not all substitution studies have found such patterning in the use of e-mail. In fact a recent review of studies of e-mail (Garton and Wellman 1995) concludes that there is no clear pattern concerning process or function substitution of face to face by e-mail across studies. Nor are there clear patterns of substitution associated with other electronic means of communication (Shulman et al. 1990). And some researchers are suggesting that one possible reason why no clear pattern has emerged is that other more established electronic modes, such as video and audio conferencing and fax, are now creating 'conditions more like face to face conversation' (Kiesler and Sproull 1992: 97). That is, the mixed results are in part due to the ability to use the modes to achieve the same purposes that can be achieved in ongoing face to face communication, but to do it in different ways. Such explanations

of equifinality are consistent with McGrath's (1991) time, interaction and performance (TIP) theory of groups. Unfortunately, the problematic 'social and temporal context' themes that were summarized in the first section of this chapter are compounded when we further limit the literature to incidences where the potential evolution of patterns of mode use across meetings and episodes has been studied. There are, however, models and anecdotal evidence that when group members recognize that they have a future, that there will be other encounters, they modify their behaviors, depending upon the urgency of task demands and the modes that are anticipated to be available (Shulman and Steinman 1978). Further support for the view that people's anticipation of future encounters on different modes matters at least in terms of group processes is reviewed in Walther (1994); however, almost all of the work has concentrated on well-being or satisfaction and not on task performance outcomes.

For other researchers who appear to follow a substitution of group activity as opposed to the previous process substitution approach, information technologies are often regarded as input tools for structurally determining and eliminating/adding to functions of group processes either positively or negatively, and therefore indirectly affecting work group outputs. These researchers regard the technologies as exerting unidirectional influence over the group. There are those, described variously as optimists (Hirschheim 1985) or utopians (Bryant 1988), who view information technology as the solution to all, or almost all, group coordination problems. An example of this can be found in work on group decision support systems (GDSSs) by DeSanctis and Gallupe, who state: 'A GDSS aims to improve the process of group decision making by removing communication barriers, providing techniques for structuring decision analysis, and systematically directing the pattern, timing and content of discussion' (1987: 589). Here, we have an example that not only perpetuates the belief in substitutability, but introduces the added element that technology will improve the organizational communication process. At no point in their argument do DeSanctis and Gallupe question the tenability of their optimistic assumption.

At the other extreme are those described as pessimists (Hirschheim 1985). From this doom-laden position, the electronic information technologies are seen as the source or exacerbation of control of the workers by management. For example, Duran (1990) describes a case where the implementation of information systems removed problem solving activities from task execution, leading to the disintegration of work teams. Allen (1994) suggests that increased mutual access to electronically conveyed information about others' performance can lead to excessive pressure for tighter monitoring and control. Although this belief predicts the opposite of the first, it is in fact based on a similar technocratic faith. In both instances, the technology is assumed to take on an existence independent of group users, but one that still determines group behavior.

Others take a more circumspect view. Some suggest that the technology does determine outcomes but the effects are likely to be of a second order. Some question it on grounds that studies of the cost/benefit of such systems have yielded marginal results on return on investment, at best (*The Economist*, 1991). In fact, at least one information technology vendor, WANG, has acknowledged this lack of productivity gain as a selling point to encourage businesses to use their expertise to get it right (Wilde 1991). Others suggest a second order determinism that the availability and use of electronic systems in work groups leads people to shift attention to different things, have contact with different people, and do things differently (Kiesler and Sproull 1992: 99). Likewise group researchers such as McGrath (1990) put forward some interesting conjectures of how asynchronous systems, in particular, may expand possible participation from physically distant nodes and at different stages of group activity, to increase performance on well learned tasks, but at the same time suggest that they may also restrict participation and reduce the attention that the group pays to the well-being and member support functions. In contrast, Bikson et al. (1989) acknowledge that the interactive information technologies are overcoming space/time constraints, but seem to be supplementing and not replacing existing preferences, opportunities, and methods for interaction.

The above positions have not provided the manager or researcher with a pathway to bring about the innovative potential or minimize negative consequences. In other words there is no unequivocal set of conjectures or results (Kraemer and Danziger 1990; Robey 1987). As suggested by Bikson et al.: 'Successful new modes of work group collaboration will require more social and managerial innovation than has been evidenced to date' (1989: 112).

All the above models rest on certain implicit beliefs about the nature of information technologies and their use in work groups. Specifically, it has been assumed that information technologies will lead to increased efficiencies and effectiveness and that the use of information technology would be consistent with formal theories of rational choice. Neither of these

implicit assumptions about the nature and use of information technology has received convincing empirical support (Orlikowski 1992; Shulman et al. 1990).

## Mostly Open System Approaches

There are at least two open system approaches. In one the emphasis is on the group becoming more self-directed through the availability of empowering information exchanges within the group, whereas in the second the emphasis is on the empowerment coming about through electronically mediated exchanges with others outside of the group. In both open system approaches, the effects of the information technologies are not limited to their actual use, but also include the effects associated with their symbolic presence or absence. Thus some of these researchers are likely to focus on the ways people's concepts of the technology affect their behaviors and relationships with others inside and outside of the work group. Like the determinists, some of these researchers act as if the concepts of technology can be used as an excuse for bringing about other changes, but for these researchers such changes are not determined by the technology, but enable occasions for different configurations to be explored.

In the first, 'groupware' information technologies are seen as providing opportunities for group members to increase their capacity to be more self-directed and actively create and change themselves within the group. An example of this is the use of an Internet bulletin board to search for a new editor of a journal as a means of providing more equal access to the views of other members within the membership (Zuboff 1988: 371).

Followers of the second open system approach see 'collaborativeware' information systems as flexible means of creating new relationships within a dynamic context which they are both affecting and being affected by, particularly with persons outside of the work group. (Examples of this view are provided in Kiesler and Sproull 1992: 98.) Thus researchers following this second approach focus on how the electronic technology provides an opportunity for new interest groups to form over the electronic highway or how increased stakeholder access to the electronic modes changed the makeup and nature of the ways the group performed. What much of the research suggests is that enlarged groups will behave in unexpected ways. Whether such differences lead to better performance is an open question.

## Mixture of Open and Closed Systems

Many of the researchers cited above appear at times to take a mixture of open and closed system approaches, focusing on the group as an open system with persons creating enabling constructs of information technology, but also acknowledging the deterministic impacts of the hard wiring of the information system on its users. That is, what occurs within the group is somewhat determined by the technology, but the persons within the group have some agency of choice within the constraints that are imposed by the technology. Other proponents of this view often build upon the socio-technical systems school of Emery and Trist (1965) or upon Giddens's (1979) structuration theory.

Taylor and Felten (1993) provide a historical account of the development of current variations of socio-technical systems. Followers of this approach place an emphasis on the necessity of attending to the social structuring of work groups to maximize the fit between technology and human systems. Most of the humanistic oriented models on group task design (Hackman 1987; Campion et al. 1993) are consistent with this perspective. Yet as pointed out in the introduction to this section, most work group researchers following the socio-technical systems school have not focused on technology. Those that have included Gutek et al. (1986), who studied the implementation of computer-based office information technologies in fifty-five offices and their relation to organizational structure defined in terms of the primary occupational function of the unit (clerical, managerial) and the nature of the technology. The latter was defined in terms of its physical attributes (age, micro/mini). They found some support for covariation of structure and technology, but little support for a relationship between organizational outcome (in this study, productivity and satisfaction) and this covariation.

In fact, the current state of our knowledge about possible ways of maximizing technology and work group design fit is quite limited. The contingency hypothesis and related context fit hypothesis have had little empirical support. (See Markus and Robey 1988 for a review of related organizational imperative studies.) Furthermore, researchers ignore the processes by which congruence can be achieved (Gutek et al. 1986). Suffice to say that the contingency hypothesis will probably remain attractive to researchers hopeful of eventually finding the elusive key element that will make heterogeneous findings homogeneous. However, the real limitations of the contingency hypothesis become apparent when it is realized that information and the relevant technologies are not just about rational control of the organizational environment.

In structuration theory, and consistent with the more general constructionist perspective, more emphasis is placed on humans (as agents) being both enabled and constrained by technical structures, yet these very same structures are the result of previous actions (Giddens 1979). Within an agency view, human interaction is concerned with the communication of meaning. To accomplish this, interpretative schemes must be used by the actors to interact in a sense-making manner with the world. Through the use of one's interpretative scheme and communication, the structures of signification are created which represent the rules that inform and define interaction (Orlikowski 1992). The rules however are not 'fixed'. Having been created by actors who are both knowledgeable and reflexive, the rules can be challenged or reaffirmed. That is, through the use of their knowledge base, actors are able to observe and understand what they are doing whilst they are doing it. Thus actors can potentially change the existing structure, but the extent or type of change cannot be predicted with complete accuracy, in part because of attention to the notion of 'unintended consequences of action'. The usefulness of applying structuration theory to the study of information technology derives from the fundamental premise of the 'duality of structure'. Unlike closed system substitution approaches that may overemphasize the importance of technical constraints on action, and their humanist open system counterparts that may overemphasize the importance of the capability of human actors, the structural approach provides a means by which researchers (such as Fulk 1993; Robey and Azevedo 1991: 11; Orlikowski 1992) can acknowledge the tangible constraints that technology may impose as well as accounting for the phenomena of 'interpretative flexibility' and adaptation of information technology for evolving purposes.

For these researchers, because information technology is highly susceptible to reinterpretation and social construction, the impact of information technology on work groups cannot be produced independently of human action and interpretation (Robey and Azevedo 1991: 13). This is because interactive electronic information systems, more so than other technologies, can be put to varied uses and are therefore more open to reinterpretation. The studies of Kraut et al. (1989) and Nelson (1990) provide good examples of technology being put to a variety of uses that were not initially intended by the original designers. Interpretative flexibility has important consequences for group processes, as technology can be seen to be a product of human action, while it simultaneously presents a constraint on that action.

However, the concept of interpretative flexibility is not infinite. While there may be a degree of flexibility in the design, use and interpretation of technology, the level of flexibility is constrained by the physical characteristics of the technology. Apart from information technology's obvious physical constraints, it is also constrained by the organizational as well as the social and temporal structures that it is embedded in. (These latter constraints also were raised in the first section.) Consistent with the 'duality of structure' approach, Kohut (1994) has illustrated, using key informants and participants of a work group of system designers involved in the introduction and use of a new computer system, that the level of interpretative flexibility tends to taper off once the electronic information system has been in place for a while. That is, the degree to which group members take advantage of the possibilities decreases as the technology becomes institutionalized. Why this pattern of decreased exploration over time occurred isn't clear. Perhaps it is related to the tendency of groups using interactive computer technology over a period of time to decrease their use of the technology for group maintenance purposes unless they are instructed (to provide feedback) to increase it (Losada et al. 1990). Or it may be related to the group going through the mid-life transition referred to above (Gersick 1988) in which the declining use for experimentation is associated with the team members just getting on a direct path to project completion.

While the interpretations afforded through structuration theory and the assumptions of duality of infrastructures are much richer than those offered by the previous schools, we are left with little guidance as to what is good work group performance or how its occurrence is facilitated by the symbolic or actual use of information technology.

In this section, I have presented closed system, open system and a combination of open and closed system stances that have been taken on the role and impact of information technology on group performance. It appears that the same seven themes raised in the previous section, that characterized current research of good work group performance, are also applicable to researchers who have been examining the nexus between work groups and electronic information technology. The impact of information technologies varies from study to study. For every research study that shows a particular impact of information technology, there is either another study that shows the reverse or a study that concludes that the impacts are more complex

than had been previously assumed. This is a pattern of results that occurred with the information technologies of the 1980s, and still holds today (see Markus and Robey 1988; Robey 1986; 1987; Siegel et al. 1986). Put another way, the impacts of information technology on work group performance are organizationally, socially and temporally dependent.

One can also conclude from this review, that work group research has neither significantly helped nor hindered the introduction of information technology into groups. Although there are numerous reasons why this came about (see Rice 1984), an obvious practical reason is that by the time researchers produced results, the users were already onto the next generation of technology. For the researchers, the technologies themselves became moving targets (Tomarzky 1986). For work group members, the ongoing updating of information technology has become a fact of life. For most researchers, these technology changes are yet to be seen as part of the dynamic ongoing episodes of work groups.

There are suggestions in the above reviews that the failure of researchers to focus on this dynamic can be traced to the inappropriateness of the models and methods of study used – models and methods based on an empiricist tradition. As pointed out in the first section, the inappropriateness of this tradition has been well argued by Hackman (1987) for work group research. Others, such as Shulman et al. (1990) and Orlikowski (1992), have raised parallel concerns for information technology research. For these researchers, the models and methods commonly employed within the empiricist tradition do not distinguish methodologically between the work group and technological infrastructure. As such, researchers operating in that tradition are inadvertently led to adopt some kind of technological determinism. The empiricist tradition does have its place as a symbolic way of acting as if people were technology.

But there are important lessons that emerge from the information-technology/work-group research that can lead to a better understanding of good work group performance. This is because those interested in the impacts of the information technologies have articulated their assumptions about the roles of information and communication much more sharply than those directing their research efforts at work group performance in general. In the next section, these insights build upon categorizations of how researchers of information technology have portrayed information and communication (Shulman et al. 1990) and recent advances in communication theory by Penman (1995). These give rise to a different conception of communication that in turn leads us to ask new questions about information technologies and good group performance. These new questions also allow us to put information technology in its place – as a potential aid to the real business of work groups, not as a substitute for it. The next section concludes with a different view of the duality of infrastructures that can address the moral question of what is good work group performance.

## RECONSIDERING INFORMATION TECHNOLOGY, COMMUNICATION AND WORK GROUP PERFORMANCE

Perhaps the most striking feature of all the literature reviewed here is its faith that work group members understand and share the same view (symbolic or otherwise) of information and communication. With the exception of the dualistic position taken by constructionists, researchers of information technology took the communication process for granted. (See Shulman et al. 1990 for a review of definitions of information and communication used by information technology researchers.) Most seem to follow Shannon and Weaver's (1949) definition of communication, that is, information is the signal sent or received, with communication being a process of sending and receiving information or messages. This definition was originally developed to deal with electronic systems but is commonly applied to human systems. The key elements still remain in contemporary work group researchers' definitions of communication (McGrath 1990; Kiesler and Sproull 1992).

With the new information technologies we are presumably able to speed up the transmission and to increase the storage of ideas much more than we could if we were relying on simple human 'connections' and the fallible human mind (Guzzo and Shea 1992: 307). But as the research demonstrates, there is little evidence that information technology can act as a substitute for human communication, let alone do it better. As described elsewhere (Shulman and Penman 1992; Sless 1986b), the major consequence of the introduction of new information technologies within organizations has not been better communication, only faster misunderstandings.

The belief that communication and therefore the information technology is a tool – an instrument for getting your message across – has led to false and exaggerated expectations about what information technology can do. And as such it has also led many practitioners and researchers alike along an unproductive pathway with substantial hidden costs. Ineffective and costly management decisions based on false expectations about information technology as a tool for getting a message across are shown in studies demonstrating that new computer systems can result in lower profitability and reduce production (Dougherty 1988).

In other words, how we think about information technology and communication is not simply a matter of scholarly indulgence; it determines the decisions and actions we all take in our practical communicative activities. As pointed out in the previous section, there is an emerging recognition that there is a need to use different models for the human versus mechanical-technological infrastructure. Researchers who adhere to the transmission view of work group communication treat the technological and human aspects of the infrastructure of communication as if they were part of the same phenomenon.

The key point so far, then, is that most contemporary research has failed to make the distinction between these two infrastructures and has applied a technical means of knowing to human problems. This is well illustrated by the assumptions of causality that underlie most research in this area (see the review by Markus and Robey 1988). Strictly speaking, causality is a concept that belongs only to the technical realm, where external events can directly cause or determine other events. When we enter the human realm and attribute humans with any agency or intention in their communicative actions, then we cannot assume simultaneously that those actions are caused by external events. From this constructionist position, causality has no place in the human infrastructure. When inappropriate technical concepts, such as causality, continue to be used to understand the human realm, the real problems will never be addressed, let alone resolved. And the real problems can never be addressed until we discard the technical, instrumental view of communication.

### New Conceptions of Information and Communication

Communication is a messy and uncertain business. Communication is always partially ineffective, potentially wasteful, and to some degree beyond the control of any one individual or organization. Here, I am concerned with developing a description of communication that can account for these practical observations which reinforce the seven themes raised in the first section. Much of the confusion in the work group research literature, as well as in practice, rests on the failure to make a critical conceptual distinction between information and communication. Sless (1981) has developed an extensive argument regarding the differences and I draw heavily on this here as I have done elsewhere (Shulman et al. 1990).

## Information

In the commonsense view of information as an entity, all things that exist in the physical world are potential sources of information. As such, information has the properties of the physical world and exists regardless of our perception of it. In other words, information is something independent of humans. It is inanimate, incapable of acting or exhibiting agency. When the human agent enters the scene and reads the information a fundamental change takes place. In the relationship between human agent and information something new is created that we usually call meaning. Information does not contain meaning *per se*. Meaning is brought about in the relationship between the reader and the information being read.

The concept of information has some similarities with common sense views that also see information as an entity. But Sless's view does not falsely attribute the 'entity' with meaning independent of the human reader. Those views that equate information and meaning are making a category mistake in the same way that Ryle (1963) argued for the mind/body dualism. Similarly, those who expect meaning to be a property of information mistakenly believe meaning to be a part that can be separately identified, rather than the outcome of an interaction between information and human agent. The problem of a category mistake in the field of information technology is that meaning is taken as belonging to the category of the physical world, when it actually belongs in the human world (Shulman et al. 1990).

When meaning is assumed to exist independent of humans, it is easy (although false) to conceive of technical/mechanical means for storing, transferring, and transforming this meaning, as Guzzo and Shea (1992) have done. When meanings are seen as stored in words or other signals, then the more signals we can create and preserve, presumably the more ideas we transfer and store. This very mistaken view has, according to Reddy (1979), significant social consequences. If we do not cultivate our abilities to create and reconstruct meanings we will end up with a culture less sophisticated rather than more. On the other hand, if we take meaning to be a process in the human infrastructure, we are correctly placing the responsibility for meaning creation and manipulation in human hands, not mechanical ones.

## Communication

For communication to occur, a further condition is necessary: a communicative intent must be inferred in the information being read. By this I mean that if we believe the information in our environment was generated by someone else in order to communicate then the necessary and sufficient conditions exist to describe the phenomenon as communication. It is important to note here that it is the inference of the 'other' and their intent that is critical, not the physical presence, nor that the 'other' really had a communicative intent.

Communication then is also a relational phenomenon, but one involving more than one person, whether assumed or real. Thus, the communication process incorporates the meaning generation process, but in a particular way. The communication process incorporates more than one 'reader' and this adds complexity to the meaning generation process. It is the way in which these people are in relation with each other that provides the basis for our conception of communication. Moreover, this process not only creates its own internal structure but also sets its own boundaries. Communication, as an autopoietic process (Maturana and Varela 1980), is self-generating, structure-creating, and boundary-setting. In acting in this process we find ourselves in a rather more difficult place than conventionally proposed. Communication activity is not only self-generating, it is also self-specifying. It is self-specifying in the sense that our past activities point to the directions of our present activities. 'Rather than acting "out of" an inner plan or schema, we can think of ourselves as acting "into" our own present situation' (Shotter 1986: 203).

The meanings generated in this process arise from unique patterns of interaction between the participants – patterns beyond the control or intention of any individual party. The meanings are also subject to continual modification with the evolving temporal context. As we act into our communicative situation we are at the same time changing it by that action. In continually bringing about a new state of affairs, joint communicative actions and the implicated meanings are always emergent and never finished.

The meanings generated in this process are also position specific. In this sense everyone is in a unique position, shaped by both history and the perceived future: hence the meanings generated in this process cannot be identical, and 'shared' understandings are at best transitory. David Sless has poignantly captured this momentary, changing nature of understanding: 'Understanding is the dead spot in our struggle for meaning: it is the momentary pause, the stillness before incomprehension continues. . . . Thus understanding is a temporary state of closure' (1986a: i).

A critical point in this argument, then, is that meaning is inherently indeterminate. We cannot guarantee, predict or fully control the direction of the process or the nature of the meaning inferred. Instead, the 'organized settings' we are led into by our past actions and implicated meanings act as constraints (in contrast to determinants) on the range of possible future meanings. These constraints provide temporary closure in an otherwise unstable and indeterminate social world. In this way, although there may be potential for an infinite range of meanings, in practice this is limited by the closure we impose. Thus, our key concern is one not of determining (or even believing in) the stability of meaning, but of understanding the points and procedures for closures. Meaning cannot be controlled or predicted, but it can be managed and constrained.

The essential indeterminacy of meaning logically leads us to challenge the metaphysics of foundationalism (see Rorty 1980) – a metaphysics that assumes there can be a stable foundation, a certain objective and unchangeable knowledge base. From our point of view, it is logically impossible to establish foundations for, and derive predictable long term generalizations from, anything as inherently unstable as human social life (see MacIntyre 1985). This, then, is the real key to the failure of past research on information technology reviewed in this chapter. The past research attempted to predict the impact of technology on work group activity, when that activity itself is inherently unstable.

From the point of view of the management of the work group information and technology nexus, our major concern is with generating and managing better expectations. Better expectations are those that are based on a realistic conception of the communication process and its inherently problematic nature. When we take misunderstandings to be the norm rather than the exception we are more alert for the problems and more able to manage them. In this sense, then, better expectations take the technology to be both an enabling and a constraining device, depending on how well it is designed, implemented and used.

When we are concerned with strictly information-based activities (cf. communication), information technology systems provide us with a range of opportunities for modeling and rehearsal of information activities. When we are concerned with communication activities *per se*, the technology once again provides us with certain opportunities. In particular, the various technologies offer people opportunity for

greater access, different types of access – such as voice, data, and graphics – and facility for faster access. But technology only provides us with more and faster opportunities for communication. It does not provide us with communication *per se*, let alone better communication. The problems inherent in the communication process are not removed by that technology. In fact, given the state of user unfriendliness of many of these technologies, problems in the communication process are more likely to be exacerbated than minimized. (See Shulman et al. 1990 for a review of information technology design faults.)

Given this indeterminacy and instability, the management of meaning can be construed as one of autopoietic deviation, amplification, and counteraction. As Nord (1985) has pointed out, managing involves understanding both the conditions where small deliberate changes – as in bringing in a new information technology in a complex system – can produce a self-sustaining (deviation amplifying) change in the complex system, and the conditions where the change will be overwhelmed by the system (deviation counteracting) (Nord 1985: 188–9). When new technology is managed as if it were an innovation, then deviation amplification occurs. When new technology is managed as if it were a substitution, then deviation counteraction occurs. Either style of management depends on managing meanings.

When we are concerned with the role of information technology in work groups we need to be concerned with questions of how the meanings attributed to information technologies are maintained and amplified by organizational members. We need also to be concerned with how these meanings change with the physical characteristics and distribution of the technology from different positions and with how these meanings are related to changing patterns of technology use. Thus, in our account gathering we are not gathering the truth in any objective or absolute sense. Instead, our accounts indicate a range of possible interpretations, including our own.

I have suggested that some of the problematics of work group performance research that were highlighted in the first section can be associated with the proclivity of researchers to examine human work groups as if they were technology. In the second section I pointed towards the advances made by researchers who are using dualistic approaches that recognize both the human and the technology aspects of work group performance. In the third section I developed the theme that many of these research efforts are still limited, in part because they still hold onto a transmission view of information and communication. This transmission view has constrained the recognition that the performance of groups can never be completely determined. Once recognized, new possibilities for management of the nexus of information technologies and work groups emerge. However, recognition of this has not provided a direct insight into what is good work group performance. In order to make that connection, in the next section I draw on recent work by Penman (1995; 1997) where in the very process of acting into our communicative practices we are acting into some moral order.

## INFORMATION TECHNOLOGY AND GOOD WORK GROUP PERFORMANCE: FUTURE DIRECTIONS

Any question of what is 'good' – including what is good work group performance – is a moral one. As social scientists, we have tended to treat 'morality' as ideas that exist independent of the participants involved. However, in the previous section I have argued that ideas do not exist independently of the participants involved, nor can the meanings be completely determined. In this section I draw on Penman's (1995; 1997) development of the implications of the constructionist view for addressing the question of what is good.

Penman (1997) uses the arguments of two twentieth-century authors drawing on different, but compatible, traditions: Hans-Georg Gadamer and John Shotter. Gadamer's (1992) major philosophical concern was with elucidating the hermeneutical nature of the human sciences and human experience generally. As pointed out by Penman, Gadamer's argument relies on Aristotle's major distinction between technical or theoretical knowledge and moral knowledge. 'For moral knowledge, as Aristotle describes it, is clearly not objective knowledge. The knower is not standing over against a situation that he merely observes; he is directly confronted with what he sees. It is something that he has to do' (Gadamer 1992: 314). For Gadamer, moral knowledge is in the domain of the full human experience; moral knowledge is always incipient in practice.

John Shotter (1990; 1993) uses three distinctions to arrive at a similar understanding. Taking Ryle's distinction between 'knowing that' (facts or theoretical principles) and 'knowing how' (technique), he adds a third, moral, kind that he calls 'knowing from' (Shotter 1990: 12). This knowing of the moral kind is a form of practical knowledge, as Aristotle and later Gadamer would characterize it. But Shotter, drawing on Vico, Vygotsky and Mead, emphasizes the social realm of this moral knowing; it is knowing that comes from our relations with others.

Shotter makes the same point as does Gadamer – that moral knowledge is about doing. But Shotter expands on this by arguing that it is something that is about doing with other people. Moral knowing does not exist independently of a social situation, it is brought about within it. You cannot reiterate a long list of professional ethics for this form of 'knowing from'; it emerges from what you do. The point that these authors make that is relevant to the argument here is that moral knowing is immanent in our practice of communicating within work groups.

Penman (1995) points out that most studies do not incorporate 'knowing from', but reflect the conventional wisdom of the past three centuries: that communication is immaterial; it is merely a trivial vehicle for something far more important. This 'wisdom' is reflected in arguments about the need to investigate how the electronic information system can be best 'shaped' and manipulated in order to best 'transmit' the ideas it 'contains' and to bring about desired effects on others.

This approach to communication, that treats the very process as immaterial, has been directly linked to the moral order of the twentieth century by Alasdair MacIntyre (1985) in his important book, *After Virtue*. His conclusion is that the prevalent moral order in our Western world is an amoral one. It is an amoral order in which the distinction between manipulative and non-manipulative relations between people has been obliterated in such a way that it seems impossible for people to conceive of communication as anything but a manipulative tool, as a means of predictability and control (Penman 1995).

For Penman, once the limitations of the conventional, Enlightenment wisdom and its amoral consequences are recognized we have three choices: to accept, to reject or to deny. To accept the conventional wisdom is to do what much of what is called communication or cultural studies has done, however unknowingly. To reject the conventional wisdom we also have to reject the basic division between material and immaterial. This approach is exemplified by Rorty's (1980) anti-foundational arguments. For Rorty, the profound error of the Enlightenment scholars was to base all their arguments on the belief that there was a true, immutable foundation to knowledge, and the scientific task was to seek this foundation. In arguing against this belief, however, Rorty chose to reject all foundations and thus all materiality, and to embrace everything as immaterial. With his choice, communication is everything and nothing. There are serious problems associated with this choice, particularly moral ones. Accepting a view of communication, along with everything else, as immaterial is to celebrate the insignificance of Being itself (Shepherd 1993). In such a celebration notions of good or right are replaced with an amoral stance of anything goes (e.g. Feyerabend 1975).

The third choice is to deny the conventional wisdom and to assert that communication is material. It is only this choice that offers the possibility of a communication view (as distinct from any other disciplinary view). It is a view that says communication is foundational to our being, it is material and it does matter (Sless 1991). While this goes against the last three centuries of mainstream philosophical tradition, it is a view that nevertheless has had its own advocates for centuries (e.g. Vico in the 1700s: Vico 1986). And these advocates for the materiality of communication are now coming to the fore again. As many recent authors who have made this last choice argue, there is a general transformation under way in the humanities and social sciences based on the recognition of the role communication plays in constructing our lives (e.g. Craig 1993; Gergen 1982; Penman 1988; 1992). And it is only in working within this transformation that questions of the broad moral dimension are possible.

## Communicating in a Moral Frame

Penman (1992; 1995) suggests that in reconstruing communication as material, because our knowing is not independent of ourselves and our communicative actions, all of our knowing and our actions have a valuational base. As such we have incorporated, by implication, what we believe is good and desirable. Following Penman's argument, then, all communicative practices, by virtue of their being communicative, have a moral dimension. 'In the very process of acting into our communicative practices we are acting into some moral order or another' (Penman 1995).

As work group researchers we could well ask in what ways are moral orders indicated and acted out in communicative action. The work of Harré (1983), Pearce and Cronen (1987), Cronen (1986) and Penman (1991) provide recent examples of approaches to this question, by specifying characteristics of moral orders in action. But even these approaches operating within the new paradigm are not exempt from having to come to terms with the second aspect of the moral issue: the moral dimension to research and theory. If all theory and research is

invention and not neutral discovery, then all research is also value based. If all research is intervention, then it is in some way or another intervention into a moral order.

The above argument has major implications for future research about good work group performance and the role of information technology. It strongly suggests that a researcher's understandings of the possibilities and constraints of electronic information technologies can best be advanced by actively engaging in the communicative activity of work groups and not just studying them at a distance. Penman (1997) has construed this as the primary research position: one where the researchers are directly participating in conversations with others as the generative source of their consequent understandings. For Penman this does not mean researchers can or should avoid retrospective analysis. She extends Dewey's (1981) argument that both participation and reflection are necessary – but that one precludes the other. 'You cannot be looking back – to study antecedents – while looking forward – to understand the possibilities – within the same communication process' (Penman 1997). For understanding the possibilities of information technology to foster good work group performance, we need to look forward. In looking forward we are presented with the unfolding of options and the closing off of others. The episodic nature of work groups, documented through participant observation by McGrath and O'Connor (1996), provides an opportunity for researchers to sequentially act in, and reflect on, work group processes.

Throughout this chapter, I have provided a snap-shot of the contributions and limitations of current research into work group performance and its relationship with information technologies. The review relied heavily on the writings of researchers that took a neutral – 'passive' – role. I suggest that recent advances have been made where researchers have taken at least a slightly active participatory role in their engagement with groups (for instance, Hackman 1990). The argument developed here has attempted to provide a conceptual base for extending this participation. What possibilities will emerge by engaging more directly into the conversations of work groups are dependent, in part, on the tools we use to move the conversations forward. Given the increasing avalanche of the use of work groups and their access to others through information technologies, it is likely that new understandings will emerge – not because the information technologies are a substitute for the conversations, but because they provide an opportunity for engaging within the conversations.

## Notes

The themes that are presented within this chapter emerged within conversations with my colleagues at the Communication Research Institute. The insights constructed within these interactions with Robyn Penman, David Rogers and David Sless guided the arguments. Other insights emerged from my participation in the R&D work teams led by Jenny Bellamy, Peter Cox and Neil MacLeod of CSIRO. I thank them for allowing me to engage with them in exploring these themes in practice, and the LWRRDC, GRDC and RIRDC Australia for partially funding these activities.

## References

Allen, J.P. (1994) 'Mutual control in newly integrated work environments', *Information Society*, 10(2): 129–38.

Ancona, Deborah G. and Caldwell, David F. (1988) 'Beyond task and maintenance: defining external functions in groups', *Group and Organization Studies*, 13(4): 468–94.

Ancona, Deborah G. and Caldwell, David F. (1990) 'Beyond boundary spanning: managing external dependence in product development teams', *The Journal of High Technology Management Research*, 1(2): 119–35.

Beer, M., Eisenstat, R.A. and Spector, B. (1990) *The Critical Path to Corporate Renewal*. Boston: Harvard Business School Press.

Bikson, Thomas K., Eveland, J.D. and Gutek, Barbara A. (1989) 'Flexible interactive technology for multi-person tasks: current problems and future prospects', in Margrethe H. Olson (ed.), *Technological Support for Work Group Collaboration*. Hillsdale, NJ: Lawrence Erlbaum. pp. 89–112.

Brooks, John (1976) *Telephone*. New York: Harper & Row.

Bryant, A. (1988) 'The information society: computopia, dystopia, myopia', *Prometheus*, 6: 61–77.

Campion, M.A. and McClelland, C.L. (1993) 'Follow-up and extension of the interdisciplinary costs and benefits of enlarged jobs', *Journal of Applied Psychology*, 78: 339–51.

Campion, M.A., Medsker, G.J. and Higgs, A.C. (1993) 'Relations between work group characteristics and effectiveness: implications for designing effective work groups', *Personnel Psychology*, 46: 823–50.

Craig, R. (1993) 'Why are there so many communication theories?', *Journal of Communication*, 43(3): 26–33.

Cronen, V. (1986) 'The individual in a systemic perspective'. Paper presented at the 15th Anniversary of Interaktie Akademie, Antwerp, 30 May.

Daboub, A.J., Rasheed, A.M., Priem, R.L. and Gray, D.A. (1995) 'Top management team characteristics and corporate illegal activity', *Academy of Management Review*, 20(1): 138–70.

Daft, R.L., Lengel, R.H. and Trevino, L.K. (1987) 'Message equivocality, media selection and manager performance', *MIS Quarterly*, 11(3): 355–66.

DeSanctis, G. and Gallupe, R.B. (1987) 'A foundation for the study of decision support systems', *Management Science*, 33: 589–609.

Dewey, J. (1981) *The Philosophy of John Dewey*, 2nd edn. New York: Crossroad.

Dougherty, B. (1988) 'DEC warns of hidden costs', *Financial Review*, 18 July: 63.

Duran, J.P. (1990) 'Information technology and the legacy of Taylorism in France', *Employment and Society*, 4(3): 407–27.

Emery, F. and Trist, E. (1965) 'The causal texture of organizational environments', *Human Relations*, 18: 21–31.

Feyerabend, P. (1975) *Against Method*. London: NLB.

Fulk, J. (1993) 'Social construction of communication technology', *Academy of Management Journal*, 36: 921–50.

Gadamer, H.G. (1992) *Truth and Method*, 2nd edn. New York: Crossroad.

Garton, Laura and Wellman, Barry (1995) 'Social impacts of electronic mail in organizations: a review of the research literature', in *Communication Yearbook 18*. pp. 434–53.

Gergen, K. (1982) *Toward Transformation in Social Knowledge*. New York: Springer-Verlag.

Gersick, C.J.G. (1988) 'Time and transition in work teams: toward a new model of group development', *Academy of Management Journal*, 31: 9–41.

Giddens, A. (1979) *Central Problems in Social Theory*. London: Macmillan.

Ginnett, R.C. (1990) 'The airline cockpit crew', in J.R. Hackman (ed.), *Groups that Work (and Those that Don't): Creating Conditions for Effective Teamwork*. San Francisco: Jossey-Bass.

Gutek, B.A., Sasse, S.H. and Bikson, T.K. (1986) 'The fit between technology and work group structure: the structural contingency approach and office automation'. Paper presented at Conference on Technology: its Meaning, Measurement and Impact in the Age of Computerized Work, Academy of Management, Chicago.

Guzzo, R.A. and Dickson, M.W. (1996) 'Teams in organizations: recent research on performance and effectiveness', *Annual Review of Psychology*, 47: 307–40.

Guzzo, R.A. and Shea, G.P. (1992) 'Group performance and intergroup relations in organizations', in M.D. Dunnette and L.M. Hough (eds), *Handbook of Industrial and Organizational Psychology*, vol. 3. Palo Alto: Consulting Psychologists Press. pp. 269–313.

Hackman, J.R. (1986) 'The psychology of self-management in organizations', in M.S. Pallack and R.O. Perloff (eds), *Psychology and Work: Productivity, Change and Employment*. Washington,

DC: American Psychological Association. pp. 86–136.

Hackman, J.R. (1987) 'The design of work teams', in J.W. Lorsch (ed.), *Handbook of Organizational Behavior*. Englewood Cliffs, NJ: Prentice-Hall. pp. 315–42.

Hackman, J.R. (ed.) (1990) *Groups that Work (and Those that Don't): Creating Conditions for Effective Teamwork*. San Francisco: Jossey-Bass.

Hackman, J.R. and Oldham, G.R. (1980) *Work Redesign*. Reading, MA: Addison-Wesley.

Harré, R. (1983) *Personal Being*. Oxford: Blackwell.

Hirschheim, R.A. (1985) *Office Automation: a Social and Organizational Perspective*. London: Wiley.

Katzenbach, Jon R. and Smith, Douglas K. (1993) 'The discipline of teams', *Harvard Business Review*, March–April: 111–20.

Kiesler, Sara and Sproull, Lee (1992) 'Group decision making and communication technology', *Organizational Behavior and Human Decision Processes*, 52: 96–123.

Kohut, Thomas, L. (1994) 'The mutuality of influence: using the theory of structuration to explore organisations and information technology'. Dissertation for Bachelor of Commerce with Honours, Griffith University.

Kraemer, K.L. and Danziger, J.N. (1990) 'The impacts of computer technology on the work life of information workers', *Social Science Computer Review*, 8(4): 592–613.

Kraut, R., Dumais, S. and Koch, S. (1989) 'Computerisation, productivity and quality of work-life', *Communications of the ACM*, 32: 220–38.

Lawler, E.E., Mohrman, S.A. and Ledford, G.E. Jr (1992) *Employee Involvement and Total Quality Management: Practices and Results in Fortune 1000 Companies*. San Francisco: Jossey-Bass.

Levine, J.M. and Moreland, R.L. (1990) 'Progress in small group research', *Annual Review of Psychology*, 41: 585–634.

Losada, Marcial, Sánchez, Pedro and Noble, Elizabeth E. (1990) 'Collaborative technology and group process feedback: their impact on interactive sequences in meetings', in *Proceedings of the Conference on Computer-Supported Cooperative Work*, 7–10 October, Los Angeles. New York: Association for Computing Machinery. pp. 53–64.

MacIntyre, A. (1985) *After Virtue*. London: Duckworth.

Markus, M.L. and Robey, D. (1988) 'Information technology and organizational change: causal structure in theory and research', *Management Science*, 34: 583–98.

Maturana, H. and Varela, F. (1980) *Autopoiesis and Cognition*. Dordrecht, Holland: D. Reidel.

McGrath, Joseph E. (1984) *Group: Interaction and Performance*. Englewood Cliffs, NJ: Prentice-Hall.

McGrath, Joseph E. (1990) 'Time matters in groups', in J. Galegher, R.E. Kraut and C. Egido (eds), *Intellectual Teamwork: Social and Technological Foundations of Cooperative Work*. Hillsdale, NJ: Lawrence Erlbaum. pp. 23–62.

McGrath, Joseph E. (1991) 'Time, interaction, and performance (TIP): a theory of groups', *Small Group Research*, 22(2): 147–74.

McGrath, J.E. and O'Connor, K.M. (1996) 'Temporal issues in work groups', in M.A. West (ed.), *Handbook of Workgroup Psychology*. Chichester, UK: John Wiley. pp. 25–52.

McKenny, James L., Zack, Michael H. and Doherty, Victor S. (1992) 'Complementary communication media: a comparison of electronic mail and face-to-face communication in a programming team', in N. Hohria and R.G. Eccles (eds), *Networks and Organizations: Structure, Form, and Action*. Boston: Harvard Business School Press. pp. 262–87.

Nelson, D.L. (1990) 'Individual adjustment to information driven technologies: a critical review', *MIS Quarterly*, Special Issue, 79–98.

Nohria, Nitin and Eccles, Robert (1992) 'Face-to-face: making network organizations work', in N. Nohria and R.G. Eccles (eds), *Networks and Organizations: Structure, Form, and Action*. Boston: Harvard Business School Press. pp. 288–308.

Nord, W. (1985) 'Can organizational culture be managed? A synthesis', in P. Frost, L. Moore, M. Louis, L. Lundberg and I. Martin (eds), *Organizational Culture*. Beverley Hills, CA: Sage. pp. 187–96.

Orlikowski, W.J. (1992) 'The duality of technology: rethinking the concept of technology in organisations', *Organisation Science*, 3(3): 398–427.

Pearce, W.B. and Cronen, V. (1987) 'Intervention: technologies for changing social systems'. Paper presented at Conflict Intervention Conference, Temple University, 26–28 March.

Penman, Robyn (1988) 'Communication reconstructed', *Journal for the Theory of Social Behaviour*, 18: 301–10.

Penman, Robyn (1991) 'Goals, games and moral orders: a paradoxical case in court', in K. Tracy (ed.), *Goals and Discourse*. Hillsdale, NJ: Lawrence Erlbaum.

Penman, Robyn (1992) 'Good theory and good practice: an argument in progress', *Communication Theory*, 2(3): 234–50.

Penman, Robyn (1995) 'Communicating: a moral frame(up)', *Australian Journal of Communication*, 22(2): 48–58.

Penman, Robyn (1997) 'The researcher in communication: the primary position', in J. Owen (ed.), *Context and Communication*. Reno, NV: Context Press. pp. 337–51.

Philp, M. (1985) 'Michel Foucault', in Q. Skinner (ed.), *The Return of Grand Theory in the Human Sciences*. Cambridge: Cambridge University Press. pp. 65–82.

Polley, Douglas and Van Dyne, Linn (1994) 'The limits and liabilities of self-managing work teams', *Advances in Interdisciplinary Studies of Work Teams*, 1: 1–38.

Reddy, M. (1979) 'The conduit metaphor', in A.

Ortony (ed.), *Metaphor and Thought*. London: Cambridge University Press. pp. 301–22.

Rice, R.E. (1984) 'Development of new media research', in R.E. Rice (ed.), *The New Media*. Beverley Hills, CA: Sage. pp. 15–31.

Rice, R.E. (1992) 'Task analyzability, use of new media, and effectiveness: a multi-site exploration of media richness', *Organization Science*, 3(4): 475–98.

Robey, D. (1986) *Designing Organizations*, 2nd edn. Homewood, IL: Richard D. Irwin.

Robey, D. (1987) 'Implementation and the organizational impacts of information systems', *Interfaces*, 17: 72–84.

Robey, D. and Azevedo, A. (1991) 'Information technology and organisational culture'. Paper presented to the College of Business Administration, Florida International University, Miami, Florida.

Rorty, R. (1980) *Philosophy and the Mirror of Nature*. Oxford: Blackwell.

Ross, Jerry and Staw, Barry M. (1986) 'Expo 86: an escalation prototype', *Administrative Science Quarterly*, 131: 274–9.

Ross, Jerry and Staw, Barry M. (1993) 'Organizational escalation and exit: lessons from the Shoreham nuclear power plant', *Academy of Management Journal*, 36(4): 701–32.

Ryle, G. (1963) *The Concept of Mind*. Harmondsworth: Penguin.

Shannon, C.E. and Weaver, W. (1949) *Mathematical Theory of Communication*. Urbana, IL: University of Illinois Press.

Shepherd, G. (1993) 'Building a discipline of communication', *Journal of Communication*, 43(3): 83–91.

Shotter, J. (1986) 'A sense of place: Vico and the social production of social identities', *British Journal of Social Psychology*, 25: 199–211.

Shotter, J. (1990) *Knowing of the Third Kind*. Utrecht: ISOR.

Shotter, J. (1993) *Cultural Politics of Everyday Life*. Toronto: University of Toronto Press.

Shulman, A.D. and Steinman, J.I. (1978) 'Interpersonal teleconferencing in an organizational context', in M. Elton (ed.), *The Evaluation and Planning of Interpersonal Telecommunication Systems*. New York: Plenum. pp. 399–424.

Shulman, A.D., Penman, R. and Sless, D. (1990) 'Putting information technology in its place', in J. Carroll (ed.), *Applied Social Psychology and Organizational Settings*. Hillsdale, NJ: Lawrence Erlbaum. pp. 155–92.

Shulman, A.D. and Penman, R. (1992) 'Developing information infrastructures that work', in *Service Delivery Communications in the 1990s*. Canberra: Department of Transport and Communication. pp. 1–7.

Siegel, J., Dubrovsky, V., Kiesler, S. and McGuire, T.O. (1986) 'Group processes in computer mediated communication', *Organizational Behavior and Human Decision Processes*, 37: 157–87.

Sless, D. (1981) *Learning and Visual Communication*. London: Croom Helm.

Sless, D. (1986a) *In Search of Semiotics*. London: Croom Helm.

Sless, D. (1986b) 'Repairing messages: the hidden cost of inappropriate theory', *Australian Journal of Communication*, 9(10): 82–93.

Sless, D. (1991) 'Communication and certainty', *Australian Journal of Communication*, 18(3): 19–31.

Smith, Ken G., Carroll, Stephen J. and Ashford, Susan J. (1995) 'Intra- and interorganizational cooperation: toward a research agenda', *Academy of Management Journal*, 38(1): 7–23.

Steiner, I.D. (1972) *Group Process and Productivity*. New York: Academic Press.

Sundstrom, E., De Meuse, K.P. and Futrell, D. (1990) 'Work teams: applications and effectiveness', *American Psychologist*, 45: 120–33.

Taylor, James C. and Felten, David F. (1993) *Performance by Design: Sociotechnical Systems in North America*. Englewood Cliffs, NJ: Prentice-Hall.

Tomarzky, L.G. (1986) 'Technological change and the structure of work', in M.S. Pallak and R.O. Perloff (eds), *Psychology and Work: Productivity, Change and Employment*. Washington, DC: American Psychological Association. pp. 53–84.

Vico, G. (1986) *The New Science of Giambattista Vico*, translated and edited by T. Bergin and M. Fisch. Ithaca, NY: Cornell University Press.

Walther, Joseph B. (1994) 'Anticipated ongoing interaction versus channel effects on relational communication in computer-mediated interaction', *Human Communication Research*, 20(4): 473–501.

Wilde, W. (1991) *Office 2000: Business Process Management*. Waltham, MA: Wang Laboratories.

Zuboff, S. (1988) *In the Age of the Smart Machine*. New York: Basil Books.

# 7

# Metaphors of Communication and Organization

## LINDA L. PUTNAM, NELSON PHILLIPS AND PAMELA CHAPMAN

Perhaps no other construct pervades organizational studies more than the term *communication*. The ubiquitous nature of the term, however, contributes to its elusiveness and to the difficulty in distinguishing it from such related terms as *information, channel*, and *media* and from the myriad of organizational concepts that incorporate nuances of the term. Classical organizational theorists have equated communication with written documents and the authority to give commands (Weber 1947), the upward flow of messages and the persuasion of workers (Taylor 1947), the horizontal flow of information (Fayol 1949), listening and informal communication (Roethlisberger 1941), feedback and circular behavior (Follett 1941), decision premises (Simon 1957), and formal channels of communication (Barnard 1968). Contemporary organizational theorists treat communication as synonymous with such constructs as information processing (Galbraith 1973), social networks (Rogers and Kincaid 1981; Tichy and Fombrun 1979), coordination (Hage 1974), and participation (Likert 1967; Miller and Monge 1986). Communication, then, has become a catch-all term that infuses most topics in organization studies and crosses most chapters in this *Handbook*.

Confusion also exists, at both the theoretical and the practical level, concerning the relationship between organization and communication (Smith 1993; Taylor 1995; Taylor and Van Every 1993). Do organizations determine the type and flow of communication or does communication shape the nature of organizing? Does message flow follow organizational structure or do communication patterns develop structures and shape task-related coordination? In effect, how does the organizational context affect communication and how does communication shape the organizational context?

Smith (1993) sets forth three ways that organization and communication are related: containment, production, and equivalency. The *containment* relationship treats communication as located within a reified, materialistic organizational structure. Thus, the structural-functional elements of communication are critical to the maintenance of the organizational container. The second type of relationship, *production*, examines the way organizations produce communication, or communication produces organization, or the two co-produce each other. That is, organizations are not simply containers in which communication activities occur, but rather communication and organization may produce each other. For example, the sharing of rituals enacts organizational culture as it operates from the residual of past communication practices. The production relationship, then, wrestles with the dilemma of whether one has *a priori* existence over the other or do they develop concomitantly. The third approach, *equivalence*, posits an even more radical turn in this relationship. It treats communication and organization as a monastic unity or as the same phenomenon expressed in different ways. That is, communicating is organizing and organizing is communicating: the two processes are isomorphic (Smith 1993; Taylor 1995).

This dilemma on the relationship between organizing and communicating calls into question the metaphors that we use to depict organizations (Morgan 1986). In these metaphors, organization is placed in the role of *figure* or principal subject, and communication assumes the position of *ground* or secondary subject (Black 1962; Taylor 1995). Thus, traditional images of organizations are influenced by relationships in which communication plays a non-existent or tangential role. But, if we take communication theory as central and equivalent to organizing, new metaphors emerge that represent the organization–communication relationship in different ways. Thus, for the purpose of exploring this relationship, the organizing scheme of this chapter positions communication as the producer of organizations. However, even though this chapter privileges communication, it examines metaphors that exemplify all three of Smith's (1993) orientations. These metaphors reveal alternative ways of thinking about the origin and nature of organizing, its processes, and the constructs that form its ontological roots.

Beginning with a brief overview of organizational communication, this chapter tracks the history and chronology of research domains within the field. Then it discusses how the study of metaphor has surfaced in the organizational literature. We then examine seven metaphor clusters that represent different threads of organizational communication research: conduit, lens, linkage, performance, symbol, voice, and discourse. Each of these metaphors introduces alternative ways of seeing organizations which emerge from the communication–organization relationship. The conclusion then unpacks the nuances of this relationship for these metaphors, discusses the contributions and omissions of each, and explores the implications of this analysis for developing organizational theories.

This chapter is not an exhaustive review of the organizational communication literature, as it appears in Jablin et al. (1987), Goldhaber and Barnett (1988), or Jablin and Putnam (forthcoming). Readers searching for reviews of the extensive body of organizational communication research should consult these volumes. Instead, this chapter casts a broad stroke across the canvas of this literature to highlight studies that illustrate the various metaphors. Thus, the literature cited within each section serves primarily as exemplars of the field. Criteria for selecting exemplars include: relevance to the metaphor cluster, recency of the work, and representation of a wide array of research domains. This chapter, then, reviews and integrates a complex body of communication literature, not only to show its relevance to organization studies, but also to explain how different streams of this work can illuminate our understanding of what organizations *are*.

## HISTORY AND DEVELOPMENT OF ORGANIZATIONAL COMMUNICATION RESEARCH

The early work in organizational communication was shaped by interests in business and industrial communication from the 1920s to the 1950s and the human relations movement from the 1950s to the mid 1970s. The writings of Dale Carnegie and texts on business rhetoric focused on the persuasive strategies of top management, the accuracy and readability of reports, and the effectiveness of different communication media (Putnam and Cheney 1985; Redding 1985). In the 1960s and 1970s, the dominant perspective shifted to the study of messages that flowed through organizations and the way communication climates influenced the adequacy and effectiveness of these transmissions. Throughout this work, communication was treated as a variable that influenced individual and organizational performance.

Two dominant interests, then, formed the foundation of the field: (1) the skills that made individuals more effective communicators on the job; and (2) the factors that characterized system-wide communication effectiveness (Redding and Tompkins 1988). This period, called the *modernist* orientation, depicted the majority of work conducted prior to the 1980s (Putnam and Cheney 1985; Redding and Tompkins 1988). It also subsumed psychological studies that focused on such topics as superior–subordinate interaction, communication climate, and information processing as well as sociological studies that centred on communication networks, work group coordination, and adoption and use of new communication technologies.

In the modernist tradition, organizations were rational, instrumental entities; thus, communication embodied a utilitarian or instrumental bias. Both organizations and communication were objective realities that could be measured and tested under controlled research conditions with methodological tools borrowed from the natural sciences. Modernists also embraced the idea of objective boundaries that separated hierarchical levels, departmental units, and organizational parameters (Redding and Tompkins 1988).

The early 1980s marked a radical shift in organizational communication scholarship, although not necessarily a complete break with the past. Concomitant with similar critiques in organizational studies, scholars challenged the research traditions in organizational communication, particularly the absence of theoretical frameworks and the nature of organizational reality embedded in modernist work (Putnam and Cheney 1983; Redding and Tompkins 1988). Nested within these critiques were challenges to the treatment of communication as a variable or a linear transmission (Putnam 1983). Organizational communication became defined as 'the study of messages, information, meaning, and symbolic activity' that constitutes organizations (Putnam and Cheney, 1985: 131). New research domains began to focus on the meanings of organizational events (Donnellon et al. 1986; Gray et al. 1985); strategic ambiguity (Eisenberg 1984); language, symbols, and organizational culture (Frost et al. 1985; Pacanowsky and O'Donnell-Trujillo 1983; Pondy et al. 1983; Rosen 1985; Smircich 1983); organizational identification and unobtrusive control (Tompkins and Cheney 1983; 1985); communication rules and scripts (Harris and Cronen 1979; Schall 1983); corporate public discourse (Cheney 1983; Cheney and Vibbert 1987; Grunig 1984); and the exercise of power and control through distorted communication (Conrad 1983; Deetz and Kersten 1983; Edwards 1979; Riley 1983).

One stream of research, *naturalistic*, centred on making interpretations grounded in context and situation. Naturalists adopted a stance that was pluralistic by viewing organizational life from multiple perspectives, not just managerial ones. Since organizational boundaries and structures were socially constituted, they were permeable and negotiable. Another orientation was that of the *critical* approach, which appeared in the mid to late 1980s. This orientation extended social constructivist views by centering on power and control. It purported that individuals and groups had differential control in constructing the meanings that mattered in organizations. Since dominant groups had more access to information and more opportunities to construct broad-ranged interpretations than did other groups, communicative processes in organizations were not neutral (Deetz 1985; Deetz and Kersten 1983). Discourse, symbolic actions, and meaning were the ways that ideology became natural and legitimate in organizations and the way subordinate groups participated in their own domination (Deetz and Kersten 1983; Mumby 1988).

This overview provides a framework for thinking about topics and research domains in organizational communication, but it fails to uncover the subtle and complex ways that communication and organization are interrelated. Moreover, it does not account for new developments in discourse and language analysis that set forth what communication is and how it operates as organizing. One of the ways to unpack these complexities is to probe into the metaphors of organizational communication that represent research domains in the field. In particular, this chapter centers on the subtle features of metaphor clusters that reveal diverse representations of communication and organization.

## METAPHORS AND IMAGES OF ORGANIZATIONS

Metaphor has become a common topic in organizational studies (Brink 1993; Deetz 1986; Deetz and Mumby 1985; Krefting and Frost 1985; Koch and Deetz 1981; Manning 1979; Morgan 1980; 1983; 1986; Pinder and Bourgeois 1982; Pepper 1995; Pondy 1983; Smith and Eisenberg 1988; Smith and Turner 1995; Stohl 1995; Trice and Beyer 1984). Although originally examined as a literary trope, metaphors are more than ornaments that decorate language. They operate at multiple levels of analysis to provide insights into how we understand organizational life.

A metaphor is a way of seeing a thing as if it were something else (Lakoff and Johnson 1980). It is a particular linguistic expression that provides a cognitive bridge between two dissimilar domains. For some theorists, metaphors link abstract constructs to concrete things (Ortony 1979), while for others, metaphors tie the familiar to the unknown (Hawkes 1972). Perhaps even more significantly, metaphors legitimate actions, set goals, and guide behaviors (Lakoff and Johnson 1980). Metaphors are also constitutive in that they facilitate the creation and interpretation of social reality. In effect, metaphors shape how we see and make sense of the world by orienting our perceptions, conceptualizations, and understanding of one thing in light of another.

Metaphor is probably best understood as a system of beliefs about figure and ground relationships which serve to highlight certain features while suppressing others. For example, to treat organizational mergers as 'ambushes and shootouts' highlights the surprise attack, hostile takeover, winners and losers, and hired guns who orchestrate the deal (Hirsch and Andrews 1983). This imagery, however, conceals the wooing, matchmaking, and compatibility issues that a courtship metaphor might reveal. In this chapter, different elements of communication surface as figure for some metaphors and ground for other ways of thinking. What becomes highlighted about organizational communication reveals the nature of the metaphor.

## Functions of Metaphor Analysis

Metaphors facilitate theory building by examining images at multiple levels of analysis. In organizational theory, metaphor analysis contributes to theory construction through: (1) articulating the ontological assumptions of different views of organizations (Morgan 1980; 1986); (2) revealing the assumptive ground of key organizational constructs (Alvesson 1993a; Buzzanell and Goldzwig 1991; Smith and Turner 1995; Stutman and Putnam 1994); and (3) generating new constructs such as a garbage can model of decision-making (Cohen et al. 1972). Organizational members also use metaphors to depict their own organizations. Metaphors such as families, zoos, savage tribes, and sporting games are ways that members construct implicit theories of organizing (Deetz 1986; Koch and Deetz 1981). Of these approaches, the most cited study of metaphors is Morgan's (1986) *Images of Organizations*. By examining dominant theories and research domains in organizational studies, Morgan uncovers diverse images that depict different ways that individuals conceive of organizations. Each image is partial, highlights different features of organizations, finds roots in diverse organizational assumptions, and embodies different strengths and weaknesses. His analysis delineates dominant or root metaphors of organizations such as machines, organisms, cultures, psychic prisons, brains, political systems, and instruments of domination. These metaphors are referenced extensively in both the communication and the management literatures (May 1993; Miller 1995; Stohl 1995).

## METAPHORS OF COMMUNICATION AND ORGANIZATION

This chapter calls into question the traditional metaphors used to depict organizations by exploring relationships between communication and organization represented in the research literature (Smith 1993; Taylor 1995). By taking communication as figure and organization as ground, we hope to unearth new ways of thinking about organizations, as well as alternative metaphors that lie in the spaces between figure and ground and within the schisms inherent in the field. In effect, this project moves away from such universal metaphors as machines and organisms as cornerstones of organizational theory.

This chapter also departs from earlier work by developing metaphor clusters within the organizational communication literature. A cluster refers to groups of metaphors or submetaphors that can be arrayed as distinct but interrelated categories. Within each cluster, metaphors subsume other metaphors, including ones that embody different assumptive ground about organizations.

A major weakness of traditional metaphor analysis is a tendency to lock categories into fixed meanings and relationships. Smith and Turner (1995) overcome this problem by employing chains of figure–ground relationships in which the ground, once presented, becomes the figure for the next metaphor. Through continual reflexivity in their analysis, they uncover the assumptions that underlie relationships among metaphors. Even though this chapter relies on traditional metaphor analysis, it tries to avoid freezing metaphorical relationships by tracking chains of metaphors between the categories.

First, we identify seven metaphor clusters that direct or guide research programs in organizational communication. Next, we describe the central features of these metaphors; note streams and schools of metaphor clusters that stem from these images; illustrate how these metaphors are employed in recent organizational communication studies; and describe how they cast the communication–organization relationship in very different ways. In the conclusion, we track chains of metaphors between the categories and clusters. The seven metaphor clusters are conduit, lens, linkage, performance, symbol, voice, and discourse. This list of metaphors is neither exhaustive nor mutually exclusive. In many respects, metaphors represent 'blurred genres' (Geertz 1973) and mutations (Weick 1979). The conclusion of this chapter, then, explores the ways that these seven metaphors overlap and contradict.

The *conduit metaphor* encompasses orientations to communication that treat organizations as *containers* or channels for amount, type, direction, and structure of information flow. Research domains that embrace this perspective focus on communication as *transmission*, and include studies on information overload and adequacy; comparisons among communication media; communication technology as media choice; communication as a tool for accomplishing organizational goals; directionality of communication flow; and organizational units as communication hubs or nodes. Metaphor clusters subsumed in this category include tool, channel, and media.

The *metaphor of lens* provides a different slant on the conduit view of communication. This cluster centers on the literature that treats organizations as perceptual systems or *eyes* that scan the environment, filter data, distort and delay information, screen or gatekeep, route messages, and disseminate innovation and change. Thus communication is *filtered* and often distorted as it passes through the various 'membranes' between organization and environment, between departments, and between individuals. Metaphors subsumed within this category include gatekeeper, sensor, and shield. The *linkage metaphor* treats organizations as *networks* or systems of interconnected individuals in which communication acts to *connect* by forming relational bonds; patterns of contacts and interconnectedness; global integration; and ties among work, home, and community (Stohl 1995). Metaphors that appear in this cluster include web, bridge, bonds, and relationships.

The next cluster of metaphors shifts from the transmission roots of communication to highlight meaning, interpretation, and sensemaking as the nature of organizing. Drawn from social constructivist roots, the *metaphor of performance* casts communication as *social interaction*, as seen in the work on jamming and improvisation, performing managerial roles, shared meanings, and theatrical productions. In this metaphor, organizations emerge as *coordinated actions*. Metaphors subsumed in this category include enactments, co-production, drama, and storytelling. The *metaphor of symbol* draws from organizational culture to cast communication as interpretation of literary forms such as narratives, metaphors, rites and rituals, and paradoxes. These symbols are not simply artifacts of cultures; instead they operate as a means of public persuasion, as ways of knowing, as options for managing identities, and as political control. Thus, the organization emerges as a *novel* jointly authored by organizational members as they create and interpret a range of symbolic activities. Metaphors subsumed in this category are semiotics, sign, culture, and shared meanings.

Drawing from critical and postmodern views of organizations, the *metaphor of voice* encompasses a number of related clusters, including distorted voices; voices of domination through ideology and unobtrusive control; a different voice through feminist perspectives; and access to voice through participatory and democratic practices. Metaphor clusters that surface within the category of voice include communication distortion and conflict suppression (Redding and Tompkins 1988). Communication is *expression* and the organization becomes a *chorus* of stilled or singing voices. Finally, the *metaphor of discourse* is equally diverse in its underpinnings and representations of communication. It highlights communication as *conversation*, in which organizations surface as *texts* that consist of genres and dialogues. Metaphor clusters subsumed within this category include language, talk, linguistics, speech acts, emotions, and discursive practices.

These metaphors serve as alternative frames for examining the organizational communication literature and the relationship between communication and organization. They are not paradigms or discrete categories; rather they serve as perspectives to facilitate understanding the diverse and multifaceted field of organizational communication. This chapter, then, is not trying to unify divergent research metaphors, nor to embrace pluralism for pluralism's sake. Nor do we advocate that researchers borrow from a pot-pourri of metaphors, unconscious of the assumptions and obligations embedded in each. Indeed, immersion in one or several closely related submetaphors typically provides the most coherent and logically congruent line of research. Instead, this chapter seeks to generate new ways of thinking about the origins and nature of organizations by exposing readers to a body of literature than can yield new insights about organizing.

## The Conduit Metaphor

As developed from early studies on communication 'within' the organization, the most common view of communication is a conduit in which messages are transmitted throughout the organization (Axley 1984; Reddy 1979). A *conduit* is a channel through which something is conveyed, such as a tube, cable, or cylinder (Axley 1984). In this metaphor, communication is equated with *transmission* and organizations appear as *containers*, physical systems, or passageways for the conduit.

Words that signal the use of a conduit metaphor are 'send', 'exchange', 'relay', and 'convey' (Axley 1984). The conduit metaphor treats transmission as figure and message and sender/receiver as ground. Communication within this metaphor is primarily a one-way, linear flow (Shannon and Weaver 1949), even though amendments to this approach add feedback, two-way flow, and process (Rogers 1994). But the centrality of transmission remains constant, even with variations in directionality of information flow. According to this perspective, a manager who communicates 'effectively' is transferring ideas to his or her subordinates with minimal spillage (Eisenberg and Phillips 1991). Words contain information, language transfers thoughts and feelings, and listeners extract ideas from transmission (Axley 1984). The conduit metaphor evokes an image of communication as easy, effortless, and linear. Miscommunication occurs when no information is received or when the information received is not what the sender intended (Eisenberg and Phillips 1991). According to this view, receivers are typically passive and reactive.

Examples of organizational research that incorporates this metaphor include studies on: (1) the links between organizational structure and the amount of communication (Jablin 1987; Katz and Kahn 1966); (2) the uses of formal and informal communication channels (Downs 1967); (3) communication as task coordination (Allen and Hauptman 1990; Fulk et al. 1987; Tushman 1979); (4) comparisons among communication media (Rice 1993; Short et al. 1976); (5) the adoption of new communication technology (Rice and Shook 1988; 1990); (6) information overload and adequacy (Miller 1960; O'Reilly 1980); and (7) organizational units as hubs through which information passes (Zmud 1990; Rice and Aydin 1991; Zmud et al. 1990). Since the concept of communication as a conduit is so ubiquitous, other reviews cover the many domains subsumed under this metaphor (Allen et al. 1993; Fulk and Boyd 1991; Jablin 1987; Rice and Gattiker forthcoming; Redding and Tompkins 1988; Wert-Gray et al. 1991).

An image of communication that falls within this category is the tool metaphor. A *tool* is an instrument, a device, a function, or a means of accomplishing an instrumental goal. Researchers who treat communication as a tool focus on how communication influences work effectiveness, improves performance feedback, diffuses organizational innovations, and fosters organizational change (Earley 1988; Rice and Gattiker forthcoming). The tool metaphor includes research on communication technologies such as electronic mail, voice mail, audio and video conferencing, and computer conferencing. These technologies differ from face-to-face interactions in their speed, ability to span distance, asynchronous links between individuals at different points in time, and retrieval systems. It also incorporates studies of computer-assisted decision aids, such as group decision support systems (GDSS), expert systems, and management information systems (Miller 1995). Although GDSS studies on decision quality, satisfaction, and effectiveness are contradictory (Fulk and Boyd 1991), they demonstrate how scholars use communication technology as an instrument for organizational ends.

Some of the work under the tool metaphor overlaps with other metaphors. For example, work on communication technologies that emphasizes social network formation, connectedness, and task dependencies (Bikson and Eveland 1990) converges with the linkage metaphor. The work of authors like Poole and DeSanctis (1990), whose model of GDSS shows how group members interact about information technologies, and Yates and Orlikowski (1992), who examine communication media as genres, moves away from the tool metaphor toward a view of organizational communication as discourse.

The conduit and tool metaphors treat communication as an object that flows from a source to a receiver. Communication is a channel, a technology, or a task that organizational members have or must do. If information is adequate and accurate in transmission (message fidelity), communication is effective. Communication media are effective if the technologies aid in reaching organizational goals. The conduit metaphor depicts an organization as a *container* or a hollow physical object that houses communication and information systems. Containers have discrete boundaries, barriers that block information flow, and physical separation that may cause breakdowns and omissions. Thus, organizations function like telephone switchboards, computer memory banks, or television signal systems (Morgan 1986). Even research which aims to stretch the physical boundaries of organizations, for example, new communication technologies, unknowingly reifies the borders of both organization and communication.

## The Lens Metaphor

A second metaphor that complements and overlaps with the conduit view of communication is a lens. A *lens* is a screen that *filters*, protects, shields, and guides transmission. Studies that center on 'distortion', 'gatekeeping', 'blocking', 'information search and acquisition', and 'accessibility' typically exemplify the lens metaphor. In this metaphor, communication is equated with a *filtering process*: searching, retrieving, and routing information. Thus the organization, as it appears in this metaphor, is an *eye* that scans, sifts, and relays.

The lens metaphor shares some assumptions of the conduit perspective. It relies on transmission and is rooted in the transfer of ideas, but, unlike the conduit metaphor, senders and receivers are active agents in the process. Distortion and filtering occur naturally, as in the game of 'telephone' in which messages change in content and form as they travel from individual to individual and unit to unit. Message simplification, the most general level of distortion, encompasses 'abbreviations, condensations, and loss of detail that occur through message flow' (Stohl and Redding 1987: 479). Reception plays a significant role in the lens metaphor whereas sending is the critical element in the conduit perspective.

Both the eye and lens metaphors are housed in containers. Just as the lens overlaps with the conduit metaphor of communication, the eye is encased in a socket. The socket or skull has physical structure, membranes, and eyelids that control access to light. Thus, organizational boundaries and structures aid in sensing and filtering stimuli. The lens metaphor also supports a containment relationship between communication and organization. The eye contains the lens that filters and screens information.

The research in organizational communication influenced by the lens metaphor ranges from studies of information flow and superior–subordinate communication to recent work on perceived environmental uncertainty, information acquisition and decision-making, media richness, and communication technology. Early studies include how employees: suppress unpleasant messages (Tesser and Rosen 1975); distort and withhold information that travels up the channel (O'Reilly and Roberts 1974); sharpen and assimilate messages through serial transmission (Davis and O'Conner 1977; Ackoff and Emery 1972); and provide access to information sources (O'Reilly 1978). These studies concentrate primarily on what senders believe that receivers want to hear.

Research on performance feedback that focuses on the timing and the delivery of messages exemplifies the lens metaphor (Cusella 1987). Studies on information sources, perceptions of ambiguity, accessibility and decision-making, and consequences of information seeking behaviors also employ themes drawn from the lens metaphor (Miller and Jablin 1991; O'Reilly et al. 1987; Stohl and Redding 1987). In these studies, the organization functions visually to open and close access to information and to route internal and external stimuli.

Two research domains that adopt a lens metaphor merit further consideration. Media richness, as one domain, purports that some communication channels which limit natural language use filter or screen out more verbal and nonverbal cues more than do others. The richest media convey the greatest amount of information (Daft and Lengel 1984; Trevino et al. 1987). Media richness theorists contend that managers will be more effective if they choose a communication medium that matches the ambiguity of their task. Although some research supports this hypothesis (Daft et al. 1987; Russ et al. 1990), other studies claim that managers are not rational in their media use and that the

characteristics of media are not necessarily objective or stable (Rice 1993; Rice et al. 1989).

The second domain guides the research on information environments, contributing not just to the ways that organizations process external cues, but also to conceptions of the environment itself. The lens metaphor underlies research on strategy formulation and implementation, image making and public relations, and stakeholder interaction. These studies examine how organizations process and interpret external information and how they influence stakeholders through external information flow.

When organizations act as sensors, top managers scan the environment and construct images or visual pictures of external stimuli (Daft et al. 1993; Huber 1991; Pfeffer and Salancik 1978). They attend to particular stimuli more closely if they are addressing broad-based, nonroutine problems than if they are just scanning (Glick et al. 1993). Organizations that engage in intense scanning and high levels of performance monitoring are more effective at handling environmental problems than are those that lack routine monitoring (Eisenhardt 1989; Huber 1991).

In addition to scanning environments, organizations manage external information flow to organizational publics (Grunig 1984; Grunig and Grunig 1992). Strategic public relations employs the lens metaphor to examine one-way (inside–outside) and two-way (inside–outside, outside–inside) dissemination between organizations and stakeholders. Two-way dissemination models preempt problems and ascertain risks by actively defining stakeholder relationships (Heath 1988). Two-way models, then, spill over into the performance metaphor of communication in which environments are enacted rather than perceived.

A basic assumption of the lens metaphor is that information is incomplete. In transmitting a message, different backgrounds and goals of senders and receivers increase the likelihood that information will be converted, simplified, reduced, or summarized (Smith 1973; Stohl and Redding 1987). The inevitability of misperception challenges traditional notions of accuracy, clarity, and communication effectiveness by introducing meaning and interpretation into message transmission.

Ambiguity and misunderstanding of messages are not necessarily breakdowns in communication as the conduit metaphor would suggest (Eisenberg and Phillips 1991; Eisenberg and Witten 1987). Rather they result from message modification and the need to balance relational and political goals. Ambiguity, defined as the failure to understand the link between a symbol and a referent, may be intentional. In this respect, the lens metaphor plays an important symbolic role in promoting surveillance, fostering legitimation, and providing evidence of rationality (Feldman and March 1981). The lens metaphor overlaps with the performance metaphor through using ambiguity strategically to unify diverse goals, protect confidentiality, build camaraderie, and facilitate organizational change (Eisenberg 1984). Misperception, then, is inevitable and information acquisition is slow. Consequently, the issue is no longer accuracy but plausibility (Sutcliffe forthcoming). Thus, taking action provides a better test for plausibility and learning than does continual scanning and filtering (Weick 1990).

The image of organizations for the lens metaphor is the *eye*, or the visual organ of sight. The eye represents perception, point of view, the center of visual processing. Even though it is part of the brain's information processing system (Morgan 1986), the eye is the center or the core in which perception activities function, like the 'eye of the storm', or 'the eye of a flower'. Information processing in organizations, although linked to cognition, is a visual process in that the eye performs the critical perceptual functions. The lens metaphor, however, highlights the boundaries and structural properties of organizations; scanning and screening occur across static borders. Perception, the locus of organizing, alters the way that information is conceived.

## The Linkage Metaphor

The conduit and lens metaphors of organizational communication share an interest in transmission and in treating organizations as containers. The linkage metaphor shifts the focus from transmission to *connection*. Thus, the communication is the connector that links people together and constitutes organizations as *networks* of relationships. In the linkage metaphor, organizations are not entities with fixed structures and boundaries. Interactants are intertwined through dyadic processes that reside within relationships rather than perceptual systems. Thus, the relationship between communication and organization moves from one of containment to one of production. Network studies, however, vary as to whether organizations produce communication or communication produces organizations. In research on network roles and structures, organizations produce linkages; while in the studies on emergent networks, communication produces organizations.

The metaphor of linkage, however, continues to rely on a conduit view of communication in that transmission and amount of communica-

tion are the key elements that connect individuals and units together. Recent work on semantic networks depart from this tradition (Stohl 1993). Linkages define network roles, create patterns and structures, determine the strength or weakness of ties, and shape interorganizational networks (Monge and Eisenberg 1987). The degree of participation or inclusion in networks stems from the presence or absence of a link, the amount of communication exchanged, the directionality of messages, and the kinds of content that flow through a link. Propensity to form communication links emanates from structural properties of networks, interpersonal attraction, proximity and contextual factors, and social activity patterns (McPhee and Corman 1995). A few studies explore linkages formed through vocabularies and interpretations rather than frequency of contacts (Monge and Eisenberg 1987). These studies move toward a symbol rather than a conduit metaphor.

The metaphor of linkage underlies research on *network roles*, the structural positions of individuals within a network. Isolates are individuals who have few communication links. Bridges, liaisons, and linking pins connect individuals and groups (Farace et al. 1977); while stars are individuals who have many linkages, both inside and outside the network (Tushman and Scanlan 1981). Stars may also be boundary spanners, ambassadors, or guards who survey, monitor, and exchange information with groups outside the network (Ancona and Caldwell 1988). Role configurations also emerge from interaction strategies and task activities. Barley's (1986; 1990) research demonstrates how communication links based on expertise, technology, and task activity shape informal roles that counter formal organizational positions of medical personnel. This positional approach to the study of networks differs from the relational or emergent perspective by treating organizational boundaries as *a priori* and by treating organizations as producing communication networks.

*Network patterns and structures* also vary in centrality, formality, content, and density (Monge and Eisenberg 1987). Centralized networks have a high degree of vertical differentiation, many isolates, and few liaisons, while decentralized networks involve more participation and information sharing (Pearce and David 1983). Centrality, however, is determined by arrangements of individuals in formal positions (Bavelas 1950; Leavitt 1951) and it is criticized for presuming that roles and structures are stable and for assuming that formal arrangements such as organizational charts determine information flow (Monge and Eisenberg 1987).

Studies of centralized/decentralized networks also examine discrepancies between the formal and the informal patterns. For example, Davis (1953) notes how the grapevine or rumor mill travels diagonally across the organizational hierarchy. Both the informality and the dynamic quality of the grapevine contribute to its speed and kernels of accuracy (Hellweg 1987). Studies that track who talks to whom, how often, and about what topics map configurations of cliques, groups, and isolates (Monge and Contractor 1988). The properties that aid in forming these configurations include numbers of contacts per week (frequency of communication), agreement on type of linkage shared (reciprocity), and one-way versus two-way communication (symmetry/asymmetry).

Network configurations also vary in content of communication, with organizational members developing different networks for task, innovation, and social support activities (Albrecht and Ropp 1984; Albrecht and Hall 1991). If individuals talk only about one function, they develop a uniplex network; if they deal with multiple topics in their interactions, they form multiplex linkages. Multiplex linkages provide richer information, are more enduring and stable, and are more influential and supportive than are relationships that share only one or two topics (Albrecht and Hall 1991; Stohl 1995).

Research on the function and content of communication casts linkages as producing organizations. Organizations move from uniplex to multiplex relationships by extending the function of work teams to innovation, social support, and occupational networks (Stohl 1995). As work teams develop complex networks among employees, they typically increase concertive control and reduce dependence on authority structures (Barker 1993). Linkages among church members also develop informally from the number, size, and type of communication activities of individuals (McPhee and Corman 1995).

Network patterns also vary in density, defined as the ratio of actual contacts to the total number of possible linkages in the system. Density of a network plays a key role in adopting new ideas. Close connections among employees make people feel more comfortable with an innovation (Albrecht and Hall 1991) and facilitate positive attitudes toward new communication technologies (Fulk 1993; Rice et al. 1990). In fact, having a critical mass of users in a dense network is vital for the adoption of e-mail and voice mail systems (Ehrlich 1987; Fulk et al. 1990; Rice and Danowski 1993). Drawing from a social influence theory, Schmitz and Fulk (1991) attribute this pattern to the support that coworkers provide, vicarious learning of the new media, and norms for how the new media should be used (Fulk and Boyd 1991).

Dense or tightly interconnected links form *strong ties* in which frequent communication links endure for long periods of time. Individuals joined through strong ties experience greater pressure to adopt norms, values, and expectations than do employees who are loosely coupled (Stohl 1995). Although dense networks are supportive, they become self-conforming and may inhibit opportunities for risk, change, and adaptability (Papa 1990). Thus, *weak ties* maintain an organization's stability and help it adapt to environmental changes. As a whole, organizational members acquire more information from multiple, loosely connected links than from dense, tightly coupled ones (Granovetter 1973).

Patterns of loose and tight couplings also affect *interorganizational networks*. Interorganizational networks are fields or systems of organizations; thus, an organization's environment can be viewed as a network (Perrow 1986). Jolts or rapid changes within this network can disrupt an entire industry of tightly coupled linkages (Eisenberg and Goodall 1993). Organizations communicate with each other through interlocking boards of directors, interaction among boundary spanners (Adams 1980), and exchanging personnel (Eisenberg et al. 1985). Organizations form interdependent and complementary services, for example providing parts for assembling an engine, or passing clients to each other. They develop linkages through joint ventures, agency-sponsored projects, and trade associations (Oliver 1990). These connections allow organizations to enhance their legitimacy and meet legal and regulatory requirements. Many linkages form through contacts outside of work, for example at professional and occupational meetings (Stohl 1995).

The study of interorganizational linkages treats communication as a connector or a contact system. In most studies, communication is implicit, defined as a tool for building the network. One type of research, however, departs from this approach by treating communication as sensemaking formed through relationships. Rather than focusing on information flow, a sensemaking perspective highlights the symbolic nature of communication, reinforcing the position that communication produces organizations. In particular, research on semantic networks examines the connections between people who hold similar interpretations of key organizational events (Monge and Eisenberg 1987). In a study of mission statements, dense semantic networks indicate that employees share perceptions of the organization's goals and its culture (Stohl 1993).

Rogers and Kincaid's (1981) convergence model of network analysis contends that individuals converge on shared meanings through network participation. Studies of memorable messages illustrate how particular phrases hold significance for network members. Individuals recall them readily, share them privately, and use them to determine the appropriateness of behaviors (Stohl 1986; 1993). For some postmodernists, who aim to move organizations beyond hierarchical and exploitative structures, the linkage metaphor offers opportunities for voice, democracy, and multiplicity (Rosenau 1992). Information networks focus on a plurality of voices and reduce dependence on instrumental rationality.

In the linkage metaphor, organizations consist of multiple, overlapping networks with permeable boundaries. Members are interlocked in a variety of relationships that 'transcend office walls' through community projects, child care concerns, informal friendships, neighbourhood activities, and company socials (Stohl 1995). Since communication serves as a building block that connects individuals, group, and inter-organizational levels, organizations are clusters or constellations of task activities, social interactions, innovations, and a variety of organizational processes (McPhee and Corman 1995; Mintzberg 1979).

Connections among people imply collaboration and interdependence; linkages promote coordinated action and extend webs of social influence. Since communication alters network patterns, linkages shift with issues, topics, and context. Thus, network roles and patterns are fluid and dynamic. Treating organizations as networks challenges traditional notions of static boundaries, unidimensional functions, and immobile structures.

## The Metaphor of Performance

A major factor that distinguishes the conduit, lens, and linkage metaphors from the next four perspectives is an emphasis on interaction and meaning. In the performance metaphor, *social interaction* becomes the focal point for organizational communication research. Performance refers to process and activity, rather than to an organization's productivity or output. Performance combines Turner's (1980) view of 'accomplishment' with Goffman's (1959) notion of 'presentation'. In this metaphor, 'organizational reality is brought to life in communicative performance' (Pacanowsky and O'Donnell-Trujillo 1983: 131). Communication consists of interconnected exchanges, for example, message–feedback–response, action–reaction–adjustment, symbolic action–interpretation–reflection, and action–sensemaking. Social interaction is

rooted in the sequences, patterns, and meanings that stem from exchanging verbal and nonverbal messages.

The key features that distinguish social interaction from the conduit and lens metaphors are dynamic processes, interlocking behaviors, reflexivity, sensemaking, and collaboration (Fisher 1978). Performances, then, are interactional, contextual, episodic, and improvisational (Pacanowsky and O'Donnell-Trujillo 1983). Communication becomes part of an ongoing series of cues, without a clear beginning and ending. Individuals bracket or punctuate streams of experience to make sense of their interactions (Watzlawick et al. 1967; Weick 1979). Communicative acts form patterns of contiguous acts, interlocked behaviors, episodes, and incidents. Rather than centering on task activities, organizational communication functions as passion developed through organizational storytelling, sociality through performing small talk, and politics through displaying personal strength (Pacanowsky and O'Donnell-Trujillo 1983). The flow of actions and interpretations reflects back on and constrains previous message activities.

In the performance metaphor, organizations emerge as *coordinated actions*, that is, organizations enact their own rules, structures, and environments through social interaction. Performance, however, serves as an umbrella for perspectives that stem from such diverse roots as cybernetic theory, self-referential systems, dramaturgy, symbolic interaction, phenomenology, and hermeneutics. These schools form different approaches to the metaphor of performance: those rooted in *enactment* (Weick 1979); in co-constructing or *co-production* (Boje 1991; Eisenberg 1990); and in *storytelling*, folklore, and symbolic convergence (Boje 1991; 1995; Bormann 1983; Jones et al. 1988). Social interaction is both behavioral and symbolic, with a simultaneous emphasis on action and sensemaking. Storytelling in this metaphor is not monologic but is interactionally achieved through discourse (Boje 1991). Storytellers and listeners serve as co-authors to simultaneously construct and make sense of their interactions. Researchers act as organizational detectives who engage in storytelling through constructing plots based on organizational talk (Goodall 1989) and through writing and staging organizations as theatrical productions (Mangham and Overington 1987).

*Enactment*, the first major school in the performance metaphor, emanates from Weick's (1979) model of organizing. Communication in this approach is a double interact, the basic building block of organizations. A double interact consists of an action–reaction–adjustment which forms interlocked behaviors or behavioral cycles. Individuals make sense of double interacts through retrospective analysis and causal maps. Enactment is the way individuals bracket or punctuate the streams of ongoing organizational experiences; selection is the process of interpreting these experiences through constructing causal maps or developing collective sensemaking; and retention is the storing of causal maps and routines for future action. Drawn from evolutionary theory, Weick's (1979) double interacts are triggered by organizational equivocality, which occurs when individuals interpret organizational events in multiple, plausible ways. Organizations reduce equivocality through coordinated action rather than through planning, goal-setting, or calculated decisions. People act and then reflect on their actions to make sense of organizing.

Weick's conception of organizing underlies empirical studies on the way message equivocality influences information processing (Bantz and Smith 1977; Daft and MacIntosh 1981; Kreps 1980; Putnam and Sorenson 1982); how meanings are enacted and changed as events unfold (Donnellon et al. 1986; Isabella 1990); and how media industries produce news through organizational sensemaking (Bantz 1990). Enactment also serves as a heuristic in which organizational scholars theorize about the role of communication in organizational culture (Bantz 1989; 1993); strategic management (Gioia 1986; Smircich and Stubbart, 1985); negotiation and conflict management (Putnam 1989); and public relations (Sproule 1989).

Weick's (1979) view of enactment liberates communication from its bondage as an object that is stored and transmitted. Enactment also liberates organizational environments from being objective events assessed through measures of turbulence, complexity, and load. In the enactment perspective, organizational environments are constructions. Organizations enact their environments which they, in turn, rediscover and use to constrain or to enable future actions.

In Weick's (1979) model, organizations surface as charades, improvisational theater, orchestras, and soliloquies. *Soliloquy* serves as the forerunner of self-organizing systems (Lotman 1977; Luhmann 1990). Organizations talk to themselves to clarify their surroundings and they act to discover what they are doing. The application of self-referential or auto-communication systems to organizations provides new insights into the ways that organizations develop identities and markets through interactions with stakeholders and publics (Cheney and Christensen forthcoming; Steier and Smith 1992). Both the enactment and the soliloquy approaches treat communication as producing organizations.

In Weick's (1979) model, enactment continues to ground social interaction and sensemaking in

individuals rather than collaborative processes or cultural performances (Taylor and Robichaud 1992). A variation on this approach captures the *co-productive process* in which communication arises collectively rather than through an individual's cognitive experience. Co-productions are collaborative performances that stem from the way participants come together to produce social practices and coordinate local agreements. For example, improvisations of jazz performances are not simply in the minds of the musicians who created their environments; they are worked out through mutual responsiveness, complex verbal and nonverbal cues, shared focus and attention, and altercasting (Bastien and Hostager 1988; 1992). The dynamic and simultaneous flow of performance and the joint cueing of meanings of the event leads to co-constructing improvisations.

In like manner, *jamming* is a co-production in which participants experience a transcendence through suspending self-consciousness, co-orienting to each other, and surrendering to the experience (Eisenberg 1990). Jamming reflects those moments in which organizing magically comes together, as in the 'flow and zone' of street basketball or a serendipitous encounter of guitarists. As the metaphor of performance suggests, jamming and improvisation treat communication and organizations as co-constructing each other. Communication produces organizations while organizations produce communication.

Another way in which organizational members co-construct performances is through *storytelling*. Storytelling is how members dramatize organizational life and transform mundane events into passions and zeal (Pacanowsky and O'Donnell-Trujillo 1983). This approach focuses on the way organizational members introduce stories in conversations; how listeners co-produce them through prompting the teller; how stories unravel through subsequent performances of sharing them (Boje 1991). Stories, then, are not simply cultural artifacts or monologues; rather they emerge as performances that are never complete. Storytelling is often challenged by the listener who interrupts and adds elements to the narrative. Individuals often tell bits and pieces of stories with elaboration developed through pattern fitting. The chaining out of a story is adapted to different audiences through highlighting, eliminating, or modifying the narrative.

Symbolic convergence theory also emanates from storytelling, particularly through the way narratives chain out over time. Rooted in dramaturgical theory, this approach centers on how meanings, values, and motives converge through forming group narratives (Bormann

1983; 1985). As organizational members get caught up in a story, they participate in the drama and feel psychologically invested in its plot, motives, and characters. Research on teacher–administrator negotiations reveals that both sides converged on common enemies and contract issues through co-constructing stories of the accounts, past negotiators, and third-party mediators (Putnam et al. 1991). Convergence on the value of reaching a settlement was reinforced through chaining out stories on impasse and past failures to reach agreement. Symbolic convergence theory shows how organizational members come to stand on common ground through an emotional climate and an identity with the enacted drama (Bormann 1983).

At the macro level of analysis, organizations are also storytellers. Their images and identities emerge, in part, from the narratives that they construct with different publics (Alvesson 1990). In a postmodern world in which the presence of grand narratives is problematic (Lyotard, 1984), images become hyper-real: that is, many competing narratives surface, become disassociated from their signifiers, and vie for representational space (Baudrillard 1983). Images represent a world of flickering images that play upon other images, making it difficult to distinguish between the real and the pseudo-events (Boorstin 1961). Storytelling about organizations entails a plurality of narratives with multiple voices and interpretations (Boje 1995). An organization such as Disney Studios aims to write its own historical narrative, but in trying to tell its story it conflicts with and marginalizes some discourses while privileging others.

Enactment, co-constructing, and storytelling represent three diverse but related threads of the performance metaphor. This approach treats communication as an outgrowth of a collaborative process in which social and symbolic interaction is dynamic, interconnected, reflexive, and simultaneous. Meaning surfaces through retrospective sensemaking, co-constructing interpretations, and collaborative storytelling. Organizations emerge from *coordinated actions*: hence, social interaction is both the process and the product of organizing. Performance is not, however, a univocal metaphor. Multiple approaches surface through pluralistic constructions of enactments, improvisations, jamming, and storytelling. Performance, then, provides an interactive view of organizational communication, one that treats it as joint production.

## The Symbol Metaphor

Storytelling in the performance metaphor has a direct tie to organizational symbols. In this metaphor, communication functions as the creation, maintenance, and transformation of meanings (Bantz 1993; Carey 1989). In effect, the symbolic aspect of communication becomes the figure while social interaction become the ground. A symbol is something that stands for or suggests something else through association or convention (Saussure 1983). Symbols are complex signs in that they suggest cultural, historical, or political interpretations; that is, they go beyond signaling a particular response, like a traffic light indicating stop. The meaning of a symbol is typically rooted in cultural significance, for example, an emblem that represents the values and history of a nation.

In this metaphor, communication is *interpretation* through the production of symbols that make the world meaningful. Communication becomes a process of representation. Organizational members use language, exhibit insight, produce and interpret ideas, vest meaning in events, and make sense of their lives: in short, they act symbolically (Morgan et al. 1983). The organization is a complex collection of representations that define a symbolic milieu; it is a *novel* or a *literary text* that organization members inscribe as they construct their reality (Calás and Smircich 1985; Czarniawska-Joerges 1995). Researchers who embrace this perspective emphasize the complex meanings that members construct rather than the formal and rational aspects of organization (Alvesson and Berg 1992; Czarniawska-Joerges 1992). Life in organizations becomes a literary activity in which members interpret the symbols that they inscribe on the organizational landscape.

Studies that focus on the construction and maintenance of organizational cultures (Alvesson and Berg 1992; Bantz 1993; Goodall 1989; Wuthnow and Witten 1988), organizational identification and commitment (Cheney 1991); organizational folklore (Bell and Forbes 1994; Jones et al. 1988); and shared meanings (Kelly 1985; Young 1989) rely on the symbol metaphor. Studies of organizational symbols encompass a broad range of forms, from institutional architecture to company logos to reports, charts, and documents (Berg and Kreiner 1990; Daft 1983; Johnson 1977). To illustrate the symbol metaphor, however, this chapter highlights the forms linked to literature, namely, narratives, metaphors, rites and rituals, and paradox and irony.

*Narratives* are ubiquitous symbols that are prevalent in all organizations (Martin 1982). Also referred to as stories, scripts, myths, legends, and sagas, narratives are accounts of events, usually developed chronologically and sequentially to indicate causality. Action, as revealed through intentions, deeds, and consequences, holds a central place in narratives

(Czarniawska-Joerges 1995). Narratives are produced and reproduced in organizations as members make sense of a sequence of events, its causes, and its significance for the organization.

In an organizational context, narratives function to socialize newcomers (Brown 1985), to solve problems (Mitroff and Kilmann 1976), to legitimate power relationships (Mumby 1987; Clair 1993a; Witten 1993), to enhance bonding and organizational identification (Kreps 1989; Trujillo 1985), and to reduce uncertainty (Brown 1990). They are the vehicles through which organizational values and beliefs are produced, reproduced, and transformed (Smircich 1983). They shape organizational meanings through functioning as retrospective sensemaking (Wilkins 1983), serving as premises of arguments and persuasive appeals (Browning 1992; Weick and Browning 1986), acting as implicit mechanisms of cultural control (Clegg 1993; Kunda 1992), and constituting frames of reference for interpreting organizational actions (Shrivastava and Schneider 1984). Wilkins (1984), for example, argues that organizations high in performance have more concrete action stories than do their less successful counterparts. They also act as repositories of organizational intelligence for employees to update collective sensemaking (Kreps 1989).

Several empirical studies illustrate how narratives are enacted to manage organizational meanings. In a study of a hospital organization, narratives function as symbols of ideological positioning in a struggle to define quality medical care among administrators, nurses, and doctors. Through sharing stories of quality care, organizational members challenge the hospital's political structures and negotiate an alternative ideology (Geist and Hardesty 1990). Just as narratives construct ideology, stories also constitute individual and organizational identities. Czarniawska-Joerges's (1994) research in the Swedish public sector shows how identity construction is a process of narrative production between an actor and an audience.

A second important symbol for understanding *interpretation* in organizations is *metaphor*. Just as metaphors contribute to theory construction, as exemplified in this chapter, they also help organizational members structure their beliefs and behaviors. Metaphors enable individuals to express abstract ideas, convey vivid images, transfer information, and structure coherent systems (Ortony 1979). For example, the phrase that 'life is a game' provides a simple and well understood framework of rules, players, moves, winners, and losers to understand a complex phenomenon. Thus, metaphors are enacted and surface through everyday language use. Phrases like 'waging campaigns', 'gathering intelligence',

'conferring with the brass' may symbolize a military metaphor in which bypassing the 'chain of command' becomes 'insubordination' (Deetz 1986; Weick 1979). Some metaphors become so sedimented in everyday use that their status as metaphors becomes obscured. These conventional or literal metaphors may become root metaphors that subsume other metaphors and provide rich summaries of worldviews (Smith and Eisenberg 1987).

Researchers also use metaphors as analytic tools to gather data about specific organizations. In particular, scholars use metaphor as 'a master detective' (Manning 1979) to infer norms, motives, and meaning in studying organizational cultures (Bantz 1993; Pondy 1983; Trice and Beyer 1984). Research on conflicting metaphors reveals the nature of struggles between competing ideologies (Hirsch and Andrews 1983; Smith and Eisenberg 1987) and covert practices that mask power relationships (Deetz and Mumby 1985). By isolating the predominant metaphors in organizations, researchers can describe organizational reality and the relation of power to metaphor structure. Through what metaphors hide, they support the status quo by treating routine practices as natural and immutable. For example, when organizational members treat human labor as a resource to be 'invested' and 'measured', the distinctions between meaningful and meaningless work become erased (Lakoff and Johnson 1980).

Practitioners often employ metaphor analysis to help organizational members diagnose problems, manage cultures, and enhance organizational effectiveness (Brink 1991; Broms and Gahmberg 1983; Coffman and Eblen 1987; Krefting and Frost 1985). Through the use of metaphors, practitioners can critique current understandings, note possibilities for organizational change, and introduce alternative metaphors. Metaphor, then, is a flexible analytical tool that can be used to understand an organization's culture and to evoke change in past practices.

Unlike metaphor, rites and rituals center on events and behavioral practices that enact organizational meaning. *Rites* are elaborate, dramatic activities that consolidate cultural expressions into one event, while *rituals* are the norms and behaviors that enact the rites (Trice and Beyer 1984). Rites and ceremonies are public events like retirement dinners, new member orientations, and award ceremonies, whereas rituals are less scripted behaviors like handshakes, coffee breaks, gift giving, and staff meetings. Although these symbols are commonplace in organizations (Siehl et al. 1992; Trice and Beyer 1984; 1985), they lack conceptual rigor and systematic distinction (Alvesson and

Berg 1992; Knuf 1993). While their exact nature remains contested, researchers acknowledge that patterned and repeated social activities serve an important role in maintaining an organization's infrastructure.

In particular, rites and ceremonies make public the private values of a group. They perform both instrumental and expressive functions that confer status, evaluate performance, anoint membership, and recognize commitment. But in enacting routines and annual events, they reaffirm the status quo and the power relations of dominant groups. In his analysis of a corporate awards breakfast and an annual Christmas party, Rosen (1985; 1988) illustrates how these seemingly routine performances reaffirm patterns of dominance, reward performance, and admonish failure. Rites, rituals, and ceremonies are communicative acts performed as part of the accomplishment of organizing. As Knuf argues, this performance is tantamount to a single symbol or sign (1993: 85). Hence, rites and rituals overlap with enactment in the performance metaphor.

Paradoxes and ironies differ from other literary forms in focusing on relationships among messages rather than on the meanings of a particular symbol. *Paradoxes* are statements and actions that are self-contradictory but seemingly true (Putnam 1986), while *irony* arises when intended meanings contradict customary meanings (Brown 1977). Paradoxes are common features of organizations. Paradoxical goals can lead to enacting reward structures and operating procedures that violate the overall mission of the organization. For instance, orphanages that develop stringent rules to limit adoptions work against their goal of getting children placed in homes; seniority systems that reward longevity contradict the goal of meritorious performance (Kerr 1975). Paradoxes are evident in double-loop learning and organizational changes (Argyris 1988; Ford and Backoff 1988; O'Connor 1995); incongruities between individual and group goals (Smith and Berg 1987); dialectical tensions rooted in the 'deep structures' of organization life (Benson 1977; Putnam 1986); and double-bind messages in superior–subordinate communication (Putnam 1986; Tompkins and Cheney 1983). They appear in the interwoven but oppositional forces that evoke organizational change, namely through struggles between action and structure, internal and external, and stability and instability (Van de Ven and Poole 1988).

Paradoxical situations cause tensions and feelings of paralysis. Individuals can choose to live with a paradox and conform to one of the contradictory messages (Wood and Conrad 1983); or to step outside of the paradoxical frame and comment on it (Putnam 1986); or to abide by one aspect of the paradox at one time and the other at a different time (Van de Ven and Poole 1988); or to change levels of analysis to address the problem (Quinn and Cameron 1988). In another vein, individuals can introduce a new logic and transcend the contradictions through reframing the experience, transforming the situation, or integrating the oppositions (Bartunek 1988). This second type of response resembles a second-order change and involves a discontinuous shift in an organization's culture, ideology, or deep structure.

Another response to contradictions and paradoxical situations stems from research on irony (Filby and Willmott 1988; Hatch and Ehrlich 1993; Kunda 1992). Ironic remarks and ironic humor acknowledge the contradictory and paradoxical nature of organizing by disrupting historical frames through reversals in meanings. Irony transforms organizational experiences by providing members with an opportunity to confront new versions of social reality and grasp unthinkable propositions (Hatch and Ehrlich 1993).

Communication as organizational interpretation lies at the core of creating and responding to paradoxes. Irony as a play on actual versus expected meanings is a form of communication. In a postmodern world characterized by rapid changes and fragmentation, the management of ironies and paradoxes becomes particularly vital. Although individuals can reduce contradictions and understand the puzzles in organizational paradoxes, they cannot eliminate or escape from them (Handy 1994). The central dilemma that organizations face is learning to survive and flourish in a world defined by the paradoxical situations that they themselves have created (Smith and Berg 1987).

The metaphor of symbol provides a direct link between representation and interpretation. Symbols such as narratives, metaphors, rites and rituals, and paradoxes and ironies are literary tropes used to inscribe organizational texts. Symbols constitute the novel and novels reflect symbolic forms. Hence, the relationship between communication and organization is one of production, with symbols producing texts. Analyzing the elements of the novel is the way that organizational members interpret events, position themselves in the organizational scenario, and understand the motives and values in their everyday lives. Symbols provide ways for organizational members to negotiate scripts but they also serve as subtle means of preserving the status quo and re-create traditional modes of control. Symbols are more than manifestations of an organization's culture; they are the means through which organizing is accomplished.

## The Metaphor of Voice

The metaphor of voice appears in different forms in the organizational literature, but each form shares an interest in the practices and structures that affect who can speak, when, and in what way. Understanding this metaphor entails focusing on communication as the *expression* or *suppression* of the voices of organizational members. To have a voice is to be able to speak in the context of the organization; organizations, then, exist as a *chorus* of member voices. But not all the members of an organization have an equal voice and not all members of the chorus sing the same tune. This metaphor focuses our attention on the ability of members to make their experiences heard and understood; on the existence of an appropriate language of expression; on the availability of occasions to speak; on the willingness of others to listen; and on the values, structures, and practices that suppress voice.

Each of these perspectives, however, emanates from different theoretical traditions, including rhetorical theory, critical theory, and feminist theory. The metaphor of voice clusters into the subcategories of distorted voices, voices of domination, different voices, and access to voice. In *distorted voices*, members are able to speak, but not in ways that represent their interests (Alvesson 1993b; Deetz 1992a; Haslett 1990; Thompson 1984; 1990). Such ideological aspects (Eagleton 1991; Therborn 1980; Thompson 1984) of communication draw attention to the role that meaning plays in the service of power (Fairclough 1992; Thompson 1990). Thus, the study of ideology generally focuses on the ways that powerful groups use communication for organizational control (Tompkins and Cheney 1985; also see Alvesson 1993b; Barker 1993). When particular understandings of the world become naturalized and taken-for-granted, other modes of knowing are excluded, resistance to authority is limited, and communication supports the status quo rather than each member's genuine interests (Clair 1993a; 1993b).

Communication distortion shapes members' ways of speaking, their understandings, and the structures and practices that constitute the organization (Mumby 1988). Power and meaning join together to distort voices so that even though voices may be heard, they echo the sentiments of the elite. However, since multiple coalitions often exist in complex organizations, theorists argue that resistance is typically present in some form and the ideological landscape reflects struggles between competing rather than univocal positions (Haslett 1990). Despite the limits to this perspective, distortion and suppression of voice

result in highly undemocratic organizations, in which resistance is problematic.

When meaning mystifies relations of power, the only voice left is the *voice of domination*. Speaking, then, becomes hegemonic in that patterns of activity and institutional arrangements culminate in common sense, thus concealing the choices and interests of the dominant group (Deetz 1992a; 1992b; Deetz and Mumby 1990; Fairclough 1992; Mumby forthcoming). Hegemony exists in everyday activities and influences the way dominant coalitions control organizations through political, cultural, and economic actions (Deetz 1992b).

Deetz's (1992a) study of the role of the corporation in modern society illustrates how the political ideology of managerialism has become hegemonic in that no other solution to organizational problems seems conceivable. As a result, the corporation as the primary institution in society continues to encroach on activities traditionally organized in other ways. Corporations control everything from personal identity to the use of natural resources to definitions of value and distribution of goods and services (Deetz 1992a: ix).

This concern with the ability to speak arises in other forms. The voice metaphor finds perhaps its most direct and common usage in feminist organizational studies (e.g. Bullis 1993; Buzzanell 1994; Fine 1993; Marshall 1993). This work highlights the fact that some people need to speak in a *different voice*. Because their voices are unique, they are often ignored, silenced, or misunderstood.

The idea of speaking in a different voice appears in two guises. First, researchers must speak differently (Mumby 1993) to uncover the bias inherent in the way we talk about gender and organizations (see Calás and Smircich, Chapter 8 in Volume 1 of this work). Feminist scholars are developing ways of speaking that challenge the unexamined assumptions about patriarchal organizations and that represent women's experiences in organizations. Since the voice that expresses women's experience is often silenced (Clair 1993a; Marshall 1993), researchers must work against the backdrop of patriarchy in trying to communicate authentically about women's organizational experiences. Dominant academic forms that shape writing styles and research methods limit efforts to undo the gendered pattern of theorizing (Marshall 1993: 140). Feminist literature, then, addresses issues of gaining a voice for academic writers and 'unlearning to not speak' (Piercy in Marshall 1993).

A second way in which the concept of a different voice guides organizational scholarship is concern about the patriarchal bias in organizations. Researchers center on the way this bias limits opportunities for women to participate as women in organizational activities (Bullis 1993; Marshall 1993; Rakow 1986). Organizational communication practices which range from conversational turn-taking to storytelling enact gendered organizations and re-create gender inequality (Bullis 1993). These studies question the role of communication in constructing gendered organizations and the need for research to move away from treating gender as a variable to conceive of it as a fundamental organizing principle (Marshall 1993).

This notion of a different voice extends to issues of race and ethnicity in organizations (see Nkomo and Cox, Chapter 5 in this volume, for a discussion of race and organizations; see Kim 1994 for a discussion of race and communication). Work in this area examines the communication practices through which race and ethnicity are accomplished (Frankenberg 1993; Kim 1994; Nakayama and Kriziek 1995) and the role of race and ethnicity in organizations (Nkomo 1992). In each case, a central concern is that minority groups are marginalized because they speak in a different voice.

Another metaphor in the cluster of voice is *access to voice*. In traditional, hierarchical organizations, voice typically increases as one moves up the organizational ladder. Organizational members near the bottom of the ladder have little or no access to voice. While most research that studies access to voice targets traditional bureaucratic organizations, other work focuses on alternative organizational forms such as democratic institutions (Cheney 1995; Deetz 1992a; Harrison 1994; Rothschild-Whitt 1986). These organizations take specific steps to provide members with access to voice. Alternative organizational forms demonstrate how communication develops interdependence and provides a balanced understanding of institutions (Harrison 1994: 249). Democratic organizations also provide a basis upon which to critique traditional bureaucratic forms.

Another alternative for investigating access to voice is through participative management programs that vary from ones aimed at improving organizational efficiency to ones driven by a belief in the collective good (Gordon 1994: 293). In each case, the success of the democratization program depends on the development of alternative patterns of communication (Eisenberg 1994; Harrison 1994). But the rationale behind them and the approach to studying them is quite different.

For some scholars the empowerment of individuals and the democratization of organizations is a way *to make a difference through voice*, which aims to improve both work experience and effectiveness. To be empowered means that a person believes that he or she can direct organizational events toward desired ends (Albrecht 1988: 380). Organizational members who are empowered feel that they are partners with others in influencing their organizations and being influenced by them (Pacanowsky 1988: 371). Empowerment depends on communication structures that give individuals voice and that provide broad frameworks for understanding sagas that interpret the organization and its goals (Bormann 1988).

Empowerment is the use of voice to provide active participation and commitment to organizational members. For example Pacanowsky's (1988) study of empowerment at W.L. Gore & Associates describes a lattice structure that embodies decentralized power structures and produces what Pacanowsky calls a 4,500 member improvisational jazz group. He outlines six characteristics of empowering firms: (1) power and opportunity are distributed widely; (2) a full, open and decentralized communication system is maintained; (3) integrative problem solving is used; (4) a climate of trust is maintained; (5) people are rewarded and recognized in ways that encourage high performance and self-responsibility; and (6) people learn from organizational ambiguity, inconsistency, contradiction, and paradox. These characteristics incorporate a full, open, and decentralized communication system that allows direct participation by organizational members and transmits a strong enabling culture (1988: 374). Empowerment is therefore inextricably linked to communication (Bormann 1988).

An alternative view of organizational democracy returns to the metaphor of distorted voices. In any movement towards democratization, employees face the asymmetry of power based on managerial possession of capital (Gordon 1994: 286). Consequently, workers find it difficult to develop ways of 'making a difference through voice'. For example, Barker (1993) provides an ethnographic account of 'self-regulated work teams' designed to free employees from bureaucratic control. But rather than freeing workers, the system of concertive control that was developed was more powerful, more invisible, and more difficult to resist than the former managerial control (Barker 1993: also see the concluding chapter of this *Handbook*). In this example, voice overlaps with the metaphor of symbol as managers use unobtrusive controls to distort communication (Tompkins and Cheney 1985). The metaphor of voice overlaps with the metaphor of discourse when ideological practices and discipline undermine efforts to make a difference through voice. These efforts stem from cultural-ideological control as Alvesson (1993b) sets forth in his fourfold theory: (1)

*collective control*, based on a sense of community; (2) *performance-related control*, based on norms for collective performance; (3) *ideological control*, based on values, norms, and ideas about what is good or important; and (4) *perceptual control*, based on the management of beliefs about what exists and how things are (see also McPhee 1993; Kersten 1993). In each case, modes of control move away from focusing on the labor process itself toward the ideological frame in which work is accomplished.

The metaphor cluster of voice brings together different orientations to the issues of speaking, hearing, and making a difference in organizations. The voice metaphor centers on implicit factors that shape the role of communication, namely, ideology, hegemony, legitimation to speak, and unobtrusive control. It connects the issues of power and meaning with communication, although in very different ways. In this metaphor communication functions simultaneously to express and suppress voice; that is, voices may be heard but they are distorted or dominated; new voices may be added to change existing asymmetries, but they result in merely echoing them. The organization constitutes a chorus of diverse and often muted voices; the tune they sing is not always clear.

## The Metaphor of Discourse

One major critique of the voice metaphor is its failure to account for the micro processes that contribute to the origin and development of organizational arrangements. The performance metaphor centers on these dynamic, ongoing processes, but fails to demonstrate how organizations emerge as institutional forms. The *discourse* metaphor provides alternatives that address the weaknesses in both the performance and the voice metaphors.

Discourse refers to language, grammars, and discursive acts that form the foundation of both performance and voice. In the discourse metaphors, communication is a *conversation* in that it focuses on both process and structure, on collective action as joint accomplishment, on dialogue among partners, on features of the context, and on micro and macro processes (Taylor 1993). Conversation, in this metaphor, is a simile for organizations as sequential interactions among people. Bergquist (1993) contends that conversations are both the essence and the product of organizations. In many ways, conversations lay the groundwork for community.

Conversation is immediate in its claim on attention, instantaneous in its moment to moment occurrence, and fleeting or ephemeral in its form, yet it relies on patterns that become culturally sanctioned, frames that presuppose prior knowledge, and macro processes in which individuals speak as representatives for others. Conversations embody many of the elements that characterize communication as symbols, performance, and voice; however, discourse foregrounds language as the nexus for untangling relationships among meaning, context, and praxis. Unlike the symbol metaphor, discourse centers less on cultural forms such as narratives and rituals and more on the co-production of language in situated practice. Thus, text and context are intertwined with action and meaning.

In the discourse metaphor, communication casts organizations as *texts* (Barthes 1981; Geertz 1983; Ricoeur 1979). Texts are sets of structured events or ritualized patterns of interaction that transcend immediate conversations (Taylor 1993). However, scholars differ in the various senses in which they use texts: (1) as the discursive acts inscribed in institutions, (2) as the interpretations of organizational life, and (3) as the ways that organizations are written or authored (Cheney and Tompkins 1988).

Research within the discourse metaphor, however, is very disparate and ranges from studies that treat language as a reflection of culture and society to ones that view language as ongoing conversations and discursive practices. These studies differ markedly in their orientation to language. Thus, the use of discourse as a metaphor serves as a category under which a number of separate and disparate perspectives reside. These perspectives fall into the arenas of (1) discourse as artifacts, (2) discourse as structure and process, and (3) discourse as discursive acts. In the artifact category, words represent 'fixed' objects; whereas in the discursive acts category, language is a 'fluid' negotiation of meanings through interplays among texts (actions performed at any given moment) and context (the circumstances in which those actions take place). In the first two categories, language is unidimensional and goal-oriented; while as a discursive act, language is multifaceted and situated in everyday interaction. Some perspectives of language locate meaning in relational, organizational, and socio-cultural context while others situate meaning at the intersection of conversation, text, and praxis.

The orientation that casts *discourse as an artifact* treats language as representing objects and as signaling particular meanings. Meanings reside in words, syntax, systems of codes, and social orders reflected in language use. Work on structural semiotics, general semantics, and sociolinguistics adopts these assumptions of language and meaning. Through analyzing surface and deep structures, studies of common codes uncover subtleties of organizational life, tacit understandings developed through complex systems of meaning, and the way social systems constrain language use (Barley 1983; Fiol 1989; Manning 1992). Discourse facilitates organizational processes by developing structural arrangements as in Barley's (1983) analysis of the themes of 'naturalness' and 'familiarity' in funeral parlors or Tway's (1976) study of code systems among factory workers. Labels function as control systems that enhance organizational understanding (Czarniawska-Joerges and Joerges 1988). Analysis of code systems reveals how rules, underlying orders, and language patterns work against each other, as in Manning's (1988) analysis of communication technology in two police departments and Fiol's (1989) study of oppositional tensions in CEO letters to stockholders about organizational boundaries. Code systems can reveal unstable images of firms and their internal relations.

In like manner, research on the way language classifies and reflects social structures falls into the category of discourse as artifact. In this perspective, language becomes a fixture of reified social systems such as occupations, departments, and administrative roles. Meaning, then, is embodied in social orders and represented through language use. Taylor's (1987) study of slang in a British financial institution shows how bank tellers avoid the use of words that refer to monetary denominations to distract attention from money. The use of technical terms adheres to geographic proximity, departmental boundaries, and common task operations (Tway 1975), while slang terms in hospitals provide emotional distance between patients and caretakers (Gordon 1983). In a merger and acquisition situation, changes in language codes and dress signal willingness to integrate employees, accommodation to the aggressive firm, and social differentiation of subgroups (Bastien 1992).

A second major orientation centers on the study of *discourse as structure and process*. In this perspective, language reflects the intent or functions of what is said and meaning resides in the structure of ongoing conversations. Meaning is located in discourse patterns rather than in semantics, semiotics, or word choice. This perspective includes the research on speech acts, conversational analysis, and interaction patterns in organizations. Speech act theory treats discourse as spoken or written utterances accomplished through being uttered. Such actions as promising, requesting, demanding, and apologizing occur through the form and rules of language use. In speech act research, language performs relational and organizational functions, such as exercising control, executing influence, reaching agreements, expressing

politeness, and managing impressions (Donohue and Diez 1985; Gioia et al. 1989).

Speech act research also underlies studies on the ethnography of speaking and the appropriateness of language use in organizational settings. For example, Van Maanen's (1973; 1978) classic investigations on the language of policemen and Spradley and Mann's (1975) seminal work on the cocktail waitress examine norms and functions of interactions in particular organizations. Gregory (1983) identifies lexical and semantic fields of native views in subcultures among Silicon Valley employees. Investigations of humor and informal interactions in organizations illustrate how language relieves tensions, defines status relationships, sabotages work processes, and forms informal groups (Duncan 1983; Duncan and Feisal 1989; Ullian 1976).

Conversational analysts center on talk turns, interruptions, talkovers, topic switching, and questions/answers (McLaughlin 1984). When organizational members violate implicit rules, individuals engage in conversational repairs, accounts, and disclaimers. Organizational researchers use conversational analysis to study superior–subordinate communication, organizational control (Barley 1986), selection interviews (Morris 1988; Ragan 1983; Ragan and Hopper 1981), and group decision-making. Drawing from research on powerful and powerless speech, Fairhurst and Chandler (1989) show how topic control, disclaimers, and hedges distinguish conversational patterns of in-group from out-group members. Fairhurst (1993) extends this work to female managers to reveal the way moves of alignment differ for pairs of high, medium, and low leader–member relationships. In like manner, Gronn (1983) describes how a school principal controls issues of staffing through everyday talk that tightens and loosens administrative reins. In a study of decision-making in a psychiatric health care facility, Geist and Chandler (1984) note that conversational accounts serve as arguments for and against group proposals and signal organizational identification. The decision to take a common organizational action may emerge from linguistic indirectness and dissimilar meanings among members of different departments (Donnellon et al. 1986).

Interactional analysis focuses on coding verbal messages in organizational settings. As such it derives meaning from the structures of messages that evolve in organizational contexts, such as performance behaviors (Komaki et al. 1986; Komaki 1986; Komaki and Citera 1990), leader behaviors and perceptions of power (Gioia and Sims 1983; Sims and Manz 1984), managerial control (Fairhurst et al. 1987; 1995; Watson-Dugan 1989), and labor–management negotiations (Putnam and Roloff 1992).

One particular type of interaction analysis that moves toward an interpretative model is adaptive structuration theory, drawn from Giddens's (1979) principles of structuration. This approach focuses on the way interactions among organizational group members appropriate technology and decision support systems (DeSanctis and Poole 1994). Basically, the effects of GDSS on decision-making and group process vary depending on how each group makes sense of the technology (DeSanctis et al. 1992; Poole and DeSanctis 1992). Structuration theory can move interaction analysis beyond micro levels of talk to global considerations of genres and institutional texts (DeSanctis and Poole 1994).

A third stream of research within the discourse metaphor centers on *discourse as discursive practices*. It subsumes research on language as social construction, as emotional expressions, as knowledge, as genres, and as dialogue. Discourse, in this orientation, is the way that organizational understanding is produced and reproduced. In the *social construction* perspective, discourse not only reflects language use, but also creates social meanings in organizations. Labels such as 'ideal patient' and 'health care provider' are not simply terms that classify occupational groups. Rather they define expectations, forms of knowledge, and task activities for organizational groups. Adjustments to new organizational experiences may stem from the way that discourse reconstitutes these institutional labels (Loseke 1989; Sigman 1986).

In like manner, *emotions* as discursive acts center on the way that members regulate, interpret, control, and resist organizational actions (Conrad and Witte 1994; Fineman 1993; Waldron 1994). Regulation occurs through display rules that translate emotions into acceptable organizational forms (Hochschild 1983; Rafaeli and Sutton 1987; Waldron and Krone 1991). Rules for expressing feelings may yield positive organizational outcomes while simultaneously creating estrangement and emotional numbness (Van Maanen and Kunda 1989). Emotional expression is intertwined with dichotomies that privilege a rational view of work and marginalize the private, feminine, and informal side of organizational life (Mumby and Putnam 1992; Putnam and Mumby 1993).

Most of these studies, however, treat emotional language as an artifact of organizational culture rather than as a social construction of reality. In effect, labeling an emotion as anger, fear, pride, or surprise is an ambiguous and complex process. Both the display and the interpretation of emotion hinge on the way that feelings are legitimated and on the social costs for displaying emotions (Conrad and Witte 1994). The control of emotional expression, even in strong cultures, acknowledges that affect rules are complex and malleable. Thus, the study of emotional expressions in organizations needs to consider how interactions shape the way feelings emerge, develop, and transform.

Emotional expression also functions as a discursive practice when it is treated as *knowledge*. That is, language is the depository of reconstructed discourses that legitimate particular practices (Deetz 1992a). Discourse in this orientation overlaps with the voice metaphor and centers on historically situated thoughts, expressions, and actions (Foucault 1980). Through embedding discursive practices in history, language functions as an institutional text. Genres or technologies such as interviews, therapeutic discourse, and legal discourse embody social and institutional conventions. Hence, the selection interview is not simply a language game of questions and answers; it is a genre that incorporates bureaucratic placement, market demands, and employee relationships into its discursive practice (Fairclough 1989).

The study of *communication genres* as discursive practices centers on the form, audience, and socio-historical situation (Yates and Orlikowski 1992). Developed from structuration theory, genres are recurring patterns of communicative practices that form types of interaction, for example, reports, memos, meetings, and e-mail. Organizational members enact genres for particular purposes; hence, they become institutional templates for social interaction (Orlikowski and Yates 1994). However, member actions can deviate from genre templates and change an organization's discourse (Yates 1993); thus, as people interact, they draw on rules developed through tradition to produce, reproduce, and change genres. Orlikowski and Yates (1994) show how the presence and the absence of genres such as memos, reference manuals, and dialogue establish an organization's identity as temporary, accountable to a professional community, and flexible in work processes.

Another type of communication genre, *dialogue*, merits separate attention as a discursive practice. Participants who engage in dialogue suspend defensive exchange, share and learn from experiences, foster deeper inquiry, and resist synthesis or compromise (Eisenberg and Goodall 1993). Drawn from Bakhtin (1981) and Buber (1985), dialogue strives for a balance between individual autonomy and organizational constraint through incorporating diverse voices. Dialogue can transform action and promote organizational learning through developing synergy, empathy, and authentic deliberation among individuals (Evered and Tannenbaum 1992; Isaacs 1993). Dialogue legitimates each person's experience from connecting with others to determine what counts as knowledge and how it is valued. Self-recognition and transformation arise from the additive nature in which each person's experience contributes to the whole (Eisenberg 1994).

Although dialogue places humanism at the forefront of organizing, it often misses the politics of experience by grounding discourse in individual identity. When dialogue incorporates postmodernism, it emphasizes how discourse decenters subjects and fragments identities, situates meanings, and locates power in systems that normalize discursive practices (Deetz forthcoming). By rejecting the notion of autonomous, self-determined individuals, theorists treat discourse as producing identity and as spoken by different selves; thus, the individual is fragmented. Fragmentation provides an opportunity for dialogue, as Townley (1993) illustrates in his essay on discourses of human resource management.

In this poststructuralist treatment of dialogue, meaning is fragmented and localized rather than being universal or fixed. Even phrases like 'the bottom line' and 'profit and loss', and particular accounting practices, have meaning only within the localized, situated discourses that create them (Miller and O'Leary 1987). A deconstruction of management theories demonstrates how organizational texts are localized meanings that often marginalize the voices of those who are absent in these works (Mumby and Putnam 1992). Finally, consistent with the metaphor of distorted voices, power resides in discourse, not through dominant coalitions, but through the way discursive practices like discipline and surveillance become normalized in social interactions (Foucault 1977; Knights 1992).

Treating organizational communication as a discursive practice clarifies the relationship between discourse and texts. A text is the structured sets of events that comprise the organization. These events, created and reconstituted through discourse, have symbolic meaning to participants. A text as symbolic meaning substitutes for treating organizations as objects or entities. Texts are the *Gestalt* meanings aligned with the underlying frames of discursive practices (Strine 1988; Taylor 1993).

The organizational text, however, should not be treated as a social fact or as a 'fixed' meaning. Rather texts are symbolic forms, open to multiple and unlimited readings, frequently ruptured displays, reflexivity between authors and texts, and concerns for transcendence and transformation (Strine 1988). Researchers serve as authors who produce both the texts and the readings of the texts as they engage in organizational studies (Cheney and Tompkins 1988).

## DISCUSSION AND CONCLUSIONS

This chapter sets forth seven metaphor clusters drawn from the organizational communication literature. By reversing the figure–ground relationship between organization and communication, these metaphors recast our images of organizations to adhere to the linguistic turn in social sciences. In many ways this chapter responds to Pondy and Mitroff's (1979) appeal to embrace language-based conceptions of organizations. Boje echoes this appeal by claiming that 'it is time to heed Pondy and Mitroff's advice and move [organizational theory] to discursive metaphors, such as Lyotard's (1984) "conversation," Bakhtin's (1981) "novel," and Thachankary's (1992) "text"' (1995: 1000). This chapter, through its examination of metaphors of communication, takes a step in this direction.

The metaphor clusters included in this chapter present different alternatives for conceptualizing communication and organization. As perspectives, researchers can examine any organizational topic from one of these clusters. In particular, this review demonstrates how communication technology, typically treated as a *tool* in the conduit metaphor, can also be viewed as a *lens* in media richness research, as dense *networks* in the social influence model of media adoption and use, as a *symbol* in studying how social meanings are managed through media use, as the *voice* of domination that enables certain groups to control decision-making processes, as *discourse* or social interaction that structures communication technology, and as *genre* through the historical and habitual use of communication media. The criteria for choosing a particular metaphor are the researcher's goals, the ontological basis of both communication and organization, and the phenomenon that is most central to the organizing process.

Some metaphors include more aspects of the communication process than do others. For example, the discourse, performance, and voice metaphors draw their insights from examining the relationship among messages, meaning, and context, while the conduit, lens, and linkage metaphors, in their pure forms, typically exclude key elements of communication. In effect, some metaphors are more complete and complex than are others.

In this section, we explore the communication–organization relationship embedded in each metaphor, show how the metaphor clusters are interwoven through related chains, and review the contributions and omissions embedded in each metaphor. The end of this section explores the implications of this analysis for theory building in organizations.

In general, the relationship that surfaces from the conceptions of communication and organization within each metaphor is equivalency. That is, a closer examination of each metaphor shows how the two constructs are isomorphic. At first glance, the conduit and the lens metaphors point to a containment relationship between communication and organization. A deeper examination, however, reveals that the two constructs are similar in structure and function. In the conduit metaphor, both communication and organization are containers. Just as communication functions as a channel to contain messages, so organizations act as containers of tasks, technologies, and job functions. In this metaphor, both constructs are defined instrumentally: communication is the way to attain message fidelity; organization is the means of attaining productivity and efficiency. As containers, both processes appear as material objects that isolate form from substance through reliance on discrete boundaries.

In the lens metaphor, both communication and organization are forms of selective perception; that is, the lens and the eye define the boundaries of the system, control access to it, and open and close the system. The lens and the eye identify the parameters of an organization through selecting, screening, and routing information. In this metaphor, communication and organization become synonymous with information management.

In the linkage metaphor, communication contacts are the building blocks of organizational networks. Linkages, then, form the web or structural framework of the organization. Organizations, as networks of relationships, are communication systems defined through the presence or absence of interlocked activities. In contrast, the performance metaphor supports a production relationship between communication and organizations. Either communication produces organizations as in enactment, or the two co-produce each other as in storytelling and collaborative performance. Close examination, however, reveals an equivalency relationship in that organization as coordinated actions parallels communication through social interaction.

In the symbol metaphor, communication is sensemaking through the use of a set of literary tropes that inscribe a novel. Even though this process suggests a production relationship, a novel becomes isomorphic with its symbolic forms. The metaphors of voice and discourse are so multifaceted that it is difficult to isolate the relationship between communication and organization. Production seems paramount in developing the organizational chorus. However, close examination indicates that the presence or absence of voice is consistent with hegemony and unobtrusive control. Speaking in a different voice and access to voice can alter the gendered practices of organizing and enhance democratization of organizational life; hence, the relationship between organizing and communicating is equivalence.

The discourse metaphor includes subgroups that support all three types of relationships between communication and organization. Language as artifact operates from the containment metaphor while language as structure and process emphasizes the co-productive relationship. Discourse as discursive practices, however, casts the relationship as equivalence. Conversations are texts and texts embody conversations (Taylor 1993). Discourse is organizing in that language shapes discursive practices that, in turn, constitute knowledge, genres, and dialogue. In effect, then, metaphors of communication suggest an equivalency relationship between communication and organization, even though assumptions of social reality may differ within and between metaphor clusters.

Each metaphor in this chapter subsumes clusters of related metaphors. These categories then are not locked into particular labels or modes of meaning. Threads from each cluster extend to metaphors in other categories and reveal interrelationships. The conduit, lens, and network metaphors chain together through their foci on transmission. Network research that centers on meanings and relationships overlaps with the symbol metaphor.

Performance chains into discourse metaphors through an emphasis on grammars and recipes for organizing. Speech acts and conversational analysis in the discourse metaphor are performative in nature. Discursive practices in the discourse metaphor are linked to improvisations through routines that form communicative structures and collective moves. Jamming and dialogue are interrelated, providing a chain between the performance and discourse metaphors. Many threads tie the voice to the discourse metaphors through discursive practices, knowledge, and language as ideology. Speaking in a different voice, although not logically tied to the linkage metaphor, treats relationships and connections as the fundamental processes of organizing. In effect, overlaps among these seven clusters suggest new metaphors that might emerge as research develops.

Studies that mix metaphors, however, run the risk of confounding the assumptive ground of both communication and organization. For instance, research on the way leaders transmit organizational narratives combines the conduit with symbol metaphors. However, in this type of research, symbols become transformed into signals sent to receivers. Hence, meanings are relayed and 'exchanged' through channels, rather than being socially constructed. Chaining across metaphors, then, can lead to converting one type of organizational communication research into another and confound the assumptions that underlie the nature of communication.

The concluding chapter of this *Handbook* illustrates how theories of organizations are really different representations. In like manner, metaphor clusters described in this chapter are different representations of communication and organizations. Being aware of what each metaphor captures – and what it neglects – adds insights to organizational studies and reflexiveness to research. The conduit and lens metaphors, with their concern for transmission, instrumentality, and message fidelity, highlight the container images of organizations and neglect meaning, context, and social interaction. The linkage metaphor captures elements that the conduit and lens metaphors miss, namely, the give and take of transactions, organizations as relationships, and the erosion of physical boundaries. Without a physical structure, communication becomes even more central to the essence of organizing.

Both the network and the performance metaphors emphasize patterns of organizing, but performance moves to the collective production of interlocked behaviors. Meaning and sense-making become the basis for coordinated actions. The symbol metaphor adds representation to the process of organizing, but it often reproduces the meanings that service organizational elites. The voice metaphor introduces power and control as factors that influence who can speak and who can be heard in organizations. This metaphor, however, fails to capture the way resistance influences the micro processes that constitute organizing. The discourse metaphor incorporates these micro processes through research on language, but many of these studies neglect the critical role of nonverbal communication and silence in organizing and of authors who write and read organizational texts. Research on communication genres, discursive practices, and dialogue provides notable exceptions to some of these shortcomings. In effect, each image is partial and highlights different elements of organizational communication. Somewhere in the crevices within and schisms between these metaphors, other metaphors reside, ones that account for missing elements and synthesize critical factors in each perspective.

In concluding this chapter, three implications for organizational studies stem from this analysis. First, the conduit and the lens metaphors are the primary ways that organizational scholars treat communication. These metaphors limit not only the way communication is conceived, but also the way organizations are cast. To study language as an artifact of culture or communication technology as an organizational tool limits the complexity and completeness of both communication and organization. Hence, in selecting a particular metaphor, scholars should note the contributions and omissions that a perspective holds. For example, when a crisis like an oil spill occurs, it may seem appropriate to focus on effective transmission of information. However, sending information about an oil spill is a rhetorical process rooted in concerns for audience analysis, persuasive appeals, social and political context, and ethical considerations (Heath 1988). A discourse or symbol metaphor includes more of these factors and can still probe for issues of effectiveness in message transmission. Effectiveness, however, is no longer message fidelity; it is understanding the rhetorical circumstances that govern sending messages to particular audiences. Moreover, to force the study of language or symbols into a transmission metaphor alters the way that both communication and organizations are conceived.

Second, although organizational theorists like Barnard (1968) and Weick (1979) imply that communication and organization are equivalent, a close examination of the metaphors in this chapter provides even stronger support for this supposition. If, indeed, the two constructs are isomorphic, then all organizational theories contain implicit notions about communication and all communication theories, in turn, provide important insights about organizing. Weick (1987) illustrates this point through a deconstruction of the principles of communication embodied in Burns and Stalker's (1961) description of mechanistic and organic organizations. Perhaps, more importantly, theorists could embellish ways of thinking about organizations through applying metaphors of communication. This chapter takes a step in this direction.

Third, the field of organizational communication, like that of organizational studies, faces a crisis of representation. Communication no longer mirrors or reflects reality, rather it is formative in that it creates and represents the process of organizing. The range of metaphors reviewed in this chapter attests to the scope of this crisis. This crisis is also evident in recent challenges to orthodox views of organizations and in critiques of modernism in all its forms. This crisis is also apparent in the fluidity of new organizational forms such as chains, clusters, and strategic alliances (see the introduction to this volume) and in dynamic collaborative relationships between competitors, often developed through linkages in cyberspace.

Other signs of this crisis appear in postmodern approaches to organizations, often described as 'communication-intensive organizations' (Galbraith et al. 1993). These organizations are decentralized in activities, fluid in boundaries, hybrid in forms, cyclical in order and chaos, and integrative in embracing diversity (Bergquist 1993). Their images are fragmented and inconsistent, characterized by paradoxes and contradictions in a global world of shifting visions. Metaphors of organizations as conversations, texts, and voice become increasingly viable.

This chapter explores a body of literature that many writers in organizational studies have previously ignored. The nature of communication and the links between communication and organization suggest that these metaphors are viable alternatives for rethinking organizational theories. If organizational reality is determined, in part, by the perspectives that we take rather than the phenomena we observe (Bergquist 1993), then this chapter responds to the plea for new perspectives and alternative metaphors of organizing.

## REFERENCES

Ackoff, R.L. and Emery, F.E. (1972) *On Purposeful Systems*. Chicago: Aldine/Atherton.

Adams, J. (1980) 'Interorganizational processes and organizational boundary activities', in Larry L. Cummings and Barry Staw (eds), *Research in Organizational Behavior*, vol. 2. Greenwich, CT: JAI Press. pp. 321–55.

Albrecht, Terrance L. (1988) 'Communication and personal control in empowering organizations', in James A. Anderson (ed.), *Communication Yearbook 11*. Newbury Park, CA: Sage. pp. 380–90.

Albrecht, Terrance L. and Hall, Bradford (1991) 'Facilitating talk about new ideas: the role of personal relationships in organizational innovation', *Communication Monographs*, 58: 273–88.

Albrecht, Terrance L. and Ropp, V.A. (1984) 'Communicating about innovation in networks of three U.S. organizations', *Journal of Communication*, 34: 78–91.

Allen, Myria Watkins, Gotcher, J. Michael and Seibert, Joy Hart (1993) 'A decade of organizational communication research: journal articles 1980–1991', in Stanley A. Deetz (ed.), *Communication Yearbook 16*. Newbury Park, CA: Sage. pp. 252–330.

Allen, Thomas J. and Hauptman, Oscar (1990) 'The substitution of communication technologies for organizational structure in research and development', in Janet Fulk and Charles W. Steinfield (eds), *Organizations and Communication Technology*. Newbury Park, CA: Sage. pp. 275–94.

Alvesson, Mats (1990) 'Organization: from substance to image'?, *Organization Studies*, 11(3): 373–94.

Alvesson, Mats (1993a) *Cultural Perspectives on Organizations*. Cambridge: Cambridge University Press.

Alvesson, Mats (1993b) 'Cultural-ideological modes of management control: a theory and a case study of a professional service company', in Stanley A. Deetz (ed.), *Communication Yearbook 16*. Newbury Park, CA: Sage. pp. 3–42.

Alvesson, Mats and Berg, Per Olof (1992) *Corporate Culture and Organizational Symbolism*. Berlin: Walter de Gruyter.

Ancona, Deborah and Caldwell, D.F. (1988) 'Beyond task and maintenance: defining external functions in groups', *Group and Organizational Studies*, 13: 468–94.

Argyris, Chris (1988) 'Crafting a theory of practice: the case of organizational paradoxes', in Robert E. Quinn and Kim S. Cameron (eds), *Paradox and Transformation: Toward a Theory of Change in Organization and Management*. Cambridge, MA: Ballinger. pp. 255–78.

Axley, Stephen (1984) 'Managerial and organizational communication in terms of the conduit metaphor', *Academy of Management Review*, 9: 428–37.

Bakhtin, M. (1981) *The Dialogic Imagination*, translated by Caryl Emerson and Michael Holquist. Austin, TX: University of Texas Press.

Bantz, Charles R. (1989) 'Organizing and the social psychology of organizing', *Communication Studies*, 40(4): 231–40.

Bantz, Charles R. (1990) 'Organizational communication, media industries, and mass communication', in James A. Anderson (ed.), *Communication Yearbook 13*. Newbury Park, CA: Sage. pp. 503–10.

Bantz, Charles R. (1993) *Understanding Organizations: Interpreting Organizational Communication Cultures*. Columbia, SC: University of South Carolina Press.

Bantz, Charles R. and Smith, David H. (1977) 'A critique and experimental text of Weick's model of organizing', *Communication Monographs*, 44: 171–84.

Barker, James (1993) 'Tightening the iron cage: concertive control in self-managing teams', *Administrative Science Quarterly*, 38: 408–37.

Barley, Steve (1983) 'Semiotics and the study of occupational and organizational culture', *Administrative Science Quarterly*, 23: 393–413.

Barley, Steve (1986) 'Technology as an occasion for structuring: evidence from observations of CT scanners and the social order of radiology departments', *Administrative Science Quarterly*, 31: 78–108.

Barley, Steve (1990) 'The alignment of technology and structure through roles and networks', *Administrative Science Quarterly*, 35: 61–103.

Barnard, Chester (1968) *The Functions of the Executive* (1938). Cambridge MA: Harvard University Press.

Barthes, R. (1981) 'Theory of the text', in R. Young (ed.), *Untying the Text: a Post-Structuralist Reader*. Boston: Routledge & Kegan Paul. pp. 31–47.

Bartunek, Jean M. (1988) 'The dynamics of personal and organizational reframing', in Robert E. Quinn and Kim S. Cameron (eds), *Paradox and Transformation: Toward a Theory of Change in Organization and Management*. Cambridge, MA: Ballinger. pp. 137–62.

Bastien, David T. (1992) 'Change in organizational culture: the use of linguistic methods in corporate acquisition', *Management Communication Quarterly*, 5: 403–42.

Bastien, David T. and Hostager, Todd J. (1988) 'Jazz as a process of organizational innovation', *Communication Research*, 15: 582–602.

Bastien, David T. and Hostager, Todd J. (1992) 'Cooperation as communicative accomplishment: a symbolic interaction analysis of an improvised jazz concert', *Communication Studies*, 43: 92–104.

Baudrillard, J. (1983). *Simulations*. New York: Semiotext.

Bavelas, A. (1950) 'Communication patterns in task-oriented groups,' *Acoustical Society of America Journal*, 22: 727–30.

Bell, Elizabeth and Forbes, Linda C. (1994) 'Office folklore in the academic paperwork empire: the interstitial space of gendered (con)texts', *Text and Performance Quarterly*, 14(3): 181–96.

Benson, J. Kenneth (1977) 'Organizations: a dialectical view', *Administrative Science Quarterly*, 22: 1–26.

Berg, Per Olof and Kreiner, K. (1990) 'Corporate architecture: turning physical settings into symbolic resources', in P. Gagliardi (ed.), *Symbols and Artifacts: Views of the Corporate Landscape*. Berlin: Walter de Gruyter.

Bergquist, William (1993) *The Postmodern Organization: Mastering the Art of Irreversible Change*. San Francisco, CA: Jossey-Bass.

Bikson, T. and Eveland, J.D. (1990) 'The interplay of work group structures and computer support', in J. Galegher, R. Kraut and C. Egido (eds), *Intellectual Teamwork: Social and Technological Bases of Cooperative Work*. Hillsdale, NJ: Erlbaum. pp. 245–90.

Black, Max (1962) *Models and Metaphors*. New York: Cornell University Press.

Boje, David M. (1991) 'The storytelling organization: a study of story performance in an office-supply firm', *Administrative Science Quarterly*, 36: 106–26.

Boje, David M. (1995) 'Stories of the storytelling organization: a postmodern analysis of Disney as "Tamara-Land"', *Academy of Management Journal*, 38(4): 997–1035.

Boorstin, D. (1961) *The Image: a Guide to Pseudo-Events in America*. New York: Atheneum.

Bormann, Ernest G. (1983) 'Symbolic convergence: organizational communication and culture', in Linda L. Putnam and Michael E. Pacanowsky (eds), *Communication and Organization: an Inter-pretative Approach*. Beverly Hills, CA: Sage. pp. 99–122.

Bormann, Ernest G. (1985) 'Symbolic convergence theory: a communication formulation based on *homo narrans*', *Journal of Communication*, 35: 128–39.

Bormann, Ernest G. (1988) '"Empowering" as a heuristic concept in organizational communication', in James A. Anderson (ed.), *Communication Yearbook 11*. Newbury Park, CA: Sage. pp. 391–404.

Brink, T.L. (1991) 'Corporate cultures: a color coding metaphor', *Business Horizons*, September/October: 39–44.

Brink, T.L. (1993) 'Metaphor as data in the study of organizations', *Journal of Management Inquiry*, 2(4): 366–71.

Broms, H. and Gahmberg, H. (1983) 'Communication to self in organizations and cultures', *Administrative Science Quarterly*, 28: 11–21.

Brown, Mary Helen (1985) '"That reminds me of a story": speech action in organizational socialization', *Western Journal of Speech Communication*, 49: 27–42.

Brown, Mary Helen (1990) 'Defining stories in organizations: characteristics and functions', in James A. Anderson (ed.), *Communication Yearbook 13*. Newbury Park, CA: Sage. pp. 162–90.

Brown, Richard H. (1977) *A Poetic for Sociology*. Cambridge: Cambridge University Press.

Browning, Larry D. (1992) 'Lists and stories as organizational communication', *Communication Theory*, 4: 281–302.

Buber, M. (1985) *Between Man and Man*, 2nd edn. New York: Macmillan.

Bullis, Connie (1993) 'At least it is a start', in Stanley A. Deetz (ed.), *Communication Yearbook 16*. Newbury Park, CA: Sage. pp. 145–54.

Burns, T. and Stalker, G.M. (1961) *The Management of Innovation*. London: Tavistock.

Buzzanell, Patrice M. (1994) 'Gaining a voice: feminist organizational communication theorizing', *Management Communication Quarterly*, 7: 339–83.

Buzzanell, Patrice M. and Goldzwig, Steven R. (1991) 'Linear and nonlinear career models', *Management Communication Quarterly*, 4: 466–505.

Calás, Marta B. and Smircich, Linda (1985) 'The metaphor of the text/the paradigm of reading: interpretive organization', Paper presented at the Academy of Management Meeting.

Carey, James W. (ed.) (1989) *Communication as Culture: Essays on Media and Society*. New York: Routledge.

Cheney, George (1983) 'The rhetoric of identification and the study of organizational communication', *Quarterly Journal of Speech*, 69: 143–58.

Cheney, George (1991) *Rhetoric in Organizational Society: Managing Multiple Identities*. Columbia: University of South Carolina Press.

Cheney, George (1995) 'Democracy in the workplace: theory and practice from the communication perspective', *Journal of Applied Communication Research*, 23: 167–200.

Cheney, George and Christensen, Lars Thoger (forthcoming) 'Identity at issue: linkages between "internal" and "external" organizational communication', in Fred M. Jablin and Linda L. Putnam (eds), *The New Handbook of Organizational Communication*. Thousand Oaks, CA: Sage.

Cheney, George and Tompkins, Phillip K. (1988) 'On the facts of the text as the basis of human communication research', in James A. Anderson (ed.), *Communication Yearbook 11*. Newbury Park, CA: Sage. pp. 455–81.

Cheney, George and Vibbert, Steven L. (1987) 'Corporate discourse: public relations and issue management', in Fredric M. Jablin, Linda L. Putnam, Karlene H. Roberts and Lyman W. Porter (eds), *Handbook of Organizational Communication: an Interdisciplinary Perspective*. Newbury Park, CA: Sage. pp. 165–94.

Clair, Robin (1993a) 'The use of framing devices to sequester organizational narratives: hegemony and harassment', *Communication Monographs*, 60: 113–36.

Clair, Robin (1993b) 'The bureaucratization, commodification, and privatization of sexual harassment through institutional discourse', *Management Communication Quarterly*, 7: 123–57.

Clegg, Stewart R. (1993) 'Narrative, power, and social theory', in Dennis K. Mumby (ed.), *Narrative and Social Control: Critical Perspectives*. Newbury Park, CA: Sage. pp. 15–45.

Coffman, S.L. and Eblen, A.L. (1987) 'Metaphor use and perceived managerial effectiveness', *Journal of Applied Communication Research*, 1–2: 53–66.

Cohen, M., March, J. and Olsen, J. (1972) 'A garbage can model of organizational choice', *Administrative Science Quarterly*, 17: 1–25.

Conrad, Charles (1983) 'Organizational power: faces and symbolic forms', in Linda L. Putnam and Michael E. Pacanowsky (eds), *Communication and Organizations: an Interpretive Approach*. Beverly Hills, CA: Sage. pp. 173–94.

Conrad, Charles and Witte, Kim (1994) 'Is emotional expression repression oppression? Myths of organizational affective regulation', in Stanley A. Deetz (ed.), *Communication Yearbook 17*. Thousand Oaks, CA: Sage. pp. 417–28.

Cusella, Louis P. (1987) 'Feedback, motivation, and performance', in Fredric M. Jablin, Linda L. Putnam, Karlene E. Roberts and Lyman W. Porter (eds), *Handbook of Organizational Communication: an Interdisciplinary Perspective*. Newbury Park, CA: Sage. pp. 624–78.

Czarniawska-Joerges, Barbara (1992) *Exploring Complex Organizations: a Cultural Perspective*. Newbury Park, CA: Sage.

Czarniawska-Joerges, Barbara (1994) 'Narratives of individual and organizational identities', in Stanley A. Deetz (ed.), *Communication Yearbook 17*. Thousand Oaks, CA: Sage. pp. 193–221.

Czarniawska-Joerges, Barbara (1995) 'Narration or science? Collapsing the division in organization studies', *Organization*, 2(1): 11–33.

Czarniawska-Joerges, Barbara and Joerges, B. (1988) 'How to control things with words: organizational talk and control', *Management Communication Quarterly*, 2(2): 170–93.

Daft, Richard L. (1983) 'Symbols in organizations: a dual-content framework of analysis', in Louis R. Pondy, Peter J. Frost, Gareth Morgan and Thomas C. Dandridge (eds), *Organizational Symbolism*. Greenwich, CT: JAI Press. pp. 199–206.

Daft, Richard L., Bettenhausen, K.R. and Tyler, B.B. (1993) 'Implications of top managers' communication choices for strategic decisions', in George P. Huber and William H. Glick (eds), *Organizational Change and Redesign: Ideas and Insights for Improving Performance*. New York: Oxford University Press. pp. 112–46.

Daft, Richard L. and Lengel, R.H. (1984) 'Information richness: a new approach to managerial information processing and organizational design', in Larry L. Cummings and Barry M. Staw (eds), *Research in Organizational Behavior*, vol. 6. Greenwich, CT: JAI Press. pp. 191–234.

Daft, Richard L., Lengel, R.H. and Trevino, Linda K. (1987) 'Message equivocality, media selection, and manager performance: implications for information systems', *MIS Quarterly*, 11: 355–66.

Daft, Richard L. and MacIntosh, N. (1981) 'A tentative exploration into the amount and equivocality of information processing in organizational work groups', *Administrative Science Quarterly*, 26: 207–24.

Davis, Keith (1953) 'A method of studying communication patterns in organizations', *Personnel Psychology*, 6: 301–12.

Davis, W.L. and O'Conner, J.R. (1977) 'Serial transmission of information: a study of the grapevine', *Journal of Applied Communication Research*, 5: 61–72.

Deetz, Stanley A. (1985) 'Ethical considerations in cultural research in organizations', in P. Frost, L. Moore, L. Louis, C. Lundberg and J. Martin (eds), *Organizational Culture*. Newbury Park, CA: Sage. pp. 251–69.

Deetz, Stanley A. (1986) 'Metaphors and the discursive production and reproduction of organizations', in Lee Thayer (ed.), *Organization–Communication: Emerging Perspectives I*. Norwood, NJ: Ablex. pp. 168–82.

Deetz, Stanley A. (1992a) *Democracy in an Age of Corporate Colonization*. Albany, NY: State University of New York Press.

Deetz, Stanley A. (1992b) 'Disciplinary power in the modern corporation', in Mats Alvesson and Hugh Wilmott (eds), *Critical Management Studies*. Newbury Park, CA: Sage. pp. 21–45.

Deetz, Stanley A. (forthcoming) 'Conceptual foundations for organizational communication studies', in Fredric M. Jablin and Linda L. Putnam (eds), *The New Handbook of Organizational Communication*. Thousand Oaks, CA: Sage.

Deetz, Stanley A. and Kersten, Astrid (1983) 'Critical models of interpretive research', in Linda L. Putnam and Michael E. Pacanowsky (eds), *Communication and Organizations: an Interpretive Approach*. Beverly Hills, CA: Sage. pp. 147–71.

Deetz, Stanley, A. and Mumby, Dennis K. (1985) 'Metaphors, information and power', *Information and Behavior*, 1: 369–86.

Deetz, Stanley A. and Mumby, Dennis K. (1990) 'Power, discourse, and the workplace: reclaiming the critical tradition', in James A. Anderson (ed.), *Communication Yearbook 13*. Newbury Park, CA: Sage. pp. 18–47.

DeSanctis, G. and Poole, Marshall Scott (1994) 'Capturing the complexity in advanced technology use: adaptive structuration theory', *Organizational Science*, 5: 121–47.

DeSanctis, G., Poole, M.S., Lewis, H. and Desharnais, G. (1992) 'Using computing in quality team meetings: initial observations from the IRS–Minnesota Project', *Journal of Management and Information Systems*, 8: 7–26.

Donnellon, Anne, Gray, Barbara and Bougon, M. (1986) 'Communication, meaning, and organized action', *Administrative Science Quarterly*, 31: 43–55.

Donohue, William A. and Diez, Mary E. (1985) 'Directive use in negotiation interaction', *Communication Monographs*, 52: 305–18.

Downs, Anthony (1967) *Inside Bureaucracy*. Boston: Little Brown.

Duncan, W.J. (1983) 'The superiority theory of humor at work: joking relationships as indicators of formal and informal status patterns in small, task-oriented groups', *Small Group Behavior*, 16: 556–64.

Duncan, W.J. and Feisal, J.P. (1989) 'No laughing matter: patterns of humor in the work place', *Organizational Dynamics*, 17(4): 18–30.

Eagleton, Terry (1991) *Ideology: an Introduction*. London: Verso.

Earley, P.C. (1988) 'Computer-generated performance feedback in the magazine-subscription industry', *Organizational Behavior and Human Decision Processes*, 41: 50–64.

Edwards, Richard (1979) *Contested Terrain: the Transformation of the Workplace in the Twentieth Century*. New York: Basic Books.

Ehrlich, S. (1987) 'Strategies for encouraging successful adoption of office communication systems', *ACM Transactions on Office Information Systems*, 5: 340–57.

Eisenberg, Eric M. (1984) 'Ambiguity as strategy in organizational communication', *Communication Monographs*, 51: 227–42.

Eisenberg, Eric M. (1990) 'Jamming: transcendence through organizing', *Communication Research*, 17: 139–64.

Eisenberg, Eric M. (1994) 'Dialogue as democratic discourse: affirming Harrison', *Communication Yearbook 17*. Thousand Oaks, CA: Sage. pp. 275–84.

Eisenberg, Eric M., Farace, R., Monge, P., Bettinghaus, E., Kurchner-Hawkins, R., Miller, K. and Rothman, L. (1985) 'Communication linkages in interorganizational systems: review and synthesis', in Brenda Dervin and M. Voight (eds), *Progress in the Communication Sciences*, vol. 6. Norwood, NJ: Ablex. pp. 231–58.

Eisenberg, Eric M. and Goodall, H.L. Jr. (1993) *Organizational Communication: Balancing Creativity and Constraint*. New York: St Martin's Press.

Eisenberg, Eric M. and Phillips, Steven R. (1991) 'Miscommunication in organizations', in N. Coupland, H. Giles and J. Wiemann (eds), *'Miscommunication' and Problematic Talk*. Newbury Park, CA: Sage. pp. 244–58.

Eisenberg, Eric M. and Witten, M. (1987) 'Reconsidering openness in organizational communication', *Academy of Management Review*, 12: 418–26.

Eisenhardt, K.M. (1989) 'Making fast strategic decisions in high-velocity environments', *Academy of Management Journal*, 32: 543–76.

Evered, R. and Tannenbaum, R. (1992) 'A dialog on dialog', *Journal of Management Inquiry*, 1: 43–55.

Fairclough, Norman (1989) *Language and Power*. New York: Longman.

Fairclough, Norman (1992) *Discourse and Social Change*. Cambridge: Polity Press.

Fairclough, Norman (1993) 'Critical discourse analysis and the marketization of public discourse: the universities', *Discourse and Society*, 4: 133–68.

Fairhurst, Gail T. (1993) 'The leader–member exchange patterns of women leaders in industry: a discourse analysis', *Communication Monographs*, 60: 321–51.

Fairhurst, Gail T. and Chandler, Teresa A. (1989) 'Social structure in leader–member interaction', *Communication Monographs*, 56: 215–39.

Fairhurst, Gail T., Green, Stephen and Courtright, John (1995) 'Inertial forces and the implementation of a socio-technical systems approach: a communication study', *Organizational Science*, 6(2): 168–85.

Fairhurst, Gail T., Rogers, E. and Sarr, R. (1987) 'Manager–subordinate control patterns and judgments about the relationship', in Margaret McLaughlin (ed.), *Communication Yearbook 10*. Beverly Hills, CA: Sage. pp. 395–415.

Farace, R., Monge, P. and Russell, H. (1977) *Communicating and Organizing*. Reading, MA: Addison-Wesley.

Fayol, H. (1949) *General and Industrial Management* (1925). New York: Pitman.

Feldman, Martha and March, James (1981) 'Information in organizations as signal and symbol', *Administrative Science Quarterly*, 26: 171–86.

Filby, Ivan and Willmott, Hugh (1988) 'Ideologies and contradictions in a public relations department: the seduction and impotence of living myth', *Organization Studies*, 9(3): 335–49.

Fine, Marlene (1993) 'New voices in organizational communication: a feminist commentary and critique', in S.P. Bowen and Nancy Wyatt (eds), *Transforming Visions: Feminist Critiques in Communication Studies*. Cresskill, NJ: Hampton Press. pp. 125–66.

Fineman, Stephen (1993) 'Organizations as emotional arenas', in Stephen Fineman (ed.), *Emotion in Organizations*. London: Sage. pp. 9–35.

Fiol, C.M. (1989) 'A semiotic analysis of corporate language: organizational boundaries and joint venturing', *Administrative Science Quarterly*, 34: 277–303.

Fisher, B. Aubrey (1978) *Perspectives on Human Communication*. New York: Macmillan.

Follett, Mary Parker (1941) 'Constructive conflict', in H.C. Metcalf and L. Urwick (eds), *Dynamic Administration: the Collected Papers of Mary Parker Follett*. New York: Harper. pp. 30–49.

Ford, Jeffrey D. and Backoff, Robert H. (1988) 'Organizational change in and out of dualities and paradox', in Robert E. Quinn and Kim S. Cameron (eds), *Paradox and Transformation: Toward a Theory of Change in Organization and Management*. Cambridge, MA: Ballinger. pp. 81–121.

Foucault, Michel (1977) *Discipline and Punish: the Birth of the Prison*, translated by A. Sheridan Smith. New York: Random House.

Foucault, Michel (1980) *Power/Knowledge: Selected Interviews and Other Writings, 1972–1977*. New York: Pantheon.

Frankenberg, R. (1993) *White Women, Race Matters: the Social Construction of Whiteness*. Minneapolis, MN: University of Minnesota Press.

Frost, Peter J., Moore, Larry L., Louis, Meryl Reis, Lundberg, Craig C. and Martin, Joanne (eds) (1985) *Organizational Culture*. Beverly Hills, CA: Sage.

Fulk, Janet (1993) 'Social construction of communication technology', *Academy of Management Journal*, 36: 921–50.

Fulk, Janet and Boyd, Brian (1991) 'Emerging theories of communication in organizations', *Journal of Management*, 17(2): 407–46.

Fulk, Janet, Steinfield, Charles and Schmitz, Joseph (1990) 'The social influence model of technology use', in Janet Fulk and Charles Steinfield (eds), *Organizations and Communication Technology*. Newbury Park, CA: Sage. pp. 117–40.

Fulk, Janet, Steinfield, Charles, Schmitz, Joseph and Power, J.G. (1987) 'A social information processing model of media use in organizations', *Communication Research*, 14: 529–52.

Galbraith, J.R. (1973) *Designing Complex Organizations*. Reading MA: Addison-Wesley.

Galbraith, J.R., Lawler, E.E. and Associates (1993) *Organizing for the Future*. San Francisco: Jossey-Bass.

Geertz, Clifford (1973) *The Interpretation of Cultures*. New York: Basic Books.

Geertz, Clifford (1983) *Local Knowledge: Further Essays in Interpretive Anthropology*. New York: Basic Books.

Geist, Patricia and Chandler, Teresa (1984) 'Account analysis of influence in group decision making', *Communication Monographs*, 51: 67–78.

Geist, Patricia and Hardesty, Monica (1990) 'Ideological positioning in professionals' narratives of quality medical care', in Norman K. Denzin (ed.), *Studies in Symbolic Interaction*, vol. 2. Greenwich, CT: JAI Press. pp. 257–84.

Giddens, Anthony (1979) *Central Problems in Social Theory: Action, Structure and Contradiction in Social Analysis*. Berkeley: University of California Press.

Gioia, D.A. (1986) 'Symbols, scripts, and sensemaking: creating meaning in the organizational experience', in Hank P. Sims, Jr., Dennis A. Gioia, and Associates (eds), *The Thinking Organization*. San Francisco. Jossey-Bass. pp. 49–74.

Gioia, Dennis A. and Sims, Hank P. (1983) 'Perceptions of managerial power as a consequence of managerial behavior and reputation', *Journal of Management*, 9: 7–26.

Gioia, Dennis A., Donnellon, Anne and Sims, Hank P., Jr. (1989) 'Communication and cognition in appraisal: a tale of two paradigms', *Organization Studies*, 10(4): 503–30.

Glick, William H., Miller, C.C. and Huber, George P. (1993) 'Upper-echelon diversity in organizations: demographic, structural, and cognitive influences on organizational performance', in George W. Huber and William H. Glick (eds), *Organizational Change and Redesign: Ideas and Insights for Improving Performance*. New York: Oxford University Press. pp. 176–214.

Goffman, Erving (1959) *The Presentation of Self in Everyday Life*. New York: Doubleday Anchor.

Goldhaber, Gerald M. and Barnett, George A. (eds) (1988) *Handbook of Organizational Communication*. Norwood, NJ: Ablex Publishing.

Goodall, H.L., Jr. (1989) *Casing A Promised Land: The Autobiography of an Organizational Detective as Cultural Ethnographer*. Carbondale, Ill.: Southern Illinois University Press.

Gordon, David Paul (1983) 'Hospital slang for patients: crocks, gomers, gorks, and others', *Language in Society*, 12: 173–85.

Gordon, William I. (1994) '"Wego" comes in several varieties and is not simple', in Stanley A. Deetz (ed.), *Communication Yearbook 17*. Thousand Oaks, CA: Sage. pp. 285–97.

Granovetter, M. (1973) 'The strength of weak ties', *American Journal of Sociology*, 78: 1360–80.

Gray, Barbara, Bougon, M. and Donnellon, Anne (1985) 'Organizations as constructions and destructions of meaning', *Journal of Management*, 11: 83–98.

Gregory, K.L. (1983) 'Native-view paradigms: multiple cultures and culture conflicts in organizations', *Administrative Science Quarterly*, 28: 359–76.

Gronn, P.C. (1983) 'Talk as the work: the accomplishment of school administration', *Administrative Science Quarterly*, 28: 1–21.

Grunig, James E. (1984) 'Organizations, environments, and models of public relations', *Public Relations Research and Education*, 1: 6–29.

Grunig, James E. and Grunig, Laura A. (1992) 'Models of public relations and communication', in James E. Grunig (ed.), *Excellence in Public Relations and Communication Management*. Hillsdale, NJ: Erlbaum. pp. 285–325.

Hage, J. (1974) *Communication and Organizational Control: Cybernetics in Health and Welfare Agencies*. New York: Wiley.

Handy, C. (1994) *The Age of Paradox*. Boston: Harvard Business School Press.

Harris, Linda and Cronen, Vernon E. (1979) 'A rules-based model for the analysis and evaluation of organizational communication', *Communication Quarterly*, 27: 12–18.

Harrison, Teresa M. (1994) 'Communication and interdependence in democratic organizations', in Stanley A. Deetz (ed.), *Communication Yearbook 17*. Thousand Oaks, CA: Sage. pp. 246–74.

Haslett, Beth (1990) 'Discourse, ideology, and organizational control', in James A. Anderson (ed.), *Communication Yearbook 13*. Newbury Park, CA: Sage. pp. 48–58.

Hatch, M.J. and Ehrlich, S.B. (1993) 'Spontaneous humor as an indicator of paradox and ambiguity in organizations', *Organization Studies*, 14: 505–26.

Hawkes, D.F. (1972) *Metaphor*. London: Methuen.

Heath, R.L. (ed.) (1988) *Strategic Issues Management: How Organizations Influence and Respond to Public Interests and Policies*. San Francisco: Jossey-Bass.

Hellweg, Susan (1987) 'Organizational grapevines: a state of the art review', in Brenda Dervin and M. Voight (eds), *Progress in the Communication Sciences*, vol. 8. Norwood, NJ: Ablex.

Hirsch, Paul M. and Andrews, John A.Y. (1983) 'Ambushes, shootouts, and knights of the roundtable: the language of corporate takeovers', in Louis R. Pondy, Peter J. Frost, Gareth Morgan and Thomas C. Dandridge (eds), *Organizational Symbolism*. Greenwich, CT: JAI Press. pp. 145–55.

Hochschild, A. (1983) *The Managed Heart: Commercialization of Human Feeling*. Berkeley: University of California Press.

Huber, George A. (1991) 'Organizational learning: the contributing processes and literatures', *Organizational Science*, 2: 88–115.

Isaacs, William N. (1993) 'Taking flight: dialogue, collective thinking, and organizational learning', *Organizational Dynamics*, 22(2): 24–39.

Isabella, Lynn A. (1990) 'Evolving interpretations as a change unfolds: how managers construe key organizational events', *Academy of Management Journal*, 33: 7–41.

Jablin, Fredric M. (1987) 'Formal organizational structure', in Fredric M. Jablin, Linda L. Putnam, Karlene H. Roberts and Lyman W. Porter (eds), *Handbook of Organizational Communication: an Interdisciplinary Perspective*. Newbury Park, CA: Sage. pp. 389–419.

Jablin, Fredric M., Putnam, Linda L., Roberts, Karlene H. and Porter, Lyman W. (eds) (1987) *Handbook of Organizational Communication: an Interdisciplinary Perspective*. Newbury Park, CA: Sage.

Jablin, Fredric M. and Putnam, Linda L. (eds) (forthcoming) *The New Handbook of Organizational Communication*. Thousand Oaks, CA: Sage.

Johnson, Bonnie (1977) *Communication: the Process of Organizing*. Boston: Allyn-Bacon.

Jones, Michael O., Moore, Michael D. and Snyder, Richard C. (eds) (1988) *Inside Organizations: Understanding the Human Dimension*. Newbury Park, CA: Sage.

Katz, D. and Kahn, Robert (1966) *The Social Psychology of Organizations*. New York: Wiley.

Kelly, Jan W. (1985) 'Storytelling in high tech organizations: a medium for sharing culture', *Journal of Applied Communication Research*. 13: 45–58.

Kerr, S. (1975) 'On the folly of rewarding A, while hoping for B', *Academy of Management Journal*, 47: 469–83.

Kersten, Astrid (1993) 'Culture, control, and the labor process', in Stanley A. Deetz (ed.), *Communication Yearbook 16*. Newbury Park, CA: Sage. pp. 54–60.

Kim, Young Yun (1994) 'Interethnic communication: the context and the behavior', in Stanley A. Deetz (ed.), *Communication Yearbook 17*. Thousand Oaks, CA: Sage. pp. 511–38.

Knights, D. (1992) 'Changing spaces: the disruptive impact of a new epistemological location for the study of management', *Academy of Management Review*, 17: 514–36.

Knuf, Joachim (1993) 'Ritual in organizational culture theory: some theoretical reflections and a plea for greater terminological rigor', in Stanley A. Deetz (ed.), *Communication Yearbook 16*. Newbury Park, CA: Sage. pp. 61–103.

Koch, Susan and Deetz, Stanley A. (1981) 'Metaphor analysis of social reality in organizations', *Journal of Applied Communication Research*, 9: 1–15.

Komaki, Judith L. (1986) 'Toward effective supervision: an operant analysis and comparison of managers at work', *Journal of Applied Psychology*, 71: 270–8.

Komaki, Judith L. and Citera, M. (1990) 'Beyond effective supervision: identifying key interactions between superior and subordinate', *Leadership Quarterly*, 1: 91–106.

Komaki, Judith L., Zlotnick, S. and Jensen, M. (1986) 'Development of an operant-based taxonomy and observational index of supervisory behavior', *Journal of Applied Psychology*, 71: 260–9.

Krefting, Linda A. and Frost, Peter J. (1985) 'Untangling webs, surfing waves, and wildcatting: a multiple-metaphor perspective on managing organizational cultures', in Peter J. Frost, Larry F. Moore, Meryl Reis Louis, Craig C. Lundberg and Joanne Martin (eds), *Organizational Culture*. Beverly Hills, CA: Sage. pp. 155–68.

Kreps, Gary L. (1980) 'A field experimental test and revaluation of Weick's model of organizing', in Dan Nimmo (ed.), *Communication Yearbook 4*. New Brunswick, NJ: Transaction Books. pp. 389–98.

Kreps, Gary L. (1989) 'Stories as repositories of organizational intelligence: implications for organizational development', in James A. Anderson (ed.), *Communication Yearbook 13*. Newbury Park, CA: Sage.

Kunda, Gideon (1992) *Engineering Culture: Control and Commitment in a High-tech Corporation*. Philadelphia: Temple University Press.

Lakoff, George and Johnson, Mark (1980) *Metaphors We Live By*. Chicago: University of Chicago Press.

Leavitt, Harold (1951) 'Some effects of certain communication patterns on group performance', *Journal of Abnormal and Social Psychology*, 46: 38–50.

Likert, R. (1967) *The Human Organization: Its Management and Value*. New York: McGraw-Hill.

Loseke, D.R. (1989) 'Creating clients: social problems work in a shelter for battered women', *Perspectives on Social Problems*, 1: 173–93.

Lotman, J.M. (1977) 'Two models of communication', in D.P. Lucid (ed.), *Soviet Semiotics: an Anthology*. London: Johns Hopkins. pp. 99–101.

Luhmann, N. (1990) *Essays on Self-Reference*. New York: Columbia University Press.

Lyotard, J.-F. (1984) *The Postmodern Condition: a Report on Knowledge*, translated by G. Bennington and B. Massumi. Minneapolis: University of Minnesota Press.

Mangham, I.L. and Overington, M.A. (1987) *Organizations as Theatre: a Social Psychology of Dramatic Appearances*. New York: Wiley.

Manning, Peter K. (1979) 'Metaphors of the field: varieties of organizational discourse', *Administrative Science Quarterly*, 24: 660–71.

Manning, Peter K. (1988) *Symbolic Communication: Signifying Calls and the Police Response*. Cambridge, MA: MIT Press.

Manning, Peter K. (1992) *Organizational Communication*. New York: Aldine De Gruyter.

Marshall, Judi (1993) 'Viewing organizational communication from a feminist perspective: a critique and some offerings', in Stanley A. Deetz (ed.), *Communication Yearbook 16*. Newbury Park, CA: Sage. pp. 122–43.

Martin, Joanne (1982) 'Stories and scripts in organizational settings', in A. Hastorf and A. Isen (eds), *Cognitive Social Psychology*. London: Routledge. pp. 255–305.

May, Steven K. (1993) 'A communication course in organizational paradigms and metaphors', *Communication Education*, 42: 234–54.

McLaughlin, Margaret (1984) *Conversation: How Talk Is Organized*. Beverly Hills, CA: Sage.

McPhee, Robert D. (1993) 'Cultural-ideological modes of control: an examination of concept formation', in Stanley A. Deetz (ed.), *Communication Yearbook 16*. Newbury Park, CA: Sage. pp. 43–53.

McPhee, Robert D. and Corman, Seven R. (1995) 'An activity-based theory of communication networks in organizations, applied to the case of a local church', *Communication Monographs*, 62: 132–51.

Miller, J.G. (1960) 'Information input, overload, and psychopathology', *American Journal of Psychiatry*, 116: 695–704.

Miller, Katherine I. (1995) *Organizational Communication: Approaches and Processes*. Belmont, CA: Wadsworth.

Miller, Katherine I. and Monge, Peter R. (1986) 'Participation, satisfaction, and productivity: a meta-analytic review', *Academy of Management Journal*, 29: 727–53.

Miller, P. and O'Leary, T. (1987) 'Accounting and the construction of the governable person', *Accounting, Organizations, and Society*, 12: 235–65.

Miller, Vernon D. and Jablin, Fredric M. (1991) 'Information seeking during organizational entry: influences, tactics, and a model of the process', *Academy of Management Review*, 16: 92–120.

Mintzberg, Henry (1979) *The Structuring of Organizations*. Englewood Cliffs, NJ: Prentice-Hall.

Mitroff, Ian I. and Kilmann, Ralph H. (1976) 'On organizational stories: an approach to the design and analysis of organizations through myths and stories', in Ralph H. Kilmann, Louis R. Pondy and D.P. Slevin (eds), *The Management of Organizational Design*, vol. 1. New York: Elsevier North-Holland. pp. 189–207.

Monge, Peter R. and Contractor, Noshir (1988) 'Communication networks: measuring techniques', in C.H. Tardy (ed.), *A Handbook for the Study of Human Communication*. Norwood, NJ: Ablex. pp. 107–38.

Monge, Peter R. and Eisenberg, Eric (1987) 'Emergent communication networks', in Fredric M. Jablin, Linda L. Putnam, Karlene H. Roberts and Lyman W. Porter (eds), *Handbook of Organizational Communication*. Newbury Park, CA: Sage. pp. 304–42.

Morgan, Gareth (1980) 'Paradigms, metaphors and puzzle solving in organizational theory', *Administrative Science Quarterly*, 25: 605–22.

Morgan, Gareth (1983) 'More on metaphor: why we cannot control tropes in administrative science', *Administrative Science Quarterly*, 28: 601–7.

Morgan, Gareth (1986) *Images of Organizations*. Beverly Hills, CA: Sage.

Morgan, Gareth, Frost, Peter J. and Pondy, Louis R. (1983) 'Organizational symbolism', in Louis R.

Pondy, Peter J. Frost, Gareth Morgan and Thomas C. Dandridge (eds), *Organizational Symbolism*. Greenwich, CT: JAI Press. pp. 3–35.

Morris, G.H. (1988) 'Accounts in selection interviews', *Journal of Applied Communication Research*, 15(2): 82–98.

Mumby, Dennis K. (1987) 'The political function of narrative in organizations', *Communication Monographs*, 54: 113–27.

Mumby, Dennis K. (1988) *Communication and Power in Organizations: Discourse, Ideology, and Domination*. Norwood, NJ: Ablex.

Mumby, Dennis K. (1993) 'Feminism and the critique of organizational communication studies', in Stanley A. Deetz (ed.), *Communication Yearbook 16*. Newbury Park, CA: Sage. pp. 155–66.

Mumby, Dennis K. (forthcoming) 'Power, politics and organizational communication: theoretical perspectives', in Fredric M. Jablin and Linda L. Putnam (eds), *The New Handbook of Organizational Communication*. Thousand Oaks, CA: Sage.

Mumby, Dennis K. and Putnam, Linda L. (1992) 'The politics of emotion: a feminist reading of bounded rationality', *Academy of Management Review*, 17: 465–86.

Nakayama, T. and Kriziek, Robert (1995) 'Whiteness: a strategic rhetoric', *The Quarterly Journal of Speech*, 81: 291–309.

Nkomo, Stella (1992) 'The emperor has no clothes: rewriting "race in organizations"', *Academy of Management Review*, 17: 487–513.

O'Connor, Ellen S. (1995) 'Paradoxes of participation: a textual analysis of case studies on organizational change', *Organization Studies*, 16(5): 769–803.

Oliver, C. (1990) 'Determinants of interorganizational relationships: integration and future directions', *Academy of Management Review*, 15: 241–65.

O'Reilly, Charles A. (1978) 'The intentional distortion of information in organizational communication: a laboratory and field approach', *Human Relations*, 31: 173–93.

O'Reilly, Charles A. (1980) 'Individuals and information overload in organizations: is more necessarily better?', *Academy of Management Journal*, 23: 684–96.

O'Reilly, Charles A., Chatman, Jennifer A. and Anderson, John C. (1987) 'Message flow and decision making', in Fredric M. Jablin, Linda L. Putnam, Karlene H. Roberts and Lyman W. Porter (eds), *Handbook of Organizational Communication: an Interdisciplinary Perspective*. Newbury Park, CA: Sage. pp. 600–23.

O'Reilly, Charles A. and Roberts, Karlene H. (1974) 'Information infiltration in organizations: three experiments', *Organizational Behavior and Human Performance*, 11: 253–65.

Orlikowski, Wanda J. and Yates, JoAnne (1994) 'Genre repertoire: the structuring of communicative practices in organizations', *Administrative Science Quarterly*, 39: 541–74.

Ortony, A. (ed.) (1979) *Metaphor and Thought*. Cambridge: Cambridge University Press.

Pacanowsky, Michael E. (1988) 'Communication in the empowering organization', in James A. Anderson (ed.), *Communication Yearbook 11*. Newbury Park, CA: Sage. pp. 356–79.

Pacanowsky, Michael E. and O'Donnell-Trujillo, Nick (1983) 'Organizational communication as cultural performance', *Communication Monographs*, 50: 126–47.

Papa, Michael (1990) 'Communication network patterns and employee performance with new technology', *Communication Research*, 17: 344–68.

Pearce, M. and David, J. (1983) 'A social network approach to organizational design-performance', *Academy of Management Journal*, 26(3): 436–44.

Pepper, Gerald L. (1995) *Communicating in Organizations: a Cultural Approach*. New York: McGraw-Hill.

Perrow, Charles (1986) *Complex Organizations: a Critical Essay*, 3rd edn (1st edn 1972). New York: Random House.

Pfeffer, J. and Salancik, G.R. (1978) *The External Control of Organizations: a Resource Dependence Perspective*. New York: Harper & Row.

Pinder, C.C. and Bourgeois, V.W. (1982) 'Controlling tropes in administrative sciences', *Administrative Science Quarterly*, 27: 641–52.

Pondy, Louis R. (1983) 'The role of metaphors and myths in organizations and in the facilitation of change', in Louis R. Pondy, Peter J. Frost, Gareth Morgan and Thomas D. Dandridge (eds), *Organizational Symbolism*. Greenwich, CT: JAI Press. pp. 157–66.

Pondy, Louis R. and Mitroff, Ian (1979) 'Beyond open systems models of organization', in Barry M. Staw (ed.), *Research in Organizational Behavior*, vol. 1. Greenwich, CT: JAI Press. pp. 3–39.

Pondy, Louis R., Frost, Peter J., Morgan, Gareth and Dandridge, Thomas C. (eds) (1983) *Organizational Symbolism*. Greenwich, CT: JAI Press.

Poole, Marshall S. and DeSanctis, G. (1990) 'Understanding the use of group decision support systems: the theory of adaptive structuration', in Janet Fulk and Charles Steinfeld (eds), *Organizations and Communication Technology*. Newbury Park, CA: Sage. pp. 173–93.

Poole, Marshall S. and DeSanctis, G. (1992) 'Microlevel structuration in computer-supported group decision-making', *Human Communication Research*, 19: 5–49.

Putnam, Linda L. (1983) 'The interpretive perspective: an alternative to functionalism', in Linda L. Putnam and Michael E. Pacanowsky (eds), *Communication and Organizations: an Interpretive Approach*. Beverly Hills, CA: Sage. pp. 31–54.

Putnam, Linda L. (1986) 'Contradictions and paradoxes in organizations', in Lee Thayer (ed.), *Organization–Communication: Emerging Perspectives I*. Norwood, NJ: Ablex. pp. 151–67.

Putnam, Linda L. (1989) 'Negotiating as organizing: two levels within the Weickian model', *Communication Studies*, 40: 249–57.

Putnam, Linda L. and Cheney, George (1983) 'A critical review of the research traditions in organizational communication', in Mary S. Mander (ed.), *Communication in Transition*. New York: Praeger. pp. 206–24.

Putnam, Linda L. and Cheney, George (1985) 'Organizational communication: historical development and future directions', in Thomas W. Benson (ed.), *Speech Communication in the Twentieth Century*. Carbondale, IL: Southern University Press. pp. 130–56.

Putnam, Linda L. and Mumby, Dennis K. (1993) 'Organizations, emotion, and the myth of rationality', in Stephen Fineman (ed.), *Emotions in Organizations*. London: Sage. pp. 36–57.

Putnam, Linda L. and Roloff, Michael E. (eds) (1992) *Communication and Negotiation*. Newbury Park, CA: Sage.

Putnam, Linda L. and Sorenson, Ritch L. (1982) 'Equivocal messages in organizations', *Human Communication Research*, 8: 114–32.

Putnam, Linda L., Van Hoeven, Shirley A. and Bullis, Connie A. (1991) 'The role of rituals and fantasy themes in teachers' bargaining', *Western Journal of Speech Communication*, 55: 85–103.

Quinn, Robert E. and Cameron, Kim S. (eds) (1988) *Paradox and Transformation: Toward a Theory of Change in Organization and Management*. Cambridge, MA: Ballinger.

Rafaeli, A. and Sutton, Robert I. (1987) 'Expression of emotion as part of the work role', *Academy of Management Review*, 12: 23–37.

Ragan, Sandra L. (1983) 'A conversational analysis of alignment talk in job interviews', in Robert Bostrum (ed.), *Communication Yearbook 7*. Beverly Hills, CA: Sage. pp. 502–16.

Ragan, Sandra L. and Hopper, Robert (1981) 'Alignment talk in the job interview', *Journal of Applied Communication Research*, 9: 85–103.

Rakow, Lana F. (1986) 'Rethinking gender research in communication', *Journal of Communication*, 36: 11–26.

Redding, W. Charles (1985) 'Stumbling toward identity: the emergence of organizational communication as a field of study', in Robert D. McPhee and Phillip K. Tompkins (eds), *Organizational Communication: Traditional Themes and New Directions*. Beverly Hills, CA: Sage. pp. 15–54.

Redding, W. Charles and Tompkins, Phillip K. (1988) 'Organizational communication – past and present tenses', in Gerald M. Goldhaber and George A. Barnett (eds), *Handbook of Organizational Communication*. Norwood, NJ: Ablex. pp. 5–33.

Reddy, M. (1979) 'The conduit metaphor – a case of frame conflict in our language about language', in A. Ortony (ed.), *Metaphor and Thought*. Cambridge: Cambridge University Press. pp. 284–324.

Rice, Ron E. (1993) 'Media appropriateness: using social presence to compare traditional and new organizational media', *Human Communication Research*, 19: 451–84.

Rice, Ron E. and Aydin, C. (1991) 'Attitudes toward new organizational technology: network proximity as a mechanism for social information processing', *Administrative Science Quarterly*, 36: 219–44.

Rice, Ron E. and Danowski, James (1993) 'Is it really just like a fancy answering machine? Comparing semantic networks of different types of voice mail users', *Journal of Business Communication*, 30(4): 369–97.

Rice, Ron E. and Gattiker, Urs E. (forthcoming) 'New media and organizational structuring: the sublimation of boundaries in meaning and relations', in Fredric M. Jablin and Linda L. Putnam (eds), *The New Handbook of Organizational Communication*. Thousand Oaks, CA: Sage.

Rice, Ron E., Grant, A., Schmitz, J. and Torobin, J. (1990) 'Individual and network influences on the adoption and perceived outcomes of electronic messaging', *Social Networks*, 12(1): 27–55.

Rice, Ron E., Hughes, D. and Love, G. (1989) 'Usage and outcomes of electronic messaging at an R&D organization: situational constraints, job level, and media awareness', *Office: Technology and People*, 5(2): 141–61.

Rice, Ron E. and Shook, D. (1988) 'Access to, usage of, and outcomes from an electronic message system', *ACM Transactions on Office Information Systems*, 6(3): 255–76.

Rice, Ron E. and Shook, D. (1990) 'Relationships of job categories and organizational levels to use of communication channels, including electronic mail: a meta-analysis and extension', *Journal of Management Studies*, 27: 195–229.

Ricoeur, P. (1979) 'The model of the text: meaningful action considered as a text', in P. Rabinow and W.M. Sullivan (eds), *Interpretive Social Science: a Reader*. Berkeley: University of California Press. pp. 73–102.

Riley, Patricia (1983) 'A structurationist account of political culture', *Administrative Science Quarterly*, 28: 414–37.

Roethlisberger, F.J. (1941) *Management and Morale*. Cambridge, MA: Harvard University Press.

Rogers, Everett M. (1994) *A History of Communication Study: a Biographical Approach*. New York: Free Press.

Rogers, Everett M. and Kincaid, D. (1981) *Communication Networks: Toward a New Paradigm for Research*. New York: Free Press.

Rosen, M. (1985) 'Breakfast at Spiro's: dramaturgy and dominance', *Journal of Management*, 11(2): 31–48.

Rosen, M. (1988) 'You asked for it: Christmas at the bosses' expense', *Journal of Management Studies*, 25: 463–80.

Rosenau, P. (1992) *Post-Modernism and the Social*

*Sciences: Insights, Inroads, and Intrusions*. Princeton, NJ: Princeton University Press.

Rothschild-Whitt, J. (1986) *The Cooperative Workplace: Potentials and Dilemmas of Organizational Democracy and Participation*. London: Cambridge University Press.

Russ, G.S., Daft, R.L. and Lengel, R.H. (1990) 'Media selection and managerial characteristics in organizational communications', *Management Communication Quarterly*, 4: 151–75.

Saussure, Ferdinand de (1983) *Course in General Linguistics*. La Salle, IL: Open Court.

Schall, M.S. (1983) 'A communication-rules approach to organizational culture', *Administrative Science Quarterly*, 28: 557–81.

Schmitz, Joseph and Fulk, Janet (1991) 'Organizational colleagues, media richness, and electronic mail: a test of the social influence model of technology', *Communication Research*, 18: 487–523.

Shannon, Claude E. and Weaver, Warren (1949) *The Mathematical Theory of Communication*. Urbana, IL: University of Illinois Press.

Short, J., Williams, E. and Christie, B. (1976) *The Social Psychology of Telecommunications*. London: Wiley.

Shrivastava, P. and Schneider, S. (1984) 'Organizational frames of reference', *Human Relations*, 37: 795–809.

Siehl, Caren, Bowen, David E. and Pearson, Critine M. (1992) 'Service encounters as rites of integration: an information processing model', *Organizational Science*, 3(4): 537–55.

Sigman, Stewart, J. (1986) 'Adjustment to the nursing home as a social interactional accomplishment', *Journal of Applied Communication Research*, 14: 37–58.

Simon, Herbert A. (1957) *Administrative Behavior*. New York: Free Press.

Sims, Hank P. and Manz, C.C. (1984) 'Observing leader verbal behavior: toward reciprocal determinism in leadership theory', *Journal of Applied Psychology*, 69: 222–32.

Smircich, Linda (1983) 'Concepts of culture and organizational analysis', *Administrative Science Quarterly*, 28: 339–58.

Smircich, Linda and Stubbart, Charles (1985) 'Strategic management in an enacted world', *Academy of Management Review*, 10: 724–36.

Smith, A.G. (1973) 'The ethic of the relay men', in Lee Thayer (ed.), *Communication: Ethical and Moral Issues*. London: Gordon & Breach. pp. 313–24.

Smith, Kenwyn K. and Berg, David N. (1987) *Paradoxes of Group Life*. San Francisco: Jossey-Bass.

Smith, Ruth C. (1993) 'Images of organizational communication: root-metaphors of the organization–communication relation'. Paper presented at the International Communication Association Conference, Washington, DC.

Smith, Ruth C. and Eisenberg, Eric M. (1987) 'Conflict at Disneyland: a root-metaphor analysis', *Communication Monographs*, 54: 367–80.

Smith, Ruth C. and Eisenberg, Eric M. (1988) 'Root metaphor analysis: a heuristic method for studying organizational change. Paper presented at the Academy of Management Meetings, Anaheim, California.

Smith, Ruth C. and Turner, Paaige (1995) 'A social constructionist reconfiguration of metaphor analysis: an application of "SCMA" to organizational socialization theorizing', *Communication Monographs*, 62: 152–81.

Spradley, J.P. and Mann, B.J. (1975) *The Cocktail Waitress*. New York: Wiley.

Sproule, J. Michael (1989) 'Organizational rhetoric and the public sphere', *Communication Studies*, 40: 258–65.

Steier, Fred and Smith, K. (1992) 'The cybernetics of cybernetics and the organization of organization', in Lee Thayer (ed.), *Organization–Communication: Emerging Perspectives III*. Norwood, NJ: Ablex.

Stohl, Cynthia (1986) 'The role of memorable messages in the process of organizational socialization', *Communication Quarterly*, 34: 231–49.

Stohl, Cynthia (1993) 'European managers' interpretations of participation: a semantic network analysis', *Human Communication Research*, 20: 97–117.

Stohl, Cynthia (1995) *Organizational Communication: Connectedness in Action*. Thousand Oaks, CA: Sage.

Stohl, Cynthia and Redding, W. Charles (1987) 'Messages and message exchange processes', in Fredric M. Jablin, Linda L. Putnam, Karlene H. Roberts and Lyman W. Porter (eds), *Handbook of Organizational Communication: an Interdisciplinary Perspective*. Beverly Hills, CA: Sage. pp. 451–502.

Strine, Mary S. (1988) 'Constructing "texts" and making inferences: some reflections on textual reality in human communication research', in James A. Anderson (ed.), *Communication Yearbook 11*. Newbury Park, CA: Sage. pp. 494–500.

Stutman, Randall K. and Putnam, Linda L. (1994) 'The consequences of language: a metaphorical look at the legalization of organizations', in Sim B. Sitkin and Robert J. Bies (eds), *The Legalistic Organization*. Thousand Oaks, CA: Sage. pp. 281–302.

Sutcliffe, Kathleen M. (forthcoming) 'Organizational environments and organizational information processing', in Fredric M. Jablin and Linda L. Putnam (eds), *The New Handbook of Organizational Communication*. Thousand Oaks, CA: Sage.

Taylor, Frederic W. (1947) *Principles of Scientific Management* (1912). New York: Harper.

Taylor, James R. (1993) *Rethinking the Theory of Organizational Communication: How to Read an Organization*. Norwood, NJ: Ablex.

Taylor, James R. (1995) 'Shifting from a heteronomous to an autonomous worldview of organizational communication: communication theory on the cusp', *Communication Theory*, 5(1): 1–35.

Taylor, James R. and Robichaud, Daniel (1992) 'A

new look at enactment'. Paper presented at the International Communication Association Conference, Miami, Florida.

Taylor, James R. and Van Every, Elizabeth J. (1993) *The Vulnerable Fortress: Bureaucratic Organization and Management in the Information Age*. Toronto: University of Toronto Press.

Taylor, M.E. (1987) 'Functions of in-house language: observations on data collected from some British financial institutions', *Language in Society*, 16: 1–7.

Tesser, A. and Rosen, S. (1975) 'The reluctance to transmit bad news', in Leonard Berkowitz (ed.), *Advances in Experimental Social Psychology*, vol. 8. New York: Academic Press. pp. 193–232.

Thachankary, T. (1992) 'Organizations as "texts": hermeneutics as a model for understanding organizational change', *Research in Organizational Change and Development*, 6: 197–233.

Therborn, G. (1980) *The Ideology of Power and the Power of Ideology*. London: Verso.

Thompson, John B. (1984) *Studies in the Theory of Ideology*. Berkeley, CA: University of California Press.

Thompson, John B. (1990) *Ideology and Modern Culture*. Stanford, CA: Stanford University Press.

Tichy, N. and Fombrun, C. (1979) 'Network analysis in organizational settings', *Human Relations*, 32: 923–65.

Tompkins, Phillip K. and Cheney, George (1983) 'Account analysis of organizations: decision making and identification', in Linda L. Putnam and Michael E. Pacanowsky (eds), *Communication and Organizations: an Interpretive Approach*. Beverly Hills, CA: Sage. pp. 123–46.

Tompkins, Phillip K. and Cheney, George (1985) 'Communication and unobtrusive control in contemporary organizations', in Robert D. McPhee and Phillip K. Tompkins (eds), *Organization Communication: Traditional Themes and New Directions*. Beverly Hills, CA: Sage. pp. 179–210.

Townley, B. (1993) 'Foucault, power/knowledge, and its relevance for human resource management', *Academy of Management Review*, 18: 518–45.

Trevino, Linda K., Lengel, R.H. and Daft, Richard L. (1987) 'Media symbolism, media richness, and media choice in organizations: a symbolic interactionist perspective', *Communication Research*, 14: 553–74.

Trice, Harrison M. and Beyer, Janice M. (1984) 'Studying organizational culture through rites and ceremonies', *Academy of Management Review*, 9: 653–69.

Trice, Harrison M. and Beyer, Janice M. (1985) *Using Six Organizational Rites to Change Culture*. San Francisco: Jossey-Bass.

Trujillo, Nick (1985) 'Organizational communication as cultural performance: some managerial considerations', *Southern Speech Communication Journal*, 50: 201–24.

Turner, Victor (1980) 'Social dramas and stories about them', *Critical Inquiry*, 7: 141–68.

Tushman, Michael L. (1979) 'Work characteristics and subunit communication structure: a contingency analysis', *Administrative Science Quarterly*, 24: 82–98.

Tushman, Michael L. and Scanlan, T.J. (1981) 'Boundary spanning individuals: their role in information transfer and their antecedents', *Academy of Management Journal*, 24: 289–305.

Tway, P. (1975) 'Workplace isoglosses: lexical variation and change in a factory setting', *Language in Society*, 4: 171–83.

Tway, P. (1976) 'Verbal and nonverbal communication of factory workers', *Semiotica*, 16: 29–44.

Ullian, J.A. (1976) 'Joking at work', *Journal of Communication*, 26: 479–86.

Van de Ven, Andrew H. and Poole, Marshall Scott (1988) 'Paradoxical requirements for a theory of organizational change', in Robert E. Quinn and Kim S. Cameron (eds), *Paradox and Transformation: Toward a Theory of Change in Organization and Management*. Cambridge, MA: Ballinger. pp. 19–64.

Van Maanen, John (1973) 'Observations on the making of policemen', *Human Organization*, 32: 407–18.

Van Maanen, John (1978) 'The asshole', in Peter K. Manning and John Van Maanen (eds), *Policing*. New York: Random House.

Van Maanen, John and Kunda, Gideon (1989) 'Real feelings: emotional expression and organizational culture', in Larry L. Cummings and Barry M. Staw (eds), *Research in Organizational Behavior*, vol. 6. Greenwich, CT: JAI Press. pp. 287–365.

Waldron, Vincent R. (1994) 'Once more, with feeling: reconsidering the role of emotion in work', in Stanley A. Deetz (ed.), *Communication Yearbook 17*. Thousand Oaks, CA: Sage. pp. 388–416.

Waldron, Vincent R. and Krone, Katherine (1991) 'The experience and expression of emotion in the workplace: a study of a corrections organization', *Management Communication Quarterly*, 4: 287–309.

Watson-Dugan, K.W. (1989) 'Ability and effort attributions: do they affect how managers communicate performance feedback information?', *Academy of Management Journal*, 32: 87–114.

Watzlawick, Paul, Beavin, Janet Helmick and Jackson, Don D. (1967) *Pragmatics of Human Communication: a Study of Interactional Patterns, Pathologies, and Paradoxes*. New York: W.W. Norton.

Weber, Max (1947) *The Theory of Social and Economic Organization*. New York: Free Press.

Weick, Karl E. (1979) *The Social Psychology of Organizing* (1969). Reading, MA: Addison-Wesley.

Weick, Karl E. (1987) 'Theorizing about organizational communication', in Fredric M. Jablin, Linda L. Putnam, Karlene H. Roberts and Lyman W. Porter (eds), *Handbook of Organizational Communication*. Newbury Park, CA: Sage. pp. 97–122.

Weick, Karl E. (1990) 'Cartographic myths in organizations', in Anne S. Huff (ed.), *Mapping Strategic Thought*. New York: Wiley. pp. 1–10.

Weick, Karl E. and Browning, Larry (1986) 'Arguments and narration in organizational communication', *Journal of Management*, 12: 243–59.

Wert-Gray, S., Center, C., Brashers, Dale and Meyers, Renee (1991) 'Research topics and methodological orientations in organizational communication. A decade in review', *Communication Studies*, 42: 141–54.

Wilkins, Alan L. (1983) 'Organizational stories as symbols which control the organization', in Louis R. Pondy, Peter J. Frost, Gareth Morgan and Thomas C. Dandridge (eds), *Organizational Symbolism*. Greenwich, CT: JAI Press. pp. 81–92.

Wilkins, Alan L. (1984) 'The creation of cultures: the role of stories and human resource systems', *Human Resource Management*, 23: 41–60.

Witten, Marsha (1993) 'Narrative and the culture of obedience at the workplace', in Dennis K. Mumby (ed.), *Narrative and Social Control: Critical Perspectives*. Newbury Park, CA: Sage. pp. 97–118.

Wood, Julia T. and Conrad, Charles (1983) 'Paradox in the experiences of professional women', *Western Journal of Speech Communication*, 47: 305–22.

Wuthnow, Robert and Witten, Marsha (1988) 'New directions in the study of culture', *Annual Review of Sociology*, 14: 49–67.

Yates, JoAnne (1993) 'Co-evolution of information processing technology and use: interaction between the life insurance and tabulating industries', *Business History Review*, 67: 1–51.

Yates, JoAnne and Orlikowski, Wanda (1992) 'Genres of organizational communication: an approach to studying communication media', *Academy of Management Review*, 17: 299–326.

Young, Ed (1989) 'On the naming of the rose: interests and multiple meanings as elements of organizational culture', *Organizational Studies*, 10(2): 187–206.

Zmud, Robert W. (1990) 'Opportunities for strategic information manipulation through new information technology', in Janet Fulk and Charles W. Steinfield (eds), *Organizations and Communication Technology*. Newbury Park, CA: Sage.

Zmud, Robert W., Lind, M. and Young, F. (1990) 'An attribute space for organizational communication channels', *Information Systems Research*, 1(4): 440–57.

# 8

# *Organizations, Technology and Structuring*

## KARLENE H. ROBERTS AND MARTHA GRABOWSKI

Everywhere one looks technology seems to rapidly advance. As just one example, when the University of Hawaii's eighty-eight inch telescope on Mauna Kea (on the state's 'big island' of Hawaii) was commissioned in 1970, it was the fourth largest telescope in the world. Today it isn't even the fourth largest telescope on Mauna Kea. In the organizational literature, there is a great deal of overlap in discussions of technology, technological systems, and environment. A whole raft of issues are conceptualized and studied under the rubric of technology.

Historically, discussions of technology have involved descriptions of technology and problems with technology. Little has been written about difficulties associated with measuring or assessing technology. Exploration of technology characteristics and challenges develops *descriptive* pictures of what technology is, how it grew, and its role in organizations. In contrast, *relational* approaches focus on relationships between technology and organizations, and incorporate problems of assessment because it is difficult to assess fluid concepts and relationships.

This chapter adopts the dual challenge of providing a descriptive view of technology and organizations followed by a relational examination of technology and organization structure. The descriptive picture is an important first step that sets the context for the rest of the chapter. The relational view develops for us the continuous, changing, and interactive nature of technology and organizations, a perspective both related to and distinct from the impacts technology has on organizations. These relational constructs between organizations and technology are particularly useful for managing

organizations in the post-industrial age (Huber 1984).

Organizational constructs give us important insights into the role of technology in organizations, and highlight the importance of considering technology as a process as well as a product in our examination. Given the development of such a descriptive and relational picture, it is worthwhile considering whether technology is still a useful construct in organizational studies. We answer in the affirmative, but caution that such an affirmative answer is contingent upon two important findings of this chapter:

- Technology's dual nature as a product and a process suggests that sociotechnical frameworks need to change significantly to accommodate longitudinal, temporal views of technology.
- Technology has increasingly become the *structuration process* by which tasks and people in an organization change in response to demands in the post-industrial age.

We consider each of these points in turn. In this chapter, we first examine definitions of technology, technological growth, and the role of technology in organizations as descriptive views of technology. We next note problems with those views, particularly in a changing world. We then focus on the technology organizational relationship most frequently studied, the relationship of technology and structure, and move from considering organizations taken one at a time to thinking about systems of organizations. We conclude with a discussion of the utility of technology as a construct and provide suggestions for further research.

## Descriptive Approaches to Technology

### Definitions

Definitions of technology in the literature focus our attention on different issues. Some examples are:

1  In contemporary society, the most powerful engines of change are human invention, innovation, and the applications of scientific knowledge. Collectively, we call these functions 'technology'. (Wenk 1989: 6)

2  In defining my concept of technology I restrict its *scope* to material artifacts (various configurations of hardware and software). I wish to sustain a distinction – at least theoretically – between the material nature of technology and the human activities that design or use those artifacts. (Orlikowski 1992: 403)

3  To focus on the technology of an organization is to view the organization as a place where some type of work is done, as a location where energy is applied to the transformation of inputs into outputs. The concept is broadly defined by organization theorists and includes not only the hardware used in performing work but also the skills and knowledge of workers, and even the characteristics of the objects on which work is performed. (Scott 1992: 20, 227)

4  We define technology as the physical combined with the intellectual or knowledge processes by which materials in some form are transformed into outputs used by another organization or subsystem within the same organization. (Hulin and Roznowski 1985: 47)

5  Organizations have two other characteristics that might provide a basis for a typology: raw materials (things, symbols, or people), which are transformed into outputs through the application of energy; and tasks or techniques, or techniques of effecting the transformation . . . 'Technology' is not used here in its commonplace sense of machines or sophisticated devices for achieving high efficiency, as in the term, 'technologically advanced society', but in its generic sense of the study of techniques or tasks. (Perrow 1986: 141)

6  Technology refers to a body of knowledge about the means by which we work on the world, our arts and our methods. Essentially, it is knowledge about the cause and effect relations of our actions. . . . Technology is knowledge that can be studied, codified, and taught to others. (Berniker 1987: 10)

7  The central idea is captured by the phrase *technology as equivoque*. An *equivoque* is something that admits of several possible or plausible interpretations and therefore can be esoteric, subject to misunderstandings, uncertain, complex, and recondite. (Weick 1990: 2)

Definition 1 focuses attention on the knowledge and scientific aspects of innovation. The invention of the wheel added to mankind's knowledge base but certainly did not reflect applications of science as today's technological innovations frequently do. Definition 2 severely limits technology's focus. Definition 3 brings the organization into the picture, adding hardware and workers' skills and knowledge to definition 1's focus on knowledge. It includes the components discussed by most organizational researchers interested in technology.

Definition 4 is consistent with definition 3 but, according to Weick:

> in contrast to many other definitions, however, explicit mention is made of raw materials and a transformation process, items that are often implicit in other definitions. Also novel to this definition is the mention that output might also be used within the same organization. Inclusion of this contingency makes it possible to talk about multiple, diverse technologies within the same organization. Finally, this definition is noteworthy because of its emphasis on process rather than on static knowledge, skills, and equipment. By equating technology with process, the authors alert us to the importance of changes over time and sequence. (1990: 3)

Definition 5 introduces yet other components of the definitional space of technology. The notions of energy application and specific tasks or techniques are highlighted. Perrow also positions the conceptual definition of technology away from the layman's definition. Definition 6 focuses on the knowledge aspects of technology, and provides an important distinction when coupled with the author's definition of a technical system as 'a specific combination of machines, equipment, and methods used to produce some valued outcome. . . . Every technical system embodies a technology. It derives from a large body of knowledge which provides the basis for design decisions' (Berniker 1987: 10; cited in Weick 1990). As Weick notes:

> By differentiating between the opportunities provided by knowledge ('technology') and the choice of one combination from this larger set as 'the' technical system, Berniker makes the design of technology a more explicit, more public process that need not be left to engineers . . . the very complexity and incomprehensibility of new technologies may warrant a new reexamination of our knowledge of cause–effect relations in human actions and the choice of a different combination of machines, equipment, and methods to produce the outcomes for which new technologies are instrumental. (1990: 4)

Definition 7 puts a whole new twist on the notion of technology. It says that technology has multiple meanings. 'Complex systems . . . make limited sense because so little is visible and so much is transient, and they make many different kinds of sense because the dense interactions within them can be modelled in so many different ways' (1990: 2).

Integrating these distinct views of technology is difficult. For instance, several of them contradict one another (e.g. Orlikowski and everyone else), and one definition includes almost everything (Weick). In and of themselves, these factors make the development of common conceptual models and empirical studies of technology and organizations difficult. In one attempt to integrate such views, Collins et al. (1986) provide an overarching paradigm for technology, suggesting that such systems are 'the set of mechanical, knowledge, and human technologies used to convert inputs into outputs in the production sector' (1986: 82).

*Mechanical technologies* refer to the physical machines, tools and equipment used to produce goods and are featured in most approaches to technology. *Human technologies* consist of the skills and physical energy involved in producing goods and can be substituted for mechanical technologies. *Knowledge technologies* refer to the abstract meanings and concepts used in production. Because knowledge technologies may constrain or facilitate the development and utilization of the mechanical and human technologies, many writers consider them the most important technologies (e.g. Perrow 1967). Interestingly, each of these technologies is interdependent: they coexist and covary in systems and organizations, which has significant impact for current and future organizations.

## Technological Growth

Current lay thinking about technological change often assumes that technological development is analogous to natural selection in the sense that the best technology survives. But we all know the story of the QWERTY typewriter keyboard and its competitor. In reality, the technological developer comes to his or her work with as many prejudices as anyone else, influenced by his or her culture, career considerations, intellectual enthusiasm, incentives, etc. The full range of technologies is never considered because these prejudices determine the range of real possibilities. Technological development may, in fact, have more to do with interaction of technical options with organization and interorganization dynamics (Tushman and Rosenkopf 1992), or with evolutionary

'technology cycles' of reciprocal interactions among 'researchers' beliefs, the artifacts they create, and the evaluation routines they foster' (Garud and Rappa 1994: 346).

The growth and consolidation of technology are often explained by two factors (Hughes 1987). One is the drive for high diversity and load factors, and a good economic mix. The load factor concept, now applied in many industries, was derived in the electric power industry. It refers to the ratio of average output to maximum output over a specified period. In an electric power system, the load factor is desirably diverse when customers make demands evenly across the twenty-four hour day. When this does not happen, managers try to expand the system to acquire a more desirable load or diversity. Thus, in northern California, when the demand factor exceeds the ability of the current mix of power plants (e.g. hydro, nuclear), managers might bring on power generated in a fossil fuel plant or buy power from another geographical area. The mix they choose depends on power availability and cost.

The other factor often cited as contributing to technological development is the effect of 'reverse salients' (Hughes 1987). 'A salient is a protrusion in a geometric figure, a line of battle, or an expanding weather front. As technological systems expand, reverse salients develop . . . components in the system that have fallen behind or are out of phase with the others' (Hughes 1987: 73). Attention is given to the reverse salient often through invention to bring it, once again, into line with other characteristics of the technological system. Other explanations of the shaping of technology focus on science's role in shaping technology, technology's role, the role of economics, political interests, and the social shaping of technology (MacKenzie and Wajcman 1985; Piore and Sabel 1984). The difficulty with each of these diagnoses of technological growth is that they are easy to describe, and challenging to assess: few metrics or standards exist, and little empirical or other work has been conducted that might develop such measures.

## The Role of Technology in Organizations

Weick reminds us that technology in organizations is a source of stochastic events, continuous events, and abstract events, and each type of event presents difficulties. Technologies are a source of *stochastic events* in organizations. Because they are not deterministic, with clear cause and effect relationships between what is to be done, how it is to be done, and when it is to be done, organizations face a variety of problems:

- A large repertoire of skills must be maintained, even though the skills are infrequently used.
- Special attention must be paid to start-ups in
  systems, and to anticipating faults that may
  lead to downtime.
- Distinctions between operators and maintenance skills become blurred, and skills in
  monitoring and diagnosis become critical
  skill sets (Weick 1990: 4).

Stochastic events pose difficulties for organizations, as they provide moving targets for
learning, because environmental changes occur
more quickly than people in organizations can
learn about them. Since recurrence is scarce,
learning is scarce, and stochastic events become
repetitive patterns and 'permanent fixtures' in
organizations (1990: 6).

People in such organizations face further
problems:

- Routine tasks become automated and non-
  routine tasks are left to human judgment,
  resulting in humans being faced with a
  complex task composed of an unbroken
  string of tough decisions.
- A reliability imperative develops, which
  places a premium on maintenance and
  integrity responsibilities, rather than responsibility.
- People must be committed to do what is
  necessary on their own, and be autonomously motivated to act on their own, at the
  same time that they assume the role of
  'variance absorber', dealing with counteracting the unexpected (Davis and Taylor
  1976: 388–9; Weick 1990: 4).

*Continuous events* precipitated by technology
also cause difficulties. Whereas reliability is the
hallmark of the industrial era (populated by
stochastic events), efficiency is the hallmark of
the post-industrial era, which is characterized by
continuous events, especially over disparate
geographical areas. New technologies knit
people, transactions, and locations together in
a continuous process, and they combine both
craft and continuous processing in the same
enterprise. The result of continuous events is that
the required people skills are different from
those required by discontinuous events: emphasis is given to work processes, rapid response to
emergencies, the ability to stay calm in tense
environments, and attempts to detect early
malfunctions in such continuous systems. As a
result, supervisors often pay more attention to
processes and products than to people.

If individuals lose a sense of cause and effect
with the advent of continuous process technology, the resulting systems can become much

more interactively complex and more prone to
failure. Since buffers may be eliminated (in the
form of mental models in operators' heads of
safe and unsafe operations), these continuous
processes and events compound the difficulties
associated with stochastic events and higher
mental workloads (Weick 1990).

Technology is increasingly a source of *abstract
events*, as more and more work associated with
new technologies has disappeared into machines.
The result is inadequate sampling of displayed
information, inattention to information on the
periphery, and distractions when building problem representations. New technologies have
essentially dual characters: they involve self-
contained, invisible unfolding *material processes*,
and equally self-contained, invisible *imagined
processes* that mentally unfold in the mind of the
individual or team (Weick 1990). As noted
before, these technologies exist as much in the
head of the operator as on the plant floor. The
result is that both managers and operators
experience increasing cognitive demands for
inference, imagination, integration, problem
solving and mental mapping to understand
what is going on out of sight. People thus need
sufficient understandings of abstract events so
they can intervene at any time, pick up the
process, and assemble a recovery (1990: 8).

By 1992, there seemed to be three perspectives
on the role of technology in organizations
(Orlikowski 1992). The first body of work (to
which comparative research belongs) is the *technological imperative* model. This model 'treats
technology as an independent influence on
human behavior or organizational properties,
that exerts unidirectional, causal influences over
humans and organizations similar to those
operating in nature' (Giddens 1984; Orlikowski
1992: 400). This is a very mechanical view of
technology and structure.

The second perspective is the *strategic choice*
model. From this perspective, technology is not
an external object but a product of ongoing
human action. Three streams of research are
within this perspective. One stream focuses on
how a particular technology is constructed
through social interactions. 'Particularly relevant here are socio-technical studies, which are
premised on the belief that outcomes such as job
satisfaction and productivity of workers can be
manipulated by jointly "optimizing" the social
and technical factors of jobs [Davis and Taylor
1976; Trist et al. 1963]' (Orlikowski 1992: 400).
These analyses rely too heavily on the capability
of humans, assuming that once managers are
committed to the right strategy, good things will
come for their organizations and the people in
them. The second stream within this second
perspective examines how shared interpretations

around a certain technology arise and affect interaction with that technology (e.g. Bijker 1987; Wynne 1988). This research tends to downplay the material and structural aspects of interacting with technology, but implicitly recognizes structure as a social construction.

The third stream is represented in Marxist accounts of technology (e.g. Braverman 1974; Noble 1984). These studies focus on how technology is devised and deployed to serve the purposes of political and economic interests of powerful capitalists, but fail to consider the person in the workplace. It is characteristic of these writers 'to emphasize the unevenness and unexpectedness of change and the diversity of causes and connections' (Scott 1992: 245). Of concern to them is 'roads not taken'.

The third model views *technology as a trigger of structural change*. This model portrays technology as an intervention in the relationship between people and organizational structure (Barley 1986). However, this model makes no room for physical changes which may occur during technology use. This view may be appropriate to the technological subject of Barley's study, CT scanners, but may work less well for information technology.

Within each of these models there are many studies that describe the role of technology in organizations, but few measure or assess those roles. One difficulty in conducting such studies is the complete absence of metrics or standards by which to judge good or poor performance, appropriate or inappropriate roles. This was one goal of the 'Management in the 1990s' project at MIT; however, the project focused solely on the role and relationships of information technology to organizations, rather than undertaking a more broadly based examination of roles and relationships of technology in and to organizations (Morton 1991).

## TECHNOLOGY AND A CHANGING WORLD

Organizations and the world in which they exist are undergoing profound changes; consequently, many of the conceptions of technology presented here are simply inadequate. In an organizational growth scenario that includes increased knowledge, complexity, and turbulence, the attributes of technologies are expanding and no longer bear much resemblance to the definitions above. Huber suggests that, as a result, 'post industrial organizations will adopt on a widespread basis three design features: (1) advanced communication and computer ($C^2$) technologies, (2) improved decision-group technologies and structures, and (3) "decision process management"'

(1984: 934). In contrast, Barley (1988) indicates that technological attributes include semiotic properties, cybernetic controls, and radical versus incremental innovation. He suggests that work is an interpretative act and technology affects that act in three ways: by creating codes as outputs, by generating codes as a byproduct of functioning, and by circumventing existing codes. Some technologies produce codes, as in medical imaging; some may generate codes as byproducts, as in machines that emit sounds and smells that indicate their status; and some circumvent codes that have served as an occupation's source of influence, as when they alter power structures in organizations. These technological attributes seem much clearer and more precise descriptors of organizational realities in a changing world than do definitions that focus on mechanical, human, and knowledge aspects of transformation but which fail to specify transformation processes.

Much discussion in the technological literature is about the impact of the cultural milieu on technological development (e.g. Noble 1984; Barley 1988). One problem in understanding technological development is that the national political milieux in which some organizations are trying to develop and adopt technology are changing in ways that are difficult to understand. At the same time cultural aspects of organizations are also changing, through the move to diversity in some work forces. Thus, environments are turbulent and dynamic, and cause organizations in turn to be turbulent and dynamic.

What gets done in organizations is also changing. For example, American organizations are turning increasingly to creating information – information made out of nothing, and once made, difficult to destroy. Other societies are very good at taking this information and selling it back to Americans and others in the form of hard goods (Thurow 1992a; 1992b; Lucky 1991). Current discussions of technology often fail to take the invisible nature of information into account even though many of the technologies focused on are information processing technologies.

### New Technologies that Strain Old Models

One of the difficulties with technology discussions and descriptions has to do with the ever-changing nature of technology. Current technologies in many cases strain and stretch old models of technology and organizations. These technologies include, among others, advances in biomedical engineering, virtual reality, genetic and chemical process engineering, and information technology (Teich 1993; Morton 1991).

Let us consider one of these examples. Information technology comprises mechanical (i.e. computer-based hardware), human, and knowledge technologies, coexisting to greater or lesser degrees in different systems and organizations, with greater or lesser performance impacts (National Research Council 1994). Integrating Anthony's (1965) management activities and organizational functions, Davis and Olson define information systems (IS) as:

> a federation of functional subsystems, each of which is divided into four major information processing components: transaction processing, operational control information system support, managerial control information system support, and strategic planning information system support. (1985: 45)

The strategic importance of information technology (IT) has increased as computing power and communication facilities have been enhanced. Indeed, it is believed that 'more than being helped by computers, companies will live by them, shaping strategy and structure to fit new information technology' (*Fortune* 1988). Examples of strategic uses of information technology often cited in the literature include airline reservation systems (Copeland and McKenney 1988), automated teller machines (Gerstein 1987), and computer-aided design/manufacturing (CAD/CAM) (Ohara 1988; Liker et al. 1992). The resulting importance of the relationship between IT and organizational performance is evidenced by the considerable literature on the subject.

Information technology is not the only new technology to stretch and strain existing organizational models; a quick perusal of virtual reality, CAD/CAM, chemical and continuous process technologies, and the human genome project in biomedical engineering are other examples of new technologies which call for a reexamination of organizational and technological models. Each of these technologies contributes to the development of stochastic, continuous, and abstract events in organizations. Each increases and changes the nature of human mental work by reason of their introduction and adoption in organizations. Each incorporates powerful linking mechanisms that produce or facilitate the development of virtual organizations (Goldman et al. 1995), and the technologies themselves are increasingly intelligent and sophisticated, assimilating more and more 'human' processing into their domain.

Such technologies will proliferate, and be restructured and integrated as organizations mature in technology utilization. McKenney and McFarlan (1982) observe that organizations are experiencing multiple technology assimilation patterns associated with new technology. They recommend managing these assimilations in phases, since assimilation patterns are different for each system, despite their coexistence.

The magnitude of investment in technology, and particularly information technology, in the past decade has prompted questions about payoff for both the nation and the individual enterprise. Because technology is often used to automate processes, and because automation is popularly associated with efficiency and cost reduction, questions about payoff usually center on productivity. In particular, some economic studies suggest that large investments in information technology by the service sector are not associated with substantial gains in productivity as measured by national macroeconomic statistics – the so-called IT paradox (Morton 1991; Thurow 1992b; National Research Council 1994). While some studies indicate that US productivity levels themselves compare quite favorably with those of international competitors in several important service industries, others suggest little correlation between investments in IT and productivity, profitability, or return on investment at the industry or enterprise level (National Research Council 1994). Each of these concerns and developments calls us to reexamine the paradigms we historically used to examine and assess technology, organizations and structures.

## RELATIONAL VIEWS OF TECHNOLOGY AND ORGANIZATIONS

Relational views of technology focus away from snapshots of technology or its characteristics, and refocus on relationships between organizations and technology, primarily organizational structure. In this section we develop such a view and use that view to develop a research agenda.

### Organization Structure and Technology

The concept of structure is usually understood to mean the configuration of activities in an organization that is enduring and persistent and provides the organization's patterned regularity (Ranson et al. 1980). Structure is a social construction of reality, a view sometimes called the positional view of structure (Monge and Eisenberg 1987). Research on the relationship of structure and technology has only been conducted since the 1960s (Gerwin 1981), though, as previously indicated, it has been frequently studied. By the 1980s, the structure-task-technology paradigm embraced 'two major perspectives: comparative analysis contributed by sociologists, and systems design developed by sociotechnical-systems advocates and administrative theorists' (1981: 3). Both were interested in the impact of task and technology on organization structure.

*Comparative analysis* studies treat systems as wholes, and the system is usually an organization. The studies by Blau and Shoenherr (1971), Child and Mansfield's (1972) research, Hage and Aiken (1967), the Aston Group (Pugh et al. 1969), and Woodward (1965) are all examples. Comparative analysis tries to draw general conclusions across many organizations and industries, but is 'short on conceptual insights, strong on empirical work, and explanation-oriented' (Gerwin 1981: 4).

A number of cross-national comparative analysis studies have been done in the last fifteen years, several of which show that structure differs across cultures regardless of technology. For example, Maurice et al. (1980) report relatively large differences in the organization of work in France, Britain and Germany: German firms exhibited higher levels of worker expertise, flexibility, and autonomy; British firms showed intermediate levels; and French firms concentrated expertise in decision-making in top managers and staff. Lincoln and his colleagues (Lincoln et al. 1986; Lincoln and Kalleberg 1990) compared American and Japanese manufacturing plants, and reported that the impact of technology on organizations was stronger in American than Japanese firms. Japanese firms were found to be less specialized and have taller hierarchies than American firms.

In contrast to comparative analyses, *systems design* studies differ in a number of ways. One premise of these studies is that organizations cannot be understood without specifying their components and the interrelationships among components. Research by Chapple and Sayles (1961), Lawrence and Lorsch (1967), Miller and Rice (1967), and Thompson (1967) represents this position. 'Systems research is rich on insights, weak on empirical work, and normatively oriented' (Gerwin 1981: 4) because it focuses on detailed observation of one organization at a time and, consequently, does not measure technology and structure and relate them.

A number of authors note that positionally structured organizations of the nineteenth and twentieth centuries, structured around traditional functions such as marketing, accounting, and finance, are obsolete. To replace them, Miles and Snow (1978) suggest that four strategic types of organizations have risen in response to different adaptations to technology, engineering, and administrative requirements: defenders, prospectors, analyzers, and reactors. Three of the four strategic types are successful and one, reactors, is unsuccessful.

In this typology, defenders seek to create a stable entrepreneurial domain. They do this by developing a single core technology that is highly cost efficient, to corner a narrow segment of the potential market. Prospectors maintain a broad and continuously developing domain, monitoring a wide range of environmental conditions and events in search of new product and market opportunities. Analyzers are interested in locating and exploiting new product and market opportunities; while maintaining a firm base of traditional products and customers. The perpetual instability and resultant poor performance of reactors arises from their inability to respond appropriately to their environments.

Neither the comparative analysis nor the system design approach to the relationship of structure and technology represents the more variegated view of technology seen in the literature since the mid 1980s. To meet global challenges and uncertainties, a number of authors call for restructuring organizations using available technologies. Peters (1987) calls for flatter organizations that rely on information brought in by information technologies. Kanter (1989) and Senge (1990) also call for interesting structural modifications to meet global changes, with Senge focusing on appearing, changing, and disappearing boundaries in organizations. Mitroff et al. (1994) propose that to meet tomorrow's challenges, organizations must be structured around five new organizational entities: a knowledge/learning center, a recovery development center, a world service/spiritual center, a world class operations center, and a leadership institute. These organizational forms may be yet another approach to functional specialization.

If technology is sector-specific in organizations, greater structural differentiation, which we see much of in today's organizations, will result in weaker correlations between technology in one sector and the structure of another sector. Thus, studies that examine relationships among technology and structure at the organizational level fail to tell a very interesting or true story. The result is that studies of the relationships between organizational structure and technology are interesting, but not particularly helpful in managing processes in the post-industrial age.

## Organizations as Technology

Two alternatives to the positional view of organizational structure and technology have been identified: the relational and cultural views of structure (Monge and Eisenberg 1987), which view organizations as networks of systems, people, and groups. Writers in the relational tradition focus on how humans forge and maintain communication linkages, thus enacting structure. Writers in the cultural tradition emphasize the roles of symbols, their meanings, and their transmission through the social system. Some writers attempt to integrate these two perspectives with the positional tradition. Structure is then seen as a complex medium of control which is continually produced and re-created in interaction and yet shapes that interaction; structures are constituted and constitutive.

> Formal and emergent networks coexist, and each can be best understood in the context of the other. . . . This implies that the constraints imposed by an existing structure limit and shape the interactions of people who work in various roles and fulfill various status sets. It also implies the converse, that the interaction of people helps to shape and define the social networks . . . the predominance of either type of structure is to some degree a function of where the organization is in its evolutionary life cycle. In most contemporary organizations both formal and emergent networks are in constant change. This change, however, is not simply the substitution of people in positions as characterized by the positional perspective. Rather, the positions themselves are somewhat altered and the structure significantly changed as a result. (1987: 309)

Network research, which positions organizations as technology, centers around describing characteristics of networks and their linkages, including their strength or intensity, symmetricality, reciprocity, and multiplexity. The strength or intensity of a linkage is a reflection of the amount of information, affect, or resources flowing through the system. Symmetricality refers to the degree to which both people enter into the same kind of relationship with one another. Reciprocity refers to the degree that two people supposedly in a relationship report the relationship. Multiplexity refers to the degree to which the same people are involved in different networks in an organization. Content of linkages is also frequently studied because it determines what flows through the network.

Environmental, organizational, and individual influences are often examined in network studies; for instance, environmental effects such as national character have been shown to influence organizational communication patterns. French employees, for example, avoid close ties at work while Japanese employees seek such ties (Crozier 1964; Yoshino 1968); French organizational network structure patterns would thus differ from Japanese patterns. Other environmental influences include local character, changes in the business environment, and

characteristics of specific industries. The characteristics of jobs, tasks, technology, and the organization as a whole also influence emergent structures:

> In a recent review, Fulk, Power, and Schmitz (1986) presented support for four propositions linking electronic messaging to organizational communication networks. Specifically, they argue that electronic mail facilitates (1) more horizontal linkages across geographical distances thus linking a diversity of people who would otherwise not communicate; (2) more vertical linkages across status levels, leading to a flattening of the hierarchy by encouraging less social inhibition about such contacts; (3) less dense networks, in which a person's contacts are less likely to know each other; and (4) linkages that 'spill over' to the relational non-electronic communication network in the organization, this having implications for changes in friendship patterns and enduring organizational structures. (Monge and Eisenberg 1987: 320–1)

The emergence of informal structure as a result of organizations acting as technology is dependent on individual differences. People express their preferences for interacting or not interacting with others through their network behaviors. A well developed line of research at the individual level focuses on the roles people occupy: liaisons and isolates have different characteristics, with liaisons being better educated, of higher status, with higher rank and tenure (e.g. Schwartz and Jacobson 1977; Roberts and O'Reilly 1974).

Assessments of organizational networks focus on technical complexity, uncertainty, and interdependence. According to Scott (1992: 231):

- The greater the technical complexity, the greater the structural complexity.
- The greater the technical uncertainty, the less formalization and centralization.
- The greater the technical interdependence, the more resources must be devoted to coordination.

Galbraith (1973; 1977) argues that one way the varying demands of technologies on structure can be summarized is to ascertain how much information must be processed during the execution of a task sequence. Network approaches are ideally suited to this. Information requirements increase as a function of increasing diversity, uncertainty, and interdependence of work flow, and formal structures can be employed to manage work flow: rules and programs, schedules, departmentalization, hierarchy and delegation, and micro coordination.

## Technology as Structuration

Positional views of structure focus on rigid and very narrow structural and technological constructs (i.e. complexity, task definition, work flow integration, etc.). Relational and cultural views of structure add the notion of a sense of process. They also introduce other technological constructs such as complexity, uncertainty, and interdependence. Because this research primarily emanates from the body of research concerned with organizational communication, this literature is often not considered by researchers concerned with technology.

A merger of the positional and relational or cultural views of structure is a step toward developing a more comprehensive view of technology and organizations in the post-industrial age. If this were done, a more fluid approach to structure would be required. Returning to the definitions first presented in this chapter, it seems one would want as variegated a conceptualization of technology as one would have developed of structure. Collins et al. (1986) and Barley (1988) offer beginnings of that task.

Orlikowski (1992) and later De Sanctis and Poole (1994) propose a reconceptualization of technology that takes into account both the older view of technology as an objective external force and the newer view of technology as the outcome of strategic choice and social action. This view is also quite consistent with a merger of positional and relational views of structure, since such a merger combined with the world changes described previously suggests the emergence of fluid organizational forms with appearing, disappearing, and changing boundaries within and between organizations. This structuration view is also adaptable to thinking about structure and technology at the systems level. Essentially, a *structurational model of technology* collapses previous thinking about structure and technology and their interrelationship into a single set of constructs from which it is difficult, if not impossible, to separate technology and structure. In contrast to structure, the emergent property of ongoing action (Weick 1969), *structuration* is the production and reproduction of a social system through members' use of rules and resources in interaction. Structuration suggests, then, that systems are built from rules and interactions; that resources, like actions, are tools people use to enact organizations; and that structures are the medium and outcome of the interaction (Weick 1990: 18). Structuration is a particularly useful construct for technology and organizational studies, as it 'sensitizes the observer to look for ongoing redefinition among structure, action, and technology', and it suggests that

technology is both a cause and a consequence of structure (1990: 18).

> The theory of structuration recognizes that human actions are enabled and constrained by structures, yet that these structures are the result of previous actions. In Giddens' framework, structure is understood paradigmatically, that is, as a generic concept that is only manifested in the structural properties of social systems (Giddens 1979, pp. 64–65). Structural properties consist of the rules and resources that human agents use in their everyday interaction. These rules and resources mediate human actions, while at the same time they are reaffirmed through being used by human actors.
>
> In this theory, the role of human actors in reaffirming structural properties is highlighted so as to avoid reification. The recognition that actors are knowledgeable and reflective is a central premise. (Orlikowski 1992: 404)

Orlikowski introduces a recursive notion of technology as created and changed by human action and also used to accomplish some action, which is consistent with our earlier definitions. She calls this the duality of technology. Technology is interpretatively flexible (consistent with definition 7), and the interaction of technology and organization is a function of the different actors and socio-historical contexts in which it develops.

Technological development and use are often done in different organizations. Thus, much work that constitutes technology is separate in time and space from actions constituted by technology. Recognizing this time–space discontinuity helps us understand how researchers came to view technology as a fixed object *or* as a *product* of human interaction (Tyre and Orlikowski 1994). It depended on when and where they looked:

> Technology is the product of human action, while it also assumes structural properties. That is, technology is physically constructed by actors working in a given social context, and technologies are socially constructed by actors through the different meanings they attach to it and the various features they emphasize and use. However, it is also the case that once developed and deployed, technology tends to become reified and institutionalized, losing its connection with the human agents that constructed it and gave it meaning, and it appears to be a part of the objective, structural properties of the organization. (Orlikowski 1992: 406)

These arguments about technology are consistent with those we might pose about structure. Structure is both changed and used by humans. Structure can be interpretatively flexible. Structure development and use are often viewed by researchers at different times. Thus, the constituents of structure are often perceived as separate from what it constitutes. Recognizing this time–space discontinuity helps us see how researchers came to see structure as fixed (the positional view) or as a product of human interaction (the relational view).

Extending the view of the duality of technology, it becomes increasingly clear that technology and structure are thus both a *process* and a *product* of human action and interaction. Understanding this should increase our impatience with sociotechnical frameworks that fail to account for the duality, or for the increasingly important longitudinal and temporal view of technology and organizations. This duality also highlights that technology is increasingly becoming the *structuration process* by which tasks and people in organizations change in response to the demands of post-industrial society.

## Systems of Organizations

Defining technology as Wenk does in definition 1, or perhaps as Orlikowski does in definition 2, technology, and particularly information technology, is rapidly changing the nature of organizations, and the structuring of decision-making in them. Traditionally, most discussions of technology and organizations have focused on impacts of technology on an industry, an enterprise, or an organizational activity. However, the advent of several technologies also heralds the arrival of new organizational constructs:

- relatively affordable and widely distributed global telecommunications capabilities, which link together geographically dispersed parts of an organization
- decision support technologies which emulate or replicate human capabilities and allow for quick decisions based on much information
- technologies which allow decision-makers to participate in remote discussions through teleoperation, telepresence, and teleconferencing, thereby increasing interconnectedness and interdependence
- technologies which permit the development of virtual communities and participation by remote participants.

These technologies make possible the blurring of organizational boundaries and the creation of virtual organizations, tied together in pursuit of specific opportunities, or for mutually beneficial (symbiotic) relationships in a market. Many of these organizational constructs are now touted as being instrumental in defining and producing

competitive advantage in a number of industries (National Research Council 1994; Goldman et al. 1995). Vendors and suppliers, customers, and support organizations can be bound together in virtual temporary or permanent systems that can effectively defeat competitors in the marketplace, and which can provide significant added value to the host organization, as well as to the participating customers and suppliers. Thus, rather than technology and organizational constructs coexisting and covarying as in the past, organizations in the future can be expected to be much more fluid, with teaming arrangements and organizational partners defined on an opportunity, or market, basis.

New technologies and global economic development increasingly produce systems of organizations tied together through interdependencies. The notion of organization sets has been around for some time (e.g. Evan 1966). In 1979, and again in 1986, Perrow suggested using network methodology to study forces among organizations that contribute to their behavior. Such studies are non-existent in the organizational literature.

In one of the few pieces in the organizational literature that addresses issues of interorganizational linkages, Mitroff and Mohrman (1986) discuss what happened during a run on savings and loan institutions in Ohio. The fate of these organizations was tied to that of an obscure securities firm in Florida and the value of British oil stocks was linked to both. These authors point out that managers need to develop holistic or systems views of their organizations (as should researchers).

Another example of systems of organizations operating together is taken from Piers Paul Read's (1993) account of the meltdown at the Soviet power reactor at Chernobyl. This example is filled with technological overlays. In designing the Chernobyl power plant, the axiom, 'the bigger the better' was put to full use. The plant was to be the largest in the world with each of its six units having enormous generating capacity.

The framework for the development of reactor number four and nuclear power in the Soviet Union was based on deliberations by the Central Committee, the military high command, and the Ministry of Medium Machine Building. These debates were embedded in the Soviet history of nuclear development and focused on cost; safety was never an issue. In addition to this kind of interorganizational interaction, when construction of the power station was begun at Chernobyl, its manager had the awesome task of supervising the building of both the power station and the town of Pripyat. The parts specified by the plant's designer were frequently impossible to find and had to be manufactured on site. This encouraged a spirit of improvisation which can be dangerous in nuclear power generation.

In addition, many of the goods supplied by other organizations were shoddy, reflecting a spirit of low concern for quality by those organizations. The plant manager reported to both the Ministry of Medium Machine Building and the Communist Party, which acted as a shadow administration in every social, political, industrial, or cultural structure. A number of other interorganizational interactions and interdependencies characterized this situation. It is possible organizations can live without considering these kinds of interdependencies if their technological cores are unsophisticated. But as these cores become more sophisticated and as various cores become more tightly tied to one another, designers and managers must manage the linkages among organizations. To date, organizational researchers have provided no conceptual tools to help manage these linkages.

Some systems theorists have dwelled at length on the conceptualization of interdependence (e.g. Thompson 1967), but have failed to develop good operational measures of the concept. Similarly, some comparative researchers have also developed concepts of interdependence: for instance, when the performance of one or more operations has consequences for others. This research shows that as one moves from the work level, through the department level, to the organizational level, the chances of a relationship between structure and interdependence decreases (Gerwin 1981).

Each of these concepts poses interesting and unique measurement difficulties. Requirements for new metrics are emerging at the same time that current metrics explaining burgeoning technological growth are showing their age. Neither natural selection, nor load factors, nor reverse salients are adequate constructs for understanding or measuring technology, or its relationship to an organization. What is needed is a different vantage point, and along with the vantage point, different constructs, to better understand relationships between organizations and technology.

## A RESEARCH AGENDA

Before moving to specific discussion of future research, we consider the lingering and important question of whether technology is today a useful construct with which to gauge and measure organizations. With the plethora of organizational and technological changes occurring today, some of which have been catalogued in this chapter, organizations and researchers are increasingly questioning the utility of traditional paradigms and metrics. Thus, the notion of technology as a vulnerable construct is worth considering. Technology is rapidly changing, as are organizations, but neither is disappearing. Although we have difficulties in measuring and assessing technology, and although organizational researchers are searching for useful constructs with which to assess the relationships between organizations and technology, neither of these developments suggests that the concept of technology is antiquated, or that technological impacts on organizations can be expected to disappear or dissipate in the years to come. A perspective is needed that incorporates new views of useful organizational constructs (i.e. duality of technology, structuration rather than structure, etc.) to understand relationships between technology and organizations.

We have not discussed at length in this chapter such a contingency framework of organizational and technological utility; yet, such a framework clearly makes sense. Uniform or generalized descriptions of technology and organizational applicability, adaptability, or utility are increasingly artifacts of simpler technological eras. Here we call for increasing attention to the nature of temporal and longitudinal studies of organizations and technology.

The need to understand technology as a process intertwined with other processes underscores the importance of research that consider the following:

- Measurement and assessment difficulties with technology produce systemic difficulties in managing organizations.
- Technology's and organizations' dual natures as product and process suggest that sociotechnical frameworks need to change significantly to accommodate longitudinal, temporal views of technology.
- Technology has increasingly become the *structuration process* by which tasks and people in an organization change in response to demands in the post-industrial age.

Researchers need to address the immediate problem of measuring or assessing technology. Currently, technology is often measured in terms of inputs, processes, and outputs, a rather traditional systems-oriented paradigm that blurs distinctions between processes, and muddies cause and effect relationships so important to understanding technologies. Current measurements are also insensitive to sources or consequences of stochastic events, and to interactions between technology; the result is that it is difficult to envision how current approaches to measuring and assessing technology can assist in deciphering changing and complex roles of technology in organizations, and relationships between organizations and technology.

Weick (1990) suggests that understanding the importance of stochastic, continuous and abstract events in technology and in organizations highlights additional difficulties with measuring and assessing technology. For instance, if organizational members using technology 'lose the bubble' with respect to cause and effect, and the system becomes more interactively complex and more prone to failure, perhaps the concept of *operator error*, long used as a measure of how 'safe' an organization or system is, should be replaced. Since such a term is now no longer reflective of unique and sizable cognitive demands, and since operators are often blamed for designer and system errors (Perrow 1984), perhaps the term might best be replaced with the term *operator mistakes*, which emanate from a misunderstanding, a misidentification, or a misconception rather than from straying from guided or prescribed paths (i.e. an error) (Weick 1990: 7).

In addition, the measurement of *formation of intention* becomes increasingly important in abstract systems, as does the measurement of individual and organizational 'mental maps', since the relational information contained in such maps is most important. The measurement dilemmas of *technology on the floor* and *technology in the head*, as well as the measurement of the *role of emotion* in technology and in society, with proliferating continuous, stochastic, and abstract events, are equally challenging measurement difficulties (Weick 1990).

Several other research agendas are suggested by this review. More refined typologies of technology, and further study of issues of our changing world, as well as technological constructs, are traditional types of 'next steps'.

Decision settings in the future will be characterized by more and increasing knowledge, complexity, and turbulence (Huber 1984). As a result, technologies that increase the efficiency and effectiveness of meetings and interactions will be of particular significance. Some types of these technologies have already been developed for teleconferencing, video conferencing, and electronic mail services for aiding distributed groups (Hogan 1989; Johansen et al. 1979); integrating these technologies into reasoning and decision systems is a natural evolution.

Following our discussion of structure and technology, we might merge the positional and more fluid approaches to organizational structure and relate the derived structural constructs to technology. It should be clear that examining the technology–structure relationship at the level of the organization probably does not make

much sense because different technologies and different levels of technological development are represented in different parts of any organization. We do, however, need to develop conceptual ways to think about *systems of organizations*, and about *systems of advanced technologies* which reside in and coexist with organizations.

Following a structurational view of technology, we might well recognize that many notions advanced by researchers interested in structure are similar to, identical to, or subsumed under notions discussed by technology researchers. It may well be time to merge the two approaches and work toward deriving one model of structure/technology.

Thoughtful examinations of new technologies and the nature of stochastic, continuous and abstract events in organizations suggest that a number of research studies are required:

- investigations into concepts intended to differentiate among the different forms that stochastic events can take, i.e. using measures of predictability, efficacy, equivocality, clarity and task complexity, among others (Campbell 1988; Dornbusch and Scott 1975; Daft and Lengel 1986)
- examinations of differences in diagnosis, analysis, and problem solving tasks in order to account for new mental demands consequent with new technologies
- investigations that utilize multiple measures in order to assess performance of complex tasks in actual and virtual organizations
- investigations of the nature and role of interruptions and arousal in simple and complex technological organizations
- examinations of the role that increased cognitive demands, increased electronic complexity, and dense organizational interdependence over large areas have on increases in incidences of unexpected outcomes that produce unexpected ramifications
- investigations of whether such unexpected outcomes and ramifications are occasions for failure or opportunities for innovation and learning
- explorations of the nature and importance of temporal and longitudinal views of technology and organizational relationships, as well as the importance of contingency frameworks which consider organizational types as constructs in organizational and technological studies.

In short, investigations of how best organizations can compensate for the energizing, debilitating or systemic effects of technology are well intentioned and important. In designing such technologies and organizations, future researchers might do well to examine how best to make complex judgment tasks simpler, to distribute responsibility among team members, to reduce distractions and provide incentives for early reporting of error and problem solving, to reduce production pressures and heighten perceptions of control, and to add slack capacity to attention (Weick 1990: 33). These, of course, are hardly new organizational or technology challenges. However, in the wake of an environment characterized by stochastic events, continuous processing, and higher cognitive workload, increased attention to fundamental outstanding research issues such as these is ever more important.

REFERENCES

Anthony, R.N. (1965) *Planning and Control Systems: a Framework for Analysis*. Cambridge, MA: Harvard University Press.

Barley, S. (1986) 'Technology as an occasion for structuring: evidence from observation of CT scanners and the social order of radiology departments', *Administrative Science Quarterly*, 31: 78–108.

Barley, S. (1988) 'Technology, power, and the social organization of work: towards a pragmatic theory of skilling and deskilling', in P. Torbert and S. Barley (eds), *Research in the Sociology of Organizations*, vol. 6. Beverly Hills, CA: Sage. pp. 33–80.

Berniker, E. (1987) 'Understanding technical systems'. Paper presented at the Symposium on Management Training Programs: Implications of New Technologies, Geneva, Switzerland, November.

Bijker, W.E. (1987) 'The social construction of bakelite: toward a theory of invention', in W.E. Bijker, T.P. Hughes and T. Pinch (eds), *The Social Construction of Technological Systems*. Cambridge, MA: MIT Press. pp. 159–87.

Blau, P.M. and Schoenherr, R.A. (1971) *The Structure of Organizations*. New York: Basic Books.

Braverman, H. (1974) *Labor and Monopoly Capital: the Degradation of Work in the Twentieth Century*. New York: Monthly Review Press.

Campbell, D.J. (1988) 'Task complexity: a review and analysis', *Academy of Management Review*, 13: 40–52.

Chapple, E.D. and Sayles, L.R. (1961) *The Measure of Management*. New York: Macmillan.

Child, J. and Mansfield, R. (1972) 'Technology, size, and organization structure', *Sociology*, 6: 369–93.

Collins, P.D., Hage, J. and Hull, F. (1986) 'A framework for analyzing technical systems in complex organizations', in *Research in the Sociology of Organizations*, vol. 6. Greenwich, CT: JAI Press. pp. 81–100.

Copeland, D.G. and McKenney, J.L. (1988) 'Airline reservations systems: lessons from history', *MIS Quarterly*, 12(3): 353–69.

Crozier, M. (1964) *The Bureaucratic Phenomenon*. Chicago: University of Chicago Press.

Daft, R.L. and Lengel, R.H. (1986) 'Organizational information requirements, media richness and structural design', *Management Science*, 32: 554–71.

Davis, G.B. and Olson, M.H. (1985) *Management Information Systems*, 2nd edn. New York: McGraw-Hill.

Davis, L.E. and Taylor, J.C. (1976) 'Technology, organization and job structure', in R. Dubin (ed.), *Handbook of Work, Organization, and Society*. Chicago: Rand-McNally. pp. 379–419.

De Sanctis, G. and Poole, M.S. (1994) 'Capturing the complexity in advanced technology use: adaptive structuration theory', *Organization Science*, 5: 121–47.

Dornbusch, S M. and Scott, W.R. (1975) *Evaluation and the Exercise of Authority*. San Francisco: Jossey-Bass.

Evan, W.M. (1966) 'The organization set: toward a theory of interorganizational relations', in J.D. Thompson (ed.), *Approaches to Organizational Design*. Pittsburgh: University of Pittsburgh Press. pp. 175–91.

*Fortune* (1988) 'The winning organization', 26 September: 50–60.

Fulk, J., Power, J.G. and Schmitz, J. (1986) 'Communication in organizations via electronic mail: An analysis of behavioral and relational issues'. Paper presented at the Annual Meeting of the American Institute of Decision Sciences, Honolulu, HA.

Galbraith, J. (1973) *Designing Complex Organizations*. Reading, MA: Addison-Wesley.

Galbraith, J. (1977) *Organization Design*. Reading, MA: Addison-Wesley.

Garud, R. and Rappa, M.A. (1994) 'A socio-cognitive model of technology evolution: the case of cochlear implants', *Organization Science*, 5: 344–62.

Gerstein, M.S. (1987) *The Technology Connection*. Reading, MA: Addison-Wesley.

Gerwin, D. (1981) 'Relationships between structure and technology', in P.C. Nystrom and W.H. Starbuck (eds), *Handbook of Organizational Design*, vol. 2. New York: Oxford. pp. 3–38.

Giddens, A. (1979) *Central Problems in Social Theory: Action, Structure and Contradiction in Social Analysis*. Berkeley, CA: University of California Press.

Giddens, A. (1984) *The Constitution of Society: Outline of the Theory of Structure*. Berkeley, CA: University of California Press.

Goldman, S.L., Nagel, R.N. and Preiss, K. (1995) *Agile Competitors and Virtual Organizations: Strategies for Enriching the Customer*. New York: Van Nostrand Reinhold.

Hage, J. and Aiken, M. (1967) 'Program change and

organizational properties: a comparative analysis', *American Journal of Sociology*, 72: 503–19.

Hogan, N. (1989) 'Controlling impedance at the man–machine interface', in *Proceedings of the 1989 IEEE Conference on Robotics and Automation*, Scottsdale, Arizona, 14–19 May.

Huber, G.P. (1984) 'The nature and design of post-industrial organizations', *Management Science*, 30: 928–51.

Hughes, T.P. (1987) 'The evolution of large technological systems', in W.E. Bijker, T.P. Hughes, and T.J. Pinch (eds), *The Social Construction of Technological Systems*. Cambridge, MA: MIT Press.

Hulin, C.L. and Roznowski, M. (1985) 'Organizational technologies: effects on organizations' characteristics and individuals', in L.L. Cummings and B.M. Staw (eds), *Research in Organizational Behavior*, vol. 7. Greenwich, CT: JAI Press. pp. 39–86.

Johansen, R., Vallee, J. and Spangler, K. (1979) *Electronic Meetings*. Reading, MA: Addison-Wesley.

Kanter, R. (1989) *When Giants Learn to Dance: Mastering the Challenges of Strategy, Management, and Careers in the 1990s*. New York: Simon & Schuster.

Lawrence, P.R. and Lorsch, J.W. (1967) *Organization and Environment*. Boston: Graduate School of Business Administration, Harvard University.

Liker, J.K., Fleischer, M. and Arnsdorf, D. (1992) 'Fulfilling the promises of CAD', *Sloan Management Review*, Spring: 74–86.

Lincoln, J.R., Matsuo, H. and McBride, K. (1986) 'Organization structures in Japanese and U.S. manufacturing', *Administrative Science Quarterly*, 31: 338–64.

Lincoln, J.R. and Kalleberg, A. (1990) *Culture, Control, and Commitment: a Study of Work Organization and Work Attitudes in the United States and Japan*. New York: Cambridge University Press.

Lucky, R. (1991) *Silicon Dreams*. New York: Van Nostrand Reinhold.

McKenney, J.L. and McFarlan, F.W. (1982) 'The information archipelago – maps and bridges', *Harvard Business Review*, September–October: 100–17.

MacKenzie, D. and Wajcman, J. (1985) *Social Shaping of Technology*. Philadelphia, PA: Open University Press.

Maurice, M., Sorge, A. and Warner, M. (1980) 'Societal differences in organizing manufacturing units: a comparison of France, West Germany, and Great Britain', *Organization Studies*, 1: 59–86.

Miles, R.E. and Snow, C.C. (1978) *Organizational Strategy, Structure and Process*. New York: McGraw-Hill.

Miller, E.J. and Rice, A.K. (1967) *Systems of Organizations*. London: Tavistock.

Mitroff, I.I. and Mohrman, S. (1986) 'The whole system is broke and in desperate need of fixing:

notes on the second industrial revolution', *International Journal of Technology Management*, 1: 65–75.

Mitroff, I.I., Mason, R.O. and Pearson, C.M. (1994) *Framebreak*. San Francisco: Jossey-Bass.

Monge, P.R. and Eisenberg, E.M. (1987) 'Emerging communication networks', in F. Jablin, L. Putnam, K.H. Roberts and L.W. Porter (eds), *Handbook of Organizational Communication*. Beverly Hills, CA: Sage. pp. 304–42.

Morton, M.S. (ed.) (1991) *The Corporation of the 1990s: Information Technology and Organizational Transformation*. New York: Oxford University Press.

National Research Council. (1994) *Information Technology in the Service Society: a Twenty-First Century Lever*. Washington, DC: National Academy Press.

Noble, D.F. (1984) *Forces of Production: a Social History of Industrial Automation*. New York: Oxford University Press.

Ohara, M. (1988) 'CAD/CAM at Toyota Motor Company', in T. Kitagawa (ed.), *Computer Science and Technologies*. New York: North Holland.

Orlikowski, W. (1992) 'The duality of technology: rethinking the concept of technology in organizations', *Organization Science*, 3: 398–426.

Perrow, C. (1967) 'A framework for the comparative analysis of organizations', *American Sociological Review*, 32: 194–208.

Perrow, C. (1979) *Complex Organizations: a Critical Essay*, 2nd edn. New York: Random House.

Perrow, C. (1984) *Normal Accidents: Living with High Risk Technologies*. New York: Basic Books.

Perrow, C. (1986) *Complex Organizations: a Critical Essay*, 3rd edn. New York: Random House.

Peters, T. (1987) *Thriving on Chaos*. New York: Knopf.

Piore, M.J. and Sabel, C.F. (1984) *The Second Industrial Divide: Possibilities for Prosperity*. New York: Basic Books.

Pugh, D.S., Hickson, D.J., Hinings, C.R. and Turner, C. (1969) 'The context of organization structure', *Administrative Science Quarterly*, 14: 91–114.

Ranson, S., Hinings, B. and Greenwood, R. (1980) 'The structuring of organizational structures', *Administrative Science Quarterly*, 25: 1–17.

Read, P.P. (1993) *Ablaze: the Story of the Heroes and Victims of Chernobyl*. New York: Random House.

Roberts, K.H. and O'Reilly, C.A. (1974) 'Some correlates of communication roles in organizations', *Academy of Management Journal*, 22: 42–57.

Schwartz, D. and Jacobson, E. (1977) 'Organizational communication network analysis: the liaison communication role', *Organization Behavior and Human Performance*, 18: 158–74.

Scott, W.R. (1992) *Organizations: Rational, Natural, and Open Systems*. Englewood Cliffs, NJ: Prentice-Hall.

Senge, P.M. (1990) *The Fifth Discipline: the Art and Practice of the Learning Organization*. New York: Doubleday Currency.

Teich, A.H. (1993) *Technology and the Future*. New York: St Martin's Press.

Thompson, J.D. (1967) *Organizations in Action*. New York: McGraw-Hill.

Thurow, L.C. (1992a) 'Who will own the 21st century?', *Sloan Management Review*, Spring: 5–18.

Thurow, L.C. (1992b) *Head to Head: Coming Economic Battles among Japan, Europe, and America*. New York: William Morrow.

Trist, E.L., Higgin, G.W., Murray, H. and Pollock, A.B. (1963) *Organizational Choice*. London: Tavistock.

Tushman, M.L. and Rosenkopf, L. (1992) 'Organizational determinants of technological change: toward a sociology of technological evolution', in B.M. Staw and L.L. Cummings (eds), *Research in Organizational Behavior*, vol. 14. Greenwich, CT: JAI Press. pp. 311–47.

Tyre, M.J. and Orlikowski W.J. (1994) 'Windows of opportunity: temporal patterns of technological adaptation in organizations', *Organization Science*, 5(1): 98–118.

Weick, K.E. (1969) *The Social Psychology of Organizing*. Reading, MA: Addison-Wesley.

Weick, K.E. (1990) 'Technology as equivoque: sensemaking in new technologies', in P.S. Goodman and L. Sproull (eds), *Technology and Organizations*. San Francisco: Jossey-Bass.

Wenk, E. (1989) *Tradeoffs: Imperatives of Choice in a High Tech World*. Baltimore, MD: Johns Hopkins University Press.

Woodward, J. (1965) *Industrial Organization: Theory and Practice*. London: Oxford University Press.

Wynne, B. (1988) 'Unruly technology: practical rules, impractical discourses and public understanding', *Social Studies of Science*, 18: 147–67.

Yoshino, M. (1968) *Japan's Managerial System*. Cambridge, MA: MIT Press.

# 9

# *Organizing for Innovation*

## DEBORAH DOUGHERTY

The ability to develop viable new products and services is important to many organizations. Product innovation enables organizations to improve the quality of their output, revitalize mature businesses, enter new markets, react to competitive encroachment, try out new technologies, leverage investment in technologies that are so expensive that no single product can recoup them, and develop alternative applications for existing product categories, to name just a few outcomes. For organizations which must adapt to changing competition, markets, and technologies, product innovation is not simply a fad. It is a necessity (Hage 1988; Jelinek and Schoonhoven 1990; Zahra and Covin 1995).

Not surprisingly, the literature relevant to innovation includes thousands of books and articles. Just within the fields of management, many review articles have been written. See, for example, Cooper (1983), Crawford (1983), Gatignon and Robertson (1985), and Johne and Snelson (1988) in marketing; Burgelman (1983), Johnson (1988), and Day (1990) in strategy; Rothwell (1977), Roberts (1988), and Rothwell and Whiston (1990) in technology management; Downs and Mohr (1976), Kimberly (1981), Van de Ven (1986), Nord and Tucker (1987), Hage (1988), Kanter (1988), and Damanpour (1991) in organization theory.

Despite all this attention, organizations continue to have problems innovating effectively. They have difficulty shifting to new technologies (Tushman and Anderson 1986); moving away from familiar customers (Christensen and Bower 1993); changing their strategic paradigm (Johnson 1988); breaking out of prevailing patterns of decision-making (Starbuck and Milliken 1988); adjusting their product architecture (Henderson and Clark 1990); using marketing tools appro-

priately (Mahajan and Wind 1992); and learning from experience (Van de Ven and Polley 1992). According to Cooper and Kleinschmidt, 'What the literature prescribes and what most firms do are miles apart' (1986: 73).

The persistence of these problems suggests that more theory building is necessary. However, the existence of this large literature suggests that a fresh perspective is also necessary, since established conceptual views do not address all the problems. The purpose of this chapter is to build theory on organizing for innovation by changing the perspective on the topic in three ways.

The first change in perspective is to *build up from the activities of innovation*. Most organization views of innovation are not anchored on underlying activities, because 'innovation' is defined very broadly as the adoption of any device, system, process, problem, program, product, or service that is new to the organization (Downs and Mohr 1976; Kanter 1988; Damanpour et al. 1989). Within this 'anything goes' framework, research relies on broad constructs like administrative versus technical, development stage, and radical versus incremental. These constructs may correlate with various outcomes (albeit at a low level – Damanpour 1991), but researchers still find what Downs and Mohr (1976) called a 'troublesome instability' in their relationships (Takeuchi and Nonaka 1986; Nord and Tucker 1987; Day 1994). This chapter focuses on the activities of product innovation, and how to organize effectively for them. My central premise is straightforward: theories of organization should reflect the activities that are being organized. Focusing on the activities of product innovation limits the generalizability of the implications, but it allows a more thorough treatment of the particular processes, dynamics, and events underlying this kind of innovation.

My second change in perspective is to *shift the level of analysis*. Much of the innovation literature concerns either individual innovation projects (Brown and Eisenhardt 1995) or successful high technology organizations (Kanter 1983; Jelinek and Schoonhoven 1990). These theories address project management and 'best practices' for technology-centered, simple organizations, but they apply less well to organizations which have the most trouble with product innovation – the large, complex firm. In this setting, product innovation involves the re-innovation of the project and the simultaneous adaptation of the organization, not just the management of separate projects (Leonard-Barton 1988; Tyre and Orlikowski 1994). By concentrating on projects or simple organizations, theorists overlook the most problematic relationship between innovation and the organization. In addition, not all large, complex organizations are successful with innovation. By concentrating on successful practices, theorists overlook the question of how noninnovative organizations can *become* innovative (Hage 1988; Van de Ven 1986; Hedlund and Ridderstrale 1994).

The third change is to *deal with the fact that complex organizations have difficulty with innovation* (Hage 1988). Rather than simply present another normative model of 'the innovative organization', this chapter first examines why existing models are not adequate. The basic questions are how and why do large, complex organizations inhibit the activities necessary to effective product innovation? I use the metaphor 'tension' to frame the discussion. Both Pelz and Andrews (1966) and Jelinek and Schoonhoven (1990) characterize innovation as 'tensions', because the term captures very well the organizing challenges of iterating between diverse activities, working around barriers, combining insights, and resolving the conflicts of seemingly opposing forces, all of which can be found in the innovation process. Thinking of the organizing challenges of innovation as inherent tensions that must be accommodated emphasizes the dialectical nature of innovation, in which the organization and the new products are mutually constitutive (Barley 1986; Scarborough and Corbett 1992; Heller 1994).

In the following sections, findings from a number of fields of study are first synthesized into four sets of activities that are necessary for effective product innovation. Next, the organizing problems associated with each set of activities are summarized in terms of the inherent tensions which must be managed if the organization is to enable those activities. Research

suggests that people have developed ways to handle these tensions effectively at the project level, but still not at the organization level. I then go back to Burns and Stalker's (1966) classic discussion, because they provided initial insights into how these tensions might be managed across the organization. I flesh out their largely overlooked insights into possible solutions, and conclude with some new, or in fact *re*newed, directions for research.

## PROBLEMS IN ORGANIZING FOR PRODUCT INNOVATION

'Product innovation' is defined as the conceptualization, development, operationalization, manufacture, launch, and ongoing management of a new product or service (Cooper 1983; Imai et al. 1985; Dougherty 1992a). 'New' means new to the organization, and can involve new customers, new uses, new manufacturing, new distribution and/or logistics, new product technology, and any combination of these. Product innovation is inherently interfunctional, and, according to Crawford (1983), is second only to corporate strategy in the way it involves all aspects of all functions of management. It is also inherently ambiguous, and therefore involves perception and social construction (Daft and Weick 1984).

To translate product innovation into organizational terms, it helps to focus on the underlying activities of the process. Four sets of activities are described in turn: (1) conceptualizing the product to integrate market needs and technological potential; (2) organizing the process to accommodate creative problem solving; (3) monitoring the process; and (4) developing commitment to the effort. Although discussed separately, these four activities interrelate in practice.

### Market–Technology Linking

A new product is a package of features and benefits, each of which must be conceived, articulated, designed, and 'operationalized', or brought into existence. This set of activities is called market–technology linking (Burgelman 1983). To carry out market–technology linking effectively, innovators need to conceptualize the product as fully as possible as early as possible, so that its design reflects customer needs, market structure, technological capability, manufacturability, selling and distribution, and the firm's unique competencies (Bacon et al. 1994). Clark and Fujimoto use the term 'product integrity' to describe how these elements are integrated into a comprehensive package:

Product integrity has both internal and external dimensions. Internal integrity refers to consistency between the function and structure of the product – e.g., the parts fit well, components match and work well together, layout achieves maximum space efficiency. External integrity is a measure of how well a product's function, structure and semantics fit the customers' objectives, values, production system, lifestyle, use-pattern, and self-identity. (1991: 30)

Market–technology linking is multi-functional, because all functions have vital knowledge to contribute. Understanding customer needs is essential to product success (Myers and Marquis 1969; Rothwell et al. 1974), but, since these needs must be operationalized through technology, marketing must be complemented with input from other functions (Allen 1977; Cohen and Levinthal 1990). The product's design actually emerges from the development process, because both market and technological issues are ambiguous. On the market side, customers cannot articulate needs if the application is new, and needs may change in any case as the product is used (Rosenberg 1982). In addition, market information is 'sticky', or embedded in a context and not retrievable except by hands-on interaction within the context (von Hippel 1994). On the technical side, it is not always apparent to a scientist if she is working on a minor problem of adjustment or a major problem of principle (Schon 1967). Market–technology linking thus involves the creation of knowledge through hands-on learning, as innovators work with customers, experiment with new designs, and test different approaches (Freeman 1982; Kanter 1988; Nonaka 1994).

A number of techniques have been developed for market–technology linking in a specific project. One approach is to look for 'lead users', or people on the leading edge of a new market who already have experience with the problem the product will solve (von Hippel 1986). These users can provide some actual product design insights (Bailetti and Guild 1991). Another approach is 'empathetic design', through which multidisciplinary teams work in an anthropological mode with potential users to develop the product's design (Leonard-Barton 1991). Ideas on quality function deployment (Griffin and Hauser 1993) and team visits with customers also are useful (McQuarrie 1993).

## Organization-Wide Tensions for Market–Technology Linking

To advance our understanding of organizing for innovation, however, research must also reckon with the fact that many organizations do not carry out market–technology linking very well, despite the wide availability of techniques (Cooper and Kleinschmidt 1986; Mahajan and Wind 1992; Dougherty and Corse 1995). In a study which included firms that are usually considered as exemplars of the 'innovative organization', Bacon et al. conclude: 'many of the firms in our study used surprisingly rudimentary procedures to bring together the requisite product definition information' (1994: 1). The pervasiveness and persistence of problems with market–technology linking suggests that these problems are not rooted only in poor project management.

Looking at market–technology linking from the perspective of 'tension', one can see that these activities embody a tension between outside (market) and inside (the firm's operations and technology). This inherent tension can be handled within a single project, if the multi-functional team members collaborate among themselves and with users and suppliers over the product's conceptualization and operationalization. The market–technology linking activities cannot be confined within a project, however, because the necessary technology may exist in another division, while vital elements of the specific design (e.g. a sales force for distribution) might be controlled by another unit. Innovators must simultaneously relate their product to these other resources and incorporate the organization's competencies into their product (Prahalad and Hamel 1990). To be innovative, therefore, the whole organization needs to be capable of balancing this outside–inside tension.

Unfortunately, many large, complex organizations focus inward on the efficiency of their operations, thus tilting inward the balance between inside and outside. Because of the pressures of day-to-day operations, people follow standard operating procedures to ensure that the work of the organization does not grind to a halt. These procedures, however, filter out extraneous (i.e. new) information, punish people for stepping out of 'normal' work roles, and focus attention on immediate issues (March and Simon 1958; Quelsh et al. 1987; see examples by Wheelwright and Clark 1992). One department may also have more power than the others because historically it has managed more of the uncertainties in the firm (Pfeffer and Salancik 1978; Nelson and Winter 1982). Workman (1993), for example, describes how the engineering department in a high technology firm dominated product development and kept manufacturing and marketing out of the market–technology linking process, despite official integrating structures. The outcome of this internally oriented operational pressure is that different bits of information about the outside and inside are fragmented into different 'thought worlds' (Dougherty 1992b), and become difficult to integrate.

In addition, new products by definition constitute a new understanding of the firm's market and technology, so managers must reconceptualize the business (however slightly in some cases) to incorporate them into the organization. However, operational pressures lead to a fixed understanding of 'our business' which inhibits reconceptualization (Johnson 1988; Henderson and Clark 1990). Senior managers concentrate on what has been successful in the past, fixating on 'current strategy' (Burgelman 1983; Bower 1970), while know-how becomes abstracted into 'core rigidities' or simplifications which no longer adapt with market and/or technology changes (Leonard-Barton 1992; Miller 1993).

To summarize, linking customer needs with the organization's technical capabilities is necessary to create a viable new product. The ability to manage this linkage and its inherent tension between outside and inside must permeate the entire organization, since a specific product must draw on resources around the organization, and all those resources must accommodate multiple sets of market–technology linkages. However, the pressures to make operations efficient focus attention inward on day-to-day procedures, and narrow the kinds of business that are considered appropriate. These inward pressures serve the important functions of focusing attention, reducing ambiguity, and 'getting the iron out the door', but they inhibit the organization-wide market–technology linking that is necessary for innovation. A theory of organizing for innovation in large, complex organizations must explain how to manage operations efficiently *and* overcome these inward pressures.

## Organizing for Creative Problem Solving

The product's conceptualization and development require that innovators solve complex problems to overcome surprises, work around barriers, merge processes from different functions, and weave together resources from different locations. Innovators must push issues along within each function, such as setting up manufacturing processes, establishing the selling and distribution system, and working through the details of design. At the same time, they must jointly focus on problems that affect more than one function, and solve them by taking the constraints of

the other functions into account (Yang and Dougherty 1993).

Organizing for problem solving is multifunctional in that work must be coordinated, sometimes in a parallel fashion, and sometimes in a joint fashion. For example, to reduce time to market, the engineers must be designing the parts for the product at the same time that the manufacturing people are designing the production process. To coordinate such highly interdependent activities, innovators must understand the constraints in other functions, anticipate others' needs, and use dense, two-way communication to process fragmentary information (Clark and Fujimoto 1991). Relationships among the team emerge through mutual adaptation, in response to the needs of the task (Mintzberg and McHugh 1985; Leonard-Barton 1988). As well, innovators and their managers must make decisions quickly, or small problems will snowball into huge ones. This also requires hands-on experimenting both within and across functions, as people iterate across options and possibilities.

Structures have been developed to enable this complicated form of organizing at the project level. Souder (1987) found that when the technology and market are unfamiliar, the most successful structure is the 'task dominant' team approach, in which everyone focuses on the entire development process rather than one piece of it. People are functional specialists, but their interactions are continuous and frequent, and information flows freely along multiple channels. Coordination mechanisms are diffused among team members rather than clearly assigned, so there are no formal handoffs, transfer points, or transfers of personnel. Other structural elements include: (1) a variety of boundary spanning roles to handle inter-functional communication (Ancona and Caldwell 1990); (2) a 'heavyweight' project manager when it is necessary to work through conflicts with higher level functional managers (Clark and Fujimoto 1991); (3) coordination mechanisms which vary with the project's analyzability, the novelty of connection between units, and differences in development phases (Adler 1995); and (4) multi-team structures which leverage technologies across multiple products (Jelinek and Schoonhoven 1990; Cusumano and Nobeoka 1994).

### Organization-Wide Tensions for Creative Problem Solving

Despite all the insights into project management, organizations still have difficulty especially with multiple projects. From the perspective of tension, we can see that organizing for creative problem solving embodies a tension between the old and the new. For example, a new product may require new supplier relationships, new parts handling, and new selling procedures, all of which can conflict with existing procedures designed for old products. The old–new tensions can be managed within the individual project through collaborative teaming, communication, and hands-on practice. Unfortunately, many problems do not fall within the control of a project team: innovations must tap into the firm-wide budgeting process, access resources in other divisions, and compete with existing businesses for time in the tool room, space on the shop floor, or inclusion in the sales people's kits. To be innovative, the whole organization must be capable of balancing the tension between the old and the new.

Unfortunately, the tension between the old and the new is easily disrupted and tilted toward the old in the large, complex organizations. A primary source of the disruption is 'segmentalism' (Kanter 1983), which emerges from the mechanistic system that predominates in many large organizations (Burns and Stalker 1966; Mintzberg 1979; Dougherty and Corse 1995). Segmentalism reduces complexity by breaking big problems down into smaller pieces, which are separated further into product lines that are managed by different people. In such compartmentalized systems, the conduits that are needed to coordinate the creative problem solving and to process the fragmentary information between the different units do not exist. Problem solving comes to a screeching halt when a boundary is reached; action stops, problems fester, and the development languishes. The power in the organization reinforces segmentalism because it is attached to existing boundaries and established routines (Nelson and Winter 1982). The power of resources that is embedded in funds, expertise, information, and credibility is in the hands of managers who are not part of the innovative initiative, so it sustains current activities rather than solves new problems. The power of process such as agenda-setting, budgeting, and decision-making also channel attention to established businesses, not to innovation (Hardy 1994; Dougherty and Hardy 1995).

To summarize, managing the tension between the new and the old to creatively solve problems on an organization-wide basis is necessary for effective new product development. However, the complexity of work in these large organizations reinforces a tendency to separate and compartmentalize work, locates power in the established businesses, not new ones, and hinders integrated problem solving. A theory of organizing for innovation must,

then, grapple with the need to deal with complexity and also overcome the pressures to focus on established routines.

## Monitoring and Evaluation

A third set of activities essential to effective product innovation concerns monitoring and evaluating the product innovation process. New product efforts need to be evaluated throughout their development, because they can absorb enormous amounts of resources with no sure payoff. Changes in markets, technologies, or competition also can quickly turn a good idea into a bad one, so the development effort needs to be monitored to see if design premises still hold. Despite the fanciful sense of unfettered freedom for innovation sometimes found in the organization literature, evaluation is necessary for innovation, since random 'variation' will not produce comprehensive design or thorough problem solving. Indeed, Van de Ven and Polley (1992) illustrate how easily an innovation can fall into disabled learning.

Monitoring and evaluation require multi-disciplinary team work, because innovators must rely on one another to assess progress. A multi-functional 'community of practice' jointly selects possible courses of action and judges progress (Brown and Duguid 1991). Requisite collaborative skills for this activity include the ability to accept the judgement of others, to integrate diverse views without compromising the project, and to take responsibility for the choice rather than to second-guess. Criteria for evaluation emerge during the development, because product innovations cannot be evaluated by formula or algorithm (Johne and Snelson 1988). Indeed, Brock and MacMillan (1993) argue that standard controls are not just obstacles to innovation, but the primary cause of cost overruns. Evaluation also depends on hands-on, experiential learning, because useful heuristics arise from experience.

The project management, technology, and marketing literatures offer a variety of techniques for evaluation and control (Cooper 1983; Urban and Hauser 1988; Wheelwright and Clark 1992). A phase review helps to assure that necessary activities occur at the right time – for example, doing market research to establish customer needs, not to 'confirm' presumptions at the end of the development (Deshpande and Zaltman 1982). Other criteria assure that necessary modifications are made before the project moves forward, that funding is adequate, and that design premises have been verified. Budget reviews held after key milestones such as concept testing, first process design and test, or prototype provide a more realistic sense of progress (Brock and MacMillan 1993).

## Organization-Wide Tensions for Monitoring and Evaluation

Despite all the models, the monitoring and evaluation of product innovation are even more problematic than the first two activities (Griffin and Page 1993). This set of activities embodies a tension between strategic emergence and strategic determination. If new products are forced to conform to top-down plans they would not address new opportunities, but if the organization relied strictly on bottom-up emergence, its innovations would not build on one another (Day 1990). This tension between determination and emergence can be handled within a project if senior managers exert 'subtle control' by framing the domain for the innovation, and then allowing the innovators to work out the specifics (Takeuchi and Nonaka 1986; Quinn 1985). But evaluation cannot be limited to the project level, since the success of an innovation may depend on how well it embodies the firm's unique competencies (Crawford 1983; Cooper and Kleinschmidt 1987). Connecting innovations to a larger plan allows firms to leverage investments across several projects (Jelinek and Schoonhoven 1990), and to build innovations on one another in a 'rapid inch-up' process (Clark and Fujimoto 1991). To be innovative, the whole organization must balance the tension between determination and emergence.

Large, complex organizations tend to emphasize determination over emergence, however. To control the wide variety of activities under them, managers rely on abstracted and generalized criteria, but these obliterate the unique aspects of an innovation. Because senior managers are detached from the situated specifics of work, they may force a uniform development time on all innovations regardless of differences, intervene in day-to-day problem solving even though they are not familiar with the issues, and impose rigid controls when delays crop up (Rosenbloom and Abernathy 1982; Dougherty and Cohen 1995). Brown and Duguid (1991), Van de Ven and Polley (1992), and Dougherty and Heller (1994) illustrate how, by following routine procedure, the situated realities of a given innovation are ignored as team members with vital experience are transferred, new project goals are imposed midstream, and processes are formalized inappropriately. In addition, most organizations do not have the kind of forward-reaching, adaptive strategies that are described in the practitioner models (Wheelwright and Clark 1992). Strategic intent becomes the rule (Mintzberg 1994), so there is no 'umbrella

strategy' that encourages innovations to emerge and develop (Mintzberg and McHugh 1985).

To summarize, evaluating and monitoring are necessary to create a viable new product. The ability to manage the tension between determination and emergence that is inherent in these activities must permeate the entire organization, because most innovations need to be linked with the firm's resources and strategy. However, abstracted processes for control emphasize determination over emergence, and senior managers are too detached from the specifics of innovation to enable learning. A theory of organizing for product innovation must explain how large, complex organizations can control such a variety of activities and still enable emergence to co-exist with determination.

## Commitment to the Innovation Process

The three sets of activities described above require enormous investment in time, and perhaps more importantly, in psychic energy and attention. Innovation requires a deeper commitment than regular work, according to Burns and Stalker (1966), because the boundaries of responsibility must be broader and more inclusive in the rapidly changing, ambiguous conditions of innovation. An individual needs to: 'see himself as fully implicated in the discharge of any task . . . and as committed to the success of the firm's undertaking' (1966: iv). A broader, more inclusive job can create serious problems, however:

> The organic form, by departing from the familiar clarity and fixity of the hierarchic structure, is often experienced by the individual manager as an uneasy, embarrassed, or chronically anxious quest for knowledge about what he should be doing, or what is expected of him, and a similar apprehensiveness about what others are doing. (1966: 122)

Multidisciplinary teams help innovators generate commitment by providing a sense of 'inclusion', or the feeling of centrality, regardless of their official status (Van Maanen and Schein 1979). An interdisciplinary team provides a comfortable sense of accountability and commitment for participants, because innovators share the work with others who can be trusted to do their part (Dougherty and Corse 1995). Collaborative skills for this set of activities include the ability to trust others to do their part even when it may seem that they will not, and the ability to fulfil one's own part in a reliable fashion. Responsibilities vary across team member and over time, so roles emerge as the development proceeds.

A number of techniques have been proposed to help broaden commitment. One approach focuses on personality factors: finding people with the requisite independence and creativity to work as champions and sponsors, and then training and encouraging them (Roberts 1988). In addition, work roles can be defined more broadly so people do not constrain the breadth of issues they attend to (Kanter 1988; 1989). People can be given greater autonomy over the operational aspects of their work, which expands their sense of inclusiveness without overwhelming them (Bailyn 1985; Katz 1988). Career paths can be designed to accommodate people's life trajectories, which enables them to take on more responsibility at work in sync with lessening responsibility at home (Bailyn 1993).

### Organization-Wide Tensions for Commitment

Commitment is the most problematic activity of product innovation, even at the project level. It embodies the tension between freedom and responsibility, which is one of the most challenging trade-offs in theory as well as in practice (see Weber 1946; Barnard 1938; Kunda 1992). For innovation, it is desirable that people feel free to generate ideas, create possible solutions to problems, and experiment with various courses of action. It is also desirable that people feel responsible to work toward common goals, use organizational resources efficiently, and achieve budgets and milestones. Despite the difficulties, this tension can be managed within a project if managers create a high commitment 'skunkworks', and hand-pick people who are both committed to the innovation and professional enough to see it through (Peters 1983). But commitment to innovation cannot be separated from the organization as a whole. Over time, individuals will be on different teams, report to multiple supervisors, and work with people who are not willing to commit themselves totally to their job (i.e. normal people). To be innovative, therefore, the organization as a whole needs to embody the tension between freedom and responsibility.

Large, complex organizations emphasize responsibility over freedom, however, because accountability is defined in precise, legalistic ways. This impersonal governance focuses on 'doing things right', not 'doing the right things', and inhibits the sense of inclusion that is essential for commitment. Westley (1990) argues more generally that middle-level people are often excluded from strategic conversations, which demoralizes them and reduces their commitment. Such demoralization is unfortunately common for innovation, since surveys show that most innovators think their senior managers are not committed to innovation

(Gupta and Wilemon 1990). Despite all the lip service paid to it, innovation is often not legitimate within the organization, which further reduces the probability that people will commit to it.

To summarize, people throughout the organization need to feel committed to product innovation if viable new products are to be developed more than occasionally. The ability to manage the tension between freedom and responsibility inherent in commitment to innovative action must permeate the entire organization. However, because accountability is difficult to determine, people rely on precise measures and legalistic job definitions, which make innovation illegitimate, and inhibit their ability to develop the sense of inclusion that innovation requires. A theory of organizing for product innovation must explain how large, complex organizations can govern work effectively and still balance freedom and responsibility.

## A Summary of Organizational Problems

I have argued that four sets of activities underlie the development of commercially successful new products. Innovators must work with potential customers to identify needs and link those needs with technological possibilities. They must organize the flow of work to collaborate across boundaries over problems, and solve them within the context of the whole system of attributes that comprise the product. They must monitor and evaluate their progress. And they must develop a sense of commitment which enables participants to take more responsibility without feeling overwhelmed. I have also argued that one reason why the vast organization studies literature provides relatively little insight into the organizational problems of innovation is that it is not anchored in the basic activities which underlie product innovation.

Recasting the activities as tensions suggests a new perspective on the organizing problems of product innovation. Ideally: (1) market–technology linking balances outside and inside; (2) organizing for problem solving balances new with old; (3) evaluating the process balances determination with emergence; and (4) developing commitment to innovation balances freedom with responsibility. These tensions cannot be eliminated because they are inherent in the activities, and help to power the innovation process. These tensions must be balanced throughout the organization, because the activities of innovation extend beyond a project, and are inextricably bound up with the organization as a whole.

Table 1   *The tensions, what perpetuates imbalances, and how to restore balance*

| Activity | Tension | Problem of normal functioning that disrupts tension | Particular practices which perpetuate disruption | Capacities to restore the balance in the tension |
|---|---|---|---|---|
| Market–technology linking | Outside vs inside | Keeping operations efficient | Inward emphasis on dept thought worlds and units; fixed sense of business | Generate and maintain an identity based on the value provided to customers |
| Organizing for creative problem solving | New vs old | Managing complexity | Segmentalist thinking and compartmentalization of work; power based on current work | See work of organization in terms of process, focusing on relationships among parts, and changes |
| Evaluating and monitoring innovation | Determined vs emergent | Controlling multiple activities | Abstracting work into generic standards; no strategy making | Situated judgement, collective ability to be engaged in details of work but also appreciate unstructured problems |
| Developing commitment to innovation | Freedom vs responsibility | Accounting for work, results | Illegitimacy of innovation; illegitimacy of inclusion | Collective accountability, accept and share responsibility, legitimize innovation and inclusion |

Because theories focus either on the project level of analysis or on entirely innovative organizations, they do not address the fundamental organizing question identified in this chapter: how can large, complex organizations solve the problems of normal functioning (i.e. efficient operations, reduction of complexity, control, and governance), and still embody the tensions which power innovation? In other words, how can we organize *organizations* to be more effectively innovative? Continued research at the project level is important, of course, but it does not grapple with this central question of organizing for innovation. Moreover, organizations that are now trapped by the problems discussed above cannot simply snap their collective fingers to be innovative. Change theories remind us of how difficult managing change can be: current practices must be 'unfrozen'; new 'mindsets' must be developed along with new practices through which the mindsets can be fleshed out and put into practice; and the new system of action must be stabilized or refrozen, or practices will revert to the old system (Schein 1990; Mintzberg and Westley 1992). In the next section, I sketch out possible mindsets to restore the balance in the tensions, along with some behavioral repertoires through which organizations can implement the new approach to organizing.

## RENEWED DIRECTIONS FOR RESEARCH

Table 1 summarizes the four tensions, the problems of normal functioning that disrupt them, and the particular practices which perpetuate the disruptions. These tensions are not new to organization theory, since the problems of responsiveness, complexity, control, commitment, and so forth have been central to organizational analysis since the inception of the field (Weber 1946; Barnard 1938; Gouldner 1954). Most classic discussions of these problems have not connected them directly to the practice of innovation, however, or to the question of how to change the organization. Work by Burns and Stalker (1966) is an exception, because their study combined the classic concerns with tensions such as the ones outlined above with managing innovation. Indeed, they argued that organizations need to be able to combine mechanistic and organic systems, but this aspect of their work has been largely overlooked. Starting with Burns and Stalker's forgotten insights is a way to *re*new theory on the innovative organization.

One of Burns and Stalker's forgotten insights is that many firms in their study did not become organic, even though their environment had become more complex (see preface and p. 4 of

1966 edition). Much of their book was devoted to exploring why the organic form was tenuous, and what managers could do about that. Burns and Stalker explained that few organizations became organic because people did not know how to organize, except for the bureaucracy:

> The ideology of formal bureaucracy seemed so deeply ingrained in industrial management that the common reaction to unfamiliar and novel conditions was to redefine, in the most precise and rigorous terms, the roles and working relationships obtaining within management along orthodox lines . . . and to reinforce the formal structure. In these concerns, the efforts to make the orthodox bureaucratic system work (because it was seen as the only possible way to organize . . .) produced dysfunctional forms of the mechanistic system. (1966: ix)

A second lost insight is that culture, not just structure, is central to organizing for innovation. Burns and Stalker argued that before an organization could become organic, it was necessary to develop 'codes of conduct' which would enable people to 'comprehend more eventualities and more information . . . and [in which] the limits of feasible action could be set more widely' (1966: 11). Codes of conduct were defined as an expression of a shared system of belief, or culture (1966: 119).

To build on Burns and Stalker, it is necessary to clarify the nature of 'code of conduct', and to describe the codes of conduct that would enable organizations to balance the tensions inherent in innovation. Swidler's (1986) discussion of cultural capacities addresses the nature of codes of conduct. She argues that culture affects behavior by providing people with a 'tool kit' of cultural material such as symbols, stories, habits, categories, and skills, which become a set of general 'capacities'. People draw on these cultural capacities to construct larger assemblages of action within which particular choices make sense, and for which certain culturally shaped skills and habits are useful. Established capacities persist because people come to value ends for which their cultural equipment is well suited (Geertz 1973). Established cultures also suppress alternative capacities. For example, Swidler suggests that people raised in impoverished urban ghettos fail to adopt a middle class life style, not because they lack the necessary values or have a bad attitude toward work, but because they lack the capacities for such a life style:

> One can hardly pursue success in a world where the accepted skills, style, and informal know-how are unfamiliar. . . . To adopt a line of conduct, one needs an image of the kind of world in which one is trying to act, a sense that one can read reasonably accurately (through one's own feelings and through the responses of others) how one is doing, and a capacity to choose among alternative lines of action. (1986: 275)

In the same fashion, organizations may not innovate well because the people lack the requisite codes of conduct, or capacities, that would enable them to carry out the four activities of innovation. Organizations therefore must develop capacities which provide an image of an organization which can manage the four tensions throughout. Otherwise, the existing capacities which concentrate attention inward on current, standardized operations will persist. In the next subsections, I outline some of the themes from theory on organizing for innovation, suggest that they do not quite provide a way to restore the balance in the four areas, and then suggest four capacities that fill in the gaps. These capacities are purely speculative, and my goal in suggesting them is to prompt others to develop ideas to replace, challenge, or elaborate them.

## A Capacity for Organization-Wide Market–Technology Linking

Research in marketing and in technology development indicates that a capacity for market–technology linking will involve the development and exploitation of knowledge. First, the idea of being 'customer oriented', defined as having a set of norms that put customer interest first, has been around at least since Drucker (1954). Recent research in marketing confirms that a customer orientation relates to improved product innovation (Narver and Slater 1990; Deshpande et al. 1992; Moorman 1995). Second, the idea of having core competencies or resources has been around at least since Penrose (1959), and recent research confirms that developing technological knowledge also relates to improved performance (Cohen and Levinthal 1990; Henderson and Cockburn 1994). It seems clear that an organization must develop thorough knowledge of its markets and technologies, and be able to apply this knowledge, if it is to develop new products successfully.

While necessary to innovativeness, these two sets of knowledge are not sufficient, because in most theories the two sides remain separated, so the capacity for linking is still missing (Gatignon and Xeureb 1995). I propose that organizations must also develop a capacity to generate an organizational identity that combines internal and external issues. According to Fiol (1991), an organization identity describes what people define as central, distinctive, and enduring about their organization. If people understood their organization's identity in terms of *the value* it provides to customers, they could bridge inside technology and outside customers. To provide value, an organization must solve actual customer problems and fulfil needs, so value, by definition, is grounded in specific customer issues. Technologies can be seen as solutions to problems, so value is also grounded in specific technical possibilities.

An identity based on value would help organizations break out of the strong inward pull of internal operations and still meet efficiency needs. Bureaucratic efficiency is based on economies of scale, which are increasingly inefficient when markets are fragmenting (Hage 1988). Defining the collective organizational self in terms of providing value shifts attention to alternative kinds of efficiency based on economies of scope (the ability to produce an array of products), or economies of substitution (the ability to substitute modules of technology in an overall system, see Garud and Kumaraswamy 1995). The capacity to combine inside and outside in an identity enables the organization to become an 'enacting organization' (Daft and Weick 1984) rather than stay mired in a rigid view of 'our business'.

Generating and maintaining a value-based identity will be challenging, especially for organizations whose identity is now centered internally on technologies or products. However, a number of behavioral repertoires can be implemented concurrently with an emphasis on customer orientation and R&D competence, to unfreeze the day-to-day practices which reinforce the imbalance between inside and outside. First, value is a common language that can bridge the departmental thought worlds. If people in all departments interact with potential customers, they can learn the common language and begin to see how to apply their technical solutions to customer problems. People can extend this experience to the management of established businesses by learning how to track emerging trends in both markets and technologies, and then relating those changes to specific changes in businesses (Wheelwright and Clark 1992). Within the umbrella of organizational identity as value, a business unit can define itself in terms of how it contributes to the creation of the organization's value, strengthening the inside–outside thinking throughout the organization. Organizing business units into product families reinforces the combined thinking by embodying market–technology linking into the management processes.

## A Capacity for Organization-Wide Creative Problem Solving

The organization studies literature suggests that a capacity for organization-wide problem solving will involve teams and networks. The innovative organization is usually described as comprising small, autonomous work units, which proliferate as the variety of products proliferates (Galbraith 1982; Peters 1983; Van de Ven 1986; Kanter 1988). To connect all these teams, communication in the innovative organization is based on consultation rather than command, and its content consists of information and advice rather than instructions and decisions (Burns and Stalker 1966). Different networks exist to handle: (1) the production process, extending both backward to suppliers and forward to customers; (2) joint ventures with other firms; (3) venture capital with former employees; and (4) various research consortia (Hage 1988).

Replacing the hierarchy with networked teams seems necessary for continual problem solving, but not sufficient. As noted in Table 1, the pressures of complexity have pushed many large, complex organizations to break down tasks and compartmentalize action. If anything, multiple teams would heighten complexity and segmentalism. I suggest that a capacity to see the organization as process – thus focusing on *organizing* – is also a necessary ingredient that is missing from our understanding of organizing for innovation. The capacity to see the organization as a process would enable people to shift the boundaries of their work over time more comfortably, and to accommodate the multi-paced, emergent processes of innovation. Seeing the organization as a process manages complexity without eliminating the ability to solve cross-boundary problems, so this capacity can restore the balance between the old and the new.

With the capacity to understand work as process, people still consider sets of work, but, rather than bracketing a particular set of work out of the whole, people would emphasize relationships among the sets. Effective management of complexity comes not from sticking to the tried and true, but from changing different aggregates of action at different times. For example, managers can shift smaller sets of work such as job definitions or pilot production processes, while holding larger sets constant, such as the strategy or manufacturing regime, and then reverse the focus (Leonard-Barton 1988). Time itself can also segment work without separating it. Tyre and Orlikowski (1994) argue that the implementation of new technologies is best managed by iterating bursts of innovative activity with stable periods during which people focus on normal operations. They recommend that managers deliberately punctuate adaptation with routine rather than focus only on one or the other, because problems are more likely to be surfaced and solved effectively. Gersick (1994) also shows how the manager of a new venture used temporal pacing to set the speed of development, and event planning to regulate attention.

'Process' is not new, since it underlies emergent strategy, total quality management, and process re-engineering. The idea of process as a shared image of organizing can be difficult to implement, however, since it violates the established image of organization as boxes or states of being (Pettigrew 1992). Shifting to the process-based image of organizing may be possible if teams and networking are coupled with day-to-day practices which reinforce thinking in terms of processes and relationships over time. For example, Jelinek and Schoonhoven (1990) describe organizing around development of technology. In this context, individuals can see their work in terms of how it flows into other people's work. Business unit managers can see product lines in terms of how they flow into generations or product revolutions. In manufacturing, planning and thinking concerns *changing* the manufacturing processes to fit with shifts in products and customer trends. In technology, planning and thinking concerns *developing* competencies. With the process as central, power can be aligned to orient the flows of resources, decision-making, reporting, and communication around integrating innovation into the organization, not around protecting turf (Hardy 1994).

## A Capacity for Organization-Wide Monitoring and Evaluation

The organization studies literature indicates that organization-wide monitoring and evaluation for innovation involves senior management leadership and a risk-taking culture. In innovative organizations, senior managers must translate market needs for organization members, work closely with customers in order to stay on top of shifting needs, and channel innovation by setting goals, selecting key people, and establishing a few critical limits (Burns and Stalker 1966; Jelinek and Schoonhoven 1990; Quinn 1985; Imai et al. 1985). A cultural context which values change, risk-taking, and learning reinforces the need to take innovative action (Peters 1983; Quinn and Pacquette 1990).

The insights of senior managers must be grounded in the everyday business of the organization and must frame and guide the actions of others in order to achieve effective monitoring and evaluation. However, leadership and culture *per se* do not address the problems of control in large, complex organizations, where managers come to rely on predetermined standards. I suggest that a capacity for situated judgement is a necessary ingredient that must be added to effective leadership and culture if organization-wide monitoring and evaluation are to enable innovation. Relying on situated judgement fills the need for control, but still enables innovation.

'Situated' refers to being engaged in the details of the innovation and its relationship to the organization's value, because these are complex, often tacit issues that must be 'visceralized' to be understood (Brown and Duguid 1991; Dougherty 1992a; Eisenhardt and Zbaracki 1992). 'Judgement' refers to the capability to use insights and heuristics developed from know-how and experience, and to 'appreciation', which Vickers (1965) uses to refer to sizing up unstructured situations and making judgements about the significance of various facts (see also Schon 1983). The capacity for situated judgement gives people throughout the organization the skills for and orientation to evaluating complex, fuzzy problems, making difficult choices, quickly reassessing choices and adjusting as necessary. This capacity restores the balance between determination and emergence, because it enables people to decide how and when to use rules, not to apply them unthinkingly.

Implementing the capacity for situated judgement would also be difficult, because it violates the premises of optimization and precision which underlie many views of management. However, if strong strategic leadership can be combined with several behavioral repertoires, perhaps this capacity can be developed. First, situated judgement is a collective version of Eisenhardt's (1990) high velocity decision-making. She found that to make high velocity decisions, managers used lots of real-time information on the firm's operations and competitive environment, and built on multiple alternatives simultaneously. Eisenhardt also found considerable collaboration, as managers relied on counsellors, continually sought advice, and made decisions using 'consensus with qualification'. Jelinek and Schoonhoven's (1990) description of the 'operations reviews' used in electronics organizations to evaluate multiple innovations also illustrates situated judgement. These organizations have a strong norm that employees will both develop and exercise their ability to judge the viability of innovations. During the actual review process, managers work closely with teams, and everyone

studies detailed operational data, focuses relent-
lessly on problem solving, and uses the reviews
as a forum in which to discuss problems and
consider alternatives. Situated judgement can be
further developed through the recognition of
'communities of practice' with the firm, which
emphasize learning in working, and the circula-
tion of knowledge across various boundaries
(see Brown and Duguid 1991).

## A Capacity for Organization-Wide Commitment to Innovation

The organization studies literature suggests that
different understandings of work and of governance are important to commitment to innovation. To paraphrase Burns and Stalker (1966:
121–2), innovative work roles emphasize the
contributive nature of special knowledge and
expertise, not its differentiation into separate
tasks; tasks are understood realistically as part
of the business as a whole rather than abstracted
out; tasks are adjusted through interaction with
others rather than through reconciliation by the
next level up; and 'the sanctions which apply to
the individual's conduct in his working role
derive more from presumed community of
interest . . . and less from a contractual relationship between himself and a non-personal corporation' (1966: 121). In addition, decision-making
is no longer part of the hierarchy but is shared
among autonomous units (Hage 1988).
Organizations must learn how to cooperate,
even with competitors, because as networks
proliferate 'they are not part of the same
hierarchy, [so] many of the standard control
mechanisms of central headquarters no longer
apply' (1988: 58). Negotiation skills will become
more important than accounting, loyalty more
important than price, and, according to Powell
(1990), trust more important than contracts.

While new understandings of work and
governance are important, they do not address
the underlying problem so clearly articulated by
Burns and Stalker – the chronic anxiety induced
in employees by the organic organization over
what they should be doing. Both managers and
employees may gladly settle for a precise,
legalistic job definition which fully accounts for
people's responsibilities. To break out of the
noninnovative mindset and generate the broader
sense of commitment required by innovation, I
suggest that the capacity for collective accountability needs to permeate the organization as a
whole. Collective accountability is similar to the
accountability developed in a well-functioning
innovation team: since all participants take on
some responsibility, the work is not overwhelming for anyone. Collective accountability

requires that innovation become legitimate. That
is, instead of following the authority of the boss,
relying on rules, and sticking to one's own area
of expertise, which are legitimate activities in
bureaucratic organizations, the four sets of
innovative activities need to be understood as
proper and appropriate activities for all employees. Collective accountability also requires that
inclusion becomes legitimate, because the sense
of inclusion seems essential to people's ability to
become more broadly committed.

I find the capacity for collective accountability
the most challenging to articulate, because
theory does not seem to relate this complex
issue to actual practice very well. However, some
suggestions for implementation can be made, at
least to point to areas for research. First, people
must be trained to take on broader roles, by
providing them with expertise as well as
experience. As well, the organization must be
free of harassment and other debilitating power
ploys (Kanter 1988). Second, asking people to
accept more accountability takes control away
from them, so they must be given more control in
return or they will slip back into mechanistic
roles. Allowing employees operational control
over how day-to-day work is done is one element
(see Bailyn 1985). Broadening people's participation in the rules of work is another – see Adler's
(1993) development of Gouldner's (1954) ideas
of the representational bureaucracy, for example.
Perhaps more importantly, senior managers need
to learn how to include middle and operating
managers in their ongoing 'strategic conversations'. As Westley (1990) illustrates, when lower-
level managers could participate in setting
framing rules for decisions, contribute their
own framing rules, and at least participate in
dominating some of the conversation, they felt
included, energized, and committed.

## CONCLUSION

In this chapter, I have argued that we have not
adequately addressed the question of how to
organize *an organization* for innovation – at least
not a large, complex organization. Most of the
theories concern projects or simple organizations, while most of the problems now concern
the practice of innovation in large organizations
that cannot be entirely innovative. By focusing
on how to carry out the essential activities of
product innovation throughout the organization, I highlighted four tensions that must be
balanced. The key problem for the theory of the
innovative organization suggested by this analysis is how can complex organizations solve the

problems of normal functioning (i.e. efficient operations, reduction of complexity, control, and governance), and still embody the tensions which power innovation?

Many organizations emphasize one side of the balance – the inside, the old, the determined, and the responsible. Interestingly, many organization theories emphasize the other side of the balance – the outside, the new, the emergent, and the free. To fill in this gap and restore balance between the sides, I recommend going back to Burns and Stalker's ideas regarding cultural codes of conduct, or capacities for action (Swidler 1986). From this framework, it seems that fundamentally new capacities for organizational action are necessary if large organizations are to actually become adept with ongoing product innovation. The innovative organization is indeed a new form, a new kind of social system. However, the new capacities suggested above are not alien, because aspects of them have already been widely discussed in the literature.

The primary insight of this chapter is that the many bits of behavior and culture which comprise the innovation literature need to be crystallized into skill sets or systematic patterns of thinking and acting – called capacities – that enable the activities of innovation throughout the organization. I do not argue that the vast literatures on tools and techniques for measuring, managing, strategizing, evaluating, organizing, and so forth are not important, since they are (see Wheelwright and Clark 1992; Griffin and Page 1993). I do argue that organizations cannot simply adopt all these tools and techniques. Rather, they must *also* develop underlying capacities for action which enable people to use these tools effectively for innovation. The capacities sketched out here would enable people throughout complex organizations to work with customers, form teams, solve problems creatively, apply technical potential to market needs, appreciate the relationships among functions and businesses well enough to shift them as necessary, and develop an ongoing sense of how well they are doing.

Much more research is necessary, of course. These proposed capacities may not be fully or correctly articulated, or they may not exist at all. These ideas are 'testable', however, since I predict that organizations that are more adept with product innovation have these capacities. How the capacities relate to different structures, processes, tools, and techniques has been discussed only in passing, and also needs more study. Perhaps most important, how established organizations can develop these capacities needs to be examined. The alternative approach to the 'innovative organization' in this chapter chal-lenges researchers to address the organization as a whole, and the problem of changing non-innovative organizations. These issues shape the theoretical frontier for theory on organizing for innovation.

## REFERENCES

Adler, P. (1993) 'The learning bureaucracy: new United Motor Manufacturing, Inc', *Research In Organization Behaviour*, 111–94.

Adler, P. (1995) 'Interdepartmental interdependence and coordination: the case of the design/manufacturing interface', *Organization Science*, 6: 147–67.

Allen, T. (1977) *Managing the Flow of Technology*. Cambridge, MA: MIT Press.

Ancona, D. and Caldwell, D. (1990) 'Beyond boundary spanning: managing external development in product development teams', *High Technology Management Research*, 1: 119–36.

Bacon, G., Beckman, S., Mowery, D. and Wilson, E. (1994) 'Managing product definition in high-technology industries: a pilot study', *California Management Review*, 36: 32–56.

Bailetti, A. and Guild, P. (1991) 'A method for projects seeking to merge technical advancements with potential markets', *R&D Management*, 21: 291–300.

Bailyn, L. (1985) 'Autonomy in the R&D lab', *Human Resource Management*, 24: 129–46.

Bailyn, L. (1993) *Breaking the Mold: Women, Men, and Time in the New Corporate World*. New York: Free Press.

Barley, S. (1986) 'Technology as an occasion for structuring: evidence from observations of CT scanners and the social order of radiology departments', *Administrative Science Quarterly*, 31: 78–109.

Barnard, C. (1938) *The Functions of the Executive*. Cambridge, MA: Harvard University Press.

Bower, J. (1970) *Managing the Resource Allocation Process: a Study of Corporate Planning and Investment*. Boston: Graduate School of Business Administration.

Brock, Z. and MacMillan, I. (1993) *Corporate Venturing: Creating New Businesses within the Firm*. Boston: Harvard Business School Press.

Brown, J. and Duguid, P. (1991) 'Organizational learning and communities of practice', *Organization Science*, 2: 40–57.

Brown, S. and Eisenhardt, K. (1995) 'Product development: past research, present findings, and future directions', *Academy of Management Review*, 20: 343–78.

Burgelman, R. (1983) 'A process model of internal corporate venturing in the diversified major firm', *Administrative Sciences Quarterly*, 28: 223–44.

Burns, T. and Stalker, G.M. (1966) *The Management of Innovation*, 2nd edn. London: Tavistock.

Christensen, C. and Bower, J. (1993) 'Catching the next wave: why good customers make it hard'. Working paper, Harvard Business School.

Clark, K. and Fujimoto, T. (1991) *Product Development Performance*. Boston: Harvard Business School Press.

Cohen, W.M. and Levinthal, D. (1990) 'Absorptive capacity: a new perspective on learning and innovation', *Administrative Science Quarterly*, 35: 128–52.

Cooper, R. (1983) 'A process model for industrial new product development', *IEEE Transactions on Engineering Management*, 30: 2–11.

Cooper, R. and Kleinschmidt, E. (1986) 'An investigation into the new product process: steps, deficiencies, and impact', *Journal of Product Innovation Management*, 3: 71–85.

Cooper, R. and Kleinschmidt, E. (1987) 'Success factors in product innovation', *Industrial Marketing Management*, 16: 215–33.

Crawford, C.M. (1983) *New Products Management*. Homewood, IL: Richard D. Irwin.

Cusumano, M. and Nobeoka, K. (1994) 'Multi-project management: strategy and organization in automobile product development'. Paper presented at ORSA-TIMS, Boston, April.

Daft, R. and Weick, K. (1984) 'Toward a model of organizations as interpretive systems', *Academy of Management Review*, 9: 43–66.

Damanpour, F. (1991) 'Organizational innovation: a meta-analysis of effects of determinants and moderators', *Academy of Management Journal*, 34: 555–90.

Damanpour, F., Szabat, K. and Evan, W. (1989) 'The relationship between types of innovation and organizational performance', *Journal of Management Studies*, 26: 587–602.

Day, D. (1994) 'Raising radicals: different processes for championing innovative corporate ventures', *Organization Science*, 5: 148–72.

Day, G. (1990) *Market Driven Strategy: Processes for Creating Value*. New York: Free Press.

Deshpande, R., Farley, J. and Webster, F. (1992) 'Corporate culture, customer orientation, and innovativeness in Japanese firms: a quadrad analysis'. Report 92-100, Marketing Science Institute.

Deshpande, R. and Zaltman, G. (1982) 'Factors affecting the use of market research information: a path analysis', *Journal of Marketing Research*, 19: 14–31.

Dougherty, D. (1992a) 'A practice-centered model of organizational renewal through product innovation', *Strategic Management Journal*, 13: 77–92.

Dougherty, D. (1992b) 'Interpretative barriers to successful product innovation in large firms', *Organization Science*, 3: 179–202.

Dougherty, D. and Cohen, M. (1995) 'Product innovation in mature firms', in E. Bowman and B. Kogut (eds), *Resdesigning the Firm*. New York: Oxford University Press.

Dougherty D. and Corse, S. (1995) 'When it comes to product innovation, what is so bad about bureaucracy?', *Journal of High Technology Management Research*, 6: 55–76.

Dougherty, D. and Hardy, C. (1995) 'Powering innovation: problems and prospects in large bureaucracies'. Working paper, McGill University Faculty of Management, Montreal.

Dougherty, D. and Heller, T. (1994) 'The illegitimacy of successful product innovation in established firms', *Organization Science*, 5: 200–18.

Downs, G. and Mohr, L. (1976) 'Conceptual issues in the study of innovation', *Administrative Science Quarterly*, 21: 700–14.

Drucker, P. (1954) *The Practice of Management*. New York: Harper and Row.

Eisenhardt, K. (1990) 'Speed and strategic choice: how managers accelerate decision making', *California Management Review*, 32: 1–16.

Eisenhardt, K. and Zbaracki, M. (1992) 'Strategic decision making', *Strategic Management Journal*, 17–38.

Fiol, M. (1991) 'Managing culture as a competitive resource: an identity-based view of sustainable competitive advantage', *Journal of Management*, 17, 191–211.

Freeman, C. (1982) *The Economics of Industrial Innovation*. Cambridge, MA: MIT Press.

Galbraith, J. (1982) 'Designing the innovative organization', *Organizational Dynamics*, Winter: 5–25.

Garud, R. and Kumaraswamy, A. (1995) 'Technological and organizational designs for realizing economies of substitution', *Strategic Management Journal*, 16: 93–111.

Gatignon, H. and Robertson, T. (1985) 'A propositional inventory for new diffusion research', *Journal of Consumer Research*, 11: 849–67.

Gatignon, H. and Xeureb, J.M. (1995) 'Strategic orientation of the firm and new product performance'. Working paper, INSEAD and ESSEC, France.

Geertz, C. (1973) *The Interpretation of Cultures*. New York: Basic Books.

Gersick, C. (1994) 'Pacing strategic change: the case of a new venture', *The Academy of Management Journal*, 37: 9–45.

Gouldner, A. (1954) *Patterns of Industrial Bureaucracy*. New York: Free Press.

Griffin, A. and Hauser, J. (1993) 'The voice of the customer', *Management Science*, 12: 1–27.

Griffin, A. and Page, A. (1993) 'An interim report on measuring product development success and failure', *Journal of Product Innovation Management*, 10: 291–309.

Gupta, A. and Wilemon, D. (1990) 'Accelerating the development of technologically based new products', *California Management Review*, 24–44.

Hage, J. (ed.) (1988) *Futures of Organizations.* Lexington, MA: Lexington Books.

Hardy, C. (1994) *Managing Strategic Action: Mobilizing Change.* London: Sage.

Hedlund, G. and Ridderstrale, J. (1994) 'International development projects – key to competitiveness, impossible, or mismanaged?'. Working paper, Stockholm School of Economics.

Heller, T. (1994) 'Organizing for innovation: optimizing the project–organization relationship and the matter of context'. Paper presented at the Academy of Management Meetings.

Henderson, R. and Clark, K. (1990) 'Architectural innovation: the reconfiguration of existing product technologies and the failure of established firms', *Administrative Science Quarterly*, 35 (March): 9–31.

Henderson, R. and Cockburn, I. (1994) 'Measuring core competence? Evidence from the pharmaceutical industry', *Strategic Management Journal*, 15: 63–84.

Imai, K., Nonaka, I. and Takeuchi, H. (1985) 'Managing product development: how Japanese companies learn and unlearn', in K. Clark, R. Hayes and C. Lorenz (eds), *The Uneasy Alliance: Managing the Productivity–Technology Dilemma*. Boston: Harvard Business School Press. pp. 337–76.

Jelinek, M. and Schoonhoven, C. (1990) *The Innovation Marathon: Lessons from High Technology Firms.* Oxford: Basil Blackwell.

Johne, F.A. and Snelson, P. (1988) 'Success factors in product innovation: a selective review of the literature', *Journal of Product Innovation Management*, 114–128.

Johnson, G. (1988) 'Rethinking incrementalism', *Strategic Management Journal*, 9: 75–91.

Kanter, R.M. (1983) *The Changemasters.* New York: Simon and Schuster.

Kanter, R.M. (1988) 'When a thousand flowers bloom', in *Research in Organization Behaviour*. Greenwich, CT: JAI Press. pp. 169–211.

Kanter, R.M. (1989) 'The new managerial work', *Harvard Business Review*, November–December.

Katz, R. (ed.) (1988) *Managing Professionals in Innovative Organizations: a Collection of Readings.* Cambridge, MA: Ballinger.

Kimberly, J. (1981) 'Managerial innovation', in P. Nystrom and W. Starbuck (eds), *Handbook of Organizational Design*, vol 1. New York: Oxford University Press. pp. 84–104.

Kunda, G. (1992) *Engineering Culture: Control and Commitment in a High-Tech Corporation.* Philadelphia: Temple University Press.

Leonard-Barton, D. (1988) 'Implementation as mutual adaptation of technology and organization', *Research Policy*, 17: 251–67.

Leonard-Barton, D. (1991) 'Inanimate integrators: a block of wood speaks', *Design Management Journal*, 2: 61–7.

Leonard-Barton, D. (1992) 'Core capabilities and core rigidities: a paradox in managing new product development', *Strategic Management Journal*, 13: 111–26.

Majahan, V. and Wind, J. (1992) 'New product models: practice, shortcomings and desired improvements', *Journal of Product Innovation Management*, 128–39.

March, J. and Simon, H. (1958) *Organizations.* New York: Wiley.

McQuarrie, E. (1993) *Customer Visits: Building a Better Market Focus.* Newbury Park, CA: Sage.

Miller D. (1993) 'The architecture of simplicity', *Academy of Management Review*, 18: 116–39.

Mintzberg, H. (1979) *The Structuring of Organizations.* Englewood Cliffs, NJ: Prentice-Hall.

Mintzberg, H. (1994) *The Rise and Fall of Strategic Planning.* New York: Free Press.

Mintzberg, H. and McHugh, A. (1985) 'Strategy formation in an adhocracy', *Administrative Science Quarterly*, 30: 160–97.

Mintzberg, H. and Westley, F. (1992) 'Cycles of organizational change', *Strategic Management Journal*, 13: 39–60.

Moorman, C. (1995) 'Organizational market information processes: cultural antecedents and new product outcomes', *Journal of Marketing Research*, 22: 318–35.

Myers, S. and Marquis, D. (1969) *Successful Industrial Innovations.* NSF report 69-17.

Narver, J. and Slater, S. (1990) 'The effect of a market orientation on business profitability', *Journal of Marketing*, 54: 20–35.

Nelson, R. and Winter, S. (1982) *An Evolutionary Theory of Economic Change*, Boston: Belkamp Press.

Nonaka, I. (1994) 'A dynamic theory of organizational knowledge creation', *Organization Science*, 5: 14–37.

Nord, W. and Tucker, S. (1987) *Implementing Routine and Radical Innovations.* Lexington, MA: Lexington Books.

Pelz, D. and Andrews, F. (1966) *Scientists in Organizations.* New York: Wiley.

Penrose, E. (1959) *The Theory of Growth of the Firm.* New York: Wiley.

Peters, T. (1983) 'The mythology of innovation, or a skunkworks tale, Part II', *The Stanford Magazine*.

Pettigrew, A. (1992) 'The character and significance of strategy process research', *Strategic Management Journal*, 13: 39–60.

Pfeffer, J. and Salancik, G. (1978) *The External Control of Organizations: A Resource Dependence Perspective.* New York: Harper and Row.

Powell, W. (1990) 'Neither market nor hierarchy: network forms of organization', *Research in Organization Behaviour*, 12: 295–336.

Prahalad, C.K. and Hamel, G. (1990) 'The core competence of the corporation', *Harvard Business Review*, May–June.

Quelsh, J., Farris, P. and Olver, J. (1987) 'The product

management audit: design and survey findings', *The Journal of Consumer Marketing*, 3: 45–58.

Quinn, J.B. (1985) 'Managing innovation: controlled chaos', *Harvard Business Review*, 3: 78–84.

Quinn, J.B. and Pacquette, P. (1990) 'Technology in services: creating organizational revolutions', *Sloan Management Review*, Winter.

Roberts, E. (1988) 'What we've learned: managing invention and innovation', *Research Technology Management*, January–February, 11–29.

Rosenberg, N. (1982) *Inside the Black Box: Technology and Economics*. Cambridge: Cambridge University Press.

Rosenbloom, R. and Abernathy, W. (1982) 'The climate for innovation in industry', *Research Policy*, 11: 209–25.

Rothwell, R. (1977) 'The characteristics of successful innovators and technically progressive firms', *R&D Management*, 7: 191–206.

Rothwell, R., Freeman, C., Horsley, A., Jervis, V.T.P., Robertson, A. and Townsend, J. (1974) 'SAPPHO Updated – Project SAPPHO Phase II', *Research Policy*, 3: 258–91.

Rothwell, R. and Whiston, T. (1990) 'Design, innovation and corporate integration', *R&D Management*, 20: 193–201.

Scarborough, H. and Corbett, J.M (1992) *Technology and Organization*. London: Routledge.

Schein, E. (1990) *Organizational Culture and Leadership*. San Francisco: Jossey-Bass.

Schon, D. (1967) *Technology and Change*. Oxford: Pergamon.

Schon, D. (1983) *The Reflective Practitioner: How Professionals Think in Action*. New York: Basic Books.

Souder, W. (1987) *Managing New Product Innovations*. Lexington, MA: Lexington Press.

Starbuck, W. and Milliken, F. (1988) 'Challenger: finetuning the odds until something breaks', *Journal of Management Studies*, 25: 319–40.

Swidler, A. (1986) 'Culture in action: symbols and strategies', *American Sociological Review*, 51: 273–86.

Takeuchi, H. and Nonaka, I. (1986) 'The new product development game', *Harvard Business Review*, 64: 137–46.

Tushman M. and Anderson, P. (1986) 'Technological discontinuities and organizational environments', *Administrative Science Quarterly*, 31: 439–65.

Tyre, M. and Orlikowski, W. (1994) 'Windows of opportunity: temporal patterns of technological adaptation in organizations', *Organization Science*, 5: 98–118.

Urban, G. and Hauser, J. (1988) *The Design and Marketing of New Products*, 2nd edn. Englewood Cliffs, NJ: Prentice Hall.

Van de Ven, A. (1986) 'Central problems in the management of innovation', *Management Science*, 32: 590–608.

Van de Ven, A. and Polley, D. (1992) 'Learning while innovating', *Organization Science*, 3: 92–116.

Van Maanen, J. and Schein, E. (1979) 'Toward a theory of organizational socialization', *Research in Organizational Behaviour*, 1: 209–64.

Vickers, G. (1965) *The Art of Judgement*. New York: Basic Books.

von Hippel, E. (1986) 'Lead users: a source of novel product concepts', *Management Science*, 32: 791–805.

von Hippel, E. (1994) 'Sticky information and the locus of problem solving: implications for innovation', *Management Science*, 40: 429–39.

Weber, M. (1946) *From Max Weber: Essays in Sociology*, translated, edited, and introduced by H.H. Gerth and C. Wright Mills. New York: Oxford University Press.

Westley, F. (1990) 'Middle managers and strategy: microdynamics of inclusion', *Strategic Management Journal*, 11: 337–51.

Wheelwright, S. and Clark, K. (1992) *Revolutionizing Product Development*. New York: Free Press.

Workman, J. (1993) 'Marketing's limited role in new product development in one computer systems firm', *Journal of Marketing Research*, 30: 405–21.

Yang, E. and Dougherty, D. (1993) 'Product innovation: more than just making a new product', *Creativity and Innovation Management*, 2.

Zahra, S. and Covin, J. (1995) 'Contextual influences on the corporate entrepreneurship–performance relationship: a longitudinal analysis', *Journal of Business Venturing*, 10: 43–58.

# 10

# Organizational Learning: Affirming an Oxymoron

## KARL E. WEICK AND FRANCES WESTLEY

Organizing and learning are essentially antithetical processes, which means the phrase 'organizational learning' qualifies as an oxymoron. To learn is to disorganize and increase variety. To organize is to forget and reduce variety. In the rush to embrace learning, organizational theorists often overlook this tension, which explains why they are never sure whether learning is something new or simply warmed-over organizational change. Either way, the reluctance to grapple with the antithesis has led to derivative ideas and unrealized potential.

As if this were not enough trouble, there appear to be more reviews of organizational learning than there is substance to review. Most reviews now available are competent summaries of a common body of work (e.g. Dodgson 1993; Levitt and March 1988) and we see no purpose in duplicating once more what they say. Instead, this chapter extends and complements those reviews by taking seriously the hope Cohen and Sproull (1991) voiced for the concept of learning. They described the problem and the hope this way:

> better theories of learning will provide a positive alternative to rational choice assumptions. Much empirical work on both individual behaviour and organizational processes rests on a negative theme of counterevidence to rational actor assumptions (e.g. Kahneman, Slovic, and Tversky 1982; Allison 1971). This produces a peculiar intellectual schizophrenia, with rigorous theories built on rationality assumptions and substantial empirical work denying those assumptions, but not proposing a positive theoretical alternative. . . . It is essential to develop a coherent large scale alternative view, one that

satisfactorily accounts for phenomena such as culture and institutionalization. Learning is the most attractive alternative engine for such theoretical development.

The word 'affirming' in our title is tied directly to Cohen and Sproull's agenda. Existing discussions of organizational learning, especially those linked directly to information processing and indirectly to rational choice assumptions (e.g. Huber 1991), threaten to create once more an idealized sequence which is then shown to be something organizations don't follow. The potential is ripe for more 'negative themes of counterevidence'. And if the basic phenomenon is oxymoronic, then the temptation to unmask should be even stronger. If we're not careful, all we'll have to show for our efforts to grasp learning will be the assertion that, not only are organizations non-rational, they are also non-learners as well.

To consolidate an infrastructure for organizational learning in the face of an inherent oxymoron and temptations to highlight the affinity between learning and rational choice, we do several things in this chapter. First, we explore the need to ground the idea of organizational learning in concepts which connect the theoretical to the experiential. Secondly, we deal with the problem of how to distinguish between individual and organizational learning and why this is necessary. In response to both these issues we argue that theories which focus on cultural aspects of organizations can perhaps provide us with images at once social and experiential with which we can explore and ground a discussion of organizational learning.

Once having determined the context of exploration, we resume our examination of the oxymoron inherent in the concept of organizational learning in three subsystems of culture: language, artifacts and action routines. Lastly, we seek to enlarge our understanding of the set of conditions under which organizational learning is most likely to occur in these cultural subsystems. Consistent with the notion that organizational learning is oxymoronic, we treat occasions which juxtapose order and disorder as social spaces where learning is possible. These juxtapositions include moments of humour, improvisation, and small wins. The juxtaposition of order–disorder found in a joke, for example, provides no less a window to learning than a false alarm of imminent nuclear attack. A concept that is capable of spanning that range of phenomena surely does deserve attention.

In summary, our intent in this chapter is to articulate and affirm the conditions under which moments of learning occur in organizations, while remaining attentive to the many ways in which efforts to preserve the organization undermine such moments.

## IMAGES OF ORGANIZATION CONDUCIVE TO LEARNING ANALYSIS

As we hinted in the introduction, the experiential referent for the term 'organizational learning' is elusive. This is so for at least three reasons: imprecise referents for the word 'organization', misinterpretations of the achievement verb (Ryle 1949) 'learning'; and debate about whether learning is an individual or organizational phenomenon. After discussing each of these three issues, we review attempts to describe organizations as cultures, at once repositories and self-designing systems. We do so because such an approach represents a solution to the basic invisibility of organization, and carries with it a tacit theory of learning that suggests the importance of juxtaposing order and disorder.

The lack of an experiential referent for the word 'organization' is discussed by Sandelands and Srivatsan (1993). They argue that organizations cannot be perceived, which means that it is difficult to theorize about them. Organizational scientists have too often resorted therefore to theories based on metaphors, as opposed to experience, hence abandoning the healthy tension between experience and conceptualization which drives the natural sciences.

Sandelands and Srivatsan suggest that there are three ways to deal with the fact that we cannot experience organizations directly. Each of these solutions has a different set of implications for the conceptualization of learning, as it does for the conceptualization of organizations. The experience of organizations can be made a clearer object for theorizing if people use such artifacts as models or cause maps (e.g. Barr et al. 1992; Voyer and Faulkner 1989) that 'condense large tracts of organized activity into a single surveyable region' (1993: 16), or computer simulations (Lant and Mezias 1990) that reproduce the capacities or tendencies of organizations. The experience of organizations can also be made clearer if middle-range concepts are identified which can 'stand in' for the concept of organization, and which more closely correspond to experience, such as those concepts developed through grounded theory (Glaser and Strauss 1967). Finally, the experience of organizations can also be made clearer if non-traditional sensitivities are used to capture qualities of experience that are usually neglected. Thus, 'even though organizations cannot be seen, [perhaps] they can be felt' (1993: 17). Attention to feeling, emotion and affect, and methodologies which employ empathy and artistic apprehension of experience can perhaps allow us to grasp the experience of organization in ways which maintain the healthy tension between theory and experience.

Clearly, if we are not able to conceptualize organizations while maintaining a hold on experience, developing a theory of organizational learning becomes even more difficult. 'Learning', as Sandelands and Drazin (1989) point out, is an achievement verb. This means that the same word 'learning' refers to both an outcome and a process, giving it a circular, tautological sense, and concealing rather than revealing the dynamics of the process and the exact nature of the outcome. Coupled with the lack of empirical referents for organization described above, it is not surprising that, indeed, there seems very little of organization in the existing literature on organizational learning. Perhaps in response to the frustrations of grasping the nature of organization, many students of organizational learning such as March and Olsen, Argyris and Schon, and Simon simply sidestep the issue by treating organizational learning as individual learning in an organizational context. And they have no trouble pointing to individuals in a context. Others such as Hedberg, Weick, and Cyert and March argue that organizations learn the same way individuals learn, which means they too can point to individual action as the datum to be explained. When either group feels more emboldened to claim an organizational referent, they are likely to be caught reifying, confusing the map with the territory, or committing the error of hypostatization (treating that which cannot be denoted as if it could).

But such sidestepping of the issues leaves us again with the depressing lack of a truly social science of organization or of learning. Surely, if we in the organizational sciences are going to adopt the concept of learning just as the psychologists seem on the verge of abandoning it, we must proceed with the faith that social learning processes have something to teach us about individual learning, as well as vice versa. So in our effort to contribute to a greater understanding of organizational learning we now focus on 'getting the organization right', by which we mean selecting those images of organizing which are most conducive to grasping the nature of the learning experience. We then turn to vocabularies of learning which seem best designed to grasp the fundamentally 'organized' nature of that experience. Finally we reach the heart of our own argument, the oxymoron inherent in coupling learning with organizing, and its pertinence to understanding the phenomena at hand.

## IMAGES OF ORGANIZATION CONDUCIVE TO LEARNING

Those who embed knowledge in culture and its artifacts seem to be in an unusually good position to draw inferences about learning. This is illustrated in Cook and Yanow's (1993) work. They define culture as 'a set of values, beliefs, and feelings, together with the artifacts of their expression and transmission (such as myths, symbols, metaphors, rituals), that are created, inherited, shared, and transmitted within one group of people and that, in part, distinguish that group from others' (1993: 379). Hence learning is inherent in culture. Normann emphasizes this intriguing connection further:

> I would interpret the increasing interest in the concept of culture as really an increasing interest in organizational learning – in understanding and making conscious and effective as much as possible all the learning that has taken place in an organization. To be aware of culture is to increase the likelihood of learning. Only when the basic assumptions, beliefs, and success formulas are made conscious and visible, do they become testable and open to reinforcement or modification. (1985: 231)

The existing literature on organizational learning as cultural process is slim, but instructive. When researchers focus on organizations as cultures, they focus less on cognition and what goes on in individual heads, and more on what goes on in the practices of groups. This is a key shift for students of organizational as opposed to individual learning. For example Argote and McGrath

(1993: 53) observe that organizational learning 'focuses on how organizations acquire knowledge as they gain experience, how this knowledge is embedded in organizations, and what the effect of such changes in knowledge is on later performance'. The key point turns on the word 'embedded'. For Argote and McGrath, it makes a big difference whether knowledge is embedded in work group structures, roles, and procedures, or in individual workers. The difference is that turnover is less disruptive when knowledge is embedded in structures rather than people (see also Corbett and Van Wassenhove 1993). The way investigators handle the question of where and how knowledge is embedded in organizations affects how they will then handle learning.

What all of this comes down to is the conclusion that conceptualizing organizations as cultures makes it easier to talk about learning. It is less of a conceptual leap to treat an organization as a tribe, than to treat it as a brain or a person or computer (Cook and Yanow 1993: 383). Attention to culture as an organizational system helps us to grasp more not only about the nature of organizing, but also about the nature of learning.

Culture is a complex and much debated concept. However, culture has the great advantage over such concepts as organization or even structure in that it is embodied in specific, visible, tangible products of social systems. First and foremost it is embodied in the language, the words, phrases, vocabularies, and expressions which individual groups develop. Secondly, it is embodied in artifacts, the material objects a group produces, from machines to decorative objects, from buildings to paintings. Lastly, and most ephemerally, it is embodied in coordinated action routines, predictable social exchanges from highly stylized rituals to the informal (but socially structured) convention of greetings with acquaintances. Thus culture as theoretical construct meets all three of Sandelands and Srivatsan's criteria for social science of organizations: the invisible (social relations) made manifest in the tangible (artifacts as models); the middle-range concepts which offer experiential reference points; and an option of approaching the phenomena with methodologies which build on empathy and empathize feeling (such as literary analysis, ethnographic analysis and ethnomethodology).

Having underlined the value of an approach to learning which involves treating organizations as cultures, we now look at a body of literature related to a cultural approach: that of treating organizations as repositories and as self-designing systems. We note that, as with culture, these images of organizations are highly conducive to illuminating learning.

## Organizations as Repositories

The image of organizations as repositories, as found in Schon's (1983b) work, is conducive to descriptions of learning. A static rendering of the idea of repository is found in the following:

> A manager's reflection-in-action also has special features of its own. A manager's professional life is wholly concerned with an organization which is both the stage for his activity and the object of his inquiry. Hence, the phenomena on which he reflects-in-action are the phenomena of organizational life. Organizations, furthermore, are repositories of cumulatively built-up knowledge: principles and maxims of practice, images of mission and identity, facts about the task environment, techniques of operation, stories of past experience which serve as exemplars for future action. When a manager reflects-in-action, he draws on this stock of organizational knowledge, adapting it to some present instance. And he also functions as an agent of organizational learning, extending or restructuring, in his present inquiry, the stock of knowledge which will be available for future inquiry. (1983b: 242)

Schon's image of the learning organization as a stage is also found in Hedberg (1981: 6) who describes the organization as a repertory company, and in Czarniawska-Joerges (1992: 223) who feels that the theatre helps us understand the practical, the symbolic, and the political complexities of organization. Schon's description of the content in the repository (principles, maxims, images, etc.) anticipates those who discuss artifacts as the locus of learning in organizational culture. And Schon's observation that managers who draw on the repository also extend and restructure it, is reminiscent of people like March (1991) who emphasize that organizations not only socialize their members but also learn from them.

Schon portrays the organization in more dynamic images in the following description:

> Finally, managers live in an organizational system which may promote or inhibit reflection-in-action. Organizational structures are more or less adaptable to new findings, more or less resistant to new tasks. The behavioral world of the organization, the characteristic pattern of interpersonal relations, is more or less open to reciprocal reflection-in-action – to the surfacing of negative information, the working out of conflicting views, and the public airing of organizational dilemmas. Insofar as organizational structure and behavioral world condition organizational inquiry, they make up what I will call the 'learning system' of the organization. (1983b: 242)

Here we get a clearer sense of the dimensions along which organizational structures can vary in ways that affect individual learning.

## Organizations as Self-Designing Systems

The image of organizations as self-designing systems blends the image of repository with that of culture, as is seen in this description:

> Self-designing knowledge work systems are thinking and learning organizations that have well-developed self-diagnostic capacities, allowing them to question their governing assumptions and reassess their relationship to changing environmental demands. . . . Knowledge work organizations 'learn how to learn' by maintaining processes that critically examine key assumptions, beliefs, tasks, decisions, and structural issues. (Purser and Pasmore 1992: 55)

Further discussion of these systems is found in Eccles and Crane (1988), Hedberg et al. (1976), Weick (1977), and Weick and Berlinger (1989). The suitability of self-designing systems for learning is evident in Metcalfe's observation that, in a self-designing organization, 'routine interaction with the task environment should generate information about ways to improve performance' (1981: 503). Notice that, up to now, routines have been treated as collective activities that encode rather than generate improvements. Self-designing organizations use routines consisting of small continuous changes in the interest of frequent, adaptive updating rather than less frequent convulsing and crisis.

Continuous updating results from a combination of continuous redesign, underspecified structures, reduced information filtering, intentional imbalance, and cultivation of doubt. Continuous redesign consists of discarding 'even adequate old methods in order to try new ones, looking upon each development as an experiment that suggests new experiments' (Hedberg et al. 1976: 45). As Torbert (1987) suggests, self-designing systems gain their identity from their capacity to restructure. Underspecification of structure encourages both heightened sensitivity to local conditions and continuous mutual adjustment as local learnings keep changing among interdependent individuals. Self-designing systems intentionally try to undermine the seduction of Miller's (1993) architecture of simplicity by creating structures that do less filtering and less uncertainty absorption, by replacing specialists with generalists so that specialist labels do not dominate perception, and by flattening hierarchies to put more people closer to the action. Intentional imbalances, instituted in the belief that low contentment sharpens perception, are a signature of such systems: 'Ambiguous authority structures, unclear objectives, and contradictory assignments of responsibility can legitimize controversies and challenge traditions. . . . Incoherence and indecision can foster exploration, self-evaluation, and learning. Redundant task allocation can provide experimental replications and partial incongruities can diversify portfolios of activities' (Hedberg et al. 1976: 45).

Self-designing systems are also characterized by the institutionalization of doubt (Weick 1979). If organizations are repositories, they are flawed sources of guidance, both because storage is imperfect and because retrieval is an act of reconstruction. Memory is imperfect twice over, which is bad enough. Even worse, organizations face a chronically 'novel present'. To rely on a repository of built-up knowledge is to rely on approximations rather than certainties. To underscore the approximate character of prior learning, self-designing systems apply lessons of the past while simultaneously questioning their relevance.

As culture is explicated, people see more clearly the learning that has already taken place. Once they see past learning more clearly, they are in a better position to retest, modify, and/or reaffirm it. A good example of this sequence of culture explication and learning occurred when the Strategic Air Command under General Chain abandoned its motto 'peace is our profession' and replaced it with the motto 'war is our profession: peace is our product'. This culture shift away from a culture of guardians to a culture of warriors emphasized the greater necessity to maximize military power as a deterrent, and also the likelihood that safety might be traded off for readiness and risk (Sagan 1993: 271–2). Both shifts alarmed key stakeholders. The moment General Chain was replaced by a new commander (General Butler), the old motto was reinstated, peace once more became SAC's profession, the warriors became a bit less conspicuous, and the stakeholders became a bit less anxious.

Thus, we come full circle back to culture. And we complete the circle with a final description of organizing from Schon that incorporates repositories, self-design, culture, and the collective. To conceptualize an organization so that its manner of learning is more apparent, one can begin by asserting that the organization

*acts* when individual members, functioning as agents of the collectivity, carry out their parts of the larger task system. Like the individual craftsman, the collective has a theory-in-use implicit in the norms, strategies, and assumptions that govern its regular patterns of task performance. As in his case, their theory-in-use may be inferred from the evidence of intelligent action, especially from the detection and correction of errors. But in their case, intelligent action depends on a continuing mutual adjustment of individual behaviours, one to another. Their organizing depends, in turn, on each person's image of the larger system. In this sense, the organization exists in its members' heads. But the members also have access to external maps, memories, and programs, which they must continually complete through mutually adjusted actions. (Schon 1983a: 118)

Schon's description lends itself to an analysis of learning. His theory-in-use equates with cultural know-how; theories implicit in norms equate with beliefs embedded in artifacts; intelligent action equates with heedful conduct; correction and detection of error equate with feedback; mutual adjustment equates with interaction that is both artifactual and face to face; images of the larger system equate with culture; the organization in the head equates with individual learning in an organizational context; and external maps, memories and programs equate with routines, repositories, and institutions. The investigator whose thinking about organization is primed with these images is then likely to frame learning not only in ways that are truly organizational, but also in ways that recognize the tension between learning and organizing. For in both the notions of organizations as repositories and of organizations as self-designing systems there is the explicit notion of juxtaposition, the individual against the organization, the present against the past, the new against the routine. And so, in our images of organization conducive to learning, we find that learning appears to be about repunctuating the continuous experience of the organization. To make this repunctuation even a possibility, organization must be reduced and doubt and curiosity must be cultivated. In the section which follows we continue our exploration of organizational learning, viewed in the context of culture, i.e. in the context of language, artifacts and action routines. Here our emphasis shifts, however, to the oxymoron inherent in the concept.

## LEARNING AND ORGANIZING: THE OXYMORON WRIT LARGE

The relationship between learning and organizing is inherently uncomfortable, a tension rather than a compatibility. This tension has been represented in the literature as a choice between structural forms. Certain forms, such as self-designing organizations or adhocracies, are, as we have noted, particularly good at adapting to changing environments and at innovating in response to environmental demands. In terms of creativity or original thinking, this seems to be a recommended form, associated with high creativity.

Other forms, such as bureaucracies, are dedicated to efficiencies, reaping the benefits of learning curves. Bureaucracy is associated with more mechanical division of labour, more rigid chain of command, clearcut distinctions and technical rationality, qualities which are designed to repress or forget confusing or contradictory qualities.

This dichotomy suggests that self-designing organizations learn, while bureaucracies organize. However, on closer examination, the picture seems more complex. March (1991) suggests that each form learns, but the learning is of a different order. Self-designing organizations have a tendency to explore, bureaucracies to exploit. Both are a form of learning and the most resilient organizations of either form do both. The challenge is not to choose between these structures, but rather to strike a balance:

> In studies of organizational learning, the problem of balancing exploration and exploitation is exhibited in distinctions made between refinement of an existing technology and invention of a new one. . . . It is clear that exploration of new alternatives reduces the speed with which skills at existing ones are improved. It is also clear that improvements in competence at existing procedures make experimentation with others less attractive. . . . Finding an appropriate balance is made particularly difficult by the fact that the same issues occur at levels of a nested system – at the individual level, the organizational level, and the social level.

Balance is important because it is evident that either form, taken to its extreme, results in a paralysed organization, unable either to learn or to act. For example, while organizations seem to learn when they exploit routines and develop functioning 'communities of practice' (Brown and Duguid 1991), after a certain point such specialization results in a simplicity which renders the organization so rigid, and so incapable of new response, that it is prone to failure and even death (March 1991; Miller 1993), even in slowly changing environments. On the other hand, while looser, more chaotic forms seem good designs in creating alignment, clearly an important part of organizational learning (Fiol and Lyles 1985), too much alignment can also result in a loss of integrity and hence of an organization's capacity to learn. This would appear to be associated with the system theorists' conception of the totally open system, one in which the boundaries become so permeable as to lose all definition.

So it would appear that learning is associated with both exploitation and exploration, with both establishing routines and accepting disruptive, non-routine behaviour in the interests of alignment. Too much of either ultimately results in the destruction of the system. This suggests that the problem of learning should be viewed not as a choice between exploitation at the expense of exploration, or exploration at the expense of exploitation, but rather as an optimal juxtaposition of the two. Another way of looking at the problem which ties learning back to organizing is that the optimal learning point, whether for the individual or the organization, is in circumstances when order and disorder are juxtaposed, or exist simultaneously. Such moments represent the intersection of double-loop learning (discovery, exploration, proactive learning, revolutionary learning, frame breaking) and single-loop learning (exploitation, adaptation, habit formation, deviation reduction, reactive learning, evolutionary learning). The optimal juxtaposition between order and disorder is created not through alternation between the two but through the intimate and continuing connection between the two.

## Exploitation and Exploration in Cultural Systems

Existing definitions of organizational learning tend to focus either on learning as exploitative (Simon 1991: 125) or on learning as exploration (Buckley 1968). For a definitional option that begins to combine themes of exploration and exploitation we are brought again to culture and the related concepts of repository and self-designing systems. Recall Normann's (1985) earlier observation that, as culture is explicated, people see more clearly the learning that has already taken place. Normann (1985: 230) defines culture as 'the institutionalized language and values of an organization, together with their symbolic and structural manifestations'. Culture is important to learning because it acts 'as a symbol and storage of past learning', and it works as an instrument to communicate this learning throughout the organization.

If we combine these images of culture with images of exploration and exploitation, we begin to get a definition that sounds like this: organizational learning is 'the acquiring, sustaining, and changing, through collective actions, of the meanings embedded in the organization's cultural artifacts' (Cook and Yanow 1993: 384). Cook and Yanow avoid the blind spots of 'learning' as an achievement verb when they insist that observers pay attention to the acquiring, sustaining, and changing of intersubjective meanings. And they also avoid the non-experiential references to whole organizations when they use artifactual vehicles that embody collective know-how as their referent.

Cook and Yanow's definition focuses on intersubjective meanings rather than knowledge or information or behaviour as the outcome of interest. Notice, however, that the meanings that are learned are not free-standing, existential, philosophical profundities. Far from it. They are embedded in cultural artifacts, which means the meanings likely represent a tacit synthesis of knowledge, information, and behaviour. Furthermore, the definition lends itself to conceptualization of organizational learning as a capacity possessed not only by individual members, but by the aggregate itself. Language, action routines and material artifacts are both the means to produce and share meanings and the resource from which further cultural artifacts are created.

With these fundamentals and definitions in hand, we can now afford to look more closely at three cultural subsystems mentioned earlier – those of language, material artifacts and action routines – in search of a more experientially based understanding of the oxymoron of organizational learning. In each case, we discover that learning seems to be as much about reaffirmation, conservation, complication, efficacy, appreciation, community, and sometimes even self-destruction, as it is about change and improvement. Learning is not a synonym for change, and here we get our first glimpse of why that is so.

## Language and Learning

When we approach the task of examining the tension between learning and organizing, we cannot avoid looking at the role of language. As the central cultural system of any social organizing, language is vital to both learning and organizing. To learn is to use language, to communicate, both at the interpersonal and at the intrapersonal level. At the intrapersonal level, language allows for the reflection which, along with action or behaviour, is a critical part of learning as described by most organizational theorists (Fiol and Lyles 1985). Children, given the opportunity to move, will develop motor skills without the benefit of human interaction (as in the case of 'feral' children), but their ability to learn is fundamentally inhibited by failure to acquire language. Skilled athletes exhibit what Gardner (1983) has called 'physical intelligence'; it would appear that their bodies 'learn' without conscious, analytic reflection. However, the universal phenomenon of the coach is evidence that there are limits to the purely physical action-based learning, even among gifted athletes. At a certain point the coach assumes the role of reflection *vis-à-vis* the action of the athlete. So even among athletes, where much learning is physical, communication at the interpersonal and intrapersonal levels has an important place.

This becomes even more critical in team sports. Here the coach must provide the structure through which the actions of individual actors become the game of the team, and this is done through language. It is true that this metastructure becomes embedded in 'plays' which technically can be carried out wordlessly. The coach, however, is still critical to learning, as it is the coach who orchestrates how the plays are sequenced in each game and from one game to the next.

At the primary level then, all learning occurs through social interaction. Language is both the tool and the repository of learning. It is the critical tool for reflection at both the interpersonal and intrapersonal levels. And language is a social phenomenon. Stated differently, learning is embedded in relationships or relating. By this we mean that learning is not an inherent property of an individual or of an organization, but rather resides in the quality and the nature of the relationship between levels of consciousness within the individual, between individuals, and between the organization and the environment. Thus learning at the individual level (intrapersonal) and at the organizational level (interpersonal or interorganizational) evolves through a continual process of mutual adjustment.

Language has the interesting property that it is as closely linked to forgetting as it is to learning. Koestler (1964), Freud (1905), Lévi-Strauss (1963), and Leach (1972) all note that the human ability to create and use language allows finer distinctions to be made in the overall pattern of experience. Through the naming of things, however, we are not only seeing, we are suppressing awareness in order to distinguish one thing from another. The best example of this is perhaps the colour spectrum. In reality the colour spectrum represents a continuum. In order to differentiate red from orange from yellow, however, it is necessary 'not to see' the part of the spectrum which joins red to orange (Leach 1970). As a given culture places greater importance on certain parts of experience than others, words proliferate to distinguish ever greater nuances. The multiple words which Eskimos use to describe snow is often cited as an example. The irony is however that while the Eskimos seem to have a richer experience of snow than the average non-Eskimo, and a perception of greater variety, they must also work harder at not seeing, at ignoring the anomalies that threaten to blend one category with another. While they therefore see more, they must simultaneously ignore more as well. For the average non-Eskimo snow is a bland continuum, which may be sensed or felt, but is rarely explored or exploited.

And here we get our first intimation of how in language as a cultural system we may see the manifestations of exploitative or explorative learning. When we speak of articulating ideas in an organizational context, we refer to this movement from vague, unspecified sensing to increasing precision of language (highly technical, scientific or logical language being the most precise). Paradoxically we lose some awareness as we increase variety and specificity but such loss is necessary to carry on the partitioning and labelling that we conceive of as rational or logical thinking. As Bateson (1972) points out, we can deal with only a fragment of the mind's totality at any given moment. In fact, to think rationally it is necessary to isolate a figure and then ignore the background. This is in no way automatic and often requires great 'concentration'.

> All thought involves a certain mental tension. In controlled and rational thought this takes on the form of attention which serves two distinct functions. On the one hand the mind takes on a certain imperviousness, a 'hide' which protects it from irrelevant stimuli. This is called the surface tension. On the other hand, the act of attending also serves to direct the mind along certain definite channels. When a thinking process continues organized and controlled in this manner and progresses towards an end, it is termed rational. (Munro 1951: 176)

So rational, logical thinking involves a closing, a protecting of the figure from disruption by irrelevant material, be it thoughts or stimuli, through the forging and selection of words which increase variety and precision at the expense of experience. This, of course, is the linguistic equivalent of exploitative learning. We progress through rational thought processes to logical conclusions, which one assumes are different and technically superior to the vague, unformed hunches which may have triggered the process of articulation. We think of Weber's (1978) notion of the momentum of processes of technical rationality and the 'disenchantment' of the world which accompanies this movement.

However, this kind of learning might be seen as 'normal science' or single-loop learning. Creativity or original thinking seems to involve exactly opposite processes. Instead of protecting the figure from disruption, 'insight' involves the disruption of these same controlled thinking processes. According to Koestler, in the 'flash of insight' which characterizes the creative act (and which he terms bi-association), the mind 'connects previously unconnected matrices [contexts] of experience, shows a familiar situation or even in a new light and elicits a new response to it' (1964: 659). Just as conscious thought involves a

movement from generalization to specificity, creative thought 'regresses' to find its source in the 'phylogenetically and ontologically older underground layers of the mind. He (the creator) can only reach them through a regression to earlier, more primitive, less specialized levels of mentation, through a *reculer pour mieux sauter*' (1964: 659). Here we retreat from language itself, to a realm of experience beyond words.

Learning is intimately connected to the dynamics of communication and to the tension between levels of consciousness. To 'see' we must 'not see', but to learn, i.e. to see more, we must retrieve what we deliberately forgot. To communicate what we have seen anew we must again resort to words, to logics of communication, to semantics, and so 'forget' again in the interest of precision. If we forget too much or fail to allow the unseen to disrupt the order, Koestler argues, we become trapped in habit, repetitiveness, eventually dogmatism. Learning requires the ability both to see and not to see, to name and not to name, to organize our thinking and to disorganize it.

## Learning and Artifacts

Organizational identity is what members perceive as central, enduring, and unique or distinctive about their organization and believe others share as well (Dutton and Penner 1993: 95; Albert and Whetten 1985). It 'is a subset of the collective beliefs that comprise an organization's culture' (Dutton and Penner 1993: 95), and identity is created and distributed by the cultural system. Identity is described by Ring and Van de Ven (1994: 100) as an image that aids sensemaking: 'By projecting itself onto its environment, organization develops a self-referential appreciation of its own identity, which in turn, permits the organization to act in relation to its environment.' Organizations learn something about their core attributes when they see what they can and cannot enact. And more often than not, for an organization, that identity is embodied by a tangible symbol, be it logo or product. To understand the oxymoron of organizational learning we may look at efforts to juxtapose innovation and preservation at the level of the material artifacts themselves.

Cook and Yanow (1993) have provided us with an excellent example of such a juxtaposition in their study of the Powell flutemaking workshop. At Powell, people make an effort to maintain unique core patterns of activity while socializing new craftsmen and marketing to customers who have changing needs. These conflicting pulls toward innovation and preservation converged in 1974 when Albert Cooper, an independent English flutemaker, developed a new scale (a new configuration of tone holes in a flute) that flute players strongly preferred. This created a dilemma at Powell because their identity as maker of 'the best flutes in the world' was tied in part to the fact that the 'best' flute had a Powell scale that 'had been developed by Mr Powell himself and was felt to be an intimate part of the Powell flute' (1993: 382). To adopt the Cooper scale would amount to changing the identity of the company. The dilemma, recast as a learning issue, was: can Powell build a Powell flute based on a Cooper scale and still have it be a Powell flute?

To see if they could make something different without becoming a different company, the Powell craftsmen made a prototype Powell flute with a Cooper scale. Cook and Yanow catch several subtleties in this prototyping. In building the prototype, craftsmen did *not* test the Cooper scale, because that had already been done. Instead,

> making the prototype enabled Powell, almost ceremonially, to go through the motions of making a Cooper-scale Powell flute and in doing so, to assure itself that the flute and the company's style would be preserved through the Cooper innovation. Powell was not so much learning a new technology as learning – collectively, as an organization – how to maintain its identity in the face of a new undertaking. (1993: 383)

It was decided to offer the Cooper scale as an option. Unfortunately, Cook and Yanow do not unpack this decision so we are left to speculate about the exact process by which people were reassured that innovation would not erode identity. Virtually all customers chose the Cooper scale option once it was offered, yet the quality, feel, and style of Powell flutes was maintained. Cook and Yanow interpret that outcome this way: 'At root, Powell adopted a new technology to maintain and reaffirm its own self-image as makers of "the best" – that is, to sustain what the group felt, believed, and valued' (1993: 383). Learning did not change the organization and that is the measure of its success. People underwent a change, yet were able to 'maintain', 'reaffirm', and 'sustain' their feelings, beliefs, and values. If they had any doubts about whether there really was a distinctive Powell flute, this incident laid them to rest.

The larger point regarding moments of learning in organizations is that they may involve the basic oxymoron writ small. In moments of organizational learning, people may want to take on a new situation but not a new identity (1993: 385). Learning may be most likely to occur when situations are explored but

identities are exploited. People learn how to innovate, but they also learn how to reaccomplish their identity amidst a new set of threats.

When organizations fail to innovate, this may signify an inability to decouple innovation from identity. This could take one of two forms. First, an inability to decouple identity from innovation could lead to no innovation at all. The firm is unwilling to become something else. Second, the same inability could be resolved in favour of innovation rather than identity, meaning that a firm has as many identities as it has innovations: in other words, no identity at all. The Powell flutemakers show that there is a third option, namely, 'ambivalence as the optimal compromise'. They juxtapose order and disorder, exploration and exploitation, first- and second-order learning, and incremental and transformational change. In doing so, they affirm an oxymoron and grow.

## Learning and Action Routines

The image of 'a moment in a process' is Mary Parker Follett's (1924). It appears in the context of her discussion of the ways in which stimulus–response (SR) language can mislead:

> The activity of the individual is only in a certain sense caused by the stimulus of the situation because that activity is itself helping to produce the situation which causes the activity of the individual. In other words behaviour is a relating not of 'subject' and 'object' as such, but of two activities. . . . Stimulus is not cause and response the effect. Some writers, while speaking otherwise accurately of the behaviour process, yet use the word result – the result of the process – whereas there is no result *of* process but only a moment *in* process. . . . On the social level, cause and effect are ways of describing certain moments in the situation when we look at those moments apart from the total process. (1924: 60–1)

Since most ideas about learning, at least in their earliest form, contained some variant of SR language, more recent extensions may still understate the degree to which learning occurs amidst flows and cycles where responding co-defines the conditions for its own unfolding.

Efforts to capture patterns, cycles, and flows of organizational life more richly are found in the work of people like Gersick (1988), Cowan (1993), and Cohen et al. (1972). Learning in this context involves a different vocabulary. Learning amidst flows and cycles is a matter of alignment, timing, opportunities that open and then close, patterns that form and dissolve, entrainment, synchronicity, coincidence, luck, chance, rhythms of variation (Cowan), unfolding, passages, and recapitulation. Learning is not about the artificial beginnings of stimulation that end in a response. Instead, it is about punctuation, forgetting, and not-seeing portions of the flow in order to justify naming, categorizing, and protecting the remaining portions that are seen. Learning as a moment in a process draws our attention to learning as it may be seen in action routines.

If we view learning as a mindful moment in action routines when order and disorder are juxtaposed, then we look for occasions when this might occur and we count the frequency of such occasions. For example, a survivable error from which a system gets information is a learning moment. A near-miss between two aircraft flying on the same course (Tamuz 1988) mixes the order of a safe separation with the disorder of a non-fatal loss of this separation. Literally, a moment is created when the air traffic system can see what it has forgotten. But the moment is fleeting. The opportunity opens and then closes swiftly as those involved get their accounts in order. As Cohen and Gooch put it,

in the chaos of the battlefield there is the tendency of all ranks to combine and recast the story of their achievements into a shape which shall satisfy the susceptibilities of national and regimental vainglory. . . . On the actual day of battle naked truths may be picked up for the asking; by the following morning they have already begun to get into their uniforms. (1990: 44)

It is not just efforts to deflect blame that make learning moments fleeting. The very fact that there is evidence of both order and disorder thwarts conclusion drawing.

Every time a pilot avoids a collision, the event provides evidence both for the threat and for its irrelevance. It is not clear whether the learning should emphasize how close the organization came to disaster, thus the reality of danger in the guise of safety, or the fact that disaster was avoided, thus the reality of safety in the guise of danger. (March et al. 1991: 10)

If the moment is interpreted as safety in the guise of danger, then learning should be diminished because 'more thorough investigations, more accurate reporting, deeper imagination, and greater sharing of information' are all discouraged (Sagan 1993: 247). Even if it is decided later, during more formal inquiry, to reverse the interpretation, qualities of the original moment such as the preconditions that led up to it will be underdeveloped. Close inspection of the last twenty minutes before a near-miss overlooks the possibility that this is simply the last distraction set in motion much earlier, much farther away (e.g. an unresolved quarrel).

Survivable errors are prototypes of moments which juxtapose order and disorder, moments which partially disorganize the organized, and partially dismantle routines. The errors testify to the entropy that gnaws constantly at organization. The survival testifies that the entropy can be controlled. The fact that errors broke through previous controls, however, signifies the need to rework them. This is the opportunity that opens and closes abruptly. How organizations respond to such moments affects their learning.

So far we have talked most about flows and their effects on learning. More needs to be said about cycles. Adler and Cole's (1993) comparison of learning at NUMMI and Volvo-Uddevalla automobile manufacturing plants provides insight into cycles and learning. Although both plants involve labour-intensive production of relatively standardized products, the cycles are radically different. At NUMMI, teams of four or five workers perform a work cycle that is well documented in which each member has a cycle lasting about sixty seconds. The system 'is based on specialized work tasks supplemented by modest doses of job rotation and great discipline in the definition and implementation of detailed work procedures' (1993: 85). At Uddevalla, teams of ten workers perform a work cycle that is less well documented and that lasts about two hours. These greatly lengthened work cycles represent 'a return to craftlike work forms that give teams substantial latitude in how they perform their tasks and authority over what have traditionally been higher-level management decisions' (1993: 85).

Adler and Cole argue that these differences in documentation and cycle length create a distinct learning advantage for NUMMI. NUMMI is better able to identify problems in detail, define improvements, implement improvements, share improvement opportunities, and continue to improve. These learning advantages are seen to occur because NUMMI workers have a more explicit idea of what they think they already know, which facilitates re-examination. And with shorter cycles, it is easier to spot changes that may correct unwanted deviations.

It is much more difficult to learn collectively at Volvo. Individuals improve their individual skills, but not mutual adjustment. There are few shared views of what interdependencies are in place. And, when deviations occur, there are two hours' worth of activities that potentially may be their source. Learning at Volvo is a textbook case of individual learning in an organizational context, whereas NUMMI exemplifies organizational learning (1993: 92).

These seemingly straightforward findings are not as simple as they appear. We see in them echoes of several earlier themes. For example, the shorter, more precise learning cycles at NUMMI are a good example of exploitative learning. Learning which depends upon having 'a more explicit idea of what they think they already know, which facilitates reexamination . . . [and corrects] unwanted deviations' would seem to be learning highly dependent on precise articulation and exploitation of the underlying system. In contrast, the longer cycles in Volvo could allow for greater exploration. The shorter cycles at NUMMI and the more rigid procedures make it less likely that workers will 'explore' alternatives together. We should ask not only how the length of cycles impacts on learning, but perhaps when those fleeting learning opportunities occur in short cycles? in long cycles?

Furthermore, if we re-examine the Powell flutemakers in this context, they appear to have the best of both worlds. Their work has longer cycles and more craftwork than NUMMI and more group learning and more structure than Uddevalla. The level of documentation at Powell is less than at NUMMI and greater than at Uddevalla since it is carried indirectly by artifacts rather than directly by detailed methods and standards. As a result, workers at Powell have more flexibility and more personal learning opportunities than those at NUMMI, more structure and more cross-individual learning opportunities than those at Uddevalla. Powell flutemakers have broader knowledge than workers at NUMMI, deeper knowledge than those of Uddevalla. In short, Powell has more moments of juxtaposition.

Alder and Cole's findings allow us to make a point about culture and learning. The NUMMI edge could disappear if more attention were paid to the culture at Uddevalla. Recall that there was no detailed documentation available to workers at Uddevalla that 'described how to perform each work task and [specified] how long it should take' (1993: 89). But neither was such documentation available at Powell. A representative worker at Uddevalla said, 'You don't really need all that detail because you feel it when the task isn't going right; you can feel the sticking points yourself' (1993: 89). That too is no different from Powell. Then what's different? Either the culture at Volvo was not coincident with know-how as it was at Powell, or it was, but Adler and Cole missed it because of their prior assumption that 'without a well documented, standardized process, it is hard to imagine how these people could have spotted improvement opportunities or shared them across teams. You cannot sustain continual improvement in the production of products as standardized as automobiles without clear and detailed methods and standards' (1993: 89).

It may be hard for Adler and Cole to imagine how opportunities can be spotted and shared without formal documentation, but not for Cook and Yanow who argue that opportunities can be felt. The difference is that Cook and Yanow look for more artifacts of culture and therefore spot more vehicles for learning than simply those of a well-documented process. Furthermore, Cook and Yanow are attentive to identity. If workers at Uddevalla truly are slow learners, which is not proven simply by the existence of inferior documentation, they may fear that too much will change too fast if they learn too well. Such may be the Achilles heel in a self-managed team where intense interactions create vivid identities that threaten to vanish with any change whatsoever.

In summary, what we wish to emphasize here is that in looking more closely at the workings of cultural systems such as language, material artifacts and action routines we can better apprehend learning and its tension with organizing. That all three cultural systems serve to reinforce each other in situations where exploitative learning is high (as in the case of NUMMI) should not surprise us. Neither should it surprise us that conflict between the three cultural systems (as was the case at Uddevalla, where action routines did not seem to be supported by a similarly patterned linguistic protocol) may produce the ideal context for exploration. For explorative learning feeds on the idiosyncratic, the unexpected, the serendipitous and atrophies in the face of tight and centralized control.

## FACILITATORS OF
## ORGANIZATIONAL LEARNING

Improbable though learning may be in the context of imperatives towards order associated with organizing, there are moments when order is juxtaposed with disorder and people get a glimpse of the forgotten and the unseen. These are moments when learning is possible. But these are also moments that are fleeting and short-lived. Recall the 'naked truths of battle' that swiftly get back into their uniforms the next day. If moments of balance between exploration and exploitation are transient, then researchers need to look at uncommon, often inconspicuous events to spot learning. And practitioners need to be less enamoured with large-scale training programs and campaigns of transformation and more alert to places and moments where canons and dogma become suspect.

Learning moments and spaces tend not to be obvious precisely because they retain vestiges of order, routine, and expected exploitation. They are *almost* business as usual. What keeps them from being nothing but business as usual is some quirk of language embodied in a joke, or an improvised routine, or a misunderstood instruction leading to a near-miss, or a speculation that serves as an irreverent gloss on institutionalized practice. The irreverent gloss uncovers forgotten meanings, hints at flaws or limits in current practice, redirects thought toward new channels, or detects pervious areas in the impervious 'hide' of controlled thinking (recall Bateson's image of rational thought). This is not simply quantum change or brute exploration or sudden second-order learning. Those are possible, of course – but relatively rare. More common and more crucial in the determination of learning over the long haul are *approximations* to quantum change, approximations in the sense that their disorder is nested in and balanced by orderly ongoing organized practice. The limits of that ongoing practice become visible precisely because that very same ongoing practice reveals some of its own flaws. Flawed practices that generate self-criticism can't be all that flawed . . . and yet they are. That is the complex message implicit in the juxtaposition of order and disorder that precedes learning. That is the complex message conveyed by humour, improvisation, and small wins, all of which represent small moments of learning with large consequences. We conclude this chapter with brief discussions of all three.

## Humour as a Moment of Learning

Both Salman Rushdie (1992) and Michael Cole (1990) have recently discussed the relation between power and memory in the context of Milan Kundera's (1981) book *The Book of Laughter and Forgetting*. Cole (1990: vii), citing efforts by the Chinese government to deny that anyone was killed in Tienanmen Square, argues that the increasing incidence of socially organized forgetting seems to illustrate George Orwell's assertion that 'He who controls the past controls the future. He who controls the present controls the past.' Rushdie argues, therefore, that 'Redescribing a world is the necessary first step to changing it' (1992: 14).

This perspective implies that power, particularly absolute power, presents a major impediment to learning, linked as it is to rigid taboos, autocracy, impression management, sycophancy, and hubris. What the title of Kundera's book suggests is that in this 'struggle against forgetting', humour is an invaluable tool.

But how does humour provide learning or, as we have elaborated the concept above, how does humour provide identity maintenance, moments in a process, and in what way does it provide the juxtaposition of action and reflection, emotion and rationality, order and disorder in the kind of release of energy which we have categorized as 'learning as coincident with action'?

A sense of humour, according to Robertson Davies (1958), is 'a sense of anarchy, a sense of chaos'. On a purely linguistic level, studies of the joke form have indicated that it is precisely designed to name the unnamed, confuse sense with non-sense, and create disorder of our ordered thought systems.

Bateson (1972) lumps humour with art and madness under the general heading of creativity. Specifically, he describes the use of humour as a completed circuit involving a dissolution and re-establishment of the figure–ground relationship:

> in the first phase of telling a joke, the information content is on the surface, the other content types in various forms are implicit in the background. When the point of the joke is reached, suddenly this background material is brought into attention and a paradox or something like it is touched off. A circuit of contradictory notions is completed.

Koestler uses humour as the example *par excellence* of the creative act on which he based his description of other areas of creativity. The entire spectrum of creativity he divides into three: humour, discovery, and art. All three are based on the bisociation of two matrices and result in either 'a collision ending in laughter, a fusion in a new intellectual experience, or a confrontation in an aesthetic experience' (1964: 45). But, unlike art or discovery, humour is not constructive–destructive. Rather, it is a tolerated and permitted expression of the unconscious, neither a true merging, nor a suspension of consciousness. In this sense, it meets our criteria for juxtaposition.

Freud (1905) noted that jokes involve taking mental shortcuts with words or ideas: condensing, unifying, modifying to create 'double meanings'. In the process we name the unnamed and connect things previously kept separate. As Freud put it, 'Joking is the disguised priest who weds every couple . . . he likes best to wed couples whose union their relatives frown upon' (1905: 11). Freud concluded that this 'play with words' was in fact a regression to a preverbal state and that herein lay the source of our pleasure in humour. Children are not restrained by the rules of grammar. The child is permitted to talk 'non-sense.' Nevertheless, the nonsense of the joke is not the nonsense of the child. In order for the joke to be appreciated, in order for it to be intelligible, it must take a specific form. A joke, as every child must learn, is culturally defined, following a definite pattern (Sils 1972).

It is this pattern which protects and permits the regression, the release of unconscious sense to the conscious mind. The laugh, then, is one of combined relief and pleasure. The experience is that of a child who escapes unpunished with forbidden behaviour. The joke form simultaneously plays with order and maintains it. We momentarily escape 'this strict, untiring, troublesome governess, the reason', but we must, in order to feel this pleasure, acknowledge her continued authority.

Sociological and anthropological studies of humour and its function in social situations would seem to support this view; in interpersonal relations, as well as intrapersonally, humour acts to simultaneously blur and support social distinctions. Conditions most conducive to humour in groups were 'anxiety about self, submission to rigid authority structure, and adjustment to a rigid routine (Coser 1959: 175). Jokes provide an 'institutionalized means for the expression of social tensions', particularly in very structured, authoritarian situations (Daniels and Daniels 1964). In a study of joking relationships in a hospital setting, Emerson (1969) suggests that joking functions among patients and staff as a covert way of dealing with taboo subjects, in this case, death. Again, the joking form is key as 'the joking form is in itself a negation.' By choosing a joking mode, patients at once break and support a taboo.

Studies of the social role of joker or fool provide additional support. Clown or joker roles are almost universal (Charles 1945; Welsford 1935). In most situations, the clown acts as a mediator, to bring the forgotten or repressed material of the collective unconscious to the public eye in order that it may be put to use for 'further social progress' (Charles 1945: 25). However, the anarchy and disruption which the clown is allowed to create are, like the joking relationship, carefully controlled by ritual form and often restricted to certain time periods (carnival is a notable example).

So jokes, joking, and humour act both to confirm identity and to allow it to evolve our first context for learning. Dying patients can admit they are dying without negating the healing situation; friends can incorporate hostility into close relationships. Anxiety and competence can co-exist, enmity and solidarity can be juxtaposed (Coombs and Goldman 1973; Stebbins 1979; Bradney 1957).

In addition, jokes provide moments in a process in which alternative realities, 'forgotten' truths, anomalous information can, in a transitory and non-disruptive way, be introduced into the flow of events. Humour is the enemy of hubris, while being the friend of authority. In classical literature, the king needs his fool as much as his sage, as it is the fool who dares (under the cloak of foolery) to criticize authority or its rigid assumptions of omnipotence (Kets de Vries 1990). Studies of humour in organizations suggests that it is a vehicle for expressing criticism and contradiction of existing policies and procedures, of unmasking ambiguities, of making hitherto unrecognized connections (Linstead 1985; Weick and Browning 1986; Hatch and Ehrlich 1993). Organizational foolery provides a counterpoint to canonical practice (Locke 1992), and hence offers the same potential for learning as other forms of non-canonical practice described by Seeley Brown.

And humour has the fleeting, ephemeral quality that we have recognized in other learning moments. It has nothing to do with stimulus–response and everything to do with timing, synchronicity, coincidence, and luck. It is also a visceral more than rational activity, inimitably connected to the release of energy. Humour is the only form of creative activity which produces a massive physical response (laughter) which is simultaneously physical and social. The pleasure in the joke comes not from creating it but from sharing it. In this sense, humour is like jazz, 'the spontaneous joke organizes the total situation in its joke patterns' (Douglas 1975: 97). It becomes part of action, producing energy and subtly redirecting the flow of events it responds to. And when others enter into playfulness of this kind, we move from joking to improvisation.

In sum, humour provides flexibility, adjustment, insight without the loss of order. We may conclude from our discussion that learning organizations differ from highly explorative organizations, in that they retain greater integrity of structure; they differ from highly exploitative organizations in that they retain an element of slack, redundancy, disorder, and hence, flexibility. Humour is a good example of the creation of disorder within order. Starting from the other viewpoint, we must consider improvisation as a means of creating order while simultaneously maintaining disorder.

## Improvisation as a Learning Place

The joker provides one set of clues about conditions that facilitate learning, and the improvisation of the jazz musician provides another set. What is distinctive about jazz improvisation is that it requires learning co-incident with action. There is 'on-the-spot surfacing, criticizing, restructuring, and testing of intuitive understandings of experienced phenomena' while the ongoing action can still make a difference (Schon 1987: 26–7). In the case of jazz, what is surfaced on the spot is an activity rather than an object. Like cinema and dance, jazz is a performance art that cannot be grasped in an instant. The hallmark of jazz is improvisation, 'playing extemporaneously, i.e., without the benefit of written music . . . composing on the spur of the moment' (Schuller 1968: 378). Thus, the traditional distinction between composition and performance, which mirrors the rational distinction between planning and doing, disappears in jazz when the creator becomes the interpreter. Unlike an architect who works from plans and looks ahead, a jazz musician cannot 'look ahead at what he is going to play, but he can look behind at what he has just played; thus each new musical phrase can be shaped with relation to what has gone before. He creates his form retrospectively' (Gioia 1988: 61). Since intention is loosely coupled to execution, the jazz musician essentially wades in, guided by the minimal structure of a melody, and makes sensible, after the fact, whatever becomes visible in hindsight.

Improvisation is not confined to jazz. It occurs in other places such as psychotherapy and combat. First, we sample psychotherapy:

> Given the unpredictable nature of a client's communication, the therapist's participation in the theatrics of a session becomes an invitation to improvise. In other words, since the therapist never knows exactly what the client will say at any given moment, he or she cannot rely exclusively upon previously designed lines, patter, or scripts. Although some orientations to therapy attempt to shape both the client and therapist into a predetermined form of conversation and story, every particular utterance in a session offers a unique opportunity for improvisation, invention, innovation, or more simply, change. (Keeney 1990: 1)

If therapy is viewed as improvisation, then therapies are viewed as songs. The song can be played exactly as scored or with improvisation, but one would not expect an improvisational therapist to play only one song over and over, any more than one would expect a jazz musician to play only one song throughout a lifetime.

Second, we sample the combat soldier. Contrary to stereotypes, this seeming ideal model of a rule-following bureaucrat 'is not detached, routinized, and self-contained; rather his role is one of constant improvisation . . . The impact of battle destroys men, equipment, and organization, which need constantly and continually to be brought back into some form of unity through on-the-spot improvisation' (Janowitz 1959: 481).

None of these extensions portray some kind of second-class rationality practised by people who read about rational choice and missed the point. Instead, this is the activity of people who are thrown into the middle of things and play their way out by thinking while doing. In other words, this is everyday organizational life. To borrow Thayer's (1988: 254) Spanish proverb, 'No es lo mismo hablar de toros, que estar en el redondel', which translates, 'It is not the same thing to talk of bulls as to be in the bullring.' To talk of intelligent action, to talk of leadership, to prepare for war (Cohen and Gooch 1990: 236) are not the same things as acting, leading, and fighting. The trick is to learn *in* the bullring and *during* wartime conditions. Once the bull enters and the war starts, surprise is inevitable. Failure to learn how to learn, faster, can be fatal. This is why learning coincident with action is crucial.

Good jazz, like good conversation, is collective improvisation. Both mix together listening to others with listening to self, mutual elaboration, on-line invention, all within an underlying structure. 'Improvisation consists in varying, combining, and recombining a set of figures within a schema that gives coherence to the whole piece. As the musicians feel the directions in which the music is developing, they make new sense of it. They reflect-in-action on the music they are collectively making' (Schon 1987: 30).

The interesting thing about such moments and spaces is that when they truly involve learning, they are remembered as organizational 'peak experiences', when the coordinated action seemed particularly fluid and effortless, when language seemed to invent rather than merely to describe experiences, when the old was suddenly seen anew, in a blend of discovery and nostalgia. Individuals recognize the experience as social, not individual, and as a 'place' which might possibly be recaptured with the right combination of people, resources and circumstances. But such moments or places are hard to plan or design; rather they perpetually have an improvisational quality. Here we are reminded again about methodologies which emphasize feeling. When learning occurs, it may be 'felt' rather than programmed or monitored. To apprehend and duplicate an organizational learning experience may be to search for a remembered place which feels both old and new, stimulating and reassuring. Learning moments, like surprises, may only be known after they are felt.

To understand how learning is facilitated by improvisation, one needs to appreciate the role of feeling, but one also needs to appreciate the role of songs as minimal structures and the role of imperfections as aesthetic structures.

Songs provide the minimal order that is partially disordered in the interest of learning. Sudnow describes songs this way:

song is a social organizational device *par excellence*, a format of two or more individuals. Its metrical structure, with a beginning and an end and a definite number of grouped pulses, furnishes a planful means for coordinating simultaneous movement and allocating little batches of talk among various players over the course of on-going play. (1979: 105)

Songs coordinate diversity, impose order across time, provide cues for elaboration, encourage mutual adjustment, afford a continuing sense of common place and, because of their simplicity, do not get in the way of imagination. The key issue for organizational learning becomes: what is the equivalent of a song in an organization? Candidates include a vision statement, a credo (e.g. General Electric's 'speed, simplicity and self-confidence'), milestones, a role, developmental sequences, routines, past history, traditions, and rituals. Whatever the source, learning is more likely to occur when there are songs and a songbook, rather than endless variations on the same old melody. 'The energy and creativity it would take to keep one's imagination alive under the constraint of playing the same song time and time again is unimaginable' (Keeney 1990: 8).

Improvisation requires minimal structure but it also requires a capacity to tolerate and elaborate errors. This is especially true with jazz. Jazz is an imperfect art. As Gioia puts it, 'errors will creep in, not only in form but also in execution; the improviser, if he seriously attempts to be creative, will push himself into areas of expression which his technique may be unable to handle. Too often the finished product will show moments of rare beauty intermixed with technical mistakes and aimless passages' (1988: 66). The 'errors' attendant on the juxtaposition of order and disorder in jazz can be recast as opportunities rather than threats to performance. Expressions that seem not to fit with what is now under way can be seen as experiments from which people learn, oddities to be incorporated and made normal, outcomes to be isolated and localized, evidence of reaching, testing of one's limits, transient dissonance that will soon be resolved, lyrical moments for a different context, avoidance of traps and clichés, or clever solutions of an even bigger problem glimpsed after the fact. A more nuanced interpretation of what error means in improvisation heightens the chance for threats to be recast as opportunities, and for the balance between order and disorder to be sustained. With a deep appreciation of the aesthetics of imperfection, people can sustain the balance of order and disorder for a longer period and increase the chance that learning moments will materialize some time during that extended interval.

## Small Wins as Learning Moments

The organizational context within which learning occurs often works against that occurrence.

In a complex environment, major changes are hard to accomplish and even harder to control; they typically entail the manipulation of so many variables simultaneously that one must strain to learn anything from the experience. Moreover, major change is likely to be a day late and a dollar short. That is, the environment in many instances is changing faster than major planned change attempts. An alternative, then, is small change attempts started in many locations.

The moderate size, implemented outcome is a special form of change: it is manageable; its impact is not disruptive; it is designed to improve learning about the system. Moreover, it acts as part of a pattern and as such the necessary prelude to further adjustments and, finally, possibly larger changes. (Peters 1977: 358, 4)

This 'special form of change' is called a small win, and is defined as controllable opportunities of modest size that produce visible and tangible outcomes (Weick 1984). Small wins, despite their seeming embodiment of nothing but order and incremental exploitation, in fact often produce a more complex mixture of exploitation, exploration, and learning. Although there is a tangible outcome, the meaning and significance of that outcome are not fixed. Instead, it becomes an occasion that attracts unexpected allies, deters opponents for reasons that had not been foreseen, uncovers new opportunities, breaches old assumptions, and juxtaposes new symbols with old artifacts to produce new forgetting. Small wins can churn old routines into new learning.

To illustrate, consider the relative success feminists have had with the smaller win of making people more conscious of gender bias in language (e.g. chair*man*) compared to their relative failure in removing gender bias through legislation (e.g. equal rights amendments). Attempts to induce self-consciousness about gender references in speech revealed that language was more susceptible to change than people had realized; that the opponents to language change were more dispersed and less formidable than anticipated; that gender-biased language was more pervasive and therefore a stronger leverage point than people realized; and that language reform could be incorporated into a wide variety of agendas (e.g. various revisions of style manuals could feature gender-fair speech). These small language experiments uncovered entrenched sexism that had been invisible. These discoveries created disorder in taken-for-granted, orderly speech patterns and opened the possibility for learning. This disorder was relatively short-lived because the old categories of 'male' and 'female' were forgotten and the flow of experience was repunctuated into new, equally arbitrary distinctions involving 'people' and 'persons'. This reshuffling of language and routines, done in response to the co-presence of order and disorder, is a fundamental episode of learning that results in people giving a new response to an old stimulus.

To take a different example, when Greyhound of Canada was faced with a steady decline of riders there was no shortage of theories about what the problem was. Senior Vice President John Munro decided to do something, so he started with Greyhound's unclean restrooms. To launch his cleanup campaign Munro began holding candlelight dinners for management, complete with white tablecloths – in depot restrooms. Passengers were diverted to employee restrooms. The result?

> Half the [staff] thought I was crazy and half thought, 'He's serious about this,' says Munro. 'Since then we had some black tie [dinners] – with caterers. Now managers do it in their own locations.' [As a result] more than 70 percent of the 570 restrooms have been kept immaculate. Munro hired janitorial services to guide depot staff in scrubbing the offending 30 percent – and sent the depot managers the bills. . . . Female ridership has increased by 10 percent. Total ridership grew in 1989 for the first time since '82, and 1990 saw further growth. (*Tom Peters on Achieving Excellence* 1991: 12)

Munro juxtaposed the order of a banquet with the disorder of an unclean place designed for other purposes. As a result he learned about the willingness and capability for change at depots and about the distribution of zest for innovation among the management team. The depot managers themselves learned about Munro's intentions and his level of seriousness as well as about their own depots. Old meanings and labels were forgotten and replaced by new ones. Much like Follett's neighbours who treated their trees as apple-bearing trees and produced apples, Munro treated his system restrooms as locales for delight and produced renewal. Both sets of actions juxtaposed order with chaos and produced new structures. Juxtaposition created the conditions for learning, and the realignment of forgetting produced the learning itself. Social construction of a restroom as a place to dine forces people to suppress a wide variety of other constructions.

A small win is not simply a large task broken down into a series of smaller, logically related subtasks as people like Kouzes and Posner (1987: 218) argue. Decomposing a large task into a series of incremental steps is itself a precarious venture since it assumes that the steps will be carried out in a stable environment. Small wins are opportunistic as well as logical. They are local, stand-alone, completed actions that may bear little relation to one another. Each change may be an improvement, may move towards something or away from something, may demonstrate efficacy or controllability, may suggest the feasibility of a larger goal or the availability of an unexpected set of allies or affirm a key value. Small wins are experiments, as well as logically derived subtasks. Because they are opportunistic, and because opportunities are widely distributed, small wins resemble uncorrelated probes in an evolutionary system. Since they are diverse rather than homogeneous explorations, they are more likely to uncover unanticipated properties of the environment and promote learning.

Small wins are criticized by those who argue that resistance to change is countered only by changes that are dramatic, revolutionary, transformational. Small wins, as exemplified in Bateson's fable of 'the boiled frog' (Tichy and Sherman 1993: 73), encourage people to learn too little, too slowly. That fate is possible, but it overlooks three dynamics. First, small wins in large systems can occur in parallel as well as serially, which means that several small changes in the aggregate can approximate those of a radical transformation. Second, a series of small wins often precedes and paves the way for a revolution. Small wins provide the momentum and basic learnings that make revolution possible. And third, many so-called revolutions consist in part of a retrospective packaging of a series of prior small wins, all of which are interpreted as moving in a similar new direction.

Small wins embed the disorder of a non-routine event in the order of an action routine and the two are balanced in a specific setting for a relatively short period of time. A small win is *almost* business as usual in the same sense that a near-miss is *almost* business as usual. The juxtaposition is brief, local, and transient, as is the chance to learn. The chances for learning increase as more small wins are initiated by more people in more places.

## SUMMARY AND CONCLUSIONS

One reviewer of an early version of this chapter described an oxymoron as a 'language's learning'. What this reviewer meant was that paradoxes reveal the limitations of conventional grammar based on conventional logic. When these paradoxes are expressed in contradictions, ironies, and oxymorons, the resulting juxtapositions both reveal the limits of the conventions and supply the pretext for the language to renew itself. Hence, the language learns.

The language that learns is a microcosm of the organization that learns. We have argued that learning is an ongoing and implicit feature of the organizing process. By this we mean that as organizing unfolds, it does so in ways that intermittently create a set of conditions where learning is possible. We call these 'learning moments'. As organizing becomes disorganized, the forgotten is remembered, the invisible becomes visible, the silenced becomes heard. These changes create an opportunity for learning. Learning can be said to occur when forgetting, concealing, and silencing hide a *new* set of continuities and in their place create new categories, different meaning, and more organization.

These learning moments, which vary in their frequency, value, and duration, are occasions when people can renegotiate which portions of their continuing collective experience they will next forget, render invisible, and silence, and which discontinuous residuals they will treat as current meaningful artifacts of culture.

The act of repunctuating continuous experience is what we mean by learning. What people learn are intersubjective meanings embedded in culture. To make repunctuation even a possibility, organization must be reduced and doubt and curiosity must be cultivated. These changes, which mix together order and disorder, juxtapose sufficient order to sustain a learning entity and sufficient disorder to mobilize forgotten material and new alternatives. This juxtaposition is dynamic and represents a transient window of opportunity. Examples of occasions which juxtapose order and disorder are humour (an instance of culture as language), improvisation on a routine (an instance of culture as action routine), and a pocket of order in a setting of chaos which takes the form of a small win (an instance of culture as artifact).

The likelihood of learning drops quickly when invention and disorder overwhelm capacities for retention and identity, or when systems, routines, and order overwhelm capacities for unjustified variation. These tendencies towards overwhelming are a constant threat because each one represents a simpler way of dealing with the world. To learn is to dwell in the oxymoron of 'organizational learning', to be pulled simultaneously in multiple directions, and to have no assurance of success when engaged in fresh forgetting. To 'affirm the oxymoron of organizational learning' is to keep organizing and learning connected despite the fact that they pull in opposite directions.

Different forms of organizing create different problems for learning. Adhocracies explore, create, and align with changes but, in embracing disorder with disorderly forms, they risk integrity, a loss of identity, and a loss of lessons learned from the past that undergird current efficiencies. Bureaucracies exploit lessons from the past as well as past identities. Adhocracies trade away retention for variation, bureaucracies trade away variation for retention. Adhocracies embody disorder, bureaucracies embody order. Only as each form adopts some of the other, or imitates the other, is it possible to achieve repunctuation that persists.

Finally, if organization is conceptualized in terms of culture, it is easier to talk about organizational learning. It is easier because cultural artifacts and practices preserve past learning; cultural awareness and criticism may provide occasion for cultural change; organizations have multiple cultures which allows for ongoing comparison and review of what any one culture fails to see; and culture underscores that the object of most learning is intersubjective meaning.

In the final analysis all organizations are the authors and readers of their own near-miss narratives. What distinguishes the *learning* organization is its capability to confront the possibility that the story being told is simultaneously a tale of disorder in which the reality of danger masquerades as safety, and a tale of order in which the reality of safety masquerades as danger. To hold onto both possibilities long enough to restir the forgotten is to affirm the oxymoron of organizational learning.

## REFERENCES

Adler, P.S. and Cole, R.E. (1993) 'Designed for learning: a tale of two plants', *Sloan Management Review*, 34(3): 85–94.

Albert, S. and Whetten, D. (1985) 'Organizational identity', in L.L. Cummings and B.M. Staw (eds), *Research in Organizational Behavior*, vol. 7. Greenwich, CT: JAI Press. pp. 263–95.

Allison, G. (1971) *Essence of Decision*. Boston: Little Brown.

Argote, L. and McGrath, J.E. (1993) 'Group processes in organizations: continuity and change', in C.L. Cooper and I.T. Robertson (eds), *International Review of Industrial and Organizational Psychology*. New York: Wiley.

Barr, P.S., Stimpert, J.L. and Huff, A.S. (1992) 'Cognitive change, strategic action, and organizational renewal', *Strategic Management Journal*, 13: 15–36.

Bateson, G. (1972) *Steps to an Ecology of Mind.* New York: Ballentine.

Bradney, P. (1957) 'The joking relationship in industry', *Human Relations,* 10: 179–87.

Brown, J.S. and Duguid, P. (1991) 'Organizational learning and communities-of-practice: toward a unified view of working, learning, and innovation', *Organization Science,* 2: 40–57.

Buckley, W. (1968) 'Society as a complex adaptive system', in W. Buckley (ed.), *Modern Systems Research for the Behavioral Scientist.* Chicago: Aldine. pp. 490–513.

Charles, L.H. (1945) 'The clown's functions', *Journal of American Folklore,* 58: 25–35.

Cohen, M.D., March, J.G. and Olsen, J.P. (1972) 'A garbage can model of organizational choice', *Administrative Science Quarterly,* 17: 1–25.

Cohen, M.D. and Sproull, L.S. (1991) 'Editors' introduction', *Organization Science,* 2(1): i–iii.

Cole, M. (1990) 'Preface', in D. Middleton and D. Edwards (eds), *Collective Remembering.* Newbury Park, CA: Sage. pp. vii–ix.

Cook, S.D.N. and Yanow, D. (1993) 'Culture and organizational learning', *Journal of Management Inquiry,* 2: 373–90.

Coombs, R.H. and Goldman, (1973) 'Maintenance and discontinuity of coping mechanisms in an intensive care unit', *Social Problems,* 20: 342–55.

Corbett, C. and Van Wassenhove, C. (1993) 'Trade-offs? What trade-offs? Competence and competitiveness in manufacturing strategy', *California Management Review,* 35(4): 107–20.

Coser, R.L. (1959) 'Some social functions of laughter', *Human Relations,* 12: 171–8.

Cowan, D.A. (1993) 'Rhythms of variation: patterns that integrate individual and organizational learning'. Paper presented at the International Workshop on Managerial and Organizational Cognition, Brussels, Belgium.

Czarniawska-Joerges, B. (1992) *Exploring Complex Organizations: a Cultural Perspective.* Newbury Park, CA: Sage.

Daniels, A. and Daniels, R. (1964) 'The social function of the career fool', *Psychiatry,* 27: 219–30.

Davies, R. (1958) *A Mixture of Frailties.* London: Macmillan.

Dodgson, M. (1993) 'Organizational learning: a review of some literatures', *Organization Studies,* 14(3): 375–94.

Douglas, M. (1975) *Implicit Meanings.* London: Routledge and Kegan Paul.

Dutton, J.E. and Penner, W.J. (1993) 'The importance of organizational identity for strategic agenda building', in J. Hendry and G. Johnson (eds), *Strategic Thinking: Leadership and the Management of Change.* pp. 89–113.

Eccles, R.G. and Crane, D.B. (1988) *Doing Deals.* Boston: Harvard Business School.

Emerson, J. (1969) Negotiating the serious import of humour', *Sociometry,* 32: 169–81.

Fiol, C.M. and Lyles, M.A. (1985) 'Organizational learning', *Academy of Management Review,* 10: 803–13.

Follett, M.P. (1924) *Creative Experience.* New York: Longmans, Green.

Freud, S. (1905) *Jokes and their Relation to the Unconscious.* London: Hogarth.

Gardner, H. (1983) *Frames of Mind: an Outline of Interpretative Sociology.* New York: Basic Books.

Gersick, C.J.G. (1988) 'Time and transition in work teams: toward a new model of group development', *Academy of Management Journal,* 31: 9–41.

Gioia, T. (1988) *The Imperfect Art.* New York: Oxford University Press.

Glaser, B.G. and Strauss, A.L. (1967) *The Discovery of Grounded Theory.* Hawthorne, NY: Aldine.

Hatch, M.J. and Ehrlich, S.B. (1993) 'Spontaneous humour as an indicator of paradox and ambiguity in organizations', *Organization Studies,* 14: 505–26.

Hedberg, B.L.T. (1981) 'How organizations learn and unlearn', in P.C. Nystrom and W.H. Starbuck (eds), *Handbook of Organizational Design,* vol. 1. New York: Oxford University Press. pp. 3–27.

Hedberg, B.L.T., Nystrom, P.C. and Starbuck, W.H. (1976) 'Camping on seesaws: prescriptions for a self-designing organization', *Administrative Science Quarterly,* 21: 41–65.

Huber, G.P. (1991) 'Organizational learning: the contributing processes and the literatures', *Organization Science,* 2(1): 88–115.

Janowitz, M. (1959) 'Changing patterns of organizational authority: the military establishment', *Administrative Science Quarterly,* 3(4): 473–93.

Kahneman, D.P. Slovic, P. and Tversky, A. (eds) (1982) *Judgment under Uncertainty.* Cambridge: Cambridge University Press.

Keeney, B.P. (1990) *Improvisational Therapy.* New York: Guilford Press.

Kets de Vries, M. (1990) 'The organizational fool: balancing a leader's hubris', *Human Relations,* 43(8): 751–70.

Koestler, A. (1964) *The Act of Creation.* London: Hutchinson.

Kouzes, J.M. and Posner, B.Z. (1991) *The Leadership Challenge.* San Francisco: Jossey-Bass.

Kundera, M. (1981) *The Book of Laughter and Forgetting.* New York: Penguin.

Lant, T.K. and Mezias, S.J. (1990) 'Managing discontinuous change: a simulation study of organizational learning and entrepreneurship', *Strategic Management Journal,* 11: 147–79.

Leach, E. (1970) *Lévi-Strauss.* London: Fontana/Collins.

Leach, E. (1972) 'Anthropological aspects of language: animal categories and verbal abuse', in P. Maranda (ed.), *Mythology.* London: Penguin.

Lévi-Strauss, C. (1963) *Structural Anthropology.* New York: Harper and Row.

Levitt, B. and March, J.G. (1988) 'Organizational learning', *Annual Review of Sociology,* 14: 319–40.

Linstead, S. (1985) 'Jokers wild: the importance of humour in the maintenance of organizational culture', *Sociological Review*, 33(4): 741–67.

Locke, K. (1992) 'Organizational foolery: mixing canonical and carnivalesque cultures in the delivery of medicine'. Paper presented at the SCOS conference.

March, J.G. (1991) 'Exploration and exploitation in organizational learning', *Organization Science*, 2: 71–87.

March, J.G., Sproull, L.S. and Tamuz, M. (1991) 'Learning from samples of one or fewer', *Organization Science*, 2: 1–13.

Metcalfe, L. (1981) 'Designing precarious partnerships', in P.C. Nystrom and W.H. Starbuck (eds), *Handbook of Organizational Design*, vol. 1. New York: Oxford University Press. pp. 503–30.

Miller, D. (1993) 'The architecture of simplicity', *Academy of Management Review*, 18: 116–38.

Munro, D.H. (1951) *Argument of Laughter*. Melbourne: Melbourne University Press.

Normann, R. (1985) 'Developing capabilities for organizational learning', in J.M. Pennings (ed.), *Organizational Strategy and Change*. San Francisco: Jossey-Bass. pp. 217–48.

Peters, T.J. (1977) 'Patterns of winning and losing: effects on approach and avoidance by friends and enemies'. Unpublished dissertation, Stanford University, Stanford, California.

Purser, R.E. and Pasmore, W.A. (1992) 'Organizing for learning', in W.A. Pasmore and R.W. Woodman (eds), *Research in Organizational Change and Development*, vol. 6. Greenwich, CT: JAI Press. pp. 37–114.

Ring, P.S. and Van de Ven, A.H. (1994) 'Developmental processes of cooperative interorganizational relationships', *Academy of Management Review*, 19: 90–118.

Rushdie, S. (1992) *Imaginary Homelands*. New York: Penguin.

Ryle, G. (1949) *The Concept of Mind*. Chicago: University of Chicago Press.

Sagan, S.D. (1993) *The Limits of Safety*. Princeton: Princeton University Press.

Sandelands, L. and Drazin, R. (1989) 'On the language of organizational theory', *Organization Studies*, 10: 457–78.

Sandelands, L. and Srivatsan, V. (1993) 'The problem of experience in the study of organizations', *Organization Studies*.

Schon, D.A. (1983a) 'Organizational learning', in G. Morgan (ed.), *Beyond Method*. Beverly Hills, CA: Sage. pp. 114–28.

Schon, D.A. (1983b) *The Reflective Practitioner*. New York: Basic Books.

Schon, D.A. (1987) *Educating the Reflective Practitioner*. San Francisco: Jossey-Bass.

Schuller, G. (1968) *Early Jazz*. New York: Oxford University Press.

Sils, J.M. (1972) 'Two stage models for the appreciation of jokes', in J. Goldstein (ed.), *The Psychology of Humour*. New York: Academic Press.

Simon, H.A. (1991) 'Bounded rationality and organizational learning', *Organization Science*, 2(1): 125–34.

Stebbins, R.A. (1979) 'Comic relief in everyday life: dramaturgic observations on the functions of humour', *Symbolic Interaction*, 2(1): 95–104.

Sudnow, D. (1979) *Talk's Body*. New York: Knopf.

Tamuz, M. (1988) 'Monitoring dangers in the air: studies in ambiguity and information'. Unpublished doctoral dissertation, Stanford University.

Thayer, L. (1988) 'Leadership/communication: a critical review and a modest proposal', in G.M. Goldhaber and G.A. Barnett (eds), *Handbook of Organizational Communication*. Norwood, NJ: Ablex. pp. 231–63.

Tichy, N.M. and Sherman, S. (1993) *Control your Destiny or Someone Else Will*. New York: Doubleday.

*Tom Peters on Achieving Excellence* (1991), 'Terminal cleanliness leads to a new lease on life', 6(2): 12.

Torbert, W.R. (1987) *Managing the Corporate Dream*. Homewood, IL: Dow-Jones-Irwin.

Voyer, J.J. and Faulkner, R.R. (1989) 'Organizational cognition in a jazz ensemble', *Empirical Studies of the Arts*, 7(1): 57–77.

Weber, M. (1978) *Economy and Society*. Berkeley, CA: University of California Press.

Weick, K.E. (1977) 'Organizations as self-designing systems', *Organizational Dynamics*, 6(2): 30–46.

Weick, K.E. (1979) *The Social Psychology of Organizing*, 2nd edn. Reading, MA: Addison-Wesley.

Weick, K.E. and Berlinger, L. (1989) 'Career improvisation in self-designing organizations', in M.B. Arthur, D. Hall and B.S. Lawrence (eds), *Handbook of Career Theory*. New York: Cambridge University Press. pp. 313–28.

Weick, K.E. and Browning, L.D. (1986) 'Argument and narration in organizational communication', in J.G. Hunt and J.D. Blair (eds), *1986 Yearly Review of Management of the Journal of Management*, 12(2): 243–59.

Welsford, E. (1935) *The Fool*. Gloucester, MA: Faber and Faber.

# 11

# *Organizations and the Biosphere: Ecologies and Environments*

CAROLYN P. EGRI AND LAWRENCE T. PINFIELD

> Theories about nature and theories about society have a history of interconnections. A view of nature can be seen as a projection of human perception of self and society onto the cosmos. Conversely, theories about nature have historically been interpreted as containing implications about the way individuals or social groups behave or ought to behave. (Merchant 1980: 69)

A significant feature of contemporary society is the increasing concern expressed for the current and emerging quality of the natural environment. This concern has taken many forms, from the establishment of global forums on environmental issues (e.g. World Commission on Environment and Development 1987; the 1992 United Nations Conference on the Environment and Development), to formal assessments of the environmental records of large US manufacturing firms (Rice 1993), to reports of 'ecotage' by radical environmentalists determined to limit business activities which are claimed to be degrading the natural environment (Day 1989; Egri and Frost 1994). This brief sample of indicators suffusing the public media represents a significant challenge to traditional ways of thinking about societal and industrial activities, including the conceptual models of organizations which inform and direct those activities.

What are these concerns and challenges? While we have some difficulty in prioritizing or even grouping all the issues associated with the environmentalist movement, they are manifest in expressed anxieties regarding current and future life-styles, quality of life, economic prosperity, and more generally the future of *Homo sapiens* on planet earth. A number of both specific and general considerations trigger these anxieties: population growth and its consequences for the carrying capacity of planet earth; increasing aspirations for a more urban and materialistic life-style on the part of the growing number of citizens of less developed nations; the nature of industrialization which results in high levels of waste and pollution while depleting nonrenewable resources. Associated with these concerns are others such as the loss of biodiversity and the irretrievable change of bioregions and natural environments into areas forever hostile to human habitation (Brown 1991; Buchholz 1993; Commoner 1990; Daly and Cobb 1994; Paehlke 1989).

These issues are symptomatic of the deep structure of beliefs regarding the consequences of an industrialized society. Governmental and business organizations are judged not to take the interests, aspirations, and needs of their citizenry into account in their pursuit of organizational goals and objectives. From the perspective of those wishing to act on beliefs such as these, the situation is even more difficult because direct action is unlikely to be successful. The 'environmental problem' is a consequence of how society is structured, for as multiple organizations pursue their self-interests, the interstices of society become an increasingly degraded residual. The institutionalized and taken-for-granted assumptions of an organizationally based, contemporary society produce consequences that are barely discernible and actionable within the logics of that frame of reference.

Exploration of the topic of organizations and the biosphere requires a holistic approach that is multi-faceted, cross-disciplinary and contro-versial. Multi-faceted because one investigates phenomena at different levels (individual, group, organizational, societal and global) from alter-native perspectives (physical, technical, eco-nomic, social and ethical). Cross-disciplinary because one delves into both the natural sciences (ecology, biology, chemistry, physics) and the social sciences (philosophy, sociology, organ-ization theory) in a search for areas of intersections and divergence. Controversial because it is an evolving arena replete with political conflict between and among societal actors proposing alternative courses of action. As identified in the opening quote by Merchant, there are those who contend that our theories of nature and of societies are inextricably inter-twined and cannot (or should not) be regarded as separate. Alternatively, there are others such as Schnaiberg and Gould (1994) who argue that there is an 'enduring conflict' between the logic and dynamics of natural ecosystems and those of industrialized society which prevent any mean-ingful synthesis at either theoretical or practical levels. It is the latter view that appears to have been adopted by traditional organizational theorists and practitioners for both conceptual and practical convenience. However, those who challenge this traditional worldview argue that there is an urgent need to incorporate ecological principles and the natural environment into both organization theory and practice. Who are these champions of change? What is their vision and agenda for change in modern organizations and societies? What are the implications for our theories of organization? These are only a few of the questions which can be explored to develop an understanding of the theoretical and practical intersections between organizations and the biosphere.

Our exploration will start with the historical origins and current state of ecological theory and modern environmentalist perspectives. Three perspectives on eco-environments are presented to demonstrate how ecological values are intertwined with human values concerning desired social, political and economic realities. These vary from the very strong anthropocentric values of the *dominant social paradigm* which sees unlimited progress resulting from the exploitation of infinite natural resources (Catton and Dunlap 1978; Daly 1977) to the biocentric values of the *radical environmentalism* philosophy of deep ecology which advocates 'biospecies egalitarianism' in which economic advancement is forgone for harmony with nature (Devall and Sessions 1985; Naess 1973). Other radical environmentalism philosophies such as spiritual ecology (Fox 1990), social ecology (Bookchin 1990a), and ecofeminism

(Merchant 1980; 1992; Salleh 1984; Warren 1990) advocate social and biological arrange-ments in which there is a balance between the interests of humanity and nature. In this idealized conceptualization of ecocentric values, the ecological relationships among people and nature within communities are integrated with others sharing ecoregions which, in turn, cooperate to sustain the shared ecosphere of the plant (Tokar 1988). More intermediate perspectives are termed *reform environmentalism* which represents degrees of modification of anthropocentric values to include the natural environment in human endeavours. In sustain-able development proposals, all types of capital and environmental resources are considered in local and national policy development (Colby 1990; World Commission on Environment and Development 1987) and risk management emerges as a critical task (Kleindorfer and Kunreuther 1986). In addition, environmental protection policies maintain the strongly anthropocentric posture of the dominant social paradigm within a system of tradeoffs between economic growth and environmental degrada-tion (Berkes 1989; Colby 1990). Each perspective is described and then critically analysed to identify contradictions between proposals and enactment. To facilitate conceptual clarity, perspectives at the endpoints of the environmen-talist perspective continuum (i.e. the dominant social paradigm and radical environmentalism) are presented before focusing on the middle ground of reform environmentalism.

The next section of the chapter explicates how the concept of 'environment' has been treated in orthodox and more recent organization theories. How different conceptualizations of organ-izations are either compatible with or in conflict with environmentalist points of view is dis-cussed. Current and potential areas for a confluence of theories concerning eco-environ-ments and organizations are identified. In addition, the concepts of self-interest and systems theory are used to illustrate the conceptual and practical challenges of integ-rating environmentalist views of biophysical environments into organizational views of en-vironments. Finally, the chapter closes with summary conclusions and thoughts regarding future directions in both theory and research.

## ECOLOGY AND ENVIRONMENTALIST PERSPECTIVES

The historical origin of the term *ecology* can be traced back to 1866 when German zoologist Ernst Haeckel combined the two Greek words *logos* (meaning 'the study of') and *oikos* (meaning 'house' or 'place to live') (Buchholz 1993). As elaborated by Haeckel in 1870, 'ecology' was originally defined as:

> the body of knowledge concerning the economy of nature – the investigation of the total relations of the animal both to its inorganic and to its organic environment; including above all, its friendly and inimical relations with those animals and plants with which it comes directly and indirectly into contact – in a word, ecology is the study of all those complex interrelations referred to by Darwin as the conditions of the struggle for existence. (translated in Allee et al. 1949: frontispiece; as cited by McIntosh 1985: 7–8)

From its nineteenth-century conceptualization as a branch of biology, ecology has become a 'polymorphic science' accessed and extended to encompass various aspects of natural and social phenomena (McIntosh 1985). Fundamental to theoretical conceptualizations of ecology and ecosystems[1] are the principles of: holism (interconnections within and amongst systems and environments); the balance of nature (self-regulating equilibria of biological and nonbiological systems); diversity (tendency towards greater biodiversity in natural systems); finite limits of planetary life-support systems (carrying capacity to support populations and communities of organisms); and dynamic change of natural processes and cycles (Daly and Cobb 1994; Buchholz 1993; Lovelock 1979; Sarkar 1986; Serafin 1988; Wilson 1992). At its core, ecology represents the body of knowledge which is concerned with the relations between organisms and their organic and inorganic environments.

Within ecology, the term *environment* 'refers to all of the external physical and biological factors that directly influence the survival, growth, development, and reproduction of organisms' (Colby 1990: 10). *Environmentalism* is primarily concerned with the interactions between the biosphere and the technosphere and sociosphere.[2] At one level, environmentalism is the application of ecological theory to understanding the development and operation of social systems within the biosphere. At another level, environmentalism is the study of human sociopolitical values which inform the conceptualization and enactment of human relations with the natural environment (Bird 1987; Hays 1987; Paehlke 1989).

It was only after World War II that environmentalism gained sufficient grass-roots support to become the nascent social movement which presently manifests itself as a dominant social concern (Hays 1987: 3). Different origins have moulded different national movements. In Britain and other parts of Europe, most environmentalist groups originated from established nature groups which had a long tradition of access to decision-making (Rudig and Lowe 1986), whereas movements in North America and Australasia had little or no connection with previous social groups (Fox 1981; Hay and Haward 1988). In North America, environmentalism began with a focus on conservation and protection of natural environments for the purposes of outdoor recreation and preservation of wilderness. Natural resources were increasingly valued for their existential qualities in a natural state as well as their amenity for other aesthetic pursuits. Environmental concerns, especially among the younger generation, therefore became associated with deeply rooted human aspirations for a better life, and hopes for personal and social achievement. In other arenas, notably Western Europe, anti-nuclear sentiments had both a radical and an integrating impact on the green movement. In all countries, additional attention and support flowed to environmentalist causes as a consequence of increased scientific capacity to detect, measure and link environmental contaminants to human health and ecological degradation (Carson 1962; Sarkar 1986). Reports from the Club of Rome in the early 1970s also focused public attention on the insidious dangers of uncontrolled industrial growth for natural and social environments. Increasingly, the prevalent notions of the supremacy of science, technology and industrialization have come under challenge (Sarkar 1986). Although the dominant political ideology of the 1970s and 1980s, as well as the oil-cartel-induced economic crisis of the 1970s, could have restrained the growth of environmentalist movements during those decades, environmental activism has proved to be a persistent, deeply rooted, organized feature of contemporary society (Dunlap 1989; Sale 1993).

While there are commonalities in the evolution of environmentalist movements, there also exist fundamental differences. Green movements in general have been fragmented and under-organized with various subgroups independently representing more specialized interests such as preservation of wilderness, environmental policy development, toxic waste management, resource protection and conservation, animal rights, and so forth (Sale 1993; Snow 1992a). Presently, there is no clear focus to these different sub-movements other than their general association with some aspect of environmentalism which challenges in various ways the traditional conceptualizations and practices of a predominantly urban, industrial, developed and organizationally based society.

Three frameworks of environmental philosophy and concepts represent the primary schools of thoughts concerning the human–nature relationship. The dominant social paradigm is not an 'environmentalist' perspective *per se*, but rather represents the traditional worldview of industrialized society – the status quo against which other environmentalist perspectives are compared. The radical environmentalism perspective represents the worldview of those who advocate transformational change. The reform environmentalism perspective represents those occupying the middle ground in both environmental philosophy and practice. The historical origins, beliefs and assumptions of each perspective are presented and then critically discussed.

## Dominant Social Paradigm

We are the absolute masters of what the earth produces. We enjoy the mountains and the plains. The rivers are ours, we sow the seed and plant the trees. We fertilize the earth. . . . We stop, direct, and turn the rivers. In short, by our hands we endeavour, by our various operations on this world, to make, as it were, another nature. (Cicero, 106–43 BC, as quoted by Hughes 1975: 30)

The advent of ancient urban civilizations marked the emergence of anthropocentrism in spiritual and philosophical thought on humankind's relationship with nature. For ancient Mesopotamians, humans possessed a divine right to tame the 'monstrous chaos' of nature; for classical Greek humanists (Aristotle, Plato) and the early Stoics, humans claimed the resources of nature for their own exclusive use (Hughes 1975; Sessions 1987; Wall 1994). Early evidence of the ecological price of human order and domination would become apparent in the destruction of the ancient cedar forests of Lebanon, the desertification of the once Fertile Crescent of Mesopotamia, and the erosion, pollution and extinction of numerous species under imperial Rome (Hughes 1975). Judaeo-Christian teachings are also identified as promoting an anthropocentric worldview in which humanity's role was to 'be fruitful and multiply' as well as to 'have dominion over every living thing that moveth upon the earth' (Merchant 1980; White 1967).

One critical aspect of the anthropocentric worldview is the notion of dualisms such as the ideological separation of the human mind and spirit from the physical reality of existence and the division into higher and lower entities. The dualism of mind and matter was fundamental to the advocacy by seventeenth century Age of Enlightenment philosophers (in particular, Bacon, Descartes, Newton, Hobbes) of mastery over nature as essential for scientific and social

progress (Daly and Cobb 1994; Ehrenfeld 1978; Merchant 1980). Mechanistic materialism, rationality and scientific reductionism became the ideological cornerstones of the Scientific and Industrial Revolutions of Western societies and are now regarded as core elements of the dominant social paradigm (Bramwell 1989; Fox 1990).

As represented in modern industrialized society, the dominant social paradigm (DSP) represents an adherence to neoclassical economic principles and goals (economic growth and profits) with natural factors treated as either externalities or infinitely exploitable resources. If there are observable environmental problems, these can easily (or eventually) be solved through scientific and technological progress (Daly and Cobb 1994; Hawken 1993; Milbrath 1989). The DSP is most closely associated with Western capitalist societies in which the principles of 'free markets' and private property ownership reign. However, closed economic systems informed by Marxist philosophy are also included in this perspective. This apparently paradoxical ideological marriage is justified by virtue of Marxism's strong anthropocentric bias which supports the capital intensive production goals of modern industrialism (Daly and Cobb 1994; Jacobs 1993; Jung 1991; Lee 1980; Porritt 1984).[3] Additional justification is offered by the evidence of environmental degradation in modern socialist states which many assert exceeds that of unfettered capitalism (Clow 1986; Davies 1991; Feshbach and Friendly 1992; Jancar-Webster 1993).

Other facets of the dominant social paradigm concern the notion of individual self-determinism and the centralized control of societies by social, political and economic elites. In societies premised on hierarchical structures and relationships, both persons and nonhuman nature are objectified and valued only in instrumental terms (as inputs or consumers of production) rather than for their intrinsic or spiritual value (Cotgrove and Duff 1981; Devall and Sessions 1985; Drengson 1980).

## Radical Environmentalism Perspective

The politics of the Industrial Age, left, right and centre, is like a three-lane motorway, with different vehicles in different lanes, but *all* heading in the same direction. Greens feel it is the very direction that is wrong, rather than the choice of any one lane in preference to the others. It is our perception that the motorway of industrialism inevitably leads to the abyss – hence our decision to get off it, and seek an entirely different direction. (Porritt 1984: 43)

The radical environmentalism perspective promotes a vision of the biosphere and human society based on the ecological principles of holism, the balance of nature, diversity, finite limits and dynamic change (Catton and Dunlap 1978; Cotgrove and Duff 1981; Drengson 1980; Devall and Sessions 1985; among others). As identified by Donald Worster (1977), the 'idea of ecology is much older than the name.' Aspects of the radical environmentalism perspective have been shown to predate as well as to have developed in opposition to anthropocentric ideologies. Archaeological evidence of the early hunter-gatherer societies and ancient civilizations offers a picture of nature and its forces personified as deities to be worshipped and obeyed (Eisler 1987; Merchant 1980). Vestiges of nature deities were/are present in the spiritual traditions of shamanism, Egyptian, Greek and Roman pantheism (with Gaia as the Earth Mother), Eastern mysticism (Taoism, Sufism, Zen, Buddhism), Islam, and paganism (Earth Mother goddess) (Wall 1994). Underlying these conceptualizations of an all-powerful nature is the belief that human survival depends on a holistic synthesis and integration of humanity with the natural environment. The philosophical holism of the early Greek philosopher Heraclitus (c. 535–475 BC) is echoed in the work of seventeenth and eighteenth century natural philosophers and theologians (von Linné, Emerson, Malthus, Thoreau) who wrote of the interconnectedness of humans and nature in the 'web of life' (Wall 1994). The concept of organismic holism would be developed further in the early twentieth century by Jan Smuts (1926: 86) as a synthesis or 'a unity of parts which is so close and intense as to be more than the sum of its parts . . . and the whole and the parts therefore reciprocally influence and determine each other'.

The biocentric respect for other life forms can be traced back to the vegetarianism of Eastern religions, classical Greek philosophers, St Francis of Assisi of the thirteenth century, and the late eighteenth century English Romantics (e.g. Blake, Shelley, Wollstonecraft) who equated animal rights with human rights (Wall 1994). Critiques of scientific industrial society are found in the writings of the seventeenth to eighteenth century European Romantic movement as well as in the works of transcendentalist philosophers in the United States (Sessions 1987). One of the central tenets of the radical environmentalism perspective is the recapturing of a pre-Enlightenment organismic worldview in which the universe is seen as organic, living and spiritual (Cotgrove and Duff 1981; Devall and Sessions 1985; Drengson 1980; Sale 1985).

The modern radical environmentalism perspective is positioned in direct opposition to the dominant social paradigm's support of modern industrialism as the revolutionary alternative required for long-term ecological survival. The radical environmentalism perspective advocates the massive redesign of industrial and agricultural systems of production and transportation (Commoner 1990). Instead of developing large-scale capital intensive technologies for the industrial-military complex, science needs to be redirected to developing technologies which reduce human interference with the nonhuman world. This is to be accomplished through the development and use of intermediate (appropriate) technologies which reduce the depletion and pollution of natural resources as well as provide for craftsmanship in human labour (Commoner 1990; Schumacher 1973). In contrast to the DSP belief in unlimited material and economic growth, the radical perspective asserts that the limits and delicate balance of the biosphere require the preservation and conservation of natural resources through anti-consumptionist and anti-materialism ethics.

One important facet of the radical environmentalism perspective is bioregionalism as the organizing principle for decentralized social, economic and political systems (Irvine and Ponton 1988; Leopold 1949; Mumford 1938; Sale 1985). A bioregion is 'a place defined by its life forms, its topography and its biota, rather than by human dictates; a region governed by nature, not legislature' (Sale 1985: 43). While natural criteria for a bioregion's boundaries are neither mutually exclusive nor devoid of human criteria of use and perception (Alexander 1990), communities within bioregions would regain local decision-making authority to engender environmental and economic self-sufficiency of production and use.

Within the radical environmentalism perspective there are four prominent philosophies – deep ecology, spiritual ecology, social ecology, ecofeminism – which differ primarily in terms of emphasis and means rather than ends of the radical agenda for transformational change in the human–nature relationship.

## Deep Ecology

Deep ecology is a holistic perspective which integrates biological-psychological-spiritual-metaphysical dimensions of interdependent and interacting ecosystems (Devall and Sessions 1985; Naess 1973; 1984). As proposed by Norwegian philosopher Arne Naess, deep ecology questions the normative and descriptive premises (why? how?) at a more fundamental level than the everyday technical and scientific levels of ecosystems. Drawing from the philosophies of Spinoza, Gandhi and Thoreau, and various spiritual traditions (Buddhist, Christian, Native American), deep ecology proposes the moral goal of 'self-realization' which is attained through an identification with 'the interest or interests of another being [which] are reacted to as our own interest or interests' (Naess 1988: 261). The deep ecology platform posits 'biospherical egalitarianism', that is, humans have no rights to interfere with the richness and diversity of all life forms (human and non-human) which have intrinsic or inherent value. Deep ecologists identify as epistemologically problematic, but practically necessary, the application of human cultural concepts such as rights, values and ethics to the natural environment (Manes 1990; Sessions 1987). Nature is to be viewed not as an extension of humans but rather as the basic element on which human civilizations are based. The moral and ethical imperative of deep ecology is that humans have an obligation to implement (by example and by direct action) these changes in society.

## Spiritual Ecology

Spiritual ecology or transpersonal ecology (Berry 1988; Fox 1990; Hull 1993; Reason 1993) shares deep ecology's emphasis on the need for transformational changes in human consciousness as a prerequisite to changes at physical levels of existence. The alienation caused by the mechanistic and dualistic worldview of industrialized society can only be healed through a recapturing of humanity's sacred connections with all aspects of creation.

## Social Ecology

Social ecologist Murray Bookchin (1980; 1982; 1990a; 1990b) advances a more secular approach to understanding the relationship between society and nature.

> The ways in which we interact with each other as social beings profoundly influence attitudes we are likely to have toward the natural world. Any sound ecological perspective rests in great part on our social perspectives and interrelationships; hence, to draw up an ecological agenda that has no room for social concerns is as obtuse as to draw up a social agenda that has no room for ecological concerns. (Bookchin 1990b: 24–5)

As a result of both social evolution and natural evolution, human society has developed patterns of hierarchical domination which are socially and environmentally destructive. Unlike non-human species, humanity is unique in its capacity for creative and self-conscious thought to alter the course of social evolution. Bookchin (1980; 1990b) offers a vision of a reconstructed sociopolitical order premised on 'libertarian

municipalism' which involves decentralized grass-roots bioregionally based planning and governance in human settlements which mirror local ecosystems. Only through ecological community and participatory democracy can a new society free of ecological and cultural oppression be created.

## Ecofeminism

The integration of social and political change as part of ecological change is also echoed in definitions of ecofeminism:

> Ecofeminism is a term that some use to describe both the diverse range of women's efforts to save the Earth and the transformations of feminism in the West that have resulted from the new view of women and nature ... ecofeminism is not a monolithic, homogeneous ideology ... Indeed, it is precisely the diversity of thought and action that makes this new politics so promising as a catalyst for change in these troubled times. (Diamond and Forenstein 1990: ix, xii)

Ecofeminists (King 1989; Merchant 1980; Plant 1989; Warren 1990) also posit that while humans are members of the ecological community, they are different from (but not equivalent to) other life forms. The domination of nature is viewed as being interconnected with hierarchical domination of humans based on gender, race, ethnicity and social class. The central concern of ecofeminism is 'to end all forms of oppression' (Warren 1990), especially that of women within patriarchal cultures. The ecofeminist antidote to exploitative societal structures and processes is social justice based on the principles of egalitarianism, inclusiveness, communitarianism, consensual decision-making, mutual care and responsibility (Cheney 1987).

## Reform Environmentalism Perspective

> Man has too long forgotten that the earth was given to him for usufruct alone, not for consumption, still less for profligate waste. ... The earth is fast becoming an unfit home for its noblest inhabitant, and another era of equal human crime and human improvidence ... would reduce it to such a condition of impoverished productiveness, of shattered surface, of climatic excess, as to threaten the depravation, barbarism, and perhaps even extinction of the species. (George Perkins Marsh, *Man and Nature*, 1863, as cited by Strong 1988: 35)

The origins of the reform environmentalism perspective can be traced to early critics of nineteenth century industrialism who alerted the public and reformers to its side effects on human health and environmental degradation (Devall

1988). George Perkins Marsh, a nineteenth-century geographer, is viewed as instrumental in the transition of earlier romantic views of nature to advocacy for the stewardship of nature for long-term human survival. From the 1880s to the 1920s, the conservation and preservation of natural resources and habitats would become the mission of the newly founded ecological and natural history societies throughout North America, the United Kingdom and Europe (Jancar-Webster 1993; McIntosh 1985; Strong 1988). The work of the founders of the American conservation movement (John Muir, Aldo Leopold, Gifford Pinchot) continues to inform the operating philosophy of the mainstream organizations in the environmental movement to this day (McIntosh 1985; Snow 1992a; Strong 1988).

The reform environmentalism perspective represents a modification of anthropocentric values to include biocentric values to the extent that there is sustainable development, which is defined as meeting 'the needs of the present without compromising the ability of future generations to meet their own needs' (World Commission on Environment and Development 1987: 43). In this perspective, technology is the vehicle for scientific and economic progress as well as the means for detecting and managing environmental risks which threaten human survival and well-being. The operation of the mechanistic metaphor is evident in reform environmentalism's focus on the efficient use of natural resources and the minimization of negative economic effects of pollution (Dorfman and Dorfman 1977). However, unlike the dominant social paradigm perspective, the reform environmentalism perspective attempts to incorporate a systems approach and the thermodynamic laws of conservation and entropy into the calculations of environmental sustainability (Georgescu-Rogen 1971; Stead and Stead 1992).[4] The physical limits of living and economic systems necessitate the development of renewable energy resources and the conservation of nonrenewable resources.

Ecological economics and industrial ecology represent two means by which the natural environment is incorporated into industrial decision-making processes. Ecological economics may be utilized for the quantification of tradeoffs between economic and environmental benefits and costs, and for environmental risk management (the determination of optimum pollution levels and economic compensation for the depletion and/or degradation of natural resources) (Dorfman and Dorfman 1977). The methodological challenges of measuring the ecological impact of industries are demonstrated in recent studies by Schaltegger (1993) and Ilinitch and Schaltegger (1993). For example, when there are questions regarding the validity of proposed pollution measures such as the toxicity levels of different chemical pollutants, how does one accurately compare the ecological impact of lead versus ammonia versus dioxins? More generally, how does one calculate the synergy effects of combinations of pollutants in different ecosystems?

Industrial ecology is concerned with the means for achieving environmentally sustainable systems of production (Allenby 1992; Hawken 1993; Stead and Stead 1992). Industrial ecology proposes that the impact of industrial systems on the natural environment can be minimized by adopting total environmental quality management (TEQM) principles for product and process design (Callenbach et al. 1993; Cairncross 1991; Baram and Dillon 1993; Flannery and May 1994; Hawken 1993; Sharfman and Ellington 1993; Shrivastava 1994). In industrial closed systems, the use of nonrenewable natural resources is minimized and/or supplanted by renewable sources of energy and natural resources. Industrial wastes and pollutants are reduced, recycled, and/or disposed of in an ecologically safe manner. Whereas technological systems are closed, industrial environmental policy and strategy processes are open to include collaborative decision-making with multiple stakeholders (community and interest groups, government agencies, employees). Ecological auditing procedures are used to measure environmental performance and industrial activities are disclosed to employees and interested publics.

One important feature of the reform environmentalism perspective is the concept of stakeholders and stakeholder rights (McGowan and Mahon 1991; Shrivastava 1994; Stead and Stead 1992; Steger 1993; Throop 1991; Westley and Vredenburg 1991). Whilst not extending to include the natural environment and nonhuman entities as formal stakeholders, public interests in ensuring long-term environmental sustainability are recognized. Thus from the reform environmentalism perspective, the relevant question is not *whether* non-industrial stakeholders (e.g. governments, environmentalist organizations, the general public) are included in organizational decision-making but rather *how* and *to what degree* they are included in decisions concerning the natural environment (Bennett 1991; Berle 1990; Elkington and Burke 1989; Schmidheiny 1992; Scott and Rothman 1992; Steger 1993; and others). Generally, it is the large mainstream reform environmentalist organizations that have developed collaborative arrangements with industry and government (McCloskey 1991; Sale 1993; Snow 1992a).

## Managing the Environmental Commons

Reform environmentalism's goal of sustainable development represents 'an accommodation between economic growth and environmental protection' (Cairncross 1991: 26) at local, national and global levels. Proponents of sustainable development identify one major cause of environmental degradation as being the inequitable distribution of economic wealth between industrialized nations and 'Third World' countries. Economically impoverished Third World countries are unable to develop or purchase the scientific technologies to conserve and protect their natural environment. Nor can they afford to prevent the exploitation and export of their natural resources required to maintain the higher standard of living in industrialized nations (e.g. with only one-fifth of the world's population, industrialized nations consume four-fifths of fossil fuel and metal mineral resources produced). While recognizing that consumption patterns of industrialized nations are environmentally unsustainable and need to be curtailed, the eradication of poverty in Third World countries is viewed as an integral part of economic, social and political self-sustainability. In addition, alternative styles and modes of economic development appropriate to local cultures and biophysical environments need to be developed. Thus one of the concerns of sustainable development is management of the bioregional and local commons but not in isolation from the global commons – a more inclusive vision than the radical environmentalist closed bioregional concept (Keating 1993; Sitarz 1993; World Commission on Environment and Development 1987).

In that the biosphere represents a global commons, the potential for a 'tragedy of the unmanaged commons' necessitates that formal government involvement and regulation be instituted to develop and manage natural resources (Hardin 1968; 1991; *The Ecologist* 1993; Throop 1991). As proposed by Hardin (1991), informal pressures to prevent the ruination of the commons are only workable with small groups involving 50 to 150 actors. If the global commons is left unmanaged and unregulated, the motivation of individual parties to play the 'commonize the costs while privatizing the profits' (CC-PP) game inevitably leads to the degradation of the commons. Within the reform environmentalism perspective there are variations in regards to the desired nature of governments' responsibility and involvement in managing the global and local commons. Towards the anthropocentric end of the anthropocentric–ecocentric continuum, government assumes limited responsibility for the conserva-

tion and management of public natural resources (e.g. in national parks), levying taxes for the use of public resources, and regulating pollution levels. In the mid-range, government assumes a more active role by developing and administering environmental regulations, taxes and marketable permits for industrial pollution (Cairncross 1991; Hahn and Hester 1989). While there is a general preference for voluntary informal pressures to encourage environmental responsibility, policy strategists acknowledge that the potential for environmental free-ridership necessitates active government intervention. However, the record to date of such interventions has not been very encouraging as environmental regulations have proved to be expensive, unwieldy and often, ineffective (Baram and Dillon 1993; Nemetz 1986; Paehlke 1990; Schweitzer 1977; Simmons and Wynne 1993).

Another approach to management of the global commons is one based on the principle of collaboration rather than competition between public and private institutions at local, national and international levels (Colby 1990). As identified in the United Nations Conference on Environment and Development (UNCED) Agenda 21 (Keating 1993; Sitarz 1993), the global liberalization of trade and cultures necessitates a redefinition of public and private institutional roles for the protection of global and local commons. Efforts to develop international environmental regulations and enforcement mechanisms include the Montreal Protocol (signed by eighty-one nations by 1992) in which signatories have pledged to end the use of CFCs (chlorofluorocarbons, which threaten the planet's ozone layer) by the year 2000 (Cairncross 1991). Less successful have been international efforts to remedy the environmental degradation of the Canada–US Great Lakes ecosystem (Colburn et al. 1990; MacLarkey 1991). Initiated in 1972 and expanded in 1978, the International Joint Commission for the Great Lakes Water Quality Agreement was bold in its goal of involving government agencies (at federal, provincial/state and local levels), industry, academia and environmental groups to develop and implement an action plan. Despite the best of intentions, after ten years of efforts the participants agree that

> In many respects, it has been a frustrating period: new discoveries often seem to have served to extend the tangle of environmental relationships, making action more difficult and solutions seemingly ever more complex, difficult, time consuming, and perhaps ultimately impossible. (Colburn et al. 1990: 11)

As revealed in studies of other multi-stakeholder initiatives to develop environmental public policy, interorganizational collaboration to establish new sociopolitical systems of governance is much easier said than done (Crowfoot and Wondolleck 1990; Egri and Frost 1992; Feyerherm 1994; Gray 1989; Pasquero 1991). One critical issue revolves around the degree to which true collaboration is practised or even possible when the parties at the table are unequal and/or different in terms of philosophical values, resources, power and influence.

## A CRITICAL ANALYSIS OF ENVIRONMENTALIST PERSPECTIVES

In his critique of alternative ecological paradigms, Routley (1983) cautions that contemporary paradigms often contain overlapping or contradictory elements, thus failing to offer unified systems of beliefs. As identified by Colby (1990), this lack of conceptual clarity counterindicates a linear interpretation of perspectives which are still in their evolutionary stages of development. Whereas the dominant social paradigm and radical environmentalism perspectives offer a greater degree of contrasts, within the intermediate reform environmentalism perspective there is considerable variability in the degree of inclusiveness of ecological assumptions and prescribed ends and means for environmental sustainability. See Table 1 for a summary of the salient features of each perspective.

The reform environmentalism perspective is the least clear conceptually because it represents the current state of flux and change in human society in regards to the natural environment. It is also the site of political and social contests regarding the ends, forms and means of resolving ecological concerns. From the radical environmentalism perspective, reform environmentalism is an incremental (and some would assert superficial or shallow) response to ecological issues (Devall 1988), whereas from the dominant social paradigm perspective, reform environmentalism is a progressive response (Cairncross 1991; Schmidheiny 1992). The merits of each position in this debate concerning environmental philosophy and practice are examined next.

## Critiques of the Dominant Social Paradigm

In many respects, the DSP perspective has been positioned as the 'straw man' in the ecological debate (Fox 1990; Routley 1983; Wexler 1990). In its pure form, the DSP exists primarily in the abstract principles of neoclassical and Marxist economic theories or as an incomplete historical representation of industrialized society. In

reality, rational free market principles are continuously compromised and adjusted to accommodate the subjective 'irrationality' of governments, organizations and individuals in society. As identified by economic theorists and environmentalist critics alike (Cairncross 1991; Daly and Cobb 1994; Dorfman and Dorfman 1977; Friend 1992; Hawken 1993; Jacobs 1993), neoclassical economic assumptions and techniques are ill equipped to accurately reflect environmental externalities, qualitative costs and benefits, public goods and resources, limits to substitutions, resource depletion costs, long-term projected costs and benefits, complex systems, and so forth. One oft-cited example used to illustrate the inadequacies of neoclassical economics is the paradox that the cleanup of environmental disasters is accounted for as growth in a country's GNP while the preservation and conservation of environmental resources are regarded as costs (Cairncross 1991; Daly and Cobb 1994). Given these contradictions in practice, the dominant social paradigm can be most accurately regarded as an ideological perspective which serves as a conceptual endpoint against which other environmentalist perspectives and actions can be measured.

### Critiques of the Radical Environmentalism Perspective

As the most extreme set of these alternative perspectives, radical environmentalism proposes a complete philosophical reformation of society based on DSP principles. However, it is the utopian political, social and economic agenda of deep ecology which has evoked the strongest reactions from philosophers within and outside of the environmentalist movement (Fox 1990; Jacobs 1991). Both radical and reform environmentalist critics of deep ecology highlight its disassociation of ecological issues from social problems (Bookchin 1994; Bradford 1987); its advocacy of interference with individual freedom of humans but not that of wildlife or nature (Fox 1990); and its parallel to ancient neostoicism (Cheney 1989). In addition, deep ecology is criticized for its lack of a theory of transition to a biocentric world (Fox 1990; Luke 1988) and its logically inconsistent and simplistic position (Wexler 1990). Bookchin (1994: 6) provides the most condemning critique of what he regards as the 'intellectual, cultural, and spiritual poverty' of the deep ecology approach which he says verges on 'ecofascist propaganda'. Deep ecologists who advocate that there is only 'one way', that is, 'their way' of reconstructing the human–nature relationship may be more like their DSP

Table 1   *Typology of environmentalist perspectives*

| | Dominant social paradigm | Reform environmentalism | Radical environmentalism |
|---|---|---|---|
| Human–nature relationship | Domination over nature (very strong anthropocentrism) | Stewardship of nature (modified anthropocentrism) | Cooperation and harmony with nature (ecocentrism → biocentrism) |
| Approach to natural environment | Dominionistic (mastery) Utilitarian (material) Negativistic (avoidance) | Naturalistic (conservation) Utilitarian (modified) Scientific | Moralistic (spiritual) Aesthetic (preservation) Symbolic Humanistic (affection/emotion) |
| Nature of social order | Hierarchical Centralized authority  Competitive Individualistic | Hierarchical Centralized with stakeholder consultation Competitive/collaborative Individualism/collectivist | Egalitarian Decentralized participatory (minority tradition on bioregional basis) Communalism Collectivist |
| Assumptions: Knowledge | Reductionism Rationality of means Dualism | Reductionism-systems Rational-political means/ends | Holism Rationality of ends Integrative/dialectic |
| Economic | Neoclassical economics (unlimited economic and material growth essential for human progress) | Ecological economics (neoclassical plus natural capital for optimal decision-making) | Steady state economics (homeostasis) |
| Natural resources | Infinite natural resources (unlimited substitutes available) | Nonrenewable and renewable natural resources (limits to substitutes) | Very limited natural resources ('spaceship earth') |
| Scientific technology | Technological optimism | Technological optimism | Technological scepticism |
| Dominant goals | Unlimited economic and material growth essential for human progress  Scientific and technological progress | Sustainable development of natural environment  Economic and industrial development to reduce local/global societal inequities | Holistic balance with a fragile nature (symbiosis)  Environmental and social justice |
| Environmental management Technologies and strategies | Modern industrialism  Unrestricted consumerism  Pollution dispersion  Large-scale capital intensive technologies    Unregulated free markets | Green industrialism  Green consumerism  Pollution reduction  Eco-technologies to develop and conserve natural resources (technical and environmental efficiency)  Utilitarian biodiversity  Monitoring and regulation of environmental risks in local and global commons (calculate tradeoffs) | Bioregional planning and control  Post-consumption ethic  Pollution elimination  Intermediate (appropriate) technologies    Cultural and biological diversity  Government regulation for preservation/conservation of natural environment |
| Operating metaphor | Machine | Machine-systems | Organism |

*Sources*: Catton and Dunlap 1978; Colby 1990; Cotgrove and Duff 1981; Devall and Sessions 1985; Drengson 1980; Kellert 1993; Routley 1983

opponents than they would realize or wish to acknowledge. It could be argued that deep ecologists are falling into the positivist trap of taking as natural and uncontestable sets of assumptions which are the result of political and social interaction rather than a unitary version of reality or 'truth'. Despite these criticisms, deep ecology has proved to be significantly influential in ecophilosophy discourse (Fox 1990) as well as becoming the operating philosophy of many radical environmentalists (Devall 1988; Manes 1990).

The utopian, abstract radical nature of the social and biological objectives subsumed under the label of radical environmentalism has limited the degree to which this philosophy has influenced the day-to-day affairs of modern society. Nevertheless, radical environmentalism serves as a useful philosophical umbrella for several special interest groups whose own objectives overlap only partially with other radical environmentalists. The composition of particular groups which combine to undertake action depends therefore on the specific action being contemplated. Radical environmentalism has achieved a formal political voice in the election of green party candidates in the EEC Parliament and various European governments (Fisher 1993; Jancar-Webster 1993; Spretnak and Capra 1986). Within North America, green parties have been less able to garner the support of the voting public (McCloskey 1991; Slaton 1992). Instead, radical environmentalism has been more often adopted by grass-roots advocacy organizations (Sale 1993; Snow 1992a; 1992b). For radical environmentalist organizations such as Earth First!, the Sea Shepherd Society, Friends of the Earth, Rainforest Action Network and others, deep ecology principles provide a rationale for direct action campaigns of ecotage (ecological sabotage) and civil disobedience against those they view as enemies of nature. Not all radical environmentalists condone the use of violence in the struggle for transformational change in the human–nature relationship. More numerous have been campaigns of passive resistance against governments and industrial interests such as the Chipko movement of women in northern India to prevent logging in the Himalayan foothills (Shiva 1988) and environmentalist blockades to prevent logging in the Clayoquot Sound old-growth forests of coastal British Columbia. In pre-democratic Eastern Europe, there are numerous examples of effective large-scale grass-roots protests against environmental degradation, nuclear power projects, polluting industrial projects and the damming of the Danube River (Jancar-Webster 1993). On a smaller scale, grass-roots organizations have focused on local and regional environmental crises such as the Love Canal toxic waste dump (Wallace 1993).

Nevertheless, radical environmentalists have had limited influence on social change because they clearly oppose the most powerful arrangements and institutions in modern society. Rather than working less visibly from within, and running the risk of cooptation, proponents of radical environmentalism have attempted to effect social change from outside. While they may have had some marginal effect on selected local issues such as the reduction of clear-cutting in old-growth forests (Egri and Frost 1994), they have not yet produced either a coherent social movement or a set of proposed social reforms likely to be accepted or adopted by organizational members in mainstream society.

## Critiques of the Reform Environmentalism Perspective

While the reform environmentalism perspective is not a 'pure' paradigm, it does represent a diversity of means by which industrialized society has sought to integrate the natural environment into decision-making. As observed by Gladwin (1993) the concept of 'greening' in society and its organizations is replete with ambiguity and contradictions more indicative of the garbage-can model of decision-making (March 1978) than any rational choice or planning.

Reform environmentalism has been criticized more by radical environmentalists than by the mainstream agencies it has sought to reform. While reform environmentalism proponents claim to be environmentally responsible, one critique by radical environmentalists is that the anthropocentric bias of reform environmentalists proposes only minor incremental adjustments to economic and technological systems rather than transformational changes in human society (Colby 1990).

The concept of sustainable development is perhaps the most contentious aspect of the reform environmentalism perspective for both reform and radical environmentalists (Hawken 1993; Jacobs 1993; McRobert and Muldoon 1992; Schnaiberg and Gould 1994; *The Ecologist* 1993). Intended to encompass a wide variety of approaches and initiatives, the imprecision of the term 'sustainable development' allows for a wide variety of interpretations and enactments. One position is that sustainable development is not possible given the fundamental contradictions between the principles and goals of environmental sustainability and those of economic development (Schnaiberg and Gould 1994).

Critics argue that the concept of sustainable development enables governments and industry to 'embrace environmentalism without commitment' (Jacobs 1993: 59). It is also charged that participants in high-profile public events such as the UNCED are engaging in symbolic politics – projecting the illusion of substantive environmental change while simultaneously protecting and promoting their economic self-interests and power bases. For example, the UNCED endorsement of the global liberalization of capital and trade is regarded as antithetical to the environmentalist principle of bioregionalism (Hawken 1993; McRobert and Muldoon 1992). Hawken is especially wary about the potential efficacy of international standards for environmental regulations and trade given the environmental records of multinational corporations as well as the nature of existing free trade governing bodies (such as GATT) which exclude small businesses, farms, churches, environmentalist organizations and trade unions. There is also little confidence in the ability of international bodies (such as the World Bank) to effectively institute environmentally sustainable economic policies in the face of contradictory pressures from member governments (Hawken 1993; Rich 1990).

Radical environmentalist critics also identify the Brundtland Report's and UNCED's Agenda 21 support of development of nuclear energy and biogenetic engineering technology as being environmentally destructive, not sustainable (Rifkin 1983; Shiva 1993; Women's Environment and Development Organization (WEDO) 1992). Ecofeminists find the identification of women's fertility rates as one of the major causes of environmental degradation to be particularly objectionable (WEDO 1992). Population control policies which violate the reproductive rights of women are seen as symptomatic of the continued marginalization of women and overall neglect of gender issues in the reform environmentalist agenda for change.

In regards to industrial organizations, environmental responsibility is seen as one facet of a wider range of corporate social responsibilities encompassing economic, legal, ethical and philanthropic concerns (Carroll et al. 1988). Whilst some argue that social and environmental performance objectives conflict with economic performance objectives (Buchholz 1993; Hawken 1993; Jacobs 1993), others assert that what is morally and ethically right is also economically beneficial for industrial organizations (Elkington and Burke 1989; Rice 1993; Russo and Fouts 1993; Schmidheiny 1992). However, empirical research indicates that corporate environmental responsibility is rarely voluntary and more often in response to strong regulatory and consumer pressures (Ilinitch and Schaltegger 1993; Schnai-

berg and Gould 1994; Schot 1991; Steger 1993). This would tend to support mainstream (DSP) criticisms that the reform environmentalism agenda is both economically impractical (increased costs, fewer jobs) and procedurally undesirable (increased bureaucracy, less democracy). Both radical and reform environmentalists are sceptical about the promotion of the reformist vision of a 'green consumerism' and 'green capitalism' which can be regarded as oxymorons that permit a state of false ecological consciousness (Ekins 1991; Hawken 1993; Jacobs 1993).

Within the 'hydra-headed' environmental movement (Sale 1993; Snow 1992a), radical environmentalist and grass-roots advocacy groups often charge that large institutionalized bureaucratic reform environmentalist organizations have been coopted by the industrial and government status quo. Despite growth in memberships, a wide range of activities and public support, the record of mainstream reform environmentalist organizations has been less than exemplary in terms of the enactment of environmental statutes and mobilization of support for issues other than nature protection (McCloskey 1991).

In its defence, the reform environmentalism agenda of incremental change offers several positive features. Compared to the radical environmentalism position, the reform approach is more inclusive of diverse constituencies within government, industry and the general public in both the negotiation and implementation of environmentally informed action. Transformational potential can thereby be realized by the multiple incremental initiatives of wide breadth which in total may result in a fundamental shift in the human–nature relationship. However, one essential problem in regards to the 'sustainable development' concept as currently envisioned and enacted is that it represents a reluctance to totally abandon the DSP assumptions of infinite growth, consumerism, belief in technological fixes, and hierarchical social relations. There is the fundamental risk that an incremental approach may be concerned with only solving superficial symptoms rather than addressing the root causes of environmental degradation. It may be illusory that the environmental crisis is manageable and soluble through human ingenuity.

## Summary Comments

As revealed by this review of environmentalist perspectives, there is no 'perfect' approach to envisioning and enacting the human–nature relationship. One theme for the three perspectives on eco-environments described here is their common focus on the physical environment as the lens through which each views the consequences of social, political and economic activities. At one end of the continuum, the dominant social paradigm represents an approach wherein the economic interests and needs of human society are pre-eminent over all other concerns. While it can be argued that this is a caricature of reality (both present and past), the DSP offers a useful conceptual point of departure for other perspectives which advocate changes to existing human–nature relationships. The primary strength of the radical environmentalism perspective resides in its (relative) philosophical coherence whilst its prescriptions for enactment remain largely untested. Although based on a less cohesive (and often contradictory) set of philosophical assumptions, the reform environmentalism perspective engenders a more optimistic pragmatic approach to resolving immediate environmental problems.

However, both reform and radical environmentalism challenge established conceptions we have of the purposes and consequences of modern industrial organizations. As a means of developing a further appreciation of the tensions between these perspectives, we now consider environments as seen through the lens of organization theory.

## THE ENVIRONMENT IN ORGANIZATION THEORY

Not unlike environmentalists, organization theorists claim a centrality of their worldview. 'Organizations . . . are the fundamental building blocks of modern societies' (Aldrich and Marsden 1988: 361). Even a Nobel laureate in economics has argued that when viewing earth, a mythical visitor from space would discover that 'organizations would be the dominant feature of the landscape' (Simon 1991: 27). More recently, sociologists Schnaiberg and Gould (1994) have typified the dominant worldview as being a 'treadmill of production' in which the industrial logic of firms and other economic organizations maintains '*society-wide* social and political institutions which . . . expand both production . . . and ecological extraction' (Schnaiberg and Gould 1994: 45). Alternative theories or competing modes of thought, such as those of eco-environmentalism, will have to be particularly robust if they are to modify or displace established models of organizations based on an orgocentric perspective.

Traditional orthodoxy in organization theory has been dominated by functionalist perspectives in which organizations have been viewed as either machines or organisms or some combination of each metaphor (Morgan 1980). In the machine metaphor, organizations are viewed primarily as rational instruments for the accomplishment of pre-formed and internally generated objectives. Contextual or environmental constraints which limit the attainment of goals and objectives are given scant attention as the environment is taken as immutable and given by organizational actors. Such perspectives are consistent with the economic institutions of capitalism and the social ethos of individual competition. Market environments are considered to be self-regulating. Individual and collective welfare are maximized through the pursuit of individual self-interest and social and economic competition.

When organizations are viewed as organisms, the continued survival of an organization is seen as being dependent on an appropriate interactive and interdependent relationship between the organization and its environment. Thus, environments are attended to in so far as they constrain or risk organizational survival. In the short and not necessarily glorious history of organization theory (Perrow 1973), perspectives which emphasize ideas of environmental dependence are relatively new. While there were previous scatterings of ideas regarding the consequences of this environmental dependence (Dill 1958; Burns and Stalker 1961), sustained research on the nature of organizational environments did not begin to develop fully until the latter part of the 1960s and the early 1970s (Duncan 1972; Emery and Trist 1965; Evan 1966; Jurkovich 1974; Lawrence and Lorsch 1967; Osborne and Hunt 1974; Thompson 1967). Since then, there have been scattered assessments of organizational environments which have not radically changed traditional orgocentric perspectives (Aldrich 1979; Aldrich and Marsden 1988; Aldrich and Pfeffer 1976; Carroll et al. 1988; Meyer and Scott 1983; Starbuck 1976).

Current conceptualizations of organizational environments can be traced to the seminal work of Emery and Trist (1965). Their development of the 'causal texture' of organizational environments envisaged a set of transactional dependencies among a set of organizations viewed from the perspective of a single focal organization. The first-order environment of any focal organization consists of the relationships between that organization and others with which it has direct transactions – such as suppliers and customers. The second-order environment of the focal organization consists of all other relationships, or transactional dependencies, between organizations in the first-order environment and all other organizations. The causal texture of the environment of the focal organization therefore is a conceptual map of the causal linkages in which a change in the behaviour of any organization in that environment would influence the functioning of the focal organization. In this conceptualization, the second-order rather than the first-order environment is potentially more problematic for the functioning of a focal organization. First, changes in environmental elements are less visible in second-order environments. Second, the nature of the causal interdependencies in second-order environments is rarely known or understood by representatives of the focal organization.

Emery and Trist extended this framework to develop an initial classification of organizational environments. Organizational environments are problematic as a function of the degree of uncertainty they pose for organizational decision-makers. Such uncertainty is indicated by the strength of interorganizational linkages and the rates of change of the organizational elements in an environment. Environmental conditions are most problematic and produce greatest uncertainty when interorganizational linkages are dense and rates of change are high. Such environments are characterized as being 'turbulent'. In a potentially prophetic extension of the Emery and Trist model, Terryberry (1967) examined the trends in modern society and predicted that the environments of most organizations would evolve into turbulence – a condition not unfamiliar to students of the contemporary business press or chaos theory (Gleick 1987).

In developing these conceptualizations of environments, organization and management theorists extended traditional functionalist ways of thinking beyond organizational boundaries. For example, organizations need to spend more time and energy aligning collective actions under conditions of uncertainty than when conditions are stable and known (Thompson 1967). Thus, uncertainty detracts from organizational efficiency (a machine attribute) as less energy is available to pursue agreed-upon objectives. Moreover, because environments could potentially mean everything outside the organizational boundary, attention is focused on only those environmental attributes which make the pursuit of organizational objectives problematic. Organizational decision-makers are indifferent to events having consequences for other 'environmental' stakeholders but which have little consequence for the focal organization.

There have been relatively few attempts to define environments independently of a specific single or group of focal organizations. Scott (1981: 170) identified different levels of analysis for the study of organizational environments.

His review included concepts of the organization set (Blau and Scott 1962; Evan 1966) and the related term of organizational domain (Levine and White 1961; Thompson 1967) which were both similar to Emery and Trist's (1965) ideas of first-order environments. At broader and more encompassing levels of analysis, environments can also be considered as all organizations constituting either the ecological community (Hawley 1950) or the interorganizational field (Warren 1967; Trist 1983). For example, a more recent development regarding the nature of organizational environments originated with Hannan and Freeman's (1977) population ecology theory of organizations. Although these theories apply models, theories and methods from the biological sciences to populations of organizations, environments are again defined in relational terms. Organizational environments have no definition independent of those attributes, primarily their carrying capacity, which influences the survival characteristics of a population of organizations. In fact, population ecology models of organizations and their environments are extensions of the functionalist perspectives which have dominated organization theorizing. It is both ironic and misleading that the models derived from biology, applied to the analysis of organizations and their environments, and provided with an ecological label, should have so little to do with the biosphere (Young 1988). Other attempts to arrive at independent definitions of organizational environments have been used to define attributes of organizations themselves. Thus, Scott (1992) uses economists' definitions of markets such as pure competition or oligopoly to illustrate and summarize the consequences of attributes of a firm's environment for organizational design.

In all of these instances, conceptualizations of organizational environments fail to explicitly include considerations of the natural environment. Even attempts to define environments at environmental levels of analysis rely on relational constructs. That is, environments are defined as having no character to define other than their organizationally relevant attributes. Within the dominant paradigms of organizationally defined environments, we have few, if any, means of assessing the consequences of organizational actions for the qualities of the environment(s) which contain them.

Traditional perspectives on organizations and their environments have gained acceptance because of their utility for the initiation and engagement of collective action (Starbuck 1983), especially by powerful organizational decision-makers whose personal interests were assumed to be aligned with those of the organizations they represent. In the burgeoning market of professional business education during the post World War II period, at least two generations of managers in training have been exposed to limited rationales such as these. However, other open systems views of organizations and their environments have been developed from more institutional and critical perspectives.

In open systems perspectives, the boundary between organizations and their environments is viewed as permeable. Organizations cannot be easily separated from the environments in which they are embedded. They not only adapt to their environments but also strongly influence the nature of those environments. Derived from Selznick's (1948; 1957) seminal work in organizational sociology, numerous studies have examined the processes of organizational adaptation. Perrow (1972) outlines two generic options. Less powerful organizations are 'captured' by powerful environmental elements and modify their goals and objectives to ensure both the survival of the organization and presumably a continuation of the entitlements of organizationally dependent actors. Alternatively, more powerful organizations are able to impose their worldview on other organizations and agencies. In this latter scenario, powerful organizational leaders shape the ideology and resources under their control to produce environmental exigencies that are advantageous for the members of the dominant coalition which controls that organization (Aldrich and Pfeffer 1976). It is in the latter conceptualization that the fears of some environmentalists can be found. Organizations adapt to their task-defined environments, but individual, societal and (biophysical) environmental interests are not necessarily factored into the priorities of organizational decision-makers. This view assigns large degrees of relative influence to organizations over their environments. While such characterizations are undoubtedly true of a small number of large, powerful organizations, this perspective ignores the larger proportion of organizations which are more environmentally dependent. In addition, this perspective also fails to take into account the potential for environmental beliefs, norms and values to be incorporated into the axioms, assumptions, and values of powerful organizational members (Beyer 1981).

Organizational activities are not independent of the larger social, economic, cultural, political and technical systems of which they are a part. All have outside interests and commitments which inform their behaviours inside the organization as well as their intended objectives for organizational activities. Organizations import knowledge and technologies into their internal domains. They also take in resources and supplies which are combined and transformed to provide outputs to the larger social environment. In the long run, organizations need to continue to provide valued functions to the larger society if they are to continue to survive (Fellmeth 1970; Maniha and Perrow 1965).

The net consequence of these pressures is for organizations to become more or less isomorphic with their environments as this 'fit' is required if they are to acquire the resources and legitimacy needed to operate in those environments. Conventionally, environmentally dependent organizations will have to adjust to strong environmental demands whereas more powerful organizations can shape environmental exigencies to better suit their requirements. In either case, social values will be carried by organizational participants into the direction and guidance of organizational activities. Thus organizations can be considered to adapt to their environments in at least two ways. First, within the limited perspective of a rational, mechanistic model, organizations change when it is within the limited self-interests of the organization to do so. Second, from an institutional point of view, organizations will accommodate changing social values as these are imported into the decision premises of members of the organization's dominant coalition (Meyer and Rowan 1983; Powell and DiMaggio 1991). It is quite clear, though rarely examined explicitly, that orgocentric conceptions of organizational environments have little apparent overlap with the concerns of environmentalists. None has a complete view of any other, and misconceptions are actively encouraged. The 'straw man' environmentalist perspective of the dominant social paradigm, as well as that of radical environmentalists, fails to acknowledge open systems characteristics of organizations. Advocates of the bounded rationality embedded in DSP perspectives fear the indeterminacy associated with the inclusion of humanistic values into organizational considerations. Radical environmentalists have so far only proposed romantic ideals with little thought being given to the practical manner in which their nirvana may be attained. Reform environmentalists have proposed various modifications to DSP values – but relatively few of these have been translated into orgocentric action frames.

From the perspective of organization theory, environmental degradation becomes relevant only when the performance of a focal organization and the welfare of organizational participants are affected by such concerns. Organizational actions which degrade the local environment become pertinent when future organizational survival or profitability is threatened by legislated restrictions or scarcity of natural resources. In contrast, a clear theme of many environmentalists is that the limited and shortsighted actions of organizational actors inevitably degrade the natural environment. From their perspective, there is a clear link between organizational actions and their conception of what constitutes the environment. However, the exhortations of environmentalists for organizations to modify their behaviours without framing such persuasion in terms of organizational self-interests is to misunderstand the logics of organizational action.

Despite these confusions, we believe there is a nexus for these different perspectives. We argue that functionalist abstractions of organizational environments understate the potential for aspects of the natural environment to be included in the decision premises of organizational actors. As persons who hope to continue to exist in the bounded biosphere of spaceship earth, we believe that self-interested environmental actions will be informed by the values, knowledge and experiences of organizational actors.

## INTEGRATING PERSPECTIVES ON ECO-ENVIRONMENTS AND ORGANIZATIONS

Essentially, the environmentalist debate is concerned with fundamental and transformational changes in the deep structure of society (see Elliott 1988; Egri and Frost 1994; and others). A compelling question therefore concerns the extent to which, both conceptually and practically, the present state of affairs should remain or whether there are advantages to greater overlap and synthesis of these disparate ideas. That is, to what extent can and should environmentalist views of biophysical environments be incorporated into organizational views of their environments? In this section of the chapter, we focus on two issues – self-interest and systems theory – which illustrate the challenges of integrating these disparate approaches to eco-environments.

### Self-Interest and Environmental Change

The dominant features of contemporary society are deeply embedded. Challenges to the status quo need to be based on powerful motives if they are to modify existing arrangements which may contain strong tendencies for global self-destruction. Thus, our discussion of self-interest is presented as a device for merging concerns for the environment with the possibility of organizational action.

In contemporary society, organizations are the primary means for accomplishing collective action. However, collective actions are usually framed within a hierarchy of nested systems. Individual actors confront the reality of conflicting objectives in their individual experiences of ambivalence. Individuals also experience tension between their personal objectives and the immediate social systems such as families and work groups which frame individual action. At larger and broader levels of analysis, the salience of individual perspectives diminishes as organizational, regional and possibly national interests provide the frames through which prospective collective actions are assessed. A common thread throughout the cognitions and rationalizations associated with the intentionality of action is self-interest.

Self-interests can be viewed through a number of different lenses. At its most primitive and selfish level, self-interest is short term and totally preoccupied with the physical survival of the individual. At one level removed from this primitive conceptualization is a concept of self-interest based on immediate family and progeny (cf. Simon 1993; Samuelson 1993; Wilson 1975). Individuals could consider sacrificing their well-being (their lives??) for an improved change for the survival of progeny which carry their genes. Thus parents forgo leisure and consumption to invest in the education of their children and provide them with resources which improve their life chances. At a small remove from this would be self-interest based on a loose family collectivity such as a clan or a tribe. The widest conceptualization of self-interest is one based on the species (*Homo sapiens*). Individuals and collectives forgo returns from immediately beneficial activities, such as the development of nuclear energy or the usage of fossil fuels, to improve the chances that both current and future citizens of the whole planet would be exposed to less environmental risk from increased solar radiation, proliferation of nuclear weapons, global warming or elevated sea levels.

Two aspects of competing perceptions of reality complicate assessments of self-interest which frame action perspectives. On the one hand, we can consider the immediacy or distance of environmental threat. On the other hand, environmental threats can be considered as being experienced (and therefore motivated) by individuals, genetically similar groups, or whole societies. When self-interest can be shown to be immediately at risk as a consequence of actions over which they have control, those actions will be changed. But when the consequences of current actions are problematic, unclear and not necessarily experienced until several decades or longer into the future, self-interests of those benefiting from current arrangements will lead to resistance of environmentalist advocates. In contested situations such as these, claims for legitimacy based on partial scientific evidence, normative ideology, and political contests become the currency of public debate (Pinfield and Berner 1992; Samuel and Spencer 1993; Schelling 1992).

Nevertheless, a shared appreciation of environmental issues is critical as resolution of environmental threats invariably requires interdependent collective action. Without substantial agreement regarding the nature of collaborative actions, individual actions are unlikely to serve the interests of any higher-level collectivity. Similarly, local actions taken by collectives will have little effect on global consequences unless other collectives, which also contribute to environmental degradation, modify their behaviours as well. Moreover, we should recognize that not all persons and collectivities are similarly situated either to see or to experience scarce or degraded resources.

Expression of special interests and the working through of collective actions require the agency of organizations. Attainment of the outcomes desired by any environmentalist group requires an appreciation of how special interest and collective objectives may be obtained. We live in an organizational world in which organizations are the means through which interests are realized. No matter which environmental perspective is accepted, orgocentric tradition, philosophy, and knowledge are required if goals are to be attained. Organizations are special purpose social collectivities whose activities are informed by the interests of organizational participants. These interests are circumscribed by those of other actors who operate both within and outside of organizational boundaries, and are considered to be essential to organizational functioning. Organizationally defined environments are functionally useful constructs for the accomplishment of collective actions. The environmental perspective described as the dominant social paradigm is a crude and limited interpretation of action perspectives on organizations as it ignores the relationally defined construct of organizational environments. Nevertheless, open systems models of organizations, while still problematic, permit the introduction of environmentalist concerns into organizational decision criteria. The attributions (caricatures) by environmentalists of hermetically sealed boundaries between organizations and their eco-environments as characterizations of the DSP are inaccurate representations of contemporary organizations. Moreover, contemporary organizational parallels of the DSP do encourage action perspectives which eventually could include amelioration of environmental abuses.

In contrast, the radical environmentalism perspective presents a transformational view of desired outcomes. Organizational actions required 'to get there from here' are not considered. Organizational and radical environmentalist perspectives are presently incompatible and the possibility for a synthesis of the two is minimal. In the short term, proponents of the radical environmentalist perspective need to use and master mass media if their message is to be received and accepted by mainstream members of society. We speculate that the requirements for collective action would likely produce conflict between orgocentric ideas and the coherence of the radical environmentalist position. Proponents of radical environmentalism may find their accomplishments limited by their inherent denial of self-interest in organizational actions. As have others who have argued for larger social concerns to be factored into organizational objectives, advocates of radical environmentalism may find their emotional energies sapped by lack of progress and their attention claimed by other issues (Downs 1972). The ideological pull of radical environmentalism will remain, but in a muted form that will help ground further elaborations of the reform environmentalist viewpoint.

Reform environmentalism offers a viable long-term perspective on bio-environments because it is this perspective alone which more or less accepts the collective action utilitarianism of relational definitions of organizational environments. Evaluations of environments defined in biophysical terms are relevant to organizational decision-makers when translated into terms of their self-interest. These self-interests can be defined in increasingly broad terms of societal values, informed by new information regarding the consequences of individual and collective organizational actions. While we have incomplete information regarding these consequences (Hawken 1993; Shrivastava 1994; Stead and Stead 1992), this clearly represents an opportunity for further truly interdisciplinary organizational research.

Once such information becomes available, what are the chances it will be used to inform and redirect the activities of organizational participants? For those persons whose interests are not served, or are possibly even harmed, by the activities of a focal organization, two sets of tactics are available to them to change that situation. The first is to find avenues for influence through the existing institutional superstructure (Astley and Fombrun 1987) of the community of which the focal organization is a member. If the existing institutional superstructure provides little or no recourse, then citizens (at least those in democratic societies) have opportunities to elaborate that superstructure in the form of new legislation and regulations. Such developments are not likely to occur quickly. We recognize it is possible that the long-term harm from the activities of focal organizations could be well established before any meaningful restrictions could be developed and applied. Moreover, the development of new legislation is likely to be contested by those who benefit from the absence of such legislation and those whose interests would be harmed by the passage of such legislation. Nevertheless, the formal and informal 'rules' governing the conduct and consequences of organizational activities would be subject to both scientific and political scrutiny.

Political scrutiny and evaluation occur within an existing normative ideology. As part of the process of attempting to change or elaborate existing legislation, political action necessarily involves attempts to change existing ideologies. Proponents of new legislation can attempt to apply moral suasion to the activities of a focal organization. They can attempt to change the values of the members of the dominant coalition or work to change the larger social values so that the activities of targeted firms are perceived as being less and less legitimate. In either case, the legitimacy of existing organizational arrangements becomes the trigger for change of organizational activities in which the self-interests of the dominant coalition are judged to run counter to those of other members of society. There will be continuing political conflict between social and organizational objectives and the quality of the natural environment (Schnaiberg and Gould 1994).

## The Promise of Systems Theory

Systems theory appears to be a common conceptual framework for both environmentalist and organizational domains. Indeed, one common prescription amongst environmentalist writers is for the wholesale adoption of ecological systems principles in societies and organizations as the 'only path' towards environmental sustainability (Milbrath 1989; Shrivastava 1992; 1994; Stead and Stead 1992). What is less discussed within each perspective is that reality is socially constructed with the consequence being that the temporal and spatial boundaries which both focus and limit attention are problematic. Paradoxically, these problematic features of both domains permit an optimistic, adaptive future confluence of two historically separate conceptual schemata. As information on the consequences of collective human and organizational actions on the biosphere becomes available, it will gradually be enacted into the beliefs of social actors (Gamson et al. 1992). Individuals, whether through self-interest or through a cultivation of ecological consciousness, will modify collective conceptualizations of organizations and their environments.

There are a number of theoretical issues which remain largely unresolved in the sociological and organization theory literatures about social systems, and within ecological theory about ecological systems. Open systems theory directs us to view organizations and the biosphere as dynamic phenomena which are constantly adjusting to changing environments. Systems comprise subsystems and individual units which are also in states of dynamic change in relation to each other. However, the linkages between individual action and system-level consequences (the micro–macro relationship) and linkages between system-level changes and individual consequences (the macro–micro relationship) remain largely unexplored by social scientists (Ashmos and Huber 1987; Coleman 1986; Namboodiri 1988). One important exception is the exploration of the nature of connections between social and ecological systems in terms of tight and loose coupling (Weick 1979).

In general, loosely coupled systems have often been regarded as a positive feature of organizations, with tightly coupled systems being regarded as less desirable in modern organizations. As determined by Perrow (1984), tightly coupled technological systems are prone to 'normal accidents'. More recently, Weick and Roberts (1993) have proposed that tightly coupled *social* systems can mediate or neutralize the dangers inherent in tightly coupled *technological* systems. Conceptualizing the collective mind as 'the pattern of heedful interrelations of actions in a social system', Weick and Roberts (1993: 357), propose that individual actions in high reliability (dangerous) systems need to be both representative of, and subordinate to, mutually shared meanings and communities of practice. Cooperation, rather than individualism, is essential for heedful (careful) action in systems of interactive complexity. This introduces more complexity to developing an appreciation of the dynamics of tight and loose coupling between organizational and ecological systems.

Within the reform environmentalism perspective, industrial ecology proposes that environmental safety is enhanced through the development of closed tightly coupled industrial systems of production. The underlying assumption is that industrial activity is inherently dangerous to ecological systems, therefore industrial systems need to be heedful but disengaged from wider eco-environments. Consistent with Weick and Roberts's observations regarding tightly coupled social systems under such conditions, individual actions are informed and subordinate to that of the collective value of environmental sustainability.

More problematic for concerted environmental action are what Weick and Roberts identify as conditions where there is an undeveloped collective mind. As learned in the analysis of the reform environmentalism perspective, there remain significant contradictions between espoused environmentalist values and visible actions concerning the natural environment. While part of this can be attributed to the early stage of the sustainable development concept, much can be traced to the lack of willingness to totally abandon the values of individualism and competitive free market principles of Western industrialized societies. These values inform loose coupling within and between social, technological and ecological systems. As identified by Weick and Roberts (1993: 378): 'A culture that encourages individualism, survival of the fittest, macho heroics, and can-do reactions will often neglect heedful practice of representation and subordination.' To the degree that these cultural values remain within the reform environmentalism perspective, heedful environmental action will continue to be compromised and incremental changes may remain isolated or absorbed into the status quo. Systems theory also offers an alternative hypothesis concerning the outcome of incremental actions. Consistent with the underlying premise of the environmentalist credo 'Think globally, act locally', what may appear to be incremental change in one small part of a system may, over time, amplify to effect a large-scale transformation in macro-level systems. Irrespective, traditional research methodologies which limit the spatial and temporal scope of inquiry appear to be ill suited to addressing questions concerning multi-faceted systems phenomena. Organizational research needs to further develop a diversity of approaches to studying organizations and their eco-environments.

## CONCLUDING THOUGHTS

The more we get out of the world the less we leave, and in the long run we shall have to pay our debts at a time that may be inconvenient for our own survival. (Wiener 1954: 2)

The 'issue–attention cycle' of social issues would suggest that current concern with environmental issues is only temporary and will fade away as problems are resolved and a bored public turns its attention to other issues (Downs 1972). However, historical and empirical evidence is proving otherwise (Dunlap 1989). Concern with the natural environment has a long history and has proved to be remarkably resilient despite temporary detours and lulls in activity. One reason why the environmental challenge to society and its organizations promises to remain and become more prominent is that humans are witnessing and experiencing the deleterious effects of the degradation of the natural environment on a scale and scope unprecedented in human history.

Another reason can be found in the concept of biophilia, which is defined as the 'innately emotional affiliation of human beings to other living organisms' (Wilson 1984: 31). The biophilia hypothesis proposes that humans' relations with the natural environment are simultaneously concerned with the material, emotional, cognitive, aesthetic and spiritual dimensions of human existence (Kellert 1993). The three alternative perspectives on eco-environments identified in this chapter represent degrees of emphasis on each interconnected dimension. While the dominant social paradigm emphasizes humans' dominionistic and utilitarian relations with nature, the radical environmentalism perspective emphasizes humans' emotional, aesthetic and spiritual connections with the natural environment. The mid-range reform environmentalism perspective represents a more cognitive (or scientific) approach to integrating and balancing these sometimes contradictory dimensions. The central tenet of the biophilia hypothesis is that each approach has a place and role to play in the evolutionary history of humanity. Overemphasis on one or a few to the exclusion of other facets can have destructive consequences for both humans and the natural environment. For example, focusing solely on the material value and benefits to be derived from the natural environment (as per the dominant social paradigm) informs environmentally unsustainable actions and will ultimately threaten humans' long-term needs for sustenance, protection and security. Similarly, preserving the natural environmental purely for its aesthetic value (as per deep ecology) to the exclusion of other relations with the natural environment denies the development of material relations necessary for human physical existence. In the end, there is a need for a balance among these disparate and sometimes conflicting relationships with the natural environment – not a static final balance, but a dynamic balancing between evolving human and natural systems of existence.

A similar argument can be made concerning the introduction of the natural environment into the discourse of organization theory and practice. As learned in our discussion of organization theory, orthodox conceptualizations of organizational interests and actions have been largely devoid of considerations of the human–nature connection. And yet, there is increasing evidence that changes in the biophysical environment will clearly bring societal change. From environmentalist perspectives, biophysical and social change is imminent and inevitable. Thus adhering to the status quo in both organizational theory and action is not a safe avenue but a destructive one for the biosphere and the human species. That change is inevitable is not at issue. It is the direction and nature of change which are the focus of the environmentalist challenge to organization science. As Lovelock (1988) proposes in his Gaia principle, the biosphere of the planet will continue to adapt and change as a result of human and nonhuman phenomena: the essential question is whether the future biosphere will be one which includes the human species.

## NOTES

1 In 1935, British plant ecologist Tansley would introduce the concept of *ecosystems* as being: 'the whole *system* (in the sense of physics) including not only the organism-complex, but also the whole complex of physical factors forming what we call the environment of the biome – the habitat factors in the widest sense' (as cited by McIntosh 1985: 193).

2 As proposed by Kassas and Polunin (1989), ecosystems comprise of three systems: the *biosphere*, which encompasses the planet's lower atmosphere, lithosphere (land), hydrosphere (aquatic) and life systems; the *technosphere*, which is composed of the systems of human structures within the biosphere; and the *sociosphere*, which is composed of the socio-political, socioeconomic and sociocultural institutions created by humans. The biosphere performs three interrelated functions in maintaining living systems, that is, it provides resources, it provides environmental services (such as life support and amenities) and it accumulates waste products (Jacobs 1993).

3 However, defenders of Marxist theory assert that the original Marxist teachings were not antagonistic to the natural environment but rather that the centralized practices of modern socialist states were based on a Stalinist interpretation of communism (Grundmann 1991; McLaughlin 1990; Raskin and Bernow 1991). As Pepper (1993: 109) contends, Marx's 'society–nature dialectic appears to be, in reality, deeply organic (seeing them both as making up one organic body) and monist (physical and mental phenomena can be analyzed in terms of a common underlying reality)'.

4 The first law of thermodynamics is the conservation law, which states that the total amount of energy is constant, is not destroyed or created but is transformed from one state to another (Stead and Stead 1992). The second is the entropy law, which posits that when energy changes state, a portion of available useful energy is lost. In respect to living systems, there is the potential for negative entropy in that the import of additional energy can forestall decline and death (Georgescu-Rogen 1971).

## REFERENCES

Aldrich, H.E. (1979) *Organizations and Environments.* Englewood Cliffs, NJ: Prentice-Hall.

Aldrich, H.E. and Marsden, P.V. (1988) 'Environments and organizations', in N.J. Smelser (ed.), *The Handbook of Sociology*. Newbury Park, CA: Sage.

Aldrich, H.E. and Pfeffer, J. (1976) 'Environments of organizations', *Annual Review of Psychology*, 27: 79–105.

Alexander, D. (1990) 'Bioregionalism: science or sensibility?', *Environmental Ethics*, 12(2): 161–73.

Allenby, B.R. (1992) 'Achieving sustainable development through industrial ecology', *International Environmental Affairs*, 4(1): 56–68.

Ashmos, D.P. and Huber, G.P. (1987) 'The systems paradigm in organization theory: correcting the record and suggesting the future', *Academy of Management Review*, 12(4): 607–21.

Astley, W.G. and Fombrun, C.J. (1987) 'Organizational communities: an ecological perspective', *Research in the Sociology of Organizations*, 5: 163–85.

Baram, M. and Dillon, P. (1993) 'Corporate management of chemical accident risks', in K. Fischer and J. Schot (eds), *Environmental Strategies for Industry: International Perspectives on Research Needs and Policy Implications*. Washington, DC: Island Press. pp. 227–41.

Bennett, S.J. (1991) *Ecopreneuring: the Complete Guide to Small Business Opportunities from the Environmental Revolution*. New York: Wiley.

Berkes, F. (ed.) (1989) *Common Property Resources: Ecology and Community-Based Sustainable Development*. London: Belhaven.

Berle, G. (1990) *The Green Entrepreneur: Business Opportunities that can Save the Earth and Make You Money*. Liberty Hall Press.

Berry, T. (1988) *The Dream of the Earth*. San Francisco: Sierra Club Books.

Beyer, J.M. (1981) 'Ideologies, values, and decision making in organizations', in P.C. Nystrom and W.H. Starbuck (eds), *Handbook of Organizational Design*, vol. 2. New York: Oxford University Press.

Bird, E.A.R. (1987) 'The social construction of nature: theoretical approaches to the history of environmental problems', *Environmental Review*, 11(4): 255–64.

Blau, P.M. and Scott, W.R. (1962) *Formal Organizations*. San Francisco: Chandler.

Bookchin, M. (1980) *Toward an Ecological Society*. Montreal: Black Rose Books.

Bookchin, M. (1982) *The Ecology of Freedom: the Emergence and Dissolution of Hierarchy*. Palo Alto, CA: Cheshire Books.

Bookchin, M. (1990a) *Philosophy of Social Ecology: Essays on Dialectical Naturalism*. Montreal: Black Rose Books.

Bookchin, M. (1990b) *Remaking Society: Pathways to a Green Future*. Boston: South End Press.

Bookchin, M. (1994) *Which Way for the Ecology Movement?* San Francisco: Ak Press.

Bradford, G. (1987) 'How deep is deep ecology? A challenge to radical environmentalism', *Fifth Estate*, 22(Fall).

Bramwell, A. (1989) *Ecology in the 20th Century*. New Haven, CT: Yale University Press.

Brown, L.R. (ed.) (1991) *The WorldWatch Reader on Global Environmental Issues*. New York: W.W. Norton.

Buchholz, R.A. (1993) *Principles of Environmental Management: the Greening of Business*. Englewood Cliffs, NJ: Prentice-Hall.

Burns, T. and Stalker, G.M. (1961) *The Management of Innovation*. London: Tavistock.

Cairncross, F. (1991) *Costing the Earth: the Challenge for Governments, the Opportunities for Business*. Boston: Harvard Business School Press.

Callenbach, E., Capra, F., Goldman, L., Lutz, R. and Marburg, S. (1993) *EcoManagement: the Elmwood Guide to Ecological Auditing and Sustainable Business*. San Francisco: Berrett-Koehler.

Carroll, G.R., Delacroix, J. and Goodstein, J. (1988) 'The political environments of organizations: an ecological view', *Research in Organizational Behaviour*, 10: 359–92.

Carson, R. (1962) *Silent Spring*. Boston: Houghton Mifflin.

Catton, W.R. Jr and Dunlap, R.E. (1978) 'Environmental sociology: a new paradigm', *The American Sociologist*, 13(February): 41–9.

Cheney, J. (1987) 'Eco-feminism and deep ecology', *Environmental Ethics*, 9(2): 115–45.

Cheney, J. (1989) 'The neo-stoicism of radical environmentalism', *Environmental Ethics*, 11(4): 293–325.

Clow, M. (1986) 'Marxism and the "environmental question": an assessment of Bahro', *Studies in Political Economy*, 20(Summer): 171–86.

Colburn, T.E., Davidson, A., Green, S.N., Hodge, R.A., Jackson, C.I. and Liroff, R.A. (1990) *Great Lakes, Great Legacy?* Washington, DC: Conservation Foundation. Ottawa: Institute for Research for Public Policy.

Colby, M.E. (1990) 'Ecology, economics, and social systems: the evolution of the relationship between environmental management and development'. PhD dissertation, University of Pennsylvania.

Coleman, J.S. (1986) 'Social theory, social research, and a theory of action', *American Journal of Sociology*, 91(6): 1309–35.

Commoner, B. (1990) *Making Peace with the Planet* (1975). New York: Pantheon Books.

Cotgrove, S. and Duff, A. (1981) 'Environmentalism, values and social change', *British Journal of Sociology*, 32(1): 92–110.

Crowfoot, J.E. and Wondolleck, J.M. (1990) *Environmental Disputes: Community Involvement in Conflict Resolution*. Washington, DC: Island Press.

Daly, H.E. (1977) *Steady-State Economics*. New York: Freeman.

Daly, H.E. and Cobb, J.B. Jr (1994) *For the Common Good: Redirecting the Economy toward Community, the Environment, and a Sustainable Future*, 2nd edn. Boston: Beacon Press.

Davies, C. (1991) 'The need for ecological cooperation in Europe', *International Journal on the Unity of the Sciences*, 4(2): 201–16.

Day, D. (1989) *The Environmental Wars: Reports from the Front Lines*. New York: St Martin's Press.

Devall, B. (1988) *Simple in Means, Rich in Ends: Practicing Deep Ecology*. Salt Lake City: Peregrine Smith Books.

Devall, B. and Sessions, G. (1985) *Deep Ecology*. Salt Lake City: Peregrine Smith Books.

Diamond, I. and Forenstein, G. (eds) (1990) *Reweaving the World: The Emergence of Ecofeminism*. San Francisco: Sierra Club Books.

Dill, W.R. (1958) 'Environment as an influence on managerial autonomy', *Administrative Science Quarterly*, 2: 409–43.

Dorfman, R. and Dorfman, N.S. (eds) (1977) *Economics of the Environment: Selected Readings*, 2nd edn. New York: W.W. Norton.

Downs, A. (1972) 'Up and down with ecology: the "issue-attention cycle"', *The Public Interest*, 28(Spring): 38–50.

Drengson, A. (1980) 'Shifting paradigms: from the technocratic to the person-planetary', *Environmental Ethics*, 2(3): 221–40.

Duncan, R.B. (1972) 'Characteristics of organizational environments and perceived environmental uncertainty', *Administrative Science Quarterly*, 17: 313–27.

Dunlap, R.E. (1989) 'Public opinion and environmental policy', in J.P. Lester (ed.), *Environmental Politics and Policy: Theories and Evidence*. London: Duke University Press. pp. 87–134.

Egri, C.P. and Frost, P.J. (1992) 'The power and politics of interorganizational collaboration to engender environmental sustainability in agriculture'. Paper presented at the 1992 Academy of Management Meeting, Las Vegas.

Egri, C.P. and Frost, P.J. (1994) 'The organizational politics of sustainable development', in H. Thomas, D. O'Neal, R. White and D. Hurst (eds), *Building the Strategically-Responsive Organization*. Chichester: Wiley. pp. 215–30.

Ehrenfeld, D. (1978) *The Arrogance of Humanism*. New York: Oxford University Press.

Eisler, R. (1987) *The Chalice and the Blade: Our History, Our Future*. San Francisco: Harper & Row.

Ekins, P. (1991) 'A strategy for global development', *Development*, 2: 64–73.

Elkington, J. and Burke, T. (1989) *The Green Capitalists: How to Make Money and Protect the Environment*. London: Victor Gollancz.

Elliott, B. (ed.) (1988) *Technology and Social Process*. Edinburgh: Edinburgh University Press.

Emery, F. and Trist, E.L. (1965) 'The causal texture of organizational environments', *Human Relations*, 18(1): 21–32.

Evan, W.M. (1966) 'The organization set: toward a theory of interorganizational relations', in J. Thompson (ed.), *Approaches to Organizational Design*. Pittsburgh: University of Pittsburgh Press.

Fellmeth, R.C. (1970) *The Interstate Commerce Commission*. New York: Grossman.

Feshbach, M. and Friendly, A. Jr (1992) *Ecocide in the USSR: Health and Nature under Siege*. New York: Basic Books.

Feyerherm, A.E. (1994) 'Leadership in collaboration: a longitudinal study of two interorganizational rule-making groups', *Leadership Quarterly*, 5(3/4).

Fisher, D. (1993) 'The emergence of the environmental movement in Eastern Europe and its role in the revolutions of 1989', in B. Jancar-Webster (ed.), *Environmental Action in Eastern Europe: Responses to Crisis*. Armonck, NY: M.E. Sharpe. pp. 89–113.

Flannery, B.L. and May, D.R. (1994) 'Prominent factors influencing environmental leadership: application of a theoretical model in the waste management industry', *Leadership Quarterly*, 5(3/4).

Fox, S. (1981) *John Muir and his Legacy*. Boston: Little, Brown.

Fox, W. (1990) *Toward a Transpersonal Ecology: Developing New Foundations for Environmentalism*. Boston: Shambhala.

Friend, A.M. (1992) 'Economics, ecology and sustainable development: are they compatible?', *Environmental Values*, 1(2): 157–70.

Gamson, W.A., Croteau, D., Hoynes, W. and Sasson, T. (1992) 'Media images and the social construction of reality', *Annual Review of Sociology*, 18: 373–93.

Georgescu-Rogen, N. (1971) *The Entropy Law and the Economic Process*. Cambridge, MA: Harvard University Press.

Gladwin, T.N. (1993) 'The meaning of greening: a plea for organizational theory', in K. Fischer and J. Schot (eds), *Environmental Strategies for Industry: International Perspectives on Research Needs and Policy Implications*. Washington, DC: Island Press. pp. 37–61.

Gleick, J. (1987) *Chaos: Making a New Science*. New York: Penguin.

Gray, B. (1989) *Collaborating: Finding Common Ground for Multiparty Problems*. San Francisco: Jossey-Bass.

Grundmann, R. (1991) *Marxism and Ecology*. Oxford: Clarendon Press.

Hahn, R.W. and Hester, G.L. (1989) 'Marketable permits: lessons for theory and practice', *Ecology Law Quarterly*, 16(2): 361–406.

Hannan, M.T. and Freeman, J. (1977) 'The population ecology of organizations', *American Journal of Sociology*, 82: 929–64.

Hardin, G. (1968) 'The tragedy of the commons', *Science*, 162(13 December): 1243–8.

Hardin, G. (1991) 'The tragedy of the unmanaged commons: population and the disguises of providence', in R.V. Andelson (ed.), *Commons without Tragedy: Protecting the Environment from Overpopulation – a New Approach*. London: Shepheard-Walwyn. pp. 162–85.

Hawken, P. (1993) *The Ecology of Commerce: A Declaration of Sustainability*. New York: Harper Business.

Hawley, A.H. (1950) *Human Ecology*. New York: Ronald.

Hay, P.R. and Haward, M.G. (1988) 'Comparative green politics: beyond the European context?', *Political Studies*, 36: 433–48.

Hays, S.P. (1987) *Beauty, Health, and Permanence: Environmental Politics in the United States 1955–1985*. New York: Cambridge University Press.

Hughes, J.D. (1975) *Ecology in Ancient Civilizations*. Albuquerque: University of New Mexico Press.

Hull, F. (ed.) (1993) *Earth and Spirit: the Spiritual Dimension of the Environmental Crisis*. New York: Continuum.

Ilinitch, A.Y. and Schaltegger, S.C. (1993) 'Eco-integrated-portfolio analysis: a strategic tool for managing sustainably'. Paper presented at the 1993 Academy of Management Meeting, Atlanta.

Irvine, S. and Ponton, A. (1988) *A Green Manifesto*. London: Macdonald Optima.

Jacobs, M. (1993) *The Green Economy: Environment, Sustainable Development and the Politics of the Future*. Vancouver, BC: UBC Press.

Jacobs, R. (1991) 'Deep ecology: a philosophy for the twenty-first century?', *Tijdschrift voor Sociale Wetenschappen*, 36(4): 364–99.

Jancar-Webster, B. (ed.) (1993) *Environmental Action in Eastern Europe: Responses to Crisis*. Armonck, NY: M.E. Sharpe.

Jung, H.Y. (1991) 'Marxism and deep ecology in postmodernity: from *Homo oeconomicus* to *Homo ecologicus*', *Thesis Eleven*, 28: 86–99.

Jurkovich, R. (1974) 'A core typology of organizational environments', *Administrative Science Quarterly*, 19(3): 380–90.

Kassas, M. and Polunin, N. (1989) 'The three systems of man', *Environmental Conservation*, 16(1): 7–11.

Keating, M. (1993) *The Earth Summit's Agenda for Change: a Plain Language Version of Agenda 21 and the Other Rio Agreements*. Geneva: Centre for Our Common Future.

Kellert, S.R. (1993) 'The biological basis for human

values of nature', in S.R. Kellert and E.O. Wilson (eds), *The Biophilia Hypothesis*. Washington, DC: Island Press. pp. 42–69.

King, Y. (1989) 'The ecology of feminism and the feminism of ecology', in J. Plant (ed.), *Healing the Wounds: The Promise of Ecofeminism*. Santa Cruz, CA: New Society. pp. 18–28.

Kleindorfer, P.K. and Kunreuther, H.C. (eds) (1986) *Insuring and Managing Hazardous Risks: from Seveso to Bhopal and Beyond*. Berlin/New York: IIASA and Springer-Verlag.

Lawrence, P.R. and Lorsch, J.W. (1967) *Organization and Environment*. Boston: Harvard University Press.

Lee, D.C. (1980) 'On the Marxian view of the relationship between man and nature', *Environmental Ethics*, 2(1): 3–16.

Leopold, A. (1949) *A Sand County Almanac with Essays on Conservation from Round River*. New York: Ballantine Books, 1966.

Levine, S. and White, P.E. (1961) 'Exchange as a conceptual framework for the study of interorganizational relationships', *Administrative Science Quarterly*, 5: 583–601.

Lovelock, J.E. (1979) *Gaia: a New Look at Life on Earth*. Oxford: Oxford University Press.

Lovelock, J.E. (1988) *The Ages of Gaia: a Biography of Our Living Earth*. Oxford: Oxford University Press.

Luke, T. (1988) 'The dreams of deep ecology', *Telos*, 76(Summer): 65–92.

MacLarkey, R.L. (1991) 'The emergence of environmental legislation and policy in the Great Lakes ecosystem', *International Review of Modern Sociology*, 21(2): 93–111.

Manes, C. (1990) *Green Rage: Radical Environmentalism and the Unmaking of Civilization*. Boston: Little, Brown.

Maniha, J.K. and Perrow, C. (1965) 'The reluctant organization and the aggressive environment', *Administrative Science Quarterly*, 10: 238–57.

March, J.G. (1978) 'Bounded rationality, ambiguity, and the engineering of choice', *Bell Journal of Economics*, 9: 587–608.

McCloskey, M. (1991) 'Twenty years of change in the environmental movement: an insider's view', *Society and Natural Resources*, 4(3): 273–84.

McGowan, R.A. and Mahon, J.F. (1991) 'Multiple games multiple levels: the greening of strategy on environmental issues'. Paper presented at the Strategic Management Society Annual Conference, Toronto.

McIntosh, R.P. (1985) *The Background of Ecology: Concept and Theory*. Cambridge: Cambridge University Press.

McLaughlin, A. (1990) 'Ecology, capitalism and socialism', *Socialism and Democracy*, 10 (Spring–Summer): 69–102.

McRobert, D. and Muldoon, P. (1992) 'Towards a bioregional perspective on international resource-use conflicts: lessons for the future', in M. Ross and J.O. Saunders (eds), *Growing Demands on a Shrinking Heritage: Managing Resource-Use Conflicts: Essays from the Fifth Institute Conference on Natural Resources Law*. Calgary: Canadian Institute of Resources Law. pp. 187–215.

Merchant, C. (1980) *The Death of Nature: Women, Ecology, and the Scientific Revolution*. New York: Harper & Row.

Merchant, C. (1992) *Radical Ecology: the Search for a Livable World*. New York: Routledge.

Meyer, J.W. and Rowan, B. (1983) *Organizational Environments: Ritual and Rationality*. Beverly Hills, CA: Sage.

Meyer, J.W. and Scott, W.R. (1983) *Organizational Environments: Ritual and Rationality*. Beverly Hills, CA: Sage.

Milbrath, L.W. (1989) *Envisioning a Sustainable Society: Learning Our Way Out*. Albany, NY: State University of New York Press.

Morgan, G. (1980) 'Paradigms, metaphors, and puzzle solving in organizational theory', *Administrative Science Quarterly*, 25: 605–22.

Mumford, L. (1938) *The Culture of Cities*. New York: Harcourt Brace Jovanovich.

Naess, A. (1973) 'The shallow and the deep, long-range ecology movements: a summary', *Inquiry*, 16: 95–100.

Naess, A. (1984) 'A defense of the deep ecology movement', *Environmental Ethics*, 6(3): 265–70.

Naess, A. (1988) 'Identification as a source of deep ecological attitudes', in M. Tobias (ed.), *Deep Ecology*. San Marcos, CA: Avant Books. pp. 256–70.

Namboodiri, K. (1988) 'Ecological demography: its place in sociology', *American Sociological Review*, 53(August): 619–33.

Nemetz, P.N. (1986) 'Federal environmental regulation in Canada', *Natural Resources Journal*, 26(Summer): 551–608.

Osborne, R.N. and Hunt, J.G. (1974) 'Environment and organizational effectiveness', *Administrative Science Quarterly* 19(2): 231–46.

Paehlke, R.C. (1989) *Environmentalism and the Future of Progressive Politics*. New Haven, CT: Yale University Press.

Paehlke, R.C. (1990) 'Regulatory and non-regulatory approaches to environmental protection', *Canadian Public Administration*, 33(1): 17–36.

Pasquero, J. (1991) 'Supraorganizational collaboration: the Canadian environmental experiment', *Journal of Applied Behavioral Science*, 27(1): 38–64.

Pepper, D. (1993) *Eco-socialism: from Deep Ecology to Social Justice*. London: Routledge.

Perrow, C. (1972) *Complex Organizations: a Critical Essay*. Glenview, IL: Scott, Foresman.

Perrow, C. (1973) 'The short and glorious history of organization theory', *Organizational Dynamics*, 2(1): 2–15.

Perrow, C. (1984) *Normal Accidents: Living with High-Risk Technologies*. New York: Basic Books.

Pinfield, L. and Berner, M. (1992) 'The greening of the press: a case study of stakeholder accountability and the corporate management of environmentalist publics', *Business Strategy and the Environment*, 1(3): 23–33.

Plant, J. (ed.) (1989) *Healing the Wounds: the Promise of Ecofeminism*. Santa Cruz, CA: New Society Press.

Porritt, J. (1984) *Seeing Green: The Politics of Ecology Explained*. Oxford: Blackwell.

Powell, W.W. and DiMaggio, P.J. (eds) (1991) *The New Institutionalism in Organizational Analysis*. Chicago: University of Chicago Press.

Raskin, P.D. and Bernow, S.S. (1991) 'Ecology and Marxism: are green and red complementary?', *Rethinking Marxism*, 4(10): 87–103.

Reason, P. (1993) 'Reflections on sacred experience and sacred science', *Journal of Management Inquiry*, 2(3): 273–83.

Rice, F. (1993) 'Who scores best on the environment', *Fortune*, 128(2): 114–22.

Rich, B. (1990) 'The emperor's new clothes: the World Bank and environmental reform', *World Policy Journal*, 7(2): 305–29.

Rifkin, J. (1983) *Algeny: a New Word – a New World*. New York: Penguin.

Routley, R. (1983) 'Roles and limits of paradigms in environmental thought and action', in R. Elliot and A. Gare (eds), *Environmental Philosophy*. St Lucia, Queensland, Australia: University of Queensland Press. pp. 260–93.

Rudig, W. and Lowe, P.D. (1986) 'The withered "greening" of British politics: a study of the Ecology Party', *Political Studies*, 34: 262–84.

Russo, M.V. and Fouts, P.A. (1993) 'The green carrot: Do markets reward corporate environmentalism?'. Paper presented at the Academy of Management Annual Meeting, Atlanta.

Sale, K. (1985) *Dwellers of the Land: the Bioregional Vision*. San Francisco: Sierra Club.

Sale, K. (1993) *The Green Revolution: the American Environmental Movement 1962–1992*. New York: Hill and Wang.

Salleh, A.K. (1984) 'Deeper than deep ecology: the eco-feminist connection', *Environmental Ethics*, 6: 339–45.

Samuel, P. and Spencer, P. (1993) 'Facts catch up with "political" science', *Consumer's Research*, May: 1–14.

Samuelson, P.A. (1993) 'Altruism as a problem involving group versus individual selection in economics and biology', *AEA Papers and Proceedings*, 83(2): 143–8.

Sarkar, S. (1986) 'The green movement in West Germany', *Alternatives*, 11: 219–54.

Schaltegger, S.C. (1993) 'Strategic management and measurement of corporate pollution. Ecological accounting: a strategic approach for environmental assessment'. Discussion paper 183, Strategic Management Research Center, University of Minnesota.

Schelling, T.C. (1992) 'Some economies of global warming', *American Economic Review*, 82(1): 1–14.

Schmidheiny, S. (1992) *Changing Course: a Global Business Perspective on Development and the Environment*. Cambridge, MA: MIT Press.

Schnaiberg, A. and Gould, K.A. (1994) *Environment and Society: the Enduring Conflict*. New York: St Martin's Press.

Schot, J. (1991) 'Credibility and markets as greening forces for the chemical industry'. Paper presented at the Strategic Management Society Annual Conference, Toronto.

Schumacher, E.F. (1973) *Small is Beautiful: a Study of Economics As If People Mattered*. London: Sphere.

Schweitzer, G.E. (1977) 'Regulations, technological progress, and societal interests', *Research Management*, 20(1): 13–17.

Scott, M. and Rothman, H. (1992) *Companies with a Conscience: Intimate Portraits of Twelve Firms that Make a Difference*. New York: Birch Land Press.

Scott, W.R. (1981) *Organizations: Rational, Natural and Open Systems*. Englewood Cliffs, NJ: Prentice Hall.

Scott, W.R. (1992) *Organiztions: Rational, Natural and Open Systems*, 3rd edn. Englewood, NJ: Prentice Hall.

Selznick, P. (1948) 'Foundations of a theory of organizations', *American Sociological Review*, 13: 25–35.

Selznick, P. (1957) *Leadership in Administration*. Evanston, IL: Row, Peterson.

Serafin, R. (1988) 'Noosphere, Gaia, and the science of the biosphere', *Environmental Ethics*, 10(2): 121–37.

Sessions, G. (1987) 'The deep ecology movement: a review', *Environmental Review*, 11(2): 105–25.

Sharfman, M. and Ellington, R.T. (1993) 'Management for total environmental quality: antecedents and organizational implications'. Paper presented at the 1993 Academy of Management Annual Meeting, Atlanta.

Shiva, V. (1988) *Staying Alive*. London: Zed Books.

Shiva, V. (1993) *Monocultures of the Mind: Perspectives on Biodiversity and Biotechnology*. London: Zed Books.

Shrivastava, P. (1992) 'Corporate self-greenewal: strategic responses to environmentalism', *Business Strategy and the Environment*, 1(3): 9–22.

Shrivastava, P. (1994) *Greening Business: towards Sustainable Corporations*. Cincinnati: Thompson Executive Press.

Simmons, P. and Wynne, B. (1993) 'Responsible care: credibility, trust and environmental management in the British chemical industry', in K. Fischer and J. Schot (eds), *Environmental Strategies for Industry: International Perspectives on Research Needs and Policy Implications*. Washington, DC: Island Press. pp. 201–26.

Simon, H.A. (1991) 'Organizations and markets', *Journal of Economic Perspectives*, 5(2): 25–44.

Simon, H.A. (1993) 'Altruism and economics', *AEA Papers and Proceedings*, 83(2): 156–61.

Sitarz, D. (ed.) (1993) *Agenda 21: the Earth Summit Strategy to Save Our Planet*. Boulder, CO: Earth-Press.

Slaton, C.D. (1992) 'The failure of the United States

greens to root in fertile soil', *Research in Social Movements, Conflicts and Change*, Supplement 2: 83–117.

Smuts, J. (1926) *Holism and Evolution*. London: Macmillan.

Snow, D. (1992a) *Inside the Environmental Movement: Meeting the Leadership Challenge*. Washington, DC: Island Press.

Snow, D. (ed.) (1992b) *Voices from the Environmental Movement: Perspectives for a New Era*. Washington, DC: Island Press.

Spretnak, C. and Capra, F. (1986) *Green Politics*. Santa Fe, NM: Bear.

Starbuck, W.H. (1976) 'Organizations and their environments', in M.D. Dunnette (ed.), *Handbook of Industrial and Organizational Psychology*. Chicago: Rand McNally.

Starbuck, W.H. (1983) 'Organizations as action generators', *American Sociological Review*, 48: 91–102.

Stead, W.E. and Stead, J.G. (1992) *Management for a Small Planet: Strategic Decision Making and the Environment*. Newbury Park, CA: Sage.

Steger, U. (1993) 'The greening of the board room: how European companies are dealing with environmental issues', in K. Fischer and J. Schot (eds), *Environmental Strategies for Industry: International Perspectives on Research Needs and Policy Implications*. Washington, DC: Island Press. pp. 147–66.

Strong, D.H. (1988) *Dreamers and Defenders: American Conservationists*. Lincoln, NE: University of Nebraska Press.

Terryberry, S. (1967) 'The evolution of organizational environments', *Administrative Science Quarterly*, 12(4): 590–613.

*The Ecologist* (1993) *Whose Common Future? Reclaiming the Commons*. Philadelphia: New Society Publishers.

Thompson, J.D. (1967) *Organizations in Action*. New York: McGraw-Hill.

Throop, G.M. (1991) 'Strategy in a greening environment: supply and demand matching in U.S. and Canadian electricity generation'. Paper presented at the Strategic Management Society Annual Conference, Toronto.

Tokar, B. (1988) 'Social ecology, deep ecology, and the future of green political thought', *The Ecologist*, 18(4/5): 132–45.

Trist, E.L. (1983) 'Referent organizations and the development of interorganizational domains', *Human Relations*, 36: 247–68.

Wall, D. (1994) *Green History: a Reader in Environmental Literature, Philosophy and Politics*. New York: Routledge.

Wallace, A. (1993) *Eco-Heroes: Twelve Tales of Environmental Victory*. San Francisco: Mercury House.

Warren, K.J. (1990) 'The power and the promise of ecological feminism', *Environmental Ethics*, 12(2): 125–46.

Warren, R.L. (1967) 'The interorganizational field as a focus for investigation', *Administrative Science Quarterly*, 12: 396–419.

Weick, K.E. (1979) *The Social Psychology of Organizing*, 2nd edn. Reading, MA: Addison-Wesley.

Weick, K.E. and Roberts, K.H. (1993) 'Collective mind in organizations: heedful interrelating on flight decks', *Administrative Science Quarterly*, 38: 357–81.

Westley, F. and Vredenburg, H. (1991) 'Strategic bridging: the collaboration between environmentalists and business in the marketing of green products', *Journal of Applied Behavioral Science*, 27(1): 65–90.

Wexler, M. (1990) 'Deep ecology: grounding a contemporary argument field', *International Journal of Sociology and Social Policy*, 10(1): 47–70.

White, L. Jr (1967) 'Historical roots of our ecologic crisis', *Science*, 155: 1203–7.

Wiener, N. (1954) *The Human Use of Human Beings: Cybernetics and Society*. Boston: Houghton Mifflin.

Wilson, E.O. (1975) *Sociobiology: the New Synthesis*. Cambridge, MA: Harvard University Press.

Wilson, E.O. (1984) *Biophilia: the Human Bond with Other Species*. Cambridge, MA: Harvard University Press.

Wilson, E.O. (1992) *The Diversity of Life*. Cambridge, MA: Belknap Press of Harvard University Press.

Women's Environment and Development Organization (WEDO) (1992) *Official Report: World Women's Congress for a Healthy Planet*. New York: Women's Environment and Development Organization.

World Commission on Environment and Development (1987) *Our Common Future*. New York: Oxford University Press.

Worster, D. (1977) *Nature's Economy: the Roots of Ecology*. San Francisco: Sierra Club Books.

Young, R.C. (1988) 'Is population ecology a useful paradigm for the study of organizations?', *American Journal of Sociology*, 94(1): 1–24.

# 12

# Evolution and Revolution: from International Business to Globalization

## BARBARA PARKER

There is a growing sense that events occurring throughout the world are converging rapidly to shape a single, integrated world where economic, social, cultural, technological, business, and other influences cross traditional borders and boundaries such as nations, national cultures, time, space, and industries with increasing ease. The resulting dissolution of traditional boundaries of every kind has blurred distinctions that once seemed clear. Business activities, for example, are conducted or shaped by enterprises outside the business sector such as nongovernmental organizations. Activities such as these blur the borders between sectors that once were more clearly defined: it is no longer so easy as it once was to call on visual or verbal cues to distinguish between advertisements and content; between men and women; between what is real and what is virtual; between what organizations can do and what they should do. The implications of such changes are potentially *revolutionary*, leading to significant and wide-ranging changes in every sphere of life and creating new challenges and responsibilities for organizations of all types.

The conceptual and practical demands for interpreting any single aspect of global change are enormous, and these demands multiply when rapid and simultaneous change occurs in many sectors, interacts, and changes again. Global economic shifts, for example, motivated political sponsorship of the World Trade Organization and common commercial rules worldwide. Simple enough. But because trade barriers are embedded in each nation's traditions, dismantling them forces us to breach still other boundaries. Traditional practices are recast as

human rights violations; cultural traditions add up to an affront to immigration policies; diseases that afflict humans, animals and crops are exported along with consumer durables. This example illustrates that political and economic events of global scope also have cultural, political, technological and human implications; and as the economic fortunes of individuals, organizations, and nations are linked to one another, new interdependencies of many kinds also are created. Organizations are not simply affected by globalization: the combined activities of all kinds of organizations stimulate, facilitate, sustain, and extend globalization. In the search for new products and markets, business enterprises spread not only consumer goods but ideas concerning wealth creation; ideals concerning how people should live and work; ideologies concerning political and business governance. Nor are the parameters of business in the global world easily controlled: a telephone link to the Internet yields tips on guerrilla tactics or access to kiddie porn as readily as it provides the latest Dow-Jones index; mafia organizations and drug cartels operate in a worldwide arena with as much expertise as Shell, Imperial Chemical Industries or Exxon. Global business is not, then, just about business: it has cultural, legal, political and social effects as much as economic ones.

Current knowledge of such global phenomena might, however, be described as *evolutionary*. As academics and practitioners, we still know so little about globalization. Reports from business people confirm that organizational life, as well as life apart from organizations, occurs in the context of an increasingly global world. Most would doubtless agree that this global world is having a revolutionary effect on life and work; that the dissolution and permeation of boundaries of every type create both opportunities and challenges for organizations and their people. Those who manage organizations under conditions of globalization also recognize the multiplicity, variety and complexity of issues associated with it, but many are too busy coping with change either to document or to explain it. Consequently, descriptions of the practices associated with these revolutionary changes are more anecdotal than organized.

Writers disagree about the impact of globalization: some contest that globalization is a phenomenon deserving of notice (Farnham 1994); others believe globalization began some time ago (Ohmae 1985) and so now the challenge is simply to face up to it (Henzler and Rall 1986). There is a lack of consensus about what globalization is and means. In the social sciences alone, Pieterse (1995) points out there are almost as many conceptualizations of globalization as there are disciplines. Some writers have focused on globalization as the crossing of national borders; others have emphasized its effect on other boundaries as traditional concepts of time, space, scope, geography, functions, thought, cultural assumptions, and the understanding of the self in relation to others are redefined and reduced (Rhinesmith 1993). Some writers have emphasized the permeation of boundaries between organizations as new alliances are formed; others have pointed to changes with organizations as vertical boundaries of level and rank are razed, and horizontal boundaries of function and discipline are merged (Ashkenas et al. 1995).

These definitional differences are more than semantic; each shapes assumptions about what the other is saying or should be allowed to say, and directs and limits the further exploration of globalization. For example, a sociological approach to globalization represents this phenomenon as 'the compression of the world and the intensification of consciousness of the world as a whole' (Robertson 1992: 8). Globalization is more usually described in the business literature as shifts in traditional patterns of international production, investment, and trade (Dicken 1992); or as interconnections between overlapping interests of business and society (Brown 1992; Renesch 1992). A popular view of globalization is as the absence of borders and barriers to trade between nations (Sera 1992; Ohmae 1995).

This conceptualization of globalization as national 'borderlessness' might lead some to conclude that globalization is producing a worldwide trend towards homogeneity and uniformity. Others, however, have pointed out that as boundaries dissolve, as barriers are permeated, as the world compresses, as we become interdependent, we become more aware of cultural *difference* and diversity (Kahn 1995; Robertson 1995):

> one paradoxical consequence of the process of globalization, the awareness of the finitude and boundedness of the planet and humanity, is not to produce homogeneity but to familiarize us with greater diversity, the extensive range of local cultures. (Robertson 1995: 86)

Thus the call to 'act global, think local' and become part of the 'global village' worldwide is hindered by the tendency to define, describe and envision globalization in quite different ways.

If we are confused about what globalization means now, we are also perplexed about what it will mean for the future. Some observers argue that the domestic and international diversity promoted by globalization will be 'the engine that drives the creative energy of the corporation of the 21st century' (Rhinesmith 1993: 4). According to this view, globalization will create worldwide opportunities for growth and development by expanding options for both organizations and people across the world; create employment opportunities for thousands of impoverished people; help forge entrepreneurial infrastructure for developing countries; contribute to the process of democratization; and address global social problems (e.g. Pieterse 1995; Cooperrider and Passmore 1991; see Gergen 1995). Others believe that the same activities will lead to the exploitation of foreign workers; limit choices to unappealing options like 'McWorld' and 'Jihad'; and destroy natural resources and local cultures (e.g. Lavipour and Sauvant 1976; Barber 1992).

So, despite the magnitude of the global 'revolution'; despite the complexities, uncertainties, and rapid rates of change that it has brought about; despite the degree to which business is implicated in and affected by globalization, it remains difficult, from an academic perspective, to say what is occurring and why. And it is even more difficult to say which tools and techniques are appropriate when managing the global enterprise, particularly since globalization makes it possible for organizations of every size and type and from any geographic location to participate in business activities. These changes suggest that current theories of markets and organizations bear reexamination and possible revision in the light of globalization. For example, while some writers proclaim that bureaucracy in its various forms is, or ought to be, dead, there is evidence to show that principles of bureaucracy may have as much currency today as ever. But in a new form: coexisting alongside newer organizational forms, some of which are distinctly counter-bureaucratic. The expanding choices for organizations involve more complex, hybrid structures and processes capable of surviving and thriving in the global marketplace. This, in turn, requires more sophisticated research 'which combines a comprehensive overview of the systems in which firms operate with examination of specific inner workings of the systems themselves' (Earley and Singh 1995: 337), research that can deal with the complexity of the global enterprise (see Melin 1992).

There is, then, a need for a comprehensive, interdisciplinary look at globalization and its effects on late twentieth century life. This chapter structures this task by looking at the nature of globalization in the business context: what causes it; what it looks like; how business drives it; how business is affected by it; and what it might mean, not just for business, but for those of us, all of us, who make up the global world. The first section describes how international business research has changed over the last fifty years. The second discusses the characteristics of the global enterprise, showing how it engages in a different set of activities than the international or multinational business. The third section shows how globalization is a phenomenon which embraces far more than just the global enterprise: it involves far more fundamental and broadly based changes. It explores how five particular contexts are affected by these changes: economy; politics; culture; technology; and natural resources. Finally, some of the implications of globalization for business and other organizations are discussed.

In the end, this chapter asks more questions than it answers. Rather than document what we know about the comparatively evident field of international business, it points out what we do not know about globalization. It tries to clarify some of the profound implications that globalization has for all societies. In pointing out these implications and the tensions they involve, we may be better prepared to consider how a new research agenda might evolve.

## THE PATH FROM INTERNATIONAL TO GLOBAL BUSINESS

There is not yet a clear answer to the question: what is globalization? Global challenges traditionally have been those that impact the planet and its people as a whole, because 'virtually all human activity is confined to the biological and physical boundaries of the Earth' (Stead and Stead 1994: 369). Air and water, for example, have long been identified as a global common because the earth's population equally depends on these resources for survival, and all are affected by activities that degrade or alter availability for these commonly held resources. Today, concern for use of natural resources is joined by other global concerns, concerns not nearly so visible but just as important to the future. This section starts the examination of what globalization is, making particular reference to the business world by showing how business research has evolved. In the following section, a closer look is given to the global enterprise, and it is argued that the global firm engages in a different set of activities and creates additional responsibilities for organizations than does international business. In particular, we stress that business enterprises operate in a world with more permeable borders along national, spatial, and cultural divides as interconnections between business and other activities increase, but that organizational borders are themselves more permeable than they once were.

The academic study of international business (IB) is a fairly recent phenomenon, beginning with formal IB studies that appeared after World War II as US exports and foreign direct investment (FDI) came to play an important role in world reconstruction and development. Until the 1960s, the bulk of IB research focused on economic explanations for trade flows between countries, reflecting its roots in macroeconomic theory and a heavy emphasis on the theory of comparative advantage (Bartlett and Ghoshal 1991; also see Grosse and Behrman 1992; Dunning 1993).

From the 1960s on, the field grew and diversified (Melin 1992). An impetus was Hymer's (1976) thesis, originally published in 1960, on patterns of FDI triggered by the post-war expansion of multinational enterprises (MNEs), which led to the development of different, complementary streams of research: on the link between FDI and oligopolistic competition (e.g. Caves 1971); on the relationship between the product life cycle and internationalization (e.g. Vernon 1966); and, by the late 1970s, on the existence and behavior of MNEs using Williamson's (1975) work on transaction costs (e.g. Buckley and Casson 1976; Rugman 1980; Hennart 1982; see Bartlett and Ghoshal 1991). Another stream of research stemmed from the Uppsala School, which studied how firms gradually increase their international involvement (e.g. Johanson and Vahlne 1977; also see Melin 1992).

By the 1970s, a field of IB, separate from economics, had been established. First, it concentrated on:

firm-level business activity that crosses national boundaries or is conducted in a location other than the firm's home country. (This activity may be the movement of goods, capital, people, and know-how, or it may be manufacturing, extraction, construction, banking, shipping, advertising, and the like.) Second, it [was] concerned in some way with the interrelationships between the operations of the business firm and international or foreign environments in which the firm operates. (Nehrt et al. 1970)

During this time, the focus shifted from the international economy to include the firm and internal processes within the firm, as synthesized by Dunning's (1988) 'eclectic paradigm' of FDI, which included ownership-specific, localization and internationalization explanatory variables of an MNE's pattern of FDI. Work in this growing field was published in newly founded journals: nineteen journals publishing IB research were introduced in the 1970s, a 50 per cent increase in the number of outlets previously available for IB research, and another eighteen were added in the 1980s (Pierce and Garven 1995). The growing importance of trade and investments to firms and the increased complexity of their operating environments also made it possible to publish IB research in non-IB journals, although its impact was still limited: Adler's (1983) review of publishing trends in cross-cultural management throughout the 1970s showed that less than 5 per cent of articles appearing in the top management journals looked at organizational behavior issues from a cross-cultural or international perspective. Consistent with the definition provided by Nehrt et al. (1970), this IB research did *not* include studies of economic development, foreign trade, or the international monetary system (because they 'belonged' to academic fields in development and international economics); or foreign legal, political, economic and social environments (because they fell under the purview of academic disciplines like law, political science, economics and behavioral science).

At the same time as formal studies of IB were emerging, international management (IM) research also developed with an emphasis on a stronger administrative focus following the work of writers like Aharoni (1966), who explored the process of FDI from a managerial perspective; Fayerweather (1969) who discussed MNE responsiveness to the cultural, political and economic characteristics of individual countries; and Perlmutter (1969) who described the evolution of the structures of MNEs. Stopford and Wells (1972), Franko (1976) and Dyas and Thanheiser (1976) extended Chandler's (1962) strategy/structure work to the international organization. Over time, other writers such as

Prahalad, Doz, Bartlett and Hedlund started to examine management actions and strategic processes in MNEs (see Bartlett and Ghoshal 1991; Melin 1992).

The 1970s also marked a change in the types of issues tackled by researchers, as host countries started to question MNEs' ethnocentric stances and, in some cases, reject the role multinationals played (Robinson 1981). Growing nationalism and concerns about the political roles of MNEs led to nationalization of some industries and firms, and increased regulations for others. At the same time, competition was increasingly coming from Europe and from Japan. Accordingly, research started to examine links between the firm and its political environment; political risk analysis and bargaining represented two approaches to understanding the political environment of international business (e.g. Moran 1973; 1974; Rummel and Heenan 1978). Competitive strategy analyses focused on the relationship between industry conditions and organizations (e.g. Porter 1980; 1985). The growing importance of cultural sensitivity to international business success was demonstrated by Hofstede's (1980; 1983) comparative studies of national culture traits, and Ronen and Shenkar's (1985) clustering of countries on the basis of work values and attitudes. In as much as many of the new powerhouse competitors were Japanese firms, interest also developed in studies of Japanese firms and business techniques unique to Japan, particularly total quality concepts and their implications for non-Japanese firms (Reitsperger and Daniel 1990). The structures first suggested by Stopford and Wells (1972) were further explored to identify structural forms appropriate to a variety of multi-national strategies (Daniels et al. 1984) or to include contingencies as a factor in explaining MNE choices (Lemak and Bracker 1988). The interest in structural forms and formal control mechanisms in the 1970s shifted towards less formal forms of coordination (Melin 1992; see Martinez and Jarillo 1989). A more sophisticated and process-oriented view of international strategy replaced the work on strategy/structure 'fit' (e.g. Beamish et al. 1991; Melin 1992), focusing attention on the need to achieve a broader congruence between strategy, structure, and systems (Ghoshal and Bartlett 1995). Other researchers focused on network approaches to understanding international business (e.g. Hedlund 1986); designing global strategies (e.g. Kogut 1989); global alliances (Hamel 1991; Hedlund and Rolander 1990); and learning (Bartlett and Ghoshal 1989; Hamel 1991).

Much of the early research in IB had exhibited a belief in US superiority expressed by Henry Luce when he called this time period 'the

American century'. Research had been characterized by 'American researchers focused on American firms, American perspectives, and those questions most salient to American managers' (Boyacigiller and Adler 1991: 264). Economic success and both public and academic reinforcement doubtless confirmed an impression that bureaucratic management practices as developed by US firms were superior, an impression Robinson (1971) referred to in his presidential address to the Association for Education in International Business. Despite some changes, IB research continues to be produced primarily by scholars in the US (Pierce and Garven 1995) focusing on a small group of countries and explicitly or implicitly reinforcing Western business practices as a norm (Boyacigiller and Adler 1991). For example, a twenty-five year review of the *Journal of International Business Studies* revealed that published studies primarily examined G-7 nations with fully 40 per cent featuring the US (Thomas et al. 1994).

IB research has also developed, primarily, along disciplinary lines. Originally, many distinguished international scholars were lodged in existing departments. Today, although many departments of international business exist, IB research continues to be functionally oriented (Inkpen and Beamish 1994). Melin (1992) identifies seven fairly distinct areas of IB built on relatively narrow disciplinary lines, including finance, cross-cultural management, human resource management, and foreign direct investment. In addition, international business research has often been viewed as peripheral and less important than 'mainstream' disciplinary research (Thomas et al. 1994).

The disciplinary basis and the Western orientation that continue to characterize much of the research in the field of IB hamper comprehensive international research and teaching. In addition, the experience of globalization presents further challenges, to which IB research also must respond. One concerns the complexity of the global enterprise: a weakness in the understanding of *processes* has made it difficult for researchers to explain and document the new and different practices that are emerging in these organizations (Melin 1992). As individual, autonomous organizations are evolving into complex global networks, the organization as a unit of analysis is no longer the most useful way to study them. As the intricacies of diffusing learning across a spatially dispersed, culturally diverse enterprise become apparent, the focus on formal structure and coordination seems misplaced. As the complexity of sustaining a global strategy becomes more difficult, the need for a more sophisticated examination of the link between structure, strategy, systems and processes within an environment becomes apparent (see Bartlett and Ghoshal 1991; Melin 1992). The next section examines the complexity and confusion concerning the global enterprise in more detail.

## THE GLOBAL ENTERPRISE

The global enterprise is not well defined. There has been a strong research emphasis on large organizations, and large organizations have been important actors in internationalization as well as globalization. Either of these facts might lead some to conclude that globalization affects only large organizations from economically developed countries. This section will demonstrate how inconsistent use of the term 'global' has led to this misconception; it will define the global enterprise and identify those core competencies that appear to be most important to success and survival in a globalizing world. In so doing, it will demonstrate that the potential to engage in global activities is not confined to large organizations, but that many different types of organizations are 'going global' and they face similar challenges as a result.

The global enterprise is associated with both different activities and a different attitude from its more circumscribed, international predecessor.

> internationalization connotes expanding interfaces between nations sometimes implying political invasion or domination. Internationalization of business, therefore, is a concept of an action in which nationality is strongly in people's consciousness. It means the flow of business, goods or capital from one country into another. Globalization, by contrast, looks at the whole world as being nationless and borderless. Goods, capital, and people have to be moving freely. (Sera 1992: 89)

The international firm is one whose business activities cross national boundaries (Ball and McCullough 1990), or that is involved in business in two or more countries (Daniels and Radebaugh 1992). According to Hordes et al. (1995) its headquarters are almost always based in a single country, although it might establish partial or complete operations in others. Its culture and organizational structure are consistent with the practices and norms of the home or headquarters country. It adopts standardized technologies and business processes throughout its operations, regardless of where they are located, and it relies on similar policies, especially regarding human resources, worldwide.

Despite what is likely to be a consensus that the global enterprise differs from the international enterprise, the exact nature of the former and its distinction from, say, the multi-national enterprise is far less clear and particularly less clear to practitioners (Leong and Tan 1993). Research has tended to produce different and often confusing definitions. For example, Bartlett and Ghoshal (1989) differentiate between the international organization, which is a coordinated federation in which the parent company transfers knowledge and expertise to foreign markets; the multinational organization, which is a 'decentralized federation of assets and responsibilities' (1989: 49) that allows foreign operations to respond to local differences; and the global organization, which is a centralized hub where most assets and decisions are centralized. Bartlett and Ghoshal (1989) found empirical evidence for all three types but maintained that each encountered problems in dealing with globalization. They proposed an ideal form called the transnational organization, an integrated network where efficiency is balanced with local responsiveness to obtain both global competitiveness and flexibility in an organization dedicated to organizational learning and innovation. Thus, according to these and other authors (Adler and Bartholomew 1992) it is the transnational organization, which was not derived from empirical evidence, that offers the solution to the complex problems of globalization. In other quarters, however, transnational corporations are viewed as 'synonymous with multinational enterprises' (Daniels and Rade-baugh 1992: G-21) or simply as those that see the world as a single market (Ohmae 1989).

Global companies have also been defined as those with global strategies where economies of scale are realized from worldwide integration and standardization (Hout et al. 1982; Levitt 1983; Bartlett and Ghoshal 1989). For example, worldwide integration of design groups as well as other restructuring at Ford Motor Company led to production of a 'world car' able to enjoy scale economies and earning Ford the sobriquet of a global company (Kerwin 1995). However, as Yip (1995) notes, a global strategy is not necessarily synonymous with a global firm since the latter can sustain an integrated standard for one business line and be locally responsive in other business lines. This suggests that the global enterprise might be more or less global depending on the amount of its business that has a worldwide presence. Efforts to balance worldwide standards with demands for the localization of products and services have also been called a global strategy (Hamel and Prahalad 1985), although Yip describes this approach as *multi-local* (1995: 8), and Phatak (1992) and Ashkenas et al. (1995) call it *glocal*.

In summary, different uses of the word 'global' may be diluting any specific meaning it has in describing a strategy (Yip 1995: 8). Such definitional differences are one legacy of growing awareness of complex, and often intractable, changes occurring in the world that put new emphasis on internal coordination among firm functions and also generate greater awareness of the need to analyze events occurring throughout the world. Paradoxically, while definitions vary, the focus on the world's largest firms in the research is consistent. Public ownership and size make the world's largest 37,000 MNEs identifiable, and their control over 206,000 affiliates worldwide and combined assets in the trillions of dollars underscore their contributions to economic growth and development around the world. The world's largest 100 MNEs (not including those in banking and finance) held over US$3 trillion in global assets in 1992 (United Nations 1994a: 5). They include firms like Daimler Benz, Hanson, Glaxo, McDonald's, Siemens, Saint Gobain, Sony, Itochu, Amoco, Michelin, and Grand Met; all are from economically developed countries. It is these types of organizations that usually are thought of as 'global'.

Firms of many other types also may be considered global. Many small and medium-sized firms are breaking with existing business traditions within nations to go global, spearheading what it means to be global (Bannon 1994; *Business Week* 1995a; Shrivastava 1995). Firms of small and medium size play a growing role in global exports, and in 1995 small US businesses are for the first time expected to have sent more exports abroad than big business (Barrett 1995). Small and medium-sized firms also play a role in foreign direct investment (FDI). Examples from the developed world show that FDI on the part of small and medium-sized firms in 1992 contributed $43 billion or about 7.5 per cent of total direct investments by developed European nations, $40 billion (15 per cent) of total Japanese foreign direct investment abroad, and $15 billion in FDI (3 per cent) of total US FDI abroad. Looked at another way, about 28 per cent of small to medium-sized US firms have some direct investment abroad, but as many as 60 per cent of similarly sized Japanese firms participate in some way in equity investments abroad (Bleakley 1993). Family-owned businesses from South and Central America, Portugal, Spain, Asia, and India also are focused on global growth. Kim Woo-choong, founder of Daewoo, asserts that the firm's goal 'is to become a company without borders' (*Forbes* 1995). The growing influence of 'overseas' Chinese and Indians demonstrates that there is more than one model for family-owned enterprise. As a group, the overseas Chinese generate an estimated annual economic output equivalent to $500 billion, comparable to mainland China's 1993 gross national product; as individuals, most of the billionaires in South East Asia are ethnic Chinese living outside of China. And these ethnic Chinese business people are believed to command only a portion of the growing wealth of the overseas Chinese worldwide, and especially in South East Asia (Drucker 1994). Whether they are independently owned or run by a close-knit or far-flung 'family', enterprises like these contribute to the diversity of management practices and business objectives in the global sphere, but as yet little is known about them.

Government/business ventures as well as businesses established by global start-ups (Oviatt and McDougall 1995) are a part of global business growth, and many disenfranchised by modern business tradition now are finding it possible to become part of the global business scene (Hymowitz 1995). Nonprofit organizations increasingly contribute to economic activities (Salamon and Anheier 1994) as do nongovernmental organizations (Commission on Global Governance 1995). Finally, global gangs, pirates, warlords and others of their ilk also populate the landscape for global business. To the extent that global markets are characterized by these multiple competitors of varying size and shapes operating with differing competitive motives, global management may be said to be both more complex and less certain than when market competitors share similarities of size and motives.

This chapter argues that globalization is not confined to large organizations: it lies in 'virtually every industry' (Yip 1995), making it difficult for any firm to remain totally unaffected by global conditions. But, while virtually all organizations may be affected by globalization of business and all firms increasingly operate in a global business sphere, this is not to say that every firm is a global one. Global enterprises might more generally be described as those that establish or maintain a *worldwide presence* in one or more businesses. Firms like Pepsi Cola, CNN ('the global news network') and Benetton can be readily identified as global enterprises because they establish a global presence in virtually all their businesses. Although smaller, firms like Britain's R. Griggs (maker of Doc Martens boots), Israel's VocalTech (developer of software facilitating long-distance telephone calls over the Internet), or the Netherlands' Digicash (developer of the digital equivalent of cash for electronic purchases) also can be described as global enterprises because they are committed to establishing a worldwide presence in most or all of their product lines. Whether large or small, these firms face the same managerial challenge:

creating organization-wide processes and structures in support of their global commitment. Large firms like Nestlé and Unilever also have a significant global presence, although not in every business line – just as independent Washington State fruit growers often sell one but not all fruit lines worldwide. These firms also face managerial challenges in creating organization-wide processes and structures capable of achieving balance between what could become competing interests.

These examples demonstrate that organizations of any size can establish a global presence and can be thought of as global enterprises, and also show that establishing global presence in one, many, or all businesses creates unique challenges for organizational leaders. We can, then, think of 'global' as a worldwide view of business markets, using descriptors such as 'multilocal' to refer to strategies that firms employ when they combine worldwide standards with local responsiveness, or 'worldwide standardization' when referring to integration and standardization of products and services on a worldwide basis. For firms with a global presence, either of these strategies could be one measure of the degree to which a firm is global.

The global enterprise may also be described according to its abilities to transcend existing boundaries of three kinds. First, global enterprises cross external boundaries of nations (Ohmae 1995), space and time, or responsibilities (Brown 1992) that are in some sense measurable. Second, less tangible boundaries like culture, thought, or the relationship between self (organization) and others (Rhinesmith 1993) must also be crossed if global opportunities are to be reached. Third, some boundaries internal to the global organization have to be bridged, including vertical and horizontal barriers (Ashkenas et al. 1995), those pertaining to task or rank (Ghoshal and Bartlett 1995), and even more amorphous barriers like attitude. The importance of breaking down boundaries between departments, shifting hierarchical to contractual management, and sharing values to successful global activity was noted long ago by Stopford and Wells (1972) and Franko (1976) although, as Melin (1992) notes, these observations were not taken up by researchers at the time. More recently, they have been explored in the context of global networks, global alliances and global learning (e.g. Hedlund 1986; Hedlund and Rolander 1990; Hamel 1991).

To this point, the global enterprise has been defined as one that establishes a worldwide presence in one or more businesses, one that adopts a worldwide strategy, and one that is able to cross external and internal boundaries. We have shown that firms of any size can be defined as global enterprises, and suggested that all face significant and distinct challenges. Hordes et al. (1995) describe one form that a global firm might take: it is organized around a few core values; although it has a headquarters, it is most often managed by a team operating in diverse locations; it adopts an organizational culture that values diversity; except for a few standardized policies, its processes, policies, and technologies are diverse. A combination of mission, vision, education and training is combined with an emphasis on processes of global corporate culture (Evans et al. 1990). Knowledge (D'Aveni 1995; Senge 1990) and diversity of people, processes, or structures (Hoecklin 1995; Rhinesmith 1993; Trompenaars 1994) are essential to sustain flexibility and adapt quickly to opportunities and threats in a rapidly globalizing world. 'The ability to link and leverage knowledge is increasingly the factor that differentiates the winners and the losers and the survivors' (Bartlett and Ghoshal 1989: 12). Global firms often take unconventional approaches, developing 'a strategic innovation to change the rules of the competitive game in its particular industry' (Hout et al. 1982: 100).

The global enterprise thus organizes itself along lines different from the internally focused international firm of the 1960s and 1970s and even from the multinational enterprise that responded to a limited number of political, competitive or cultural challenges in the 1970s and early 1980s. The global firm develops a worldwide presence; it does not hesitate to cross traditional boundaries, whether these are attempts to break through national borders and nationalistic thinking more deliberately as it reconceptualizes its activities to integrate worldwide perspectives and capitalize on both global and local advantages, or internal barriers that impede its ability to leverage knowledge and diversity to sustain a global position. The importance of these internal and external boundaries may vary according to size, industry or other factors and individual firms might prioritize them in different ways. For example, a start-up in an Internet-dependent industry might place highest priority on leveraging knowledge technology; whereas an established firm might see a greater need to break down internal barriers to diversity in order to leverage knowledge. In this context, it is important to note that diversity is represented not only by visible differences like gender or ethnicity, but also by differences in rank, functional assignments, or role. While there is considerable debate and differences in opinion concerning the global organization, it seems clear that such activity is not confined simply to large organizations with a physical presence in different countries, but also includes more flexible arrangements that allow smaller organizations to benefit from global opportunities.

## GLOBALIZATION: A PERVASIVE PHENOMENON

While globalization may be driven and shaped by the activities of business, it extends well beyond the individual and collective boundaries of global organizations, regardless of how broadly they are defined. Globalization is a pervasive phenomenon, and interest should not be confined to business activities alone. In this section, interest expands to five arenas that extend beyond business organizations and a business focus. They include: the economy; politics; culture; technology; natural resources. Separating them is somewhat artificial since they interact naturally and synergistically, but doing so clarifies the content of each and provides a way to illustrate national and organizational tensions that result from globalization.

### Global Economy

The world economy is growing, with the world gross domestic product likely to increase from $26 trillion in 1994 to $48 trillion in 2010 (Richman 1995). Funds can be transferred worldwide electronically and instantly via computer technology; in 1995 Citibank alone moved over $500 billion per day through electronic transfers. Trade in equities need never stop since trading bourses now span the world. In the last decade trading has expanded from the established financial centers of New York, Tokyo, and London to include Egypt, Namibia, China, Kenya, Hungary, and Bermuda, to name a few.

While this global economy offers opportunities, it also produces increased challenges. For example, the central banks now face the force of the independent traders who manage over $1 trillion per day. Efforts by the US, Japanese and German central banks to shore up the dollar poured $30 billion into global markets between January and May of 1995. Nevertheless, the dollar fell 17 per cent against the yen and 11 per cent against the mark (Sesit 1995), proving that it may be currency speculators who increasingly play the dominant role in determining the values of currency (Millman 1995). While Millman (1995) believes these traders provide discipline for global financial markets, others suggest they undermine world economic order by making it difficult for government officials to maintain the public's interest (Solomon 1995). As a senior Canadian official attending a 1994 G-7 meeting reportedly said, 'with one trillion dollars flowing through the markets daily, there's little governments can do except stop the momentum for one day, one hour – or more like 10 minutes' (Gumbel and Davis 1994).

Where once the banks managed capital assets, today's capital markets are increasingly dominated by mutual and hedge-fund investors from the US who control about $3 trillion in assets. The global search for increasing returns on these investments creates 'hot' money that funds rapid economic growth, job creation and political stabilization, but just as easily can be withdrawn from these investments in the pursuit of higher returns elsewhere (Kwan 1991). Private capital also is displacing the need for capital from institutions like the World Bank and the IMF, and leading to questions about the continuing viability of these kinds of financial institutions in the current global milieu (Bello and Cunningham 1994; Owen 1994).

Increased globalization of economic activity is also drawing more organizations into the marketplace, stimulating trade and dispersing production facilities throughout the world (Dicken 1992). Whereas once industrialized countries were the major sources of world economic growth, today it also comes from 'reverse linkages' with the developing world, as foreign direct investment is transferred from the developing to the developed world. Whereas North America, Europe, and Japan accounted for about 65 per cent of world GDP in 1993, the figure will have dropped to 55 per cent by 2010 as China and countries in Asia and South America develop (World Bank 1995). In the last decade, firms from newly industrialized countries like South Korea, Taiwan, Thailand, and Singapore have increased their roles in the global economy from 4 per cent in the 1960s to 25 per cent in the 1990s (Farrell 1994). Moreover, the speed of development is quickening. Britain doubled its per capita income in fifty-eight years following the Industrial Revolution in 1789; then, starting in 1839, America took forty-seven years; Japan took thirty-four years from 1885; South Korea managed it in the eleven years after 1966; and more recently still, China has done it in less than ten years (*The Economist* 1994). Thus, while a global economy has the capacity to correct current economic imbalances between the developed and the developing world, this development does not come without a price. Newly industrialized countries have had to learn in a relatively short time what countries like Britain and the US took one hundred or more years to master. So economic growth incurs

penalties such as child labor, dangerous workplaces, and degraded environments.

It is important to note that it is not only the legal, the legitimate and the respectable who participate in this global arena. For example, freer access to the global arena is also enjoyed by scam artists and others who live outside the law of both domestic and global business activities, as hackers prowl throughout the Internet looking for the electronic equivalent of an unlocked door or an unguarded vault. Mafia-type organizations, gangs, pirates, and drug cartels also have emerged to carve out territory in the fertile economic realm for world trade, responding to opportunities in what Interpol estimates is a $400 billion illegal drug market; providing illegal papers to smuggle human beings willing to work; or responding to growing global demand for all manner of illicit goods and services.

The increased economic activity associated with globalization focuses attention on previously unquestioned economic assumptions. It becomes more difficult to ignore economic activities outside the paid sector, since unpaid labor worldwide has an uncounted value of $16 trillion, $11 trillion of which is generated by women (United Nations 1995). Self-interest assumptions of free market capitalism also bear re-examination in light of evidence showing that in the US the individual person or organization is expected to be the self-interested actor, while in Japan national economic interests motivate and, in Western Europe, quality of life is important (Hampden-Turner and Trompenaars 1993; Sharp 1992). While measures like gross domestic product (GDP) once were considered almost universal standards of a nation's economic development, the applicability of this measure is increasingly suspect in a global world. GDP does not adjust for varying costs of living, for differences between rich and poor within the same nation, or for those intangibles that also contribute to quality of life (Ibbotson and Brinson 1993).

Thus a globalizing economy requires a re-examination of many of our assumptions concerning wealth, in particular: whether the world economy must be played according to a zero-sum game; how resources can be allocated fairly within market systems that differ; whose and what labor 'counts' as a productive factor; even how economic criteria should be evaluated. While economic globalization can create convergence between self-interest and collective or community interests (Naisbitt 1994), self-interested economies do not operate in a vacuum, but are instead shaped by global politics (Sorenson 1995) and other national, regional, and global factors.

## Global Politics

The political sphere encompasses a tension between autonomy and dependency in so far as national governments attempt to dismantle trade barriers. Economist Robert Reich (1991) emphasizes that globalization will not only cause businesses leaders to think of themselves less as autonomous actors and more as participants inextricably linked to one another in global industries, but also reduce national autonomy. As the dismantling of boundaries opens up opportunities, it also creates dependencies that curtail autonomy. Seeking an economic payoff, few recognize that bilateral, multilateral and unilateral trade agreements necessarily reduce national autonomy through special arrangements like foreign economic zones and city-states within nations; industry alliances such as OPEC; regional alliances such as the EU, ASEAN, MEROCUR and NAFTA; or worldwide alliances such as GATT and its successor the World Trade Organization (WTO) and APEC.

These groups reduce not only barriers to trade, but also national autonomy. For example the WTO promises to phase in a common set of worldwide commercial rules. Unlike GATT, which tended to favor larger countries, the WTO promises a more level playing field, benefiting smaller countries more than in the past (*Wall Street Journal* 1995d) and encouraging more countries to join (Becker 1994) which will, in turn, place additional restraints on countries previously accustomed to more latitude. The leveling process does not come without costs. After the ten year phase-in for the WTO, sub-Sarahan Africa will suffer a net trade loss of $2.6 billion per year due mainly to increases in costs of food imports to Africa as subsidies are erased for the developed world. While the costs of the WTO incurred by countries in Africa could be met with increased aid, and while debt relief measures generate benefits to the developed world, such an occurrence is by no means a certainty. Countries in the developed world also face challenges in the form of job losses to cheaper labor elsewhere, and a possible decline in living standards if worldwide wages fall to meet global supply rather than rise to meet current standards (*World Bank Policy Research Bulletin* 1995).

Another global theme affecting the political arena concerns a change in government responsibilities: privatization all over the world has brought business into industries such as prisons, transportation, and infrastructure projects previously managed or controlled by governments. In North America, eroding confidence in the welfare state and a heightened awareness of the inefficiencies of nationalized firms have been important triggers for privatization. In Western Europe, government policies have emphasized extensive privatization, particularly in Britain. In parts of the developing world, privatization has resulted from government inability to address perceived gaps in needed products and services. The volume of privatization has been greatest in Western Europe followed by the Asian/Pacific region, Eastern Europe, and Latin America, and sales of previously state-owned enterprises climbed dramatically from just under $20 billion in 1989 to just under $70 billion in 1994 (*Wall Street Journal* 1995c). In Eastern Europe, the end of communism and the Cold War led to a reduction of government influence on many business activities, as private enterprises have attempted to respond to and profit from new entrepreneurial initiatives.

Globalization has thus moved influence from the hands of national political leaders and concentrated it in the business domain, weakening the ability of policy-makers to control key economic processes (Simai 1994). Accordingly there are growing expectations for businesses to adapt roles previously played by government entities (Brown 1992; Drucker 1989; Renesch 1992). While some global firms like The Body Shop, Levi Strauss, and Canon embrace, and even lead, new demands for social stewardship, others resist, obstruct, and willfully exploit both natural and human resources. There is now a global market for child prostitution, both male and female, fuelled by tourists and a tour industry to exploit others sexually (Shoup 1994). These activities raise concerns about the role business can, should or will play on the world's political stage: whether the authority of governments is eroding (Korten 1995), making it more difficult to regulate activities of firms (MacEwen 1994); whether, as the economic and social power of business increases, a few hundred corporations will become world empires in the twenty-first century, amassing sufficient resources to become powerful shadow governments (Barnet and Cavanagh 1994); and whether, as businesses exercise their power, a new form of imperialism will emerge as stronger economic entities use their strength to exact concessions from weaker ones (Wanniski 1995).

At the same time that global trade agreements reduce the role of national governments in global affairs, they may free up resources which governments can use to develop the nation. So, there is evidence to suggest that globalization will not phase out the role of national government completely but create a reason for its transformation. The national resources saved by the diminishing need to monitor and enforce global commercial regulations may provide opportunities for politicians to redeploy resources in education, training, or other modes of knowledge creation (Marshall and Tucker 1992). In so far as the latter leads to creativity, it may be a source of the national innovativeness needed for economic success (McRae 1995; Porter 1990).

## Global Culture

As globalization calls into question the concept of nation-state, it also focuses attention on culture. Business organizations operating solely in a domestic environment traditionally derive their cultural habits and values from the nation of origin. Although regional or ethnic variations might arise, for the most part such organizations subscribed to the values of the dominant culture. Even as firms became international, they continued to derive their cultural habits and values from their nation of origin, as Hofstede's (1980) work illustrates. But when organizations increasingly operate across borders, their members are exposed to additional cultures and adopt some measure of norms, habits, and even values from them. As sales and profits increasingly depend on foreign markets, it makes sense to hire employees who have knowledge of those markets, and managers may decide it is no longer possible or desirable to remain entirely congruent with the home culture.

Such changes in organizational practices create other changes in organizational culture, which, in the world of global business, are fed back to the parent culture as it too changes. In this way business enterprises construct and are constructed by business activities in which they and others engage. For example, organizational changes among giant conglomerates or *chaebol* like Samsung, Sunkyong, and Daewoo focus on quality improvement initiatives, all of which call for some individual initiative and accountability instead of the deference to authority more traditional to Korean culture. Changes like this then presage national change as business enterprises become conduits for a 'global' culture as well as recipients of multiple national cultures. This suggests that in a globalizing world, the nation-state is not necessarily the main source of culturally acceptable behaviors or beliefs as behaviors, norms, assumptions, and values emerge from outside national boundaries. In this sense, culture becomes 'boundaryless' as business activities transcend national borders.

Through global information and communication technologies, people throughout the world witness cultural norms, values, and behaviors reflective of many nations, and many now think and behave in ways that are increasingly global.

Business promotes, across the world, both a global language that is English, and a proliferation of consumer goods that range from cola beverages to blue jeans, from television entertainment to rock stars. Some argue that such cultural invasion provides teens and young adults with global habits that include similar modes of dress, jargon, music, entertainment preferences, and even converging values from environmental stewardship (Tully 1994) to individualism (Rohwedder 1994). Television reached 800 million homes in 1995, conveying fantasy images like 'Mighty Morphin Power Rangers' and 'Dynasty' as readily as CNN reports. Images of real and imagined violence, from a martial arts tradition filtered through the Hong Kong film industry (Dannen 1995) as well as from Hollywood, foster a culture for violence around the world that is particularly attractive to young men (Appadurai 1990).

Some writers view these influences as potential sources of cultural corruption (Finel-Honigman 1993). They see cultural convergence as a form of neo-imperialism capable of eliminating cultural variety (Tomlinson 1991), and producing cultural pressures that lead to destructive forms of conflict (Barber 1992; Huntington 1993). Others challenge these assumptions, arguing that the cultural borrowing associated with 'creolization', 'mestizaje', 'orientalization' and the like enhance, but do not redefine, culture (Pieterse 1995). 'Glocalization' or loose connections between what is local and what is global are forged (Robertson 1995), leading to the multiplication of cultural differences rather than their reduction (Kahn 1995). Instead of globalization leading to a predominantly Westernized culture, where business language, values and behaviors are standardized and homogenized on a worldwide basis, Robertson (1995) argues that cultural influences *from* East *to* West have been seriously underestimated, as, for example, values concerning religion, home and community, have become more rather than less important (Abu-Lughod 1994).

Those who categorize culture as either a global phenomenon or a series of diverse national cultures may be taking a limited view. Rather than this either/or approach we see instead a tension between homogeneity and heterogeneity played out by nations, organizations, and individuals, as demonstrated by armed conflict based on ethnicity, by public dialogue over immigration, and in private debates over religious fundamentals. While estimates suggest that the number of nations could grow from 300 to 1,000 in the twenty-first century (*Outlook* 1994), partly because of cultural differences (Davis 1994), heterogeneous countries are also coming together to form homogeneous trading blocs. The signals are mixed: as ethnic conflict has broken out in the former Yugoslavia, religious violence subsides in Northern Ireland; as political, religious and ethnic divisions fragment the Middle East, racial differences are put aside in South Africa; as Czechoslovakia, reacquainted with the democratic process, votes to separate, Quebec narrowly votes to stay part of Canada.

## Global Technologies

Digital electronics, miniaturization, telecommunications, computers, robotics, artificial intelligence, genetic engineering, low-flying satellites, and laser conductors are only a few of many technologies revolutionizing relationships between people, organizations, and nations worldwide. Medical breakthroughs from birth control to disease control bring more people to the workplace; product and process breakthroughs constantly alter the nature of their work; and information-based technologies have made people and information critical resources for organizations. Unlike the land, labor, and capital so important to economic growth during the Industrial Revolution, the driving force behind the Information Revolution is an intangible: knowledge. Because individuals own knowledge, it becomes an organizational asset only when people share it (Handy 1994), and this characteristic of knowledge creates a potential for greater equality and for worse inequality.

Telecommunication technology, capable of transmitting information almost instantaneously throughout the world, has made it possible for people and businesses to communicate and operate twenty-four hours a day, seven days a week. Moreover, the unit cost of computing power has declined rapidly in recent years. As the cost comes down, proliferation of digital technologies may encompass the globe, providing computing power, far advanced of what is available today, to users of every income level. The low cost and worldwide availability of this technology offer extraordinary potential for opportunity and equity (Negroponte 1995), but only to those with access to education and the occasion to use it. Otherwise technology may present threats rather than opportunities, by deskilling work (Rifkin 1995), and creating a greater divide between people and the activities that enrich their lives (Stoll 1995).

The digital revolution has distributed powerful tools across a huge sweep of humanity, and relocated sources of technical innovation from developed to developing world as Indian, Bulgarian, or Israeli scientists participate in technological development. Since mathematics is the foundation of all digital advances, nations well versed in that discipline, including nations like China, India, and those of South East Asia, could turn their homelands into formidable technological powers. Individual entrepreneurs and small businesses now have access to technologies previously available only to larger firms. Almost any firm can gain access to technical expertise and to knowledge workers throughout the world. Yet there are fears of what this redistribution of knowledge may mean for developed countries if companies withdraw resources there to invest them in lower-cost wages elsewhere (Rifkin 1995).

The potential for new opportunities created by these technologies is balanced by fears that those without access to the Internet will become the 'road kill' of the information highway as new categories of 'haves' and 'have-nots' emerge. The advantages of easy access to information may be offset by the loss of privacy (Gandy 1995), and information thus gained can be used to harm rather than help. Problems with 'peepers' reading one's private mail, or 'hackers' obtaining banking and credit information are now obvious. Less obvious to the general public are rising threats to intellectual property as digitalization makes it easier to pirate software, to photocopy or plagiarize copyrighted works, to reverse engineer. The Software Publishers Association estimated that software pirates illegally copied over $8 billion in software in 1994; while the London-based Business Software Alliance claimed the costs of software piracy in Europe alone totalled $6 billion in 1994 (Pope 1995).

Information associated with video and entertainment industries also offers advantages and disadvantages to equitable globalization. Video conferencing with built-in language translation across national borders may become as common as today's word-processing programs and spreadsheets; this technology would make it possible for people to 'meet' without the added costs of spatial travel. By 1997, low earth orbiting satellites will make it possible to communicate with underserved areas of Africa, Latin America, Asia and elsewhere (Boyd 1995), but those without telephones and other equipment will find this technology to be of little use. In publishing and entertainment, readers and viewers will pull news, movies, or documents directly from the 'bitstream', but these vast galaxies of digitized video, sound, and data swirling in cyberspace remain far from the reach of those who cannot read or do not have electricity. Moreover, as in other fields, technology development reflects the interests of the developer. Thus, ASCII characters are English-language characters; many computer games have greater appeal for boys than for girls (Bulkeley 1994); computer icons represent Western, and more particularly, US cultural experiences; and the format of computer games and programs reflects a Western bias for action, linear thinking, and self-determination (Goulet 1977; Magnet 1994).

## Globalization of Natural Resources

The natural environment is another arena of globalization. It intertwines people with the natural environment of which they are a part (also see Chapter 11 by Egri and Pinfield). Existing inequities between North and South, and along ethnic and gender lines, are often increased by globalization practices that exploit both natural and human resources.

Oil spills, nuclear disasters and similar accidents destroy natural resources, while industrialization consumes or depletes them. For example, water consumed during industrial production can pollute water worldwide just as airborne emissions reduce air quality or reduce the ozone layer. According to scientific testimony at the 1995 UN Climate Conference, by 2000 anticipated ozone reductions and global warming are expected to displace 95 million people who live at sea level, cause ecosystems to disappear, deserts to expand, and storms to become more violent and frequent. While industrialization creates jobs and a standard of living that individuals as well as nations seek, it also gathers people into densely populated areas where urban problems of garbage, water treatment, and noise pollution further affect the environment. Industrialization is a mixed blessing in improving world prosperity at the same time that it increases the potential for ecological disruption.

Ecological disruption increases as business activities transport plants and animals greater distances. For example, brown tree snakes introduced to Guam thirty years ago have killed off virtually all species of birds and many other animals; zebra mussels travelling on Russian ships clog intake pipes in the Great Lakes; rainbow jellyfish that entered Black Sea waters in 1982 are destroying plankton, fish eggs, and the larvae of flora and fauna. Diseases that afflict both people and plants also are going global. For example, the A2 strain of potato virus recently migrated from central Mexico to US potato fields, devastating crops and costing farmers millions of dollars (Winslow 1995). WTO reduction in agricultural trade barriers is likely to increase similar opportunities for agricultural diseases to spread.

The AIDS virus has been perhaps the first to earn the epithet of a 'global' disease, even though African adults have borne its brunt as entire generations have been wiped out, leaving grandparents to raise children, and no one to provide financial support to either. Lethal epidemics like tuberculosis, Ebola fever and dengue are expected to increase worldwide along with global interconnections among people (Garrett 1994; Preston 1994). Even natural disasters confined to one part of the world have worldwide implications because of global connections. For example, floods in Europe and an earthquake in Japan in early 1995 disrupted world trade flows throughout the world because so many goods flow through Rotterdam and Kobe.

Some argue that economic development along free market lines must be replaced with principles of sustainable development that ensure a viable future for succeeding generations (Gore 1992; Hawken 1993). Proposals for sustainable development call for fundamental changes. For example, while markets often create divisions between rich and poor, sustainable development calls for a greater degree of world economic equity. This is not to say that the world's wealth will be redistributed, but that long-standing inequities between richer and poorer nations must be overcome, providing poorer nations with better economic opportunities than in the past. According to authors of the United Nations (1994b) *Human Development Report*, 'the concept of one world and one planet simply cannot emerge from an unequal world. . . . Global sustainability without global justice will always remain an elusive goal.'

Ironically, even as some argue that lifestyles in the rich nations must be altered to consume less, many in developing countries advocate the opposite change to adopt the habits of materialism consistent with a consumption-based society. Some are willing to trade their land or raw materials for consumer goods, while others find it impossible to survive unless they exploit resources available to them. As these resources disappear, forests and water disappear and desertification grows. Given a competitive business environment, and a world population anxious or forced to join the world economy, business organizations unwilling to compromise the natural environment may lose opportunities; while those that take active steps to preserve the environment may be accused of imposing their own values on host countries anxious to develop economically. Thus, one of the challenges of sustainable development is to manage the paradox of exploiting current economic growth against protection of the natural environment and the people who live in it.

Individuals throughout the world, because of globalization, have changed their expectations concerning wealth. Labor has begun to move more freely in response to employment needs throughout the world, and because people's expectations cannot be met in emerging countries, they look elsewhere for work. Labor shortages in industrializing countries like Japan and South Korea, and limited opportunities in other parts of Asia, have led over 2 million men and women from East and South East Asia to leave home for work in nearby nations (Pura 1992). China's rural poor migrate to cities or pay large sums for illegal exit to countries where jobs are to be found. Worldwide immigration, both legal and illegal, is increasing. In the US, immigration accounted for 39 per cent of US growth in the last decade, and large population increases in Europe have occurred in the last twenty years due to economic integration and to immigration. At the same time as immigration occurs and, in some cases, is actively encouraged, barriers such as the Schengen agreement are erected to prevent some migration flows, individuals are returned to their countries of origin, and immigrants have been subjected to violent attacks against them, their property and their rights in Europe, the US, Japan (Fernandez 1991) and throughout the world.

The tradeoff between human and economic investment is greatest for those who have least. Often the people who lose the most from an emphasis on growth and development are women. The UN *Human Development Report* finds that among those countries providing gender-based statistics, no country treats women as well as it treats men. In many countries, differential treatment for women includes poor access to basic safety, security, nutrition, educational opportunities or health care resources. Women from emerging countries increasingly are sent abroad to work in menial jobs that provide opportunities for abuse. Some are sold into slavery or prostitution to become the lure for global sex tours. Accordingly, economic development is often built upon only half of the population, robbing future generations of opportunities to reach a full potential. Without education, women tend to remain net recipients of national goods rather than contributors in the form of labor or taxes paid, and less attractive to global companies seeking workers.

In industrialized nations, differential treatment toward women often is reflected in unequal pay and status inequities between women and men. The female-to-male weekly wage ratio ranged from 80 to 90 per cent in Australia, Denmark, France, New Zealand, Norway, and Sweden, while other countries in Western Europe also had ratios of roughly 65–75 per cent. Women in the US earn about 76 per cent of what men earn, while Japanese women earn about 61 per cent of what a Japanese man would earn in a similar job (*Wall Street Journal* 1995a). However, there is some evidence that women are making progress in achieving managerial positions. For example, between 1985 and 1991, the percentage of women managers increased in 39 of the 41 countries that report comparative labor statistics (*World of Work – US*, 1993). As these inequities reach resolution, they simultaneously raise awareness of other forms of inequity. For example, educational improvements for women in the developing as well as the developed world go first to those with economic resources. The poor remain poor.

Globalization often results in inequities, whether they occur between richer Northern countries and poorer Southern countries, between men and women, or within and between ethnic groups. Organizations and especially business organizations are often expected to address these inequities but, in so doing, they face a tension between capitalizing on the potential for growth and protecting and redressing such inequities.

In summarizing this section, we can say that globalization involves revolutionary changes in economic, political, cultural, technological, and natural spheres. A global pursuit of the benefits of wealth creation has altered traditional relationships among and between business, government, and society (Hawken 1993). Political responsibilities are increasingly met by consumer advocacy groups and business enterprises; while some business responsibilities have been taken on by government and nongovernmental organizations. Organizations in all sectors are under increased pressure to be more efficient, to measure the relationship between input and outcome, to be more 'business-like'. At the same time, business enterprises are implored to be more socially responsible in the way they globalize, to accommodate homogeneity and heterogeneity, to reduce inequities while maintaining internal profitability, to sustain as well as exploit. Thus globalization, in permeating far beyond the confines of business, creates significant new challenges for all parts of society.

## IMPLICATIONS FOR ORGANIZATIONS

The strategy/structure/systems approach to managing multinationals yielded efficiencies realized through hierarchical structures supported by complex and sophisticated management systems (Ghoshal and Bartlett 1995). The value of hierarchical structures and the strategy/ structure/systems approach to practice is eroding in a world populated with firms of every size, and a global environment characterized by rapid change, but the need to generate efficiencies remains great. This managerial challenge is but one of many paradoxes challenging organizations as they face increasing demands to be many things to many people all at the same time (Handy 1994). Within the firm, the paradox may be managed by increased focus on organizational processes like entrepreneurship, competence building, and renewal (Ghoshal and Bartlett 1995), and by change champions with two capabilities: anticipating the future and willingness to swim up-stream against internal tides of resistance (Handy 1994). Champions of change throughout the world can be found in every type of organization, in business, government, and academic circles. The many questions they raise about the role of business and other types of organizations in the world today give rise to still other questions about the strategy, structures and processes appropriate to organizations in a global world. The nature of globalization raises a number of important implications concerning the social responsibility of the global organization, whether business or otherwise. It also creates new demands for organizational strategy and structure. These implications are discussed in this section.

## Social Responsibility

As they assume roles previously played by government entities, e.g. via privatization (Drucker 1989), business organizations are expected to behave more as a community member than a corporate entity alone (Brown 1992); as they globalize, the costs of large, powerful worldwide organizations *not* acting responsibly increase. On the other hand, some writers believe that business may be the only mechanism strong enough to reverse many of the social problems that currently exist (Hawken 1993). In view of slowing economic growth in the industrialized world and rapid growth in the developing world, organizations have greater motivation to participate in activities that result in economic development (Handy 1994).

Regulations are one means of forcing socially responsible behavior from organizations, although the difficulties of regulating on a worldwide scale are tremendous. The Parliament of World's Religions produced a *Global Ethic,* calling for the reduction of environmental and human abuses throughout the world; the UN has produced many statements on individual and organizational rights; and in 1995 the US government introduced a voluntary code of corporate behavior. The global business community itself produced the Caux Round Table *Principles for Business* by combining basic Eastern ideals of *kyosei* (living and working for the common good) and human dignity (referring to the sacredness or value of each person) into a set of common ethical principles. Developed in 1994 through collaboration among business leaders in Japan, Europe, and the US, these principles suggest that some business leaders have the will to assume greater social responsibility. Also in 1995, forty-one major nations founded Transparency International, a group patterned after Amnesty International, and funded by European aid agencies and some multinationals, to combat large-scale corruption involving corporations and holders of public offices around the world.

Any attempt to develop global ethical codes has to address at least two key problems. The first concerns the problems inherent in policing activities that can easily cross boundaries and disappear from view. These difficulties are compounded when governments of developing countries, anxious for hard currency and economic development, are willing to tolerate, and in some cases encourage, business practices that are illegal elsewhere and which may involve dangers for a population either ignorant of them or unable to resist them. A second difficulty concerns the fact that ethical standards vary widely throughout the world: what is bribery in one country might be viewed as standard business practice in another. Values vary tremendously across the world (Hofstede 1980; Hampden-Turner and Trompenaars 1993; Kanter 1991; Schwartz 1992), leading to differences in work behaviors and attitudes (Hofstede 1983). Even Kanter's (1991) survey of 12,000 managers, which showed commonly held views on world problems, did not indicate common solutions.

Other means to encourage socially responsible behavior do exist. For example, consumer groups have assumed a new role in encouraging social responsibility from firms. According to *The Economist* (1995b), consumer pressure motivated firms like IKEA, Levi, and Nike to tackle human rights issues. Supra-national organizations like the United Nations and the International Labor Organization attempt to transcend national politics to promote a democratic society organized around values such as justice, equality, and mutual respect (Commission on Global Governance 1995) in the face of growing gaps between rich and poor, armed conflict around the world, minimal legal protection in some parts of the world, and corrupt regimes (Kennedy 1993). While business and government can be expected to assume responsibility for filling some of these gaps, partnerships among groups of business people, governmental officials, and nongovernmental representatives are most likely to lead to results that achieve some degree of balance or equity. Politicians anxious to realize advantages of something like the WTO for their countries or regions may overlook the transitional costs borne by others; markets are unlikely to pay the full or long-term costs of unanticipated change; consumers may be underinformed; or businesses may be unable to foresee the outcome of decisions they are pressured to make. For example, legitimate efforts to alleviate labor abuses of children could result in change for the worse if children suspended from factory work are forced into worse jobs or families starve. Partnerships of interest play an important role in seeing that one correction does not lead to another higher cost.

Nongovernment organizations (NGOs) have also taken on a global mandate, dubbed a global 'associational revolution' (Salamon 1994) because of the size and effect NGO activities have had on business practices worldwide. For example, consumer boycotts in Germany led by Greenpeace resulted in worldwide protest, and led to a reversal by Royal Dutch Shell of its earlier decision to bury the oil rig *Brent Spar* at sea. Less successfully, Greenpeace has played a key role in the global protest against French nuclear testing in the Pacific. NGOs also conduct global business activities such as providing seed money to the informal work sector (*World of Work* 1994); organizing workers (Frenkel 1993); or underwriting economic development (Hymowitz 1995). These activities question traditional assumptions about where business interests are served. For example, Grameen Bank loans to 3 million women in thousands of small Bangladeshi villages not only lifted half the recipients from poverty, but provided Grameen with resources to expand globally. The resulting surge in micro banks (*Wall Street Journal* 1995b) challenges traditional assumptions about the ability of the poor to repay loans and, since many of these loans go to women, they also shift traditional assumptions about the economic roles women can play.

As NGOs play business roles, expectations increase for them to be more business-like in managing money and even people. Just as business organizations face calls for social responsibility, nonprofit organizations are urged to think of people as 'customers' and to adopt accounting practices mirroring those used in business (Greenberger 1995). These demands for accountability blur the distinction between human need and business practice; between the

economic and the social; between business and politics.

There are, then, many questions concerning the social role of global organizations of all types. Many observers have expressed concern about the potential for social irresponsibility on the part of these organizations and the inability of governments and other actors to regulate them. Gergen (1995), on the other hand, argues that the postmodern attributes of the global organization: the dispersion of intelligibilities; disruptions in chains of authority; the erosion of rationality; a reduction in centralized knowledge; and undermined autonomy, provide the potential for 'ethically generative practices'. Clearly, then, this is one area where more research has much to offer.

## Organizational Strategy

Globalization calls for new approaches to strategy-making compared to traditional models. Global strategies must, for example, be informed by political, legal and social, as well as economic, considerations (Buckley 1990; Boddewyn and Brewer 1994; Earley and Singh 1995). In a global world, where it is difficult to sustain competitive advantage (D'Aveni 1995), being competitive involves rethinking many of the basic strategy concepts (Hamel and Prahalad 1989). Unanticipated opportunities arise only when traditional assumptions are challenged: organizational survival depends on seeing the future first and in a different way (Hamel and Prahalad 1994). Consequently, planning techniques must rely less on historical data to aid scenario planning or competitive analysis, and more on those that yield industry foresight and leverage global knowledge (Ghoshal and Bartlett 1995). The global organization represents a major departure from the more traditional strategy-making practices of both East and West, as organizations from different nations participate in international business activities and contribute to changes concerning how and why business is conducted. For example, in contrast to 'bigger is better' philosophies of Westernized firms, Taiwan's Acer Inc. has established itself as a global power in the personal computer market by becoming more compact. The company reorganized from a centralized structure into small business units whose managers have autonomy to make business decisions in their own markets. So, while the family-based nature of many Chinese enterprises encourages family hiring, Acer has taken an opposite tack by keeping family members out of management and giving workers a financial stake in the company (*Wall Street Journal* 1994).

The global organization also depends upon organizational learning (Bartlett and Ghoshal 1989), which has been described as the ability to develop insight and knowledge of the relationships between past actions, their effectiveness, and future actions (Lyles 1988). This learning is expected to come not just from personal mastery but from shared vision and team work (Senge 1990). As knowledge is unleashed through team as well as individual efforts, a tenuous balance is generated between flexibility and efficiency; between collaboration and autonomy; between consensus and risk. Individuals trained in the context of a collectivistic culture face a challenge in becoming individually competitive; while people from individualistic societies may find it difficult to operate as a member of a team. Organizational challenges come from nurturing and rewarding the type of learning sought, and coping with anger when learning needs change more rapidly than people.

Unlike more tangible factors of production like equipment or capital, the knowledge that stems from organizational learning is more difficult to monopolize and measure (Handy 1994). Because knowledge need not be concentrated in one place, business activities can be redistributed throughout the world to take advantage of highly skilled and educated workforces. International Data Solutions, for example, scans case and client files for US law firms and transmits them in digital form via satellite to the Philippines. There, workers organize and index the documents so they can be readily retrieved by a computer network in the US. An emphasis on everyone being both a learner and a teacher represents a profound change from traditional management principles which more clearly allocated the job of thinking and teaching to top managers alone.

Thus global strategies have profound implications for human resource strategies (e.g. Adler and Bartholomew 1992; Schuler et al. 1993). The successful global manager is less likely to be the international specialist than a generalist who can cope with complex cross-border strategies, develop appropriate personnel, and integrate across and between people and functions (Bartlett and Ghoshal 1992). According to Adler and Bartholomew (1992) these skills transcend those traditionally required from expatriate managers but are nonetheless crucial to managing an increasingly diverse workforce within and between countries whose skills, interests, and work motivations vary on the basis of gender, nationality, work role, and background (Gibson 1995; Laurent 1986; Parker 1991; Welsh et al. 1993).

There is, then, scope for further study of the different strategies that are evolving in the global marketplace: not only those adopted by Western enterprises, but also those of other countries; not only those spearheaded by business organizations, but also those in other sectors; and not only those of large, well-known multinationals, but also those of smaller and different types of global organizations.

## Organizational Structure

Bureaucracy creates organizations in the form of tall pyramids; it removes managerial expertise from the shop floor; and it emphasizes the importance of a clearly defined, autonomous entity. Although organizations from the West tend to prefer operating autonomously (Janger 1980) globalization makes different demands: there is evidence of a growing need for various forms of partnership between organizations such as spider webs (Harrigan 1985), global webs (Reich 1991), networks (Ghoshal and Bartlett 1990), or joint ventures (Kanter 1991). In international joint ventures, greater diversity between partners' societal and corporate cultures or managerial practices requires learning to bridge those gaps (Parkhe 1991). Internally, organizations may be structured less as pyramids or hierarchies, directed from the top, and more as networks guided by the shared purpose of interdependent and diverse teams (Brown 1992); by common values (Hordes et al. 1995); or by core organizational processes (Ghoshal and Bartlett 1995). The shift from hierarchical organizations to flatter or 'horizontal' structures and the move from functional to cross-functional thinking may require new structures instead of the pure form of bureaucracy. Often these new structures involve some form of hybrid that enables the global firm to be price competitive, efficient and able to compete with other global firms as well as local and regional firms.

The knowledge revolution associated with globalization has a potential to restructure not only existing organizations but also how work is organized. It is possible for some people to 'telecommute', on a long-distance, international basis, and accomplish work from home or other locales. More localized, flexible working arrangements in different countries may offer community-based groups the means to combine business opportunities with local social needs. Business activities transacted between countries and at arm's length via fax, e-mail, and computers may hide color, gender, nationality or similar factors, freeing groups from some of the discriminating effects that they might encounter inside more traditional organizational arrangements. These opportunities may be leading increasing numbers of women in Europe to leave traditional organizations to establish companies that better suit their interests and needs (Conference Board Europe 1991). A similar pattern in the US has led to an increase in female-controlled businesses: 9.1 per cent of all businesses in 1994, with recent gains found in traditionally male industries such as finance, transportation, construction and manufacturing (*Business Week* 1995b). A third to a half of small entrepreneurs in Latin America are believed to be women (Santiago 1994); and micro bank loans throughout Asia stimulate business growth, particularly for women (*Wall Street Journal* 1995b).

This is not to say that the global organization represents a transformation in the organization of work (Whitaker 1992). We should not forget that in a global world competition is high, and old principles still apply: the new core may cluster around providing service, but the old imperatives continue to emphasize the need to deliver that service at the least cost; notions of efficiency are not dead; financial pressures continue to curtail innovation and experimentation; new organizational forms as well as other 'take charge' initiatives meet needs for creating 'illusions of managerial control' (Salancik and Meindl 1984) even as they undermine morale or lead to dead-ends; the interest in cooperative links does not signal an end to competition since alliance partners may collaborate on one product line but compete on another; and, while some multinational organizations have incorporated diversity into top management, most have few women or foreign nationals in top managerial positions or on boards (*The Economist* 1995a).

In summary, the global organization often represents a hybrid of the old and the new, of the modern and the postmodern organization. It certainly is a demanding and difficult organization to manage (Melin 1992). Without profound changes in thinking throughout the organization, the changes associated with globalization may be perceived as little more than fads. The process of adapting organizational structure to globalization requires not only incremental changes in how organizations function, but a fundamental rethinking of how organizational participants think about their relationship with the organization and the organization's role in a global world.

## CONCLUSION

The challenge for research on globalization is not whether progress is being made, but whether it is being made quickly enough (Dunning 1989; Inkpen and Beamish 1994). For example, Ricks et al. (1990: 219) noted that while 'virtually every area of management has an international dimension . . . many of these areas are [only] just beginning to be investigated.' Adler and Bartholomew's (1992) data base search of publications in seventy-three academic and professional management journals from 1985 to 1990 revealed growing interest and focus on cross-cultural interactions of many kinds, but also found publications on international organizational behavior and human resource management had not increased in two decades. One particular demand is for more interdisciplinary research (Dunning 1989; Inkpen and Beamish 1994), and Dunning (1993) warns that future scholars will reach their full potential only by combining the knowledge of disciplinary scholarship with insights provided by other disciplines. Multinational organizations are believed to have developed beyond the relevance and legitimacy of single academic disciplines to explain them (Sundaram and Black 1992). Others underscore an apparent need to move away from emphasis on quantitative research to incorporate more qualitative research (Wright and Ricks 1994) and engage in more flexible forms of theorizing that can accommodate the diversity and scope of global practices.

Such a research agenda is not without problems, as the efforts of one multinational, multicultural, interdisciplinary research consortium to generate multiple perspectives and levels of analysis bear witness (Teagarden et al. 1995). Such research requires considerable collaboration and time if scholars are to understand multiple academic fields; is difficult to carry out unless resources are made available; and journals are not always geared to such multidisciplinary, qualitative work. Since few scholars have infinite resources of time or money, and many operate in systems that reward frequent annual productivity in top disciplinary journals, the academic system may discourage interdisciplinary research even as the business world needs it more.

An interdisciplinary approach invites academicians to take on additional complexity, to learn new skills, and to question assumptions. It also invites individuals to step outside comfort zones and blur customary distinctions: between disciplines; between those who theorize and those who practice; between many of the other traditional boundaries observed in knowledge generation. By developing global practices in academia, however, we may be in a better position to study them: business organizations may provide some of the resources to fund this research; global technologies undoubtedly help build worldwide academic networks; collaboration between schools and scholars that span the globe will help provide a more supportive, sensitive global culture that both facilitates and improves research. If students of organizations do not rise to the study of globalization in this way, an important chapter in business history will not be written and the lessons that could have been learned will be lost.

## NOTE

The author would like to acknowlege the help of Cynthia Hardy, McGill University and Sue Jones, Sage Publications, in writing this chapter, and to thank Anne Smith, McGill University for contributing several valuable ideas.

## REFERENCES

Abu-Lughod, J. (1994) 'Diversity, democracy, and self-determination in an urban neighorhood: the East Village of Manhattan', *Social Research*, 61(1): 181–204.

Adler, N.J. (1983) 'Cross cultural management research: the ostrich and the trend', *Academy of Management Review*, 8(2): 226–32.

Adler, N.J. and Bartholomew, S. (1992) 'Academic and professional communities of discourse: generating knowledge on transnational human resource management', *Journal of International Business Studies*, 23(3): 551–69.

Aharoni, Y. (1966) *The Foreign Investment Decision Process*. Boston: Division of Research, Harvard University.

Appadurai, A. (1990) 'Disjunctures and difference in the global cultural economy', in M. Featherstone (ed.), *Global Culture*. Newbury Park, CA: Sage. pp. 295–310.

Ashkenas, R., Ulrich, D., Jick, T. and Kerr, S. (1995) *The Boundaryless Organization*. San Francisco: Jossey-Bass.

Ball, D.A. and McCullough, W.J. Jr (1990) *International Business*, 4th edn. Homewood, IL: Irwin.

Bannon, L. (1994) 'Natuzzi's huge selection of leather furniture pays off', *Wall Street Journal*, 17 November: B4.

Barber, Benjamin. (1992) 'Jihad vs. McWorld', *Atlantic Monthly*, 269(3): 53–61.

Barnet, R.J. and Cavanagh, J. (1994) *Global Dreams: Imperial Corporations and the New World Order*. New York: Simon & Schuster.

Barrett, A. (1995) 'It's a small (business) world', *Business Week*, 17 April: 96–101.

Bartlett, C.A. and Ghoshal, S. (1989) *Managing Across Borders: the Transnational Solution*. Boston: Harvard Business School Press.

Bartlett, C.A. and Ghoshal, S. (1991) 'Global strategic management: impact on the new frontiers of strategy research', *Strategic Management Journal*, 12: 5–16.

Bartlett, C.A. and Ghoshal, S. (1992) 'What is a global manager?', *Harvard Business Review*, September/October: 124–32.

Beamish, P., Killing, J.P., Lecraw, D.J. and Crookell, H. (1991) *International Management*. Burr Ridge, IL: Irwin.

Becker, G. (1994) 'Why so many mice are roaring', *Business Week*, 7 November: 20.

Bello, W. and Cunningham, S. (1994) 'Reign of error: the World Bank's wrongs', in *Real World International*, 2nd edn. pp. 26–30.

Bleakley, F.R. (1993) 'Smaller US firms lag counterparts overseas in setting up business abroad', *Wall Street Journal*, 8 August: A2.

Bleakley, F.R. (1995) 'Foreign investment in the US surged in 1994', *The Wall Street Journal*, 15 March: A2, A10.

Boddewyn, J.J. and Brewer, T.L. (1994) 'International-business political behavior: new theoretical directions', *Academy of Management Review*, 19(1): 119–43.

Boyacigiller, N. and Adler, N.J. (1991) 'The parochial dinosaur: organizational science in a global context', *Academy of Management Review*, 16(2): 262–90.

Boyd, R.S. (1995) 'Satellites spur new space race', *Seattle Times*, 1 February: A3.

Brown, J. (1992) 'Corporation as community: a new image for a new era', in J. Rensch (ed.), *New Traditions in Business*. San Francisco: Berrett-Koehler. pp. 123–39.

Buckley, P. (1990) 'Problems and developments in the core theory of international business', *Journal of International Business Studies*, 21(1): 657–65.

Buckley, P. and Casson, M. (1976) *The Future of the Multinational Enterprise*. London: Macmillan.

Bulkeley, W.M. (1994) 'A tool for women, a toy for men', *Wall Street Journal*, 16 March: B1, B3.

*Business Week* (1995a) 'The *Mittelstand* takes a stand', 10 April: 54–5.

*Business Week* (1995b) 'The big picture: where women are making great strides', May: 8.

Caves, R. (1971) 'International corporations: the industrial economics of foreign investment', *Economica*.

Chandler, A. (1962) *Strategy and Structure*. Cambridge, MA: MIT Press.

Commission on Global Governance (1995) *Our Global Neighbourhood*. Oxford: Oxford University Press.

Conference Board Europe (1991) 'Europe's glass ceiling'. RM5, Conference Board Europe, Brussels.

Cooperrider, D. and Passmore, W. (1991) 'The organizational dimension of global change', *Human Relations*, 44: 763–87.

Daniels, J.D., Pitts, R.A. and Tretter, M.J. (1984)

'Strategy and structure of U.S. multinationals: an exploratory study', *Academy of Management Journal*, 6(3): 223–7.

Daniels, J.D. and Radebaugh, L.H. (1992) *International Business*, 6th edn. Reading, MA: Addison-Wesley.

Dannen, F. (1995) 'Hong Kong Babylon', *New Yorker*, 7 August: 30–8.

D'Aveni, R.A. (1995) *Hypercompetitive Rivalries*. New York: Free Press.

Davis, B. (1994) 'Growth of trade binds nations, but it also can spur separatism', *Wall Street Journal*, 20 June: A1, A6.

Dicken, P. (1992) *Global Shift*, 2nd edn. London: Guilford Press.

Drucker, P. (1989) *The New Realities*. New York: Harper & Row.

Drucker, P. (1994) 'The new superpower: the overseas Chinese', *Wall Street Journal*, 20 December: A16.

Dunning, J. (1988) 'The eclectic paradigm of international production: a restatement and some possible extensions', *Journal of International Business Studies*, 1–31.

Dunning, J. (1989) 'The study of international business: a plea for a more interdisciplinary approach', *Journal of International Business Studies*, 20(3): 411–36.

Dunning, J. (1993) *The Globalization of Business*. London: Routledge.

Dyas, G. and Thanheiser, H. (1976) *The Emerging European Enterprise*. London: Macmillan.

Earley, P.C. and Singh, H. (1995) 'International and intercultural management research: what's next?', *Academy of Management Journal*, 38(2): 327–40.

*Economist, The* (1994) 'A game of international leapfrog', in 'Survey: the global economy', 1 October: 6–9.

*Economist, The* (1995a) 'Who wants to be a giant?', in 'Multinationals survey', 24 June: 4.

*Economist, The* (1995b) 'Human rights', 3 June: 58–9.

Evans, P., Doz, Y. and Laurent, A. (eds) (1990) *Human Resource Management in International Firms: Change, Globalization, Innovation*. New York: St Martin's Press.

Farnham, A. (1994) 'Global – or just globaloney?', *Fortune*, 27 June: 97–100.

Farrell, C. (1994) 'The triple revolution', *Business Week*, bonus issue: 16–25.

Fayerweather, J. (1969) *International Business Management*. New York: McGraw-Hill.

Fernandez, J.P. (1991) *Managing a Diverse Work Force: Regaining the Competitive Edge*. Lexington, MA: Lexington Books.

Finel-Honigman, I. (1993) 'Popular culture in the global economy: antithesis or reconcilation?', in R.R. Sims and R.F. Dennehy (eds), *Diversity and Differences in Organizations*. Westport, CT: Quorum. pp. 123–33.

*Forbes* (1995) 'Index to foreign billionaires', 17 July.

Franko, L.G. (1976) *The European Multinationals: a Renewed Challenge to American and British Big Business*. Stamfort, CT: Greylock.

Frenkel, S. (1993) 'Organized labor in the Asia-Pacific region'. Cornell International Industrial and Labor Relations Report 24, Cornell University, Ithaca, NY.

Gandy, O.H. Jr (1995) 'It's discrimination, stupid', in J. Brook and I.A. Boal (eds), *Resisting the Virtual Life*. San Francisco: City Lights Books. pp. 35–48.

Garrett, L. (1994) *The Coming Plague: Newly Emerging Diseases in a World out of Balance*. Farrar Straus Giroux.

Gergen, K.J. (1995) 'Global organization: from imperialism to ethical vision', *Organization*, 2(3/4): 519–32.

Ghoshal, S. and Barlett, C. (1990) 'The multinational corporation as an interorganizational network', *Academy of Management Review*, 15(4): 603–25.

Ghoshal, S. and Barlett, C. (1995) 'Changing the role of top management: beyond structure to processes', *Harvard Business Review*, January/February: 86–96.

Gibson, C.B. (1995) 'An investigation of gender differences in leadership across four countries', *Journal of International Business Studies*, 26(2): 255–79.

Gore, A. (1992) *Earth in the Balance: Ecology and the Human Spirit*. Boston: Houghton Mifflin.

Goulet, D. (1977) *The Uncertain Promise: Value Conflicts in Technology Transfer*. New York: North America.

Greenberger, R.S. (1995) 'Developing countries pass off tedious job of assisting the poor', *Wall Street Journal*, 6 June: A1, A9.

Grosse, R. and Behrman, J.N. (1992) 'Theory in international business', *Transnational Corporations*, 1(1): 93–126.

Gumbel, P. and Davis, B. (1994) 'G-7 countries show limits of their powers', *Wall Street Journal*, 11 July: A3, A4.

Hamel, G. (1991) 'Competition for competence and inter-partner learning within international strategic alliances', *Journal of Strategic Management*, 12: 83–104.

Hamel, G. and Prahalad, C.K. (1985) 'Do you really have a global strategy?', *Harvard Business Review*, July/August: 139–48.

Hamel, G. and Prahalad, C.K. (1989) 'Strategic intent', *Harvard Business Review*, May/June: 63–75.

Hamel, G. and Prahalad, C.K. (1994) *Competing for the Future*. Cambridge, MA: Harvard Business School Press.

Hampden-Turner, C. and Trompenaars, F. (1993) *The Seven Cultures of Capitalism*. New York: Doubleday.

Handy, C. (1994) *The Age of Paradox*. Cambridge, MA: Harvard Business School Press.

Harrigan, K. (1985) *Strategies for Joint Ventures*. Lexington, MA: Lexington Books.

Hawken, Paul (1993) *The Ecology of Commerce*. New York: Harper Business.

Hedlund, G. (1986) 'The hypermodern MNC: a

heterarchy?', *Human Resource Management*, 25: 9–35.

Hedlund, G. and Rolander, D. (1990) 'Action in heterarchies: new approaches to managing the MNC', in C. Bartlett, Y. Doz and G. Hedlund (eds), *Managing the Global Firm*. London: Routledge. pp. 15–46.

Hennart, J.F. (1982) *A Theory of Multinational Enterprise*. Ann Arbor: University of Michigan Press.

Henzler, H. and Rall, W. (1986) 'Facing up to the globalization challenge', *McKinsey Quarterly*, Winter: 52–68.

Hoecklin, L. (1995) *Managing Cultural Differences: Strategies for Competitive Advantage*. Wokingham: Addison-Wesley.

Hofstede, G. (1980) *Culture's Consequences*. Beverly Hills, CA: Sage.

Hofstede, G. (1983) 'The cultural relativity of organization practices and theories', *Journal of International Business Studies*, 14(2): 75–90.

Hordes, M.W., Clancy, J.A. and Baddeley, J. (1995) 'A primer for global start-ups', *Academy of Management Executive*, 9(2): 7–11.

Hout, T., Porter, M. and Rudden, E. (1982) 'How global companies win out', *Harvard Business Review*, 60(2): 98–108.

Huntington, S. (1993) 'The clash of civilizations', *Foreign Affairs*, Summer: 22–49.

Hymer, S.H. (1976) *The International Operations of National Firms*. Cambridge, MA: MIT Press.

Hymowitz, C. (1995) 'World's poorest women advance by entrepreneurship', *Wall Street Journal*, 5 September: B1, B2.

Ibbotson, R.G. and Brinson, G.P. (1993) *Global Investing*. New York: McGraw-Hill.

Inkpen, A. and Beamish, P. (1994) 'An analysis of twenty-five years of research', *Journal of International Business Studies*, 25(4): 703–13.

Janger, A.R. (1980) *Organization of International Joint Ventures*. New York: Conference Board.

Johanson, J. and Vahlne, J. (1977) 'The internationalisation process of the firm: a model of knowledge development on increasing foreign commitments', *Journal of International Business Studies*, 8: 23–32.

Kahn, J.S. (1995) *Culture, Multiculture, and Postculture*. Beverly Hills, CA: Sage.

Kanter, R.M. (1991) 'Transcending business boundaries: 12,000 world managers view change', *Harvard Business Review*, May/June: 151–64.

Kennedy, P. (1993) *Preparing for the Twenty-First Century*. New York: Vintage Books.

Kerwin, K. (1995) 'Getting "two big elephants to dance"', *Business Week*, special issue: '21st century capitalism': 83.

Kogut, B. (1989) 'A note on global strategies', *Strategic Management Journal*, 10(4): 383–9.

Korten, David C. (1995) *When Corporations Rule the World*. San Francisco: Berrett-Koehler.

Kwan, R. (1991) 'Foot loose and country free', in *Real*

World International, 2nd edn. Somerville, MA: Dollars and Sense.

Laurent, A. (1986) 'The cross-cultural puzzle of international human resource management', *Human Resource Management*, 25(1): 91–102.

Lavipour, F.G. and Sauvant, K. (1976) *Controlling Multinational Enterprises: Problems, Strategies, Counterstrategies*. Boulder, CO: Westview.

Lemak, D. and Bracker, J. (1988) 'A strategic contingency model of multinational corporate structure', *Strategic Management Journal*, 9(5): 521–6.

Leong, S.M. and Tan, C.T. (1993) 'Managing across borders: an empirical test of the Bartlett and Ghoshal [1989] organizational typology', *Journal of International Business Studies*, 24(3): 449–64.

Levitt, T. (1983) 'The globalization of markets', *Harvard Business Review*, May/June: 92–102.

Lyles, M.A. (1988) 'Learning among joint venture-sophisticated firms', in F.J. Contractor and P. Lorange (eds), *Cooperative Strategies in International Business*. Lexington, MA: Lexington Books. pp. 301–16.

MacEwen, A. (1994) 'Markets unbound: the heavy price of globalization', in *Real World International*, 2nd edn. Somerville, MA: Dollars and Sense.

McRae, H. (1995) *The World in 2020*. Cambridge, MA: Harvard Business School Press.

Magnet, M. (1994) 'The productivity payoff arrives', *Fortune*, 27 June: 79–84.

Marshall, R. and Tucker, M. (1992) *Thinking for a Living: Education and the Wealth of Nations*. New York: Basic Books.

Martinez, J.I. and Jarillo, J.C. (1989) 'The evolution of research on coordination mechanisms in multinational corporations', *Journal of International Business Studies*, 20(3): 489–514.

Melin, L. (1992) 'Internationalization as a strategy process', *Strategic Management Journal*, 13: 99–118.

Millman, G. (1995) *The Vandal's Crown: How Rebel Currency Traders Overthrew the World's Central Banks*. Cambridge, MA: Free Press.

Moran, T.H. (1973) 'Transnational strategies of protection and defense by multinational corporations: spreading the risk and raising the cost for nationalization in natural resources', *International Organization*, 27: 273–89.

Moran, T.H. (1974) *Multinational Corporations and the Politics of Dependence*. Princeton, NJ: Princeton University Press.

Naisbitt, John (1994) *Global Paradox*. New York: William Morrow.

Negroponte, N. (1995) *Being Digital*. New York: Alfred A. Knopf.

Nehrt, L.C., Truitt, J.F. and Wright, R.W. (1970) *International Business Research: Past, Present, and Future*. Bloomington, IN: Indiana University Bureau of Business Research.

Ohmae, Kenichi (1985) *Triad Power: the Coming Shape of Global Competition*. New York: Free Press.

Ohmae, Kenichi (1989) 'The global logic of strategic alliances', *Harvard Business Review*, March/April: 143–54.

Ohmae, Kenichi (1995) *The End of the Nation State*. Cambridge, MA: Free Press.

*Outlook* (1994) 'World affairs', September/October: 42.

Oviatt, B. and Phillips McDougall, P. (1995) 'Global start-ups: entrepreneurs on a worldwide stage', *Academy of Management Executive*, 9(2): 30–43.

Owen, H. (1994) 'The World Bank: is 50 years enough?', *Foreign Affairs*, 73(5): 97–108.

Parker, B. (1991) 'Employment globalization', *Journal of Global Business*, 39–46.

Parkhe, A. (1991) 'Interfirm diversity, organizational learning, and longevity in global strategic alliances', *Journal of International Business Studies*, 22(4): 579–601.

Perlmutter, H.V. (1969) 'The tortuous evolution of the multinational corporation', *Columbia Journal of World Business*, 9–18.

Phatak, A.V. (1992) *International Dimensions of Management*, 3rd edn. Boston: PWS-Kent.

Pierce, B. and Garven, G. (1995) 'Publishing international business research: a survey of leading journals', *Journal of International Business Studies*, 26(1): 69–89.

Pieterse, J.N. (1995) 'Globalization as hybridization', in M. Featherstone, S. Lash and R. Robertson (eds), *Global Modernities*. London: Sage. pp. 45–68.

Pope, K. (1995) 'Software piracy is big business in East Europe', *Wall Street Journal*, 4 April: A10.

Porter, M.E. (1980) *Competitive Strategy*. New York: Free Press.

Porter, M.E. (1985) *Competitive Advantage*. New York: Free Press.

Porter, M.E. (1990) *The Competitive Advantage of Nations*. New York: Free Press.

Preston, R. (1994) *The Hot Zone*. New York: Random House.

Pura, R. (1992) 'Many of Asia's workers are on the move', *Wall Street Journal*, 5 March: A10.

Reich, R. (1991) *The Work of Nations: Preparing Ourselves for 21st Century Capitalism*. New York: Alfred A. Knopf.

Reitsperger, W.D. and Daniel, S.J. (1990) 'Japan vs Silicon Valley: quality–cost tradeoff philosophies', *Journal of International Business Studies*, 21(2): 289–300.

Renesch, J. (ed.) (1992) *New Traditions in Business*. San Francisco: Berrett-Koehler.

Rhinesmith, S.H. (1993) *A Manager's Guide to Globalization*. Homewood, IL: Business One Irwin.

Richman, L.S. (1995) 'Global growth is on a tear', *Fortune*, 20 March: 108–14.

Ricks, D., Toyne, B. and Martinez, Z. (1990) 'Recent developments in international management research', *Journal of Management*, 16(2): 219–53.

Rifkin, J. (1995) *The End of Work*. New York: G.P. Putnam's Sons.

Robertson, R. (1992) *Globalization: Social Theory and Global Culture*. London: Sage.

Robertson, R. (1995) 'Glocalization: time–space and homogeneity–heterogeneity', in M. Featherstone, S. Lash and R. Robertson (eds.), *Global Modernities*. London: Sage. pp. 25–44.

Robinson, R. (1971) 'The future of international management', *Journal of International Business Studies*, 2(1): 60–70.

Robinson, R. (1981) 'Background concepts and philosophy of international business from World War II to the present', *Journal of International Business Studies*, Spring/Summer: 13–21.

Rohwedder, C. (1994) 'Youths in Germany put individualism ahead of politics', *Wall Street Journal*, 18 Oct: A12.

Ronen, S. and Shenkar, O. (1985) 'Clustering countries on attitudinal dimensions: a review and synethesis', *Academy of Management Review*, 10(3): 435–54.

Rugman, A. (1980) 'A new theory of the multinational enterprise: internationalization versus internationalization', *Columbia Journal of World Business*, 15: 23–9.

Rummel, R.J. and Heenan, D.A. (1978) 'How multinationals analyze political risk', *Harvard Business Review*, January/February: 67–76.

Salamon, L.M. (1994) 'The rise of the nonprofit sector', *Foreign Affairs*, July/August: 109–22.

Salamon, L.M. and Anheier, H.K. (1994) *The Emerging Sector*. Baltimore: Johns Hopkins University Institute for Policy Studies.

Salancik, G.R. and Meindl, J.R. (1984) 'Corporate attributions as strategic illusions of management control', *Administrative Science Quarterly*, 29(2): 238–54.

Santiago, F. (1994) 'Latin American women to forge agenda for change', *Seattle Times*, 4 April: A11.

Schuler, R.S., Dowling, P.J. and De Cieri, H. (1993) 'An integrative framework of strategic international human resource management', *Journal of Management*, 19(2): 419–59.

Schwartz, S.H. (1992) 'Universals in the content and structure of values: theoretical advances and empirical tests in 20 countries', *Advances in Experimental Social Psychology*, 25: 1–62.

Senge, P. (1990) *The Fifth Discipline: the Art and Practice of the Learning Organization*. New York: Doubleday.

Sera, Koh (1992) 'Corporate globalization: a new trend', *Academy of Management Executive*, 6(1): 89–96.

Sesit, M.R. (1995) 'Central banks' efforts to bolster the dollar spur mostly decline', *Wall Street Journal*, 25 April: C1.

Sharp, Margaret (1992) 'Tides of change: the world economy and Europe in the 1990s', *International Affairs*, 17–35.

Shoup, Mike (1994) 'Tourism's ugly side: child prostitution', *Seattle Times*, 18 September: K10–11.

Shrivastava, A. (1995) 'Smaller firms lead German push to East', *Wall Street Journal*, 14 June: A10.

Simai, Mikaly (1994) *The Future of Global Governance*. New York: US Institute of Peace Press.

Solomon, S. (1995) *The Confidence Game*. New York: Simon & Schuster.

Sorenson, G. (1995) 'Four futures', *Bulletin of the Atomic Scientists*, July/August: 69–72.

Stead, W.E. and Stead, J.G. (1994) 'Strategic decisions and not-so-natural disasters: understanding the way in and the way out', *Organization*, 1(2): 369–73.

Stoll, C. (1995) *Silicon Snake Oil: Second Thoughts on the Information Highway*. New York: Doubleday.

Stopford, J.M. and Wells, L.T. (1972) *Managing the Multinational Enterprise*. New York: Basic Books.

Sundaram, A.K. and Black, J.S. (1992) 'The environment and internal organization of multinational enterprises', *Academy of Management Journal*, 17(4): 729–57.

Teagarden, M.B. and 13 others (1995) 'Toward a theory of comparative management research: an idiographic case study of the best international human resources management project', *Academy of Management Journal*, 38(5): 1261–87.

Thomas, A.S., Shenkar, O. and Clarke, L. (1994) 'The globalization of our mental maps: evaluating the geographic scope of JIBS coverage', *Journal of International Business Studies*, 25(4): 675–86.

Tomlinson, J. (1991) *Cultural Imperialism*. Baltimore: Johns Hopkins University Press.

Trompenaars, F. (1994) *Riding the Waves of Culture*. Burr Ridge, IL: Irwin.

Tully, S. (1994) 'Teens, the most global market of all', *Fortune*, 16 May: 90–6.

United Nations (1994a) *World Investment Report*. New York and Geneva: United Nations, UNCTC.

United Nations (1994b) *Human Development Report*. New York and Geneva: United Nations.

United Nations (1995) *Human Development Report*. New York and Geneva: United Nations.

Vernon, R. (1966) 'International trade and international investment in the product cycle', *Quarterly Journal of Economics*, June: 190–207.

*Wall Street Journal* (1994) 'Acer emerges as global PC power and Asian pacesetter', 1 December: B4.

*Wall Street Journal* (1995a) 'Comparing women around the world', 26 July: B1.

*Wall Street Journal* (1995b) 'Women's banks stage global expansion', 30 September: A10.

*Wall Street Journal* (1995c) 'What is privatization, anyway?', 2 October: R4.

*Wall Street Journal* (1995d) 'US may be losing its trade-bully status', 13 October: A7.

Wanniski, J. (1995) 'The new American imperialism', *Wall Street Journal*, 6 July: A8.

Welsh, D.H.B., Luthans, F. and Sommer, S.M. (1993) 'Managing Russian factory workers: the impact of US-based behavioral and participative techniques', *Academy of Management Journal*, 36(1): 58–79.

Whitaker, A. (1992) 'The transformation in work: post-Fordism revisited', in M. Reed and M. Hughes (eds), *Rethinking Organization*. London: Sage. pp. 182–206.

Williamson, O. (1975) *Markets and Hierarchies*. New York: Free Press.

Winslow, Ron (1995) '"Fungus fatale" poses a threat to potato crop', *Wall Street Journal*, 1 January: B1, B5.

World Bank (1995) 'Reverse linkages – everybody wins', Development brief, May. Additional information is available in *Global Economic Prospects and the Developing Economies 1995*. Washington, DC: World Bank.

*World Bank Policy Research Bulletin* (1995) 'Targeting the impact', 6(1): 4.

*World of Work* (1994) 'Women shoulder the burden of Cambodia's economy', 9: 24–5.

*World of Work – US* (1993) 'Unequal race to the top', 2: 6–7.

Wright, R.W. and Ricks, D.A. (1994) 'Trends in international business research: twenty-five years later', *Journal of International Business Studies*, 25(4): 687–701.

Yip, G.S. (1995) *Total Global Strategy*. Englewood Cliffs, NJ: Prentice-Hall.

# Epilogue: Now That It Has Been Said – What Do We Think?

The purpose of this epilogue is to make explicit the general message that we hope the careful reader has taken away from the foregoing chapters. The title is derived from Karl Weick's famous question: 'How can I know what I think until I see what I say?' (1979: 5). Weick's invitation to retrospective sensemaking provides a highly appropriate frame for this epilogue. Now that leading scholars on the traditional 'micro' side of organization studies have said what they deemed appropriate for a chapter in a book intended to summarize recent developments in each of their fields, 'What are we to think?'

It should come as no surprise that what we think is similar to what we wrote in the introduction since like many introductions it too was written after the editors (we) had studied the chapters. However, our decision to group the chapters in this volume was based on expectations we held *prior* to reading the chapters. The contrast between what we thought before reading and after reading the chapters provides the key general message of this epilogue.

Before going further a brief methodological note may be instructive. The chapters in this book were based on the recent literature on topics that have traditionally been on the so-called 'micro' side of the field. Except for three commonalties: (1) the fact that all the authors drew on the recent academic literature; (2) the high intellectual regard the editors have for all of the authors; and (3) the light editorial touches we made on some of the manuscripts when they were submitted, to our knowledge no other coordination among the authors took place. Thus, except for the constraints that the fore-mentioned commonalties may introduce, any common themes across the chapters are primarily due to recent developments in academic understanding in each of the special areas. The most glaring general theme is the breakdown of any previously existing barriers between micro and macro.

For a long time students of organizations have sought ways to overcome barriers between the micro and macro sides of the field. This quest led many of them to search for overarching frameworks such as general systems theory. To date, none of these frameworks really solved the barriers problem.

Based on our understanding of what the authors of the chapters in this volume have said, we think the barrier problem is now more likely to dissolve than to be solved. This conclusion is based on material from all of the chapters. We saw strongest support for this trend in Bryman's discussion of leadership. Not only did Bryman suggest that the study of leadership has increasingly shifted to the management of meaning, an approach that places heavy emphasis upon topics often discussed under the heading of a macro topic such as organization culture, but his call in the chapter's overview to link treatments of leadership with such macro perspectives as population ecology and institutional theory pointed in a similar direction.

A related although weaker trend towards blurring of boundaries also appeared in the literature treated by Tenbrunsel, Galvin, Neale and Bazerman in their study of cognitions in organizations. Although these authors devoted most of their attention to consideration of how behavioural decision theory has changed micro OB, before concluding their chapter they called attention to the fact that recently cognitive concepts have been used to describe behaviour of organizations.

The blurring trend is even stronger in the related chapter on decision-making by Miller, Hickson and Wilson; the authors began with the assertion that organization decision-making is part of organization theory (a term that traditionally has been almost synonymous with 'macro') and throughout the chapter called attention to the fact that much of what we think we know about decision-making could be culture-bound because our information base has been almost exclusively in Western individualistic culture. Clearly a key element of their message was a call for greater awareness of context and understanding of decision-making as an *organizational* process.

The blurring of the micro and macro boundary was also apparent in Shulman's chapter on groups, especially in his demonstration of how the contemporary study of groups demands attention to technology, morality, organizational contexts and the understanding that groups are open systems.

Finally, Nkomo and Cox's chapter on diversity revealed another sort of boundary blurring that is only partially related to the micro/macro division. Since diversity was never a traditional micro topic anyway, this partial relationship might make their position irrelevant to our basic theme of the micro/macro blurring. However, their chapter revealed another way that categories we have previously used to organize our knowledge are becoming inadequate for recent and anticipated future developments. In the context of the micro/macro blurring thesis, Nkomo and Cox's analysis helps us to understand a general way we may respond to the shifting terrain. Specifically, their treatment of identity indicates the value of simultaneously examining process and recognizing the need to treat context.

This call to study processes in the light of contexts may represent the basic orientation that, taken together, the contributors to this volume seem to be sensing as the wave of the future.

As the value of the traditional categories wanes, our attention will increasingly, at least in the short run, emphasize the ways that what might once have been thought to be separate entities mutually determine each other. However, the starting point for this trend in previously institutionalized categories means that these traditional divisions are likely to continue to play a role as new categories and theories are developed to treat the processes of mutual determination. In short, the emerging theories about process are likely to be rooted in the categories of the past.

Then too, it is likely that the processes which are treated will themselves introduce boundaries that separate them from each other. Nevertheless, if we extrapolate the pattern revealed by the foregoing chapters, we now think it is likely that, if not the *next Handbook of Organization Studies*, some future one will be structured around processes, and the micro–macro division on which the current work rests will have dissolved.

## References

Weick, Karl (1979) *The Social Psychology of Organizing* (2nd edition). New York: McGraw-Hill.

# Index

Abercrombie, N., 57
Abernathy, W., 17–18, 179
Abrams, D., 91
abstract events, 3, 162, 170
Abu-Lughod, J., 244
Acker, J., 98
Ackoff, R.L., 131
action, 95; capacities, 181–6; decision process, 53–5; routines, 191–2, 194, 196, 198–200
Adams, J., 133
adhocracies, 194, 206
Adler, N., 93, 237–9, 250, 251
Adler, P., 177, 185, 199–200
Agenda 21, 220
Aharoni, Y., 237
Aiken, M., 165
Albert, S., 197
Albrecht, T.L., 133, 140
Aldag, R.J., 71
Alderfer, C.P., 92
Aldrich, H.E., 221, 223
Alexander, D., 213
Allen, J.P., 114
Allen, M., 130
Allen, T., 130, 176
Allenby, B.R., 215
Allison, G.T., 47, 54, 57, 190
Allport, G.W., 94
Alpert, M., 71
Alston, J.P., 59
Alvesson, M., 35, 38–9, 128, 136, 138–40
Amado, G., 59
Amnesty International, 248
analysis levels, 19
Ancona, D.G., 93, 107–8, 132, 177
Anderson, P., 174
Andrews, F., 175
Andrews, J.A.Y., 127, 137
Andrews, K., 13
Anheier, H.K., 240
*Annual Review of Psychology*, 63
Ansoff, H., 11
Antal, A.B., 94
Anthony, R.N., 164
Anthony, T., 15
anthropocentrism, 4, 8, 210, 212–16
APEC, 243
Appadurai, A., 244
Appleby, J., 23
Argote, L., 76, 192
Argyris, C., 138, 191
Aristotle, 120, 212
Arnold, H.J., 73

artifacts, 141, 145–6, 160; learning and, 192, 194–8, 206
Asch, S.E., 45, 67
ASEAN, 243
Ashforth, B.E., 91
Ashkenas, R., 235, 239, 240
Ashmos, D.P., 226
Astley, W.G., 225
Aston Studies, 165
attitudes, 68–9
Attiyah, H.S., 59
attribution theory, 65–6, 72–4
Austin, N., 31
Avolio, B.J., 31, 32–3
Axelsson, R., 58
Axley, S., 129–30
Aydin, C., 130
Azevedo, A., 115

Bachrach, P., 47–8, 54–5
Backoff, R.H., 138
Bacon, F., 212
Bacon, G., 175, 176
Badran, M., 59
Bagozzi, R.P., 73
Bailetti, A., 176
Bailyn, L., 180, 185
Baker, D., 98, 100
Bakhtin, M., 143, 144
Balkin, D.B., 73–4
Ball, D.A., 238
Bannister, B.D., 73–4
Bannon, L., 239
Bantel, K.A., 93
Bantz, C.R., 135, 136, 137
Baram, M., 215, 216
Baratz, M.S., 47–8, 54–5
Barber, B., 235, 244
Bar-Hillel, M., 71
Barker, J.R., 133, 139, 140
Barley, S., 34, 36, 132, 142, 163, 167, 175
Barnard, C., 125, 146, 180–1
Barnet, R.J., 243
Barnett, G.A., 126
Barney, J.B.,12, 17, 19
Baron, J., 93
Barr, P.S., 191
Barrett, A., 239
Barrett, G.V., 73
Barry, D., 8
Barthes, R., 141
Bartholomew, S., 239, 250, 251
Bartlett, C.A., 12, 15, 22, 236–41, 247–50
Bartol, K.M., 94

Bartunek, J.M., 138
Bass, B.M., 27, 30–4, 38, 39, 78
Bassford, G., 72
Bastien, D.T., 135, 142
Bateman, T.S., 78
Bateson, G., 197, 201, 205
Baudrillard, J., 136
Bavelas, A., 132
Bazerman, M.H., 63–4, 67, 69–71, 75–6, 77, 79
Beamish, P., 237, 238, 251
Beck, V., 48
Becker, G., 243
Beer, M., 110, 112
behavioural decision theory, 2, 64, 65, 69–71, 75–80, 257
Behrman, J.N., 236
Bell, D., 70
Bell, E., 94, 136
Bello, W., 242
Bennett, S.J., 215
Bennis, W.G., 30–1, 38
Bensimon, E.M., 38
Benson, J.K., 138
Berg, P.O., 136, 138
Berger, J., 91
Bergquist, W., 141, 147
Berkes, F., 210
Berle, G., 215
Berlinger, L., 193
Bernardin, H.J., 74
Berner, M., 225
Berniker, E., 160
Berry, J.W., 96
Berry, T., 214
Best, M., 15
Bettis, R.A., 78–9
Bettman, J.R., 78
Beyer, J.M.,34–5, 127, 137, 223
Bhavnani, K.K., 98
Bijker, W.E., 163
Bikson, T.K., 114, 130
bioregionalism, 209, 213, 216, 220
biosphere, 4, 8, 209–28
Bird, E.A.R., 211
Black, J.S., 251
Black, M., 126
Blake, S., 88
Blau, P., 91, 165, 222
Bleakley, F.R., 239
Blunt, P., 59
Boddewyn, J.J., 249
Boje, D.M., 134–6
Bookchin, M., 210, 214, 217
Boons, A., 19

Boorstin, D., 136
Borman, W.C., 73
Bormann, E.G., 134, 135–6, 140
Boston Box, 15, 20
bounded rationality, 2, 45, 69, 223
Bourgeois, L.J., 12, 14, 16, 52
Bourgeois, V.W., 127
Bower, J., 174, 177
Boyacigiller, N., 238
Boyd, R.S., 130, 133, 245
Bracker, J., 237
Bradford, G., 217
Bradford Studies, 49–51
Bradley, R.T., 38
Bradney, P., 202
Bramwell, A., 212
Brasil, H.V., 59
Braverman, H., 163
Braybrooke, D., 49
Brenner, O.C., 94
Brewer, M.B., 71, 89, 91
Brewer, T.L., 249
Brief, A.P., 71, 77
Brink, T.L., 127, 137
Brinson, G.P., 242
Brock, Z., 178–9
Brodwin, D.R., 52
Broms, H., 137
Brooks, J., 112
Brown, J., 178–9, 184–5, 235, 240, 243, 248, 250
Brown, J.S., 195
Brown, L.R., 209
Brown, M.H., 137
Brown, R., 89
Brown, R.H., 138
Brown, S., 175
Browning, L.D., 137, 202
Brundtland Report, 220
Brunsson, N., 53
Bryant, A., 113
Bryman, A., 30, 32–3, 37–9
Buber, M., 143
Buchholz, R.A., 209, 211, 220
Buckley, P.J., 236, 249
Buckley, W., 195
Bulkeley, W.M., 246
Bullis, C., 139–40
bureaucracy, 194–5, 206
Burgelman, R.A., 174, 175, 177
Burke, T., 215, 220
Burns, J.M., 30, 31, 33
Burns, T., 7, 146, 175, 178, 179, 181–6, 221
Burrell, G., 14, 21, 23, 48
business (globalization), 234–52
Business Software Alliance, 245
Butler, R.J., 51, 54, 56, 57
Buzzanell, P.M., 128, 139

Cahoon, A.R., 94
Cairncross, F., 215, 216, 217
Calas, M., 98–9, 136, 139
Caldwell, D.F., 93, 107–8, 132, 177
Callenbach, E., 215
Cameron, K., 138
Campbell, D.J., 170
Campion, M.A., 107, 109, 110, 115
Cann, A., 77
Cantor, N., 68
capital, 21
capitalism, 9, 22
Capra, F., 219
Cardy, R.L., 74
Carey, J.W., 136

Carlzon, J., 31
Carnegie, Dale, 126
Carroll, B.W., 58
Carroll, G.R., 220, 221
Carroll, J.S., 67, 75
Carson, R., 211
Carter, R.T., 98
Cascio, W.F., 77
Cass, V.C., 98
Casson, M., 236
categorization, 6, 67–8, 100
Catton, W.R., 210, 213, 218
causal attribution theory, 66, 73
Caux Round Table, 248
Cavanagh, J., 243
Caves, R.E., 12, 236
Cellar, D.F., 73
CEO (role/personality), 78
Cervone, B., 77
*chaebol*, 244
Chaffee, E., 16–17
Chaiken, S., 69
chains, 19
champions, 52, 248
Chandler, A., 11, 14, 16, 18, 237
Chandler, T.A., 142
change, 52; time problem, 19–20
chaos theory, 53, 55
Chapman, J.P., 70
Chapman, L.J., 70
Chapple, E.D., 165
charismatic leaders, 2, 31, 38
Charles, L.H., 202
Cheney, G., 126–7, 135–6, 138–41, 144
Cheney, J., 214, 217
Child, J., 21, 57, 59, 165
Chittipeddi, K., 36, 38
Choudhury, N., 7
Christensen, C., 174
Christensen, L.T., 135
Cicero, 212
Citera, M., 142
Clair, R., 137, 139
Clark, C., 18, 21
Clark, K., 174–9, 183, 186
Clark, L.F., 67
Clegg, S.R., 1, 7, 56, 137
closed system approach, 108–9, 112–17
Clow, M., 212
Club of Rome, 211
co-production, 134, 135, 136
Cobb, J.B., 209, 211, 212, 217
Cockburn, C., 100
Cockburn, I., 182
code systems, 141–2
codes of conduct, 7, 182, 186
Codol, J.P., 65
Coffman, S.L., 137
cognitions in organizations, 2, 5–6, 63–80, 257
cognitive revolution, 63
Cohen, M.D., 53, 55, 57, 58, 128, 179, 190, 198, 199, 203
Cohen, W.M., 176, 182
Colburn, T.E., 216
Colby, M.E., 210–11, 216–17, 218, 219
Cole, M., 201
Cole, R.E., 199–200
Coleman, J., 226
collaboration, 52
collectivism, 51, 185
Collier, P.D., 161, 167
Collins, S., 94
Collinson, D., 100
commander model, 52

Commission on Global Governance, 240, 248
commitment (to innovation), 179–80, 185
Commoner, B., 209, 213
commons (management of), 216–17
communication, 245–6; metaphors, 3, 6–7, 125–47; work group performance, 3, 6, 107–21
comparative analysis studies, 165
competition, 17–19
competitive advantage, 7, 110
complexity (decision-making), 50–1
computer-aided design, 164
Condor, S., 100
conduit metaphor, 128, 129–30, 144–6
Conference Board Europe, 251
Conger, J.A., 30, 31
Conrad, C., 127, 138, 143
consumerism/consumption, 36–7
context, 5–9, 109–10
contingency approach, 1–2, 8, 27, 29–30
contingency theory, 115
contingent rewards, 32
continuous events, 162, 170, 171
Contractor, N., 133
control, 29–30
convergence model, 133–4
conversation, 6–8, 129, 141–2
Cook, S.D.N., 192, 195, 197–8, 200
Cool, K., 13
Coombs, R.H., 202
Cooper, A., 197–8
Cooper, R., 174–6, 178–9
Cooperrider, D., 235
coordination, 110, 134, 136, 177
Copeland, D.G., 164
Corbett, C., 192
Corbett, M.J., 175
Corman, S.R., 132, 133, 134
corporate culture, 20, 52
corporate strategy, 56
Corse, S., 176, 178, 179
Coser, R.L., 202
Cote, J.A., 95
Cotgrove, S., 212, 213, 218
Cotton, J., 94
Covin, J., 174
Cowan, D.A., 198
Cox, T. Jr., 88, 89, 93–7
Craig, C.R., 28
Craig, R., 121
Crane, D.B., 193
Crawford, C.M., 174, 175, 179
Cray, D., 49
creative deconstruction, 1, 7–8, 11–23
creative problem-solving, 177–8, 181, 183–4
crescive model, 52
critical analysis, 127, 217–21
critical theory, 127
Cronen, V., 121, 127
Cross, E.Y., 88, 98
Crowfoot, J.E., 217
Crozier, M., 46–7, 166
cultural: difference, 57–9, 235, 244; systems, 192, 195–6
culture: ethnology, 90, 95–6; global, 5, 244–5; imaginative consumption of, 36–7; leadership and, 34–7
Cummings, L.L., 71–2, 74
Cunningham, S., 242
Cusella, L.P., 131
Cusumano, M., 177
Cyert, R., 45, 47, 54, 56–7, 191

Czajka, J.M., 77
Czarniawska-Joerges, B., 136–7, 142, 193

Daboub, A.J., 111
Daft, R., 78, 112, 131, 135–6, 170, 175, 183
Dailey, R.C., 74
Daley, D., 74
Dalton, D.R., 77
Daly, H.E., 209, 210, 211, 212, 217
Damanpour, F., 174
Daniel, S.J., 237
Daniels, A., 202
Daniels, J.D., 237, 238, 239
Daniels, R., 202
Dannen, F., 244
Danowski, J., 133
Danziger, J.N., 114
D'Aveni, R.A., 241, 249
David, J., 132
Davidson, M.N., 95
Davies, C., 212
Davies, R., 201
Davis, B., 242, 244
Davis, G.B., 164
Davis, K.E., 65, 66, 133
Davis, L.E., 162
Davis, W.L., 131
Davis-Blake, A., 78
Dawes, R.M., 70
Day, D.V., 79, 174, 209
Day, G., 174, 179
decision-making, 2, 6, 43–59, 257–8
deconstructionism, 1, 11–23
deep ecology, 210, 213–14, 217, 219
Deetz, S., 127–8, 137, 139–40, 143–4
DeLorean, J., 35
De Meuse, K.P., 75
democratization process, 140, 235
demographic process, 6, 90, 93–4
DeNisi, A.S., 74, 77
Derrida, J., 99
DeSanctis, G., 113, 130, 143, 167
Descartes, R., 212
descriptive approach, 160–3
Deshpande, R., 91, 178, 182
Devall, B., 210, 212–14, 217, 218, 219
Devanna, M.A., 30–1, 38
De Vries, S., 95
Dewey, J., 121
dialogue, 143–4
Diamond, I., 214
Dicken, P., 235, 242
Dickson, M.W., 107, 111
Diez, M.E., 142
differentiation perspective, 34–5, 46
Dill, W.R., 221
Dillon, P., 215, 216
DiMaggio, P.J., 39, 223
Dipboye, R.L., 77
discourse, 8–9, 100; metaphors, 7, 129, 141–5, 146
discursive approach, 7–8
dispersed leadership, 5, 33–4
diversity, 2–3, 6, 88–101, 258
Dobbins, G.H., 72
Dodgson, M., 190
dominant social paradigm, 4, 8, 210, 212–13, 215, 217–18, 220–1, 223, 225, 227
domination, 139
Donaldson, L., 14
Donnellon, A., 127, 135, 142
Donohue, W.A., 142

Dorfman, N.S. and R., 215, 217
Doria, J.R., 76
Dornbusch, S.M., 170
double-loop learning, 195
Dougherty, B., 117
Dougherty, D., 175–9, 184
Douglas, M., 202
Downs, A., 130, 225, 227
Downs, G., 174
Drake, B., 73
Drazin, R., 191
Drengson, A., 212–13, 218
Drucker, P., 182, 240, 243, 248
Duff, A., 212, 213, 218
Duguid, P., 178–9, 184–5, 195
Duhaime, I.D., 79
Duncan, R.B., 221
Duncan, W.J., 142
Dunlap, R.E., 210–11, 213, 218, 227
Dunning, J., 236, 237, 251
Duran, J.P., 113
Durand, T., 21
Dutton, J.E., 49, 78–9, 197
Duveen, G., 98
Dyas, G.P., 237

e-mail, 112–13
Eagleton, T., 139
Eagly, A.H., 69, 94, 101
Earley, P.C., 130, 236, 249
Eblen, A.L., 137
Eccles, R., 112, 193
ecofeminism, 214, 220
ecology: biosphere, 4, 8, 209–28; population, 39, 64, 222
economies of scale, 183
Edmondson, A., 20
Edwards, R., 127
Edwards, W., 69
efficiency, 183
Egri, C.P., 209, 217, 219, 224
Ehrenfeld, D., 212
Ehrlich, S.B., 72, 133, 138, 202
Einhorn, H.J., 71
Eisenberg, E.M., 127, 129–35, 137, 140, 143–4, 164, 165–6
Eisenhardt, K.M., 45, 79, 131, 175, 184
Eisler, R., 213
Ekins, P., 220
El-Ashker, A., 59
Elbaum, B., 18
electronic information technologies, 111–17
Elkington, J., 215, 220
Ellington, R.T., 215
Elliott, B., 224
Elmes, M., 8
embedded group theory, 3, 90, 92
emergent theory, 184
Emerson, J., 202
Emery, F.,111, 115, 131, 221–2
emotion, 143
empowerment, 140
enactment metaphor, 134–6
Enlightenment, 120, 212
enterprise culture, 57
environment, 9; biosphere, 4, 8, 209–28
environmental sustainability, 4, 8, 215–17, 219–20, 226–7, 246
epistemology, 37–9
Essed, P., 95
ethnicity, 91, 140
ethnology, 3, 90, 95–6
ethnomethodology, 100
EU, 243

evaluation (of product innovation), 178–9, 184–5
Evan, W.M., 168, 221, 222
Evans, P., 241
Eveland, J.D., 130
Evered, R., 143
evolutionary theory, globalization and, 4–5, 9, 234–52
excellence, 20, 52
expectancy theory, 64
expectation-states theory, 91
explanations (decision-making), 48–51
exploitation (in cultural systems), 4, 195–6
exploration (in cultural systems), 4, 195–6

Fairclough, N., 139, 143
Fairhurst, G.T., 142
false consciousness, 48
Farace, R., 132
Farh, J.L., 95
Farnham, A., 235
Farrell, C., 242
Faulkner, R.R., 191
Fayerweather, J., 237
Fayol, H., 125
feedback, 74
Feisal, J.P., 142
Feldman, D.C., 73, 74
Feldman, M., 132
Fellmeth, R.C., 223
Felten, D.F., 115
feminist theory, 139, 204–5; ecofeminism, 214, 220
Ferdman, B., 88
Fernandez, John, 94, 247
Ferris, G.R., 75
Feshbach, M., 212
Feyerabend, P., 121
Feyerherm, A.E., 217
Fiedler, F.E., 29–30, 31
Filby, I., 138
Fine, M., 139
Finel-Honigman, I., 244
Fineman, S., 143
Finley-Nickelson, J., 96
Fiol, M., 142, 182, 195–6
Fischhoff, B., 71
Fisher, B., 134
Fisher, D., 219
Fiske, S.T., 65, 66, 67–8, 69
Flannery, B.L., 215
Fletcher, G.J.O., 66
flexible specialization, 16
focal organization, 221–2
Follett, M.P., 125, 198
Fombrun, C.J., 57, 125, 225
Forbes, L.C., 136
Ford, J., 94, 138
Fordism, 19
foreign direct investment, 236–7, 239
Forenstein, G., 214
Foucault, M., 143–4
Fouts, P.A., 220
Fox, S., 6, 211
Fox, W., 210, 212, 214, 217, 219
fragmentation perpective, 35–6, 39
Frankenberg, R., 98, 140
Franko, L.G., 237, 240
Frederickson, J., 15
Freedman, S.M., 94
Freeman, C., 176
Freeman, J., 39, 64, 222
Frenkel, S., 249

Freud, S., 196, 201
Frey, D., 68
Friedberg, M., 47
Friend, A.M., 217
Friendly, A. Jr., 212
Friends of the Earth, 8
Friesen, P.H., 19
Frost, P.J., 127, 137, 209, 217, 219, 224
Fry, L.W., 29
Fujimoto, T., 175, 177, 179
Fukuyama, F., 18
Fulk, J., 110, 115, 130, 133, 166
Fullerton, H.N., 88
functional specialization, 165, 177
functionalism, structural, 43

Gadamer, H.G., 120
Gahmberg, H., 137
Gaia principle, 228
Galbraith, J.R., 125, 147, 166, 183
Gallupe, R.B., 113
Gamson, W.A., 226
Gandy, O.H. Jr., 245
Garb, H.N., 71
garbage-can model, 53, 55, 58–9, 128, 219
Garcia, J.C., 29–30
Gardner, H., 196
Gardner, W.L., 72
Garrett, L., 246
Garton, L., 112, 113
Garud, R., 161, 183
Garven, G., 237, 238
Gatignon, H., 174, 182
GATT, 220, 243
Gattiker, U.E., 130
Geertz, C., 128, 141, 182
Geist, P., 137, 142
gender, 3, 90, 94–5
Georgescu-Rogen, N., 215
Gergen, K., 121, 235, 249
Gersick, C.J.G., 109, 116, 184, 198
Gerstein, M.S., 164
Gerwin, D., 164, 165, 169
*Gestalt*, 144
Ghoshal, S., 12, 15, 22, 236–41, 247–50
Gibb, C.A., 27
Gibson, C.B., 250
Giddens, A., 16, 48, 115, 143, 162, 167
Gilbert, N., 16
Gilbert, X., 17
Giles, W.D., 52
Ginnett, R.C., 109
Gioia, D.A., 36, 38, 63, 73–4, 135, 142
Gioia, T., 203, 204
Gladwin, T.N., 219
Glaser, B.G., 191
Gleick, J., 222
Glick, W., 131
global: commons, 216–17; culture, 5, 244–5; discourse, 8–9; economy, 5, 9, 241–2; local debate, 5, 8–9; politics, 5, 243–4; technologies, 5, 245–6
globalization, 4–5, 9, 234–52
Goffman, E., 56, 134
Goldhaber, G.M., 126
Goldman, S.L., 164, 168, 202
Goldzwig, S.R., 128
Gooch, 199, 203
Goodall, H.L. Jr., 133, 134, 136, 143
Goodman, P., 77
Gordon, D.P., 142
Gordon, W.I., 140
Gore, A., 246
Gospel, H., 18

Gould, K.A., 210, 219–21, 226
Gouldner, A., 181, 185
Goulet, D., 246
Grafton-Small, R., 36–7
Graham, R.J., 95
Grameen Bank, 249
Granovetter, M., 133
Gray, B., 127, 217
Green, S.G., 72
green movements, 211, 219, 220
Greenberger, R.S., 249
Greene, C.N., 28
Greenhalgh, L., 75
Greenhaus, J., 94
Greenpeace, 8, 249
Greenwald, A.G., 68
Greenwood, R., 19, 57
Gregory, K.L., 142
Griffin, A., 176, 179, 186
Grinyer, P.H., 57
Gronn, P.C., 142
Grosse, R., 236
group: decision-making, 76; decision support systems, 113, 130, 143; identity, 89, 93, 95–6, 98–101; information technology, 3, 6, 107–21, 258
Grunig, J.E., 127, 131
Grunig, L.A., 131
Guild, P., 176
Gumbel, P., 242
Gupta, A., 180
Gutek, B.A., 115
Guzzo, R.A., 107–8, 111–12, 117–18

Hackman, J.R., 73, 107–9, 111, 115, 116, 121
Haeckel, E., 210–11
Haefner, J.E., 77
Hage, J., 125, 165, 174–5, 183, 185
Hahn, R.W., 216
Hall, B., 133
Hall, E.T., 95, 96
Hall, M., 94
Hall, S., 98–9
Hamel, G., 15, 19, 22, 176, 237, 239–40, 249
Hamilton, D.L., 67, 68
Hammer, T.H., 73
Hampden-Turner, C., 242, 248
Handy, C., 138, 245, 248, 250
Hannan, M., , 39, 64, 222
Hardesty, M., 137
Hardin, C., 94
Hardy, C., 7, 178, 184
Harrigan, K.R., 250
Harris, C., 74, 94
Harris, L., 127
Harrison, P.D., 74
Harrison, T.M., 140
Harvey, J.H., 66
Haslett, B., 139
Hastie, R., 75
Hatch, M.J., 36, 138, 202
Hauptman, O., 130
Hauser, J., 176, 178
Haward, M.G., 211
Hawken, P., 212, 215, 217, 219–20, 225, 246–8
Hawkes, D.F., 127
Hawley, A.H., 222
Hay, P.R., 211
Hayes, R., 17
Hays, S.P., 211
Hazuda, H., 96

Heath, R.L., 131, 146
Hedberg, B., 191, 193–4
Hedlund, G., 175, 237, 240
Heenan, D.A., 237
Heider, F., 65–6, 67
Heller, F.A., 49, 54, 57, 58
Heller, T., 175, 179
Hellgren, B., 21
Hellweg, S., 133
Helms, J.E., 98
Henderson, R., 174, 177, 182
Heneman, H.G., 75
Heneman, R.L., 72, 74
Hennart, J.F., 236
Henriques, J., 98
Henry, R.A., 76
Henzler, H., 235
Heshusis, L., 38
Heskett, J.L., 34–5
Hester, G.L., 216
heuristics, 70–1, 76–7, 80
Hewstone, M., 89
Hickson, D., 46, 49, 50–1, 54–6, 57, 58
Higgins, E.T., 65, 68
Highhouse, S., 74
Hinings, B., 59
Hinings, C.R., 19, 46, 57
Hirsch, P.M., 127, 137
Hirschheim, R., 113
Hobbes, T., 212
Hochschild, A., 143
Hodgson, G., 17, 18
Hoecklin, L., 241
Hofer, C., 13
Hofstede, G., 58–9, 95–6, 237, 244, 248
Hogan, N., 170
Hogarth, R.M., 71
Hogg, M., 91
Homans, G.C., 35
Hopper, R., 142
Hordes, M.W., 238, 241, 250
Horwitz, M., 89
Hosking, D.M., 33
Hostager, T.J., 135
House, R.J., 28, 64
Hout, T., 239, 241
Huber, G., 131
Huber, G.P., 159, 163, 170, 190, 226
Huber, V.L., 73–4, 75, 77
Huff, A., 21
Hughes, J.D., 212
Hughes, T.P., 161
Hulin, C.L., 160
Hull, F., 214
human relations school, 126
human resource management, 76–7, 144
humour (learning role), 201–2
Hunt, J.G., 26, 221
Huntington, S., 244
hybrid structures, 236
Hymer, S.H., 236
Hymowitz, C., 240, 249

Iacocca, L., 31
Ibarra, H., 94
Ibbotson, R.G., 242
identity: diversities, 2–3, 6, 88–101, 258; embedded group theory, 90, 92; measurement of, 100–1; social identity theory, 3, 6, 89–92, 98
Iles, P., 94
Ilgen, D.R., 63, 73, 74, 77
Ilinitch, A.Y., 215, 220
images, 127–8; learning role, 191–4; of organizations, 3, 127–8, 191–4

'imaginative consumerism', 36–7
Imai, K., 175
immigration, 247
improvisation (learning role), 202–4
incrementalism, 49, 58
indeterminacy (research), 20
individual, 5–6
individualism (leadership), 31
industrial/organizational psychology, 17
industrial ecology, 215, 226–7
industrial revolution, 8, 242, 245
information, 118, 131, 164
information revolution, 245
information technology, 22, 163–4;
  electronic, 111–17; group, 3, 6,
  107–21, 258
Inkpen, A., 7, 238, 251
Inn, A., 77
innovation, organizing for, 3–4, 7,
  174–86
interaction analysis, 142–3
interactional model of cultural diversity
  (IMCD), 96–7
interests, 46, 55
internal market, 17, 19
international business (globalization),
  4–5, 9, 234–52
International Data Solutions, 250
International Joint Commission for the
  Great Lakes Water Quality
  Agreement, 216
International Labour Organization, 248
International Monetary Fund, 242
interorganizational relations, 133
investment, 164; foreign direct, 236–7,
  239
Irvine, S., 213
Isaacs, W.N., 143
Isabella, L.A., 135
Izraeli, D., 94

Jablin, F.M., 126, 130, 131
Jackson, D.N., 77
Jackson, S.E., 79, 88, 89, 93, 96, 97
Jacobs, M., 217, 219–20
Jacobs, R., 212
Jacobson, E., 166
Jaeger, A.M., 59
Jain, S., 17
James, L.R., 72, 74
Jamieson, D., 88
jamming (performance), 135, 145
Jancar-Webster, B., 212, 215, 219
Janger, A.R., 250
Janis, I.L., 45, 76
Janowitz, M., 203
Jarillo, J.C., 237
jazz (improvisation), 202–3, 204
Jeffcutt, P., 56
Jelinek, M., 174–5, 177, 179, 184
Jermier, J.M., 72
job: evaluation, 77; satisfaction, 72
Joerges, B., 142
Johansen, R., 170
Johanson, J., 236
Johne, F.A., 174, 178
Johnson, B., 136
Johnson, B.T., 94
Johnson, C., 68
Johnson, G., 20, 174, 177
Johnson, M., 127, 137
Johnston, W., 88, 99
joint ventures, 250
jokes/joking (role), 202
Jolly, J.P., 73

Jonas, K., 69
Jones, E.E., 65, 66
Jones, M.I., 59
Jones, M.O., 134
Jung, H.Y., 212
Jurkovich, R., 221

Kagel, J.H., 71
Kahn, J.S., 235, 244
Kahn, R.L., 78, 130
Kahneman, D., 70–1, 75, 190
Kalb, L.S., 74
Kalleberg, A., 165
Kanter, R.M., 19, 95, 165, 174–6, 178,
  180, 183, 185, 248, 250
Kanungo, R.N., 59
Karl, K.A., 73
Katerberg, R., 73
Katz, D., 78, 130
Katz, R., 130, 180
Katzenbach, J.R., 33, 108
Kay, J., 14, 15, 20
Keat, R., 57
Keating, M., 216
Keeney, B.P., 203, 204
Kehoe, J.F., 74
Keller, R.T., 32
Kellert, S.R., 218, 227
Kelley, H.H., 65–6, 77
Kelly, J.W., 136
Kennedy, J.K., 30
Kennedy, P., 248
Kerr, S., 28, 72, 138
Kersten, A., 127, 141
Kerwin, K., 239
Kets de Vries, M., 202
Kiesler, S., 112–13, 114, 117
Kiggundu, M.N., 59
Kilmann, R.H., 137
Kim, Y.Y., 140
Kimberly, L., 174
Kincaid, D., 125, 133
King, Y., 214
Kirby, P.C., 39
Kirk, D.J., 74
Kirsch, M.P., 74
Klein, H.J., 63, 73, 77
Kleindorfer, P.K., 210
Kleinschmidt, E., 174, 176, 179
Knights, D., 8, 13–14, 15, 20, 33, 54–5,
  57, 144
Knouse, S.B., 94
knowledge: power and, 8; structures,
  67–8; technologies, 160, 161
Knowlton, W.A., 72, 74
Knuf, J., 138
Koch, S., 127, 128
Koestler, A., 196, 197, 201
Kogut, B., 237
Kohut, T.L., 116
Komaki, J.L., 142
Korman, A.K., 28
Korten, D.C., 243
Kotter, J.P., 27, 30, 34–5, 38
Kouzes, J.M., 33, 205
Kozlowski, S.W., 74
Kraemer, K.L., 114
Kraiger, K., 94
Kramer, R.D., 71, 89
Kraut, R., 115
Krefting, L.A., 127, 137
Kreiner, K., 136
Kreps, G.L., 135, 137
Kriziek, R., 140
Krone, K., 143

Kuhn, T., 23
Kumaraswamy, A., 183
Kunda, G., 20, 137–8, 143, 180
Kundera, M., 201
Kunreuther, H.C., 210
Kwan, R., 242
*kyosei*, 248

labour, 247; process, 3, 163
Lachman, R., 59
Lakoff, G., 127, 137
Langlois, R.N., 18
language, 100; artifacts, 141, 145, 146;
  discourse metaphor, 7, 129, 141–5,
  146; global discourse, 8–9; learning
  and, 7, 191–2, 194, 196–7, 205–6
Lant, T.K., 191
Larson, J.R., 72, 74
Lash, S., 22
Laurent, A., 95, 96, 250
Lavipour, F.G., 235
Lawler, E.E., 64, 73, 108
Lawrence, P., 43, 58, 165, 221
Lazonick, W., 18
Leach, E., 196
leadership, 64, 72, 94; in organizations,
  1–2, 5, 26–40, 257; stages, 27–34
learning, 4, 7, 190–206, 239
least preferred coworkers scale, 20
Leavitt, H.J., 132
Leavy, B., 32
Lee, D.C., 212
Leithwood, K., 38
Lemak, D., 237
Lengel, R.H., 131, 170
lens metaphor, 129, 130–2, 144, 145, 146
Lenz, R., 17
Leonard-Barton, D., 175–7, 183
Leong, S.M., 239
Leopold, A., 213, 215
Levesque, René, 31
Lévi-Strauss, C., 196
Levine, D., 71
Levine, J.M., 65, 107–9, 111
Levine, S., 222
Levinthal, D.A., 176, 182
Levitt, B., 190
Levitt, T., 15, 239
Lewchuk, W., 18
Leyens, J.P., 65
Lichtenstein, S., 71, 77
Liden, R.C., 72
Liker, J.K., 164
Likert, R., 125
Likert scales, 68
Lilja, K., 21
Lincoln, J.R., 59, 165
Lindblom, C.E., 49, 54, 56, 57–8
Lindblom, L., 15
linkage metaphor, 129, 132–4, 144–6
Linstead, S., 36–7, 202
Lipset, S.M., 58
local: commons, 216; global debate, 5,
  8–9
Locke, E.A., 28, 77
Locke, K., 202
Loden, M., 88
Lodge, G., 18
Loewenstein, G.F., 75
loose-coupling, 226–7
Lord, R.G., 27, 29, 73, 79
Lorenzi, P., 33
Lorsch, J., 29, 43, 165, 221
Losada, M., 116
Loseke, D.R., 143

Lotman, J.M., 135
Louis, M.R., 37
Lovelock, J.E., 211
Lowe, P.D., 211
Lowe, T.R., 77
Lowin, A., 28
Luce, H., 237–8
Lucky, R., 163
Luhmann, N., 135
Luke, T., 217
Lukes, S., 48, 54
Lyles, M., 13, 20–1, 23, 78–9, 195–6
Lyotard, J., 136, 144

Macan, T.M., 77
McArthur, L.Z., 77
McBride, K., 59
McClelland, C.L., 109, 110
McClelland, D.A., 94
McCloskey, M., 215, 219, 220
McCullough, W.J. Jr., 238
McDougall, P., 240
McElroy, J.C., 73
McEwen, A., 243
McFarlan, F.W. 164
McGowan, R.A., 215
McGrath, J.E., 108–10, 112–14, 117,
    121, 192
McGuire, W.J., 91
McHugh, A., 177, 179
McIntosh, N., 135
McIntosh, R.P., 211, 215
MacIntyre, A., 119, 120
McKenney, J.L., 112–13, 164
MacKenzie, D., 161
Mackie, D.M., 68, 69
McKinsey Report (1993), 15
MacLarkey, R.L., 216
McLaughlin, M., 142
MacMillan, I., 178–9
McNulty, T., 17, 22
McPhee, R.D., 132, 133, 134, 141
McQuarrie, E., 176
McRae, H., 244
macro organizational research, 5–6,
    78–80
McRobert, D., 219, 220
Mael, F., 91
Magnet, M., 246
Mahajan, V., 174, 176
Maher, K.J., 27, 29
Mahon, J.F., 215
Malekzadeh, A., 96
Mallory, G.R., 58
management: by exception, 32; strategic,
    43
managerial rationality, 2, 44–5
managerialism, 139
Manes, C., 214, 219
Mangham, I.L., 134
Maniha, J.K., 223
Mann, B.J., 142
Mann, L., 76
Mann, R.D., 27
Manning, P.K., 127, 137, 142
Mannix, E.A., 76
Mansfield, R., 165
Manz, C.C., 29, 33, 142
mapping decision studies, 53–5
March, J.G., 1, 15, 45–7, 53–4, 56–8, 69,
    79, 132, 176, 190–1, 193, 195, 199,
    219
market, 17–19; technology links, 175–7,
    181–3
Marks, G., 66

Markus, H., 63, 67, 68
Markus, M.L., 115, 116, 117
Marquis, D., 176
Marsden, P.V., 221
Marsden, R., 3
Marsh, G.P., 214–15
Marshall, H., 99, 100–1
Marshall, J., 139–40
Marshall, R., 244
Martin, J., 34–5, 94, 99, 136
Martin, L.L., 67
Martinez, J.I., 237
Martinko, M.J., 72
Marx, K., 48
Marxism, 3, 163, 212, 217
Mason, R.O., 78
Maturana, H., 118
Maurice, M., 165
May, D., 49, 215
May, S.K., 128
Mead, M., 120
meaning, 118–19, 139, 141–4;
    management of, 26–7
mechanical technologies, 161
mechanistic organizations, 146, 178,
    181–2, 185
media richness, 131, 144
Meindl, J.R., 72, 78, 251
Melin, L., 21, 236–8, 240, 251
memory, 66–7, 72, 74, 80
mental: control, 69; maps, 170; models,
    17, 162
Merchant, C., 209, 210, 212–13, 214
MERCOSUR, 243
mergers and acquisitions, 142
Messick, D.M., 68, 89
meta-analysis, 27, 30
metaphors,3, 6–7, 125–47
Metcalfe, B., 193
Meyer, J.W., 39, 221, 223
Mezias, S.J., 191
Michael, M., 98
Michela, J.L., 66
micro organizational behaviour, 71–8,
    257
Milbrath, L.W., 212, 226
Miles, R., 12, 16, 165
Miller, D., 19, 177, 193, 195
Miller, E.J., 165
Miller, J.G., 130
Miller, K.I., 125, 128, 130
Miller, N., 66
Miller, P., 144
Miller, V.D., 131
Milliken, F., 174
Millman, G., 241
Mills, A.J., 98
Miner, J.B., 26
Mintzberg, H., 14, 15, 16, 20, 30–1, 43,
    49, 54–6, 57, 58, 134, 177–9, 181
Mirvis, P.H., 73, 96
Mitchell, T.R., 72–4
Mitroff, I.I., 78, 137, 144, 165, 168
modernism, 126–7
Moghaddam, M., 89
Mohr, L., 174
Mohrman, S., 168
Monge, P.R., 125, 132–3, 164–6
monitoring (product innovation), 178–9,
    181, 184–5
Montreal Protocol, 216
Moorman, C., 182
moral orders, 120, 121
Moran, T.H., 237
Moreland, R.L., 107–9, 111

Morgan, G., 8, 13–14, 15, 20, 26, 37–8,
    48, 55, 126–8, 130, 132, 136, 221
Morris, G.H., 142
Morrison, A.M., 88, 94
Morton, M.S., 163, 164
motivation (social cognition), 72–3
Mowday, R.T., 78, 79
Muir, J., 215
Muldoon, P., 219, 220
Mullen, B., 68
multi-functional work groups, 108–9
multinational enterprises, 9, 236, 237,
    239
Mumby, D., 127, 137, 139, 143–4
Mumford, L., 213
Muna, F.A., 59
Munro, D.H., 197
Munro, J., 205
Munyard, T., 94
Murphy, K.R., 74, 95
Murray, F., 55
Myers, S., 176
Myrdal, G., 94

Naess, A., 210, 213–14
NAFTA, 243
Nahavandhi, A., 96
Naisbitt, J., 242
Nakayama, T., 140
Namboodiri, K., 226
Nanus, B., 30–1, 38
narratives, 136–7
Narver, J., 182
nation-state, 244
National Research Council, 164, 168
natural resources, 5, 246–7
naturalistic research, 127
Neale, M.A., 63, 75, 76
negotiation, 75–6
Negroponte, N., 245
Nehrt, L.C., 237
Nelson, D.L., 115
Nelson, R.R., 176, 178
Nemetz, P.N., 216
neo-classical economics, 14, 20, 44, 212,
    217
neo-liberal theories, 12
networks, 95, 166, 168, 183;
    communication and, 129, 132–4
New Leadership, 2, 27, 30–4, 36–40
Newton, I., 212
Nisbett, R., 70
Nkomo, S.M., 94, 140
Nobeoka, K., 177
Noble, D.F., 163
Nohria, N., 112
non-decisions, 47–8
non-governmental organizations, 240,
    249
non-profit organizations, 240, 249
Nonaka, I., 174, 176, 179
Nord, W.R., 5, 6, 119, 174
normal science, 3
Normann, R., 192, 195
Northcraft, G.B., 75, 76, 77
NUMMI, 199–200
Nutt, P.C., 49, 51, 54, 57

O'Conner, J.R., 131
O'Connor, E.S., 138
O'Connor, K.M., 121
O'Donnell-Trujillo, N., 127, 134, 135
Ohara, M., 164
Ohio Studies, 28–9, 30, 32
Ohmae, K., 235, 139, 240

Okamura, J.Y., 91
Oldham, G.R., 111
O'Leary, T., 144
oligopoly, 236
Oliveira, B., 59
Oliver, C., 133
Olsen, J.P., 15, 53, 58, 191
Olson, J.M., 68–9
Olson, M.H., 164
O'Mara, J., 88
Omni, M., 98
OPEC, 243
open systems approach, 108–9, 114–17
O'Reilly, C.A., 63, 77, 93, 94, 130–1, 166
organic organizations, 126, 181–2, 185
organization: as conversation, 6–8;
   groups, 92; metaphors, 3, 6–7,
   125–47; structure, 159–71
organization studies, individual in, 5–6
organizational behaviour (cognitions in
   organizations), 2, 63–80
organizational change, 3, 163–4
organizational communication research,
   126–7
organizational culture, leadership and,
   34–7, 257
organizational democracy, 3, 140
organizational demography, 90, 93–4
organizational environments, 222–5
organizational learning, 4, 7, 190–206,
   239
organizational research, 5–6, 78–80
organizational structure, 250–1; and
   technology, 159–71
organizations: biospheres and, 4, 8,
   209–28; cognitions in, 2, 5–6, 63–80,
   257; decision-making, 2, 6, 43–59,
   257–8; diverse identities, 6, 88–101;
   images of, 3, 127–8, 191–4; leadership,
   1–2, 5, 26–40, 257; as repositories,
   193; strategy and, 11–23; systems,
   168–9, 193; as technology, 165–6
Orlikowski, W., 7, 107, 114–16, 130, 143,
   160–2, 167–8, 175, 193
Ortony, A., 127, 137
Orwell, G., 201
Osborne, R.N., 221
Ostrom, T.M., 67
outcomes (decisions), 51–3
Overington, M.A., 134
Oviatt, B., 240
Owen, A.A., 52
Owen, H., 242

Pacanowsky, M.E., 127, 134, 135, 140
Packer, A., 88, 99
Pacquette, P., 184
Padilla, A.M., 96
Paehlke, R.C., 209, 211, 216
Page, A., 179, 186
Plamer, I.C., 10
Papa, M., 133
paradigms, dominant social, 4, 8, 210,
   212–13, 215, 217–18, 220–1, 223, 225,
   227
Park, R.E., 94
Parker, B., 250
Parker, I., 100
Parkhe, A., 250
Parliament of World's Religions, 248
Pasquero, J., 217
Passmore, W., 193, 235
path–goal theory, 64
patriarchy, 139, 214
Pazy, A., 75

Peake, P.K., 77
Pearce, J.L., 74
Pearce, M., 132
Pearce, W.B., 121
Pelz, D., 175
Penman, R., 116, 117, 120, 121
Penner, W.J., 197
Penrose, E., 182
Pepper, G.L., 127
Peppers, L., 72
perception, 67–8, 74–5
performance: appraisals, 73–5;
   metaphors, 129, 134–6, 144, 145, 146;
   work groups, 3, 6, 107–21, 258
Perlmutter, H.V., 237
Perrow, C., 8, 133, 160–1, 168, 170, 221,
   223, 226
person perception, 67–8, 74–5
personality, 29; trait approach, 1, 5,
   27–8
Peters, L.H., 30
Peters, T., 14–15, 30–1, 34–6, 52, 165,
   180, 183–4, 204–5
Pettigrew, A., 15, 19, 46, 54, 55–6, 57–8,
   184
Pettigrew, T.F., 94
Pfeffer, J., 6, 23, 26, 46, 78, 93, 131, 176,
   221, 223
Phatak, A.V., 239
Phillips, J.S., 72, 94
Phillips, S.R., 129–30, 131
Philp, M., 107
Phoenix, A., 98
Pierce, B., 237, 238
Piercy, N., 52, 139
Pieterse, J.N., 235, 244
Pinchot, G., 215
Pinder, C.C., 127
Pinfield, L., 225
Piore, M., 161
Plant, J., 214
Plato, 9, 212
Podsakoff, P.M., 29, 30, 38
politicality (decision-making), 50–1
politics (global), 5, 243–4
Polley, D., 111, 174, 178, 179
pollution, 9, 215, 216, 219
Pondy, L.R., 78, 127, 137, 144
Ponton, A., 213
Poole, M., 130, 138, 143, 167
Pope, K., 245
population ecology, 39, 64, 222
Porac, J., 21
Porritt, J., 212
Porter, L.W., 74
Porter, M.E., 12, 14, 15, 17, 19, 21, 237,
   244
portfolio matrix, 15
Posner, B.Z., 33, 205
postmodernism, 144
poststructuralist theory, 144
Potter, J., 100
Powell, G.N., 94
Powell, W.W., 39, 185, 223
Powell flute (case study), 197–8, 200
Power, J.G., 166
power: decision-making, 43, 45–8;
   knowledge and, 8; relations, 3, 100
Prahalad, C.K., 15, 19, 22, 78–9, 176,
   239, 249
Pratkanis, A.R., 68
prescriptions (decisions), 48–51
Pressman, J.L., 51
Preston, R., 246
privatization, 243

problem solving, 55; creative, 177–8, 181,
   183–4
process (innovation), 184
product: innovation, 174–86; integrity,
   175–6; life-cycle, 15, 20
psychological approach (cognitive
   research), 63, 65–7
psychotherapy (improvisation), 203
Pugh, D., 58, 165
Pulakos, E.D., 72
Pura, R., 247
Purser, R.E., 193
Putnam, L.L., 126–7, 128, 135–6, 138,
   142–4

qualititative research, 37–9
quantitative research, 37–9
Quelsh, J., 176
Quinn, J., 15, 49, 54, 57, 179, 184
Quinn, R., 138
Quintana, D., 96

Rabbie, J.M, 89
race, 91, 140
racioethnicity, 3, 90, 94–5
Radebaugh, L.J., 238, 239
radical environmentalism perspective, 4,
   210, 212–14, 217–19, 220, 221, 223,
   225, 227
Rafaeli, A., 143
Ragan, S.L., 142
Ragins, B.R., 94
Raiffa, H., 64, 71, 75
Rakow, L.F., 140
Rall, W., 235
Ranson, S., 164
Rappa, M.A., 161
Rasanen, K., 21
rational: choice, 2, 44–5, 48, 190; legal
   authority, 43, 46
rationality, 2, 197; decisions, 43–5, 47,
   54–5; *see also* bounded rationality
re-engineering, 184
Read, P.P., 168
Reason, P., 214
Redding, S., 59
Redding, W.C., 126–7, 129–30, 131
Reddy, M., 118, 129
Reed, M., 39
reflection-in-action, 193, 203
reflexivity, 20
reform environmentalism, 4, 210, 212,
   214–21, 223, 225, 226–7
Reich, R.B., 33, 243, 250
Reitsperger, W.D., 237
Renesch, J., 235, 243
repository image, 193
research: cognitive, 63–71; decision
   process, 53–5; directions
   (innovations), 181–5; leadership,
   27–34; location, 57–9; organizational,
   5–6, 78–80; organizational
   communication, 126–7; technology
   and organizations, 169–71; work
   group performance, 107–11
researcher (in decision-making process),
   57–9
resource: dependence, 46; *see also* natural
   resources
Rhinesmith, S.H., 235, 240, 241
Rice, A.K., 165
Rice, F., 209, 220
Rice, R.E., 112–13, 116, 130–1, 133
Rich, B., 220
Richman, L.S., 241

Ricks, D., 251
Ricoeur, P., 141
Ridderstrale, J., 175
Ridgeway, C., 91
Rifkin, J., 220, 245
Riley, P., 127
Ring, P.S., 197
*ringi* system, 59
risk, 184
Roberts, E., 174, 180
Roberts, H., 19
Roberts, K.H., 131, 166, 226–7
Roberts, K.M., 94
Roberts, N.C., 31, 38
Robertson, R., 235, 244
Robertson, T., 174
Robey, D., 114, 115, 116, 117
Robichaud, D., 135
Robinson, R., 237, 238
Rockhart, J., 22
Roediger, D., 98
Roethlisberger, F.G., 125
Rogers, E.M., 125, 129, 133
Rogers, T.B., 68
Rohwedder, C., 244
Rolander, D., 237, 240
Roloff, M.E., 142
Ronen, S., 237
Ropp, V.A., 133
Rorty, R., 119, 120
Rose, G.L., 74, 77
Rosen, M., 127, 138
Rosen, S., 131
Rosenau, P., 134
Rosenberg, N., 176
Rosenbloom, R., 179
Rosener, J.B., 88, 94
Rosenkopf, L., 161
Rosenthal, U., 49
Ross, J., 109–10
Ross, L., 66, 70, 77
Ross, M., 66
Rothman, H., 215
Rothschild-Whitt, J., 140
Rothwell, R., 174, 176
Routley, R., 217–18
Rowan, B., 39, 223
Rowney, J., 94
Roznowski, M., 160
Rudig, W., 211
Rugman, A.M., 236
Rumelt, R.P., 12
Rummel, R.J., 237
Rush, M.C., 29
Rushdie, S., 201
Russ, G.S., 131
Russell, J.M., 72
Russo, M.V., 220
Ryan, J., 72
Ryle, G., 118, 120, 191

Sabel, C., 161
Sagan, S.D., 194, 199
St George, A., 12, 13
Salamon, L.M., 240, 249
Salancik, G.R., 46, 78, 131, 176, 251
Sale, K., 211, 213, 215, 219, 220
Sales, A.L., 96
Salleh, A.K., 210
Samuel, P., 225
Samuelson, P., 224
Sandelands, L.E., 191–2
Santiago, F., 251
Sarkar, S., 211
Sashkin, M., 30

satisficing, 57
Saussure, F. de, 136
Sauvant, K., 235
Sayles, L.R., 165
Scanlan, T.J., 132
Scarborough, H., 175
Schall, M.S., 127
Schaltegger, S.C., 215, 220
Schattsneider, E.F., 47
Schein, E.H., 34–6, 179, 181
Schelling, T.C., 225
schemata, 67–8
Schendel, D., 13
Schmidheiny, S., 215, 217, 220
Schmitz, J., 133, 166
Schnaiberg, A., 210, 219, 220–1, 226
Schneider, D.J., 65, 67, 69
Schneider, S., 137
Schoemaker, P.J.H., 45
Schoenherr, P.A., 165
Schon, D., 176, 184, 191, 193–4, 202, 203
Schoonhoven, C.B., 174–5, 177, 179, 184
Schot, J., 220
Schotter, A., 18
Schuler, R.S., 250
Schuller, G., 203
Schumacher, E.F., 213
Schumpeter, J.A., 17
Schwab, D.P., 75
Schwartz, D., 166
Schweitzer, G.E., 216
Schwenk, C., 78–9
Scott, M., 215
Scott, R., 18
Scott, W.R., 160, 163, 166, 170, 221–2
Scott-Poole, M., 22
'segmentalism', 178
self: concepts, 68, 72–3, 80; designing systems, 191–5; identity, 89, 91; realization, 214;
self-interest, 69; environmental change and, 4, 209–10, 220–1, 224–6
Selznick, P., 30, 223
Senge, P.M., 165, 241, 250
Sera, K., 235, 238
Serafin, R., 211
Sesit, M.R., 241
Sessions, G., 210, 212–13
Shamir, B., 73
Shanley, M., 57
Shannon, C.E., 117, 129
Sharfman, M., 215
sharing (work groups), 110
Sharp, M., 242
Shea, G.P., 107–8, 111–12, 117–18
Shenkar, O., 237
Shepherd, G., 121
Sherif, C. and M., 89
Sherman, S.J., 65–9, 205
Shiva, V., 219, 220
Shook, D., 130
Short, J., 22, 130
Shotter, J., 118, 120
Shoup, M., 243
Shrivastava, P., 20, 78, 137, 215, 225–6, 239
Shulman, A.D., 107, 112–14, 116–19
Siegel, J., 116
Siehl, C., 35, 137
Sigman, S.J., 143
silences (absences), 19–20
Sils, J.M., 201
Silverman, D., 56
Simai, M., 243

Simmons, P., 216
Simon, H.A., 2, 6, 43–6, 54–7, 69, 79, 125, 176, 191, 195, 221, 224
Sims, H.P., 29, 33, 63, 74, 142
Singh, H., 236, 249
single-loop learning, 195, 197
Sitarz, D., 216
situational control, 29–30
Sivanandan, A., 94
Skevington, S., 98, 100
Skinner, B.F., 97
'skunkworks', 180
Skvoretz, J., 91
Slater, S., 182
Slaton, C.D., 219
Sless, D., 117–18, 121
Slovic, P., 71, 77, 190
small wins (learning role), 204–5
Sminia, H., 23
Smircich, L., 26, 37–8, 98, 127, 135–7, 139
Smith, A.G., 131
Smith, D.H., 135
Smith, D.K., 33, 108
Smith, G., 49
Smith, J.E., 73
Smith, J.K., 38
Smith, K., 135
Smith, K.G., 110, 112
Smith, K.K., 92, 138
Smith, R.C., 125–6, 127–8, 137
Smuts, J., 213
Snelson, P., 174, 178
Sniezek, J.A., 76
Snow, C., 12, 16, 165
Snow, D., 211, 215, 219, 220
social cognition, 2, 64–9, 71–5, 78–80
social constructionism, 91, 98, 143
social contexts, 109
social ecology, 214
social identity theory, 3, 6, 89–92, 98
social institutions, 18
social interactions, 129, 134–6, 143
social networks, 21, 91
social responsibility, 248–9
social system, 226–7
socialism, 9
socio-technical systems, 3, 115, 164–9
Software Publishers Association, 245
Solomon, S., 242
songs (learning function), 203–4
Sorenson, G., 242
Sorenson, R.L., 135
Souder, W., 177
specialization (functional), 165, 177
speech, 142, 145
Spencer, P., 225
Spender, J., 21, 57
spiritual ecology, 214
Spradley, J.P., 142
Spretnak, C., 219
Sproule, J.M., 135
Sproull, L., 112–14, 117, 190
Srivatsan, V., 191, 192
Srull, T.K., 67
Stacey, R., 56
Stahlberg, D., 68
stakeholders, 215, 222
Stalker, G.M., 7, 146, 175, 178–9, 181–6, 221
Stamp, G., 95
Starbuck, W.H., 174, 221–2
Staw, B.M., 73, 78–9, 109–10
Stayman, M.H., 91
Stead, J.G., 215, 225–6, 236

Stead, W.E., 215, 225–6, 236
Stebbins, R.A., 202
Steger, U., 215, 220
Steier, F., 135
Steinbach, R., 38
Steiner, I.D., 112
Steinman, J.I., 113
stereotypes, 67–8, 74–5, 77
Stewart, R., 43
Stillinger, C., 75
stimulus-response (SR), 198, 202
stochastic events, 161–2, 169–71
Stogdill, R.M., 26, 27–8
Stohl, C., 127–9, 131, 132, 133–4
Stoll, C., 245
Stone, E.F., 94
Stoner, J.A.F., 76
Stopford, J.M., 237, 240
storytelling metaphor, 134, 135–6
strategic choice, 3, 162–3
strategic groups, 12
strategic intent, 15, 19, 179
strategic management, 43
strategic planning, 14–15, 23
strategy:creative deconstruction, 1, 7–8,
    11–23; organizational, 249–50
Strauss, A., 47, 191
Strebel, P., 17
Strine, M.S., 144
Stroebe, W., 69
Stroh, L.K., 94
Strong, D.H., 214–15
Strube, M.J., 30
structural change, 3, 159–71
structural functionalism, 43
structuration, 3, 115, 143, 159, 167–70
structure, organizational, 159–71,
    250–1
Stubbart, C., 135
Stutman, R.K., 128
style approach (leadership), 27, 28–9
substitution process, 112–13
Sudnow, D., 56, 203–4
Sujan, H., 73
Sullivan, J.J., 73
Sundaram, A.K., 251
Sundstrom, E., 107, 108
SuperLeadership, 2, 33
sustainable development, 4, 8, 215–17,
    219–20, 226–7, 246
Sutcliffe, K.M., 132
Sutton, R., 78–9, 143
Swidler, A., 7, 182, 186
symbol metaphor, 129, 136–8, 141, 144,
    145–6
symbolic convergence, 135–6
systems theory, 4, 168–9, 210, 226–7

Tajfel, H., 67, 89
Takeuchi, H., 174, 179
Tamuz, M., 199
Tan, C.T., 239
Tancred, P., 98
Tannenbaum, R., 143
Tansuhaj, P.S, 95
'task dominant' team approach, 177
Taylor, D.M., 76, 89
Taylor, F.W., 125
Taylor, J.C., 115, 162
Taylor, J.R., 125–6, 128, 135, 141, 144,
    145
Taylor, M.E., 142
Taylor, S.F., 65, 66, 67–8, 69
Teagarden, M.B., 251
Teas, R., 73

technological determinism, 116
technological growth, 161
technological innovation, 17–18
technological systems, 226
technology: descriptive approaches,
    160–3; global, 245–6; market linkage,
    175–7, 181–3; role (in organizations),
    161–3; structuring and, 3, 7, 159–71
technosphere, 211
Teece, D.J., 18
Teich, A.H., 163
temporality, 109–10
tensions, 175–8, 180–1, 186
Terryberry, S., 222
Tesser, A., 131
text, 129, 141, 144
Thachankary, T., 144
Thanheiser, H.T., 237
Thayer, L., 203
theory: critical, 127; in-use, 194
Therborn, G., 139
Third World, 216
Thomas, A.B., 78
Thomas, A.S., 238
Thomas, D.A., 92, 94
Thomas, H., 13, 21
Thomas, R.R., 88
Thompson, J.B., 139
Thompson, J.D., 51, 165, 169, 221–2
Thompson, L.L., 75
Throop, G.M., 215, 216
Thurow, L.C., 163, 164
Tichy, N.M., 30–1, 38, 125, 205
Tierney, W.G., 35–6, 38
tight-coupling, 226–7
time, 19–20, 109–10; interaction and
    performance (TIP) theory, 113
Tinsley, E.A., 98
Tjosvold, D., 72
Todor, W.D., 77
Tokar, B., 210
Tomarzky, L.G., 116
Tomkiewcz, J., 94
Tomlinson, J., 244
Tompkins, P.K., 126–7, 129–30, 138–41,
    144
tool metaphor, 130
Torbert, W.R., 193
total environmental quality management
    (TEQM), 215
Townley, B., 3, 144
trade (globalization), 234–52
training, 28
trait approach , 1, 5, 27–8
transactional leadership, 5, 30–2
transformational:leadership, 2, 30–2
transmission (conduit metaphor), 128,
    129–30, 144–5
transnational corporations, 239
Transparency International, 248
transpersonal ecology, 214
Trevino, L.K., 131
Triandis, H.C., 89, 94, 96–7
triangulation, 39
Trice, H., 34–5, 127, 137
Trist, E., 111, 115, 162, 221–2
Trompenaars, F., 241, 242, 248
Trujillo, N., 137
Tsui, A.S., 93
Tucker, M., 244
Tucker, S., 5, 174
Tuden, A., 51
Tully, S., 244
Tung, R.L., 95–6
Turner, J., 89

Turner, P., 127, 128
Turner, V., 134
Tushman, M.L., 130, 132, 161, 174
Tversky, A., 70–1, 75, 190
Tway, P., 142
Tyre, M.J., 167, 175, 183

Ullian, J.A., 142
uncertainty, 46
Ungson, G.R., 79
United Nations, 239, 242, 248; Climate
    Conference, 246; Conference on
    Environment and Development, 209,
    216, 220; Human Development
    Report, 246–7
Uppsala School, 236
Urban, G., 178
Urry, J., 22

Vahlne, J., 236
value-based identity, 183
value chains, 19
values (cognitive perspective), 64–5
Vanderslice, V.J., 34
Van de Ven, A.H., 14, 22, 138, 174–5,
    178–9, 183, 197
Van Dyne, L., 111
Van Every, E.J., 125
Van Maanen, J., 142–3, 179
Van Wassenhove, C., 192
Varela, F., 118
Vecchio, R.P., 30
Vernon, R., 236
vertical integration, 21
Vibbert, S.L., 127
Vickers, G., 184
Vico, G., 120, 121
visionary leadership, 2
voice metaphor, 129, 139–41, 144–6
Volvo-Uddevalla, 199–200
von Hippel, E., 176
Voyer, J.J., 191
Vredenburg, H., 215

Wajcman, J., 161
Waldron, V.R., 143
Wall, D., 212, 213
Wallace, A., 219
Walsh, J.P., 79
Walther, J.B., 113
Wanniski, J., 243
Warren, K.J., 210, 214
Warren, R.L., 222
Wason, P.C., 71
Waterman, R.H., 14–15, 30, 34–6, 52
Waters, J.A., 55–6
Watson, E.E., 88
Watson-Dugan, K.W., 142
Watzlawick, P., 134
wealth, 247
Weaver, C.N., 94
Weaver, W., 117, 129
Webb, E.J., 39
Weber, M., 31, 43, 46, 58, 125, 180–1,
    197
Weick, K.E., 5, 7, 14, 53, 64, 78, 128, 132,
    134–5, 137, 146, 160–2, 167, 170–1,
    175, 183, 191, 193–4, 202, 204, 226–7,
    247
Weiner, B., 66
Weitz, B.A., 73, 78
Wellman, B., 112, 113
Wells, L.T. Jr., 237, 240
Welsford, E., 202
Welsh, D.H.B., 250

Wendelken, D.J., 77
Wenk, E., 160, 168
Wensley, R., 17
Wert-Gray, S., 130
Westley, F.R., 30–1, 180–1, 185, 215
Wetherell, M., 99, 100–1
Wexler, M., 217
Wexley, K.N., 72, 73
Wharton, A.S., 91, 93, 98
Wheelwright, S., 176, 178–9, 183, 186
Whetten, D.A., 197
Whipp, R., 18, 19–20, 21, 34
Whiston, T., 174
Whitaker, A., 251
White, H.C., 72
White, J.F., 72, 74
White, L., 212
White, P.E., 222
White, S.B., 76
Whitley, R., 12, 21
Whittington, R., 19
Whyte, G., 76
Wiener, N., 227
Wildavsky, A., 51
Wilde, W., 114
Wilemon, D., 180
Wilkins, A.L., 137
Williams, K.J., 74
Williams, R., 11, 13
Williamson, O.E., 44, 236
Willmott, H., 20, 23, 33, 34, 36, 138
Wilson, D., 20, 32, 46, 50, 53, 57

Wilson, O.E., 211, 224, 227
Winant, H., 98
Wind, J., 174, 176
Winslow, R., 246
Winter, S.G., 176, 178
Witte, K., 143
Witten, M., 131, 136, 137
Wittgenstein, L., 8
women, 247; ecofeminism, 214, 220;
    feminism, 138, 204–5
Women's Environment and
    Development Organization (WEDO),
    220
Wondolleck, J.M., 217
Wong-Reiger, D., 96
Wood, J.T., 138
Woods, J.D., 94
Woodward, J., 165
work group: performance, 3, 6, 107–21,
    258
Workforce 2000 Report, 88
Workman, J., 176
World Bank, 220, 242–3
World Commission on Environment and
    Development, 209–10, 215, 216
World Trade Organization, 234, 243,
    246, 249
*World of Work*, 247, 249
Worster, D., 213
Wright, R.W., 251
Wurf, E., 68
Wuthnow, R., 136

Wyer, R.S., 67
Wynne, B., 163, 216

Xuereb, J.M., 182

Yancey, W.L., 91
Yang, E., 177
Yanow, D., 192, 195, 197–8, 200
Yates, J., 130, 143
Yeager, S.J., 74
Yip, G.S., 239, 240
Yoshino, M., 166
Young, E., 136
Young, R.C., 222
Yu, J., 95

Zahra, S., 174
Zajac, E.J., 79
Zajonc, R.B., 63, 67–8
Zalesny, M.D., 74
Zaleznik, A., 27,30
Zaltman, G., 178
Zan, L., 16, 20
Zanna, M.P., 68–9
Zbaracki, M.J., 45, 79, 184
*Zeitgeist*, 12
Zeithaml, C.P., 78
Zelditch, M. Jr., 91
Zey, M., 44
Zmud, R.W., 130
Zuboff, S., 114
Zuckerman, M., 66